# *Machines, Languages, and Computation*

**Peter J. Denning**
*Purdue University*

**Jack B. Dennis**
*Massachusetts Institute of Technology*

**Joseph E. Qualitz**
*Artisan Industries, Inc.*

***Prentice-Hall, Inc., Englewood Cliffs, New Jersey 07632***

*Library of Congress Cataloging in Publication Data*

DENNING, PETER J (date)
Machines, languages, and computation.

Includes index.
1. Machine theory. 2. Formal languages. I. Dennis, Jack Bonnell, joint author. II. Qualitz, Joseph E., (date) joint author. III. Title.
QA267.D45 621.3819'52 77-18128
ISBN 0-13-542258-2

***To Dorothy, David, and Donna***



Printed in the United States of America

10 9 8 7 6 5 4 3 2

PRENTICE-HALL INTERNATIONAL, INC., *London*
PRENTICE-HALL OF AUSTRALIA PTY. LIMITED, *Sydney*
PRENTICE-HALL OF CANADA, LTD., *Toronto*
PRENTICE-HALL OF INDIA PRIVATE LIMITED, *New Delhi*
PRENTICE-HALL OF JAPAN, INC., *Tokyo*
PRENTICE-HALL OF SOUTHEAST ASIA PTE. LTD., *Singapore*
WHITEHALL BOOKS LIMITED, *Wellington, New Zealand*

# Contents

# *Preface*

Theoretical computer science has evolved from three disciplines: mathematics, engineering, and linguistics. The mathematical roots of computer science date from the 1930s when Turing's work exposed fundamental limits on mechanical computation. This work, an outgrowth of mathematical logic, predates stored computers by more than a decade. Turing's discovery was reinforced by the work of Church, Kleene, and Post on recursive functions and the formalization of mathematical logic. The origins in engineering began with Shannon's observation, in 1938, that the functions of relay switching networks could be represented in the symbolic notation of Boolean algebra. In the mid-1950s, Caldwell and Huffman extended this work to obtain a formal approach to sequential switching circuits, which evolved into the theory of finite-state machines. The linguistic contribution to computer science came in the late 1950s with Chomsky's characterization of formal grammars and languages. Interest in formal specification of programming languages led many computer scientists to study Chomsky's work and build it into an important theory of artificially constructed languages.

This book explores these three underlying themes of the theory of computation, and is intended for computer science undergraduates at the senior level—especially those planning to pursue graduate study. Several selections of material may be chosen for a one-semester course, according to the emphasis desired by the instructor. Alternatively, the book may be used for a comprehensive two-semester course at a less intensive pace, or for sophomores or juniors with a good mathematics background. (Suggested chapter selections are discussed on page xiii, under *Advice for Instructors.*)

Study of the theory of computation is an essential component of any computer science curriculum. For its further evolution, modern computer science depends on new methodologies for the construction of computers, systems, languages, and application programs so that we may be confident in their ability to perform as intended by their designers. The need for accurate descriptions of computers, languages, and programs, and for precise characterization of their behavior, has spurred the development of theoretical science. This includes work on the formal specification of programs, languages, and systems, and on methods of proving their correctness; on semantic formalisms that provide a sound foundation in mathematics for basing theories of program and system behavior; and on computational complexity—the study of the structure and space/time requirements of algorithms. Since entire books are devoted to these areas,† we devote the present volume to the fundamental knowledge—abstract machines and languages, and computability—essential to understanding and contributing to these developing areas of computer science.

This book had its genesis in an MIT course taught continuously since 1965, and has seen many years of evolution and refinement. It differs from major related texts‡ in several ways. First, we have emphasized the integrated development of the main results in each of the three major conceptual threads (machines, languages, computability), showing the relations and equivalences among them. Second, we appeal to the student's knowledge of programming by using program-like descriptions of control units and algorithms. Third, we have tried to develop the material in a way that has intuitive appeal. Though our arguments are rigorous, every concept is carefully developed and well illustrated through examples.

## Content

Figure 1.4 shows the hierarchy of machines and languages studied in this book, and the chapters in which each topic is treated. The following paragraphs summarize the contents of each chapter.

Chapter 1 introduces abstract machines, and presents abstract languages as sets of strings over finite alphabets. Chapter 2 briefly reviews elements of set theory and logic, which provide concepts and notation relied on throughout the book; it also introduces terminology for strings of symbols and the important operations on strings and languages.

In Chapter 3, we begin the formal study of languages with the concept of

†Aho, Hopcroft, Ullman [1974]; Borodin & Munro [1975]; Braffort & Hirschberg [1967]; Stoy [1977]; Yeh [1977].

‡Arbib [1969;] Hennie [1968]; Hermes [1965]; Hopcroft & Ullman [1969]; Kain [1972]; Minsky [1967]; Stoll [1963].

representing an infinite set of sentences by a finite set of grammatical rules that generate the sentences of the language. The structural description of languages is illustrated by examples from English and the programming language Algol. Chomsky's hierarchy of grammars (and corresponding languages) is defined. Syntax trees are defined for context-free languages, and derivation diagrams for the more expressive language classes. Ambiguous derivations are defined.

Chapter 4 begins the study of abstract machines with a physically-motivated discussion of the finite automaton, a machine built from a finite number of elementary parts. The concept of "state" is introduced to formalize the description of a machine's internal configuration. Two common methods of assigning machine outputs (to transitions or to states of the machine) are shown to be equivalent. Equivalent machines and states are studied, and a procedure for reducing a finite-state machine to minimal canonical form is developed. The chapter treats briefly the characterization of a machine by equivalence classes of input sequences, grouped according to the states in which they leave the machine.

Chapter 5 combines concepts from Chapters 3 and 4 in the study of finite-state languages—sets of strings recognizable by finite state machines. Nondeterministic machines are introduced and are shown to be reducible to deterministic machines (usually at the cost of greater machine complexity). Methods of converting between Chomsky's linear grammars and nondeterministic machines are given. Kleene's regular expressions are introduced, and methods of transforming between regular expressions and finite-state machines are developed. The chapter ends by discussing closure properties, ambiguity, and decision problems for finite-state languages.

Chapter 6 studies the limitations of finite-state machines. It exhibits languages for which there exist no finite-state accepters. It characterizes the limitations of finite-state accepters, generators, and transducers. It characterizes the ultimately periodic behavior of finite-state machines, and proves, based on this behavior, that certain arithmetic operations (for example, multiplication) are beyond the capabilities of finite automata.

Chapter 7 introduces tape automata. In a first attempt to define a class of automata more powerful than the finite-state machines, we study tape automata with read-only input and no external writeable stores. It is shown that, even with two-way motion on their input tapes, these automata have no more computing power than finite-state machines; we conclude that additional storage is required to increase their computational power.

Chapter 8 studies pushdown automata, a class of tape automata having a restricted, but unbounded, external store: items can be retrieved from the store only in reverse order of entry. The unbounded store endows these machines with more power than finite automata—for example, they can recognize languages that are not finite state—but we show that the restriction on their store access method limits the ultimate power of these machines also. Using a concept of traverse sets—sets of input strings that lead a machine to the same control state and store configuration—we show how to transform between context-free languages and nondeterministic pushdown accepters. This equivalence is exploited to develop the closure properties of the context-free languages. We discover languages which cannot be recognized by any pushdown machine; we also discover languages which can be recognized by pushdown automata only if nondeterministic behavior is permitted. (That the deterministic languages are a proper subset of all context-free languages implies that, in practice, syntax analyzers for some context-free languages require backtracking, and thus may be slow; this implication is studied in Chapter 10.) Finally, we consider the effect of limiting the number of distinct symbols in an automaton's tape alphabet. Two symbols are shown to be sufficient for general behavior, a single symbol is shown to define a class of counting automata intermediate in power between the finite-state machines and the pushdown automata.

Chapter 9 presents properties of context-free languages which derive readily from a study of their grammars. After showing how to eliminate needless productions from a grammar, we prove that these grammars can be reduced to either of two canonical forms: the Chomsky normal form and the Greibach standard form. These forms are frequently useful for simplifying proofs and, sometimes, syntax analyzers for context-free languages. Two important characterizations of context-free languages are proved: the pumping lemma shows that, when a sufficiently long string is in a context-free language, an infinity of related strings must also be there; the self-embedding theorem characterizes the possible substring matchings in context-free languages. These theorems are used to prove that certain languages are not context free.

Chapter 10 deals with syntax analysis of context-free languages. Most modern compilers use parsing techniques based on context-free languages; this chapter develops the most important methods. Top-down and bottom-up analyses are defined and compared. Two forms of deterministic bottom-up analysis are studied: (simple mixed strategy) precedence analysis, and $LR(k)$ analysis. In each case, we show how to construct an appropriate parser and show that the corresponding grammars generate all deterministic context-free languages.

In Chapter 11 we study Turing machines, the simplest models of general mechanical computation. A variety of possible Turing machines are shown equivalent to a simple form of Turing machine which has unrestricted access to a single, singly-infinite storage tape. (The linear-bounded automaton, a machine similar to the Turing machine but with a storage tape whose length is bounded linearly by the length of its input, is discussed briefly.) A variety of Turing machine programs for simple operations are developed, and are used as procedures in a universal machine capable of simulating any other Turing machine. We state and explain Turing's thesis: the solution procedure for any problem that can be solved effectively can be programmed on a Turing machine. The universal machine partly supports this claim. Additional support is provided by the equivalence of Turing machines to two other, seemingly unrelated, models of effective computation: recursive functions and Post string manipulation systems. These equivalences are demonstrated in Chapters 13 and 14. Finally, we define the concepts of enumeration, recursive sets, and recursively enumerable sets.

Chapter 12 deals with unsolvable problems, well-defined classes of problems for which, by Turing's thesis, there exist no effective solution procedures. These include program-termination problems, word problems, and a variety of decision problems concerning context-free languages. The existence of mechanically unsolvable problems is one of the most fundamental results of the theory of computation.

In Chapter 13 we study recursive functions, a class of number-theoretic functions used to model computation. We study three classes of recursive functions: the primitive recursive functions, the $\mu$-recursive functions, and the multiple-recurisve functions. The latter two classes are shown to be equivalent, and each is shown equivalent to the Turing machines. Specifically, we show how to construct a Turing machine that evaluates a given multiple-recursive function; we show how to construct a $\mu$-recursive function that simulates a given Turing machine; and we show that the class of multiple-recursive functions contains the class of $\mu$-recursive functions.

Chapter 14 deals with Post string manipulation systems, a third model of computation. Post systems are a formalization of the processes by which humans solve problems symbolically, as in mathematical logic. We show how to represent a few common algorithms with these systems, and then show how any Turing machine may be encoded as a Post system and vice versa—thus demonstrating the equivalence between Turing machines and Post systems, and completing our study of the evidence supporting Turing's thesis.

## Advice for Instructors

Covering the entire content of this book in a one-semester course is possible for students with a strong background in basic set theory and logic, and experience in proving theorems; however, a fast pace is necessary. Many teachers will likely prefer either to cover the material in two semesters or to teach a one-semester course emphasizing some portion of the material.

Chapter 2 reviews the essential mathematical background and introduces the operations on strings used extensively throughout this book; all but Section 2.7 may be skipped for students with prior study in set theory and logic. Other parts of the book that are of secondary importance and may be skipped without loss of continuity include Sections 6.4, 6.5, 7.3, 8.6.2, and 8.7. Chapter 9 develops properties of context-free languages and grammars useful for the study of parsing methods in Chapter 10. (The theorems in Section 9.3, although useful for establishing the level of a language in the Chomsky hierarchy, are not used later in the book.) Chapter 10 itself may be omitted if a treatment of parsing algorithms is not desired.

Sections 13.5, 13.6, and 14.2 contain the detailed developments that establish simulation results in support of Church's thesis. They are included for completeness, and may be treated briefly if time is short.

For a one-semester course on language concepts (in preparation, for example, for the study of program language implementation), Chapters 3, 5, and 8 through 10 should be emphasized. For a one-semester course based on Church's thesis, Chapters 11 through 14 should be covered in depth, using selected material from Chapters 3 through 8 as background.

## Problems and References

Each chapter ends with a selection of Problems. Many of these are designed as exercises to give the student confidence in his understanding of the material and practice in applying procedures developed in the chapter. Others call for the proof of results not proved in the text, or extend, in some way, material developed in the text. These often call for some creativity on the part of the student, and are marked in boldface. Problems marked with an asterisk are more difficult and are included to challenge the student.

A bibliography of books and papers cited in the text appears on pages 584-592. At the end of each chapter, we include remarks on the origin and historical development of the major concepts treated in the chapter. Similar remarks are included in some of the Problems.

## Acknowledgements

We are grateful to Marsha Baker and Anne Rubin, whose typing of (countably) many versions of the manuscript nurtured it from a small set of lecture notes in 1967 to a manuscript four times larger in 1977.

We are indebted to our course instructors over the years who, in their quest for perfection, reproved us for every blemish and error thay could find; on their account, we have reproved many theorems. These people are: John DeTreville, Kennith Dritz, Peter Elias, Irene Greif, D. Austin Henderson, Carl Hewitt, Suhas Patil, and Richard Spann.

Seven senior computer scientists were especially influential in guiding us to the important concepts and showing us, all too frequently, simpler ways of doing things. They are: Manuel Blum, Frederick Hennie, Richard Kain, David Kuck, David Martin, Robert McNaughton, and Albert Meyer. Of these seven, two deserve special note. Professor David Kuck, now of the University of Illinois, shared with Jack Dennis the responsibility for this course when it was instituted in 1965; his influence on the structure of the course and the book was considerable. Professor Robert McNaughton, now of Rensselaer Polytechnic Institute, was a walking encyclopedia of automata theory and formal linguistics; he generously gave of his time and knowledge during the formative stages of this work, and led us to an early appreciation of the research in formal linguistics at Harvard and MIT.

We cannot omit our admiration for Karl Karlstrom, our humble and faithful servant as Senior Editor at Prentice-Hall. His interest in our work began in 1967, when Denning and Dennis agreed to deliver a manuscript the following year. Qualitz, who had instructed the course at MIT several times, rescued the project from oblivion by completing the manuscript and making needed revisions to the work which had languished as the other authors took up other interests. Karl, whose patience and encouragement did not sag for a decade, tells his friends that he knew all along: his secretary meant to type "78", not "68", in the delivery date. Thanks, Karl, for your confidence and support.

PETER J. DENNING
JACK B. DENNIS
JOSEPH E. QUALITZ

## About the Authors

*Peter J. Denning is Professor of Computer Science at Purdue University where his primary research interests are modeling and analysis of computer performance, design of operating systems, memory management and program behavior, data security and protection, secure data communication, fault tolerant software, and parallel computation. His work has led to many publications including the book* Operating Systems Theory *with E. G. Coffman, Jr. He has served the Association for Computing Machinery (ACM) in many official positions, and is very active in editorial work, including serving as Editor-in-Chief of ACM's* Computing Surveys. *Peter Denning was born in New York City, and grew up in Darien, Connecticut. He received the Ph.D degree from MIT in 1968, and joined the Purdue faculty after spending four years as Assistant Professor of Electrical Engineering at Princeton University. He has received two best paper awards, and a teaching award from Princeton. He is an inveterate jogger and wine connoisseur.*

*Jack B. Dennis is Professor of Computer Science and Engineering at MIT where he leads a research group in work on advanced concepts of computer system architecture in the MIT Laboratory for Computer Science. Jack Dennis earned his doctorate from MIT in 1958 for work relating mathematical programming and the theory of electric circuits. Since then he has been involved in developing new course offerings in basic computer science at MIT, in working with a number of successful doctoral research students, and in organizing professional conferences. He was elected Fellow of the Institute of Electrical and Electronic Engineers for his contributions to the design of computer memory systems. He is a New Jersey native and received his early education in Darien, Connecticut. He now resides in Belmont, Massachusetts and enjoys tennis, hiking, and singing with choral groups.*

*Joseph E. Qualitz is a native of Waltham, Massachusetts. He received an SB and SM in Electrical Engineering from MIT in 1972, and a Ph.D in Computer Science in 1975. He served as Instructor in the MIT Department of Electrical Engineering from 1972 to 1975, and in 1973 received a teaching award as outstanding instructor. Dr. Qualitz is currently Chief Computer Engineer of Artisan Industries, Inc., of Waltham, Mass., where he is engaged in the design and implementation of microcomputer development and support systems.*

# Table of Major Theorems

## Chapter 4: Finite-State Machines

**Theorem 4.1:** For each state-assigned machine there exists a similar transition-assigned machine. Conversely, for each transition-assigned machine there exists a similar state-assigned machine.

**Theorem 4.4:** There is an effective procedure for partitioning the states of a finite-state machine into blocks of equivalent states.

**Theorem 4.5:** The state graphs of reduced, connected finite-state machines are isomorphic if and only if the machines are equivalent.

## Chapter 5: Finite-State Languages

**Theorem 5.1:** For each finite-state accepter $\mathbf{M}_n$, one can construct a deterministic finite-state accepter $\mathbf{M}_d$ such that $\mathbf{L}(\mathbf{M}_d) = \mathbf{L}(\mathbf{M}_n)$.

**Theorem 5.2:** For any finite-state accepter **M**, one can construct a right-linear grammer **G** such that $\mathbf{L}(\mathbf{G}) = \mathbf{L}(\mathbf{M})$.

**Theorem 5.3:** For any right-linear grammar **G**, one can construct a finite-state accepter **M** such that $\mathbf{L}(\mathbf{M}) = \mathbf{L}(\mathbf{G})$.

**Theorem 5.5:** Each finite-state accepter recognizes a language that can be described by some regular expression.

**Theorem 5.6:** For any regular expression $\alpha$, one can construct a finite-state accepter $\mathbf{M}$ such that $\mathbf{L(M)} = \mathbf{R}$, where $\mathbf{R}$ is the set described by $\alpha$.

**Theorem 5.7:** The class of finite-state languages is closed under the operations of set union, intersection, complementation, difference, concatenation, closure, and reversal.

**Theorem 5.8:** There is a finite procedure for deciding whether an arbitrary right-linear grammar is ambiguous, and, if so, for finding an ambiguous sentence generated by the grammar.

**Theorem 5.9:** For any regular grammar $\mathbf{G}$, it is possible to construct an unambiguous grammar $\mathbf{G}'$ such that $\mathbf{L(G')} = \mathbf{L(G)}$.

**Theorem 5.10:** Let $\mathbf{L}_1$ and $\mathbf{L}_2$ be arbitrary finite-state languages, and let $\mathbf{G}$ be an arbitrary regular grammar. Then it is decidable whether

1. $\mathbf{L}_1 = \mathbf{L}_2$.
2. $\mathbf{L}_1 = \varnothing$.
3. $\mathbf{L}_1$ is finite; $\mathbf{L}_1$ is infinite.
4. $\mathbf{L}_1 \cap \mathbf{L}_2 = \varnothing$.
5. $\mathbf{L}_1 \subseteq \mathbf{L}_2$.
6. $\mathbf{G}$ is ambiguous.

## Chapter 6: Limitations of Finite Automata

**Theorem 6.1 (Finite-State Language Theorem):** Let $\mathbf{L}$ be a regular set, and suppose that there is an integer $p \geq 0$ such that

$$\mathbf{X} = \{\alpha_1(\alpha_2)^k\alpha_3(\alpha_4)^k\alpha_5 \mid k \geq p\}$$

is contained in $\mathbf{L}$, where $\alpha_1, \ldots, \alpha_5$ are strings with $\alpha_2$ and $\alpha_4$ nonempty. Then there exist strings $\beta_1, \ldots, \beta_5$ such that

$$\mathbf{Y} = \beta_1(\beta_2)^*\beta_3(\beta_4)^*\beta_5$$

is a subset of $\mathbf{L}$, and

$$\beta_1 \in \alpha_1\alpha_2^*$$

$$\beta_2 \in \alpha_2^* - \lambda$$

$$\beta_3 \in \alpha_2^*\alpha_3\alpha_4^*$$

$$\beta_4 \in \alpha_4^* - \lambda$$

$$\beta_5 \in \alpha_4^*\alpha_5$$

**Theorem 6.2:** A language is regular if and only if it is generated by some (nondeterministic) finite-state generator.

**Theorem 6.3:** The transduction of a regular set by a finite-state transducer is a regular set. That is, the class of regular sets on a given alphabet is closed under finite-state transducer mappings.

**Theorem 6.4:** (1) Let $\mathbf{M}$ be an $n$-state deterministic finite-state generator. Then $\mathbf{M}$ generates an ultimately periodic language $\mathbf{L(M)} = \mathbf{T} \cup \tau\rho^*\mathbf{P}$, where $|\tau| + |\rho|$

$\leq n$. (2) Conversely, each ultimately periodic language $\mathbf{L} = \mathbf{T} \cup \tau\rho^*\mathbf{P}$ is generated by some deterministic finite-state generator with no more than $|\tau\rho|$ states; moreover, if $\tau$ and $\rho$ are respectively the basic transient and basic period of $\mathbf{L}$, then no deterministic generator for $\mathbf{L}$ has fewer than $|\tau\rho|$ states.

**Theorem 6.5:** Let $\mathbf{X} \subseteq \mathbf{S}^*$ be an ultimately periodic language, and let $\mathbf{M}_t$ be a deterministic finite-state transducer with input alphabet $\mathbf{S}$. Then the transduction of $\mathbf{X}$ by $\mathbf{M}_t$ is an ultimately periodic language $\mathbf{Y}$. Furthermore, if $\tau$ and $\rho$ are the basic transient and basic period of the input $\mathbf{X}$, and $\alpha$ and $\beta$ are the basic transient and basic period of the output $\mathbf{Y}$, then

$$|\alpha\beta| \leq |\tau| + n_t|\rho|$$

where $n_t$ is the number of states in $\mathbf{M}_t$.

## Chapter 7: Tape Automata

**Theorem 7.1:** The class of regular sets is closed under transduction by a generalized sequential machine.

**Theorem 7.2:** The class of regular sets is closed under inverse transduction by a generalized sequential machine.

**Theorem 7.3:** From any deterministic two-way accepter $\mathbf{M}$, one can construct a finite-state accepter $\mathbf{M}'$ such that $\mathbf{L}(\mathbf{M}') = \mathbf{L}(\mathbf{M})$.

## Chapter 8: Pushdown Automata

**Theorem 8.1:** For any context-free grammar $\mathbf{G}$, one can construct a pushdown accepter $\mathbf{M}$ such that $\mathbf{L}(\mathbf{M}) = \mathbf{L}(\mathbf{G})$. Moreover, the accepting move sequences in $\mathbf{M}$ are in one-to-one correspondence with leftmost derivations in $\mathbf{G}$.

**Theorem 8.2:** For any pushdown accepter $\mathbf{M}$, one can construct a context-free grammar $\mathbf{G}$ such that $\mathbf{L}(\mathbf{G}) = \mathbf{L}(\mathbf{M})$.

**Theorem 8.4:** The class of context-free languages is closed under the operations union, concatenation, closure, reversal, transduction by a generalized sequential machine, and intersection and difference with a regular set.

**Theorem 8.5:** The deterministic context-free languages are a proper subclass of all context-free languages. In particular, the language $\mathbf{L}_{nd} = \{a^k b^m \mid m = k$ or $m = 2k, k \geq 1\}$ is context free but not deterministic.

**Theorem 8.6:** The class of deterministic context-free languages is closed under the operations complement, intersection with a regular set, and difference with a regular set. It is not closed under the operations union, intersection, concatenation, reversal, set closure, or (deterministic) transduction by a finite-state machine.

**Theorem 8.7:** Counting accepters are intermediate in power between finite-state accepters and pushdown accepters. In particular, there is a counting accepter that recognizes the parenthesis language $\mathbf{L}_p$, but no counting accepter that recognizes the double parenthesis language $\mathbf{L}_{dp}$.

**Theorem 8.8:** The class of deterministic context-free languages is a proper subclass of the unambiguous context-free languages.

## Chapter 9: Context-Free Languages

**Theorem 9.1 (Emptiness Test):** For any context-free grammar **G**, one can decide whether $\mathbf{L}(\mathbf{G}, A) = \varnothing$ for any nonterminal symbol $A$ in **G**. In particular, one can decide whether the grammar generates any strings at all [that is, whether $\mathbf{L}(\mathbf{G}) = \mathbf{L}(\mathbf{G}, \Sigma) = \varnothing$].

**Theorem 9.3 (Normal-Form Theorem):** From any context-free grammar, one can construct a strongly equivalent grammar in normal form.

**Theorem 9.4 (Standard Form Theorem):** From any context-free grammar, one can construct a strongly equivalent grammar in standard form.

**Theorem 9.5 (Structure Theorem):** Let $\mathbf{G} = (\mathbf{N}, \mathbf{T}, \mathbf{P}, \Sigma)$ be a well-formed context-free grammar. For any $A$ in $\mathbf{N} \cup \{\Sigma\}$, $\mathbf{L}(\mathbf{G}, A)$ is infinite if and only if **G** permits the following derivations for some nonterminal $B$:

1. $A \overset{*}{\Longrightarrow} \alpha B \beta,\ \alpha, \beta \in \mathbf{T}^*$.
2. $B \overset{*}{\Longrightarrow} \varphi B \psi,\ \varphi\psi \in \mathbf{T}^* - \boldsymbol{\lambda}$.
3. $B \overset{*}{\Longrightarrow} \sigma, \quad \sigma \in \mathbf{T}^* - \boldsymbol{\lambda}$.

**Theorem 9.6:** For any context-free grammar **G**, one can decide whether $\mathbf{L}(\mathbf{G})$ is finite or infinite.

**Theorem 9.7 (Pumping Lemma):** If **L** is a context-free language, there exists a positive integer $p$ with the following properties: whenever $\omega$ is in **L** and $|\omega| > p$, there exist strings $\alpha$, $\varphi$, $\sigma$, $\psi$, and $\beta$, with $\varphi\psi$ and $\sigma$ nonempty and $|\varphi\sigma\psi| \leq p$, such that $\omega = \alpha\varphi\sigma\psi\beta$ and $\alpha\varphi^k\sigma\psi^k\beta$ is in **L** for all $k \geq 0$.

**Theorem 9.8:** The class of context-free languages is properly contained in the class of context-sensitive languages. In particular, $\mathbf{L}_{dm} = \{a^n b^n c^n \mid n \geq 1\}$ is context sensitive but not context free.

**Theorem 9.9 (Self-embedding Theorem):** A context-free language is nonregular if and only if every grammar generating the language is self-embedding.

## Chapter 10: Syntax Analysis

**Theorem 10.2:** A context-free language is deterministic if and only if it is generated by a generalized precedence grammar.

**Theorem 10.3:** Given any context-free grammar **G**, one can determine, for any $k \geq 0$, whether **G** is an $LR(k)$ grammar.

**Theorem 10.4:** (1) Every deterministic context-free language is generated by some $LR(1)$ grammar. (2) Every $LR(k)$ language is deterministic.

## Chapter 11: Turing Machines

**Theorem 11.1:** The domain of the relation realized by any nondeterministic Turing machine is a Turing-recognizable language.

**Theorem 11.2:** The class of Turing-recognizable languages properly includes the class of context-free languages.

**Theorem 11.3:** One can construct a universal Turing machine **U** that realizes a function

$$f_{\mathbf{U}}: \mathbf{A}^* \longrightarrow \mathbf{A}^*$$

such that for any Turing machine **M** with tape alphabet **T** and any string $\omega \in \mathbf{T}^*$, we have

$$f_{\mathbf{U}}(D(\mathbf{M}) \# T(\omega)) = \begin{cases} C(\alpha) & \text{if } \mathbf{M} \text{ has a halted computation } \alpha_0 \Longrightarrow \alpha \\ \text{undefined} & \text{otherwise} \end{cases}$$

where $\alpha_0 = (\lambda, q_I, \#, \omega)$, and $D(\mathbf{M})$, $T(\omega)$, and $C(\alpha)$ are specific encodings of $\mathbf{M}$, $\omega$, and $\alpha$ in the finite alphabet **A**.

**Theorem 11.4:** A set $\mathbf{X} \subseteq \mathbf{N}$ is Turing enumerable if and only if **X** is the domain of a Turing computable function.

**Theorem 11.5:** A set $\mathbf{X} \subseteq \mathbf{N}$ is Turing semidecidable if and only if it is Turing enumerable.

**Theorem 11.6:** A set is Turing recognizable if and only if it is Turing enumerable.

**Theorem 11.7:** There exists a Turing computable function

$$W: \mathbf{N} \times \mathbf{N} \longrightarrow \mathbf{N}$$

such that for all $z, x, y$

$$W(z, x) = y$$

if and only if machine $\mathbf{M}_z$ in an enumeration of Turing machines computes

$$f_z(x) = y$$

## Chapter 12: Unsolvable Problems

**Theorem 12.1:** The halting problem for Turing machines is unsolvable.

**Theorem 12.2:** The busy-beaver function is noncomputable.

**Theorem 12.3:** The word problem for type 0 grammars is unsolvable.

**Theorem 12.4:** The correspondence problem is unsolvable.

**Theorem 12.5:** The problem of deciding, for arbitrary context-free languages **L** and **L′**, whether **L** ∩ **L′** is empty (or infinite) is unsolvable.

**Theorem 12.6:** The problem of deciding, for an arbitrary context-free language **L**, whether $\mathbf{L}^c$ is empty (or infinite) is unsolvable.

**Theorem 12.7:** There is no effective procedure for deciding whether a given context-free language is regular.

**Theorem 12.8:** There is no effective procedure for determining whether a given context-free language is deterministic.

**Theorem 12.9:** There is no effective procedure for deciding, given any context-free grammar **G**, whether **G** is ambiguous.

**Theorem 12.10:** The problem of deciding whether **L(G)** = **L(G′)** for arbitrary context-free grammars **G** and **G′** is unsolvable.

## Chapter 13: Recursive Functions

**Theorem 13.1:** The $\mu$-recursive functions, the multiple-recursive functions, and the Turing-computable functions are equivalent classes of functions.

**Theorem 13.2:** Let $\mathbf{A} \subseteq \mathbf{N}$ and $\mathbf{A}^c = \mathbf{N} - \mathbf{A}$. Then:
(1) **A** is recursive if and only if $\mathbf{A}^c$ is recursive.
(2) **A** is recursive only if **A** is r.e.
(3) **A** is recursive just if both **A** and $\mathbf{A}^c$ are r.e.

**Theorem 13.3:** A set **A** is recursively enumerable if and only if **A** is the domain of a Turing-computable function. Equivalently, **A** is recursively enumerable if and only if **A** is the domain of a (partial) recursive function.

**Theorem 13.4:** The class of total recursive functions cannot be effectively enumerated.

**Theorem 13.5:** No recursively enumerable class of recursive sets contains every recursive set.

## Chapter 14: Post Systems

**Theorem 14.1:** Post systems and Turing machines are equivalent representations of effective computability. That is, the deductions of a given Post system can be represented as the computations of some Turing machine, and the computations of a given Turing machine can be represented as the deductions of some Post system.

# 1

# *Introduction*

## 1.1 Information Machines

In the past, much of man's intellectual curiosity focused on the transformation and utilization of energy. With the advent of the digital computer, his attention has shifted toward the utilization of information. Switching circuits, telephone exchanges, computers—all are examples of *information machines*. Since these machines have played a role in nearly all facets of human life (and are sure to play an increasingly important role in the future), a thorough understanding of information machines and the computations that they can perform has motivated workers in many diverse fields. The field of computer science is an outgrowth of their studies.

The remarkable versatility of the modern computer has raised questions of the ultimate power of information machines: What, if any, are the bounds on the tasks these machines can perform? To understand the limitations of information machines, we study two principal abstractions of these devices: the abstract machine, or *automaton*, and the abstract language. Automata have been used to model a variety of practical systems, ranging from digital circuits to the human nervous system, as well as mathematical systems such as logic systems and the recursive functions. Abstract languages have been used to model programming languages, simple subsets of the natural languages, and the operation sequences of physical machines. A study of the relationship between abstract machines and languages provides insights about both kinds of models, and aids our understanding of practical information machines and their computations.

Our study begins with the simplest abstract models and proceeds toward models of increasingly greater capability. The more elementary models have important application to computer programming languages and digital systems; the most powerful models enable us to characterize the classes of problems realizable machines can hope to solve. The methods of our study are set theory and mathematical logic; the objectives of our study are an understanding of these specific abstractions, and a familiarity with the mathematical techniques needed to study arbitrary formal models.

## 1.2 Abstract Machines and Algorithms

The notion of an abstract information machine, or automaton, was conceived by A. M. Turing [1936] for the purpose of exploring limits on man's ability to formalize methods of solving problems. He proposed that one take, as a precise definition of the term "algorithm," a procedure that can be carried out by a specific type of automaton that has come to be known as a *Turing machine.* Since the publication of Turing's work, many other mathematical systems, such as the production systems of Post [1936], the logical systems of Church [1936], and the recursive functions of Kleene [1936], have been shown to yield concepts of algorithm equivalent to Turing's concept. That all these independent studies have produced essentially the same results is a persuasive argument for what is often called *Church's thesis: The computing power of the Turing machine represents a fundamental limit on the capability of realizable computing devices.*

The Turing machine may be viewed as an abstract model of a physical machine having an infinite number of functionally distinguishable *states of existence.* Although the number of states in an electronic computer is finite, this number is generally so large that the Turing machine is a suitable model of its computational power. There are many other systems, however, for which the Turing machine is far too powerful a model. For these systems, we must study models that more closely approximate their capabilities. Two such models, the finite-state machine and the pushdown automaton, have proved to be suitable for a variety of practical systems. An understanding of these important types of automata, together with that of the Turing machine, will motivate much of our study.

## 1.3 Abstract Languages

Linguists have long searched for adequate formal grammars of natural languages to help explain the remarkable ability of human beings to interpret sentences they have never before heard. While their studies have thus far failed to produce grammars of natural languages, they have provided us with considerable knowledge about classes of abstract languages.

What is an abstract language? Workers concerned with the relation of languages to automata have found it useful to view a language as a collection of *sentences* satisfying given properties or construction rules; the sentences themselves are finite sequences of symbols chosen from a set called the *alphabet* of the language. A language might be, for example, the collection of all computer programs properly written according to the rules of some programming language. Or a language might be as simple as a given sequence of 0's and 1's.

Interest in the relationship between abstract languages and automata began with an important paper by Kleene in 1956, in which he neatly and precisely characterized the languages in which membership of a sentence can be decided by a finite-state machine. Since the time of Kleene's work, persons concerned with the formal definitions of programming languages and the methods of specifying processing programs for these languages have joined in the study of these relationships.

As a result of these studies, much has been learned about the ability of automata to recognize, generate, and translate abstract languages. The work of Noam Chomsky, published in 1959, established the relation of abstract language classes to a hierarchy of abstract machine types. This work has guided the organization of this book.

## 1.4 Accepters, Generators, and Transducers

The relationships between abstract languages and machines are established through a study of three types of automata: accepters, generators, and transducers. Figure 1.1 shows a language *accepter*. The symbols of the sequence

$$s(1)s(2)\ldots s(i)\ldots s(t)$$

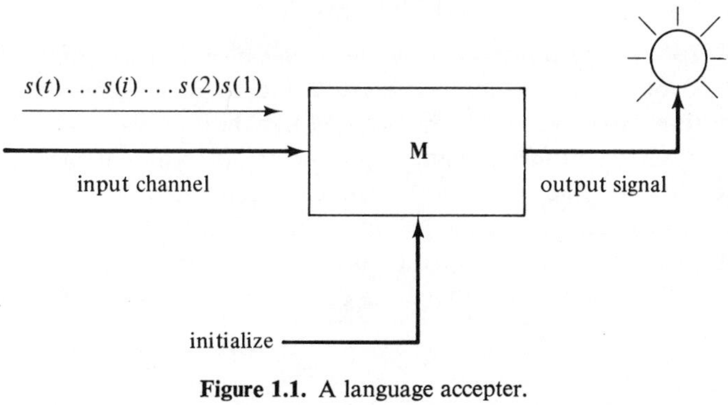


**Figure 1.1.** A language accepter.

are presented sequentially to a machine **M**, which responds to each symbol with a binary signal (shown in the figure as a lamp, which **M** may turn ON or OFF). The symbols are chosen from a finite set known as the *input alphabet* of **M**, and we suppose that **M** is placed in a predetermined state of existence (by the *initialize* input) before an input string is presented. In addition, we suppose that the machine operates *deterministically*; that is, its response depends uniquely on its initial state and the input sequence presented.

The machine **M** will divide the set of all possible sequences of symbols (sentences) into two classes, according to the indication of the lamp just after the last symbol of a sequence is presented:

1. Those sentences to which **M** responds with the lamp ultimately ON.
2. Those sentences to which **M** responds with the lamp ultimately OFF.

We say that **M** *accepts* each sentence in the first class, and *rejects* each sentence in the second. If **M** accepts precisely the sentences of some language **L**, we say that **M** *recognizes* **L**.

Figure 1.2 shows a language *generator*. When the generator **M** is started

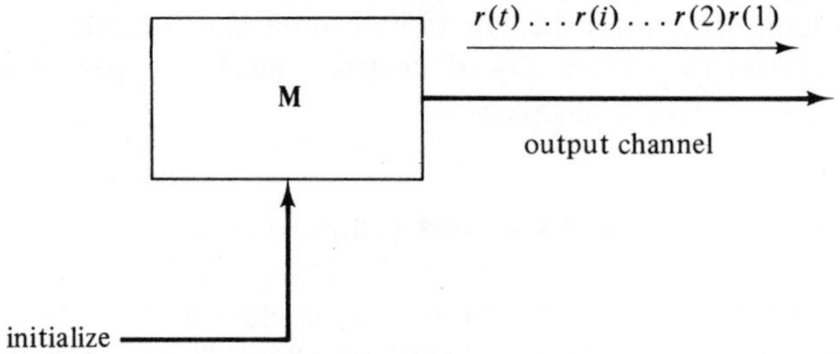


**Figure 1.2.** A language generator.

from its initial state, it emits a sequence of symbols

$$r(1)r(2) \ldots r(i) \ldots r(t)$$

selected from a set known as its *output alphabet*. Of course, if **M** produces the same sequence each time it is started, the language generated is rather uninteresting. However, we might allow **M** to exhibit *nondeterministic* behavior (e.g., to act according to chance), producing different sequences each time it is operated. We then take as the language generated by **M** the set of all different sequences the machine might ever produce.

Abstract machines that operate as *transducers* are of interest in connection with the translation of languages. In Figure 1.3, transducer **M** produces a sentence

$$r(1)r(2) \ldots r(n)$$

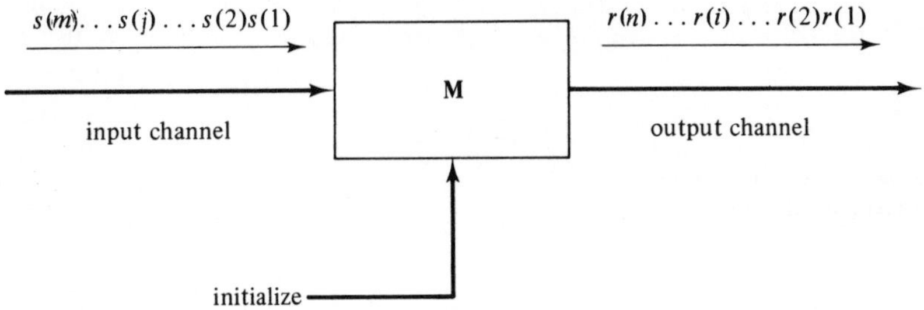


**Figure 1.3.** A language transducer.

in response to presentation of a sentence

$$s(1)s(2)\ldots s(m)$$

Such a machine (operating deterministically) translates each sentence of an input language into a specific sentence of an output language. If **L** is the input language of **M**, the set of sentences produced by **M** in response to sentences in **L** is the *transduction* of **L** by **M**.

## 1.5 Hierarchy of Abstract Machines and Languages

A hierarchy of automata and the corresponding hierarchy of language classes that they define are shown in Figure 1.4. (Included in the figure are references to the chapters in this book in which the principal discussion of each class of languages or machines is to be found.) In this pairing of machine and language classes, one would expect a more powerful machine model to be associated with a less restricted class of languages, and this is indeed the case.

The topics are studied as indicated in the figure, starting with finite-state machines and regular languages and progressing toward more powerful machines and less restricted languages. At each level, we discover problems or languages beyond the power of the machine of that level. Except for the level of the Turing machine, there is a natural generalization in each case that leads to the next higher level of machines and languages. For Turing machines, no generalization has been devised that extends their capabilities. Nevertheless, there is yet a rich class of problems beyond the power of Turing machines.

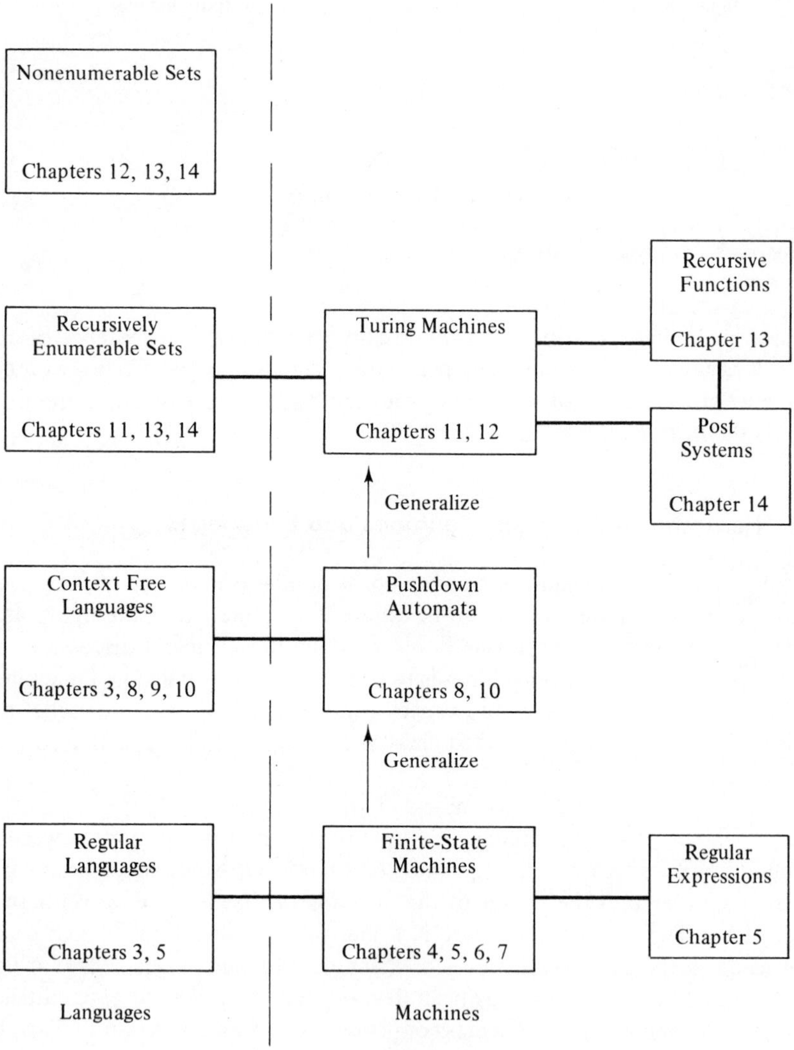


**Figure 1.4.** Hierarchy of abstract machines and languages.

# 2

# *Logic, Set Theory, and Languages*

The study of abstract machines and languages attempts to model certain real-world situations with mathematical systems. By formulating precise statements about properties of interest and relating them through rigorous deduction, mathematical systems can be used to augment one's judgment of the computing capabilities of machines and the descriptive abilities of languages.

The branches of mathematics relevant to our subject are logic, set theory, and algebra: logic provides a precise framework for proving statements, set theory provides a formalism in which discrete systems may be described with precision, and algebra gives us methods for characterizing relationships among sets. This chapter is a brief introduction to the essential concepts from these areas of mathematics.

## 2.1 Propositional Logic

### 2.1.1 Propositions

Rigorous deduction is the process of inferring the validity of one statement from the assumed validity of other statements. By a *statement*, or *proposition*, we mean a declarative sentence that can be classified either true or false. The following are examples of propositions:

1. The integer 8 is greater than the integer 5.
2. The integer 3 is equal to the integer 4.

3. $x$ is a letter in the alphabet **A**.
4. The sentence $\omega$ contains the letter $x$.
5. The sentence $\omega$ is accepted by the machine **M**.

With each proposition we can associate one of the two *truth values* {*true*, *false*} according to the *interpretation* of the proposition in the mathematical system to which it pertains. According to the usual interpretation of integers, proposition 1 is true, but proposition 2 is false. The truth of proposition 3 depends on what symbols constitute the alphabet **A**. The truth of propositions 4 and 5 depends on an understanding of such terms as "sentence" and "machine."

Propositions such as the following are called compound propositions:

6. (5 is less than 8) and (8 is less than 9) implies (5 is less than 9).
7. (2 equals 3) if and only if it is not true that (2 is greater than 3) or (3 is greater than 2).

They are formed from *primitive*, or *atomic*, propositions by means of the connecting words or phrases *and*, *or*, *implies*, *if and only if*, and *it is not true that*. We use the following notation for these connectives ($p$ and $q$ stand for arbitrary propositions):

| Formal notation | Informal meaning |
|---|---|
| $p \vee q$ | *p or q* |
| $p \wedge q$ | *p and q* |
| $p \Rightarrow q$ | *p implies q*, or *if p then q* |
| $p \Leftrightarrow q$ | *p if and only if q*, or *p just if q* |
| $\neg p$ | *not p* |

Truth values are assigned to compound propositions based on the truth values of their constituents, according to the following *truth tables:*

| $p$ | $q$ | $p \vee q$ | $p \wedge q$ | $p \Rightarrow q$ | $p \Leftrightarrow q$ |
|---|---|---|---|---|---|
| T | T | T | T | T | T |
| T | F | T | F | F | F |
| F | T | T | F | T | F |
| F | F | F | F | T | T |

| $p$ | $\neg p$ |
|---|---|
| T | F |
| F | T |

The assignment of truth values to the propositions $p \vee q$, $p \wedge q$, and $\neg p$ corresponds to the usual interpretation of the words *or*, *and*, and *not*.

The assignment of truth values to the proposition $p \Rightarrow q$ deserves explanation. If $q$ is true, then it is reasonable to say that $p \Rightarrow q$ is true independent of the truth of $p$; that is, (*true* $\Rightarrow$ *true*) and (*false* $\Rightarrow$ *true*) are both true propositions. It is also reasonable to say that (*false* $\Rightarrow$ *false*) is a true proposition. However, it is not intuitively reasonable to say that (*true* $\Rightarrow$ *false*) is a true proposition.

The assignment of truth values to the proposition $p \Leftrightarrow q$ follows from the usual understanding that $p \Leftrightarrow q$ has the same meaning as $(p \Rightarrow q) \wedge (q \Rightarrow p)$; that is, we may assert that $p \Leftrightarrow q$ is true just when $p$ and $q$ agree in truth value.

The truth value of any compound proposition can be determined from the truth values of its component propositions through repeated use of the truth tables.

**Example 2.1:** Let $p$, $q$, $r$, and $s$ be primitive propositions with truth values

$$p = \textit{true} \qquad r = \textit{false}$$
$$q = \textit{false} \qquad s = \textit{true}$$

and consider the proposition

$$p \wedge \neg(q \Rightarrow (r \vee s))$$

From the truth table $(r \vee s)$ is *true*, so that $q \Rightarrow (r \vee s)$ is *true*. Then $\neg(q \Rightarrow (r \vee s))$ is *false*, and the entire proposition is *false*.

If $p$ and $q$ are compound propositions and $p \Leftrightarrow q$ is true for all choices of truth values for the primitive propositions composing $p$ and $q$, then we say that $p$ and $q$ are *equivalent* propositions.

The reader should verify that the two compound propositions

$$p \wedge (q \vee r)$$

and

$$(p \wedge q) \vee (p \wedge r)$$

are equivalent by evaluating both for each of the eight choices of validity of $p$, $q$, and $r$. Thus it follows that the proposition

$$p \wedge (q \vee r) \Leftrightarrow (p \wedge q) \vee (p \wedge r)$$

is true for all truth values of $p$, $q$, and $r$. Such a proposition, which is always true regardless of the choice of truth values for its primitive components, is called a *tautology*. Similarly, a proposition that is always false, regardless of the choice of truth values for its primitive components, is called a *contradiction*. For example, $p \vee (\neg p)$ is a tautology, and $p \wedge (\neg p)$ is a contradiction. We note that for any tautology $p$, $\neg p$ is a contradiction.

A conventional set of precedence rules is often assumed to govern the interpretation of unparenthesized compound propositions. In order of decreasing precedence, the logical connectives are

$$\neg, \wedge, \vee, \Rightarrow, \Leftrightarrow$$

Thus all subexpressions of the form $\neg p$ are to be evaluated first, then expressions of the form $p \wedge q$, and so on. To avoid confustion, logical expressions in this book are written with parentheses whenever they might otherwise be misinterpreted.

### 2.1.2 Predicates

A predicate is a statement that contains one or more *variables,* so that its truth value depends on the values of the variables. For example, let $x$ be an integer, and consider the predicate

$$p(x) = (x < 4) \wedge (x > 2)$$

This predicate is true if and only if $x = 3$. When values are substituted for variables in a predicate, it becomes a proposition. For example,

$$p(2) = (2 < 4) \wedge (2 > 2)$$

is a proposition, which is false. A predicate, then, stands for a collection of propositions, one for each combination of variable values. For example, the predicate

$$p(x, y, z) = (x < y) \wedge (y > z)$$

represents 1000 distinct propositions if $x$, $y$, and $z$ are each restricted to be one of the integers 0, 1, . . . , 9. If $x$, $y$, and $z$ may be any integers, $p(x, y, z)$ represents an infinity of propositions.

A predicate such as

$$(x > y) \Rightarrow (x \neq y)$$

which becomes a true proposition for every choice of integer values for the variables, is said to be a *valid* predicate.

A predicate of one variable is sometimes called a *property*. If $p(x)$ is true, then we say that $x$ has the property $p$; if $p(x)$ is false, then we say that $x$ does not have the property $p$.

Compound predicates may be formed from primitive predicates in exactly the same way that compound propositions are formed from primitive propositions. In addition, propositions may be formed from predicates through the following constructions†:

†The phrase "for all $x$, $p(x)$" is often abbreviated $\forall x, p(x)$, the symbol $\forall$ being called the *universal quantifier*. The phrase "for some $x$, $p(x)$" is often abbreviated $\exists x, p(x)$, the symbol $\exists$ being called the *existential quantifier*. In this book we avoid the use of these symbols, preferring instead to use the English phrases.

1. For all $x$, $p(x)$.
2. For some $x$, $p(x)$.
   There exists $x$ such that $p(x)$.

Proposition 1 is true if and only if the predicate $p(x)$ becomes a true proposition for every choice of the variable $x$. Proposition 2 is true if any only if there is at least one choice for $x$ that makes the predicate $p(x)$ a true proposition. These propositions are closely related to each other. In fact, the proposition

$$(\text{for all } x, p(x)) \Leftrightarrow \neg(\text{for some } x, \neg p(x))$$

is a tautology.

### 2.1.3 Proofs

The *axiomatic method* is familiar to us from the study of plane geometry. We start with a set of *axioms* (propositions that we agree to accept as true without proof) and some *rules of inference*. The rules of inference specify how the truth of new propositions, *theorems*, can be deduced from the axioms and other theorems already established. By a *logic* we mean a particular set of axioms together with the appropriate rules of inference.

A *proof* of a proposition $p_k$ in a logic is a sequence of propositions

$$p_1, p_2, \ldots, p_k$$

in which each proposition $p_i$ is an axiom or else may be deduced from propositions among $p_1, p_2, \ldots, p_{i-1}$ through the use of some rule of inference in the logic. A *theorem* in a logic is any proposition (including any axiom) for which the logic provides a proof.

The rules of inference most frequently used in proving theorems are discussed below. Illustrations of these methods of proof will be seen in the remaining sections of this chapter and throughout the book.

1. *Direct proof:* If the two propositions (premises) $p$ and $(p \Rightarrow q)$ are theorems, we may deduce that the proposition $q$ is also a theorem. This fundamental rule of inference is called *modus ponens* by logicians.

2. *Proof by contradiction:* To establish the truth of proposition $q$ as a consequence of premise $p$, we may hypothesize that $q$ is false and deduce that $p$ is false. The rule of inference used is that from theorems $p$ and $(\neg q \Rightarrow \neg p)$ we may deduce the theorem $q$.

3. *Conjunction:* If statements $p$ and $q$ are theorems, we may conclude that $p \wedge q$ is a theorem.

4. *Proof by cases:* A proof may consist of separate arguments that deduce the theorem from several hypotheses, one of which must always be true. This method of proof is based on the tautology $(a \Rightarrow q) \wedge (b \Rightarrow q) \Rightarrow (a \vee b \Rightarrow q)$.

5. *If and only if proof:* A theorem of the form $p \Leftrightarrow q$ ($p$ if and only if $q$) is usually established by proving $p \Rightarrow q$ and $q \Rightarrow p$ separately, and using the tautology $(p \Rightarrow q) \wedge (q \Rightarrow p) \Rightarrow (p \Leftrightarrow q)$. In such a proof, the deduction $q \Rightarrow p$ is called the *if part*, and the deduction $p \Rightarrow q$ is called the *only if part*.

6. *Proof by induction:* Induction is a method for proving propositions of the form

$$\text{for each integer } x, p(x)$$

where the integers are the objects 0, 1, 2, . . . . Such a proposition asserts the truth of each of the propositions

$$p(0), p(1), p(2), \ldots$$

The rule of inference for induction is the following:

The validity of a predicate $p(x)$ for all integers $x = 0, 1, 2, \ldots$ may be deduced from the two propositions

***Basis:*** $p(0)$

***Induction:*** for each integer $x$, $(p(x) \Rightarrow p(x + 1))$.

Induction is essential for establishing the validity of predicates that represent infinite sequences of propositions.

## 2.2 Set Theory

For the study of abstract machines, we need to represent formally such entities as the different conditions of existence of a machine, the instructions or rules of behavior that govern its operation, and the classes of inputs that elicit certain behavior. For the study of languages, we need to formalize the notions of alphabet, sentence, and grammar. Each is a collection of objects conveniently represented using the concepts and notation of set theory.

### 2.2.1 Basic Concepts

Intuitively, a *set* is an arbitrary collection of objects. We use the boldface capital letters **A**, **B**, **C**, . . . to designate sets.

There are three basic concepts in set theory: *membership*, *extension*, and *abstraction*.

*Membership* is a relation that holds between a set and an object. We interpret the proposition

$$x \in \mathbf{A}$$

to mean "the object $x$ is a *member* of the set **A**", or "the object $x$ is an *element* of the set **A**", or "$x$ *belongs to* **A**". The negation of this assertion is written

$$x \notin \mathbf{A}$$

as an abbreviation for the proposition $\neg(x \in \mathbf{A})$.

One way to specify a set is to list its elements. For example, the set

$$\mathbf{A} = \{a, b, c\}$$

consists of three elements. For this set **A**, it is true that $a \in \mathbf{A}$ and that $d \notin \mathbf{A}$. Sets may also contain other sets as members. For example, let

$$\mathbf{A} = \{a, b\}$$
$$\mathbf{B} = \{a\}$$
$$\mathbf{C} = \{\mathbf{A}, \mathbf{B}\}$$

The set **C** has sets **A** and **B** as members. That is,

$$\mathbf{C} = \{\{a, b\}, \{a\}\}$$

In this case we cannot assert that $a \in \mathbf{C}$, but we can assert that $\{a\} \in \mathbf{C}$. That is, $\{a\} \neq a$. This distinction between the *object* $a$ and the *singleton set* $\{a\}$ is important.

The concept of *extension* is that two sets are identical if and only if they contain the same elements. Thus we write $\mathbf{A} = \mathbf{B}$ to mean

$$\text{for all } x, (x \in \mathbf{A}) \Leftrightarrow (x \in \mathbf{B})$$

This concept has two important consequences. First, it means that the elements of a set are distinct. Thus $\{a, a\}$ is not a set. Second, it means that there is no ordering of the elements of a set. Thus $\{a, b\} = \{b, a\}$.

In most cases, it is either inconvenient or impossible (in the case of infinite sets) to list the elements of a set explicitly. An alternative is to specify a set as being all objects that satisfy a given predicate. If $p(x)$ is a predicate, we write

$$\{x \mid p(x)\}$$

to mean "the set of all objects $x$ such that $p(x)$," or "the set of all objects having the property $p$." The notation $\mathbf{A} = \{x \mid p(x)\}$ stands for the proposition

$$\text{for all } x, (x \in \mathbf{A}) \Leftrightarrow p(x)$$

This proposition expresses the concept of *abstraction*: each property defines a set, and each set defines a property.

It should be noted that the phrases "of all objects" and "for all $x$" can lead to difficulty. For example, assuming that the sign $>$ represents a relationship among integers, the statement

$$\mathbf{A} = \{x \mid x > 8\}$$

says nothing about membership in **A** for objects $x$ that are not integers. To avoid these difficulties, we usually confine attention to a *universe* **U** of objects (the set of all integers, say), which is either explicitly stated or is understood from the context of the discussion. If restriction to a portion of the universe **U** is required, we shall use the notation

$$\mathbf{A} = \{x \in \mathbf{B} \mid p(x)\}$$

to mean

$$\text{for all } x \in \mathbf{U},\ (x \in \mathbf{A}) \Leftrightarrow ((x \in \mathbf{B}) \wedge p(x))$$

The theory of sets built on the intuitive concepts of membership, extension, and abstraction is known as *intuitive set theory*. As an axiomatic theory of sets, it is not entirely satisfactory, because the principle of abstraction leads to contradictions when applied to certain simple predicates. In illustration, consider the following well-known paradox: "In our village, the barber shaves just those men who do not shave themselves." Does the barber shave himself? If we assume so, we contradict the statement since it asserts that the barber shaves only those men who do not shave themselves. If we assume not, we contradict the statement since it asserts that the barber shaves all those men who do not shave themselves.

In terms of the intuitive set theory, we can express the paradox formally as follows: Let $p(\mathbf{X})$ be the predicate

$$p(\mathbf{X}) = (\mathbf{X} \notin \mathbf{X})$$

This predicate represents a true proposition for each set **X** that is not a member of itself. Let **R** be the set defined by this predicate according to the principle of abstraction:

$$\mathbf{R} = \{\mathbf{X} \mid p(\mathbf{X})\}$$

Is $p(\mathbf{R})$ true? That is, is **R** a member of **R**? If so, we conclude that $p(\mathbf{R})$ is false, and thus that **R** is not a member of **R**. If not, we conclude that $p(\mathbf{R})$ is true, and thus that **R** is a member of **R**.

This contradiction is the famous *Russell's paradox*, and exposes the difficulty implicit in assuming the existence of sets such as the set **R** defined above. Although formulations of set theory have been devised to remove the contradictions present in intuitive set theory, they are complex. Fortunately, the simpler formulation presented here is sufficient for our objectives.

### 2.2.2 Inclusion

An important relation among sets is that of *inclusion*. If each element of a set **A** is also an element of a set **B**, we write

$$\mathbf{A} \subseteq \mathbf{B} \quad \text{or equivalently} \quad \mathbf{B} \supseteq \mathbf{A}$$

which stands for the proposition

$$\text{for all } x,\ (x \in \mathbf{A}) \Rightarrow (x \in \mathbf{B})$$

In this case we say that **B** *contains* **A**, or **B** *includes* **A**, or **A** *is a subset of* **B**. If

$$\mathbf{A} \subseteq \mathbf{B} \quad \text{but} \quad \mathbf{A} \neq \mathbf{B}$$

then **B** contains at least one element that is not in **A**. In this case we write

$$\mathbf{A} \subset \mathbf{B}$$

and say that **A** *is a proper subset of* **B**. The idea of set inclusion is suggested pictorially in Figure 2.1.

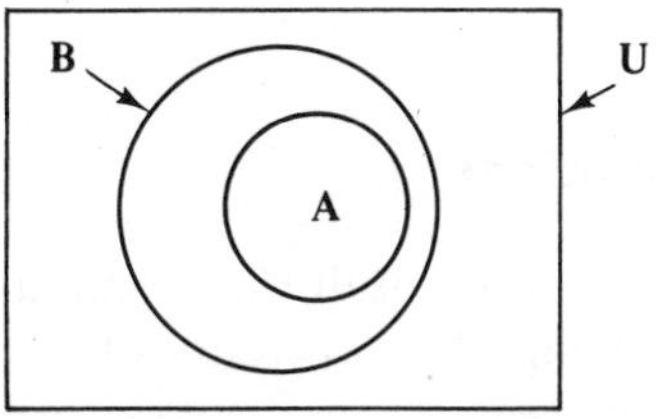


**Figure 2.1.** Inclusion.

Among the properties of the inclusion relation are the following:

1. $\mathbf{A} \subseteq \mathbf{A}$.
2. $\mathbf{A} \subseteq \mathbf{B}$ and $\mathbf{B} \subseteq \mathbf{C}$ implies $\mathbf{A} \subseteq \mathbf{C}$.
3. $\mathbf{A} \subseteq \mathbf{B}$ and $\mathbf{B} \subseteq \mathbf{A}$ implies $\mathbf{A} = \mathbf{B}$.

Property 3 formulates, in terms of the inclusion relation, a method of proving that two sets are equal. That is, to show $\mathbf{A} = \mathbf{B}$, we may show that $\mathbf{A} \subseteq \mathbf{B}$ and $\mathbf{B} \subseteq \mathbf{A}$.

The reader should be careful to distinguish the concepts of membership and inclusion. For example, if **A** is a set of integers, it is true that $\mathbf{A} \subseteq \mathbf{A}$ but not that $\mathbf{A} \in \mathbf{A}$.

Now consider the set **B** defined by a predicate $p(x)$ applied to the elements of some set **A**:

$$\mathbf{B} = \{x \in \mathbf{A} \mid p(x)\}$$

When $p(x)$ is a tautology, $\mathbf{B} = \mathbf{A}$. When $p(x)$ is a contradiction, **B** must be a set that contains no elements. By the principle of extension, there can be only such set; we call it the *empty set* and denote it by $\varnothing$.

Since the set **A** in the discussion above is arbitrary, we have shown that every set has at least two subsets, itself and the empty set. That is, if **A** is any set, then

$$\mathbf{A} \subseteq \mathbf{A} \quad \text{and} \quad \varnothing \subseteq \mathbf{A}$$

are true propositions.

The set of all subsets of a given set **A** is known as the *power set* of **A**, and is denoted by $\mathcal{P}(\mathbf{A})$:

$$\mathcal{P}(\mathbf{A}) = \{\mathbf{B} \mid \mathbf{B} \subseteq \mathbf{A}\}$$

For example, if $\mathbf{A} = \{a, b, c\}$, then

$$\mathcal{P}(\mathbf{A}) = \{\varnothing, \{a\}, \{b\}, \{c\}, \{a, b\}, \{a, c\}, \{b, c\}, \{a, b, c\}\}$$

When $\mathbf{A}$ is finite and contains $n$ elements, the power set $\mathcal{P}(\mathbf{A})$ contains $2^n$ elements (hence the term "power set"). To see this, consider how an arbitrary subset $\mathbf{B}$ may be formed from members of $\mathbf{A}$: for each $x \in \mathbf{A}$ there are two possibilities; $x$ is either chosen or not chosen as a member of $\mathbf{B}$. With $n$ elements in $\mathbf{A}$, there are $2^n$ ways to choose elements for $\mathbf{B}$; therefore, $\mathbf{A}$ has $2^n$ distinct subsets. For this reason, some authors use the notation $2^{\mathbf{A}}$ for the power set $\mathcal{P}(\mathbf{A})$.

### 2.2.3 Set Operations

The previous section dealt with relations between existing sets. We now introduce several important operations that may be used to specify new sets in terms of existing sets.

The *union* of two sets $\mathbf{A}$ and $\mathbf{B}$ is

$$\mathbf{A} \cup \mathbf{B} = \{x \mid (x \in \mathbf{A}) \vee (x \in \mathbf{B})\}$$

and consists of those elements in at least one of $\mathbf{A}$ and $\mathbf{B}$. Occasionally, we require the union of several sets. If $\mathbf{A}_1, \ldots, \mathbf{A}_n$ constitute a family of sets, their union is

$$\bigcup_{i=1}^{n} \mathbf{A}_i = \mathbf{A}_1 \cup \ldots \cup \mathbf{A}_n = \{x \mid x \in \mathbf{A}_i \text{ for some } i, 1 \leq i \leq n\}$$

The idea of union is suggested by the shaded area in Figure 2.2.

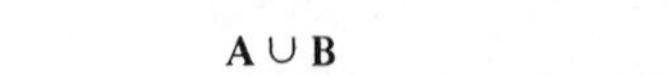

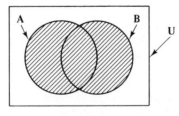

**Figure 2.2.** Union.

The *intersection* of two sets $\mathbf{A}$ and $\mathbf{B}$ is

$$\mathbf{A} \cap \mathbf{B} = \{x \mid (x \in \mathbf{A}) \wedge (x \in \mathbf{B})\}$$

and consists of those elements common to $\mathbf{A}$ and $\mathbf{B}$. The intersection of a family of sets is

$$\bigcap_{i=1}^{n} \mathbf{A}_i = \mathbf{A}_1 \cap \ldots \cap \mathbf{A}_n = \{x \mid x \in \mathbf{A}_i \text{ for all } i, 1 \leq i \leq n\}$$

If two sets have no elements in common, then

$$\mathbf{A} \cap \mathbf{B} = \varnothing$$

and we say that **A** and **B** are *disjoint*. The idea of intersection is suggested by the shaded area in Figure 2.3.

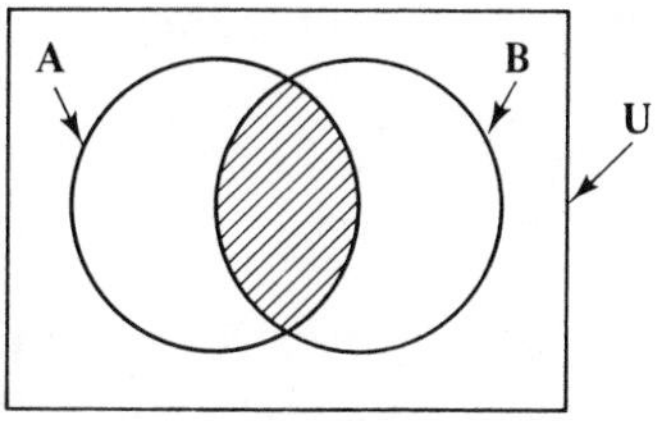


**Figure 2.3.** Intersection.

The *difference* of sets **A** and **B** is defined as

$$\mathbf{A} - \mathbf{B} = \{x \in \mathbf{A} \mid x \notin \mathbf{B}\}$$

and is suggested by the shaded area in Figure 2.4. The difference **A** − **B** is

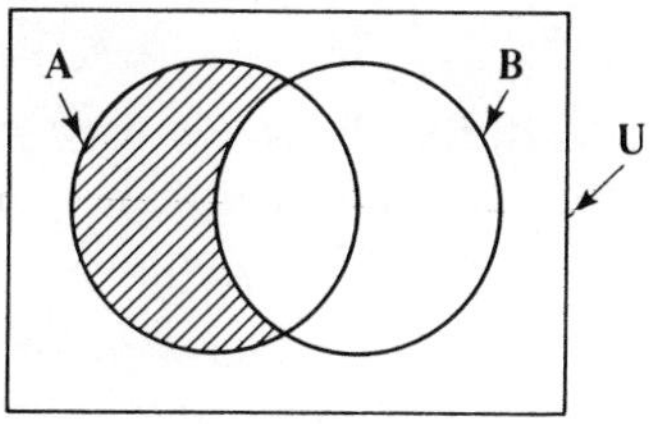


**Figure 2.4.** Difference.

also called the *complement of* **B** *with respect to* **A**. Usually, the complement of a set is taken with respect to an implicit universe **U**, in which case we merely call it the *complement* and write

$$\mathbf{A}^c = \{x \mid x \notin \mathbf{A}\}$$

Note that the complement of **A** with respect to itself is empty:

$$\mathbf{A} - \mathbf{A} = \{x \in \mathbf{A} \mid x \notin \mathbf{A}\} = \varnothing$$

**Example 2.2:** Let $\mathbf{U} = \{a, b, c, d\}$, and let

$$\mathbf{A} = \{a, b\} \qquad \mathbf{B} = \{b, c\}$$

Then these are all true propositions:

$$\mathbf{A} \subset \mathbf{U} \qquad \varnothing \subset \mathbf{A}$$

$$a \in \mathbf{A} \qquad \{a\} \subseteq \mathbf{A}$$

$$\mathbf{A} \cup \mathbf{B} = \{a, b, c\} \qquad \mathbf{A} \cap \mathbf{B} = \{b\}$$

$$\mathbf{A} - \mathbf{B} = \{a\} \qquad \mathbf{B} - \mathbf{A} = \{c\}$$

$$\mathbf{A}^c = \{c, d\}$$

$$\mathbf{A} \cup \mathbf{A}^c = \mathbf{U} \qquad \mathbf{A} \cap \mathbf{A}^c = \varnothing$$

### 2.2.4 Set-Theoretic Identities

A number of important identities follow from the definitions given above. These are summarized as Proposition 2.1.

**Proposition 2.1:** Let $\mathbf{U}$ be a universe, and let $\mathbf{A}$, $\mathbf{B}$, $\mathbf{C}$ be subsets of $\mathbf{U}$. Then the following are identities:

1. $\mathbf{A} \cup (\mathbf{B} \cup \mathbf{C}) = (\mathbf{A} \cup \mathbf{B}) \cup \mathbf{C}$ } associative laws
1'. $\mathbf{A} \cap (\mathbf{B} \cap \mathbf{C}) = (\mathbf{A} \cap \mathbf{B}) \cap \mathbf{C}$
2. $\mathbf{A} \cup \mathbf{B} = \mathbf{B} \cup \mathbf{A}$ } commutative laws
2'. $\mathbf{A} \cap \mathbf{B} = \mathbf{B} \cap \mathbf{A}$
3. $\mathbf{A} \cap (\mathbf{B} \cup \mathbf{C}) = (\mathbf{A} \cap \mathbf{B}) \cup (\mathbf{A} \cap \mathbf{C})$ } distributive laws
3'. $\mathbf{A} \cup (\mathbf{B} \cap \mathbf{C}) = (\mathbf{A} \cup \mathbf{B}) \cap (\mathbf{A} \cup \mathbf{C})$
4. $\mathbf{A} \cup \varnothing = \mathbf{A}$
4'. $\mathbf{A} \cap \mathbf{U} = \mathbf{A}$
5. $\mathbf{A} \cap \varnothing = \varnothing$
5'. $\mathbf{A} \cup \mathbf{U} = \mathbf{U}$
6. If, for all $\mathbf{A}$, $\mathbf{A} \cup \mathbf{B} = \mathbf{A}$, then $\mathbf{B} = \varnothing$.
6'. If, for all $\mathbf{A}$, $\mathbf{A} \cap \mathbf{B} = \mathbf{A}$, then $\mathbf{B} = \mathbf{U}$.
7, 7'. If $\mathbf{A} \cup \mathbf{B} = \mathbf{U}$ and $\mathbf{A} \cap \mathbf{B} = \varnothing$, then $\mathbf{A} = \mathbf{B}^c$.
8, 8'. $(\mathbf{A}^c)^c = \mathbf{A}$
9. $\varnothing^c = \mathbf{U}$
9'. $\mathbf{U}^c = \varnothing$
10. $\mathbf{A} \cup \mathbf{A} = \mathbf{A}$ } idempotent laws
10'. $\mathbf{A} \cap \mathbf{A} = \mathbf{A}$
11. $\mathbf{A} \cup (\mathbf{A} \cap \mathbf{B}) = \mathbf{A}$ } absorption laws
11'. $\mathbf{A} \cap (\mathbf{A} \cup \mathbf{B}) = \mathbf{A}$
12. $(\mathbf{A} \cup \mathbf{B})^c = \mathbf{A}^c \cap \mathbf{B}^c$ } De Morgan laws
12'. $(\mathbf{A} \cap \mathbf{B})^c = \mathbf{A}^c \cup \mathbf{B}^c$

We leave the proofs of most of these identities as exercises for the reader, but we shall prove identities 3 and 12 to illustrate the methods.

***Proof of Identity 3:*** We establish a more general result. Let

$$\mathbf{X} = \mathbf{A} \cap \left(\bigcup_{i=1}^{n} \mathbf{B}_i\right) \qquad \mathbf{Y} = \bigcup_{i=1}^{n} (\mathbf{A} \cap \mathbf{B}_i)$$

To show that $\mathbf{Y} = \mathbf{X}$, we show that $x \in \mathbf{Y}$ if and only if $x \in \mathbf{X}$. *If*: Suppose that $x \in \mathbf{X}$. Then $x \in \mathbf{A}$ and $x \in \bigcup_{i=1}^{n} \mathbf{B}_i$. For some $i$, $x \in \mathbf{B}_i$ and, for this $i$, $x \in \mathbf{A} \cap \mathbf{B}_i$. But then $x \in \mathbf{Y}$. *Only if:* Suppose that $x \in \mathbf{Y}$. Then for some $i$, $x \in \mathbf{A} \cap \mathbf{B}_i$. For this $i$, $x \in \mathbf{A}$ and $x \in \mathbf{B}_i$; therefore, $x \in \bigcup_{i=1}^{n} \mathbf{B}_i$. Hence $x \in \mathbf{X}$.

***Proof of Identity 12:*** We prove a more general identity. Let

$$\mathbf{X} = \left(\bigcup_{i=1}^{n} \mathbf{A}_i\right)^c \qquad \mathbf{Y} = \bigcap_{i=1}^{n} \mathbf{A}_i^c$$

We show that $x \in \mathbf{Y}$ if and only if $x \in \mathbf{X}$. *If*: Suppose that $x \in \mathbf{X}$. Then $x \notin \bigcup_{i=1}^{n} \mathbf{A}_i$, so for all $i$, $x \notin \mathbf{A}_i$. Therefore, for all $i$, $x \in \mathbf{A}_i^c$, and hence $x \in \bigcap_{i=1}^{n} \mathbf{A}_i^c$. *Only if*: Suppose that $x \in \mathbf{Y}$. Then $x \in \mathbf{A}_i^c$ for all $i$. Then $x \notin \mathbf{A}_i^c$ for each $i$, so $x \notin \bigcup_{i=1}^{n} \mathbf{A}_i$; hence $x \in (\bigcup_{i=1}^{n} \mathbf{A}_i)^c$.

There is a close relationship between these set-theoretic identities and the notion of logical equivalence. Suppose that the sets **A** and **B** are defined by properties $p$ and $q$:

$$\mathbf{A} = \{x \mid p(x)\}$$
$$\mathbf{B} = \{x \mid q(x)\}$$

Then $\mathbf{A} = \mathbf{B}$ if and only if $p(x) \Leftrightarrow q(x)$, because the equivalence of $p$ and $q$ guarantees that **A** and **B** have the same members. Therefore, each set-theoretic identity is true if and only if a corresponding pair of propositions is equivalent. For example, let **A** and **B** be defined as above and let **C** be a set defined by property $r$:

$$\mathbf{C} = \{x \mid r(x)\}$$

Then the associative law

$$\mathbf{A} \cup (\mathbf{B} \cup \mathbf{C}) = (\mathbf{A} \cup \mathbf{B}) \cup \mathbf{C}$$

represents the proposition

$$\text{for all } x,\ p(x) \vee (q(x) \vee r(x)) \Leftrightarrow (p(x) \vee q(x)) \vee r(x)$$

But the truth of this proposition follows directly from the fact that

$$p \vee (q \vee r) \Leftrightarrow (p \vee q) \vee r$$

is a logical equivalence. Thus each identity in Proposition 2.1 corresponds to an equivalence in propositional logic, in which $\vee$ and $\wedge$ are replaced by $\cup$ and $\cap$, and *true* and *false* are replaced by **U** and $\varnothing$.

Note that each part of Proposition 2.1 consists of two statements similar in form. Indeed, each unprimed statement is converted to the corresponding primed statement, and vice versa, by the following rules:

1. Replace $\cup$ by $\cap$.
2. Replace $\cap$ by $\cup$.
3. Replace **U** by $\varnothing$.
4. Replace $\varnothing$ by **U**.

This is known as the *principle of duality*. Statements such as 7 and 8 in Proposition 2.1, which are converted back to themselves under the above substitutions, are known as *self-dual* statements.

### 2.2.5 Ordered Sets and Set Products

In much of our subsequent work, we shall need to deal with *ordered pairs* and *ordered n-tuples*. An ordered pair of elements is written

$$(x, y)$$

where $x$ is known as the *first component*, and $y$ is known as the *second component*. We may assert $(u, v) = (x, y)$ if and only if $u = x$ and $v = y$: ordered pairs are equal if and only if their first and second components are respectively indentical.

The ordered pair $(x, y)$ is distinct from the set $\{x, y\}$.† In the set $\{x, y\}$ the ordering of the elements is not significant, whereas in the pair $(x, y)$ the ordering of the elements *is* significant. In particular, the ordered pairs $(x, y)$ and $(y, x)$ are equal if and only if $x = y$.

An *n-tuple* is an ordered sequence of elements

$$(x_1, x_2, \ldots, x_n)$$

and is a generalization of an ordered pair. Two $n$-tuples are equal if and only if they match component by component; that is,

$$(x_1, x_2, \ldots, x_n) = (y_1, y_2, \ldots, y_n)$$

if and only if $x_i = y_i$ for $i = 1, 2, \ldots, n$.

By the *Cartesian product* (or *direct product*) of two sets **A** and **B**, we mean the set

$$\mathbf{A} \times \mathbf{B} = \{(x, y) \mid x \in \mathbf{A}, y \in \mathbf{B}\}$$

which consists of all ordered pairs of elements from **A** and **B**. The notation $\mathbf{A} \times \mathbf{A}$ stands for the collection of all possible ordered pairs of elements from **A**. Similarly, the notation

$$\mathbf{A} \times \mathbf{A} \times \ldots \times \mathbf{A} \quad (n \text{ times})$$

stands for the sets of all $n$-tuples of elements from **A**.

**Example 2.3:** Let $\mathbf{A} = \{a, b\}$ and $\mathbf{B} = \{1, 2, 3\}$. Then

$$\mathbf{A} \times \mathbf{A} = \{(a, a), (a, b), (b, a), (b, b)\}$$

$$\mathbf{A} \times \mathbf{B} = \{(a, 1), (a, 2), (a, 3), (b, 1), (b, 2), (b, 3)\}$$

$$\mathbf{B} \times \mathbf{A} = \{(1, a), (1, b), (2, a), (2, b), (3, a), (3, b)\}$$

$$\mathbf{B} \times \mathbf{B} = \{(1, 1), (1, 2), (1, 3), (2, 1), (2, 2), (2, 3), (3, 1), (3, 2), (3, 3)\}$$

†But an ordered pair may be expressed in terms of unordered sets. The ordered pair $(x, y)$, where $x \neq y$, may be defined as the set $\{\{x\}, \{x, y\}\}$ in which the singleton set $\{x\}$ designates which element of the doubleton set $\{x, y\}$ is the first component of $(x, y)$.

## 2.3 Relations

The properties of abstract machines and languages concern relationships that exist between states of a machine or phrases of a sentence. The mathematical notion of *relation* and the derivative notion of *function* are the formal means of specifying relationships. Informally, a mathematical *relation* states that certain combinations of objects share some property and are to be set apart from other combinations of objects.

### 2.3.1 Definitions

Consider the universe $\mathbf{U} = \{a, b, c, d\}$ in which we may associate the objects $a$, $b$, $c$, and $d$ with the sides of a square, as shown in Figure 2.5a. Suppose that we are interested in distinguishing the edge pairs having the property, "edge $y$ is clockwise next from edge $x$." We can represent this relation by the set of ordered pairs

$$\mathbf{R} = \{(x, y) \mid y \text{ is clockwise next from } x\}$$

$$\mathbf{R} = \{(a, b), (b, c), (c, d), (d, a)\}$$

illustrated in Figure 2.5b. In the same manner, the relation "counterclock-

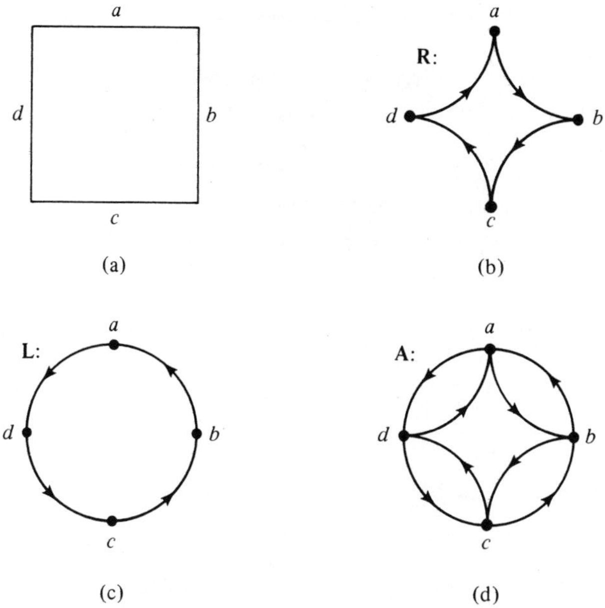


**Figure 2.5.** Relations among the edges of a square.

wise next" may be represented by

$$\mathbf{L} = \{(b, a), (a, d), (d, c), (c, b)\}$$

as in Figure 2.5c. The relation "$x$ is adjacent to $y$" is

$$\mathbf{A} = \{(x, y) \mid x \text{ is adjacent to } y\} = \mathbf{R} \cup \mathbf{L}$$

and is depicted in Figure 2.5d.

Formally, we define a *relation* $\rho$ between sets **A** and **B** to be any subset of $\mathbf{A} \times \mathbf{B}$:

$$\rho \subseteq \mathbf{A} \times \mathbf{B}$$

That is, $\rho$ is a set of ordered pairs whose first components are from **A** and whose second components are from **B**. If $(x, y) \in \rho$, we write

$$x \, \rho \, y$$

and say that "$x$ is $\rho$-related to $y$," or "$x$ is related to $y$" if $\rho$ is understood. The *domain* of $\rho$, written $\mathbf{D}_\rho$, is the set of first components of pairs in $\rho$:

$$\mathbf{D}_\rho = \{x \in \mathbf{A} \mid \text{for some } y \in \mathbf{B}, (x, y) \in \rho\}$$

The *range* of $\rho$, written $\mathbf{R}_\rho$, is the set of second components of pairs in $\rho$:

$$\mathbf{R}_\rho = \{y \in \mathbf{B} \mid \text{for some } x \in \mathbf{A}, (x, y) \in \rho\}$$

If $\rho \subseteq \mathbf{A} \times \mathbf{A}$, then $\rho$ is called a "relation on **A**."

In Figure 2.5 we used directed graphs to represent some simple relations. Any finite relation may be represented in this way. The graph of a relation $\rho$ consists of nodes that represent the elements of the domain $\mathbf{D}_\rho$ and the range $\mathbf{R}_\rho$, and a directed arc from node $x$ to node $y$ for each pair $(x, y)$ in the relation. Figure 2.6 illustrates the relation

$$\{(x_1, y_1), (x_2, y_1), (x_2, y_2)\}$$

in which the domain and range are disjoint.

Certain properties of relations on a set **A** are useful in characterizing

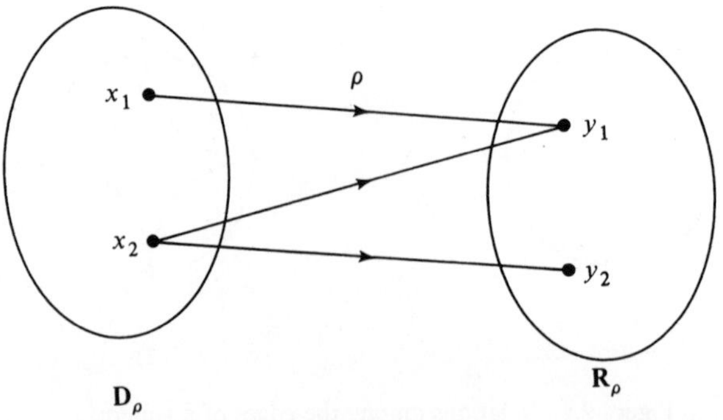


**Figure 2.6.** Graphical representation of a relation $\rho$.

important special types of relations:

1. A relation $\rho$ on a set **A** is *reflexive* if each element of **A** is related to itself:

$$x \; \rho \; x, \qquad \text{for each } x \in \mathbf{A}$$

2. A relation $\rho$ on a set **A** is *symmetric* if, for all $x, y \in \mathbf{A}$,

$$x \; \rho \; y \quad \text{implies} \quad y \; \rho \; x$$

3. A relation $\rho$ on a set **A** is *antisymmetric* if, for all $x, y \in \mathbf{A}$,

$$x \; \rho \; y \quad \text{and} \quad y \; \rho \; x \quad \text{implies} \quad x = y$$

4. A relation $\rho$ on a set **A** is *transitive* if, for all $x, y, z \in \mathbf{A}$,

$$x \; \rho \; y \quad \text{and} \quad y \; \rho \; z \quad \text{implies} \quad x \; \rho \; z$$

Although collecting objects together as a set does not imply any ordering of the objects, an order may be imposed on a set by means of a relation. A relation $\rho$ on a set **A** is called a *partial ordering* of **A** if $\rho$ is reflexive, antisymmetric, and transitive.

**Example 2.4:** Let **A** be any set and let $\mathcal{P}(\mathbf{A})$ be its power set, the set of all subsets of **A**. Let the sign $\leq$ denote the relation of set inclusion on $\mathcal{P}(\mathbf{A})$; that is, for sets **B** and **C** in $\mathcal{P}(\mathbf{A})$,

$$\mathbf{B} \leq \mathbf{C} \qquad \text{if and only if } \mathbf{B} \subseteq \mathbf{C}$$

Figure 2.7 illustrates the relation $\leq$ on the set $\mathbf{A} = \{a, b\}$. There is

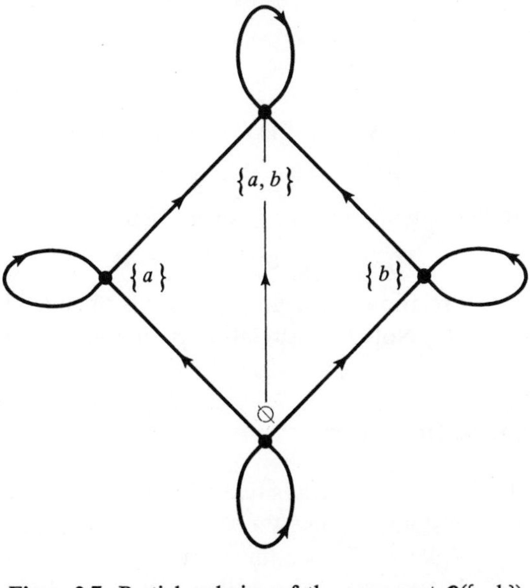


**Figure 2.7.** Partial ordering of the power set $\mathcal{P}(\{a, b\})$.

a node for each element of $\mathcal{P}(\mathbf{A}) = \{\varnothing, \{a\}, \{b\}, \{a, b\}\}$, and node $x$ is joined to node $y$ by a directed arc if and only if $x \subseteq y$. The relation $\leq$ is reflexive because each set is a subset of itself. In the graph, reflexivity appears as an arc from each node to itself. The relation is antisymmetric, because $\mathbf{B} \subseteq \mathbf{C}$ and $\mathbf{C} \subseteq \mathbf{B}$ implies that $\mathbf{B} = \mathbf{C}$. It is transitive because $\mathbf{B} \subseteq \mathbf{C} \subseteq \mathbf{D}$ implies $\mathbf{B} \subseteq \mathbf{D}$. For a graph to represent a transitive relation, there must be an arc joining each pair of nodes that are connected by a directed path. Thus the relation of set inclusion is a partial ordering of the power set of any set. The term "partial ordering" is used because some pairs of elements in $\mathcal{P}(\mathbf{A})$ are not necessarily assigned any order, for instance the sets $\{a\}$ and $\{b\}$ in Figure 2.7.

A relation $\rho$ on a set $\mathbf{A}$ is a *total ordering* of $\mathbf{A}$ if $\rho$ is a partial ordering and, for each pair of elements $(x, y)$ in $\mathbf{A} \times \mathbf{A}$, at least one of $x \; \rho \; y$ or $y \; \rho \; x$ is true. Equivalently, each pair of elements satisfies exactly one of the following conditions if $\rho$ is a total ordering:

1. $x = y$; that is, $x \; \rho \; y$ and $y \; \rho \; x$.
2. $x \neq y$ and $x \; \rho \; y$.
3. $x \neq y$ and $y \; \rho \; x$.

**Example 2.5:** Let $\mathbf{N} = \{0, 1, 2, \ldots\}$ be the set of nonnegative integers, and let $\leq$ denote the relation "is less than or equal to." Let $x < y$ mean that $x \leq y$ but $x \neq y$. The relation $\leq$ is a total ordering of $\mathbf{N}$ since, for any pair of integers $x$ and $y$, just one of

$$x < y \qquad x = y \qquad y < x$$

is true.

For any relation $\rho \subseteq \mathbf{A} \times \mathbf{B}$, the *inverse* of $\rho$ is defined by

$$\rho^{-1} = \{(y, x) \mid (x, y) \in \rho\}$$

If $\mathbf{D}_\rho$ and $\mathbf{R}_\rho$ are the domain and range of $\rho$, then

$$\mathbf{D}_{\rho^{-1}} = \mathbf{R}_\rho \quad \text{and} \quad \mathbf{R}_{\rho^{-1}} = \mathbf{D}_\rho$$

From the graph of a relation $\rho$, the graph of $\rho^{-1}$ is obtained by reversing the orientation of each arc. Note that a relation $\rho$ on a set $\mathbf{A}$ is symmetric if and only if $\rho = \rho^{-1}$.

### 2.3.2 Equivalence Relations

A reflexive, symmetric, and transitive relation on a set is called an *equivalence relation.* We customarily use the symbol $\sim$ to denote an equivalence relation. Thus $x \sim y$ is read "$x$ is equivalent to $y$," and $x \nsim y$ is read "$x$ is not equivalent to $y$."

**Example 2.6:** The relation "living in the same house" on the set of people in a given city is an equivalence relation (assuming that no person lives in more than one house):

1. It is reflexive, because each person lives in the same house as himself.
2. It is symmetric, because if $x$ lives in the same house as $y$, then certainly $y$ lives in the same house as $x$.
3. It is transitive, because if $x$ lives in the same house as $y$, and $y$ lives in the same house as $z$, then $x$ lives in the same house as $z$.

This example illustrates a central property of an equivalence relation: it *partitions* the set to which it applies into disjoint subsets, in this case households.

Formally, a *partition* of a set **A** is a collection of subsets of **A** such that each element of **A** appears in exactly one subset: a partition of **A** is a collection of disjoint sets, called *parts*, that collectively exhaust the set **A**.

As illustrated by Example 2.6, an equivalence relation induces a partition on a set. We establish this as a general result. For an equivalence relation $\sim$ on a set **A**, the notation $[x]$ represents the set of elements equivalent to $x$:

$$[x] = \{y \in \mathbf{A} \mid y \sim x\}$$

This set $[x]$ is called the *equivalence class* of $x$. Two properties of equivalence classes are obvious.

1. $x \in [x]$.
2. $x \sim y$ if and only if $[x] = [y]$.

**Proposition 2.2:** An equivalence relation on a set partitions the set.

***Proof:*** Since an equivalence relation $\sim$ on a set **A** is reflexive, each $x \in \mathbf{A}$ appears in at least one equivalence class, that is, $[x]$. Thus the equivalence classes exhaust **A**. It remains to show that each $x \in \mathbf{A}$ is in only one class; that is, if $x \not\sim y$, then $[x] \cap [y] = \varnothing$. Let $x \not\sim y$ and suppose to the contrary that $z \in [x] \cap [y]$. That $z \in [x]$ implies $x \sim z$; that $z \in [y]$ implies $z \sim y$. Thus $x \sim z \sim y$, and by transitivity $x \sim y$, a contradiction. We therefore conclude that $[x] \cap [y] = \varnothing$ unless $x \sim y$.

The reader can easily verify the converse of this proposition; that is, a partition of a set **A** defines an equivalence relation on **A**.

By the *index* of an equivalence relation, we mean the number of equivalence classes induced by the relation. In most of our work we shall deal with equivalence relations of finite index.

**Example 2.7:** Let $\mathbf{N} = \{0, 1, 2, \ldots\}$ be the set of nonnegative integers, and let $p \neq 0$ be a positive integer. Each $x \in \mathbf{N}$ can be represented as

$$x = pq + r, \qquad q \geq 0, 0 \leq r < p$$

The number $q$ is the quotient obtained in dividing $x$ by $p$; the number $r$ is the remainder, and is called the result of taking $x$ *modulo* $p$ [abbreviated $r = (x \bmod p)$].

Let the relation $\sim$ on $\mathbf{N}$ be defined by

$$x \sim y \qquad \text{if and only if } x \bmod p = y \bmod p$$

This relation is easily shown to be reflexive, symmetric, and transitive, and is therefore an equivalence relation. The equivalence classes are

$$[i] = \{x \mid (x \bmod p) = i\}, \qquad i = 0, \ldots, p - 1$$

The set $[i]$ is just the set of integers yielding the same remainder on division by $p$. This relation has finite index since the number of equivalence classes is $p$.

## 2.4 Functions

A relation $f \subseteq \mathbf{A} \times \mathbf{B}$ is a *function* if it has the property

$$(x, y) \in f \quad \text{and} \quad (x, z) \in f \quad \text{implies } y = z$$

If $f \subseteq \mathbf{A} \times \mathbf{B}$ is a function, we write

$$f\colon \mathbf{A} \longrightarrow \mathbf{B}$$

and say that $f$ *maps* $\mathbf{A}$ into $\mathbf{B}$. We use the common notation

$$y = f(x)$$

to mean $(x, y) \in f$. As before, the *domain* of $f$ is the set

$$\mathbf{D}_f = \{x \in \mathbf{A} \mid y = f(x) \text{ for some } y \in \mathbf{B}\}$$

and the *range* of $f$ is the set

$$\mathbf{R}_f = \{y \in \mathbf{B} \mid y = f(x) \text{ for some } x \in \mathbf{A}\}$$

A function, in contrast to an arbitrary relation, maps each element in its domain into exactly one element of its range. The relation of Figure 2.6 is thus not a function, whereas that of Figure 2.8 is.

When we describe a function by writing $f\colon \mathbf{A} \longrightarrow \mathbf{B}$, the set $\mathbf{A}$ is usually the domain of $f$; the range of $f$ is usually a proper subset of $\mathbf{B}$. If $\mathbf{D}_f \subseteq \mathbf{A}$, we say that $f$ is a *partial function*; if $\mathbf{D}_f = \mathbf{A}$, we say that $f$ is a *total function*. Throughout this book, *functions will always be total* unless we explicitly state

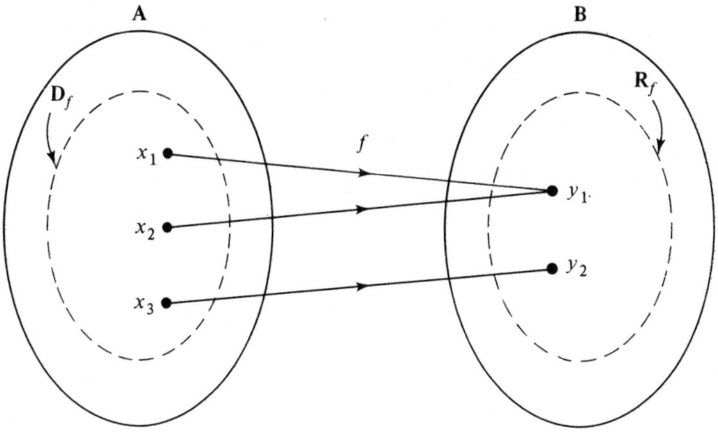


$(y_1 \neq y_2)$ implies $(x_1 \neq x_3)$ and $(x_2 \neq x_3)$

**Figure 2.8.** Graphical representation of a function $f$.

otherwise. If $x \in \mathbf{D}_f$, we say that $f$ is *defined* at $x$; otherwise $f$ is *undefined* at $x$. If $\mathbf{R}_f \subseteq \mathbf{B}$, we say that $f$ maps $\mathbf{D}_f$ *into* the set $\mathbf{B}$. If $\mathbf{R}_f = \mathbf{B}$, we say that $f$ maps $\mathbf{D}_f$ *onto* $\mathbf{B}$.

If a function $f$ has the property

$$f(x) = z \quad \text{and} \quad f(y) = z \quad \text{implies } x = y$$

then $f$ is a *one-to-one function*. If $f$: $\mathbf{A} \rightarrow \mathbf{B}$ is a one-to-one function, $f$ gives a *one-to-one correspondence* between elements of its domain and range, as illustrated in Figure 2.9.

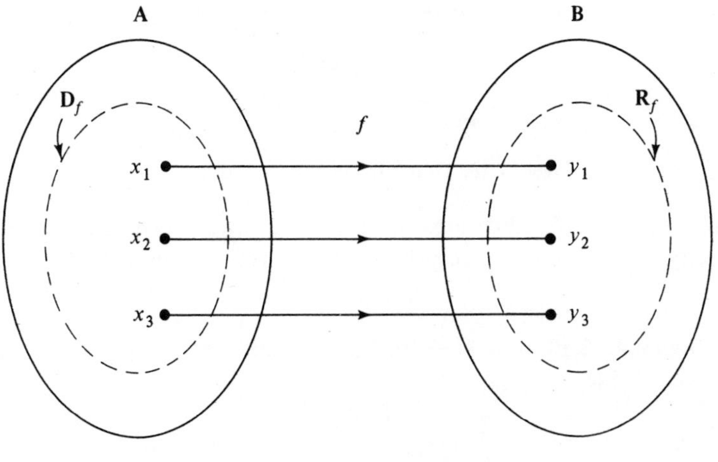


**Figure 2.9.** One-to-one correspondence.

**Example 2.8:** If $\mathbf{R}$ is the set of real numbers, then $\mathbf{R} \times \mathbf{R}$ represents the Euclidean plane. The set $\{(x, x^2) \mid x \in \mathbf{R}\}$ comprises the points in $\mathbf{R} \times \mathbf{R}$ that lie on the graph of the parabola $f(x) = x^2$. The domain of $f$ is all of $\mathbf{R}$ (thus $f$ is total), but the range of $f$ is a proper subset of $\mathbf{R}$ (thus $f$ is into, not onto).

**Example 2.9:** Let $\oplus$ be the function (called *modulo 2 addition*)

$$\oplus\colon \mathbf{S} \times \mathbf{S} \longrightarrow \mathbf{S}, \qquad \mathbf{S} = \{0, 1\}$$

defined by

$$0 \oplus 0 = 0$$
$$0 \oplus 1 = 1$$
$$1 \oplus 0 = 1$$
$$1 \oplus 1 = 0$$

We see that

$$x \oplus y = (x + y) \bmod 2$$

where $(x + y) \bmod 2$ is the remainder obtained from dividing $x + y$ by 2. The function $\oplus$ is represented by the graph in Figure 2.10. Clearly, $\oplus$ is onto but not one-to-one.

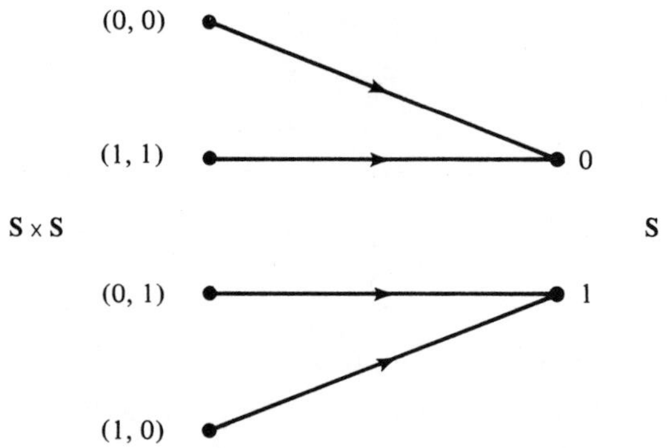


**Figure 2.10.** Graph for modulo 2 addition.

The next example illustrates the rather surprising fact that a function can specify a one-to-one correspondence of a set with itself without being onto.

**Example 2.10:** Let $\mathbf{N} = \{0, 1, 2, \ldots\}$ be the nonnegative integers, and define

$$f\colon \mathbf{N} \longrightarrow \mathbf{N}$$

by

$$y = f(x) \qquad \text{if and only if } y = x + x$$

The graph of $f$ is illustrated in Figure 2.11. This function is one-to-one, but it is not onto because its range contains only the even integers.

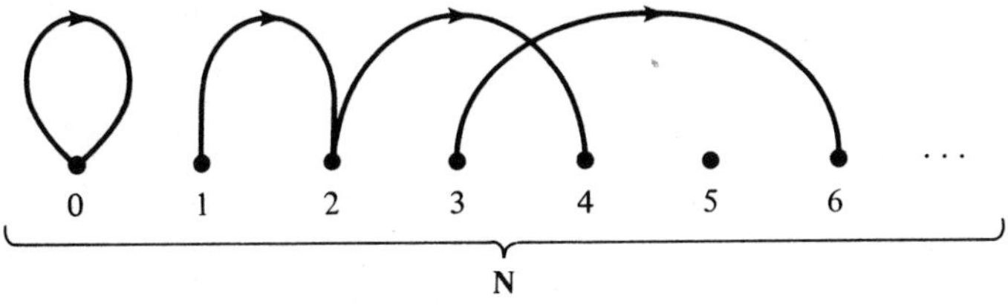


**Figure 2.11.** Graph for $f(x) = x + x$.

**Example 2.11:** Let $\mathbf{X}$ be a set and suppose that $\mathbf{A} \subseteq \mathbf{X}$. Define the function

$$C_{\mathbf{A}}: \mathbf{X} \longrightarrow \{0, 1\}$$

by

$$C_{\mathbf{A}}(x) = \begin{cases} 1, & \text{if } x \in \mathbf{A} \\ 0, & \text{otherwise} \end{cases}$$

This function $C_{\mathbf{A}}$ is known as the *characteristic function* of the set $\mathbf{A}$, since

$$\mathbf{A} = \{x \in \mathbf{X} \mid C_{\mathbf{A}}(x) = 1\}$$

This function is many-to-one and onto $\{0, 1\}$ for most choices of $\mathbf{X}$ and $\mathbf{A}$. (When is it not?)

The *inverse of a function* is defined in the same way as the inverse of a relation. If $f \subseteq \mathbf{A} \times \mathbf{B}$ is a function, then the inverse of $f$ is the set

$$f^{-1} = \{(y, x) \mid (x, y) \in f\}$$

The reader may verify that $f^{-1}$ is a function if and only if $f$ is one-to-one.

If $f(x) = y$, we speak of $y$ as the *image* of $x$ under $f$. Sometimes we are concerned with the image of a *set* of points in the domain of $f$. Let $f$: $\mathbf{A} \longrightarrow \mathbf{B}$ be a function, and suppose that $\mathbf{X} \subseteq \mathbf{A}$. Then the set

$$\mathbf{Y} = f(\mathbf{X}) = \{y \in \mathbf{B} \mid y = f(x) \text{ for some } x \in \mathbf{X}\}$$

is known as the *image* of $\mathbf{X}$ under $f$. Similarly, the *inverse image* of a set $\mathbf{Y}$ included in the range of $f$ is

$$f^{-1}(\mathbf{Y}) = \{x \in \mathbf{A} \mid y = f(x) \text{ for some } y \in \mathbf{Y}\}$$

The relationship of $f^{-1}(\mathbf{Y})$ and $\mathbf{Y} = f(\mathbf{X})$ to $\mathbf{X}$ is shown in Figure 2.12. If $f(\mathbf{X}) = \mathbf{Y}$, it is not necessarily true that $f^{-1}(\mathbf{Y}) = \mathbf{X}$, because $f$ may be many-to-one, and the set $\mathbf{X}$ need not contain all elements that map into $\mathbf{Y}$. All we may conclude is that $\mathbf{X}$ is a subset of $f^{-1}(\mathbf{Y})$.

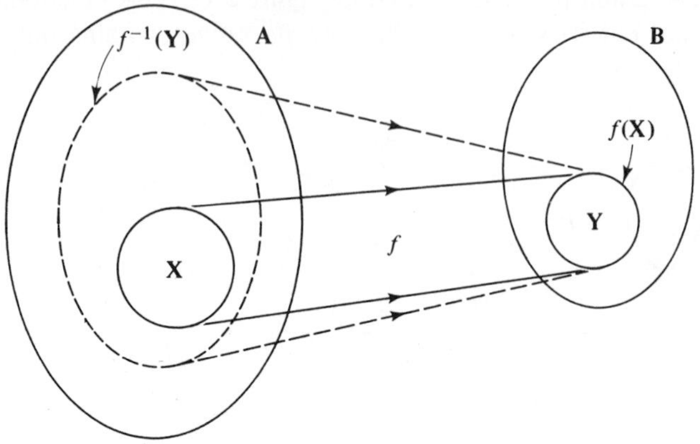


**Figure 2.12.** Images of sets defined by a function.

Because a function $f$ may be many-to-one, one must use care in writing $f^{-1}(y)$. Strictly speaking, this is only permissible if $f$ is one-to-one. In general, we may write $f^{-1}(\{y\})$ to mean the set of points in the domain of $f$ that map onto the point $y$ of its range.

**Example 2.12:** Each function determines an equivalence relation on its domain. Let $f\colon \mathbf{A} \longrightarrow \mathbf{B}$ be a function, and for each $y \in \mathbf{B}$, let $\mathbf{A}_y$ be the set of points in $\mathbf{A}$ that map onto $y$ ($\mathbf{A}_y$ is the inverse image of $\{y\}$):

$$\mathbf{A}_y = \{x \in \mathbf{A} \mid y = f(x)\}$$

Since we assume that $f$ is total, each $x \in \mathbf{A}$ appears in some set $\mathbf{A}_y$. Because a function assigns exactly one $y \in \mathbf{B}$ to each $x \in \mathbf{A}$, each element of $\mathbf{A}$ is in exactly one set $\mathbf{A}_y$. Thus the sets $\mathbf{A}_y$ form a partition of the domain of $f$. Indeed, the corresponding equivalence relation is defined by

$$u \sim v \qquad \text{if and only if } f(u) = f(v)$$

and the equivalence classes are

$$[u] = \{x \in \mathbf{A} \mid f(x) = f(u)\}$$

**Example 2.13:** A function $f\colon \mathbf{A} \longrightarrow \mathbf{A}$ is said to be a *unary operation* on $\mathbf{A}$. Let $\mathbf{I}$ be the set of all integers. Then the function

$$f\colon \mathbf{I} \longrightarrow \mathbf{I}$$

defined by

$$f(x) = -x$$

is a unary operation, that is, negation. A function $f\colon \mathbf{A} \times \mathbf{A} \longrightarrow \mathbf{A}$ is a *binary operation* on $\mathbf{A}$. The usual addition and multiplication of integers are examples of binary operations.

## 2.5 Cardinality

The concept of the *cardinal number* of a set was developed to clarify the notion of "size" as applied to infinite sets. The "number of elements" in a set is a measure of size that works for finite sets but does not carry over to infinite sets. One could conjecture, for example, that there are more integers than there are even integers. However, Example 2.10 showed that the elements of these two sets can be placed in one-to-one correspondence! In fact, any infinite set can be placed in one-to-one correspondence with a proper subset of itself. This suggests that two sets should be considered of equal size if their elements can be placed in one-to-one correspondence.

**Definition 2.1:** Two sets **A** and **B** are of *equal cardinality*, written

$$\overline{\overline{\mathbf{A}}} = \overline{\overline{\mathbf{B}}}$$

if and only if there is a one-to-one function $f$: $\mathbf{A} \longrightarrow \mathbf{B}$ that maps **A** *onto* **B**. We write

$$\overline{\overline{\mathbf{A}}} \leq \overline{\overline{\mathbf{B}}}$$

if **B** includes a subset **C** such that $\overline{\overline{\mathbf{A}}} = \overline{\overline{\mathbf{C}}}$. If $\overline{\overline{\mathbf{A}}} \leq \overline{\overline{\mathbf{B}}}$ and $\overline{\overline{\mathbf{A}}} \neq \overline{\overline{\mathbf{B}}}$, then **A** has cardinality *less than* that of **B**, and we write $\overline{\overline{\mathbf{A}}} < \overline{\overline{\mathbf{B}}}$.

It is easily seen that the relation on a universe of sets defined by [$\mathbf{A} \sim \mathbf{B}$ if and only if $\overline{\overline{\mathbf{A}}} = \overline{\overline{\mathbf{B}}}$] is reflexive, symmetric, and transitive, and therefore is an equivalence relation that partitions the universe into classes whose member sets are of equal cardinality.

For a discussion of cardinality in relation to finite and infinite sets of integers, the use of functions that define *sequences* of elements from a set is helpful. Let

$$\mathbf{J} = \{1, 2, 3, \ldots\}$$

be the set of all positive integers, and let

$$\mathbf{J}_n = \{1, 2, \ldots, n\}$$

be the set containing the first $n$ positive integers. (We take $\mathbf{J}_0 = \varnothing$.)

**Definition 2.2:** A *sequence* on a set **X** is a function $f$: $\mathbf{J} \longrightarrow \mathbf{X}$. A sequence may be represented by writing

$$f(1), f(2), f(3), \ldots, f(i), \ldots$$

However, we often use the simpler notation

$$x_1, x_2, x_3, \ldots, x_i, \ldots, \qquad x_i \in \mathbf{X}$$

A *finite sequence of length n* on **X** is a function $f$: $\mathbf{J}_n \longrightarrow \mathbf{X}$, usually written as

$$x_1, x_2, \ldots, x_n, \qquad x_i \in \mathbf{X}$$

The *sequence of length zero* is the function $f$: $\varnothing \longrightarrow \mathbf{X}$.

**Definition 2.3:** A set **A** is *finite* if $\overline{\overline{\mathbf{A}}} = \overline{\overline{\mathbf{J}}}_n$ for some integer $n \geq 0$, in which case we say that **A** has cardinality $n$. A set is *infinite* if it is not finite.

If **A** is a finite set, and $\overline{\overline{\mathbf{J}}}_n = \overline{\overline{\mathbf{A}}}$, the one-to-one correspondence required by Definition 2.1 places the elements of **A** in a repetition-free sequence of length $n$:

$$a_1, a_2, \ldots, a_n \begin{cases} a_i \in \mathbf{A} \\ a_i \neq a_j \text{ whenever } i \neq j \end{cases}$$

Since for finite sets **A** and **B**, $\overline{\overline{\mathbf{A}}} < \overline{\overline{\mathbf{B}}}$ if and only if $\overline{\overline{\mathbf{A}}} = \overline{\overline{\mathbf{J}}}_m$ and $\overline{\overline{\mathbf{B}}} = \overline{\overline{\mathbf{J}}}_n$ where $m < n$, we may represent $\overline{\overline{\mathbf{A}}}$ and $\overline{\overline{\mathbf{B}}}$ by the integers $m$ and $n$, and identify the relation $\leq$ with the usual total ordering of the nonnegative integers.

We now consider sets that have the same cardinality as the set of positive integers $\mathbf{J} = \{1, 2, 3, \ldots\}$.

**Definition 2.4:** A set **X** is *denumerable* if its elements can be placed in one-to-one correspondence with the positive integers, that is, if $\overline{\overline{\mathbf{X}}} = \overline{\overline{\mathbf{J}}}$. A set is *countable* if it is either finite or denumerable.

A set **X** is denumerable just if its elements can be arranged in an infinite sequence

$$x_1, x_2, x_3, \ldots, x_i, \ldots, \qquad x_i \in \mathbf{X}$$

in which each element of **X** appears exactly once. For example, the following sets are denumerable:

1. The integers $\{0, 1, -1, 2, -2, \ldots\}$.
2. The even natural numbers $\{0, 2, 4, \ldots\}$.
3. The odd natural numbers $\{1, 3, 5, \ldots\}$.

Many infinite sets have the same cardinality as the set of positive integers. Some of the ways in which countable sets may be constructed from other countable sets are given by the following propositions. Although the proofs are expressed in terms of the set **J**, they apply for any denumerable set **X** in view of the one-to-one correspondence that must exist between the elements of **X** and **J**. The reader may supply the additional arguments needed to apply these results to countable sets.

**Proposition 2.3:** Every subset of **J** is countable. Consequently, each subset of any denumerable set is countable.

***Proof:*** Let **X** be a subset of **J**. If **X** is finite, then **X** is countable. Suppose that **X** is infinite, and define the function $f\colon \mathbf{J} \longrightarrow \mathbf{X}$ inductively as follows:

$$f(i) = \begin{cases} \text{the smallest integer } k \text{ such that } k \in \mathbf{X},\ i = 1 \\ \text{the smallest integer } k \text{ such that } k > f(i-1) \\ \text{and } k \in \mathbf{X},\ i > 1 \end{cases}$$

The function $f$ arranges the elements of **X** in a sequence

$$f(1), f(2), \ldots, f(i), \ldots$$

and provides the required one-to-one mapping of **J** onto **X**. Therefore, $\bar{\bar{\mathbf{X}}} = \bar{\bar{\mathbf{J}}}$.

**Proposition 2.4:** A function $f\colon \mathbf{J} \longrightarrow \mathbf{Y}$ has a countable range. Hence any function on a countable domain has a countable range.

***Proof:*** Given $f\colon \mathbf{J} \longrightarrow \mathbf{Y}$, let $\mathbf{X} \subseteq \mathbf{Y}$ be the range of $f$, and define the function $g\colon \mathbf{X} \longrightarrow \mathbf{J}$ as follows:

$$g(x) = \text{smallest } n \text{ in } \mathbf{J} \text{ such that } f(n) = x$$

Then $g$ is one-to-one onto a subset of **J** and **X** is therefore countable.

**Proposition 2.5:** The set $\mathbf{J} \times \mathbf{J}$ is denumerable. Therefore, $\mathbf{A} \times \mathbf{B}$ is countable for arbitrary countable sets **A** and **B**.

***Proof:*** We construct a function $g\colon \mathbf{J} \times \mathbf{J} \longrightarrow \mathbf{J}$ that is one-to-one and onto. The idea is to consider the elements of $\mathbf{J} \times \mathbf{J}$ as forming the infinite array shown in Figure 2.13. Then it is clear that the pairs

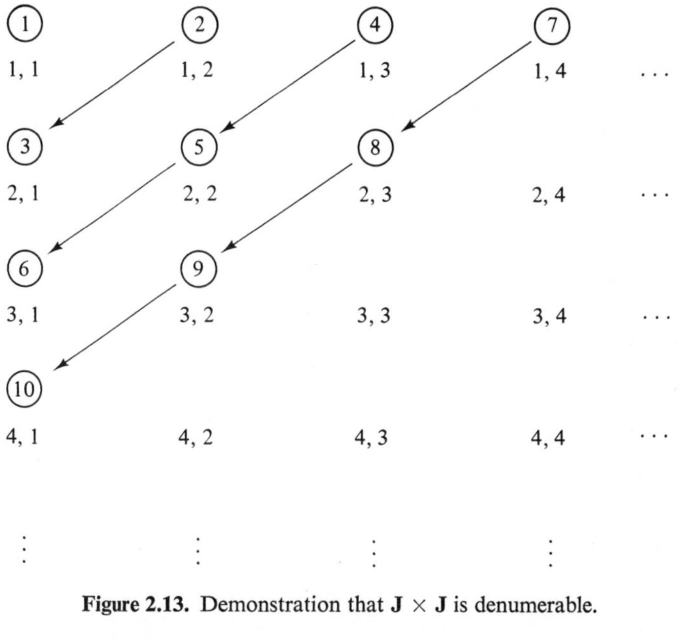


**Figure 2.13.** Demonstration that $\mathbf{J} \times \mathbf{J}$ is denumerable.

in $\mathbf{J} \times \mathbf{J}$ can be arranged in a sequence as indicated by the arrows and circled numbers in the figure. An inductive definition of the function $g$ is

$$\begin{aligned} g(1, 1) &= 1 \\ g(1, j) &= g(1, j - 1) + j - 1 \qquad j \neq 1 \\ g(i, j) &= g(i - 1, j + 1) + 1 \qquad i \neq 1, j \neq 1 \end{aligned}$$

**Proposition 2.6:** The set $\mathbf{A} \cup \mathbf{B}$ is countable whenever **A** and **B** are countable sets.

***Proof:*** Since **A** and **B** are countable, there are one-to-one and onto functions

$$f\colon \mathbf{X} \longrightarrow \mathbf{A} \qquad g\colon \mathbf{Y} \longrightarrow \mathbf{B}$$

where **X** and **Y** are subsets of **J**. Let

$$\mathbf{M} = \{2n - 1 \mid n \in \mathbf{X}\} \cup \{2n \mid n \in \mathbf{Y}\}$$

and define $h\colon \mathbf{M} \to \mathbf{A} \cup \mathbf{B}$ by

$$\begin{aligned} h(2n - 1) &= f(n) \\ h(2n) &= g(n) \end{aligned}$$

Thus $h$ maps certain odd integers onto **A** and certain even integers onto **B**, in one-to-one fashion. The domain of $h$ is a subset of **J**; the range of $h$ is $\mathbf{A} \cup \mathbf{B}$. Therefore, by Proposition 2.3, $\mathbf{A} \cup \mathbf{B}$ is countable.

Propositions 2.5 and 2.6 can be generalized by inductive arguments to show that the direct product or the union of any finite number of countable sets is a countable set.

That every subset of **J** is either finite or denumerable suggests that there are no infinite sets of cardinality less than that of **J**.

**Proposition 2.7:** Every infinite set **X** is at least denumerable; that is, $\overline{\overline{\mathbf{X}}} \geq \overline{\overline{\mathbf{J}}}$.

The proof of this proposition is left to the reader.

We now ask whether there are sets with cardinality greater than $\overline{\overline{\mathbf{J}}}$. Consider the set **R** containing all possible *infinite* sequences of 1's and 0's. A typical member of **R** might begin

$$0, 1, 1, 0, 0, 0, 1, 0, \ldots$$

**Proposition 2.8:** The set of all infinite sequences on $\{0, 1\}$ is uncountable.

***Proof:*** Let $\mathbf{R} = \{f \mid f: \mathbf{J} \longrightarrow \mathbf{S}\}$ be the set of all infinite sequences on $\mathbf{S} = \{0, 1\}$. If $\mathbf{R}$ were a countable set, we could arrange the elements of $\mathbf{R}$ in a sequence

$$\mathbf{g} = \mathbf{r}_1, \mathbf{r}_2, \mathbf{r}_3, \ldots, \mathbf{r}_i, \ldots$$

where each element is a sequence on $\mathbf{S}$:

$$\mathbf{r}_i = d_{i1}, d_{i2}, d_{i3}, \ldots, d_{ij}, \ldots, \qquad d_{ij} \in \mathbf{S}$$

We could then arrange these sequences in an array as in Figure 2.14.

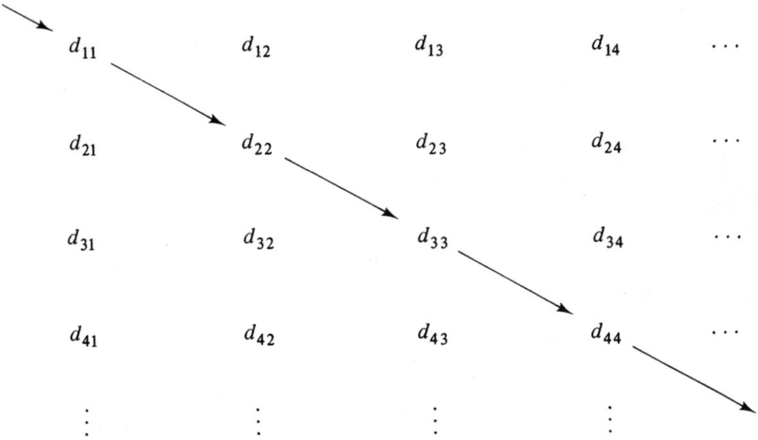


**Figure 2.14.** Diagonalization argument to show that the sequences on {0, 1} are uncountable.

Now consider the particular sequence

$$\mathbf{s} = b_1, b_2, b_3, \ldots, b_k, \ldots$$

where

$$b_k = 1 - d_{kk}$$

Thus the $k$th element of $\mathbf{s}$ is assured of having a value opposite to that of the corresponding diagonal element in the array. Chosen in this way, $\mathbf{s}$ is a sequence on $\mathbf{S}$ that differs in at least one component from each sequence in $\mathbf{g}$. Thus no sequence of elements in $\mathbf{R}$ can include every member of $\mathbf{R}$, and $\mathbf{R}$ is an uncountable set.

The method used in the above proof to construct a sequence $\mathbf{s}$ not in the collection $\mathbf{R}$ is called a *diagonalization argument*, because we can imagine the sequences of $\mathbf{R}$ as the rows of an infinite array and use the main diagonal to construct a sequence not in the array. Diagonalization occurs frequently in the theory of computability, which is introduced in Chapters 11 and 12.

The elements of $\mathbf{R}$ are in one-to-one correspondence with several important classes of objects. First, each sequence on $\{\mathbf{S} = 0, 1\}$ corresponds uniquely to a function $f$: $\mathbf{J} \longrightarrow \mathbf{S}$. Second, each function $f$: $\mathbf{J} \longrightarrow \mathbf{S}$ is the characteristic function of some subset $\mathbf{X}_f$ of $\mathbf{J}$:

$$\mathbf{X}_f = \{n \in \mathbf{J} \mid f(n) = 1\}$$

Therefore, the subsets of **J** are in one-to-one correspondence with sequences in **R**. Third, each sequence in **R** may be interpreted as the binary representation of a real number $x$ in the interval $0 \leq x < 1$. Thus the following sets all have the same cardinality, and are uncountable:

1. The collection of all functions $f$: $\mathbf{J} \longrightarrow \{0, 1\}$.
2. The power set $\mathcal{P}(\mathbf{J})$ containing each subset of the positive integers $\mathbf{J} = \{1, 2, 3, \ldots\}$. [Thus $\overline{\overline{\mathcal{P}(\mathbf{J})}} > \bar{\bar{\mathbf{J}}}$.]
3. The set of all real numbers $x$, $0 \leq x < 1$.

All infinite sets encountered in this book will have either the cardinality of the positive integers or the cardinality of $\mathcal{P}(\mathbf{J})$.

## 2.6 The Natural Numbers

An *algebraic system* consists of a set of objects **S**, a collection of functions relating the objects in **S**, and a set of axioms that specify membership in **S** or specify properties of the functions. The system of natural numbers is a simple, but extremely important, algebraic system:

**Example 2.14:** The *natural numbers* may be defined as the algebraic system $(\mathbf{N}, s)$, where **N** is a set and $s$ is a function that satisfy the following axioms:

1. There is an element *zero* in **N** (that is, $0 \in \mathbf{N}$).
2. The function $s$: $\mathbf{N} \rightarrow \mathbf{N} - \{0\}$ is a one-to-one function known as the *successor function*. We frequently write $n'$ or $(n + 1)$ instead of $s(n)$.
3. If **M** is a subset of **N** such that $0 \in \mathbf{M}$ and $n' \in \mathbf{M}$ whenever $n \in \mathbf{M}$, then $\mathbf{M} = \mathbf{N}$.

Axioms 1 and 2 assert that the objects

$$0, 0', 0'', 0''', \ldots$$

are contained in **N**. These are the natural numbers, for which we use the standard notation

$$0, 1, 2, 3, \ldots$$

Axiom 3 requires that **N** contain nothing more than the natural numbers: there must be no smaller set **M** that satisfies axioms 1 and 2.

All the familiar operations on integers may be defined in terms of the system (**N**, $s$), and their properties follow as consequences of the axioms given above. We shall see how this may be done in Chapter 13, where the properties of *recursive functions* are studied.

The system of natural numbers is the basis for the principle of inductive inference introduced in Section 2.1.3. Let $p(n)$ stand for the statement "the natural number $n$ has the property $p$." The principle of induction is as follows: *If $p(0)$ is valid and $p(k)$ implies $p(k')$ for each natural number $k$, then $p(n)$ is valid for each natural number $n$.* To see that the priniciple of induction follows from the axioms for the natural numbers, consider the set

$$\mathbf{M} = \{k \in \mathbf{N} \mid p(k)\}$$

Certainly, $0 \in \mathbf{M}$ because $p(0)$ is assumed; $k' \in \mathbf{M}$ whenever $k$ is in **M** because we assume that $p(k)$ implies $p(k')$. Hence the system (**M**, $s$) satisfies axioms 1 and 2. Since $\mathbf{M} \subseteq \mathbf{N}$, axiom 3 assures us that $\mathbf{M} = \mathbf{N}$, and $p(k)$ is valid for each natural number.

## 2.7 Strings and Languages

This section introduces the mathematical system that will serve as our abstract model of languages. The mathematical objects known as *strings* are abstractions of the familiar objects called "words" or "sentences." As an abstraction of "language," we use sets having strings as their members. The basic mathematical properties of these abstractions are developed in the following paragraphs, and are essential to all subsequent topics in this book.

### 2.7.1 Strings and String Operations

An *alphabet* is a finite set of symbols that represent the nondivisible or atomic objects used in the construction of sentences. By a *string of length k* on an alphabet **V**, we mean a sequence of $k$ symbols in **V**

$$\omega = v_1, v_2, \ldots, v_k, \qquad v_i \in \mathbf{V}$$

Ordinarily, we omit the commas and write simply

$$\omega = v_1 v_2 \ldots v_k$$

We use lowercase Greek letters to denote strings and write

$$|\omega| = k$$

to mean that $\omega$ is a string of length $k$. The unique string containing no symbols is called the *empty string* and is denoted by $\lambda$. Its length is $|\lambda| = 0$.

**Example 2.15:** Let $\mathbf{V} = (a, b, c)$. Then

$$\omega = abac$$

is a string on $\mathbf{V}$ and $|\omega| = 4$.

Let $\mathbf{W}_k$ denote the set of all strings of length $k$ on an alphabet $\mathbf{V}$:

$$\mathbf{W}_k = \{\omega \mid |\omega| = k\}$$

Then $\mathbf{W}_0$ is the set containing just the empty string; we use the boldface lambda to represent this set:

$$\boldsymbol{\lambda} = \mathbf{W}_0 = \{\lambda\}$$

The set

$$\mathbf{W} = \bigcup_{k=0}^{\infty} \mathbf{W}_k$$

is the set of all strings on $\mathbf{V}$, including the empty string. We shall show in Proposition 2.9 that $\mathbf{W}$ is a denumerable set.

The fundamental operation on strings is *concatenation* (sometimes called "string multiplication"), a binary operation on the set $\mathbf{W}$:

$$m\colon \mathbf{W} \times \mathbf{W} \longrightarrow \mathbf{W}$$

The concatenation of strings $\omega$ and $\varphi$ is the sequence of symbols formed by extending the sequence $\omega$ with the sequence of symbols $\varphi$:

$$m(\omega, \varphi) = v_1 v_2 \ldots v_m u_1 u_2 \ldots u_n$$

whenever

$$\omega = v_1 v_2 \ldots v_m \quad \text{and} \quad \varphi = u_1 u_2 \ldots u_n$$

For $m(\omega, \varphi)$ we use the notation

$$\omega \cdot \varphi$$

or simply $\omega\varphi$ where the meaning is clear. If $\omega = \varphi \cdot \psi$, we say that the string $\varphi$ is a *prefix* of $\omega$, or a *proper prefix* if $\psi$ is not the empty string. Similarly, $\psi$ is a *suffix of* $\omega$, or a *proper suffix* if $\varphi$ is nonempty.

The reader may easily verify the following properties of the concatenation operation:

1. For all $\omega, \varphi \in \mathbf{W}$, $\omega \cdot \varphi \in \mathbf{W}$. Thus the set $\mathbf{W}$ is closed under concatenation.
2. For all $\omega, \varphi, \psi \in \mathbf{W}$, $\omega \cdot (\varphi \cdot \psi) = (\omega \cdot \varphi) \cdot \psi$. Thus concatenation is associative.
3. For each $\omega \in \mathbf{W}$, $\omega \cdot \lambda = \lambda \cdot \omega = \omega$. Thus the empty string is an identity element for concatenation.
4. It is not necessarily true that $\omega \cdot \varphi = \varphi \cdot \omega$. Concatenation is not commutative.
5. For all $\omega, \varphi \in \mathbf{W}$, $|\omega \cdot \varphi| = |\omega| + |\varphi|$.

The notation $\omega^k$ is used to denote the concatenation of $k$ copies of the string $\omega$:

$$\omega^k = \underbrace{\omega \cdot \omega \cdot \ldots \cdot \omega}_{k \text{ times}}$$

The *reverse* of a string $\omega = v_1 v_2 \ldots v_n$ is the string $v_n \ldots v_2 v_1$ denoted by $\omega^R$.

It is important to keep in mind that each string on an alphabet **V** is a *finite* sequence of symbols; there is no such object as an "infinite string." (Although we sometimes use the term "sequence" to refer to a string, we will never use the term "string" to refer to an infinite sequence.) Consequently, the set of all strings on an alphabet is denumerable.

**Proposition 2.9:** If **V** is a nonempty alphabet, then the set **W** of all strings on **V** is denumerable.

***Proof:*** We construct a one-to-one and onto function

$$f\colon \mathbf{W} \longrightarrow \mathbf{J}$$

to show that $\bar{\bar{\mathbf{J}}} = \bar{\bar{\mathbf{W}}}$. Suppose that **V** contains $n$ symbols, and let $h\colon \mathbf{J}_n \longrightarrow \mathbf{V}$ be a one-to-one and onto function that associates an integer $1 \leq h(v) \leq n$ with each symbol $v$ in **V**. Define $f$ as follows:

$$f(\lambda) = 0$$

$$f(\omega \cdot v) = nf(\omega) + h(v) \begin{cases} \omega \in \mathbf{W} \\ v \in \mathbf{V} \end{cases}$$

The mapping $f$ associates with each string in **W** an integer, in base $n$ representation, in which each digit is the encoding of a letter by the transformation $h$. The reader may show that $f$ is one-to-one and onto.

A function that encodes each element of a set into a unique integer is known as a *Gödel numbering* of the set. Gödel numbering is an important method in the theory of computability, and will reappear in Chapters 11, 12, and 13.

### 2.7.2 Operations on Languages

By a *language* on an alphabet **V** we mean any set of strings on **V**. Thus each language on **V** is a subset of the set **W** of all strings on **V**, and each language is a countable set. The class of all languages on the alphabet **V** is the set of all subsets of **W**, that is, the power set $\mathcal{P}(\mathbf{W})$. Since **W** is denumerable if **V** is nonempty, the class of all languages on **V** has the cardinality of the real numbers, and is thus uncountable.

**Example 2.16:** Let $\mathbf{V} = \{a\}$ be a one-symbol alphabet. Then the language

$$\mathbf{L} = \{a^k \mid k \geq 0\}$$

contains each string of $a$'s. The language $\mathbf{L}$ is denumerably infinite even though each of its elements is a finite sequence.

The basic operations on languages include the set-theoretic operations union, intersection, and complement relative to $\mathbf{V}$. We define the concatenation of two languages $\mathbf{A}$ and $\mathbf{B}$ to be the set of strings formed by appending each string in $\mathbf{B}$ to each string in $\mathbf{A}$:

$$\mathbf{A} \cdot \mathbf{B} = \{\omega \cdot \varphi \mid \omega \in \mathbf{A}, \varphi \in \mathbf{B}\}$$

Again we often omit the dot and write simply $\mathbf{AB}$. Some important elementary properties of the concatenation of languages are illustrated by a few examples:

**Example 2.17:** Let $\mathbf{A} = \{a, ab\}$, $\mathbf{B} = \{c, bc\}$. Then

$$\mathbf{AB} = \{ac, abc, abbc\}$$

There are three strings in $\mathbf{AB}$ (not four) because two of the four possible combinations yield the same string ($abc$).

The set $\boldsymbol{\lambda} = \{\lambda\}$ is an identity element for the concatenation of languages. For instance,

$$\mathbf{A} \cdot \boldsymbol{\lambda} = \{a \cdot \lambda, ab \cdot \lambda\} = \{a, ab\} = \mathbf{A}$$

However, for any set $\mathbf{A}$,

$$\mathbf{A} \cdot \varnothing = \{\omega\varphi \mid \omega \in \mathbf{A}, \varphi \in \varnothing\} = \varnothing$$

since there are no elements in $\varnothing$. Similarly, $\varnothing \cdot \mathbf{A} = \varnothing$. Thus it is very important to distinguish between the empty set $\varnothing$ and the set $\boldsymbol{\lambda}$ containing just the empty string $\lambda$.

The reader should verify that concatenation of sets is associative, but not commutative, and that concatenation distributes over union

$$\mathbf{A} \cdot (\mathbf{B} \cup \mathbf{C}) = \mathbf{A} \cdot \mathbf{B} \cup \mathbf{A} \cdot \mathbf{C}$$

However, note that concatenation does not distribute over intersection.

Let $\mathbf{V}$ be an alphabet, and let $\mathbf{W}$ be the universe of strings generated by $\mathbf{V}$. For a language $\mathbf{A} \subseteq \mathbf{W}$, define the sets $\mathbf{A}^k$, $k \geq 0$, by

$$\mathbf{A}^0 = \boldsymbol{\lambda} \qquad \mathbf{A}^{k+1} = \mathbf{A}^k \cdot \mathbf{A}$$

Each of these sets is a subset of $\mathbf{W}$ because $\mathbf{W}$ is closed under concatenation. The union of these sets

$$\mathbf{A}^* = \bigcup_{k=0}^{\infty} \mathbf{A}^k$$

is also a subset of **W** and is called the *closure of* **A**. The unary operator * is known as the *Kleene star*, after the mathematician who first used this notation. The closure of a language contains each string that can be formed by concatenating an arbitrary number of strings chosen from the language.

**Example 2.18:** Let $\mathbf{A} = \{a, ab\}$. Then

$$\mathbf{A}^3 = \mathbf{A} \cdot \mathbf{A} \cdot \mathbf{A}$$
$$= \{aaa, aaab, aaba, aabab, abaa, abaab, ababa, ababab\}$$

Note that

$$\{a, ab\}^3 \neq \{a^3, (ab)^3\}$$

**Example 2.19:** Let $\mathbf{A} = \{a\}$, and $\mathbf{B} = \{0, 1\}$. Then

$$\mathbf{A}^* = \{\lambda, a, aa, aaa, \ldots\} = \{a^k \mid k \geq 0\}$$
$$\mathbf{B}^* = \{\lambda, 0, 1, 00, 01, 10, 11, 000, 001, 010, 011, \ldots\}$$

Note that $\mathbf{A}^*$ is the set of all possible strings on **A**, and $\mathbf{B}^*$ is the set of all possible strings on **B**.

Since the set of all strings of length $k + 1$ on an alphabet **V** may be written as

$$\mathbf{W}_{k+1} = \mathbf{W}_k \cdot \mathbf{V}$$

it follows that

$$\mathbf{W}_k = \mathbf{V}^k \quad \text{and} \quad \mathbf{W} = \mathbf{V}^*$$

Hence we shall use the notation $\mathbf{V}^*$ for the universe of strings on the alphabet **V**.

**Example 2.20:** The *reverse* of a language **L** contains the reverse of each string in **L**:

$$\mathbf{L}^R = \{\omega^R \mid \omega \in \mathbf{L}\}$$

Consider the language

$$\mathbf{L} = \{\omega\omega^R \mid \omega \in \mathbf{V}^*\}$$

Each string in **L** is the reverse of itself; for this reason **L** is known as the *mirror-image* language on the alphabet **V**. If each string of a language **L** is its own reverse, then $\mathbf{L} = \mathbf{L}^R$; but the converse is not necessarily true. For example, if $\mathbf{L} = \{01, 10\}$, then $\mathbf{L} = \mathbf{L}^R$; but **L** contains no mirror-image strings.

It is often convenient to characterize languages in terms of such operations as union, concatenation, and closure on single symbols of a given alphabet. For example,

$$\mathbf{L} = (\{0\} \cdot \{0, 1\})^*$$

is the language containing all strings obtained by repeated concatenation of the set

$$\{0\}\cdot\{0, 1\} = \{00, 01\}$$

Expressions of this sort are generally simplified by omitting the braces from singleton sets, and writing their elements as boldface symbols. Thus the expression

$$(\mathbf{0} \cdot (\mathbf{0} \cup \mathbf{1}))^*$$

is said to *denote the language* **L** above.

We also permit the use of the symbols $\boldsymbol{\lambda}$ and $\varnothing$ in such expressions. For example,

$$(\mathbf{1} \cup \boldsymbol{\lambda})(\mathbf{0} \cup \mathbf{1})$$

denotes the set

$$\{0, 1, 10, 11\}$$

whereas

$$(\mathbf{1} \cup \varnothing)(\mathbf{0} \cup \mathbf{1})$$

denotes the set

$$\{10, 11\}$$

**Example 2.21:** Unfortunately, the same set of strings may be described by a variety of different expressions, and it may not be at all obvious that the expressions describe the same set. For example, the expressions $\mathbf{0}(\mathbf{10})^*$ and $(\mathbf{01})^*\mathbf{0}$ describe the same set; similarly, the reader may verify that the expressions

$$(\mathbf{A} \cup \mathbf{1})^* \quad \text{and} \quad (\mathbf{1}^*\mathbf{A}^*)^*$$

describe the same set for any set of strings **A**.

## Notes and References

Many readers will doubtless find much of this chapter's material familiar (with the possible exception of the last section). Although our brief discussions contain enough detail for our later needs, some readers may desire a more detailed exposition of certain topics. On propositional logic, we recommend Margaris [1967], Mendelson [1964], or Stoll [1963]. On set theory, relations and functions, and algebraic systems, we recommend Birkhoff and MacLane [1967], Halmos [1960], or Stoll [1963]. (An advanced treatment of algebraic systems and language properties, with special emphasis on their relations to abstract machines, is found in Arbib [1968].) The subject of languages as string systems is considered in depth from standpoints quite different from ours by Brzozowski [1962] and by McNaughton and Yamada [1960].

## Problems

2.1. Using truth tables or other suitable means, prove that each of the following propositions is a tautology:

a. $p \lor (q \lor r) \Leftrightarrow (p \lor q) \lor r$.

b. $(p \lor q) \Leftrightarrow (q \lor p)$.

c. $p \land (q \lor r) \Leftrightarrow (p \land q) \lor (p \land r)$.

d. $p \lor \mathit{false} \Leftrightarrow p$.

e. $p \land \mathit{false} \Leftrightarrow \mathit{false}$.

f. $\neg(\neg p) \Leftrightarrow p$.

g. $p \lor p \Leftrightarrow p$.

h. $p \lor (p \land q) \Leftrightarrow p$.

i. $\neg(p \lor q) \Leftrightarrow (\neg p) \land (\neg q)$.

2.2. Consider the following six propositions:

(1) $(p \lor q \Leftrightarrow p) \Leftrightarrow (q \Leftrightarrow \mathit{false})$.

(2) $(((p \lor q) \Leftrightarrow \mathit{true}) \land ((p \land q) \Leftrightarrow \mathit{false})) \Leftrightarrow (p \Leftrightarrow \neg q)$.

(3) $((p \land q) \lor (\neg p \land \neg q)) \Leftrightarrow (\neg p \lor \neg q)$.

(4) $((p \land q) \lor (\neg p \land \neg q)) \Leftrightarrow ((\neg p \lor \neg q) \land (p \lor q))$.

(5) $\neg(\neg p \lor \neg q) \Leftrightarrow ((p \land q) \lor (\neg p \land \neg q))$.

(6) $((p \land q) \Leftrightarrow (q \lor r)) \Leftrightarrow (\neg p \land ((\neg q \land r) \lor q))$.

a. Which among the propositions are tautologies? Which are contradictions?

b. The *dual* of a compound proposition is constructed by interchanging occurrences of $\land$ and $\lor$, and occurrences of *true* and *false*, in the original proposition. Construct the dual of each proposition. Which are tautologies? Which are contradictions?

c. How does the truth table of a proposition correspond to that of its dual? In particular, must the dual of a tautology be a tautology? May it be a contradiction? May it be neither a tautology nor a contradiction?

2.3. a. Using the fundamental rules of inference and the following axioms, prove the theorem $(p \land s) \Rightarrow \neg q$.

Axiom 1: $p \Rightarrow (q \lor r)$.

Axiom 2: $q \Rightarrow \neg r$.

Axiom 3: $r \Leftrightarrow s$.

b. Using the fundamental rules of inference and the following axioms, prove the theorem $(a \land b) \Rightarrow (c \land e)$.

Axiom 1: $a \Rightarrow (c \lor d)$.

Axiom 2: $b \Rightarrow e$.

Axiom 3: $a \Rightarrow (\neg d \lor \neg e)$.

2.4. Using the fundamental rules of inference, prove the identities of Proposition 2.1. How do these relate to the identities of Problem 2.1?

2.5. Some of the following statements are false. Find counterexamples to those which are false, and prove those which are true.
a. $\mathbf{A} = (\mathbf{A} - \mathbf{B}) \cup \mathbf{A}$.
b. $\mathbf{A} = (\mathbf{A} \cup \mathbf{B}) - \mathbf{A}$.
c. $(\mathbf{A} \cup \mathbf{B})^c = \mathbf{A}^c \cup \mathbf{B}^c$.
d. $(\mathbf{A}^c \cup \mathbf{B}^c) - \mathbf{B}^c = \mathbf{A}^c$.
e. $\mathbf{B} = (\mathbf{A} \cup \mathbf{B})^c \cap (\mathbf{A} - \mathbf{B})$.
f. $((\mathbf{A} \cup \mathbf{B})^c \cap \mathbf{A}^c)^c = \mathbf{A} - ((\mathbf{A} - \mathbf{B}) \cap (\mathbf{A} \cup \mathbf{B})^c)$.
g. $\mathbf{A}^c \cup (\mathbf{B}^c - \mathbf{C}^c) = (\mathbf{A}^c \cup \mathbf{B}^c) - (\mathbf{A}^c \cup \mathbf{C}^c)$.

2.6. The *symmetric difference* $\mathbf{A} + \mathbf{B}$ of sets $\mathbf{A}$ and $\mathbf{B}$ is defined as

$$\mathbf{A} + \mathbf{B} = (\mathbf{A} - \mathbf{B}) \cup (\mathbf{B} - \mathbf{A})$$

Prove that $\mathbf{A} + \mathbf{B} = (\mathbf{A} \cup \mathbf{B}) - (\mathbf{A} \cap \mathbf{B})$.

2.7. Find a universe $\mathbf{U}$ and a property $p$ such that each set $\mathbf{S}$ can be expressed as $\mathbf{S} = \{x \in \mathbf{U} \mid p(x)\}$:
a. $\mathbf{S} = \{0, 2, 4, \ldots, 100\}$.
b. $\mathbf{S} = \{1, 2, 4, 8, 16, 32, \ldots\}$.
c. $\mathbf{S} = \{$points constituting the graph of $r^2 = x^2 + y^2\}$.

2.8. Let $\mathbf{A}, \mathbf{B}, \mathbf{C}$ be subsets of the integers defined as follows:

$$\mathbf{A} = \{k \mid 1 \leq k \leq 100\}$$

$$\mathbf{B} = \{k \mid 1 < k < 149\}$$

$$\mathbf{C} = \{k \mid 0 \leq k < 200\}$$

For each set $\mathbf{S}$, find a property $p$ such that $k$ is in $\mathbf{S}$ if and only if $p(k)$ is true:
a. $\mathbf{S} = \mathbf{A} \cup (\mathbf{B} \cap \mathbf{C})$.
b. $\mathbf{S} = (\mathbf{A} \cup \mathbf{B}) \cap (\mathbf{A} \cup \mathbf{C})$.
c. $\mathbf{S} = \mathbf{A} \cap (\mathbf{A} \cup \mathbf{B})$.
d. $\mathbf{S} = \mathbf{A}^c \cap (\mathbf{B} - \mathbf{C})^c$.
e. $\mathbf{S} = (\mathbf{A} - \mathbf{B})^c \cup (\mathbf{C} \cap \mathbf{B})$.
f. $\mathbf{S} = ((\mathbf{A} \cup \mathbf{C}) - (\mathbf{B} \cap \mathbf{A})^c \cap \mathbf{C})$.

2.9. Suppose that $\mathbf{A}$ and $\mathbf{B}$ are finite sets containing $n$ and $m$ elements, respectively. What can be said about the number of elements in $\mathbf{A} \times \mathbf{B}$? in $(\mathbf{A} \cup \mathbf{B}) \times (\mathbf{B} \cup \mathbf{A})$? in $(\mathbf{A} \cap \mathbf{B}) \times (\mathbf{B} \cup \mathbf{A})$? How do your answers change if we permit $\mathbf{B}$ to be an arbitrary countable set?

2.10. Each diagram below represents a relation $\rho$ such that $x_i \, \rho \, x_j$ if and only if a 1 marks cell $(i, j)$. Which of the represented relations are reflexive? symmetric? transitive? What characteristics of such diagrams are necessary and sufficient to ensure that the represented relations are reflexive? symmetric? transitive?

a. $\rho$:

| | $x_1$ | $x_2$ | $x_3$ | $x_4$ |
|---|---|---|---|---|
| $x_1$ | 1 | | 1 | |
| $x_2$ | | 1 | | |
| $x_3$ | 1 | | 1 | 1 |
| $x_4$ | | | 1 | 1 |

b. $\rho$:

| | $x_1$ | $x_2$ | $x_3$ | $x_4$ |
|---|---|---|---|---|
| $x_1$ | 1 | | | |
| $x_2$ | | | | 1 |
| $x_3$ | | 1 | 1 | 1 |
| $x_4$ | | | | 1 |

c. $\rho$:

| | $x_1$ | $x_2$ | $x_3$ | $x_4$ |
|---|---|---|---|---|
| $x_1$ | 1 | 1 | | |
| $x_2$ | 1 | | | |
| $x_3$ | | 1 | | 1 |
| $x_4$ | | 1 | 1 | 1 |

d. $\rho$:

| | $x_1$ | $x_2$ | $x_3$ | $x_4$ |
|---|---|---|---|---|
| $x_1$ | 1 | 1 | 1 | 1 |
| $x_2$ | 1 | | | 1 |
| $x_3$ | 1 | | | 1 |
| $x_4$ | 1 | 1 | 1 | 1 |

2.11. The inverse of a relation $\rho$, written $\rho^{-1}$, was defined in Section 2.3. Prove that $\rho$ is symmetric if and only if $\rho = \rho^{-1}$.

2.12. Consider the properties of (1) reflexivity, (2) symmetry, and (3) transitivity. Show that they are independent by describing a set **A** and eight relations on **A** such that each relation possesses a different subset of the properties.

2.13. Let $\rho$, $\rho'$ be relations such that the range of $\rho$ equals the domain of $\rho'$. Then $\rho \circ \rho'$ (the *composition* of $\rho$ and $\rho'$) is defined as

$$\rho \circ \rho' = \{(x, z) \mid (x\ \rho\ y) \wedge (y\ \rho'\ z) \text{ for some } y \text{ in the range of } \rho\}$$

a. Show that composition is associative.
b. Prove that $(\rho \circ \rho')^{-1} = \rho'^{-1} \circ \rho^{-1}$.
c. Prove that $\rho$ is transitive if and only if $\rho = \rho \circ \rho$.

2.14. a. Let $\rho$ be an equivalence relation on a set **A**. Prove that for any $x, y, z$ in **A**

$$(x\ \rho\ y) \wedge (y\ \rho\ z) \Rightarrow z\ \rho\ x$$

b. Let $\rho$ be a reflexive relation on **A** such that for all $x, y, z$ in **A** we have $(x\ \rho\ y) \wedge (y\ \rho\ z) \Rightarrow z\ \rho\ x$. Prove that $\rho$ is an equivalence relation.

2.15. Let $\rho$, $\rho'$ be equivalence relations on a set **A**. Let $n$, $n'$ be the number of equivalence classes of $\rho$, $\rho'$, respectively.

a. Define an equivalence relation $\rho''$ as follows:

$$x \, \rho'' \, y \Leftrightarrow (x \, \rho \, y) \wedge (x \, \rho' \, y)$$

What is the least number of equivalence classes of $\rho''$? What is the greatest number of equivalence classes of $\rho''$?

b. Define an equivalence relation $\rho'''$ as follows:

$$x \, \rho''' \, y \Leftrightarrow (x \, \rho \, y) \vee (x \, \rho' \, y)$$

What is the least number of equivalence classes of $\rho'''$? What is the greatest number of equivalence classes of $\rho'''$?

2.16. Prove the converse of Proposition 2.2; that is, prove that each partition of a set **A** defines an equivalence relation on **A**.

2.17. Which of the following relations $\rho$ are functions?

a. $\rho = \{(x, x^2 + x) \mid x \text{ is a real number}\}$.
b. $\rho = \{(x^2, x) \mid x \text{ is a real number}\}$.
c. $\rho = \{(x^3, x) \mid x \text{ is a real number}\}$.
d. $\rho = \{(\log x, x) \mid x \text{ is a real number}\}$.
e. $\rho = \{(x, \log x) \mid x \text{ is a real number}\}$.

2.18. Let **A** be the set $\{0, 1, 2, 3, 4\}$. For each relation $\rho$ on **A** given below, decide if $\rho$ is a (1) partial function, (2) total function, (3) one-to-one function, or (4) onto function.

a. $\rho = \{(0, 4), (3, 2), (1, 3), (2, 3), (4, 1)\}$.
b. $\rho = \{(3, 1), (2, 0), (1, 4), (4, 3), (0, 2)\}$.
c. $\rho = \{(0, 3), (1, 4), (3, 2), (2, 0), (1, 4)\}$.
d. $\rho = \{(1, 3), (3, 2), (4, 3), (0, 0), (3, 2)\}$.

2.19. Let $f$: $\mathbf{B} \longrightarrow \mathbf{C}$ and $g$: $\mathbf{A} \longrightarrow \mathbf{B}$ be functions. Then the *composition of f and g* is the function $f \circ g$: $\mathbf{A} \longrightarrow \mathbf{C}$, defined as

$$f \circ g(x) = f(g(x)), \qquad x \in \mathbf{A}$$

Show the following:

a. $(f \text{ onto}) \wedge (g \text{ onto}) \Rightarrow f \circ g \text{ onto}$.
b. $(f \text{ one-to-one}) \wedge (g \text{ one-to-one}) \Rightarrow f \circ g \text{ one-to-one}$.
c. $f \circ g \text{ onto} \not\Rightarrow g \text{ onto}$.
d. $f \circ g \text{ onto} \Rightarrow f \text{ onto}$.
e. $f \circ g \text{ one-to-one} \not\Rightarrow f \text{ one-to-one}$.
f. $f \circ g \text{ one-to-one} \Rightarrow g \text{ one-to-one}$.

2.20. Let **X** and **Y** be arbitrary sets, and let $f$ be a function from **X** to **Y**. Let $F$: $\mathcal{P}(\mathbf{X}) \longrightarrow \mathcal{P}(\mathbf{Y})$ be the function defined, for each $\mathbf{W} \subseteq \mathbf{X}$, as

$$F(\mathbf{W}) = \{y \in \mathbf{Y} \mid y = f(x) \text{ for some } x \text{ in } \mathbf{W}\}$$

Let $F^{-1}$: $\mathcal{P}(\mathbf{Y}) \longrightarrow \mathcal{P}(\mathbf{X})$ be the function defined, for each $\mathbf{V} \subseteq \mathbf{Y}$, as

$$F^{-1}(\mathbf{V}) = \{x \in \mathbf{X} \mid y = f(x), \text{ for some } y \text{ in } \mathbf{V}\}$$

Show that each of the following is a true assertion for all choices of $\mathbf{A}, \mathbf{B} \subseteq \mathbf{X}$ and $\mathbf{C}, \mathbf{D} \subseteq \mathbf{Y}$:

a. $F^{-1}(F(\mathbf{A})) \supseteq \mathbf{A}$.
b. $F(F^{-1}(\mathbf{C})) = \mathbf{C}$.
c. $F(\mathbf{A} \cup \mathbf{B}) = F(\mathbf{A}) \cup F(\mathbf{B})$.
d. $F(\mathbf{A} \cap \mathbf{B}) \subseteq (F(\mathbf{A}) \cap F(\mathbf{B}))$.
e. $F^{-1}(\mathbf{C} \cup \mathbf{D}) = F^{-1}(\mathbf{C}) \cup F^{-1}(\mathbf{D})$.
f. $F^{-1}(\mathbf{C} \cap \mathbf{D}) = F^{-1}(\mathbf{C}) \cap F^{-1}(\mathbf{D})$.

Show that containment cannot be replaced with equality in parts a and d; that is, show that the following assertions are not necessarily true:

g. $F^{-1}(F(\mathbf{A})) = \mathbf{A}$.
h. $F(\mathbf{A} \cap \mathbf{B}) = F(\mathbf{A}) \cap F(\mathbf{B})$.

Under what conditions on $f$, $\mathbf{A}$, and/or $\mathbf{B}$, will each be a true assertion?

2.21. Let $\mathbf{A}$ and $\mathbf{B}$ be sets containing $n$ and $m$ elements, respectively. How many elements are in $\mathcal{P}(\mathbf{A} \times \mathbf{B})$? How many of these elements are relations? functions? one-to-one functions?

2.22. Let $\sim$ be the relation defined as

$$\mathbf{A} \sim \mathbf{B} \qquad \text{if and only if } \bar{\bar{\mathbf{A}}} = \bar{\bar{\mathbf{B}}}$$

Show that $\sim$ is an equivalence relation on *any* family of sets.

2.23. Let $\mathbf{A}$ and $\mathbf{B}$ be finite sets. Show the following:

a. $\overline{\overline{\mathbf{A} \cap \mathbf{B}}} = \bar{\bar{\mathbf{A}}} - \overline{\overline{\mathbf{A} - \mathbf{B}}}$.
b. $\overline{\overline{\mathbf{A} - \mathbf{B}}} = \bar{\bar{\mathbf{A}}} - \overline{\overline{\mathbf{A} \cap \mathbf{B}}}$.
c. $\overline{\overline{\mathbf{A} \cup \mathbf{B}}} = \bar{\bar{\mathbf{A}}} + \bar{\bar{\mathbf{B}}} - \overline{\overline{\mathbf{A} \cap \mathbf{B}}}$.

2.24. Prove that a set is infinite just if it can be placed in one-to-one correspondence with a proper subset of itself.

2.25. Let $\mathbf{N} = \{0, 1, 2, \ldots\}$ be the set of natural numbers. A *rational* number is any number that can be expressed in the form

$$n/m, \qquad n \in \mathbf{N}, m \in \mathbf{N} - \{0\}$$

where / denotes division. Show that the set of rational numbers is countable.

2.26. Let $\mathbf{A} = \{a\}$ and $\mathbf{B} = \{b\}$. Describe informally membership in the following sets:

a. $\mathbf{A}^*$.
b. $\mathbf{A}^*\mathbf{B}^*$.
c. $(\mathbf{AB})^*$.
d. $(\mathbf{A} \cup \mathbf{B})^*$.
e. $(\mathbf{A} \cap \mathbf{B})^*$.
f. $(\mathbf{A} \cup \mathbf{B})^*\mathbf{AB}$.
g. $(\mathbf{A}^* \cup \mathbf{AB})^*\mathbf{A} \cup \mathbf{B}^*$.
h. $(\mathbf{A}^* \cup \mathbf{AB})^* - (\mathbf{BAB})^*$.

2.27. Let **A**, **B**, **C** be arbitrary languages on some alphabet **V**. Which of the following assertions are identities? Prove each identity and provide a counterexample to each assertion that is not an identity.

a. $\mathbf{A(BA)^*} = \mathbf{(AB)^*A}$.
b. $\mathbf{(AB)^*} = \mathbf{A^*B^*}$.
c. $\mathbf{A} \cdot (\mathbf{B^*} \cap \mathbf{C^*}) = \mathbf{A} \cdot \mathbf{B^*} \cap \mathbf{A} \cdot \mathbf{C^*}$.
d. $\mathbf{A^*B} = \mathbf{B} \cup \mathbf{A^*AB}$.
e. $(\mathbf{A} \cap \mathbf{B})^* = \mathbf{A^*} \cap \mathbf{B^*}$.
f. $\mathbf{A^*}(\mathbf{B} \cap \mathbf{C})^* = (\mathbf{AB} \cup \mathbf{AC})^*$.
g. $(\mathbf{A^*B^*})^* = (\mathbf{A} \cup \mathbf{B})^*$.
h. $\mathbf{A^*}(\mathbf{B} \cup \mathbf{C}) = \mathbf{A^*B} \cup \mathbf{A^*C}$.

2.28. Simplify the following expressions:

a. $\boldsymbol{\lambda}\varnothing^*$.
b. $\boldsymbol{\lambda}^*\varnothing^*$.
c. $\mathbf{A^*} \cup \varnothing^*$.
d. $(\boldsymbol{\lambda} \cup \mathbf{A})^*$.
e. $(\varnothing \cup \mathbf{A})^*$.
f. $(\boldsymbol{\lambda}^*\varnothing^*)^*$.
g. $\{\varnothing, \{\varnothing\}\} - \varnothing$.
h. $\{\varnothing, \{\varnothing\}\} - \{\varnothing\}$.
i. $\{\varnothing\} \cap \{\varnothing\}$.
j. $\{\varnothing\} \cap \varnothing$.
k. $\boldsymbol{\lambda} - \varnothing^*$.
l. $\boldsymbol{\lambda} - \{\varnothing^*\}$.
m. $\boldsymbol{\lambda}^* - \varnothing^*$.

2.29. Let $\mathbf{V} = \{0, 1\}$. Using singleton sets and the operators $\cup$, $\cdot$, and $*$, find expressions for the following languages on **V**:

a. All $\omega \in \mathbf{V}^*$ such that the string 101 appears as a substring of $\omega$.
b. All $\omega \in \mathbf{V}^*$ such that each 0 appearing in $\omega$ is immediately followed by at least two 1's.
c. All $\omega \in \mathbf{V}^*$ such that each 1 appearing in $\omega$ is immediately followed by the substring 10.
d. The set of all $\omega \in \mathbf{V}^* - \{\lambda\}$ such that 101 does not appear as a substring of $\omega$.

2.30. Let **V** be an alphabet, let $\mathbf{W} = \mathbf{V}^*$, and let $\mathbf{L} \subseteq \mathbf{W}$ be an arbitrary language on **V**. Define the relation $\sim$ on **W** as follows:

$$\alpha \sim \beta \quad \text{if and only if, for all } \omega, \varphi \in \mathbf{W},$$
$$(\omega\alpha\varphi \in \mathbf{L}) \Leftrightarrow (\omega\beta\varphi \in \mathbf{L})$$

Show that $\sim$ is an equivalence relation.

***2.31.** Let **S** be a set of strings from $\mathbf{V}^*$ for some alphabet **V**. If, for all $\alpha$, $\beta$ in **S**, we have $\alpha\beta = \beta\alpha$, then we say that **S** is *commutative*. Show that **S** is commutative if and only if $\mathbf{S} \subseteq \omega^*$ for some $\omega \in \mathbf{V}^*$. (*Hint:* Let $\omega_0$ denote the shortest nonempty string in **S** and prove that it is unique. For each integer $k \geq 1$, let $\omega_k$ be the shortest nonempty string in $\mathbf{S} - \{\omega_0, \omega_1, \ldots, \omega_{k-1}\}$, and show that $\omega_k$ is unique. Finally, show that for each $k \geq 0$, $\omega_k = \omega_0^n$ for some integer $n \geq 1$, by recalling that $\omega_k\omega_0 = \omega_0\omega_k$.)

# 3

# *Formal Grammars*

The automatic translation of text from one language to another has long been a subject of interest both to linguists and computer scientists. The years following the introduction of high-level programming languages witnessed an active and fruitful search for precise formalizations of language to aid in understanding and simplifying the description of the translation process. Although the enticing goal of quality translation of natural language texts by computer has remained elusive, the theory has had profound influence on the design and processing of computer programming languages.

We present here the fundamental concepts of formal grammars and their relation to the languages that they describe. Although many classes of grammars and languages have been studied, our attention is focused on a hierarchy of four major classes of languages, the "Chomsky hierarchy." In subsequent chapters, we relate these classes of languages to important classes of abstract automata, and use the structure of the automata to study the structure of the languages. The formalism developed in this chapter is basic to this later work and provides insights not readily obtained from consideration of abstract machines alone.

## 3.1 Representations of Languages

According to the dictionary, a language is "the aggregate of words and of methods of combining them used by a particular community, nation, or race of people." This statement is hardly specific enough to serve as an adequate mathematical description of the term "language." Linguists agree that any adequate formalism for natural language must cope with the infinity of possible sentences apparent in language use. One cannot hope to exhaustively list all possible sentences in a language, for each user of a language is able to speak sentences that have never previously been spoken and yet are intelligible to other users of the language. Similarly, one cannot hope to write down all possible Algol or Fortran computer programs, for any user is able to write programs never before written that will run perfectly well on a computer. Thus the central problem of describing a language is to provide a finite specification for an essentially infinite class of objects.

Given an alphabet **V**, the set **V*** is the totality of all possible strings on **V**, and a language **L** on **V** is an arbitrary subset of **V***. A description for **L** is sufficient for our purposes if it can be used to decide whether a given member of **V*** is or is not a member of **L**. This notion of sufficiency may appear to ignore questions concerning the "meaning" of sentences. However, we shall find that the structural descriptions of sentences provided by our representations of languages are closely related to the interpretations attached to those sentences by the language user.

For English, the alphabet might be the 26 letters in both upper- and lowercase, the ten digits, the space, and a few punctuation marks—the symbols on a typewriter keyboard. A formal grammar for English would be a finite set of rules with which one could decide whether any typed line is a legitimate sentence in English.

For a computer programming language, the alphabet is the collection of all nondivisible symbols that may appear in a program. A "sentence" in a programming language is usually considered to be any string of these symbols that represents a complete program. A satisfactory grammar for a programming language should permit one to determine by a mechanical procedure whether an arbitrary sequence of symbols is a "well-formed" program. We shall see how a grammar can provide a structural description of a well-formed program that is useful for assigning meaning to the program.

The requirement that a language representation be finite is astoundingly severe, for it means that infinitely many languages have no representations! If **V** is an alphabet, then each subset of **V*** is a language on **V**; that is, the set of languages on **V** is the power set of **V*** and is thus uncountable. On the other hand, we shall find that the number of finite representations can be at best countably infinite. Hence uncountably many languages have no finite representation. Perhaps we should not be bothered by this fact, for languages that are not finitely representable have so little order to their structure that they are likely to be of no practical interest. However, one might wonder whether the natural languages belong to this class of unrepresentable languages.

One means of representing a language has been suggested in Chapter 1: an accepter machine for the language. If the accepter has a finite number of functionally relevant states, it constitutes a finite representation. We shall find, however, that the class of languages for which such finite-state machines provide structural descriptions is rather limited. Thus we shall be led to consider other, more powerful forms of abstract machines as possible finite representations of languages.

The definition of language by an accepter machine is an *analytic* approach to language representation, since the machine directly tests an arbitrary input sentence for membership in the language. Alternatively, we may use a *generative* representation of a language—a finite set of rules which, if followed in any valid order, will construct only strings that are sentences of the language. Formal grammars are such representations.

Can a generative representation of a language be used to determine whether an arbitrary string is a member of the language? In later chapters we shall study mechanical procedures that decide whether any particular string is generated by a given formal grammar. These procedures work for all but the most general form of grammar; for that form, we shall prove that *no* mechanical procedure exists that can decide whether a given string is generated by a grammar.

## 3.2 Basic Concepts of Grammars

### 3.2.1 An Illustration from English

The essential concept in the grammatical description of language is familiar to every grammar school student of English: the construction of sentences by the successive application of grammatical *rules*. A rule specifies how a phrase may be rewritten as the concatenation of constituent phrases. For example, the sentence

Jack and Jill ran up the hill

consists of two major phrases:

| ⟨subject⟩ | ⟨predicate⟩ |
|---|---|
| Jack and Jill | ran up the hill |

This sentence construction can be described by the grammatical rule

1. ⟨sentence⟩ $\longrightarrow$ ⟨subject⟩ ⟨predicate⟩

The rule states that a phrase of type ⟨sentence⟩ may be rewritten as a phrase of type ⟨subject⟩ followed by a phrase of type ⟨predicate⟩. We have enclosed the names of phrase types in angular brackets to prevent possible confusion with words or symbols that may appear in sentences of the language being described.

The ⟨subject⟩ of the illustrative sentence is a pair of nouns connected by a conjunction. This construction could be described by the grammatical rule

$$\langle\text{subject}\rangle \longrightarrow \langle\text{noun}\rangle\,\langle\text{conjunction}\rangle\,\langle\text{noun}\rangle$$

However, we prefer to choose rules that explain the structure of as large a collection of phrases as possible. Consider the rules

2. ⟨subject⟩ ⟶ ⟨noun phrase⟩
3. ⟨noun phrase⟩ ⟶ ⟨noun⟩
4. ⟨noun phrase⟩ ⟶ ⟨noun⟩ ⟨conjunction⟩ ⟨noun phrase⟩

Rule 2 states that a phrase of type ⟨subject⟩ may be a phrase of type ⟨noun phrase⟩. Rules 3 and 4 state that a phrase of type ⟨noun phrase⟩ may take either of two forms: (1) it may be a phrase of type ⟨noun⟩ appearing alone, or (2) it may be rewritten as a phrase of type ⟨noun⟩ followed by phrases of types ⟨conjunction⟩ and ⟨noun phrase⟩ in succession. Thus a noun phrase may have a noun phrase as one of its constituents. It is this *recursive property* of grammatical rules that permits the finite representation of infinite collections of sentences.

The ⟨subject⟩ of the sample sentence is generated by one application each of rules 2 to 4 above, and one application of each of the following rules:

5. ⟨conjunction⟩ ⟶ and
6. ⟨noun⟩ ⟶ Jack
7. ⟨noun⟩ ⟶ Jill

as follows:

| | |
|---|---|
| ⟨subject⟩ | |
| ⟨noun phrase⟩ | rule 2 |
| ⟨noun⟩ ⟨conjunction⟩ ⟨noun phrase⟩ | rule 4 |
| ⟨noun⟩ and ⟨noun phrase⟩ | rule 5 |
| Jack and ⟨noun phrase⟩ | rule 6 |
| Jack and ⟨noun⟩ | rule 3 |
| Jack and Jill | rule 7 |

These lines, known as *sentential forms*, make up what is called a *derivation* of the subject phrase according to rules 2 through 7. Each line of a derivation results from rewriting the preceding line as permitted by some rule. It is often possible to represent a derivation by a tree diagram, as in Figure 3.1. The derivation above corresponds to the left part of the diagram.

The predicate of the sample sentence consists of a verb and a prepositional phrase:

8. ⟨predicate⟩ ⟶ ⟨verb⟩ ⟨prepositional phrase⟩
   ran up the hill

9. ⟨verb⟩ ⟶ ran

The structure of the prepositional phrase is described by the following rule:

10. ⟨prepositional phrase⟩ ⟶ ⟨preposition⟩ ⟨article⟩ ⟨noun⟩

in which the constituents of the right side may be replaced as follows:

11. ⟨preposition⟩ ⟶ up
12. ⟨article⟩ ⟶ the
13. ⟨noun⟩ ⟶ hill

Rules 1 through 13 constitute a *grammar*. The given sentence is one member of the language generated by this grammar. Its *structural description*, the tree diagram in Figure 3.1, shows how the productions of the grammar

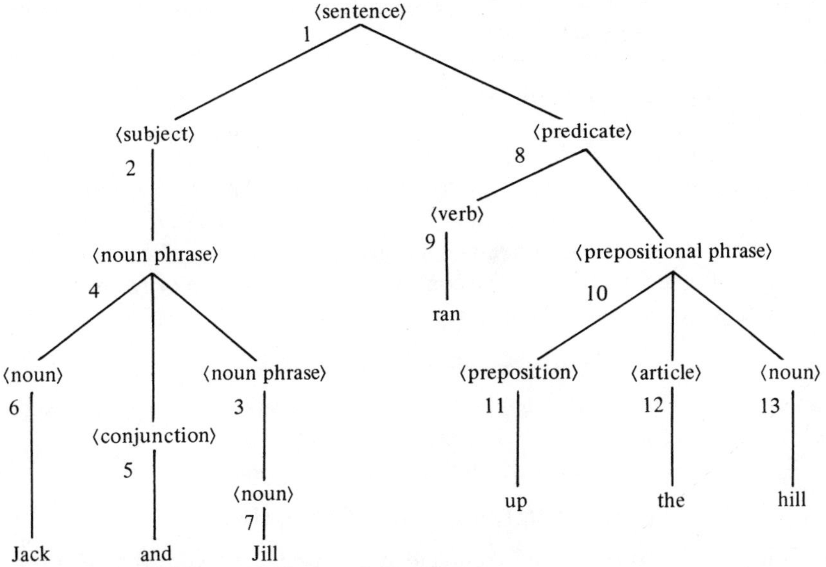


**Figure 3.1.** Structural description of an English sentence.

can be applied to generate the sentence. Each node of the tree diagram corresponds to the application of a particular grammatical rule, as indicated by the numbers in the figure. Since the productions specify how one type of phrase is formed by combining other phrase types, these grammars are often called *phrase-structure grammars*.

Any sentence for which a grammar provides a structural description is a valid sentence in the language generated by the grammar. For instance, our grammar also generates these sentences:

Jill and Jack ran up the hill

Jack and Jack and Jill ran up the hill

Jack and Jill and Jack and Jill ran up the hill

The reader should be able to construct the corresponding structural descriptions. These examples show how a finite set of rules, through repeated applications, can generate an arbitrarily large collection of sentences.

Other sentences belong to our language:

hill ran up the Jack and Jill

Jack and hill ran up the Jill and hill

We would normally regard these as nonsense sentences in English, but no constraints have been incorporated into our grammar to ensure that only sentences meaningful to a user of English are generated. Our grammar provides only that certain elementary rules concerning parts of speech be obeyed. The formulation of an adequate grammar for a natural language is a major unrealized goal of linguistic research.

### 3.2.2 An Illustration from Algol

For a second introductory example of a phrase-structure grammar, we consider a portion of the computer programming language Algol. Algol was the first practical programming language for which a complete set of grammatical rules was formulated. A program in Algol contains a sequence of phrases of type ⟨statement⟩. We consider a simplified form of Algol assignment statement, of which the phrase

$$w := \textbf{if } x < y \textbf{ then } 0 \textbf{ else } x + y + 1$$

is an example. This phrase has the following interpretation: if $x < y$, assign the value 0 to $w$; otherwise, assign the value of $(x + y + 1)$ to $w$.

This phrase is written with symbols from the alphabet

$$\{w, x, y, 0, 1, +, <, :=, \textbf{if}, \textbf{then}, \textbf{else}\}$$

which is just a portion of the complete Algol alphabet. Note that **if**, **then**, and **else** are considered single, nondivisible symbols. The overall structure of the phrase may be described by the following grammatical rule:

$$\begin{array}{llll} 1. & \langle\text{statement}\rangle \longrightarrow & \langle\text{left part}\rangle & \langle\text{expression}\rangle \\ & & w := & \textbf{if } x < y \textbf{ then } 0 \textbf{ else } x + y + 1 \end{array}$$

The meaning of an assignment statement to a programmer is that the phrase of type ⟨expression⟩ represents a numerical value which is to be assigned to the variable defined by the ⟨left part⟩ phrase. In the example, the phrase of type ⟨expression⟩ is a conditional construction formed according to the following grammatical rule:

$$\begin{array}{llllllll} 3. & \langle\text{expression}\rangle \longrightarrow & \textbf{if} & \langle\text{Boolean}\rangle & \textbf{then} & \langle\text{arithmetic}\rangle & \textbf{else} & \langle\text{expression}\rangle \\ & & & x < y & & 0 & & x + y + 1 \end{array}$$

Here the phrase type ⟨Boolean⟩ is interpreted as representing a value of either *true* or *false*. The conditional construction is to be interpreted as follows: its value is that of the ⟨arithmetic⟩ phrase if the ⟨Boolean⟩ phrase has value *true*: otherwise, its value is that of the ⟨expression⟩ phrase. The recurrence of the phrase type ⟨expression⟩ in this rule permits conditional constructions to be nested to arbitrary depth.

The structure of the phrase

$$x + y + 1$$

is described by the rules

4. ⟨expression⟩ ⟶ ⟨arithmetic⟩
7. ⟨arithmetic⟩ ⟶ ⟨term⟩ + ⟨arithmetic⟩
8. ⟨arithmetic⟩ ⟶ ⟨term⟩

The phrase type ⟨term⟩ is interpreted as being either a number or a variable-identifying letter; the value of a ⟨term⟩ is either the number itself or the value of the variable. Rule 7, recursive with respect to the phrase type ⟨arithmetic⟩, permits phrases containing an arbitrary number of ⟨term⟩ phrases separated by the symbol +.

The appearance of numbers and variable-denoting letters as ⟨term⟩ phrases requires additional rules:

9. ⟨term⟩ ⟶ ⟨identifier⟩
10. ⟨term⟩ ⟶ 0
11. ⟨term⟩ ⟶ 1
14. ⟨identifier⟩ ⟶ $x$
15. ⟨identifier⟩ ⟶ $y$

Figure 3.2 is a structural description of the phrase $x + y + 1$.

The ⟨Boolean⟩ phrase

$$x < y$$

is interpreted as a comparison of the values of two arithmetic expressions.

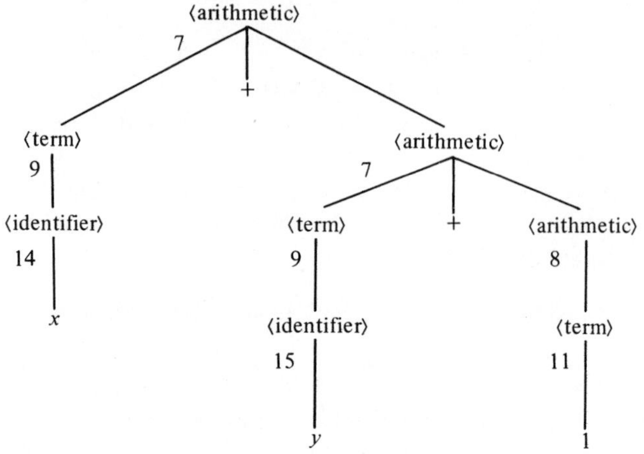


**Figure 3.2.** Structural description of an arithmetic phrase.

This construction is described by the single grammatical rule

5. ⟨Boolean⟩ ⟶ ⟨arithmetic⟩ $<$ ⟨arithmetic⟩
   $x$ $y$

That the letters $x$ and $y$ by themselves constitute phrases of type ⟨arithmetic⟩ is already established by rules 8, 9, 14, and 15. Finally, the form of the ⟨left part⟩ phrase is specified by

2. ⟨left part⟩ ⟶ ⟨identifier⟩ :=

and for the sample statement we need the additional rule

13. ⟨identifier⟩ ⟶ $w$

The complete structural description of the sample statement is given in Figure 3.3, and includes the number of the rewriting rule used in the expansion of each phrase.

To simplify further discussion, we introduce a notational convention used throughout our study of formal grammars: *capital letters will be used to denote phrase types.* For the present example, let us use the following letters:

$S$ ⟨statement⟩
$L$ ⟨left part⟩
$E$ ⟨expression⟩
$I$ ⟨identifier⟩
$B$ ⟨Boolean⟩
$A$ ⟨arithmetic⟩
$T$ ⟨term⟩

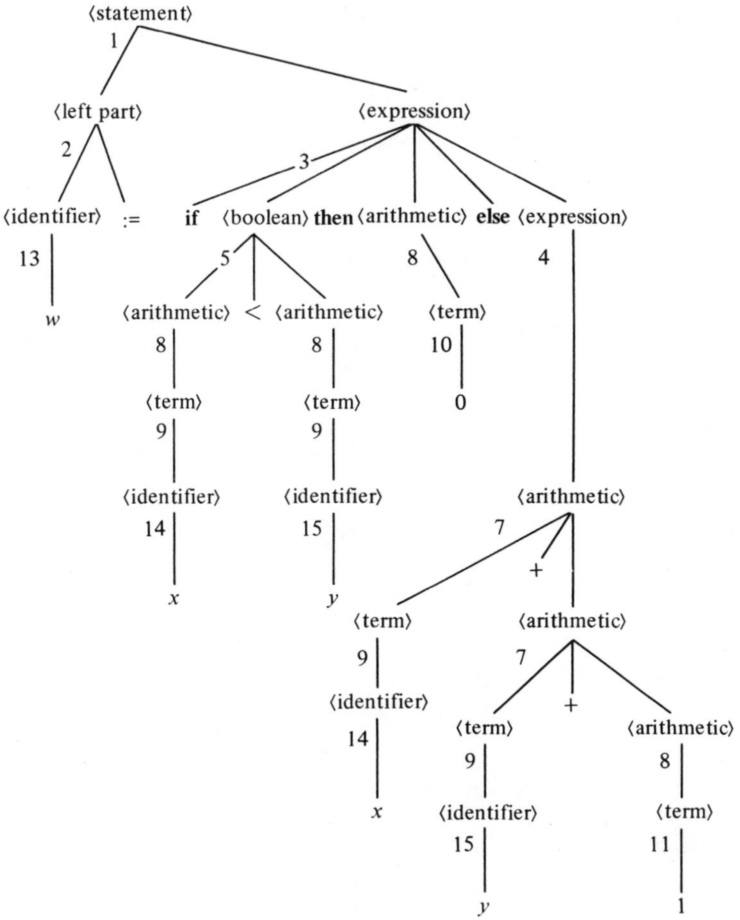


**Figure 3.3.** Structural description of the Algol statement $w$ := **if** $x < y$ **then** 0 **else** $x + y + 1$.

Expressed in terms of these letters, a more complete grammar for phrases of type ⟨statement⟩ consists of the following rules:

1. $S \longrightarrow LE$
2. $L \longrightarrow I :=$
3. $E \longrightarrow$ **if** $B$ **then** $A$ **else** $E$
4. $E \longrightarrow A$
5. $B \longrightarrow A < A$
6. $B \longrightarrow A = A$
7. $A \longrightarrow T + A$
8. $A \longrightarrow T$
9. $T \longrightarrow I$
10. $T \longrightarrow 0$
11. $T \longrightarrow 1$
12. $T \longrightarrow (E)$
13. $I \longrightarrow w$
14. $I \longrightarrow x$
15. $I \longrightarrow y$

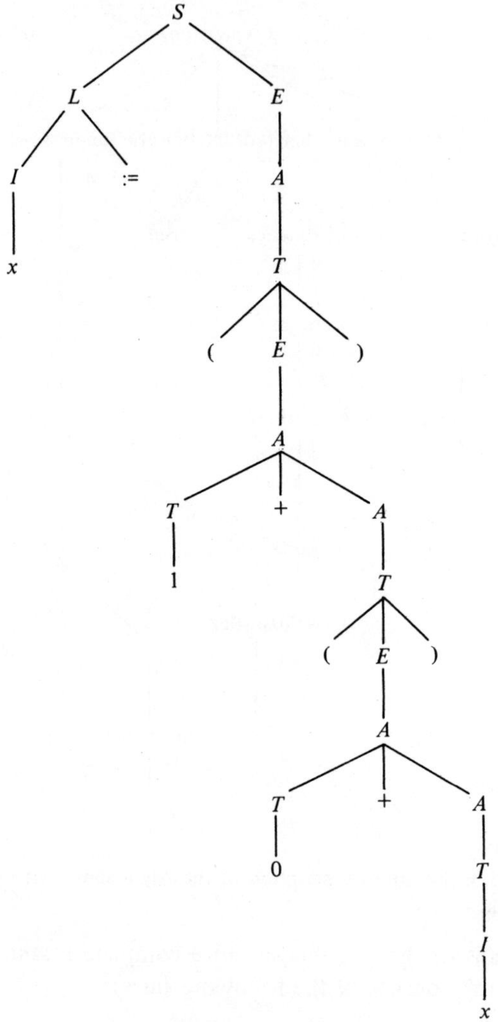


**Figure 3.4.** Structural description of the Algol statement $x := (1 + (0 + x))$.

This set of rewriting rules is a *formal grammar* in which the rules are known as *productions*. Productions 6 and 12 have been included so that forms of Algol phrases containing the symbols (,), and = may be generated. The interpretation of rule 6 should be clear. Rule 12 permits a phrase of type ⟨term⟩ to be written as an expression enclosed within parentheses. The grammar now generates a wide variety of assignment statements. Figures 3.4 and 3.5 give structural descriptions of two further examples. In each case the tree diagram shows clearly how meaning should be assigned to each phrase according to our informal discussion.

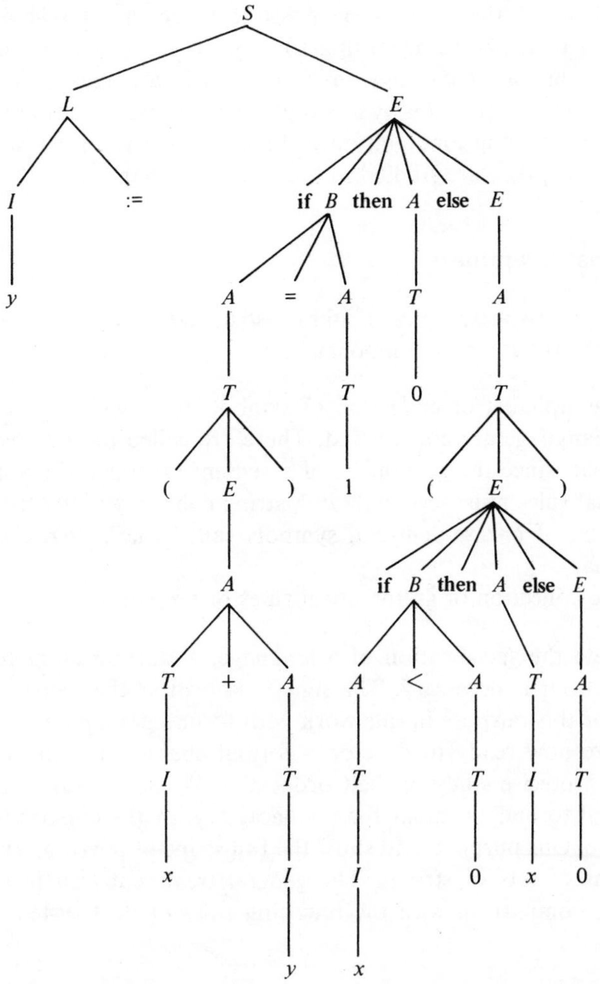


**Figure 3.5.** Structural description of the Algol statement $y :=$ **if** $(x + y) = 1$ **then** 0 **else** (**if** $x < 0$ **then** $x$ **else** 0).

Is the above grammar an adequate representation of the Algol assignment statement? Admitting that the grammar is incomplete, the answer still depends on one's objective. Each string generated by the grammar is a legal Algol phrase according to the official syntax of Algol. But the grammar generates such phrases as

$$x := x$$

and $$x := \textbf{if } w > w \textbf{ then } x + y \textbf{ else } x$$

which would be of no value in a computer program. Yet it is true that most compilers for Algol accept such statements without comment.

We shall see that it may be possible to construct several structural descriptions of a phrase according to a given set of productions. Such a grammar is then an *ambiguous* representation of a language and can easily lead to incorrect translation by a compiler or misinterpretation by a person. Questions concerning ambiguity are therefore of basic interest to the language designer; they are studied in this and later chapters.

## 3.3 Formal Grammars

From the two examples of phrase-structure grammars, we see that a grammar has three major components:

1. The alphabet or collection of symbols from which sentences of the described language are constructed. These are called the *terminal letters* of the grammar, since the generation of a sentence through the application of grammatical rules must terminate in a string containing only these symbols.
2. A set of phrase-denoting symbols called the *nonterminal letters* of the grammar.
3. The collection of grammatical rules or *productions*.

To complete the specification of a language, a starting point for applying the productions is necessary. The sign $\Sigma$, known as the *sentence symbol*, is reserved for this purpose in our work with formal grammars.

We are now ready to develop a formal characterization of grammars and begin a precise study of their properties. We start with a more general definition of formal grammar than is necessary for the illustrative examples given above. Our purpose is to show the full scope of rewriting rules as finite descriptions of sets of strings. The general treatment also provides background for comparison with the rewriting rules of Post systems studied in Chapter 14.

**Definition 3.1:** A *formal grammar* is a four-tuple

$$\mathbf{G} = (\mathbf{N}, \mathbf{T}, \mathbf{P}, \Sigma)$$

where

$\mathbf{N}$ is a finite set of *nonterminal symbols*
$\mathbf{T}$ is a finite set of *terminal symbols*
$\mathbf{N}$ and $\mathbf{T}$ are disjoint: $\mathbf{N} \cap \mathbf{T} = \varnothing$
$\mathbf{P}$ is a finite set of *productions*
$\Sigma$ is the *sentence symbol*; $\Sigma \notin (\mathbf{N} \cup \mathbf{T})$

Each production in $\mathbf{P}$ is an ordered pair of strings $(\alpha, \beta)$,

$$\alpha = \varphi A \psi$$
$$\beta = \varphi \omega \psi$$

in which $\omega$, $\varphi$, and $\psi$ are possibly empty strings in $(\mathbf{N} \cup \mathbf{T})^*$ and $A$ is $\Sigma$ or a nonterminal letter. We usually write a production $(\alpha, \beta)$ as

$$\alpha \longrightarrow \beta$$

Formal grammars as defined here are also known as *phrase-structure grammars.*

The process of generating a sentence according to a formal grammar is the successive rewriting of *sentential forms* through the use of the productions of the grammar, starting with the sentential form $\Sigma$. The sequence of sentential forms required to generate a sentence constitutes a *derivation* of the sentence according to the grammar.

**Definition 3.2:** Let $\mathbf{G}$ be a formal grammar. A string of symbols in $(\mathbf{N} \cup \mathbf{T})^* \cup \{\Sigma\}$ is known as a *sentential form.* If $\alpha \longrightarrow \beta$ is a production of $\mathbf{G}$ and $\omega = \varphi\, \alpha\, \psi$ and $\omega' = \varphi\, \beta\, \psi$ are sentential forms, we say that $\omega'$ is *immediately derived* from $\omega$ in $\mathbf{G}$, and we indicate this relation by writing $\omega \Longrightarrow \omega'$. If $\omega_1, \omega_2, \ldots, \omega_n$ is a sequence of sentential forms such that $\omega_1 \Longrightarrow \omega_2 \Longrightarrow \cdots \Longrightarrow \omega_n$, we say that $\omega_n$ is *derivable* from $\omega_1$ and indicate this relation by writing $\omega_1 \overset{*}{\Longrightarrow} \omega_n$. The sequence $\omega_1, \omega_2, \ldots, \omega_n$ is called a *derivation* of $\omega_n$ from $\omega_1$ according to $\mathbf{G}$.

**Definition 3.3:** The *language* $\mathbf{L(G)}$ generated by a formal grammar $\mathbf{G}$ is the set of terminal strings derivable from $\Sigma$:

$$\mathbf{L(G)} = \{\omega \in \mathbf{T}^* \mid \Sigma \overset{*}{\Longrightarrow} \omega\}$$

If $\omega \in \mathbf{L(G)}$, we say that $\omega$ is a *string*, a *sentence*, or a *word* in the language generated by $\mathbf{G}$.

According to the definitions, each production of a formal grammar is a grammatical rule permitting modification of a sentential form by substitution of an arbitrary string for a particular phrase-denoting letter. The application of a production $\varphi\, A\, \psi \longrightarrow \varphi\, \omega\, \psi$ to rewriting the sentential form $\omega_i$

as $\omega_{i+1}$ is illustrated in Figure 3.6. The left side of the production is matched with a substring of $\omega_i$, and the phrase letter $A$ is replaced with the string $\omega$ to yield $\omega_{i+1}$.

Two generalizations have been made beyond the concepts used in the examples of Section 3.2. First, a substitution is conditioned on the phrase symbol appearing in a particular *context* specified by strings $\varphi$ and $\psi$ of the production. Second, the string $\omega$ substituted for a phrase letter may be the empty string $\lambda$, permitting arbitrary erasure of certain nonterminals in the course of a derivation. This second generalization permits a sentential form to decrease in length in a derivation step.

It would appear possible to define more general classes of grammars. For example, we could allow productions of the form $\alpha \longrightarrow \beta$ in which

$\alpha$ may be any nonempty string in $(\mathbf{N} \cup \mathbf{T})^* \cup \{\Sigma\}$

$\beta$ may be any (possibly empty) string in $(\mathbf{N} \cup \mathbf{T})^*$

Grammars in which such rules are permitted are sometimes called *semi-Thue systems.* They can be shown to be no more general that the grammars of

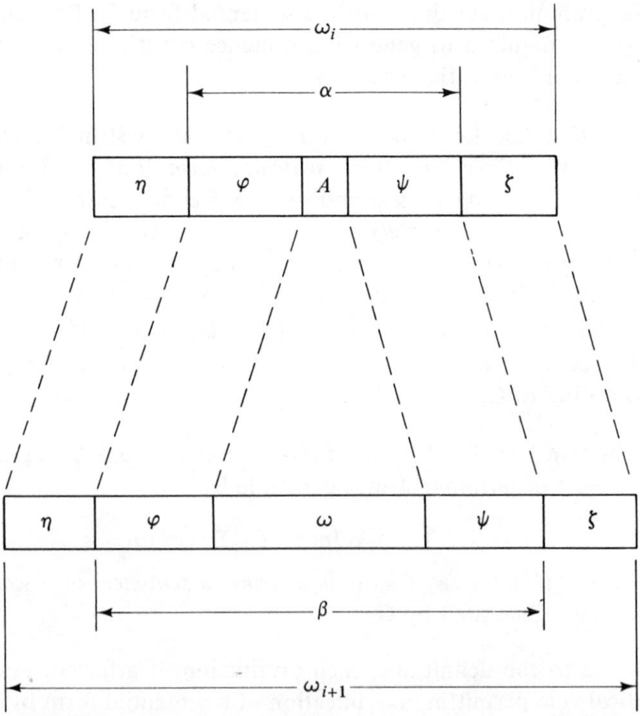


**Figure 3.6.** Application of a production $\varphi A \psi \longrightarrow \varphi\omega\psi$ in a derivation step $\omega_i \longrightarrow \omega_{i+1}$.

Definition 3.1; unrestricted rules do not permit the representation of any language that cannot be represented by our grammars. (See Problem 3.18.)

In view of the equivalence between unrestricted forms of productions and those allowed by our definitions, we will occasionally use productions like

$$AB \longrightarrow BA$$

where convenient in formal discussions. Were we to adhere strictly to the forms of Definition 3.1, these four productions would be required to interchange $A$ and $B$:

$$AB \longrightarrow XB$$
$$XB \longrightarrow XY$$
$$XY \longrightarrow BY$$
$$BY \longrightarrow BA$$

where $X$ and $Y$ are not used elsewhere in the grammar.

**Example 3.1:** Let $\mathbf{G}_1$ have $\mathbf{N} = \{A, B, C\}$, $\mathbf{T} = \{a, b, c\}$ and the set of productions

$$\begin{array}{ll} \Sigma \longrightarrow A & CB \longrightarrow BC \\ A \longrightarrow aABC & bB \longrightarrow bb \\ A \longrightarrow abC & bC \longrightarrow bc \\ & cC \longrightarrow cc \end{array}$$

Figure 3.7 is a derivation of $a^3b^3c^3$ showing the production applied at each step. The reader should convince himself that the word $a^kb^kc^k$ is in $\mathbf{L}(\mathbf{G}_1)$ for all $k \geq 1$, and that only these words are in $\mathbf{L}(\mathbf{G}_1)$. That is,

$$\mathbf{L}(\mathbf{G}_1) = \{a^kb^kc^k \mid n \geq 1\}$$

Since by convention uppercase letters and lowercase letters always stand for nonterminal symbols and terminal symbols, respectively, the alphabets of a grammar are evident from the list of productions and will no longer be specified separately.

**Example 3.2:** Grammar $\mathbf{G}_2$ is a modification of $\mathbf{G}_1$:

$$\begin{array}{lll} \mathbf{G}_2\colon & \Sigma \longrightarrow A & CB \longrightarrow BC \\ & A \longrightarrow aABC & bB \longrightarrow bb \\ & A \longrightarrow abC & bC \longrightarrow b \end{array}$$

A derivation of $a^3b^3$ is given in Figure 3.8. The reader may verify that $\mathbf{L}(\mathbf{G}_2) = \{a^kb^k \mid k \geq 1\}$. Note that the last rule, $bC \longrightarrow b$, erases

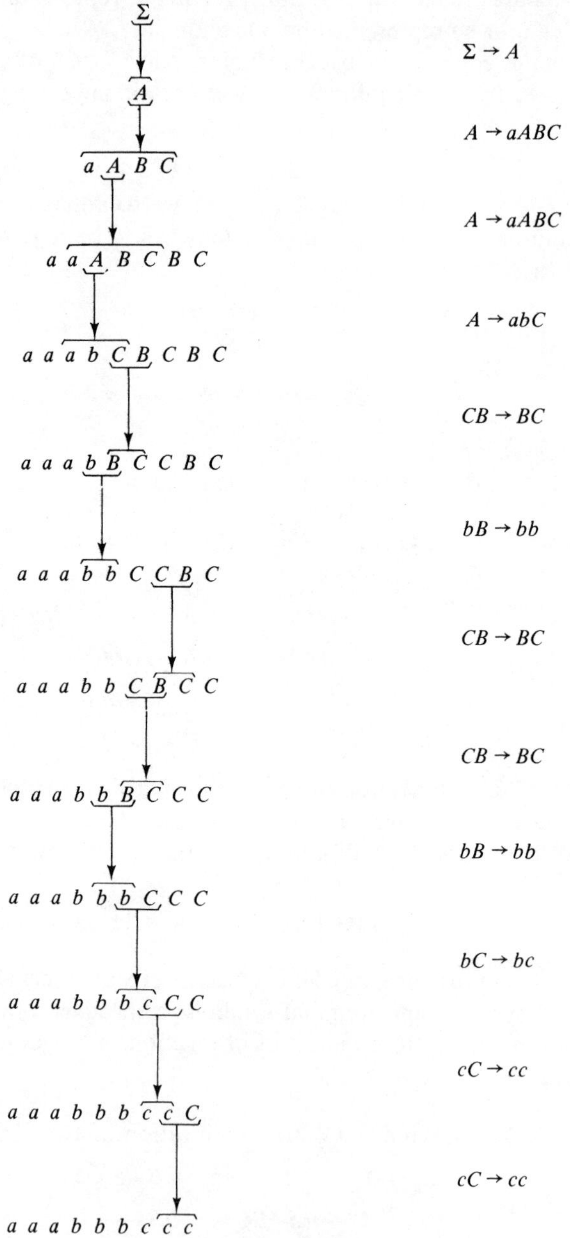


**Figure 3.7.** Derivation of $a^3b^3c^3$.

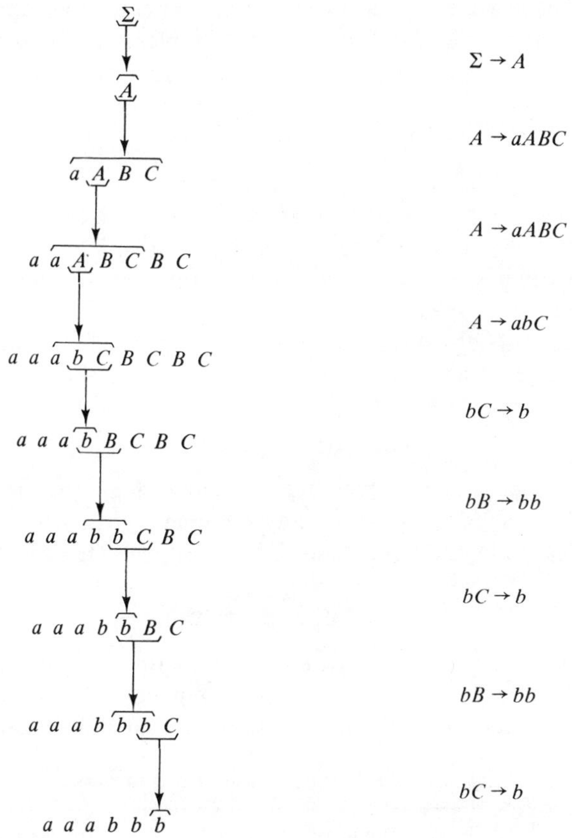


**Figure 3.8.** Derivation of $a^3b^3$.

all the $C$'s from the derivation, and that only this production removes the nonterminal $C$ from sentential forms.

**Example 3.3:** A simpler grammar that generates $\{a^kb^k \mid k \geq 1\}$ is the grammar $\mathbf{G}_3$:

$$\mathbf{G}_3\colon\ \Sigma \longrightarrow S$$
$$S \longrightarrow aSb$$
$$S \longrightarrow ab$$

A derivation of $a^3b^3$ is

$$\Sigma \Longrightarrow S \Longrightarrow aSb \Longrightarrow aaSbb \Longrightarrow aaabbb$$

The reader may verify that $\mathbf{L}(\mathbf{G}_3) = \{a^kb^k \mid k \geq 1\}$.

It is not at all obvious from examining their productions that grammars $\mathbf{G}_2$ and $\mathbf{G}_3$ generate the same language. In fact, there is no general procedure for determining whether arbitrary grammars generate the same language. We return to this problem, and study related problems, in Chapter 12.

## 3.4 Types of Grammars

By restricting the forms of productions permitted a grammar, four important types of formal grammars and corresponding classes of languages can be specified. These restrictions are given in Table 3.1, together with the names commonly used to identify the associated grammars and languages.

Proceeding down the table, the form of productions permitted is increasingly restricted. It is obvious that a grammar of one type is also a grammar of each type listed higher in the table. Using the notation $\mathcal{G}_i$ to mean a class of grammars of type $i$, we have

$$\mathcal{G}_0 \supset \mathcal{G}_1 \supset \mathcal{G}_2 \supset \mathcal{G}_3$$

Consequently, each grammar type must generate languages that are a subclass of the languages generated by any grammar type listed higher in the table. If we let $\mathcal{L}_i$ denote the class of languages generated by grammars in $\mathcal{G}_i$, then

$$\mathcal{L}_0 \supseteq \mathcal{L}_1 \supseteq \mathcal{L}_2 \supseteq \mathcal{L}_3$$

We cannot conclude from our present knowledge that any of these containments of language classes are proper containments. That they are in fact proper containments will be an important result of later chapters.

**Table 3.1** The four types of formal grammars

| Type | Format of Productions† | Remarks | | |
|---|---|---|---|---|
| 0 | $\varphi A\psi \longrightarrow \varphi\omega\psi$ | Unrestricted Substitution Rules | | Contracting |
| 1 | $\varphi A\psi \longrightarrow \varphi\omega\psi, \quad \omega \neq \lambda$<br>$\Sigma \longrightarrow \lambda$ | Context Sensitive | | Noncontracting |
| 2 | $A \longrightarrow \omega, \quad \omega \neq \lambda$<br>$\Sigma \longrightarrow \lambda$ | Context Free | | Noncontracting |
| 3 | $A \longrightarrow aB$<br>$A \longrightarrow a$<br>$\Sigma \longrightarrow \lambda$ | Right Linear | Regular | Noncontracting |
| | $A \longrightarrow Ba$<br>$A \longrightarrow a$<br>$\Sigma \longrightarrow \lambda$ | Left Linear | Regular | Noncontracting |

†$A \in \mathbf{N} \cup \{\Sigma\}$, $\left.\begin{matrix}\varphi\\ \omega\\ \psi\end{matrix}\right\} \in (\mathbf{N} \cup \mathbf{T})^*$, $B \in \mathbf{N}$, $a \in \mathbf{T}$.

In the next four sections we discuss briefly each of the four major classes of grammars and languages.

### 3.4.1 Unrestricted Grammars (Type 0)

With no restrictions, the class of formal grammars (Definition 3.1) is of surprising generality. (We have already noted that permitting a more general form of replacement rule adds nothing to the descriptive power of these formal grammars.) Sets of strings requiring this generality for their representation are not of great interest as artificial languages. Nevertheless, such systems of substitution rules are of considerable interest to logicians for studying the process of deduction. More will be said on this subject in Chapters 12 and 14.

One should note that the application of a grammatical rule $\varphi\, A\, \psi \longrightarrow \varphi\, \lambda\, \psi$ in a derivation step $\omega_i \Longrightarrow \omega_{i+1}$ produces a new sentential form $\omega_{i+1}$ shorter in length than $\omega_i$. Such rules are known as *contracting productions.* The grammar $\mathbf{G}_2$ of Example 3.2 has such a rule, the rule $bC \longrightarrow b$; its effect was displayed in Figure 3.8. A grammar containing at least one contracting production is said to be a *contracting grammar*. Only type 0 grammars may be contracting.

### 3.4.2 Context-Sensitive Grammars (Type 1)

**Definition 3.4:** A *context-sensitive grammar* $\mathbf{G} = (\mathbf{N}, \mathbf{T}, \mathbf{P}, \Sigma)$ is a formal grammar in which all productions are of the form

$$\varphi\, A\, \psi \longrightarrow \varphi\, \omega\, \psi, \qquad \omega \neq \lambda$$

The grammar may also contain the production $\Sigma \longrightarrow \lambda$. If $\mathbf{G}$ is a context-sensitive (type 1) grammar, then $\mathbf{L}(\mathbf{G})$ is a *context-sensitive* (type 1) *language*.

A production $\alpha \longrightarrow \beta$ satisfying $|\alpha| \leq |\beta|$ is known as a *noncontracting production*. Each production in a context-sensitive grammar is required to be noncontracting. As a consequence, sentential forms in any context-sensitive derivation

$$\omega_1 \Longrightarrow \omega_2 \Longrightarrow \cdots \Longrightarrow \omega_n$$

are nondecreasing in length:

$$|\omega_1| \leq |\omega_2| \leq \cdots \leq |\omega_n|$$

It follows that, if $\mathbf{G}$ is a context-sensitive grammar, $\lambda \in \mathbf{L}(\mathbf{G})$ if and only if $\mathbf{G}$ contains the production $\Sigma \longrightarrow \lambda$. Without this production, generation of the empty string would not be possible and a less elegant theory of formal languages would result.

The grammar in Example 3.1 is a context-sensitive grammar; the grammar in Example 3.2 is not because it has the contracting production $bC \longrightarrow b$.

### 3.4.3 Context-Free Grammars (Type 2)

In a context-free grammar, the context-denoting strings $\varphi$ and $\psi$ in a production $\varphi\, A\, \psi \longrightarrow \varphi\, \omega\, \psi$ are both required to be empty. Thus the possibility of replacing a nonterminal letter in a sentential form is independent of adjacent symbols; that is, it is independent of the context.

**Definition 3.5:** A *context-free grammar* $\mathbf{G} = (\mathbf{N}, \mathbf{T}, \mathbf{P}, \Sigma)$ is a formal grammar in which all productions are of the form

$$A \longrightarrow \omega \quad \begin{cases} A \in \mathbf{N} \cup \{\Sigma\} \\ \omega \in (\mathbf{N} \cup \mathbf{T})^* - \{\lambda\} \end{cases}$$

The grammar may also contain the production $\Sigma \longrightarrow \lambda$. If $\mathbf{G}$ is a context-free (type 2) grammar, then $\mathbf{L}(\mathbf{G})$ is a *context-free* (type 2) *language*.

Again, $\lambda \in \mathbf{L}(\mathbf{G})$ if and only if $\Sigma \longrightarrow \lambda$ is a production in the context-free grammar $\mathbf{G}$. The grammar $\mathbf{G}_3$ of Example 3.3 is context free, as are the two grammars of Section 3.2.

In a context-free grammar, if $A$ is $\Sigma$ or a nonterminal letter, and $\omega \in \mathbf{T}^*$ is a string derivable from $A$, we say that $\omega$ is *denoted by* $A$, or that $\omega$ is a *phrase of type* $A$. We use the notation

$$\mathbf{L}(\mathbf{G}, A) = \{\omega \in \mathbf{T}^* \mid A \stackrel{*}{\Longrightarrow} \omega\}$$

for the set of phrases denoted by $A$. If the sentential form $A$ is derivable from $\Sigma$, then $\mathbf{L}(\mathbf{G}, A) \subseteq \mathbf{L}(\mathbf{G})$, but it is not otherwise generally true that $\mathbf{L}(\mathbf{G}, A) \subseteq \mathbf{L}(\mathbf{G})$.

Context-free grammars are widely used to represent artificial languages, especially programming languages. We shall study these grammars in detail in Chapters 9 and 10.

### 3.4.4 Regular Grammars (Type 3)

Regular grammars are a highly restricted subclass of context-free grammars in which the right-hand side of a production may contain at most a single nonterminal symbol.

**Definition 3.6:** A production of the form

$$A \longrightarrow aB \quad \text{or} \quad A \longrightarrow a \quad \begin{cases} A \in \mathbf{N} \cup \{\Sigma\} \\ B \in \mathbf{N} \\ a \in \mathbf{T} \end{cases}$$

is called a *right linear* production. A production of the form

$$A \longrightarrow Ba \quad \text{or} \quad A \longrightarrow a \quad \begin{cases} A \in \mathbf{N} \cup \{\Sigma\} \\ B \in \mathbf{N} \\ a \in \mathbf{T} \end{cases}$$

is a *left linear* production. A formal grammar is *right linear* if it contains only right linear productions, and is *left linear* if it contains only left linear productions. Either form of linear grammar may contain the production $\Sigma \longrightarrow \lambda$. Left and right linear grammars are also known as *regular grammars*. If **G** is a regular (type 3) grammar, then **L(G)** is a *regular* (type 3) *language*.

The next example illustrates a general result, which will be established in Chapter 5: each regular language has both a left linear and a right linear grammar.

**Example 3.4:** A left linear grammar $\mathbf{G}_1$ and a right linear grammar $\mathbf{G}_2$ have productions as follows:

$$\begin{array}{llll} \mathbf{G}_1: & \Sigma \longrightarrow 1B & \mathbf{G}_2: & \Sigma \longrightarrow B1 \\ & \Sigma \longrightarrow 1 & & \Sigma \longrightarrow 1 \\ & A \longrightarrow 1B & & A \longrightarrow B1 \\ & B \longrightarrow 0A & & B \longrightarrow A0 \\ & A \longrightarrow 1 & & A \longrightarrow 1 \end{array}$$

The reader may verify that

$$\mathbf{L}(\mathbf{G}_1) = (\mathbf{10})^*\mathbf{1} = \mathbf{1}(\mathbf{01})^* = \mathbf{L}(\mathbf{G}_2)$$

The first two productions of grammar $\mathbf{G}_1$ or $\mathbf{G}_2$ in Example 3.4 could be replaced by the production $\Sigma \longrightarrow A$ without altering the language defined. Occasionally, it is convenient to use such a rule in a regular grammar even though it is not strictly permitted by Definition 3.6.

Regular grammars have been studied extensively since, as we shall see, their productions are related one to one with the transitions of finite-state accepter machines.

## 3.5 Derivation Trees and Diagrams

The examples developed in Section 3.2 have shown how a derivation may be displayed in the form of a tree diagram that clearly exhibits the phrase structure of a sentence. We are interested now in how such tree diagrams are related to derivations according to an arbitrary formal grammar.

By a *tree* we mean an acyclic directed graph (Figure 3.9) in which each node is connected by a unique directed path from a distinguished node called the *root node* of the tree. (The arcs in Figure 3.9 are directed downward by convention.) A node of a tree is said to be a *descendant* of any node from which it can be reached by a directed path. The root node is not the descendant of any other node, and the *leaf nodes* are those that have no descendants. A node that is neither the root node nor a leaf node is an *interior node* of the tree.

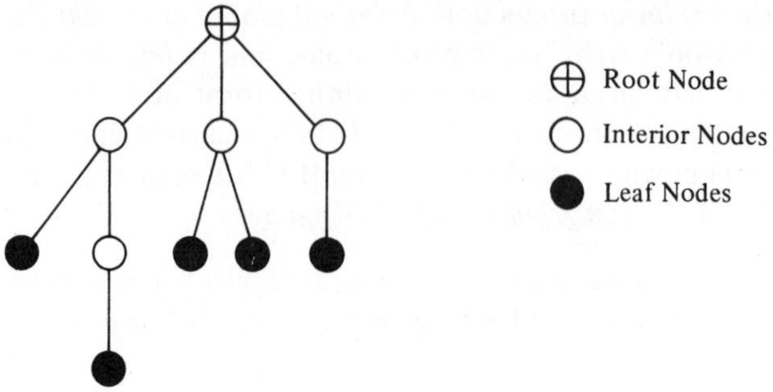


**Figure 3.9.** A tree.

A *tree diagram* for a derivation

$$\Sigma \stackrel{*}{\Longrightarrow} \omega, \qquad \omega \in (\mathbf{N} \cup \mathbf{T})^*$$

in a context-free grammar is a tree in which the root node is labeled $\Sigma$, the interior nodes are labeled with symbols in $\mathbf{N}$, and the leaf nodes are labeled with the letters of the sentential form $\omega$. To construct the tree diagram, we start with a tree consisting just of a root node labeled $\Sigma$ and extend the tree for each step of the derivation. At each stage in the construction, the leaf nodes of the tree (read from left to right) will be labeled with the letters of the corresponding sentential form. Consider any derivation step

$$\varphi\, A\, \psi \Longrightarrow \varphi\, B_1 B_2 \ldots B_n\, \psi$$

in which the production

$$A \Longrightarrow B_1 B_2 \ldots B_n \quad \begin{cases} A \in (\mathbf{N} \cup \{\Sigma\}) \\ B_i \in (\mathbf{N} \cup \mathbf{T}) \end{cases}$$

is applied. The tree constructed to this point will have leaf nodes labeled with the letters of $\varphi\, A\, \psi$. We make the leaf node labeled $A$ an interior node with descendent leaf nodes labeled $B_1, B_2, \ldots, B_n$ as shown in Figure 3.10. The

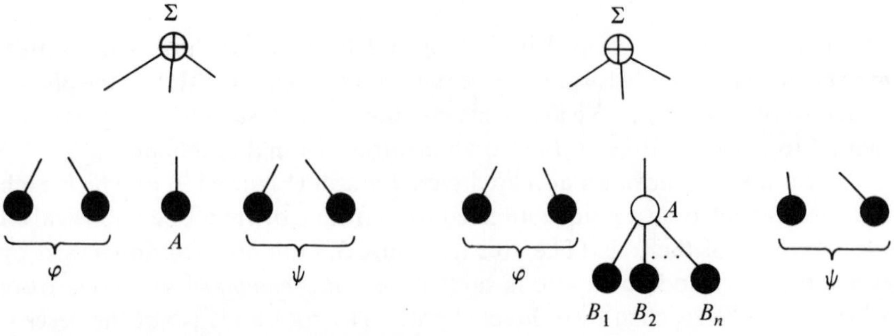


**Figure 3.10.** Extention of a derivation tree for the production $A \longrightarrow B_1 B_2 \ldots B_n$.

resultant tree diagram will have leaf nodes labeled with the letters of the sentential form $\varphi B_1 B_2 \ldots B_n \psi$.

**Example 3.5:** Consider the context-free grammar

$$\begin{aligned} \mathbf{G}:\ \Sigma &\longrightarrow S \\ S &\longrightarrow ST \\ S &\longrightarrow T \\ T &\longrightarrow (S) \\ T &\longrightarrow (\ ) \end{aligned}$$

The language generated by **G** is known as the *parenthesis language* $\mathbf{L}_p$, and consists of all well-formed strings of properly matching left and right parentheses that can occur in correctly written arithmetic expressions. Figure 3.11a gives a derivation of the string ( )(( )), and Figure 3.11b is the corresponding derivation tree. The grammar

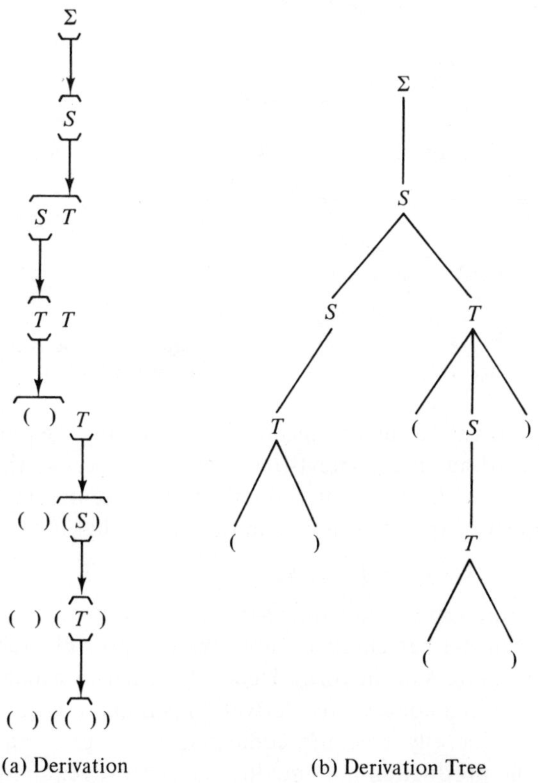


**Figure 3.11.** Derivation and derivation tree for string ( )(( )).

actually provides ten distinct derivations of this terminal string. They all correspond to the same derivation tree, but represent different orders of performing the substitutions indicated in the tree diagram. The ten derivations are shown as a *derivation diagram* in Figure 3.12. Each path from top to bottom in the diagram is a valid derivation of the string ( )(( )).

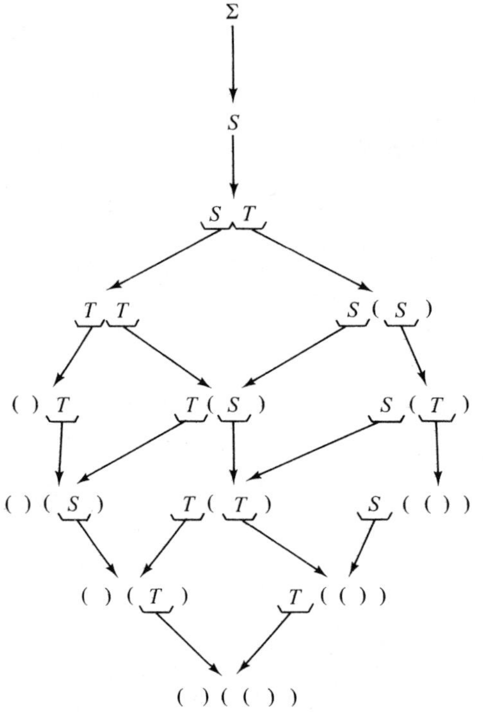


**Figure 3.12.** Derivation diagram for the string ( )(( )).

Derivation trees are a suitable means of representing the phrase structure of sentences according to a context-free grammar, because the association of a terminal string with each nonterminal letter of a sentential form is completely independent of the other letters in the form. That is, if

$$A_1A_2 \dots A_i \dots A_n, \qquad A_i \in \mathbf{N} \cup \mathbf{T}$$

is a sentential form, applying a context-free production to rewrite a nonterminal letter $A_i$ can neither eliminate nor create a possible substitution for other nonterminal letters in the form. Hence the order in which nonterminal letters are replaced in a context-free derivation is immaterial to the result.

This is not generally true for context-sensitive grammars, since the application of one production may modify the context required for application of another. For this reason, we prefer to use the derivation as our basic tool in the formal study of grammars, and to use derivation trees only for illustration.

In the case of regular grammars, there is no way of deriving from Σ a sentential form containing more than one nonterminal letter. Consequently, the derivation trees have a very simple form.

**Example 3.6:** Let **G** be the right linear grammar

$$\mathbf{G}: \quad \Sigma \longrightarrow A$$
$$A \longrightarrow 1A$$
$$A \longrightarrow 0B$$
$$B \longrightarrow 0B$$
$$B \longrightarrow 0$$

A derivation of 10000 is given in Figure 3.13. The reader may verify that **L(G)** = **1*000***.

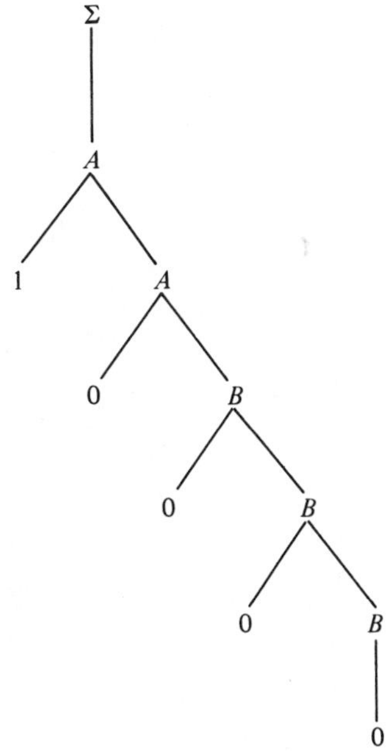


**Figure 3.13.** Derivation of 10000.

Indeed, a derivation according to a right linear grammar will always have the form shown in Figure 3.14. A derivation must start with an application of a production of the form $\Sigma \longrightarrow \lambda$, $\Sigma \longrightarrow a$, or $\Sigma \longrightarrow aA$. In the first two cases the derivation is immediately complete. In the third case, the derivation must continue, with further applications of productions of the form $A \longrightarrow aB$, and a single application of a production of the form $A \longrightarrow a$. Similar

$\Sigma \stackrel{*}{\Rightarrow} t_1 t_2 \ldots t_n$

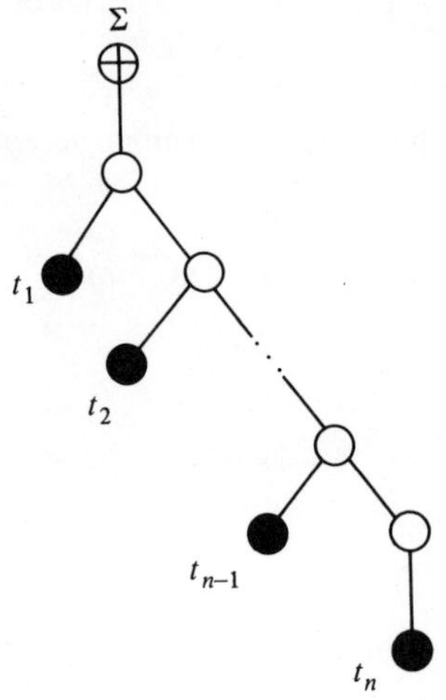


**Figure 3.14.** Right linear derivation tree.

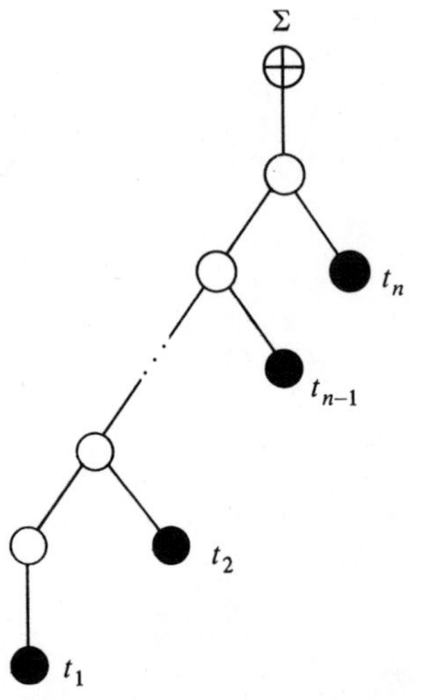


$\Sigma \stackrel{*}{\Rightarrow} t_1 t_2 \ldots t_n$

**Figure 3.15.** Left linear derivation tree.

remarks apply to the structure of derivations in a left linear grammar, as shown in Figure 3.15.

## 3.6 Ambiguity

The following example shows how a grammar may be "ambiguous" with respect to some sentence.

**Example 3.7:** Consider the context-free grammar

$$\mathbf{G}:\ \Sigma \longrightarrow S$$
$$S \longrightarrow SS$$
$$S \longrightarrow ab$$

Figure 3.16 shows two derivations of the string *ababab*. We see that the derivations correspond to *different* tree diagrams. The grammar **G** is *ambiguous* with respect to the sentence *ababab*: if the tree diagrams were used as the basis for assigning meaning to the derived string, mistaken interpretation could result.

We shall be interested in whether or not a grammar generates ambiguous sentences, so we must precisely define what is meant by an ambiguous derivation and what is meant by an ambiguous grammar. (Although the notion of ambiguity is applicable to all classes of formal grammars, our treatment of ambiguity will be limited to the class of context-free grammars: such grammars have proved most useful for representing programming languages, and questions of ambiguity, therefore, are of greatest importance for these grammars.)

**Definition 3.7:** Let **G** be a context-free grammar, and let $\omega$ be a sentence in the language generated by **G**. Then $\omega$ is *ambiguous* if there are derivations of $\omega$ that correspond to different tree diagrams.

Figure 3.17 exhibits all possible derivations of the string *ababab* according to the grammar of Example 3.7 in the form of a derivation diagram. From the sentential form *SS*, the diagram shows two paths in which the leftmost *S* is replaced first: path 1 corresponds to the tree of Figure 3.16a, and path 2 corresponds to the tree of Figure 3.16b. These two paths in Figure 3.17 have a unique property: *in each derivation step, the leftmost nonterminal letter of the sentential form is rewritten.* These derivations, known as *leftmost derivations*, permit a precise definition of ambiguous grammars.

**Definition 3.8:** Let **G** be a context-free grammar. A derivation

$$\omega_0 \Longrightarrow \omega_1 \Longrightarrow \omega_2 \Longrightarrow \cdots \Longrightarrow \omega_n$$

is a *leftmost derivation* if and only if the leftmost nonterminal letter of $\omega_i$ is replaced to obtain $\omega_{i+1}$. That is, for $0 \leq i < n$,

$$\begin{aligned} \omega_i &= \alpha\, A\, \beta \\ \omega_{i+1} &= \alpha\, \omega\, \beta \end{aligned} \qquad \begin{cases} \alpha \in \mathbf{T}^* \\ A \in \mathbf{N} \\ \beta \in (\mathbf{N} \cup \mathbf{T})^* \end{cases}$$

and $A \longrightarrow \omega$ is a production of **G**.

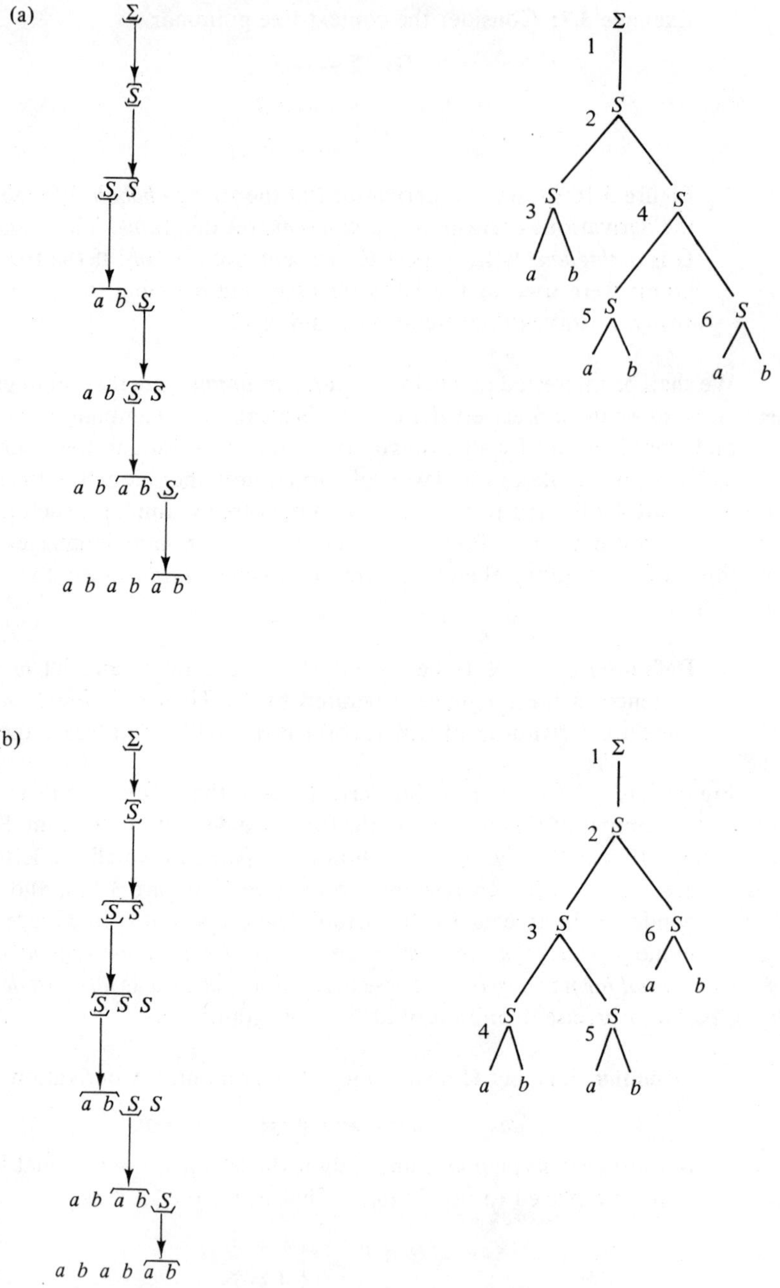


**Figure 3.16.** Ambiguous derivations in a context-free grammar.

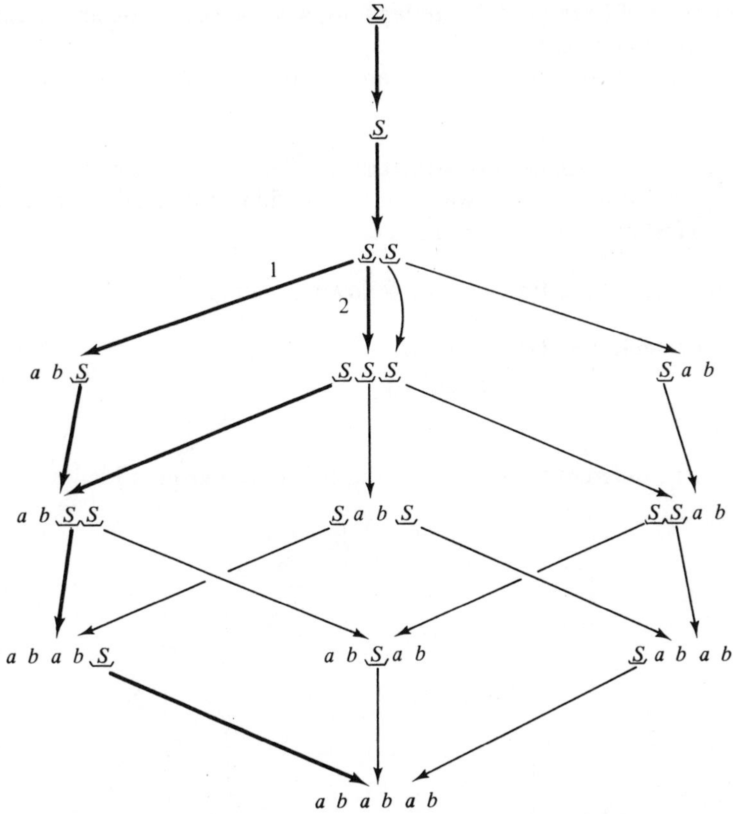


**Figure 3.17.** Derivation diagram for an ambiguous sentence.

It is easy to construct a unique leftmost derivation from a given derivation tree: Suppose that the final terminal string in the derivation is $\omega = t_1 t_2 \ldots t_n$ ($t_i \in \mathbf{T}$). For $i = 1, 2, \ldots, n$, we follow the path from the root node to the leaf node labeled $t_i$, applying the production associated with each node on the path if it has not already been applied.

The interior nodes in the trees of Figure 3.16 have been numbered to indicate the order in which the corresponding productions are applied in the leftmost derivation.

Since it is easy to obtain a derivation tree from any derivation, the correspondence between trees and leftmost derivations is one-to-one: each sentence generated by a context-free grammar has a unique leftmost derivation.

> **Definition 3.9:** A context-free grammar is *ambiguous* if and only if it generates some sentence by two or more distinct leftmost derivations.

The grammar of Example 3.7 is ambiguous, whereas the grammars of Examples 3.3 and 3.4 are not.

There are two ways in which ambiguity can arise in a context-free grammar:

1. Some sentence has two structurally different derivation trees.
2. Some sentence has two structurally similar derivation trees with different labeling of their interior nodes.

The two cases are illustrated by the following examples.

**Example 3.8:** G:
$$\Sigma \longrightarrow A$$
$$A \longrightarrow A0A$$
$$A \longrightarrow 1$$

Two different trees for the string 10101 are shown in Figure 3.18.

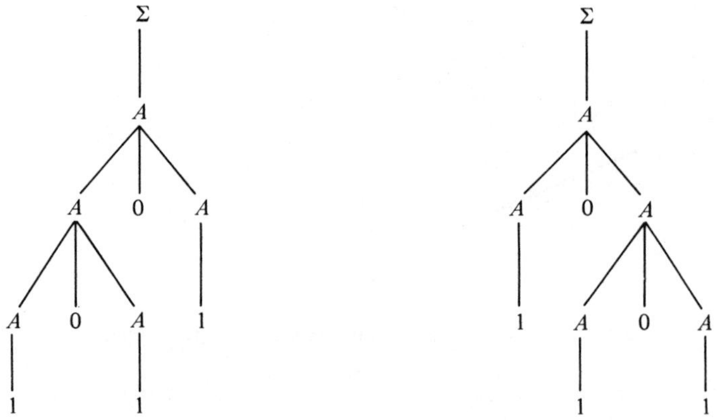


**Figure 3.18.** A structural ambiguity.

**Example 3.9:** G:
$$\Sigma \longrightarrow A$$
$$A \longrightarrow B0$$
$$A \longrightarrow A0$$
$$B \longrightarrow B0$$
$$A \longrightarrow 1$$
$$B \longrightarrow 1$$

Figure 3.19 shows two derivation trees for the string 100 that are identical apart from the nonterminal letters assigned to interior nodes.

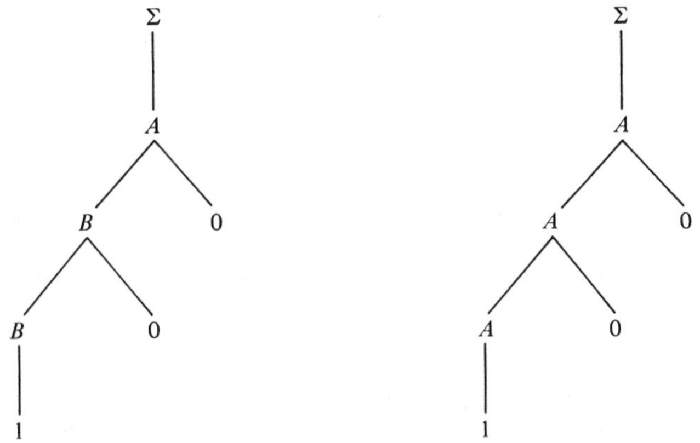


**Figure 3.19.** A labeling ambiguity.

Because each sentential form in a derivation may only contain a single nonterminal symbol, a regular grammar is ambiguous only if some string has derivation trees with different labeling of the interior nodes. We shall see how ambiguity may be removed from regular grammars in Chapter 5.

Ambiguity is important in language analysis because the analysis of a sentence with ambiguous derivations may lead to incorrect assignment of meaning. An illustration of ambiguity in English is shown in Figure 3.20.† It is this sort of ambiguity that makes natural language translation so difficult.

In programming languages, the algebraic phrase

$$a \times b + c$$

presents a similar problem of interpretation (by a compiler, for example) if a carelessly designed grammar is used. Figure 3.21 presents a grammar and two derivation trees. The familiar interpretation $(a \times b) + c$ corresponds to the lefthand tree, but the righthand tree also represents a legitimate derivation according to the grammar.

Ambiguity in context-free grammars is the subject of Chapter 9.

## Notes and References

Early descriptions of "formal grammars" for languages appear in Chomsky [1956, 1959], Chomsky and Miller [1958], and Bar-Hillel, Gaifman, and Shamir [1960]. The formalism presented in this chapter, as well as the notion of a language hierarchy, is from the 1959 publication of Chomsky.

Three classes of languages (and the corresponding grammars) are discussed more fully elsewhere in this book: type 3 languages in Chapter 5; type 2 languages in Chapters 8 to 10; and type 0 languages in Chapters 11, 12,

†This example is attributed to Noam Chomsky.

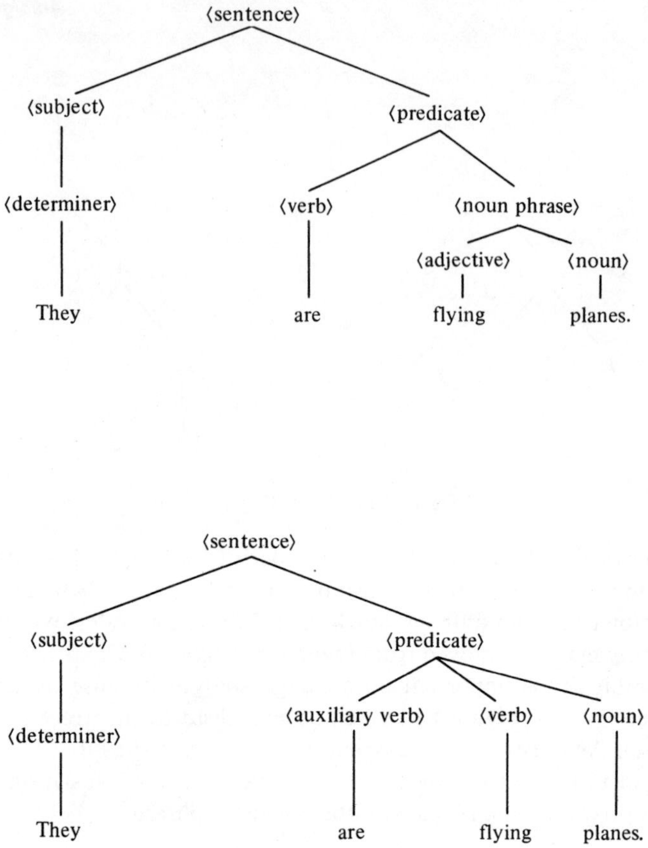


**Figure 3.20.** An ambiguity in English.

$$
\text{G:}\quad
\begin{aligned}
&A \to A\ B\ A\\
&A \to a\\
&A \to b\\
&A \to c\\
&B \to +\\
&B \to \times
\end{aligned}
$$

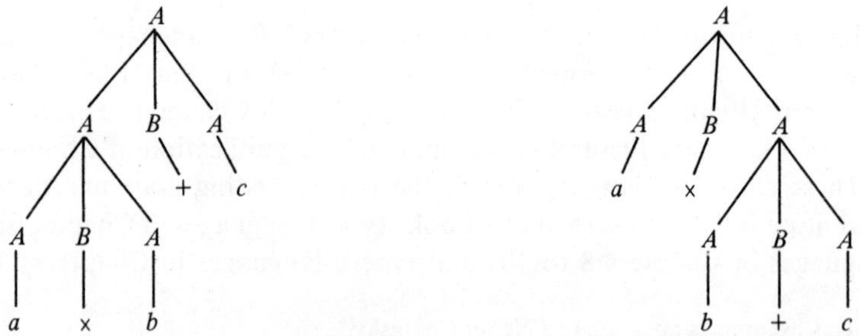


**Figure 3.21.** An ambiguity in defining arithmetic expressions.

and 14. References to supplementary material relating to these types of languages are found at the ends of those chapters.

Type 1 grammars have proved of little use in the specification either of programming languages or "natural" languages, partly because they possess certain undesirable properties (such as the ability to generate strings that cannot be readily analyzed to obtain structural descriptions), and partly because several important questions that have been resolved for other types of languages remain unresolved for type 1 languages. For this reason, such languages are not discussed in detail in this book; the reader who wishes to learn more about these languages may refer to Myhill [1960], Landweber [1963], and Kuroda [1964].

Questions of ambiguity in grammars have been studied by Cantor [1962], Floyd [1962], Parikh [1961], Ginsburg and Ullian [1966], and others. These questions are taken up again in later chapters of this book.

## Problems

3.1. Consider the following grammars:

$$\begin{array}{llll}
\mathbf{G}_1: & \Sigma \longrightarrow \lambda & \mathbf{G}_2: & \Sigma \longrightarrow \lambda \\
& \Sigma \longrightarrow S & & \Sigma \longrightarrow S \\
& S \longrightarrow SS & & S \longrightarrow cSd \\
& S \longrightarrow c & & S \longrightarrow cd \\
\mathbf{G}_3: & \Sigma \longrightarrow \lambda & \mathbf{G}_4: & \Sigma \longrightarrow cS \\
& \Sigma \longrightarrow S & & S \longrightarrow d \\
& S \longrightarrow Sd & & S \longrightarrow cS \\
& S \longrightarrow cS & & S \longrightarrow Td \\
& S \longrightarrow c & & T \longrightarrow Td \\
& S \longrightarrow d & & T \longrightarrow d \\
\mathbf{G}_5: & \Sigma \longrightarrow \lambda & & \\
& \Sigma \longrightarrow S & & \\
& S \longrightarrow ScS & & \\
& S \longrightarrow c & &
\end{array}$$

a. Describe $\mathbf{L}(\mathbf{G}_i)$ for $i = 1, 2, 3, 4, 5$.
b. Indicate any inclusions among the $\mathbf{L}(\mathbf{G}_i)$.
c. For each language, give a derivation of a length 4 string.

3.2. Construct a grammar that generates each following language:
a. $\{0^m 1^n \mid m > n \geq 0\}$.
b. $\{0^m 1^n \mid m$ odd and $n$ even, or $n$ odd and $m$ even$\}$.
c. $\{0^k 1^m 0^n \mid n = k + m\}$.
d. $\{\omega c \omega \mid \omega \in \{0, 1\}^*\}$.

3.3. Given a terminal alphabet $\mathbf{S} = \{s_1, s_2, \ldots, s_k\}$, we can define a unary operator $R$ on $\mathbf{S}^*$ as follows: (1) $R(\lambda) = \lambda$, (2) $R(s) = s$ for each symbol $s$ in $\mathbf{S}$, and (3) $R(s\varphi) = R(\varphi)s$, for $s \in \mathbf{S}$, $\varphi \in \mathbf{S}^*$. For any word $\varphi \in \mathbf{S}^*$, $R(\varphi)$ is called the *reverse* of $\varphi$ and is usually written $\varphi^R$.

A word $\omega$ is a *palindrome* if it is its own reverse, that is, if $\omega = \omega^R$. A language $\mathbf{L}$ is a *palindrome language* just if each of its elements is a palindrome.

Consider $\mathbf{G}_1$, $\mathbf{G}_2$ below:

| $\mathbf{G}_1$: | $\Sigma \longrightarrow S$ | $\mathbf{G}_2$: | $\Sigma \longrightarrow S$ |
|---|---|---|---|
| | $S \longrightarrow aSa$ | | $S \longrightarrow aS$ |
| | $S \longrightarrow aSb$ | | $S \longrightarrow Sa$ |
| | $S \longrightarrow bSb$ | | $S \longrightarrow bS$ |
| | $S \longrightarrow bSa$ | | $S \longrightarrow Sb$ |
| | $S \longrightarrow aa$ | | $S \longrightarrow a$ |
| | $S \longrightarrow bb$ | | $S \longrightarrow b$ |

a. Describe informally $\mathbf{L}(\mathbf{G}_1)$ and $\mathbf{L}(\mathbf{G}_2)$. Is either language a palindrome language?

b. The *reverse* of a language $\mathbf{L}$, written $\mathbf{L}^R$, is defined as

$$\mathbf{L}^R = \{\omega^R \mid \omega \in \mathbf{L}\}$$

Prove that if $\mathbf{L}$ is a palindrome language, $\mathbf{L}^R$ is a palindrome language. If $\mathbf{L} = \mathbf{L}^R$, must $\mathbf{L}$ be a palindrome language?

c. Suppose that $\mathbf{L}' = \mathbf{L} \cap \mathbf{L}^R$ for some language $\mathbf{L}$. If $\mathbf{L}$ is a palindrome language, must $\mathbf{L}'$ be a palindrome language? If $\mathbf{L}'$ is a palindrome language, must $\mathbf{L}$ be a palindrome language?

d. Prove that if some string $\omega$ is a palindrome, then the language $\mathbf{L} = \omega^*$ is a palindrome language.

3.4. a. Construct a left linear grammar $\mathbf{G}$ such that $\mathbf{L}(\mathbf{G}) = \mathbf{10}^*$.

b. Construct a right linear grammar $\mathbf{G}$ such that $\mathbf{L}(\mathbf{G}) = \mathbf{ab}^* \cup \mathbf{c}^*$.

3.5. Construct a context-free grammar generating the language $\mathbf{L} = \{\omega \in (\mathbf{0} \cup \mathbf{1})^* \mid N_0(\omega) = N_1(\omega)\}$, where $N_0(\omega)$ and $N_1(\omega)$ denote the number of occurrences of the symbols 0 and 1, respectively, in the word $\omega$.

3.6. Construct a context-free grammar $\mathbf{G}$ generating the language $\mathbf{L}$, where $\mathbf{L}$ is

a. $\{a^n b^k \mid 1 \leq n \leq 2k\}$.

b. $\{\omega c \omega^R \mid \omega \in (\mathbf{0} \cup \mathbf{1})^*\}$.

c. The complement of the language $\mathbf{L}'$, where $\mathbf{L}'$ is $\{a^k b^k c^k \mid k > 0\}$.

3.7. Describe the languages generated by the context-sensitive grammars $\mathbf{G}_1$ and $\mathbf{G}_2$ below:

| $\mathbf{G}_1$: | | $\mathbf{G}_2$: | |
|---|---|---|---|
| | $\Sigma \longrightarrow ACA$ | | $\Sigma \longrightarrow AcB$ |
| | $AC \longrightarrow AACA$ | | $\Sigma \longrightarrow BcA$ |
| | $AC \longrightarrow ADc$ | | $Ac \longrightarrow XAcX$ |
| | $AC \longrightarrow AcD$ | | $Bc \longrightarrow XBcX$ |
| | $D \longrightarrow AD$ | | $A \longrightarrow 1Y$ |
| | $D \longrightarrow A$ | | $B \longrightarrow 0Y$ |
| | $A \longrightarrow 0$ | | $Y \longrightarrow X$ |
| | $A \longrightarrow 1$ | | $Y \longrightarrow XY$ |
| | | | $A \longrightarrow 1$ |
| | | | $B \longrightarrow 0$ |
| | | | $X \longrightarrow 1$ |
| | | | $X \longrightarrow 0$ |

a. Describe the language $\mathbf{L} = \mathbf{L}(\mathbf{G}_1) \cup \mathbf{L}(\mathbf{G}_2)$.
*b. Find a context-free grammar generating $\mathbf{L}$.

3.8. Construct a grammar generating the language $\mathbf{L} = \{a^n b^n c^n d^n \mid n > 0\}$. (The grammar constructed must be of type 0 or 1, since it can be shown that $\mathbf{L}$ is not context free.)

3.9. Construct a type 0 grammar generating the language $\mathbf{L} = \{1^x c 1^y c 1^z \mid z = xy,\ x, y \geq 0\}$.

3.10. Let $\mathbf{N} = \{A, B\}$, and $\mathbf{T} = \{a, b\}$. Construct a context-free grammar $\mathbf{G}$ that generates all possible sets of context-free productions on terminal and nonterminal alphabets $\mathbf{T}$ and $\mathbf{N}$, respectively, that is, generates all strings of the form $\omega = \{p_1, p_2, \ldots, p_k\}$, where each substring $p_k$ is of the form $X \longrightarrow \varphi$, with $X \in \mathbf{N}$ and $\varphi \in (\mathbf{N} \cup \mathbf{T})^* - \boldsymbol{\lambda}$.

Show that a right linear grammar can be constructed that generates all right linear productions on $\mathbf{T}$ and $\mathbf{N}$.

**3.11.** Let $\mathbf{G}_1 = (\mathbf{N}_1, \mathbf{T}, \mathbf{P}_1, \Sigma)$ and $\mathbf{G}_2 = (\mathbf{N}_2, \mathbf{T}, \mathbf{P}_2, \Sigma)$ be arbitrary type $i$ grammars, $i \in \{0, 1, 2, 3\}$. Show how to construct, from $\mathbf{G}_1$ and $\mathbf{G}_2$, a type $i$ grammar for the following:
a. $\mathbf{L}(\mathbf{G}_1) \cup \mathbf{L}(\mathbf{G}_2)$.
b. $\mathbf{L}(\mathbf{G}_1)\mathbf{L}(\mathbf{G}_2)$.
c. $\mathbf{L}(\mathbf{G}_1)^*$.
For each $i$, prove that the grammars constructed in parts a through c are indeed type $i$. (This problem shows that the class of type $i$ lan-

guages, $i = 0, \ldots, 3$, is closed under the set operations of union, concatenation, and closure.)

3.12. Let **G** be a left linear grammar, let $X$ and $Y$ be symbols in its nonterminal alphabet, and let $s$ be a symbol in its terminal alphabet.

a. Show that if **G** contains the production $X \longrightarrow Ys$, then $\mathbf{L}(\mathbf{G}, Y)\mathbf{s} \subseteq \mathbf{L}(\mathbf{G}, X)$.

b. Show that the converse of part a is false; that is, show that $\mathbf{L}(\mathbf{G}, Y)\mathbf{s} \subseteq \mathbf{L}(\mathbf{G}, X)$ does not imply that **G** contains the production $X \longrightarrow Ys$. Is the converse true if $\mathbf{L}(\mathbf{G}, Y)$ is not empty?

c. Suppose that $\mathbf{L}(\mathbf{G}, Y)\mathbf{s} \nsubseteq \mathbf{L}(\mathbf{G}, X)$. If $\mathbf{G}'$ is the grammar obtained from **G** by adding the production $X \longrightarrow Ys$ to the productions of **G**, must it be the case that $\mathbf{L}(\mathbf{G}') \neq \mathbf{L}(\mathbf{G})$?

**3.13.** We say that a context-free grammar **G** is *weakly k-generative* if, whenever sentential form $\omega'$ is derivable sentential from $\omega$ in $k$ or more steps, either $\omega'$ is longer than $\omega$ or $\omega'$ contains more terminal symbols than $\omega$. We say that **G** is *k-generative* if it is weakly $k$-generative but not weakly $(k - 1)$-generative.

a. Prove that for every context-free grammar **G** there exists a $k$-generative context-free grammar $\mathbf{G}'$ (for some $k > 0$) such that $\mathbf{L}(\mathbf{G}') = \mathbf{L}(\mathbf{G})$. (*Hint:* Show that if **G** is a context-free grammar that is not $k$-generative for any $k$, then **G** permits a derivation of the form

$$A \overset{*}{\Longrightarrow} A$$

for some nonterminal $A$. In such a case, either **G** contains the production $A \longrightarrow A$, which can be discarded without altering the language generated, or **G** contains a series of productions

$$\begin{aligned} A &\longrightarrow X_1 \\ X_1 &\longrightarrow X_2 \\ &\vdots \\ X_{n-1} &\longrightarrow X_n \\ X_n &\longrightarrow A \end{aligned}$$

where $X_1, \ldots, X_n$ are nonterminals distinct from $A$. Show that in the latter case, each occurrence of a nonterminal $X_i$ in **G**, $1 \leq i \leq n$, can be replaced by an occurrence of $A$ without altering the language generated by the grammar.)

b. Prove that if **G** is a $k$-generative context-free grammar, $k > 0$, then there exists a 1-generative context-free grammar $\mathbf{G}'$ such that $\mathbf{L}(\mathbf{G}') = \mathbf{L}(\mathbf{G})$.

Parts a and b together prove that for every context-free grammar **G** there exists a 1-generative context-free grammar **G**′ such that **L**(**G**′) = **L**(**G**).

**3.14.** Describe a procedure for deciding, given an arbitrary context-free grammar **G** and an arbitrary string $\omega$, whether $\omega$ is in **L**(**G**). Does your procedure work if **G** is an arbitrary context-sensitive grammar? If not, modify the procedure so that it works for context-sensitive grammars. In Chapter 12, we show that no such procedure can be constructed for the class of type 0 grammars. Where does your procedure fail for that class of grammars?

**3.15.** Show that if we modify the definition of context-free grammars to allow productions of the form $A \longrightarrow \lambda$, where $A$ is a nonterminal, the class of languages generable by context-free grammars does not change; that is, show that for any grammar $\mathbf{G} = (\mathbf{N}, \mathbf{T}, \mathbf{P}, \Sigma)$ in which all productions are of the form

$$A \longrightarrow \alpha, \qquad A \in \mathbf{N} \cup \{\Sigma\}, \qquad \alpha \in (\mathbf{N} \cup \mathbf{T})^*$$

there exists a grammar $\mathbf{G}' = (\mathbf{N}, \mathbf{T}, \mathbf{P}', \Sigma)$ in which all productions are of the form

$$A \longrightarrow \alpha, \qquad A \in \mathbf{N} \cup \{\Sigma\}, \qquad \alpha \in (\mathbf{N} \cup \mathbf{T})^* - \lambda$$

or of the form

$$\Sigma \longrightarrow \lambda$$

such that **L**(**G**′) = **L**(**G**).

**3.16.** Let $h$: $\mathbf{S}^* \longrightarrow \mathbf{T}^*$ be a homomorphism from the set $\mathbf{S}^*$ to the set $\mathbf{T}^*$, where **S** and **T** are arbitrary sets of terminal symbols. Let $\mathbf{L} \subseteq \mathbf{S}^*$ be a type $i$ language, $i = 0, 1, 2$, or 3.

a. Prove that if $i = 0, 2$, or 3, the language $h(\mathbf{L}) = \{h(\omega) \mid \omega \in \mathbf{L}\}$ is a type $i$ language.

*b. Prove that if **L** is a type 1 language, the language $h(\mathbf{L})$ need not be type 1. (You may assume the existence of languages that are type 0 but not type 1.) Under what conditions on $h$ will $h(\mathbf{L})$ be type 1?

**3.17.** Suppose that **G** is a context-free grammar in which all productions are of the form

$$X \longrightarrow \alpha Y$$

or

$$X \longrightarrow \alpha$$

where $X$ is $\Sigma$ or a nonterminal, $Y$ is a nonterminal, and $\alpha$ is a nonempty terminal string.

a. Show that **L**(**G**) is a regular language.

*b. Suppose that we allow $\alpha$ to be any (possibly empty) terminal string. Show that **L**(**G**) is still regular. (The results of Problem 3.16 may prove helpful.)

***3.18.** A *semi-Thue system* is a grammar $\mathbf{G} = (\mathbf{N}, \mathbf{T}, \mathbf{P}, \Sigma)$ with productions of the form

$$\alpha \longrightarrow \beta, \qquad \alpha \in ((\mathbf{T} \cup \mathbf{N})^* - \lambda) \cup \Sigma, \qquad \beta \in (\mathbf{T} \cup \mathbf{N})^*$$

That is, $\beta$ can be any string and $\alpha$ any nonempty string of symbols from $\mathbf{T} \cup \mathbf{N}$; in addition, $\alpha$ can be the starting symbol. If $n$ is the length of the longest string appearing in either side of any production in $\mathbf{P}$, we say that $\mathbf{G}$ is of *order n*.

a. Let $\mathbf{G}$ be any semi-Thue system of order $k > 2$. Show that there exists a semi-Thue system $\mathbf{G}'$ such that $\mathbf{L}(\mathbf{G}') = \mathbf{L}(\mathbf{G})$ and $\mathbf{G}'$ is of order $k - 1$. Conclude that for any semi-Thue system there is a system of order 2 that generates the same language.
b. Let $\mathbf{G}$ be a semi-Thue system of order 2. Show that there exists a phrase-structure grammar $\mathbf{G}'$ of order 2 such that $\mathbf{L}(\mathbf{G}) = \mathbf{L}(\mathbf{G}')$. (The order of a phrase-structure grammar is defined in a manner analogous to that of semi-Thue systems.)
c. Prove that the class of languages generable by semi-Thue systems is precisely the type 0 languages.

**3.19.** In Problem 3.13, we defined $k$-generative context-free grammars. Suppose that $\mathbf{G}$ is a $k$-generative grammar for some $k > 0$, and $\omega$ is a word in $\mathbf{L}(\mathbf{G})$ such that $|\omega| = m$. What is the maximum number of derivation steps in any derivation of $\omega$? What is the maximum number of nodes in the corresponding derivation tree? (Note that if $\mathbf{G}$ is not $k$-generative for any $k$, we can place no bound on either the number of derivation steps or the number of nodes in the tree.) Using the results of Problem 3.13, show that if $\mathbf{L}$ is a context-free language there is a grammar $\mathbf{G}$ for $\mathbf{L}$ such that each string $\omega \in \mathbf{L}(\mathbf{G})$ is derived in no more than $2|\omega|$ steps.

3.20. Which of the grammars in Problem 3.1 are ambiguous? For each ambiguous grammar, exhibit distinct derivation trees corresponding to the derivation of some word generated by the grammar.

3.21. Let $\mathbf{T}$ be a terminal set consisting of variable-denoting elements $x, y, z$, operator-denoting elements $**, *, /, +, -$, and parentheses. Construct a context-free grammar $\mathbf{G}$ generating the set of all valid Fortran arithmetic expressions composed of elements of $\mathbf{T}$. Show derivation trees for

a. $(x + y) * z/x$.
b. $x ** y/(z - y * x - z)$.

Is the grammar $\mathbf{G}$ that you have constructed ambiguous? If so, show distinct derivation trees corresponding to the derivation of some expression.

3.22. Let $\mathbf{G}_1 = (\mathbf{N}_1, \mathbf{T}_1, \mathbf{P}_1, \Sigma)$ and $\mathbf{G}_2 = (\mathbf{N}_2, \mathbf{T}_2, \mathbf{P}_2, \Sigma)$ be unambiguous context-free grammars such that $\mathbf{N}_1 \cap \mathbf{N}_2 = \varnothing$. Let $\mathbf{G} = (\mathbf{N}_1 \cup \mathbf{N}_2, \mathbf{T}_1 \cup \mathbf{T}_2, \mathbf{P}_1 \cup \mathbf{P}_2, \Sigma)$. Prove that $\mathbf{G}$ is ambiguous if and only if $\mathbf{L}(\mathbf{G}_1)$ and $\mathbf{L}(\mathbf{G}_2)$ have some nonempty word in common.

3.23. Let $\mathbf{G} = (\mathbf{N}, \mathbf{T}, \mathbf{P}, \Sigma)$ be a context-free grammar, and let $A \in \mathbf{N}$. Suppose that there exist sentential forms $\omega_1, \omega_2, \ldots, \omega_n$ such that $A \overset{*}{\Longrightarrow} \omega_i$ for $1 \leq i \leq n$. Let $\mathbf{G}' = (\mathbf{N}, \mathbf{T}, \mathbf{P}', \Sigma)$ be the context-free grammar obtained from $\mathbf{G}$ by adding to $\mathbf{P}$ the productions $A \longrightarrow \omega_i$, $1 \leq i \leq n$.

a. Show that $\mathbf{L}(\mathbf{G}') = \mathbf{L}(\mathbf{G})$.

b. Under what conditions is $\mathbf{G}'$ ambiguous?

# 4

# *Finite-State Machines*

In this chapter we study the simplest automaton: the finite-state machine. These machines, which have been studied in such diverse disciplines as computer design, neurophysiology, communications, linguistics, and the theory of computation, are widely known and well understood. The finite-state machine model arises naturally from physical settings in which information-denoting signals are processed.

Most complex devices, whether computers, engines, or communication systems, are realized by interconnecting many simple components. Only a finite number of physical components can be enclosed in a specified volume. The "symbols" used to signal events between components are often represented by the values of physical quantities such as mechanical positions, voltages, currents, temperatures, pressures, fluid flows, or chemical compositions. Because no signal can be measured with arbitrarily high accuracy to within arbitrarily small tolerances, designers of physical devices are limited to a small number of easily distinguishable values, both for the signals themselves and for the internal conditions (*states*) of the devices. In short, physical reality imposes an inescapable, bounded *finiteness* on physical systems.

A given signal or state requires a small but nonzero interval to measure. It follows that only a finite number of operations can reliably be performed in a finite amount of time. Physical reality imposes *discreteness* on systems, not only in the symbols that they may process or the states that they may assume, but also in the times at which they may change state.

Our natural tendency to decompose problem solutions into sequences of steps is manifested in our simple machine model by *sequential action.* Indeed, designing a machine to operate one step at a time is the simplest way known to make its behavior *deterministic*, that is, not subject to uncertainty. (Of what use is a telephone number that does not reach the same party each time dialed or a computer instruction whose outcome is different each time used?)

The properties of finiteness, discreteness, sequential action, and determinism are embodied in the finite-state machine model. Because of them, the model can be (and has been) applied in diverse settings, such as the following:

1. Mechanical systems (adding machines, for example) in which signals between components are represented by the positions of moving parts.
2. Digital electronic systems (computer logic circuits, for example) in which signals are represented by "high" or "low" voltage, or by the presence or absence of current.
3. Pneumatic or hydraulic systems, comprising networks of pipes and pressure-actuated valves, in which signals are represented by the presence or absence of pressure in a pipe. (Examples are found in many types of industrial control equipment.)
4. Chemical systems, in which signals are represented by the chemical compositions of materials. (An example is the transcription of the genetic code during cell reproduction.)

The finite-state machine is also useful for modeling physical systems in which combinations of these effects are found, as in relay switching networks (electromechanical action) or the human nervous system (electrochemical action).

Despite its strong roots in physical phenomena, the finite-state machine is not limited to modeling physical processes. It is frequently applied to information-processing procedures, such as encoding and decoding messages or syntax analysis of computer programs. It plays a central role in the more powerful models of computation, where it appears as the control unit of an abstract machine having access to a storage medium of unbounded capacity.

Finiteness implies that the (finite state) machine and any storage medium to which it has access are bounded. This imposes important limitations on the capabilities of the model. We shall encounter a multitude of information-processing activities for which there is no finite-state model. Despite such limitations, this model plays an important role in the theory of computation as one absolute measure of the complexity of computational processes.

Our approach to the mathematical formulation of the finite-state machine begins from the assumptions of finite numbers of parts and permissible signals. At the end of the chapter, we shall show how the same model follows from the assumption that the machine has "finite memory" of its past experience.

## 4.1 Properties of Finite-State Machines

Consider a transducer machine **M** as shown in Figure 4.1. (Transducers were introduced in Chapter 1.) Assume that the machine operates at instants $t_0, t_1, \ldots, t_i, \ldots$, their origin ($t_0$) and spacing ($t_i - t_{i-1}, i \geq 1$) being arbitrary. For simplicity, we denote these time instants by the integers $t = 0, 1, 2, \ldots$. At $t = 0$ the parts of the machine are initialized to a known starting

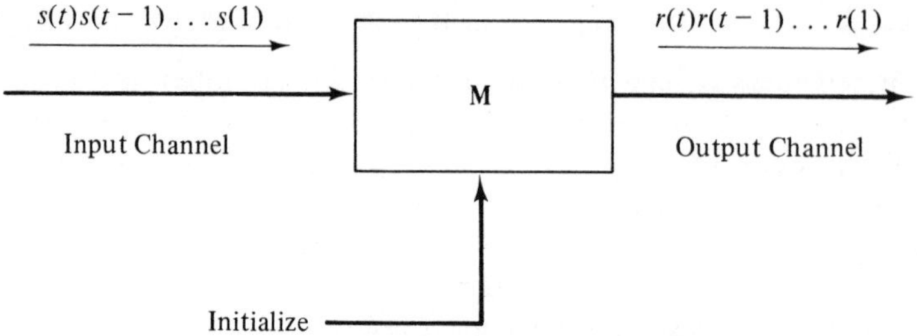


**Figure 4.1.** Finite-state transducer machine.

condition. At each subsequent moment $t$, **M** receives an input symbol $s(t)$ through its input channel and transmits an output symbol $r(t)$ through its output channel. The input symbols are chosen from a finite *input alphabet* **S**:

$$s(t) \in \mathbf{S}, \qquad t = 1, 2, \ldots$$

Similarly, the output symbols $r(t)$ are chosen from a finite *output alphabet* **R**:

$$r(t) \in \mathbf{R}, \qquad t = 1, 2, \ldots$$

A sequence of input symbols presented to the machine is called a *stimulus*; the resulting sequence of output symbols is called the *response* of **M** to the stimulus.

Suppose the transducer is constructed from a finite number of interconnected parts, each of which can assume any one of a finite number of states. The interconnections are paths along which signals pass from one part of the machine to another. Suppose that **M** has $n$ parts and that $q^{(i)}(t)$ is the state assumed by the $i$th part at moment $t$. The *total state* of **M** at time $t$ is the $n$-tuple

$$q(t) = (q^{(1)}(t), q^{(2)}(t), \ldots, q^{(n)}(t))$$

Since it is possible that each part might assume any one of its states independent of the other parts, the maximum possible number of total states of **M** is the product of the numbers of states for each part. Thus, if each part can assume no more than $k$ states, there can be no more than $k^n$ total states of **M**. From now on, we use $q(t)$ to denote the (total) *state* of **M** at moment $t$, and use **Q** to denote the finite *state set* of **M**.

Since the future behavior of **M** clearly depends on the present state of **M**, it is natural to inquire about the state of **M** prior to the presentation of any inputs. For the machine to have deterministic behavior, we must insist that its parts be placed in a fixed, known state before any stimulus is applied. The corresponding total state is called the *initial state* of **M** and is denoted $q_I$. The "initialize" input in Figure 4.1 resets the parts of **M** to the initial state, so that $q(0) = q_I$.

We make the further assumption that the machine changes state only at the moments $t = 0, 1, 2, \ldots$, so its behavior may be specified by giving the sequence of states

$$q(0), q(1), q(2), \ldots, q(t), \ldots, \qquad q(t) \in \mathbf{Q}$$

that describes the internal condition of **M** at each moment.

The input channel enters **M** and connects to certain parts of **M**. When input symbol $s(t + 1)$ arrives, it influences these parts [which are in a condition represented by state $q(t)$], and thereby establishes a new condition described by state $q(t + 1)$. The new state can depend only on the former state of **M** and the input symbol $s(t + 1)$. Thus there exists a function $f$ that specifies the next state of **M** in terms of its present state and the next arriving input symbol:

$$q(t + 1) = f(q(t), s(t + 1)), \qquad t \geq 0$$

This function is called the *state transition function* of **M**. Its domain is the set of all state–symbol pairs, and its range is a subset of the states

$$f\colon \mathbf{Q} \times \mathbf{S} \longrightarrow \mathbf{Q}$$

The output channel of the machine conveys signals from certain parts of **M**. The output symbol generated by the arrival of an input symbol depends only on which symbol arrives and on which state **M** is in just prior to its arrival. Thus there exists a function $g$ that specifies the output symbol produced by **M** in terms of its present state and the arriving input symbol:

$$r(t + 1) = g(q(t), s(t + 1)), \qquad t \geq 0$$

This function is called the *output function* of **M**. Its domain is the set of all state–input symbol pairs, and its range is the output alphabet

$$g\colon \mathbf{Q} \times \mathbf{S} \longrightarrow \mathbf{R}$$

In summary, the following are the properties of a finite-state machine:

1. The behavior of **M** is defined only at the moments $t = 0, 1, 2, \ldots$.
2. The input symbols $s(t)$ are chosen from a finite input alphabet **S**.
3. The output symbols $r(t)$ are chosen from a finite output alphabet **R**.
4. The behavior of **M** is uniquely determined by the sequence of input symbols presented.

5. The behavior of **M** carries it through a sequence of states, each of which is a member of the state set **Q**.

6. There is an initial state $q_I$ of **M** that describes the condition of the parts of **M** just before any stimulus is presented.

These properties lead to a mathematical description of a finite-state machine **M** consisting of the following:

1. The finite sets **S**, **R**, and **Q**.
2. A state transition function $f$ that gives the next state of **M** in terms of the current state and the next input symbol.
3. An output function $g$ that gives the next output symbol of **M** in terms of the current state and next input symbol.
4. A predetermined initial state $q(0) = q_I$ in which **M** is placed prior to instant $t = 0$.

These ideas are formalized in Definition 4.1.

### 4.1.1 Machines with Transition-Assigned Output

**Definition 4.1:** A *transition-assigned finite-state machine* is a six-tuple

$$\mathbf{M} = (\mathbf{Q}, \mathbf{S}, \mathbf{R}, f, g, q_I)$$

where

$\mathbf{Q}$ is a finite set of internal states
$\mathbf{S}$ is a finite input alphabet
$\mathbf{R}$ is a finite output alphabet
$f$ is the state transition function

$$f\colon \mathbf{Q} \times \mathbf{S} \longrightarrow \mathbf{Q}$$

$g$ is the output function

$$g\colon \mathbf{Q} \times \mathbf{S} \longrightarrow \mathbf{R}$$

$q_I \in \mathbf{Q}$ is the initial state

This type of machine, known in the literature as a *Mealy automaton,* is characterized by the association of output symbols with transitions between states. (Later in the chapter, machines with output symbols assigned to states are studied.) Because a finite-state machine deals with sequences of input and output symbols, and because its behavior is represented by a sequence of states, a finite-state machine is also known as a *sequential machine.* It is important to remember that *a finite-state machine includes specification of an initial state.*

To describe a particular finite-state machine, it is necessary to specify the state transition function and the output function. Two representations are standard: the *state table* and the *state diagram.*

A state table is a tabular representation of the two functions, using one row for each state and one column for each input symbol. In the tabular position for state $q$ and symbol $s$, we write the next state $q' = f(q, s)$ and the output symbol $r = g(q, s)$, as shown in Figure 4.2a.

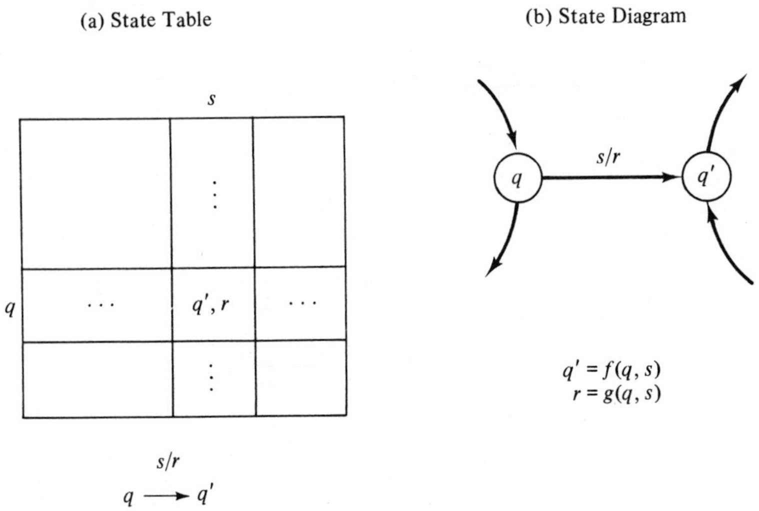


**Figure 4.2.** State table and state diagram representations for transition-assigned machines.

A state diagram is a directed graph in which each node corresponds to a state of the machine and each directed arc indicates a possible transition from one state to another. Figure 4.2b shows how the transition and output functions are represented in a state diagram. Each arc is labeled with the input symbol that causes the transition and the output symbol that is generated. We write

$$q \xrightarrow{s/r} q' \quad \text{to mean} \quad \begin{cases} f(q, s) = q' \\ g(q, s) = r \end{cases}$$

Unless otherwise specified, the first row of a state table will be assigned to the initial state of a machine. In a state diagram, the initial state is indicated by an arc having no node of origin, as shown in Figure 4.3.

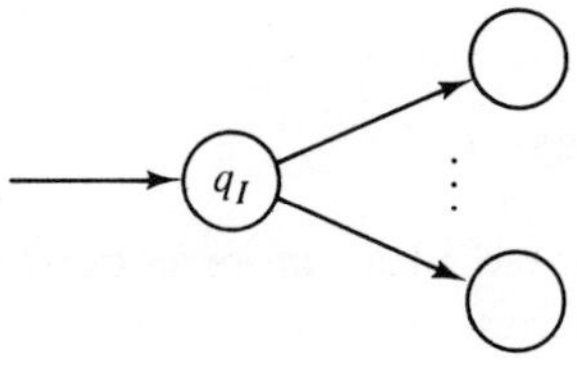


**Figure 4.3.** Initial state of a machine.

Each directed path through the state diagram shows the behavior of the machine in repsonse to the sequence of input symbols labeling the path. Suppose that $q(0)$, $q(1)$, . . . , $q(t)$ are successive nodes on a directed path (Figure 4.4) and the transitions are labeled $s(1)/r(1)$, $s(2)/r(2)$, . . . , $s(t)/r(t)$.

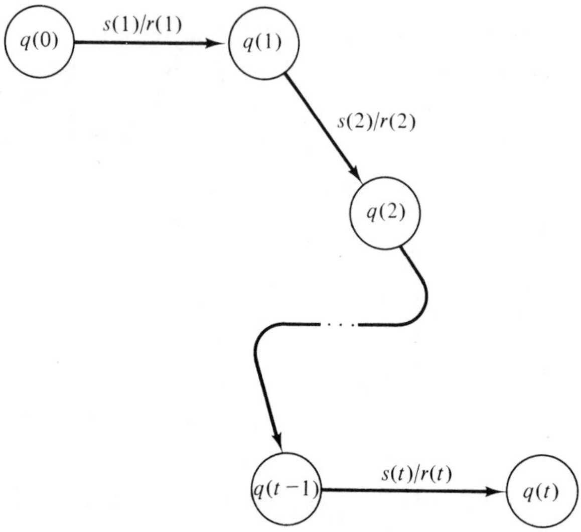


**Figure 4.4.** Path of operation corresponding to an input sequence.

Then the stimulus $s(1)s(2) \ldots s(t)$ causes the machine to trace out the state sequence $q(0)$, $q(1)$, . . . , $q(t)$ and generate the response $r(1)r(2) \ldots r(t)$. This is represented by the notation

$$q(0) \xrightarrow{s(1)/r(1)} q(1) \xrightarrow{s(2)/r(2)} \cdots \xrightarrow{s(t)/r(t)} q(t)$$

Note that the states of this sequence need not be distinct, for the path traced in the state diagram may contain loops.

If we denote the input string by $\omega = s(1)s(2) \ldots s(t)$, and the output string by $\varphi = r(1)r(2) \ldots r(t)$, then we may represent the machine's behavior by the more compact notation

$$q \xRightarrow{\omega/\varphi} q' \qquad \begin{cases} q = q(0) \\ q' = q(t) \end{cases}$$

### 4.1.2 Examples

To make these ideas more concrete, we consider some examples of finite-state machines.

**Example 4.1 (Modulo-3 Counter):** We shall design a finite-state machine $\mathbf{M}_1$ whose output tells the number of input symbols, modulo 3, that have been applied. (For integers $n \geq 0$ and $m > 0$, the value of $n$ mod $m$ is the remainder after dividing $n$ by $m$.) Let

$$\mathbf{S} = \{a\}$$
$$\mathbf{Q} = \{\mathrm{A}, \mathrm{B}, \mathrm{C}\}$$
$$\mathbf{R} = \{0, 1, 2\}$$

Let $t$ be the moment at which the last symbol of a stimulus $\omega$ is presented to $\mathbf{M}_1$. Then the state $q(t)$ will be interpreted as follows:

$$\begin{aligned} q(t) &= \mathrm{A} \text{ means } |\omega| \bmod 3 = 0 \\ &= \mathrm{B} \text{ means } |\omega| \bmod 3 = 1 \\ &= \mathrm{C} \text{ means } |\omega| \bmod 3 = 2 \end{aligned}$$

A state table and a state diagram for this machine are shown in Figure 4.5. The behavior of $\mathbf{M}_1$ for the input sequence $aaaa$, for example, is

$$\mathrm{A} \xrightarrow{a/1} \mathrm{B} \xrightarrow{a/2} \mathrm{C} \xrightarrow{a/0} \mathrm{A} \xrightarrow{a/1} \mathrm{B}$$

(a) State Diagram

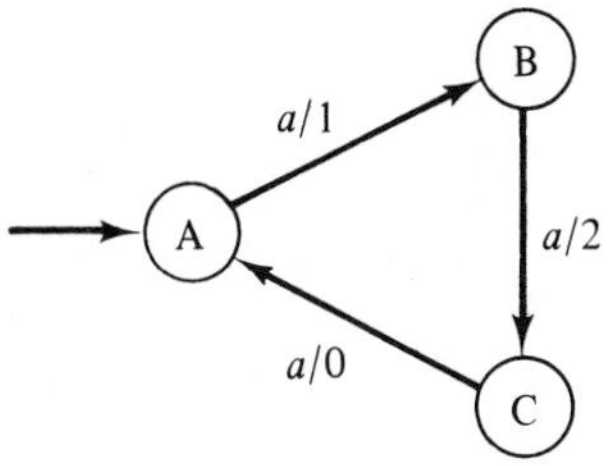


(b) State Table

| | a |
|---|---|
| A | B, 1 |
| B | C, 2 |
| C | A, 0 |

**Figure 4.5.** Modulo-3 counter.

**Example 4.2 (Parity Checker):** Let $\omega$ be a sequence of symbols in the binary alphabet $\{0, 1\}$. If $\omega$ contains an even number of 1's, it is said to have *even parity*; if $\omega$ contains an odd number of 1's, it is said to have *odd parity.*

We wish to design a finite-state machine $\mathbf{M}_2$ that produces an output 1 whenever the parity of the input sequence is odd, and an output 0 whenever the parity of the input sequence is even. Clearly, we must have $\mathbf{S} = \mathbf{R} = \{0, 1\}$.

Observe that the parity of a string $\omega s$, $s \in \{0, 1\}$, is readily determined from $s$ and the parity of $\omega$: if $s = 0$, the parity of $\omega s$ is the same as that of $\omega$; if $s = 1$, the parity of $\omega s$ is different from that of $\omega$. Thus $\mathbf{M}_2$ needs only two states, one indicating that the input sequence so far has even parity, the other indicating that it has odd parity. The machine $\mathbf{M}_2$ is shown in Figure 4.6.

(a) State Diagram

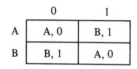

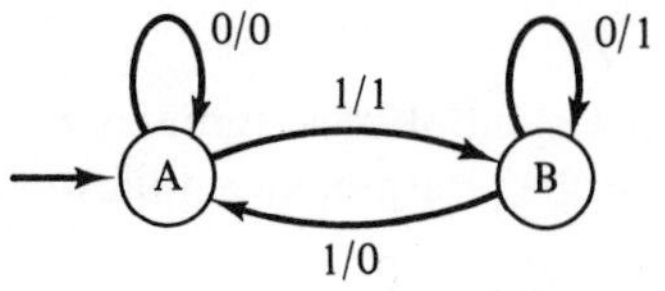


(b) State Table

| | 0 | 1 |
|---|---|---|
| A | A, 0 | B, 1 |
| B | B, 1 | A, 0 |

**Figure 4.6.** Parity checker.

For the input sequence

0 1 0 0 1 1

the behavior of $\mathbf{M}_2$ is given by

$$A \xrightarrow{0/0} A \xrightarrow{1/1} B \xrightarrow{0/1} B \xrightarrow{0/1} B \xrightarrow{1/0} A \xrightarrow{1/1} B$$

producing the output sequence

0 1 1 1 0 1

**Example 4.3 (Two-Unit Delay):** The input and output alphabets of machine $\mathbf{M}_3$ are $\{0, 1\}$. The output sequence is to be a replica of the input sequence delayed by two time units:

$$r(t) = s(t - 2), \qquad t > 2$$

We do not care what $r(1)$ and $r(2)$ are since no input symbols were applied before $t = 1$. The states of $\mathbf{M}_3$ distinguish among input sequences according to the last two symbols presented, $s(t - 1)$ and $s(t - 2)$, as follows:

| $s(t-1), s(t-2)$ | State of $\mathbf{M}_3$ |
|---|---|
| 0 0 | A |
| 0 1 | B |
| 1 1 | C |
| 1 0 | D |

The state diagram is shown in Figure 4.7. A typical stimulus and the resulting response are

Stimulus: 0 0 0 1 1 0 1 0 0
Response: 0 0 0 0 0 1 1 0 1

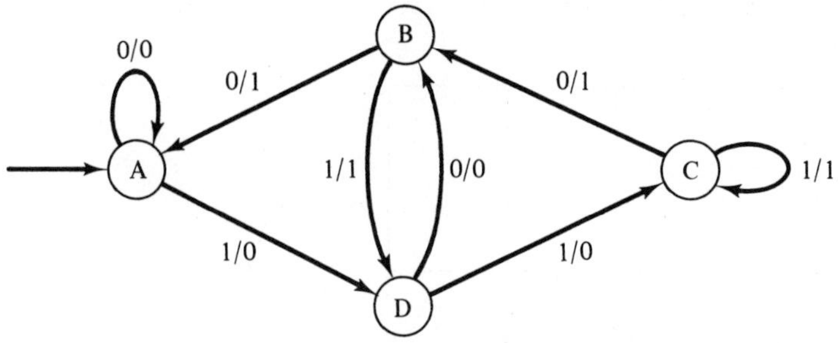


**Figure 4.7.** Two-unit delay.

for which $\mathbf{M}_3$ has the state sequence

$$A \xrightarrow{0/0} A \xrightarrow{0/0} A \xrightarrow{0/0} A \xrightarrow{1/0} D \xrightarrow{1/0} C \xrightarrow{0/1} B \xrightarrow{1/1} D \xrightarrow{0/0} B \xrightarrow{0/1} A$$

Note that an *n-unit delay* would require $2^n$ states.

### 4.1.3 Machines with State-Assigned Output

It is frequently convenient to specify the output of a finite-state machine just in terms of the state of the machine. For example, in the parity machine $\mathbf{M}_2$ the output is uniquely determined by the state to which a transition leads. In a *state-assigned* machine the output function assigns an output symbol to each state.

**Definition 4.2:** A *state-assigned finite-state machine* is a six-tuple

$$\mathbf{M} = (\mathbf{Q}, \mathbf{S}, \mathbf{R}, f, h, q_I)$$

where

$\mathbf{Q}$ is a finite set of internal states
$\mathbf{S}$ is a finite input alphabet
$\mathbf{R}$ is a finite output alphabet
$f$ is a state transition function

$$f\colon \mathbf{Q} \times \mathbf{S} \longrightarrow \mathbf{Q}$$

$h$ is an output function

$$h\colon \mathbf{Q} \longrightarrow \mathbf{R}$$

$q_I \in \mathbf{Q}$ is the initial state

This type of machine is known in the literature as a *Moore automaton.*

Figure 4.8 shows how state-assigned machines are represented by state tables and state diagrams. For state-assigned machines we write state

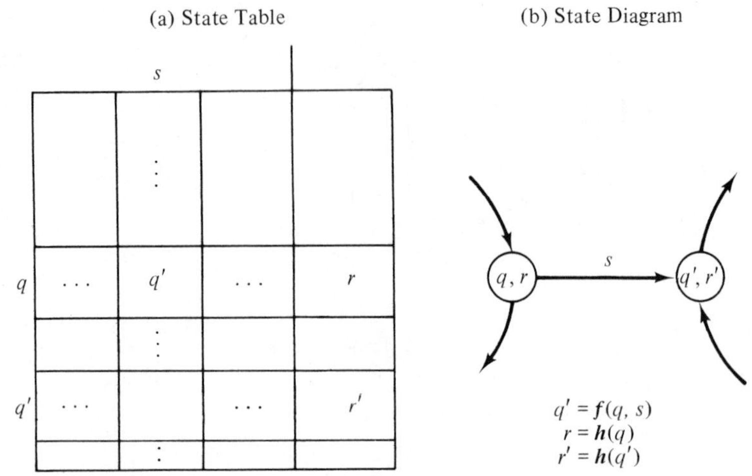


**Figure 4.8.** State table and state diagram representations for state-assigned machines.

sequences as (state, output symbol) pairs joined by arrows labeled with the input symbol causing the indicated transition:

$$(q, r) \xrightarrow{s} (q', r') \quad \text{means} \quad \begin{cases} f(q, s) = q' \\ h(q) = r \\ h(q') = r' \end{cases}$$

Later in the chapter we shall inquire whether these two models, one with transition-assigned outputs and the other with state-assigned outputs, are equivalent in computing power.

**Example 4.4: (Modulo-4 Up–Down Counter):** Machine $\mathbf{M}_4$ will analyze input sequences in the binary alphabet $\mathbf{S} = \{0, 1\}$. Let $\omega = s(1)s(2) \ldots s(t)$ be an input string and define

$$N_0(\omega) = \text{number of 0's in } \omega$$

$$N_1(\omega) = \text{number of 1's in } \omega$$

so that $|\omega| = N_0(\omega) + N_1(\omega) = t$. The last output of $\mathbf{M}_4$ is to be

$$r(t) = [N_1(\omega) - N_0(\omega)] \bmod 4$$

Hence the output alphabet is $\mathbf{R} = \{0, 1, 2, 3\}$. The machine is specified in Figure 4.9 and is called an *up–down counter* owing to the appearance of its state diagram. Typical stimulus and response sequences are

Stimulus: 1 1 0 1 1 1 0 0

Response: 0 1 2 1 2 3 0 3 2

The corresponding state sequence is

(a) State Diagram

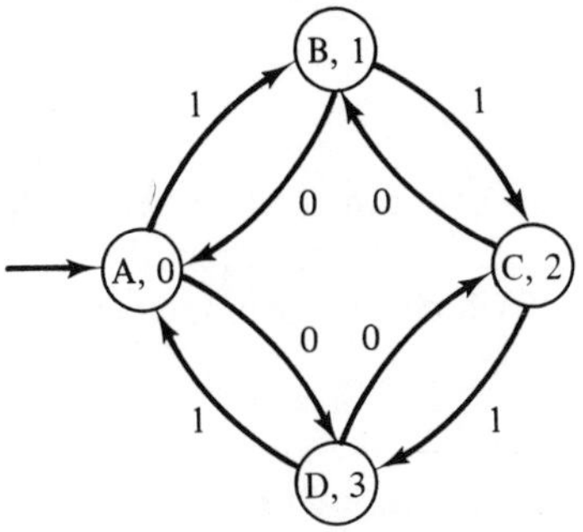


(b) State Table

| | 0 | 1 | |
|---|---|---|---|
| A | D | B | 0 |
| B | A | C | 1 |
| C | B | D | 2 |
| D | C | A | 3 |

**Figure 4.9.** Modulo-4 up-down counter.

$$(A, 0) \xrightarrow{1} (B, 1) \xrightarrow{1} (C, 2) \xrightarrow{0} (B, 1) \xrightarrow{1} (C, 2)$$
$$\xrightarrow{1} (D, 3) \xrightarrow{1} (A, 0) \xrightarrow{0} (D, 3) \xrightarrow{0} (C, 2)$$

**Example 4.5 (Language Recognizer):** Machine $\mathbf{M}_5$ is to accept a binary string if and only if it begins with a 1 and contains exactly one 0. (The set of all such strings is the set $\mathbf{X} = \mathbf{11^*\ 01^*}$.) A state diagram for $\mathbf{M}_5$ appears in Figure 4.10. The machine has an output

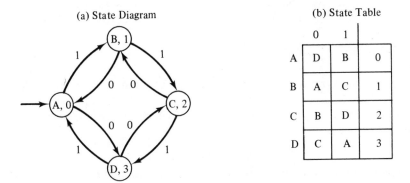

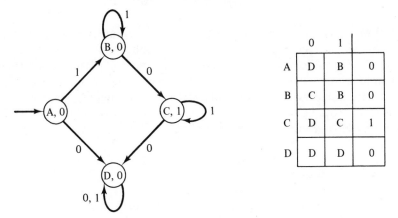

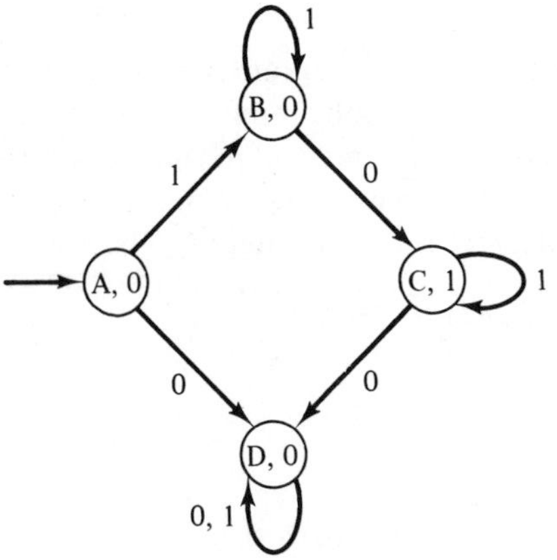


| | 0 | 1 | |
|---|---|---|---|
| A | D | B | 0 |
| B | C | B | 0 |
| C | D | C | 1 |
| D | D | D | 0 |

**Figure 4.10.** Machine to recognize $\mathbf{X} = \mathbf{11^*01^*}$.

of 1, indicating acceptance, if and only if the input string leads it into state C. Observe that once $\mathbf{M}_5$ enters state D, no subsequent sequence of input symbols can ever cause the machine to leave state D. Thus any string that is accepted must avoid leading the machine to state D. Such a state is called a *trap state*. Any input string not beginning with a 1 or having more than a single 0 leads $\mathbf{M}_5$ to the trap state. States B and C distinguish between input sequences containing no 0's and one 0, respectively. Thus each string in the set **X** leads $\mathbf{M}_5$ to its *accepting state* C, and only such strings lead $\mathbf{M}_5$ to C.

### 4.1.4 Machine Complexity

It is interesting to study the relationship between the number of states of a machine **M** and the number of physical components required to realize **M**. Suppose that **M** is built of $n$ parts, each of which can assume either of two states. Then each total state of **M** is an $n$-tuple

$$q = (q^{(1)}, q^{(2)}, \ldots, q^{(n)})$$

in which $q^{(i)}$ represents the state of the $i$th part. The number of total states is $2^n$. Therefore,

$$(\text{number of parts}) \sim \log_2 (\text{number of states})$$

Adding another two-state part to a machine doubles the number of distinct total states. Thus the number of states grows exponentially with the number of parts.

How many states does a computer have? For simplicity, let us just consider the active memory of a computer, which in certain machines is of the order of $2^{15}$ words of 32 bits apiece. Since each bit may be either 0 or 1, and the memory consists of $N = (32)(2^{15}) = 2^{20}$ bits, the memory has

$$2^N = 2^{2^{20}} \approx 2^{1{,}000{,}000} \approx 10^{300{,}000}$$

states!

It would hardly be practical to draw a state diagram for such a machine. The finite-state model, therefore, is not especially useful for studying the behavior of an entire computer. Indeed, for all practical purposes a computer has an infinite number of states, and that is why machine models that allow for infinite numbers of states are of great practical interest. The finite-state model has proved quite useful, however, in the design of subunits of a computer that have relatively few states.

## 4.2 State Sequences

We have seen that a sequence of states on a path through the state diagram of a machine corresponds to the application of a string of input symbols and the emission of a string of output symbols. We now give careful definitions for the notions of successor states and state sequences. These definitions are needed for discussing equivalence of machines and for studying their relation to languages in Chapter 5. The definitions hold for both state-assigned and transition-assigned machines.

**Definition 4.3:** Let **M** be a finite-state machine with transition function $f\colon \mathbf{Q} \times \mathbf{S} \rightarrow \mathbf{Q}$. If $f(q, s) = q'$, we say that state $q'$ is the *s-successor* of state $q$ and write

$$q \xrightarrow{s} q'$$

If a string of input symbols

$$\omega = s(1)s(2)\ldots s(t)$$

takes **M** from state $q = q(0)$ to state $q' = q(t)$, that is, if

$$q(0) \xrightarrow{s(1)} q(1) \xrightarrow{s(2)} \ldots \xrightarrow{s(t)} q(t)$$

we say that state $q'$ is the *ω-successor* of state $q$ and write

$$q \xRightarrow{\omega} q'$$

Under these conditions

$$q(0)q(1)\ldots q(t)$$

is called an *admissible state sequence* for $\omega$.

By these definitions we have effectively extended the domain of the state transition function to include all input strings, rather than just individual input symbols. That is, we now have

$$f\colon \mathbf{Q} \times \mathbf{S}^* \longrightarrow \mathbf{Q}$$

where

$$f(q, \omega) = q' \quad \text{if and only if} \quad q \xRightarrow{\omega} q'$$

and

$$f(q, \lambda) = q \qquad \text{for all } q \in \mathbf{Q}$$

Note that these four statements are equivalent:

1. There is an admissible state sequence from $q$ to $q'$ for input string $\omega = s(1)s(2)\ldots s(t)$.
2. $q \xRightarrow{\omega} q'$.
3. $f(q, \omega) = q'$.
4. There is a directed path from $q$ to $q'$ in the state diagram for **M** with transitions labeled by input symbols $s(1), s(2), \ldots, s(t)$.

**Definition 4.4:** Let **M** be a finite-state machine and suppose that

$$q_I = q(0), q(1), \ldots, q(t) = q$$

is an admissible state sequence for the input sequence

$$\omega = s(1)s(2)\ldots s(t)$$

a. If **M** is transition assigned with output function $g\colon \mathbf{Q} \times \mathbf{S} \longrightarrow \mathbf{R}$, then

$$\varphi = r(1)r(2)\ldots r(t)$$

is the *response* of **M** to *stimulus* $\omega$ where

$$r(i) = g(q(i-1), s(i)), \qquad i = 1, 2, \ldots, t$$

b. If **M** is state assigned with output function $h\colon \mathbf{Q} \longrightarrow \mathbf{R}$, then

$$\varphi = r(0)r(1)r(2)\ldots r(t)$$

is the *response* of **M** to *stimulus* $\omega$ where

$$r(i) = h(q(i)), \qquad i = 0, 1, \ldots, t$$

## 4.3 Conversion Between Transition- and State-Assigned Machines

Definition 4.4 points out an important distinction between transition- and state-assigned automata: a state-assigned machine has a response to the empty string! Our aim in this section is to show that, aside from this point, these two machine types are equivalent abstract models of computation.

How shall we decide whether the two models are equivalent? The natural question to ask is whether a machine of one type can always be designed to mimic the responses of a given machine of the other type.

**Definition 4.5:** A transition-assigned machine $\mathbf{M}_t$ and a state-assigned machine $\mathbf{M}_s$ are *similar* if, for each possible stimulus, the response of $\mathbf{M}_s$ is exactly that of $\mathbf{M}_t$ preceded by one arbitrary, but fixed, symbol.

The meaning of this definition is suggested by Figure 4.11. The same string $\omega$ is applied to both $\mathbf{M}_t$ and $\mathbf{M}_s$. The response of $\mathbf{M}_t$ is the string $\varphi$. The response of $\mathbf{M}_s$ is the string $r_0\varphi$ for some fixed symbol $r_0$ determined by $\mathbf{M}_s$.

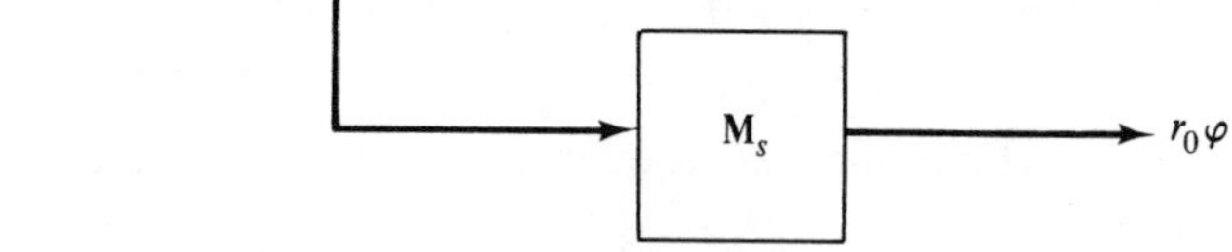

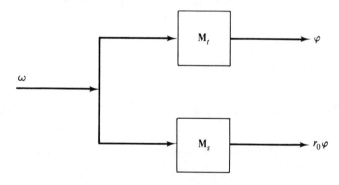

**Figure 4.11.** Illustrating the definition of similarity.

**Theorem 4.1:** For each state-assigned machine $\mathbf{M}_s$ there exists a similar transition-assigned machine $\mathbf{M}_t$. Conversely, for transition-assigned machine $\mathbf{M}_t$ there exists a similar state-assigned machine $\mathbf{M}_s$.

Proving each of these two assertions consists of constructing a machine of one type from any given machine of the other, and demonstrating that the constructed machine is similar to the original.

The simpler problem is to obtain $\mathbf{M}_t$ from $\mathbf{M}_s$. The states and transitions of $\mathbf{M}_t$ are chosen to be the same as those of $\mathbf{M}_s$. Whenever state $q$ in $\mathbf{M}_s$ has output $r$, each transition of $\mathbf{M}_t$ *into* state $q$ is labeled with output $r$. The construction is as follows: if

$$\mathbf{M}_s = (\mathbf{Q}, \mathbf{S}, \mathbf{R}, f, h, q_I)$$

then

$$\mathbf{M}_t = (\mathbf{Q}, \mathbf{S}, \mathbf{R}, f, g, q_I)$$

in which

$$g(q, s) = h(f(q, s)), \qquad \text{all } q \in \mathbf{Q},\ s \in \mathbf{S}$$

Since the states and transitions of both $\mathbf{M}_s$ and $\mathbf{M}_t$ are identical, it is clear that a state sequence is admissible in $\mathbf{M}_t$ for a stimulus $\omega$ if and only if it is admissible in $\mathbf{M}_s$ for $\omega$. The similarity of $\mathbf{M}_t$ and $\mathbf{M}_s$ follows directly from this fact and the relationship of the output functions.

> **Example 4.6:** Figure 4.12 illustrates the construction of a transition-assigned machine from a state-assigned machine. The property that $\mathbf{M}_s$ has output 1 in its initial state is lost in $\mathbf{M}_t$.

$\mathbf{M}_s$:

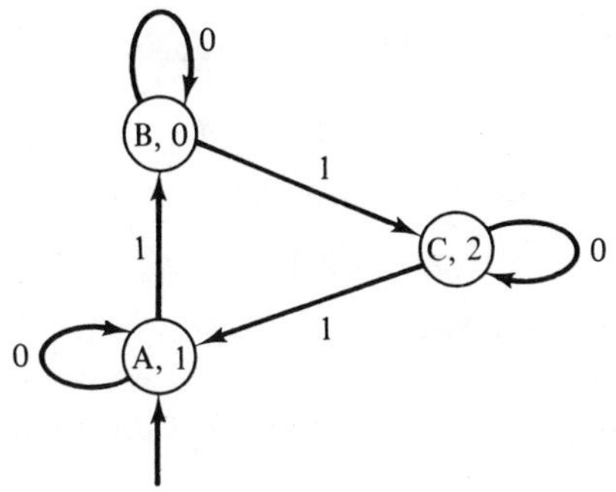


$\mathbf{M}_t$:

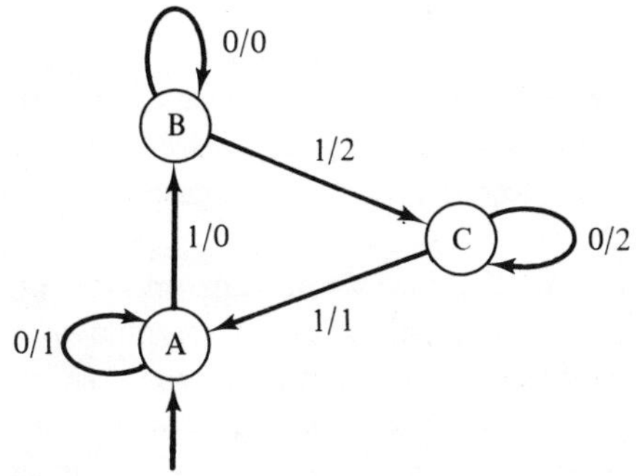


**Figure 4.12.** Construction of $\mathbf{M}_t$ from $\mathbf{M}_s$.

The construction of $\mathbf{M}_s$ from a given machine $\mathbf{M}_t$ is somewhat more complicated. We cannot simply reverse the construction given above, because $\mathbf{M}_t$ may contain a state $q$ whose input transitions are labeled by more than one output symbol. To circumvent this difficulty, we let the states of $\mathbf{M}_s$ be the set of all state–output pairs $\mathbf{Q}_t \times \mathbf{R}$ in $\mathbf{M}_t$. Machine $\mathbf{M}_s$ will enter state $(q, r)$ whenever $\mathbf{M}_t$ enters state $q$ and emits output symbol $r$. The construction is as follows: if

$$\mathbf{M}_t = (\mathbf{Q}_t, \mathbf{S}, \mathbf{R}, f_t, g, q_I)$$

then

$$\mathbf{M}_s = (\mathbf{Q}_s, \mathbf{S}, \mathbf{R}, f_s, h, (q_I, r_0))$$

where

$$\mathbf{Q}_s = \mathbf{Q}_t \times \mathbf{R}$$

The functions $f_s$ and $h$ are defined as follows: whenever $\mathbf{M}_t$ has a transition

$$q \xrightarrow{s/r} q'$$

then $\mathbf{M}_s$ has the transition

$$((q, r'), r') \xrightarrow{s} ((q', r), r)$$

for each $r' \in \mathbf{R}$. Whenever $\mathbf{M}_t$ has the transition

$$q_I \xrightarrow{s/r} q'$$

then $\mathbf{M}_s$ has the corresponding transition

$$((q_I, r_0), r_0) \xrightarrow{s} ((q', r), r)$$

where $r_0 \in \mathbf{R}$ is an arbitrarily chosen output symbol for the initial state of $\mathbf{M}_s$.

Given an input string $\omega = s(1) \ldots s(n)$ and an admissible state sequence $q(0) \ldots q(n)$ for $\omega$ in $\mathbf{M}_t$, an admissible state sequence for $\omega$ in $\mathbf{M}_s$ will consist of the pairs

$$(q(i), g(q(i-1), s(i))), \qquad i = 1, 2, \ldots, n$$

By construction, the response of $\mathbf{M}_s$ will be the same as that of $\mathbf{M}_t$ with the exception of the initial symbol $r_0$.

> **Example 4.7:** Figure 4.13 illustrates the construction of a state-assigned machine from a transition-assigned machine. We have arbitrarily chosen 0 as the output specified for the initial state of $\mathbf{M}_s$.

We conclude that the two finite-state models are of equivalent computational power, with the minor exception that a state-assigned machine has a specific response for the empty input string. Since this feature is important in connection with the study of machines as language recognizers, we shall use the state-assigned model extensively in later chapters.

$\mathbf{M}_t$:

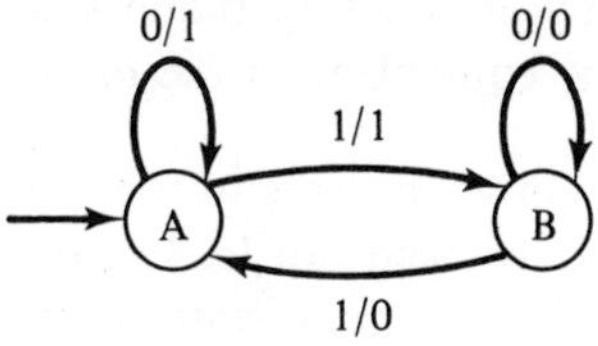


$\mathbf{M}_s$:

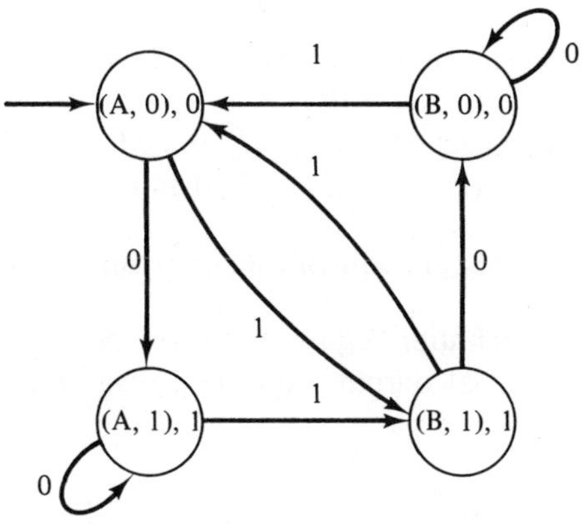


**Figure 4.13.** Construction of $\mathbf{M}_s$ from $\mathbf{M}_t$.

## 4.4 Equivalence of Finite-State Machines

An important question that recurs throughout discussions of automata is that of equivalence: under what circumstances do two automata exhibit identical behavior? Regarded as language recognizers, two automata are equivalent if and only if they recognize the same language; as generators, if and only if they generate the same language; as transducers, if and only if they produce identical transductions of each input string.

We shall see later that it is not always possible to decide whether two automata have equivalent behavior. In this section we shall find that the question *can* be answered in every case if the automata are finite-state machines. Indeed, each such automaton can be put into an essentially unique standard form.

Solving the equivalence problem for finite-state machines also resolves several issues arising naturally in the solution of design problems:

1. Given the state diagram of a machine, is it possible to detect and eliminate redundant states without altering the machine's behavior?

2. Is it possible, by eliminating redundant states, to obtain a unique minimum-state machine equivalent to the original?

We shall find affirmative answers to both questions. Although using the minimum number of states need not lead directly to a physical machine of simplest construction, the minimum-state machine is often a good starting point for hardware design.

We begin with a definition of equivalent machines:

**Definition 4.6:** Two machines $\mathbf{M}_1$ and $\mathbf{M}_2$ are *equivalent* if and only if

1. Their input alphabets and their output alphabets are the same: $\mathbf{S}_1 = \mathbf{S}_2$, $\mathbf{R}_1 = \mathbf{R}_2$.
2. For each stimulus, $\mathbf{M}_1$ and $\mathbf{M}_2$ produce identical responses. That is, if $s_1(t) = s_2(t)$, $t \geq 1$, then $r_1(t) = r_2(t)$, $t \geq 1$.

If $\mathbf{M}_1$ and $\mathbf{M}_2$ are equivalent, we write $\mathbf{M}_1 \sim \mathbf{M}_2$.

According to this defintion, equivalent machines operated as in Figure 4.14 must produce identical output sequences, regardless of the input sequence presented.

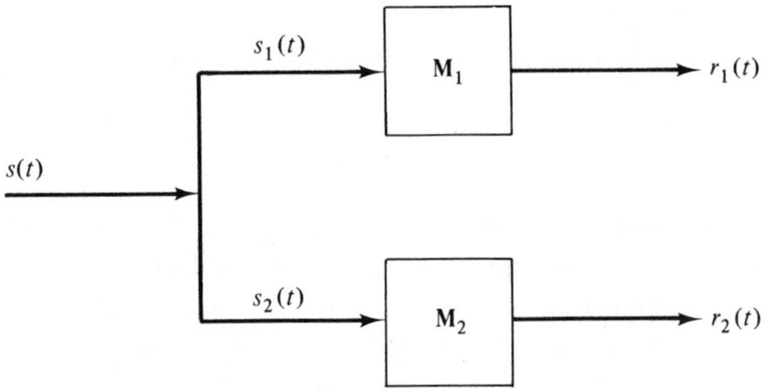


**Figure 4.14.** Conceptual test for equivalent machines.

Definition 4.6 establishes an equivalence relation on the class of finite-state automata. To confirm this, we must show that the properties of reflexivity, symmetry, and transitivity are satisfied:

1. *Reflexivity:* $\mathbf{M} \sim \mathbf{M}$. Each machine is clearly equivalent to itself.
2. *Symmetry:* If $\mathbf{M}_1 \sim \mathbf{M}_2$, then $\mathbf{M}_2 \sim \mathbf{M}_1$. Interchanging subscripts in the body of Definition 4.6 does not alter the meaning of equivalence.
3. *Transitivity:* If $\mathbf{M}_1 \sim \mathbf{M}_2$ and $\mathbf{M}_2 \sim \mathbf{M}_3$, then $\mathbf{M}_1 \sim \mathbf{M}_3$. Whenever $r_1(t) = r_2(t)$, $t \geq 1$, and $r_2(t) = r_3(t)$, $t \geq 1$, it follows that $r_1(t) = r_3(t)$, $t \geq 1$.

The relation of machine equivalence partitions the class of finite-state automata into collections of mutually equivalent machines.

## 4.5 Equivalent States

To solve the equivalence problem for finite-state automata, we must relate the equivalence of two automata to their internal structure as expressed by state diagrams or state tables. We consider two *states* of a machine to be equivalent if it is impossible to distinguish two copies of the machine, one started in each state.

> **Definition 4.7:** Two states $q_a$ and $q_b$ of a transition-assigned machine $\mathbf{M} = (\mathbf{Q}, \mathbf{S}, \mathbf{R}, f, g, q_I)$ are *equivalent states* if and only if the machines
>
> $$\mathbf{M}_a = (\mathbf{Q}, \mathbf{S}, \mathbf{R}, f, g, q_a)$$
>
> and
>
> $$\mathbf{M}_b = (\mathbf{Q}, \mathbf{S}, \mathbf{R}, f, g, q_b)$$
>
> are equivalent. An analogous statement applies to state-assigned machines. If $q_a$ and $q_b$ are equivalent states, we write $q_a \sim q_b$.

The notion of state equivalence is illustrated by Figure 4.15. If states $q_a$ and $q_b$ are equivalent in machine **M**, the two copies of **M** cannot be distinguished by presenting stimuli and comparing the responses.

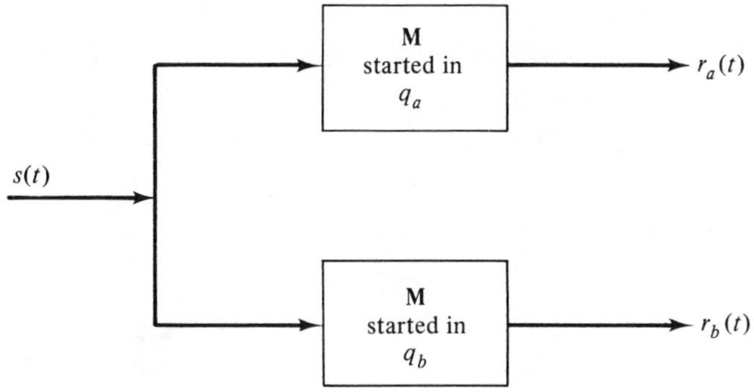


**Figure 4.15.** Conceptual test for equivalent states.

Because state equivalence is expressed in terms of machine equivalence, it is easy to see that the relation of state equivalence partitions the states of a machine into equivalence classes such that

1. All states in the same class are mutually equivalent.
2. Any two states in different classes are not equivalent.

Note that if two states are not equivalent, there must be an input sequence which, when applied to two copies of a machine as depicted in Figure 4.15, will produce different output sequences.

If two states are equivalent, one of them is clearly redundant, since all transitions into one of the states may be switched to the equivalent state without affecting the behavior of the machine. To identify redundant states in a machine, we need a method of constructing the equivalence classes of states from the state diagram or state table of the machine. Before developing such a procedure, however, we shall explore some consequences of the definition.

An interpretation of state equivalence in terms of the structure of a machine is provided by the next theorem.

**Theorem 4.2:** States $q_a$ and $q_b$ of a finite-state machine **M** are equivalent if and only if

1a. Transition-assigned: For all $s \in \mathbf{S}$, $g(q_a, s) = g(q_b, s)$. That is, the outputs for corresponding transitions from the two states are identical.

1b. State-assigned: $h(q_a) = h(q_b)$. That is, the output symbols for the two states are identical.

2. For all $s \in \mathbf{S}$, $f(q_a, s) \sim f(q_b, s)$. That is, the $s$-successors of the two states are themselves equivalent states.

***Proof:*** We give the proof for the case of transition-assigned machines, and leave the proof for state-assigned machines as an exercise for the reader.

*If:* We must show that if conditions 1a and 2 hold, then $q_a \sim q_b$. Let $s\omega$ be an arbitrarily chosen input string consisting of the single letter $s$ followed by some string $\omega \in \mathbf{S}^*$. Consider **M**'s behavior when $s\omega$ is applied:

$$q_a \xrightarrow{s/r} q_a' \xRightarrow{\omega/\varphi} q_a''$$

$$q_b \xrightarrow{s/r'} q_b' \xRightarrow{\omega/\varphi'} q_b''$$

To show that $q_a \sim q_b$, we must show that the responses are identical; that is,

$$r\varphi = r'\varphi'$$

Condition 1a asserts that $r = r'$. Condition 2 asserts that $q_a' \sim q_b'$ and thus that $\varphi = \varphi'$.

*Only if:* We must show that, if $q_a \sim q_b$, then conditions 1a and 2 hold. Again, let $s\omega$ be an arbitrarily chosen input string, as above, and consider **M**'s behavior when $s\omega$ is applied:

$$q_a \xrightarrow{s/r} q_a' \xRightarrow{\omega/\varphi} q_a''$$

$$q_b \xrightarrow{s/r'} q_b' \xRightarrow{\omega/\varphi'} q_b''$$

Since $q_a \sim q_b$, the responses to $s\omega$ must be identical. That is,

$$r\varphi = r'\varphi'$$

from which we conclude that $r = r'$ (thus condition 1a is satisfied), and that $\varphi = \varphi'$ (thus $q'_a \sim q'_b$, and condition 2 is satisfied).

In the machine of Figure 4.16 we see that states A and B are equivalent because

$$g(\text{A}, 0) = g(\text{B}, 0) = 0$$
$$g(\text{A}, 1) = g(\text{B}, 1) = 0$$

and

$$f(\text{A}, 0) = \text{B} \qquad f(\text{A}, 1) = \text{C}$$
$$f(\text{B}, 0) = \text{B} \qquad f(\text{B}, 1) = \text{C}$$

and certainly B $\sim$ B and C $\sim$ C.

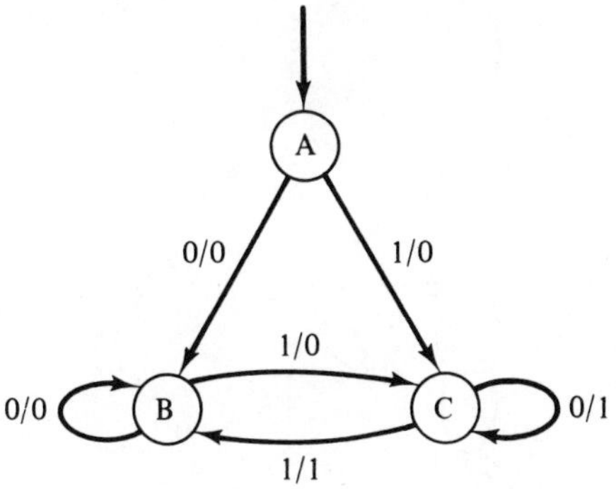


**Figure 4.16.** Machine with A $\sim$ B.

Now let us try to use Theorem 4.2 to decide if B $\sim$ C in Figure 4.17. We have

$$g(\text{B}, 0) = g(\text{C}, 0) = 0$$
$$g(\text{B}, 1) = g(\text{C}, 1) = 1$$

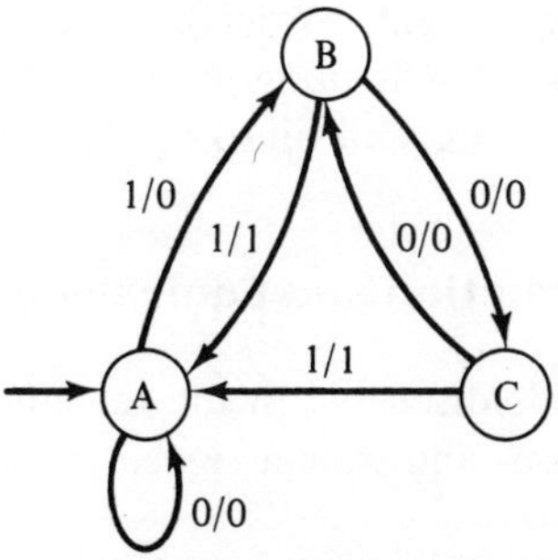


**Figure 4.17.** Machine with B $\sim$ C.

so the outputs are identical. Also

$$f(\mathrm{B}, 1) = \mathrm{A}$$
$$f(\mathrm{C}, 1) = \mathrm{A}$$

and certainly A $\sim$ A. However,

$$f(\mathrm{B}, 0) = \mathrm{C}$$
$$f(\mathrm{C}, 0) = \mathrm{B}$$

We have the result that B $\sim$ C if B $\sim$ C! This circularity reduces the value of Theorem 4.2 as a test for state equivalence: it is true that B $\sim$ C, but this does not follow directly from Theorem 4.2.

Figure 4.18 shows two copies of the same machine side by side. Viewed as a single state diagram of a machine **M**, it is obvious that

$$\mathrm{A} \sim \mathrm{C}$$
$$\mathrm{B} \sim \mathrm{D}$$

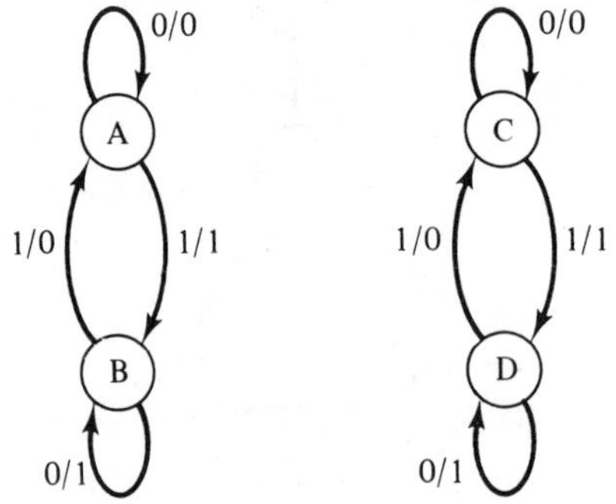


**Figure 4.18.** Machine with A $\sim$ C and B $\sim$ D.

since the behavior of **M** is the same whether it is started in either of A or C, or either of B or D. Again, these state equivalences cannot be deduced through direct application of Theorem 4.2. We need an equivalence test that will conclude that A $\sim$ C and B $\sim$ D in this type of disconnected machine, and that B $\sim$ C in a connected machine such as the one in Figure 4.17.

Theorem 4.2 is more useful for deciding when two states are *not* equivalent. In principle, we can test the states of a machine in pairs to decide which states are not equivalent, by default discovering which states are equivalent. This is precisely what is done in Section 4.6, where we develop an orderly procedure for sorting states into equivalence classes.

## 4.6 State Reduction and Equivalence Testing

The methods discussed in the remainder of this chapter are applicable to both transition- and state-assigned machines. The presentation is made in terms of the transition-assigned model. The reader should be able to supply the minor modifications required for the state-assigned model.

### 4.6.1 Reduced, Connected Machines

Intuitively, a machine is in its simplest form once all redundant and unusable states have been removed.

> **Definition 4.8:** A finite-state machine is *reduced* if it contains no pair of equivalent states.

> **Definition 4.9:** A state $q$ in a finite-state automaton is *accessible* if there is some input string $\omega$ such that $q_I \overset{\omega}{\Longrightarrow} q$. A finite-state machine is *connected* if every state is accessible from the initial state.

The reader should convince himself that if state $q$ in an $n$-state machine is accessible, there exists an input string $\omega$ such that $|\omega| < n$ and $q_I \overset{\omega}{\Longrightarrow} q$.

It should be evident that no state can be removed from a reduced and connected machine without affecting its behavior. Inaccessible states can always be removed from a machine, since the machine can never enter such states.

### 4.6.2 Distinguishing Sequences and *k*-Equivalence

If states $q_a$ and $q_b$ of machine **M** are equivalent, no input string applied to the experiment of Figure 4.15 can evoke different responses from the two copies of **M**. Conversely, if the states $q_a$ and $q_b$ are not equivalent, there is an input sequence which, when applied to the experiment of Figure 4.15, will evoke responses differing in at least one symbol. In the latter case, $q_a$ and $q_b$ are said to be *distinguishable* states.

> **Definition 4.10:** States $q_a$ and $q_b$ of a transition-assigned machine $\mathbf{M} = (\mathbf{Q}, \mathbf{S}, \mathbf{R}, f, g, q_I)$ are *k-distinguishable* if there exists a string $\omega \in \mathbf{S}^*$ with $|\omega| \leq k$, such that the responses of
>
> $$\mathbf{M}_a = (\mathbf{Q}, \mathbf{S}, \mathbf{R}, f, g, q_a)$$
>
> and
>
> $$\mathbf{M}_b = (\mathbf{Q}, \mathbf{S}, \mathbf{R}, f, g, q_b)$$
>
> to $\omega$ differ in at least one symbol. Such a string $\omega$ is called a *distinguishing sequence* for states $q_a$ and $q_b$. If states $q_a$ and $q_b$ are not $k$-distinguishable, we say that they are *k-equivalent.*

A distinguishing sequence for states $q_a$ and $q_b$, if used as input in the experiment of Figure 4.15, would enable us to decide which copy of machine **M** was started in state $q_a$ and which was started in $q_b$.

**Theorem 4.3:** Two states of a finite-state machine are $k$-equivalent if and only if

1. They are 1-equivalent.
2. For each input symbol $s$, their $s$-successors are $(k-1)$-equivalent.

The proof of Theorem 4.3 is similar to that of Theorem 4.2, except that the input string $\omega$ is restricted to being of length less than $k$; we leave it to the reader to fill in the details.

Clearly, two states of a machine are equivalent if and only if they are $k$-equivalent for all $k \geq 1$.

### 4.6.3 Partitioning the State Set

Theorem 4.3 serves as the basis for the machine-reduction procedure developed below. Our objective is to partition the machine's state set into blocks of mutually equivalent states.

Some additional terminology is useful. Recall that an equivalence relation on a set partitions the set into mutually exclusive, collectively exhaustive *blocks*. If $\mathbf{P}_1$ and $\mathbf{P}_2$ are partitions of a set $\mathbf{X}$, and if each block of $\mathbf{P}_2$ is a subset of exactly one block of $\mathbf{P}_1$, then $\mathbf{P}_2$ is a *refinement* of $\mathbf{P}_1$. That is, if

$$\mathbf{P}_1 = \{\mathbf{A}_1, \ldots, \mathbf{A}_n\} \quad \text{and} \quad \mathbf{P}_2 = \{\mathbf{B}_1, \ldots, \mathbf{B}_m\}$$

are partitions of a set $\mathbf{X}$, and $\mathbf{P}_2$ is a refinement of $\mathbf{P}_1$, then for each block $\mathbf{B}_j$ in $\mathbf{P}_2$ there is a block $\mathbf{A}_i$ in $\mathbf{P}_1$ such that

$$\mathbf{B}_j \subseteq \mathbf{A}_i$$

The number of blocks in $\mathbf{P}_2$ is never less than the number in $\mathbf{P}_1$; thus, $m \geq n$. According to this definition, a partition is a refinement of itself.

The partitioning of a state set into equivalence classes is based on the conceptual experiment depicted in Figure 4.19. Suppose that $\mathbf{M} = (\mathbf{Q}, \mathbf{S}, \mathbf{R}, f, g, q_I)$ is a machine whose state set $\mathbf{Q}$ is to be partitioned into blocks of equivalent states. Let $\mathbf{Q} = \{q_1, \ldots, q_n\}$, and let

$$\mathbf{M}_i = (\mathbf{Q}, \mathbf{S}, \mathbf{R}, f, g, q_i)$$

stand for a copy of $\mathbf{M}$ started in $q_i$. States $q_i$ and $q_j$ belong to the same block of the partition of $\mathbf{Q}$ just if no stimulus applied to the experiment will yield different responses from machines $\mathbf{M}_i$ and $\mathbf{M}_j$. We construct this partition of $\mathbf{Q}$ by forming a succession of partitions

$$\mathbf{P}_1, \mathbf{P}_2, \ldots, \mathbf{P}_m, \mathbf{P}_{m+1}$$

such that each block of partition $k$, $1 \leq k \leq m+1$, contains only states that are mutually $k$-equivalent. In terms of Figure 4.19, states $q_i$ and $q_j$ will belong to the same block of partition $\mathbf{P}_k$ if and only if machines $\mathbf{M}_i$ and $\mathbf{M}_j$ cannot be distinguished by any stimulus of $k$ or fewer symbols. Since states

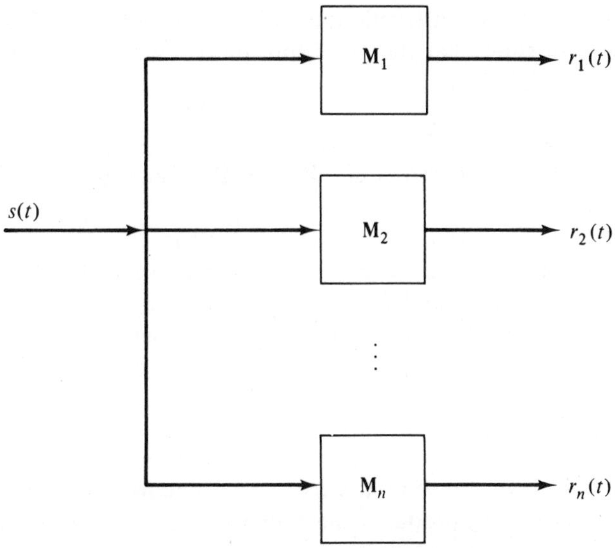


**Figure 4.19.** Conceptual experiment to partition state set **Q** of **M**.

that are $(k + 1)$-equivalent are certainly $k$-equivalent, each block of $\mathbf{P}_{k+1}$ will be contained in some block of partition $\mathbf{P}_k$. Hence each partition is a refinement of its predecessor. Theorem 4.3 provides the basis for constructing the sequence of partitions, according to the following *partitioning algorithm*:

*Step 1:* Form an initial partition $\mathbf{P}_1$ of $\mathbf{Q}$ by grouping together states that are 1-equivalent, that is, states that produce identical outputs for each input symbol. States $q$ and $q'$ are in the same block of $\mathbf{P}_1$ if and only if, for each $s \in \mathbf{S}$, $g(q, s) = g(q', s)$.

*Step 2:* Obtain $\mathbf{P}_{k+1}$ from $\mathbf{P}_k$ as follows: states $q$ and $q'$ are in the same block of $\mathbf{P}_{k+1}$ if and only if

1. They are in the same block of $\mathbf{P}_k$.
2. For each $s \in \mathbf{S}$, their $s$-successors $f(q, s)$ and $f(q', s)$ are in the same block of $\mathbf{P}_k$.

*Step 3:* Repeat step 2 until $\mathbf{P}_{m+1} = \mathbf{P}_m$ for some $m$. We call $\mathbf{P}_m$ the *final partition* of $\mathbf{Q}$.

**Theorem 4.4:** There is an effective procedure for partitioning the states of a finite-state machine into blocks of equivalent states.

***Proof:*** Theorem 4.3 guarantees that each partition $\mathbf{P}_k$ constructed during the above procedure has blocks of mutually $k$-equivalent states. Also, by construction, $\mathbf{P}_{k+1}$ is a refinement of $\mathbf{P}_k$ for all $k \geq 1$. We shall show that the procedure must terminate with a partition $\mathbf{P}_m$ such that $\mathbf{P}_k = \mathbf{P}_m$ for all $k \geq m$:

1. If $\mathbf{P}_{k+1} = \mathbf{P}_k$, then $\mathbf{P}_{k+j} = \mathbf{P}_k$, all $j \geq 0$: if $\mathbf{P}_{k+1} = \mathbf{P}_k$, then from step 2 of the procedure, $\mathbf{P}_{k+2} = \mathbf{P}_{k+1}$, and the assertion follows by induction.

2. If the machine has $n$ states, then $\mathbf{P}_{n+1} = \mathbf{P}_n$: for all $k \geq 1$, $\mathbf{P}_{k+1}$ is a refinement of $\mathbf{P}_k$. Thus the number of blocks in $\mathbf{P}_{k+1}$ is greater than the number of blocks in $\mathbf{P}_k$ unless $\mathbf{P}_k$ is final. Since the number of blocks in a partition cannot exceed the number of states in $\mathbf{M}$, partition $\mathbf{P}_n$ must be final, and therefore $\mathbf{P}_{n+1} = \mathbf{P}_n$.

### 4.6.4 Example

Figure 4.20 shows the state table of a machine $\mathbf{M}$. Applying the partitioning procedure to $\mathbf{M}$ produces the four partitions shown, as the reader

| $\mathbf{M}$: | 0 | 1 |
|---|---|---|
| A | B, 0 | C, 0 |
| B | C, 1 | D, 1 |
| C | D, 0 | E, 0 |
| D | C, 1 | B, 1 |
| E | F, 1 | E, 1 |
| F | G, 0 | C, 0 |
| G | F, 1 | G, 1 |
| H | J, 1 | B, 0 |
| J | H, 1 | D, 0 |

$\mathbf{P}_1$: $\{A, C, F\}, \{B, D, E, G\}, \{H, J\}$

$\mathbf{P}_2$: $\{A, F\}, \{C\}, \{B, D, E, G\}, \{H, J\}$

$\mathbf{P}_3$: $\{A, F\}, \{C\}, \{B, D\}, \{E, G\}, \{H, J\}$

$\mathbf{P}_4$: $\{A\}, \{F\}, \{C\}, \{B, D\}, \{E, G\}, \{H, J\}$

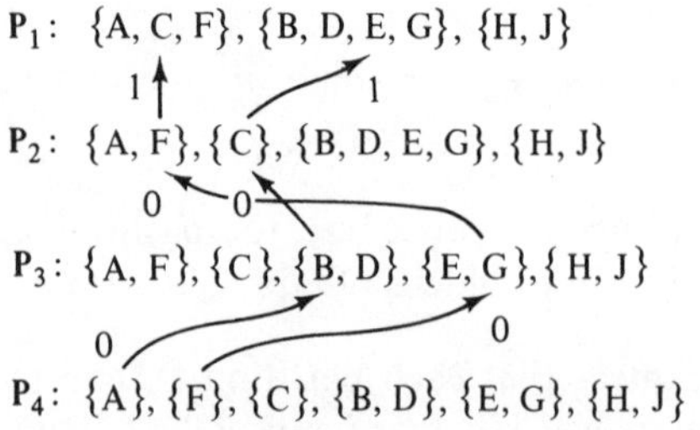

**Figure 4.20.** Example of the partitioning procedure.

should verify. The final partition $\mathbf{P}_4$ shows that B $\sim$ D, E $\sim$ G, and H $\sim$ J.

States A and F, among other pairs, are distinguishable because they are in different blocks of $\mathbf{P}_4$. How can we construct a distinguishing sequence for A and F? Since states A and F lie in the same block of $\mathbf{P}_3$, they are not 3-distinguishable, and the shortest distinguishing sequence must be of length four. Construction of the sequence $\omega = s(1)s(2)s(3)s(4)$ proceeds as follows:

1. States A and F are 4-distinguishable; hence $s(1)$ must take A and F into states that are 3-distinguishable. That is, the $s(1)$-successors of A and F must lie in different blocks of $\mathbf{P}_3$: we choose

$$s(1) = 0 \qquad \text{so that} \begin{cases} \text{A} \xrightarrow{0/0} \text{B} \\ \text{F} \xrightarrow{0/0} \text{G} \end{cases}$$

2. The $s(2)$-successors of B and G must be 2-distinguishable: we choose

$$s(2) = 0 \qquad \text{so that} \begin{cases} \text{B} \xrightarrow{0/1} \text{C} \\ \text{G} \xrightarrow{0/1} \text{F} \end{cases}$$

3. The $s(3)$-successors of C and F must be 1-distinguishable: we choose

$$s(3) = 1 \qquad \text{so that} \begin{cases} \text{C} \xrightarrow{1/0} \text{E} \\ \text{F} \xrightarrow{1/0} \text{C} \end{cases}$$

4. States E and C are 1-distinguishable, so we choose $s(4)$ to cause different outputs. Here we may choose either $s(4) = 0$ or $s(4) = 1$:

$$\text{E} \xrightarrow{0/1} \text{F} \qquad \text{C} \xrightarrow{0/0} \text{D}$$

or

$$\text{E} \xrightarrow{1/1} \text{E} \qquad \text{C} \xrightarrow{1/0} \text{E}$$

Therefore, the stimuli

$$\omega = 0\ 0\ 1\ 0$$

or

$$\omega = 0\ 0\ 1\ 1$$

are both distinguishing sequences for A and F. For the case $\omega = 0010$, we have

$$\text{A} \xrightarrow{0/0} \text{B} \xrightarrow{0/1} \text{C} \xrightarrow{1/0} \text{E} \xrightarrow{0/1} \text{F}$$

$$\text{F} \xrightarrow{0/0} \text{G} \xrightarrow{0/1} \text{F} \xrightarrow{1/0} \text{C} \xrightarrow{0/0} \text{D}$$

The machine responds with 0101 if initially in state A, and with 0100 if initially in state F. For $\omega = 0011$, we have

$$\text{A} \xrightarrow{0/0} \text{B} \xrightarrow{0/1} \text{C} \xrightarrow{1/0} \text{E} \xrightarrow{1/1} \text{E}$$

$$\text{F} \xrightarrow{0/0} \text{G} \xrightarrow{0/1} \text{F} \xrightarrow{1/0} \text{C} \xrightarrow{1/0} \text{E}$$

The machine responds with 0101 if initially in state A, and with 0100 if initially in state F. We observe that the shortest length distinguishing sequence need not be unique.

### 4.6.5 Construction of a Reduced Machine

Let $\mathbf{M} = (\mathbf{Q}, \mathbf{S}, \mathbf{R}, f, g, q_I)$ be a transition-assigned machine. We want to construct an equivalent reduced machine $\mathbf{M}' = (\mathbf{Q}', \mathbf{S}, \mathbf{R}, f', g', q'_I)$. The states of $\mathbf{M}'$ will represent the state equivalence classes of machine $\mathbf{M}$; that is, they will correspond to the blocks of the final partition $\mathbf{P}_f$ resulting from applying the partitioning procedure to $\mathbf{M}$. The initial state $q'_I$ corresponds to the block containing the intial state of $\mathbf{M}$. The state table of $\mathbf{M}'$ is obtained by applying two rules:

1. To find the $s$-successor of a state $q'$ in $\mathbf{M}'$, select any state in the block of the partition $\mathbf{P}_f$ corresponding to $q'$ and find the block containing its $s$-successor; the corresponding state of $\mathbf{M}'$ is the $s$-successor of $q'$.
2. The output for an $s$-transition from state $q'$ of $\mathbf{M}'$ is the output for an $s$-transition from any state in the block corresponding to $q'$.

Figure 4.21 shows the reduced machine equivalent to the machine in Figure 4.20. Note that state Z in the reduced machine is inaccessible when U is the initial state; thus a reduced machine need not be connected, and any inaccessible states must be eliminated separately.

### 4.6.6 Isomorphism of Equivalent Machines

The following theorem expresses the uniqueness of reduced finite-state machines. This important result means that the equivalence question for the class of finite-state automata is answerable in every case by a well-defined procedure.

> **Theorem 4.5:** Let $\mathbf{M}_1$ and $\mathbf{M}_2$ be reduced, connected finite-state machines. Then the state graphs of $\mathbf{M}_1$ and $\mathbf{M}_2$ are isomorphic if and only if $\mathbf{M}_1$ and $\mathbf{M}_2$ are equivalent.

For two state graphs to be isomorphic, we require that they be identical except for the names assigned to the states. In precise terms, the state graphs of $\mathbf{M}_1$ and $\mathbf{M}_2$ are isomorphic if and only if there exists a one-to-one correspondence

$$T\colon \mathbf{Q}_1 \longrightarrow \mathbf{Q}_2$$

between the states of $\mathbf{M}_1$ and the states of $\mathbf{M}_2$ such that the transition and output functions of $\mathbf{M}_1$ are consistent with those of $\mathbf{M}_2$:

(a)

| $P_4$: | {A} | {F} | {C} | {B, D} | {E, G} | {H, J} |
|---|---|---|---|---|---|---|
| New Names in $M'$ | U | V | W | X | Y | Z |

(b)

| New Names | Blocks | 0 | 1 |
|---|---|---|---|
| U | {A} | {B}, 0 | {C}, 0 |
| V | {F} | {G}, 0 | {C}, 0 |
| W | {C} | {D}, 0 | {E}, 0 |
| X | {B, D} | {C}, 1 | {D, B}, 1 |
| Y | {E, G} | {F}, 1 | {E, G}, 1 |
| Z | {H, J} | {J, H}, 1 | {B, D}, 0 |

(c) $M'$:

| | 0 | 1 |
|---|---|---|
| U | X, 0 | W, 0 |
| V | Y, 0 | W, 0 |
| W | X, 0 | Y, 0 |
| X | W, 1 | X, 1 |
| Y | V, 1 | Y, 1 |
| Z | Z, 1 | X, 0 |

**Figure 4.21.** Construction of a reduced machine.

$$\left.\begin{aligned} T(f_1(q, s)) &= f_2((T(q), s)) \\ g_1(q, s) &= g_2(T(q), s) \end{aligned}\right\} \begin{aligned} &\text{all } q \in \mathbf{Q}_1 \\ &\text{all } s \in \mathbf{S} \end{aligned}$$

$$T(q_{I1}) = q_{I2}$$

From Theorem 4.5 we have a procedure for testing the equivalence of two finite-state machines. We remove inaccessible states and then find reduced machines $\mathbf{M}_1$ and $\mathbf{M}_2$ from the given machines; the given machines are equivalent if and only if machines $\mathbf{M}_1$ and $\mathbf{M}_2$ are equivalent. By Theorem 4.5, this is the case if and only if the state diagrams of $\mathbf{M}_1$ and $\mathbf{M}_2$ are isomorphic.

For the proof of Theorem 4.5 it is convenient to extend the notion of equivalence to encompass states in different machines.

> **Definition 4.11:** Let $\mathbf{M}_1$ and $\mathbf{M}_2$ be finite-state machines, and assume the states are so named that $\mathbf{Q}_1 \cap \mathbf{Q}_2 = \varnothing$. The *direct-sum* machine for $\mathbf{M}_1$ and $\mathbf{M}_2$ is the result of considering the state graphs of $\mathbf{M}_1$ and $\mathbf{M}_2$ as constituting a single machine with state set $\mathbf{Q} = \mathbf{Q}_1 \cup \mathbf{Q}_2$. The initial state of the direct-sum machine is unspecified. A state $q$ in $\mathbf{M}_1$ is *equivalent* to a state $q'$ in $\mathbf{M}_2$ just if $q$ and $q'$ are equivalent in the direct-sum machine.

***Proof of Theorem 4.5***

*Only if:* If the state diagrams of $\mathbf{M}_1$ and $\mathbf{M}_2$ are isomorphic, it is obvious that $\mathbf{M}_1 \sim \mathbf{M}_2$.

*If:* We must show that, if $\mathbf{M}_1 \sim \mathbf{M}_2$ and both machines are reduced and connected, then their state graphs are isomorphic. To do this, we shall construct the required isomorphism $T$: $\mathbf{Q}_1 \longrightarrow \mathbf{Q}_2$. We apply the partitioning procedure to obtain a final partition $\mathbf{P}_f$ of the direct-sum state set $\mathbf{Q}_1 \cup \mathbf{Q}_2$. We claim that each block of $\mathbf{P}_f$ is a pair $(q, q')$ in which $q \in \mathbf{Q}_1$, and $q' \in \mathbf{Q}_2$:

First, no block of $\mathbf{P}_f$ can contain more than one state from $\mathbf{Q}_1$ because this would contradict the assertion that $\mathbf{M}_1$ is reduced. Similarly, no block of $\mathbf{P}_f$ can contain more than one state from $\mathbf{Q}_2$. Hence each block of $\mathbf{P}_f$ contains at most two states.

Second, no block of $\mathbf{P}_f$ contains exactly one state. To see this, suppose that some block of $\mathbf{P}_f$ contains exactly one state, say $q \in \mathbf{Q}_1$. Since $\mathbf{M}_1$ is connected, there exists an input sequence $\omega$ for which

$$q_{I1} \overset{\omega}{\Longrightarrow} q$$

This same sequence, applied to $\mathbf{M}_2$, must leave $\mathbf{M}_2$ in some state $q'$:

$$q_{I2} \overset{\omega}{\Longrightarrow} q'$$

Since $q$ is assumed to be alone in a block of $\mathbf{P}_f$, it must be distinguishable from $q'$, and there is a distinguishing sequence $\varphi$ for $q$ and $q'$. But then the sequence $\omega\varphi$ will distinguish $q_{I1}$ and $q_{I2}$, contradicting the assertion $\mathbf{M}_1 \sim \mathbf{M}_2$.

Thus the final partition $\mathbf{P}_f$ of $\mathbf{Q}_1 \cup \mathbf{Q}_2$ is a set of pairs of corresponding equivalent states. This establishes a one-to-one correspondence $T$: $\mathbf{Q}_1 \rightarrow \mathbf{Q}_2$. The equivalence of each pair of states in $\mathbf{P}_f$, together with Theorem 4.2, shows that the state graphs of $\mathbf{M}_1$ and $\mathbf{M}_2$ are isomorphic.

### 4.6.7 Machine Containment

The proof of Theorem 4.5 suggests that it is not necessary to construct reduced machines in order to test for equivalence.

**Definition 4.12:** Let $\mathbf{M}_1$ and $\mathbf{M}_2$ be finite-state machines. If each state in $\mathbf{M}_1$ is equivalent to a state in $\mathbf{M}_2$, we say that $\mathbf{M}_2$ *contains* $\mathbf{M}_1$.

If $\mathbf{M}_2$ contains $\mathbf{M}_1$, then for a given initial state of $\mathbf{M}_1$ we may choose an initial state for $\mathbf{M}_2$ that causes $\mathbf{M}_2$ to mimic the behavior of $\mathbf{M}_1$. If $\mathbf{M}_1$ contains $\mathbf{M}_2$ as well, then the two machines are equivalent whenever they are initialized to equivalent states.

If we apply the partitioning procedure to the direct-sum machine for $\mathbf{M}_1$ and $\mathbf{M}_2$, the final partition will group states that are equivalent in the two machines. If each block of this partition contains at least one state from $\mathbf{M}_1$, then $\mathbf{M}_1$ contains $\mathbf{M}_2$. If each block of this partition contains at least one state from $\mathbf{M}_2$, then $\mathbf{M}_2$ contains $\mathbf{M}_1$. If both these statements are true, then $\mathbf{M}_1$ and $\mathbf{M}_2$ are equivalent whenever their initial states are equivalent, and a reduced machine equivalent to both $\mathbf{M}_1$ and $\mathbf{M}_2$ can be obtained using the blocks of the final partition.

Thus the following is a procedure for deciding whether $\mathbf{M}_1 \sim \mathbf{M}_2$ and, if so, for obtaining a reduced machine $\mathbf{M}$ equivalent to $\mathbf{M}_1$ and $\mathbf{M}_2$:

1. Eliminate states of $\mathbf{M}_1$ and $\mathbf{M}_2$ inaccessible from their respective initial states.
2. Partition the state set of the direct-sum machine. Let $\mathbf{P}_f$ denote the final partition.
3. Ascertain whether each block of $\mathbf{P}_f$ contains at least one state from each of $\mathbf{M}_1$ and $\mathbf{M}_2$. If so, $\mathbf{M}_1 \sim \mathbf{M}_2$ just if the initial states of $\mathbf{M}_1$ and $\mathbf{M}_2$ are in the same block of $\mathbf{P}_f$.
4. If $\mathbf{M}_1 \sim \mathbf{M}_2$, an equivalent reduced machine $\mathbf{M}$, whose states correspond to the blocks of $\mathbf{P}_f$, is given by the construction of Section 4.6.5.

**Example 4.8:** Figure 4.22 shows the state tables of two machines $\mathbf{M}_1$ and $\mathbf{M}_2$. The state table of the direct-sum machine is given, and the partitioning procedure yields the two partitions shown. We see that

$$\text{A} \sim \text{D}, \quad \text{B} \sim \text{E}, \quad \text{and} \quad \text{C} \sim \text{F}$$

(a) $M_1$:

| | 0 | 1 |
|---|---|---|
| A | B, 0 | A, 0 |
| B | A, 0 | C, 1 |
| C | C, 1 | A, 0 |

(b) $M_2$:

| | 0 | 1 |
|---|---|---|
| D | E, 0 | D, 0 |
| E | D, 0 | F, 1 |
| F | F, 1 | D, 0 |
| G | E, 0 | H, 1 |
| H | D, 1 | G, 0 |

(c) Sum of $M_1$ and $M_2$:

| | 0 | 1 | |
|---|---|---|---|
| A | B, 0 | A, 0 | $M_1$ |
| B | A, 0 | C, 1 | $M_1$ |
| C | C, 1 | A, 0 | $M_1$ |
| D | E, 0 | D, 0 | $M_2$ |
| E | D, 0 | F, 1 | $M_2$ |
| F | F, 1 | D, 0 | $M_2$ |
| G | E, 0 | H, 1 | $M_2$ |
| H | D, 1 | G, 0 | $M_2$ |

$P_1$: {A, D}, {B, E, G}, {C, F, H}

$P_2$: {A, D}, {B, E}, {G}, {C, F}, {H}

$P_3 = P_2$

**Figure 4.22.** Testing two machines for equivalence.

Hence $M_2$ contains $M_1$. States G and H of $M_2$ are not equivalent to any states of $M_1$, so $M_1$ does not contain $M_2$, and it appears that the two machines are not equivalent. However, there is no way in $M_2$ to get from state D, E, or F to either of states G and H. If D, E, or F is specified as the starting state of $M_2$, then states G and H are inaccessible and may be eliminated from the machine. If, correspondingly, A, B, or C is made the initial state of $M_1$, the two machines will be equivalent.

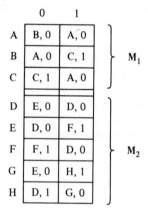

## 4.7 Machine Histories and Finite Memory

We conclude this chapter with an alternative derivation of the finite-state machine. In Section 4.1, we obtained the model by assuming that the machine comprises a finite number of interconnected parts, each capable of assuming a finite number of distinct states. We consider now another finiteness assumption, that of finite memory, and show that it leads to exactly the same machine model.

Suppose that we know these facts about a machine **M**:

1. It is deterministic.
2. It operates at discrete instants in time, at each instant receiving a symbol from an input alphabet **S** and emitting a symbol from an output alphabet **R**.

Since **M** is deterministic, its behavior is uniquely determined by its input string, which may therefore be regarded as representing **M**'s "history." Input strings $\omega$ and $\varphi$ are said to represent *equivalent* histories of **M** if it is impossible to distinguish, based on its response to a future stimulus, a copy of **M** that has received the string $\omega$ from a copy that has received the string $\varphi$.

The notion of equivalent histories can be used to define a relation on the input universe $\mathbf{S}^*$: two input strings are *equivalent* with respect to **M**'s future behavior just if they represent equivalent histories of **M**. The reader may verify that this relation is reflexive, symmetric, and transitive, and therefore partitions $\mathbf{S}^*$ into equivalence classes, which we refer to as *classes of machine histories* or simply *history classes*. These history classes are the basis of our second development of the finite-state machine model.

By saying a machine has *finite memory*, we mean that it is capable of sorting its input strings into only a finite number of distinct history classes (like the postal clerk who tosses all letters into a fixed number of bins regardless of the variety of addresses). Now suppose that we know, in addition to the two facts stated earlier, that **M** has finite memory. Let the corresponding set of history classes be

$$\mathbf{H} = \{\mathbf{H}_1, \mathbf{H}_2, \ldots, \mathbf{H}_n\}$$

These nonempty classes, being a partition of $\mathbf{S}^*$, are mutually disjoint and collectively exhaustive:

$$\mathbf{H}_i \cap \mathbf{H}_j = \varnothing, \qquad i \neq j$$

$$\bigcup_{i=1}^{n} \mathbf{H}_i = \mathbf{S}^*$$

That is, each string in $\mathbf{S}^*$ belongs to precisely one class in **H**.

Consider two strings $\omega$ and $\varphi$ that are in the same history class of $\mathbf{S}^*$, say $\mathbf{H}_i$. For any symbol $s$ in $\mathbf{S}$, the strings $\omega s$ and $\varphi s$ must also be in the same history class of $\mathbf{S}^*$: if $\omega s$ and $\varphi s$ were in different history classes, some input string (that is, the single symbol $s$) would allow us to determine whether $\mathbf{M}$ has initially received $\omega$ or $\varphi$, contradicting the assumption that $\omega$ and $\varphi$ are together in $\mathbf{H}_i$. Therefore, for each input symbol $s$ and each history class $\mathbf{H}_i$, there exists a unique class $\mathbf{H}_j$ such that

$$\mathbf{H}_i\mathbf{s} = \{\omega s \mid \omega \in \mathbf{H}_i\} \subseteq \mathbf{H}_j$$

and thus there exists a function

$$f\colon \mathbf{H} \times \mathbf{S} \longrightarrow \mathbf{H}$$

defined by

$$f(\mathbf{H}_i, s) = \mathbf{H}_j \quad \text{just if} \quad \mathbf{H}_i\mathbf{s} \subseteq \mathbf{H}_j$$

Since $f$ specifies the manner in which input symbols cause transitions of input strings from one history class to another, we refer to $f$ as the *transition function* of $\mathbf{M}$.

Because $\mathbf{M}$ is a deterministic machine, its output is determined solely by its input. In particular, the response of $\mathbf{M}$ to an input symbol $s$ depends only on $s$ and the sequence $\omega$ of symbols presented previously to $\mathbf{M}$. But the sequence $\omega$ cannot be distinguished, on the basis of $\mathbf{M}$'s response to $s$ (or any other input symbol), from the other members of its history class. Thus there exists a function

$$g\colon \mathbf{H} \times \mathbf{S} \longrightarrow \mathbf{R}$$

that specifies $\mathbf{M}$'s response to a symbol in terms of that symbol and the history class of $\mathbf{M}$'s previous input; we refer to $g$ as the *output function* of $\mathbf{M}$.

In summary, an automaton with finite memory is a five-tuple $\mathbf{M} = (\mathbf{H}, \mathbf{S}, \mathbf{R}, f, g)$, where

$\mathbf{H}$ is a finite set of *history classes*

$\mathbf{S}$ is a finite *input alphabet*

$\mathbf{R}$ is a finite *output alphabet*

$f\colon \mathbf{H} \times \mathbf{S} \longrightarrow \mathbf{H}$ is a *transition function*

$g\colon \mathbf{H} \times \mathbf{S} \longrightarrow \mathbf{R}$ is an *output function*

Note that the application of an input string to $\mathbf{M}$ leaves $\mathbf{M}$ in a state of existence that identifies the history class of the input. If we consider the classes in $\mathbf{H}$ as representing "states" of the machine $\mathbf{M}$, the definition above becomes identical to Definition 4.1, except that it does not specify explicitly an initial state. But the initial state of $\mathbf{M}$ is the state of $\mathbf{M}$ prior to the presentation of any input; that is, it is the state of the machine corresponding to the history class of the empty string. If we specify this state explicitly as a sixth component of the tuple, the definition above becomes identical to Definition 4.1. The finite-state model of this chapter can be used, therefore, to describe any model characterized by "finite memory."

## Notes and References

The notion of a finite-state device is usually attributed to McCulloch and Pitts [1943], who developed a model of "nerve nets" to aid in describing the neurological behavior of the brain. The formalisms used in this chapter were developed more than a decade later, the transition-assigned machine by G. H. Mealy in 1955, the state-assigned machine by E. F. Moore in 1956. The contributions of Moore are of particular interest to us here, since he demonstrated that the reduced form of a state-assigned machine is unique up to a labeling of states (an equivalent result follows from the study by Huffman [1954] of sequential switching circuits), and described a partitioning procedure for obtaining a reduced machine from an arbitrary state-assigned device. His procedure is essentially that described in Section 4.6. The applicability of these results to transition-assigned machines followed from a demonstration of the equivalence of the Moore and Mealy models (see, for example, Ibarra [1967]).

The characterization of finite-state machines in terms of equivalence classes is due to Myhill [1957] and Nerode [1959]. Discussions of it on our level are found in Minsky [1967] and Hopcroft and Ullman [1969]. (Minsky's work contains detailed discussions of many aspects of the theory of finite automata, and provides useful supplementary reading for this and the next three chapters.) The characterization is discussed on an abstract level by Arbib [1969] and Gunzberg [1968].

## Problems

4.1. Present the state diagram of a transition-assigned machine $\mathbf{M} = (\mathbf{Q}, \mathbf{S}, \mathbf{R}, f, g, q_I)$ with $\mathbf{S} = \mathbf{R} = \{0, 1, 2, 3\}$ and the following behavior: for $t > 2$, $r(t) = m(t) + n(t)$, where

$$m(t) = \begin{cases} 2 \text{ if } s(t-1) \text{ is 0 or 2} \\ 0 \text{ otherwise} \end{cases}$$

$$n(t) = \begin{cases} 1 \text{ if } s(t-2) \text{ is 1 or 3} \\ 0 \text{ otherwise} \end{cases}$$

Define $r(1)$ and $r(2)$ as if $s(-1) = s(0) = 0$.

4.2. Let $\mathbf{S} = \{a, b, c\}$ and define, for each symbol in $\mathbf{S}$ and any string $\omega$ in $\mathbf{S}^*$,

$$N_s(\omega) = \text{number of occurrences of symbol } s \text{ in } \omega$$

a. Display the state table of a transition-assigned machine $\mathbf{M} = (\mathbf{Q}, \mathbf{S}, \mathbf{R}, f, g, q_I)$ whose last output symbol in response to an input string $\omega$ is

$$r = (N_a(\omega) + 2N_b(\omega) - 3N_c(\omega)) \bmod 5$$

(The set $\mathbf{R}$ will be $\{0, 1, 2, 3, 4\}$.) A typical input–output pair might be

| | | | | | | | | | |
|---|---|---|---|---|---|---|---|---|---|
| Input | $a$ | $b$ | $b$ | $c$ | $c$ | $b$ | $a$ | $a$ | $b$ | $c$ |
| Output | 1 | 3 | 0 | 2 | 4 | 1 | 2 | 3 | 0 | 2 |

b. Suppose that we ask now that the last output symbol be

$$r = N_a(\omega) + 2N_b(\omega) - 3N_c(\omega)$$

Is it still possible to construct a machine $\mathbf{M}$ with the appropriate behavior? Suppose that the last output symbol is to be

$$r = \min(100, N_a(\omega) + 2N_b(\omega) - 3N_c(\omega))$$

Is it possible in this case to construct the machine $\mathbf{M}$?

4.3. Design a Mealy automaton $\mathbf{M} = (\mathbf{Q}, \mathbf{S}, \mathbf{R}, f, g, q_I)$ with $\mathbf{S} = \mathbf{R} = \{0, 1\}$ and the following output behavior:

a. $r(1) = r(2) = 0$. For $t > 2$,

$$(r(t) = 1) \Leftrightarrow ((s(t) = 0) \wedge (s(t-1) = 1) \wedge (s(t-2) = 1))$$

b. $r(1) = r(2) = 0$. For $t > 2$,

$$\begin{aligned}(r(t) = 1) \Leftrightarrow (((s(t) = 0) \wedge (s(t-1) = s(t-2) = 1))\\ \vee ((s(t) = 1) \wedge (s(t-1) = 0 \vee s(t-2) = 0)))\end{aligned}$$

4.4. Describe informally the input–output behavior and the form of the state diagram of a Mealy $n$-unit delay, for arbitrary $n$. (A 2-unit delay was constructed in Example 4.3.)

4.5. Let $\mathbf{M} = (\mathbf{Q}, \mathbf{S}, \mathbf{R}, f, h, q_I)$ be a Moore machine with $\mathbf{S} = \mathbf{R} = \{0, 1\}$. An input sequence $\omega$ is said to be *accepted* by $\mathbf{M}$ just if $\mathbf{M}$'s response to $\omega$ ends with 1. Present the state diagram of a machine $\mathbf{M}$ that accepts

a. All strings $\omega \in \mathbf{S}^*$ in which the substring 101 appears.
b. All strings $\omega \in \mathbf{S}^*$ in which the substring 101 does not appear.
c. All strings $\omega \in \mathbf{S}^*$ in which

$$(N_0(\omega) - N_1(\omega)) \bmod 4 = 0$$

(See Problem 4.2.)

4.6. Let $\mathbf{S} = \mathbf{R} = \{0, 1\}$, and let $\omega$ be a binary string. We say that $\omega$ has *property A* if each occurrence of the symbol 0 in $\omega$ is followed immediately by another 0 or by a string of at least two consecutive 1's. We say that $\omega$ has *property B* if the number of occurrences of the symbol 1 in $\omega$ is odd. Present the state table of a Moore machine $\mathbf{M} = (\mathbf{Q}, \mathbf{S}, \mathbf{R}, f, h, q_I)$ that accepts (see Problem 4.5) a string $\omega$ if and only if $\omega$ has

a. Property $A$.
b. Property $B$.
c. Both properties $A$ and $B$.
d. Either property $A$ or property $B$ or both.
e. Either property $A$ or property $B$, but not both.
f. Neither property $A$ nor property $B$.

4.7. Construct a transition-assigned machine similar (in the sense of Definition 4.5) to the following state-assigned machine:

| | 0 | 1 | |
|---|---|---|---|
| A | B | C | 0 |
| B | C | B | 1 |
| C | A | C | 0 |

Construct a state-assigned machine similar to the following transition-assigned machine:

| | 0 | 1 |
|---|---|---|
| A | B 0 | C 1 |
| B | C 1 | B 1 |
| C | A 1 | C 0 |

4.8. Find a Moore machine that accepts (see Problem 4.5) just those strings accepted by the following Mealy machine:

| | 0 | 1 |
|---|---|---|
| A | A 1 | B 1 |
| B | C 1 | D 0 |
| C | B 0 | C 0 |
| D | D 1 | A 1 |

Describe the set of strings accepted.

4.9. Consider a machine partially specified by the following table:

| | 0 | 1 |
|---|---|---|
| A | B 0 | C 1 |
| B | A 1 | D 1 |
| C | C 0 | A 1 |
| D | E 1 | ? |
| E | A 0 | E 0 |

It is known that starting in state A the machine exhibits a response ending in 0 to the input sequence 0110. Following this, application of the sequence 101 results in a response again ending in 0. What can be told about the missing entry?

4.10. The following input–output behavior was exhibited by a transition-assigned machine **M** known to contain three states. Find an appropriate state table for **M**. Is the table unique?

Input 0 0 0 0 1 0 0 0 1 0 0 0 1 0

Output 0 1 0 1 0 0 0 0 1 0 1 0 0 1

Repeat the above for the following input–output behavior, given that **M** is a transition-assigned machine with at most three states:

Input 1 1 1 0 1 1 1 0 1 0 1 0 1 0 0 0 0 1 0 0 0 1 1 0

Output 0 1 0 1 1 0 1 1 0 1 1 1 0 1 1 1 1 1 1 1 1 0 1 1

**4.11.** a. A certain four-state machine exhibits the following input–output behavior:

| | |
|---|---|
| Input | 0 1 0 1 0 1 0 1 0 1 1 |
| Output | 0 0 0 0 0 0 0 0 0 0*1 |

Prove that the state assumed by the machine at the point marked '*' must have been visited earlier in the sequence.

b. Let **M** be a three-state machine about which nothing is known except that its input alphabet contains symbols 0 and 1. Let $q$ denote the state of **M** after presentation of the input sequence $(\mathbf{01})^{100}$. What can be said about the state of **M** after presentation of the input sequence $(\mathbf{01})^{400}$?

**4.12.** Let **M** be a finite-state machine with state set **Q**. Suppose that **Q** contains $n$ states, including initial state $q_I$. For any state $q \in \mathbf{Q}$, prove that $q$ is accessible in **M** only if $q$ is the $\omega$-successor of $q_I$ for some string $\omega$ of length less than $n$.

**4.13.** We say that a finite-state machine is *strongly connected* if every state in the machine is accessible from every other state in the machine. Let **M** be an $n$-state, reduced, strongly connected, finite-state machine. Prove there exists an input string $\omega$, $|\omega| \leq n(n-1)/2$, such that **M** assumes each of its states at least once in response to $\omega$. (*Hint:* See Problem 4.12.)

4.14. A $(q, r, s)$-*machine* is a transition-assigned machine $\mathbf{M} = (\mathbf{Q}, \mathbf{S}, \mathbf{R}, f, g, q_I)$ in which

$$\bar{\bar{\mathbf{Q}}} = q$$
$$\bar{\bar{\mathbf{R}}} = r$$
$$\bar{\bar{\mathbf{S}}} = s$$

Let $\mathcal{C}(q, r, s)$ denote the class of $(q, r, s)$-machines. Show that

$$\overline{\overline{\mathcal{C}(q, r, s)}} = (rq)^{sq}$$

A *simply minimal* $(q, r, s)$-*machine* is a $(q, r, s)$-machine in which, for all $i, j$ $(i \neq j)$, there exists at least one $k$ such that

$$g(q_i, s_k) \neq g(q_j, s_k)$$

Let $\mathcal{C}'(q, r, s)$ be the class of simply minimal $(q, r, s)$-machines. Show that $\overline{\overline{\mathcal{C}'(q, r, s)}} = q^{rq}(r^s - 1)(r^s - 2) \ldots (r^s - n + 1)$. Does any simply minimal $(q, r, s)$-machine contain a pair of equivalent states?

4.15. Consider the following machine $M_1$:

| | 0 | 1 |
|---|---|---|
| A | C 0 | B 0 |
| B | E 0 | C 0 |
| C | A 0 | G 0 |
| D | G 0 | F 0 |
| E | F 1 | A 0 |
| F | E 0 | D 0 |
| G | D 0 | G 0 |

Find a minimal length distinguishing sequence for states C and G. Is the sequence unique? Is there a sequence that distinguishes C from G and also distinguishes A from D?

4.16. Consider the following machines $M_1$ and $M_2$:

$M_1$:

| | 0 | 1 | |
|---|---|---|---|
| A | B | A | 0 |
| B | C | D | 0 |
| C | E | C | 0 |
| D | F | B | 0 |
| E | G | E | 0 |
| F | H | F | 0 |
| G | I | G | 0 |
| H | J | H | 0 |
| I | A | K | 1 |
| J | K | J | 0 |
| K | A | K | 1 |

$M_2$:

| | 0 | 1 | |
|---|---|---|---|
| A | B | A | 0 |
| B | C | B | 0 |
| C | D | C | 0 |
| D | E | D | 0 |
| E | F | E | 0 |
| F | B | F | 1 |

a. Reduce $\mathbf{M}_1$. Find a minimal length distinguishing sequence for states A and B in $\mathbf{M}_1$.
b. Reduce $\mathbf{M}_2$. Find a minimal length distinguishing sequence for states A and B in $\mathbf{M}_2$.
c. $\mathbf{M}_1$ and $\mathbf{M}_2$ are started in their respective states A. Find a minimal length distinguishing sequence for machines $\mathbf{M}_1$ and $\mathbf{M}_2$.
d. In parts a and b the lengths of the distinguishing sequences were less than the number of states in the respective reduced machines. In part c, however, a sequence is needed that has a length greater than the number of states in either reduced machine. Why?

4.17. Let **M** be the following machine, and let A be its initial state:

**M:**

| | 0 | 1 | |
|---|---|---|---|
| A | B | E | 0 |
| B | C | D | 1 |
| C | B | A | 0 |
| D | B | B | 1 |
| E | B | A | 0 |
| F | G | G | 1 |
| G | F | H | 0 |
| H | I | G | 0 |
| I | G | G | 1 |

Give the state table of a reduced, connected, Moore machine equivalent to **M**. Give the state table of a reduced, connected, Mealy machine similar to **M**.

4.18. Consider the following machines $\mathbf{M}_1$ and $\mathbf{M}_2$. $\mathbf{M}_1$ has initial state A, and the initial state of $\mathbf{M}_2$ is unspecified. Can the machines be made equivalent by the correct choice of initial state for $\mathbf{M}_2$? If so, which state(s) can be chosen? (Establish the results by partitioning the states of the direct-sum machine.)

**$M_1$:**

| | 0 | 1 |
|---|---|---|
| A | G 1 | E 0 |
| B | H 1 | C 1 |
| C | H 0 | D 0 |
| D | H 0 | C 0 |
| E | F 0 | A 1 |
| F | B 0 | C 1 |
| G | H 1 | D 1 |
| H | H 1 | E 0 |

**$M_2$:**

| | 0 | 1 |
|---|---|---|
| A | F 0 | F 1 |
| B | D 1 | L 0 |
| C | G 0 | C 0 |
| D | G 1 | C 1 |
| E | J 0 | B 1 |
| F | A 0 | H 0 |
| G | G 1 | E 0 |
| H | H 0 | A 0 |
| J | D 0 | C 1 |
| K | G 1 | C 1 |
| L | M 0 | N 1 |
| M | K 0 | C 1 |
| N | K 1 | E 0 |

**4.19.** Write out the proof of Theorem 4.3.

**4.20.** Consider the following machine $\mathbf{M}_2$ with unspecified initial state.

**$M_2$:**

| | 0 | 1 |
|---|---|---|
| A | A 0 | C 0 |
| B | D 0 | E 1 |
| C | B 0 | C 0 |
| D | A 1 | B 0 |
| E | C 1 | D 0 |

a. Show that by observing only the output associated with the input sequence 011 it is possible to determine which state the machine is in after application of the sequence, without knowing its initial state. Such an input sequence is known as a *homing sequence*.

b. Devise an effective procedure to determine if a particular sequence is a homing sequence for an arbitrary finite-state machine. Use your method to find all homing sequences of length three for $\mathbf{M}_2$ above.

*c. Prove that for every reduced finite-state machine **M** there exists some homing sequence for **M**. (*Hint:* Suppose that **M** is a finite-state machine with $n$ states. Show that, if **M** has no homing sequence of length less than $n^2$, **M** must have a pair of equivalent states.)

For a detailed discussion of homing sequences and related topics the reader is referred to Hennie [1968].

**4.21.** Prove that for any integer $k \geq 1$, there exist two state-assigned machines with $k$ states that are indistinguishable by all input strings of length less than $2k - 2$.

**4.22.** Let **S** be a set of finite-state machines. If we were to apply simultaneously all input sequences of length $n$ to each machine in the set, recording all responses, we would say that we had performed an *experiment of length n* on **S**.

a. Let **M** be an $n$-state Mealy machine and, for any state $q$ in **M**, let $(\mathbf{M}, q)$ denote a copy of **M** started in state $q$. Prove that, for any states $q_i$ and $q_j$ in **M**, $(\mathbf{M}, q_i)$ and $(\mathbf{M}, q_j)$ can be distinguished by an experiment of length less than $n$ if they can be distinguished at all, that is, if they are not equivalent.

*b. Let $\mathbf{M}_1, \ldots, \mathbf{M}_k$ be finite-state machines, and let $n_1, \ldots, n_k$ be the cardinalities of their respective state sets. Find an upper bound on the maximum length of the shortest experiment that distinguishes all the machines, given that the machines are mutually distinguishable.

**4.23.** **M** is a partially specified finite-state machine. Note that the transition caused by an input of 0 while **M** is in state E is unspecified.

**M:**

| | 0 | 1 |
|---|---|---|
| A | B 0 | C 1 |
| B | A 0 | D 0 |
| C | E 1 | A 0 |
| D | B 0 | E 1 |
| E | — | D 0 |

An input sequence is *applicable to state q* if it does not cause **M**, started in state $q$, to go through an unspecified transition. We say that a state $p$ *contains* a state $q$ just if

1. Any sequence applicable to $q$ is applicable to $p$.
2. The response of **M** to a sequence applicable to $q$ is the same whether **M** is started in $q$ or in $p$.

a. Modify the partitioning procedure to obtain a procedure for determining state containment, rather than state equivalence. Is state E of the machine above contained by any other state?
b. Prove that two states in a finite-state machine are equivalent if and only if they contain each other.
c. Prove that state containment is a transitive relation; that is, prove that $p$ contains $q$ and $q$ contains $r$ only if $p$ contains $r$.
d. One way to complete a machine with unspecified transitions is to replace an unspecified transition for any state $q$ with the corresponding transition of a state containing $q$. Use this technique to complete the specification of **M**. Must this specified machine be equivalent to the original unspecified machine?
e. Repeat part d for machine **M′**:

**M′**:

| | 0 | 1 |
|---|---|---|
| A | B 0 | C 0 |
| B | A 0 | D 1 |
| C | C 1 | D 0 |
| D | D 0 | — |

**4.24.** Let $\mathbf{M}_1 = (\mathbf{Q}_1, \mathbf{S}_1, \mathbf{R}_1, f_1, g_1, q_{I1})$ and $\mathbf{M}_2 = (\mathbf{Q}_2, \mathbf{S}_2, \mathbf{R}_2, f_2, g_2, q_{I2})$ be finite-state machines such that $\mathbf{R}_1 \subseteq \mathbf{S}_2$. The *cascade machine* $\mathbf{M}_1 \bullet \mathbf{M}_2$ is diagrammed as follows:

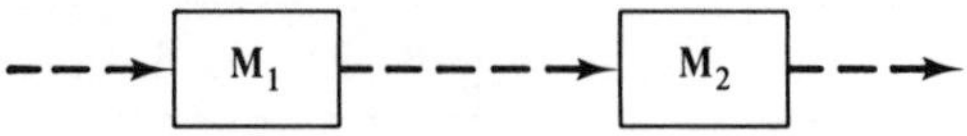


That is, the output of $\mathbf{M}_1$ is used as input to $\mathbf{M}_2$, and the output of $\mathbf{M}_2$ is the output of $\mathbf{M}_1 \bullet \mathbf{M}_2$.

a. Show that $\mathbf{M}_1 \bullet \mathbf{M}_2$ is a finite-state machine by specifying the six-tuple

$$\mathbf{M}_1 \bullet \mathbf{M}_2 = (\mathbf{Q}, \mathbf{S}, \mathbf{R}, f, g, q_I)$$

b. Given that $\mathbf{M}_1$ and $\mathbf{M}_2$ have $n_1$ and $n_2$ states, respectively, how many states are in $\mathbf{M}_1 \bullet \mathbf{M}_2$?

Let $\mathbf{M}_1$ and $\mathbf{M}_2$ be as follows:

$\mathbf{M}_1$:

| | 0 | 1 |
|---|---|---|
| A | B 1 | A 0 |
| B | B 0 | B 1 |

$\mathbf{M}_2$:

| | 0 | 1 |
|---|---|---|
| C | D 0 | D 1 |
| D | E 1 | D 0 |
| E | E 0 | E 1 |

c. Viewed as language accepters (see Problem 4.5), what strings are accepted by $\mathbf{M}_1$? by $\mathbf{M}_2$? by the cascade machine $\mathbf{M}_1 \bullet \mathbf{M}_2$?

d. Let $\mathbf{M}_1$ and $\mathbf{M}_2$ be arbitrary finite-state machines with input alphabets and output alphabets of $\{0, 1\}$. Might it be true that $\mathbf{M}_1 \bullet \mathbf{M}_2 \sim \mathbf{M}_2 \bullet \mathbf{M}_1$? *Must* it be true that $\mathbf{M}_1 \bullet \mathbf{M}_2 \sim \mathbf{M}_2 \bullet \mathbf{M}_1$?

The technique of combining machines to form a cascade machine has many useful applications. In later chapters, this technique is used in establishing closure properties of regular and context-free languages.

**4.25.** Let $\mathbf{M}_1 = (\mathbf{Q}_1, \mathbf{S}, \{0, 1\}, f_1, h_1, q_{I1})$ and $\mathbf{M}_2 = (\mathbf{Q}_2, \mathbf{S}, \{0, 1\}, f_2, h_2, q_{I2})$ be Moore machines, and consider the following *parallel machine* $\mathbf{M}_1 \cup \mathbf{M}_2$:

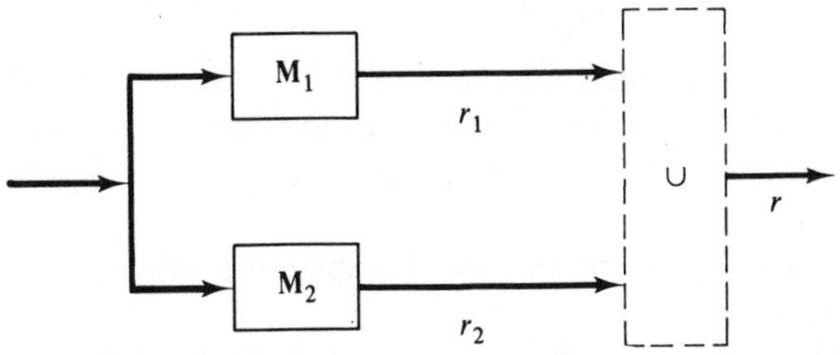


The output $r$ of the parallel machine is the Boolean sum of $r_1$ and $r_2$.

a. Show that $\mathbf{M}_1 \cup \mathbf{M}_2$ is a finite-state machine by specifying the six-tuple

$$\mathbf{M}_1 \cup \mathbf{M}_2 = (\mathbf{Q}, \mathbf{S}, \mathbf{R}, f, h, q_I)$$

b. Viewing $\mathbf{M}_1$ and $\mathbf{M}_2$ as accepters (see Problem 4.5), let $\mathbf{L}(\mathbf{M}_1)$ denote the strings accepted by $\mathbf{M}_1$, and let $\mathbf{L}(\mathbf{M}_2)$ denote the strings accepted by $\mathbf{M}_2$. In terms of $\mathbf{L}(\mathbf{M}_1)$ and $\mathbf{L}(\mathbf{M}_2)$, what strings are accepted by the parallel machine above?

c. Suppose that we replace the $\cup$-module shown in the figure with a $\cap$-module, indicating that $r$ is the Boolean product of $r_1$ and $r_2$, rather than the Boolean sum. In terms of $\mathbf{L}(\mathbf{M}_1)$ and $\mathbf{L}(\mathbf{M}_2)$, what strings are accepted by the parallel machine?
Like the cascade machines of Problem 4.24, parallel machines are often a useful tool in the study of language closure properties.

**4.26.** Any finite-state machine $\mathbf{M}$ may be regarded as a mapping $M: \mathbf{S}^* \longrightarrow \mathbf{R}^*$, defined by $M(\omega) = \varphi$, where $\varphi$ is the response of $\mathbf{M}$ to the input sequence $\omega$. A machine $\mathbf{M}$ is *information lossless* if, for each output string, it is possible to determine uniquely the corresponding input string.

a. What does information lossless mean in terms of the map $M: \mathbf{S}^* \longrightarrow \mathbf{R}^*$? In terms of the state diagram of $\mathbf{M}$?

b. Consider $\mathbf{M}_1$, $\mathbf{M}_2$ as follows:

$\mathbf{M}_1$:

| | 0 | 1 |
|---|---|---|
| A | A 0 | B 0 |
| B | C 0 | D 1 |
| C | C 1 | B 1 |
| D | D 0 | C 0 |

$\mathbf{M}_2$:

| | 0 | 1 |
|---|---|---|
| A | B 1 | C 0 |
| B | A 0 | D 1 |
| C | D 0 | B 1 |
| D | C 1 | B 0 |

Is $\mathbf{M}_1$ information lossless? Is $\mathbf{M}_2$ information lossless?

For a machine $\mathbf{M}$ that is information lossless, it is possible to construct an *inverse machine* $\mathbf{M}^{-1}$ that responds with $\varphi$ to input $\omega$ if and only if $M(\varphi) = \omega$.

c. For each information lossless machine above, construct the inverse machine.

d. Generalize the above procedure; that is, given an arbitrary information lossless machine $\mathbf{M}$, describe a procedure for constructing $\mathbf{M}^{-1}$.

For a detailed discussion of information lossless machines, the reader is referred to Hennie [1968]. The algebraic theory of these machines is treated in depth by Kurmit [1974].

**4.27.** Let $\mathbf{M}$ be a finite-state machine with input alphabet $\mathbf{S}$. Let $\sim$ be the equivalence relation on $\mathbf{S}^*$ defined in Section 4.7. For each $\omega \in \mathbf{S}^*$, let $[\omega] = \{\varphi \mid \varphi \sim \omega\}$, and let $\mathbf{T}(\mathbf{M}) = \{[\omega] \mid \omega \in \mathbf{S}^*\}$.

a. Show that

$$\alpha \in [\omega] \quad \text{and} \quad \beta \in [\varphi] \Rightarrow \alpha\beta \in [\omega\varphi]$$

Let this motivate a definition of multiplication $m$:

$$m([\alpha], [\beta]) = [\alpha\beta]$$

b. Prove that $\overline{\overline{\mathbf{T(M)}}} \leq \overline{\overline{\mathbf{Q}}}$.

c. Prove that $\overline{\overline{\mathbf{T(M)}}} = \overline{\overline{\mathbf{Q}}}$ if and only if **M** is reduced and connected.

d. Prove that (**T(M)**, $m$) is a semigroup.† Does it have an identity? The set **T(M)** is known as the *semigroup of* **M**. Note that each finite-state machine has a semigroup associated with it in this way.

**4.28.** A *semiautomaton* is a triple $\mathbf{M} = (\mathbf{Q}, \mathbf{S}, \mathbf{F})$ in which **Q** is a finite *state set*, **S** is a finite *input alphabet*, and $\mathbf{F} = \{f_s \mid f_s\colon \mathbf{Q} \longrightarrow \mathbf{Q},\ s \in \mathbf{S}\}$ is a set of transition functions, each function $f_s$ representing the transitions of **M** under symbol $s$ (that is, $f_s(q) = q'$ just if $q'$ is the $s$-successor of $q$ in **M**). Thus a semiautomaton is a finite-state machine with no specified outputs or initial state.

We may extend the transition functions from symbols to strings of symbols as follows:

1. $f_\lambda$ is the identity function.
2. $f_{rs} = f_r \circ f_s$ for any $r, s \in \mathbf{S}$, where $\circ$ denotes functional composition (see Problem 2.20).
3. $f_{\omega s}$ is $f_\omega \circ f_s$, for $s \in \mathbf{S}$, $\omega \in \mathbf{S}^*$.

Let $\mathbf{T(M)} = \{f_\omega \mid \omega \in \mathbf{S}^*\}$ be the set of extended transition mappings.

a. Show that **T(M)** is finite.

Suppose that we define a multiplication $m$ to be

$$m(f_\omega, f_\varphi) = f_{\omega\varphi}$$

b. Prove that (**T(M)**, $m$) is a semigroup with identity. (The set **T(M)** is known as the *semigroup of the semiautomaton* **M**.)

*c. Let (**X**, $m$) be any finite semigroup with identity. Describe a semiautomaton $\mathbf{M}_X$ that has semigroup **X**. [Hint: $\mathbf{M}_X$ is of the form $\mathbf{M} = (\mathbf{X}, \mathbf{X}, \mathbf{F}_X)$.]

The ideas of this problem are the starting point of the algebraic theory of automata. The beginning of the theory for finite-state automata is found in Hartmanis and Stearns [1966]. The complete theory may be found in the monograph by Ginzburg [1968].

†A *binary operation* on a set **S** is a function $f\colon \mathbf{S} \times \mathbf{S} \longrightarrow \mathbf{S}$. Such an operation is *associative* if, for all $x, y, z$ in **S**, $f(x, f(y, z)) = f(f(x, y), z)$. A *semigroup* is an ordered pair (**S**, $m$), where **S** is a set and $m$ is an associative binary operation on **S**, often referred to as a *multiplication* in **S**. If **S** contains an element $e$ such that $m(e, s) = m(s, e) = s$ for each $s \in \mathbf{S}$, then $e$ is an *identity* element and (**S**, $m$) is a *semigroup with identity*.

Arbib [1968, 1969] provides a wealth of material on semigroups, particularly as they relate to abstract machines.

**4.29.** An equivalence relation $\rho$ on a set **A** is said to be *right-invariant* if, for all $x \in \mathbf{A}$, $\alpha \rho \beta \Rightarrow (\alpha x)\rho(\beta x)$.

a. Let $[\alpha]$ denote the equivalence class of $\alpha$ with respect to the equivalence relation $\rho$. Show that $\rho$ right-invariant and $\alpha \in [\omega]$ implies $\alpha x \in [\alpha x]$, any $x \in \mathbf{A}$.

b. Let **M** be an arbitrary finite-state machine, **S** its input alphabet, and $\sim$ the equivalence relation on **S** defined in Section 4.7. Show that this relation is right-invariant.

c. Let $\rho$ be any right-invariant equivalence relation of finite index (that is, with finitely many equivalence classes) on $\mathbf{S}^*$, and let **X** be its set of equivalence classes. Show that **X** is a semigroup with identity for an appropriately chosen multiplication. Describe the construction of a finite-state machine with semigroup **X** (See Problem 4.27.)

# 5

# *Finite-State Languages*

We are ready to begin studying the intimate relationship between abstract machines and languages generated by formal grammars. In this chapter we treat this relationship at the simplest level, that of finite-state accepters and regular languages. Not only will this study add considerably to our understanding of these machines and languages, but it will unify the concepts treated in previous chapters.

Our immediate goal is to demonstrate that these three statements are equivalent:

1. The language **L** is recognized by some finite-state accepter.
2. The language **L** is generated by some regular grammar.
3. The language **L** is described by some regular expression.

## 5.1 Finite-State Accepters

We noted in Chapter 1 that a relation between abstract machines and languages can be established by means of *accepters*, machines that classify each input string as being either accepted or rejected. A finite-state machine with state assigned outputs and output alphabet {0, 1} can be viewed as such an accepter, the states of the machine being divided into two classes:

1. *Accepting states*: those with output 1.
2. *Rejecting states*: those with output 0.

The language recognized by a finite-state accepter consists precisely of those strings that take the machine from its initial state to an accepting state. Instead of specifying the accepting states by means of an output function, it is easier simply to identify the subset of the machine's states that are accepting states. In a state diagram, nodes for accepting states will be drawn as double circles.

### 5.1.1 Nondeterministic Accepters

Our first step is to relate finite-state accepters to regular grammars. A grammar contains a set of productions that may be applied in any consistent order to derive a terminal string, and is *permissive* in the sense that there are points during a derivation at which a choice must be made among several applicable productions. In contrast, the finite-state machines studied in Chapter 4 are *imperative* in the sense that each transition is uniquely determined by the preceding state and present input symbol: no alternative behavior is allowed.

To simplify the treatment of the two systems, it is convenient to introduce a generalization of the finite-state accepter that is permissive in nature. The generalization permits any number of states to be successors of a given state for a given input symbol.

**Example 5.1:** The machine shown in Figure 5.1 is a permissive machine. If it is in state A, two transitions are possible for input symbol 1:

$$A \xrightarrow{1} B \quad \text{and} \quad A \xrightarrow{1} C$$

Also, for some combinations of state and input symbol, *no* transition is specified in the figure; specifically, state A has no 0-successor and state C has no 1-successor.

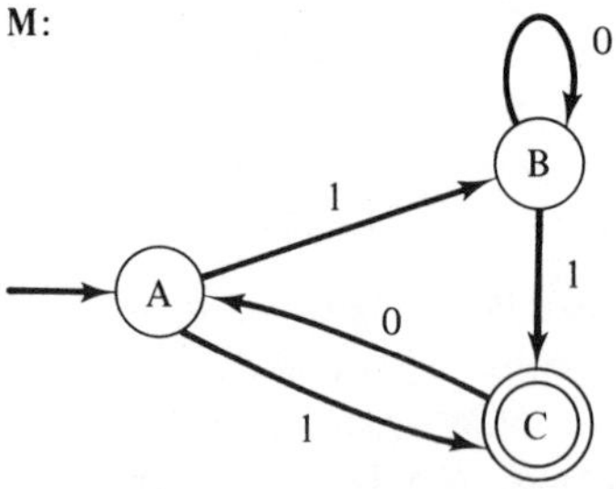


**Figure 5.1.** Nondeterministic accepter.

Because the successor of a state is not always unique, the transitions of such a generalized accepter can no longer be specified by a function $f$: $\mathbf{Q} \times \mathbf{S} \rightarrow \mathbf{Q}$. Instead we must specify which triples from the set $\mathbf{Q} \times \mathbf{S} \times \mathbf{Q}$

are transitions of the machine. Moreover, we do not require that the initial state of the accepter be unique.

**Definition 5.1:** A *finite-state accepter* (FSA) is a five-tuple

$$\mathbf{M} = (\mathbf{Q}, \mathbf{S}, \mathbf{P}, \mathbf{I}, \mathbf{F})$$

in which

$\mathbf{Q}$ is a finite set of states

$\mathbf{S}$ is a finite input alphabet

$\mathbf{I} \subseteq \mathbf{Q}$ are the initial states

$\mathbf{F} \subseteq \mathbf{Q}$ are the *final* states

$\mathbf{P} \subseteq \mathbf{Q} \times \mathbf{S} \times \mathbf{Q}$ is the *transition relation* of $\mathbf{M}$:

whenever $(q, s, q')$ is an element of $\mathbf{P}$, then

$$q \xrightarrow{s} q'$$

is a transition of $\mathbf{M}$.

Because the behavior of an FSA is not necessarily deterministic, we sometimes call an FSA a *nondeterministic finite-state accepter*. The definitions of $s$-successor, $\omega$-successor, and admissible state sequence presented in Chapter 4 apply without qualification to such accepters.

If the transition relation $\mathbf{P}$ of a finite-state accepter is a function, then each state in the accepter will have a unique successor for each input symbol. In such a case, the behavior of the machine for an input sequence depends only on the given sequence and on the state in which the machine is started. If there is only one choice of initial state, the machine will behave deterministically.

**Definition 5.2:** Let $\mathbf{M} = (\mathbf{Q}, \mathbf{S}, \mathbf{P}, \mathbf{I}, \mathbf{F})$ be a finite-state accepter. If the transitions $\mathbf{P}$ of $\mathbf{M}$ constitute a function $\mathbf{P}\colon \mathbf{Q} \times \mathbf{S} \rightarrow \mathbf{Q}$, and if $\mathbf{M}$ has exactly one initial state, then $\mathbf{M}$ is a *deterministic* finite-state accepter.

Like the finite-state machines of Chapter 4, deterministic FSA's associate a unique state sequence with each string of input symbols. In a nondeterministic accepter, however, a state may have more than one successor for a given input symbol, and there is not necessarily a unique admissible state sequence for each input string. For these machines, we can no longer think of input strings as "causing" state transitions. Instead, we must now regard input strings as specifying paths through a state diagram. For some strings there may be several paths; for others there may be none.

**Example 5.2:** The accepter **M** of Figure 5.1 has three admissible state sequences for the input string 101:

$$A \xrightarrow{1} B \xrightarrow{0} B \xrightarrow{1} C$$

$$A \xrightarrow{1} C \xrightarrow{0} A \xrightarrow{1} B$$

$$A \xrightarrow{1} C \xrightarrow{0} A \xrightarrow{1} C$$

Thus we have both

$$A \overset{101}{\Longrightarrow} C \quad \text{and} \quad A \overset{101}{\Longrightarrow} B$$

Since for a given FSA **M** we may have both

$$q \overset{\omega}{\Longrightarrow} q' \quad \text{and} \quad q \overset{\omega}{\Longrightarrow} q'', \qquad q' \neq q''$$

it is no longer appropriate to say that $\omega$ *takes* **M** from state $q$ to state $q'$. Rather, we shall say that $\omega$ *may lead* **M** from state $q$ to state $q'$ (and also that $\omega$ may lead **M** from state $q$ to $q''$). The following statements are equivalent:

1. Accepter **M** has an admissible state sequence from state $q$ to state $q'$ for input string $\omega$.
2. State $q'$ is an $\omega$-successor of state $q$:

$$q \overset{\omega}{\Longrightarrow} q'$$

3. There is a directed path from $q$ to $q'$ in the state diagram of **M** with transitions labeled by the symbols of $\omega$.

A finite-state accepter accepts a string $\omega$ just if there is an admissible state sequence for $\omega$ from some initial state of the accepter to some final state.

**Definition 5.3:** Let $\mathbf{M} = (\mathbf{Q}, \mathbf{S}, \mathbf{P}, \mathbf{I}, \mathbf{F})$ be an FSA. Then **M** *accepts* a string $\omega \in \mathbf{S}^*$ if and only if

$$q \overset{\omega}{\Longrightarrow} q'$$

for some $q \in \mathbf{I}$ and some $q' \in \mathbf{F}$. The *language* recognized by **M** is the set

$$\mathbf{L}(\mathbf{M}) = \{\omega \in \mathbf{S}^* \mid \mathbf{M} \text{ accepts } \omega\}$$

Since the final states of an accepter are those which indicate acceptance of an input string, the terms *final state* and *accepting state* are used interchangeably.

**Example 5.3:** Consider the behavior of the accepter in Figure 5.1 for the input string 1011. The allowed sequences of transitions for 1011 and its prefixes can be represented by a tree diagram (Figure 5.2).

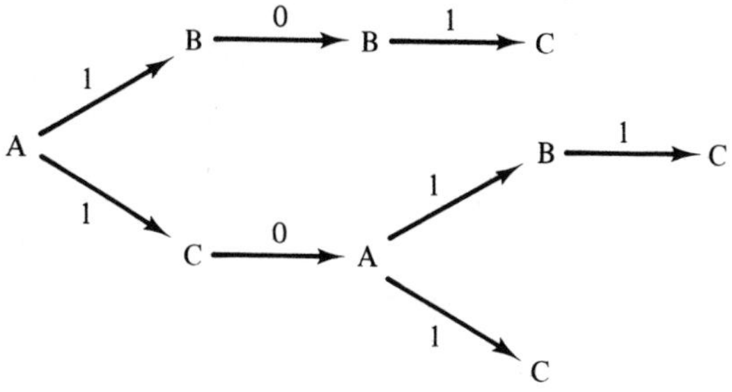


**Figure 5.2.** Tree diagram of possible state sequences for all prefixes of 1011.

Certain sequences terminate before the final input symbol because state C has no 1-successor. Since C is the accepting state, the diagram shows that strings 1, 101, and 1011 are accepted, and that the string 10 is rejected.

### 5.1.2 Conversion to Deterministic Accepters

How might we relate the behavior of a nondeterministic automaton to the operation of a physical device? We could imagine that the machine is in a definite state at each time instant and, when confronted with alternative transitions for some input symbol, makes an arbitrary choice of its next state. (A tree diagram such as Figure 5.2 represents the paths the machine could possibly follow. To determine whether a given string is accepted, we must imagine operating the machine a sufficient number of times that each route through the state diagram is attempted.) Alternatively, we might imagine that whenever several transitions are possible, the machine splits into identical copies that simultaneously pursue alternative paths. In the case of finite-state automata, there is yet a third useful point of view. We can consider the machine to be in some *combination* of states at each time instant, according to our uncertainty of the true state of the nondeterministic machine. This idea leads directly to a procedure for obtaining a deterministic machine equivalent to any given FSA.

**Example 5.4:** The information in Figure 5.2 concerning the behavior of the accepter **M** (redrawn in Figure 5.3) for the input sequence 1011 can be represented by a sequence of transitions between sets of states:

$$\{A\} \xrightarrow{1} \{B, C\} \xrightarrow{0} \{A, B\} \xrightarrow{1} \{B, C\} \xrightarrow{1} \{C\}$$

The appearance of a state set in this sequence means that there are paths in the state diagram by which the corresponding string of input

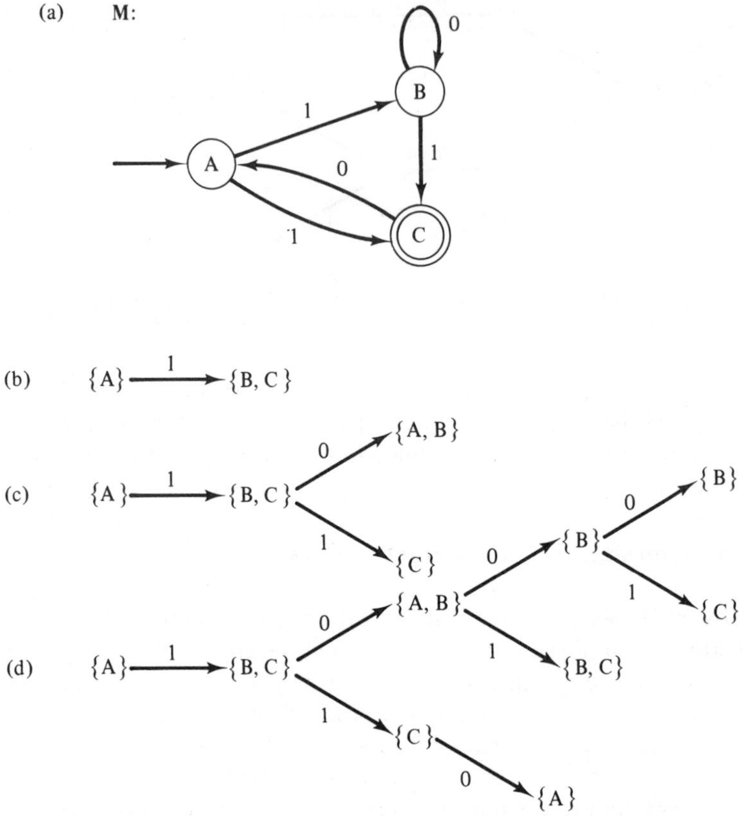


**Figure 5.3.** Reachable sets for a nondeterministic machine.

symbols leads from state A to each state in the set. For instance, the appearance of {A, B} in the sequence signifies that

$$A \overset{10}{\Longrightarrow} A \quad \text{and} \quad A \overset{10}{\Longrightarrow} B$$

are both possible.

The subset of states to which an input string can lead a machine from an initial state is called the *reachable set* for that string. Using the concept of reachable sets, we may describe the behavior of **M** for an arbitrary input string.

**Example 5.4 (continued):** Initially, **M** must be in state A. The 1-successor of A is either B or C, and there are no 0-successors of A. Thus Figure 5.3b describes the reachable sets of **M** for all strings of length 0 or 1. If **M** is in state B or C and a 0 input occurs, the successor state must be either A or B. If a 1 input occurs, the successor state can only be C. This is shown in Figure 5.3c. Continuing this procedure, we obtain the tree diagram in Figure 5.3d, in which each set of states appearing at the end of a path has already appeared elsewhere in the diagram.

The set of states that may be reached by an $s$-transition from some other set of states is determined solely by the state diagram of the machine. Therefore, recurrences of the same reachable set do not have to be distinguished in the diagram, and we may merge identical nodes in Figure 5.3d to obtain Figure 5.4a. This figure resembles the

(a)

(b)

(c)

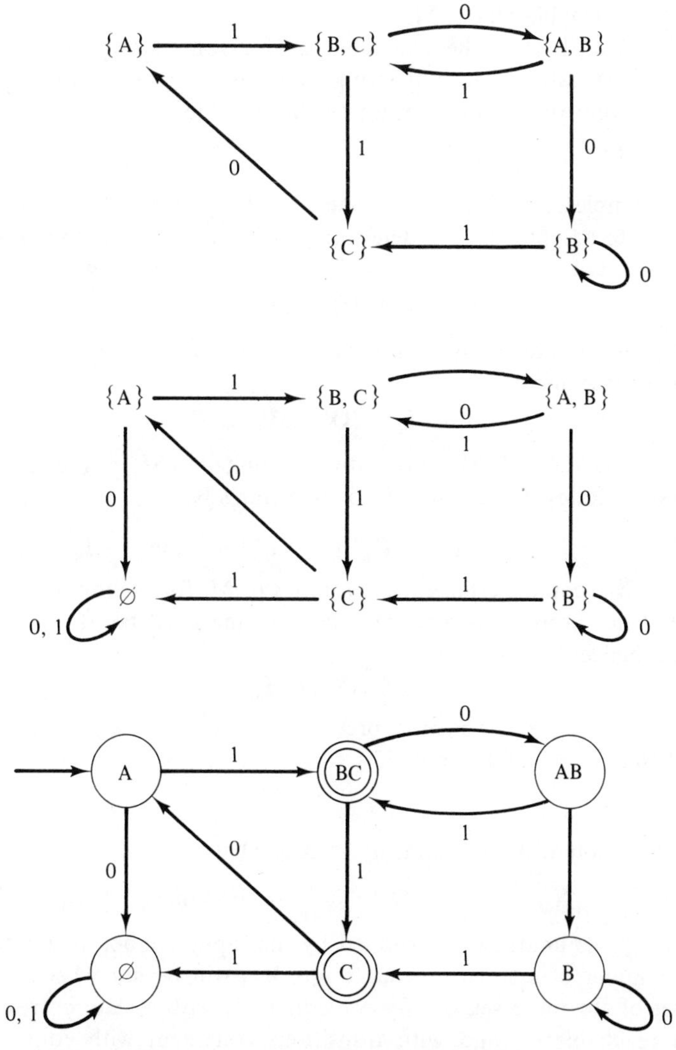


**Figure 5.4.** Construction of an equivalent deterministic accepter.

state diagram of a deterministic accepter, except that no transitions are specified for a 0 input in reachable set {A} or a 1 input in reachable set {C}. These transitions are missing because the original machine **M** specifies no states as 0-successors of A or as 1-successors of C. Strings that require the use of these missing transitions do not lead to any state of the nondeterministic accepter: the reachable set for these strings is the empty set $\varnothing$. If we include $\varnothing$ as a reachable set (Figure 5.4b), the diagram becomes the state diagram of a deterministic finite-state accepter (Figure 5.4c). The states of the deterministic machine are in one-to-one correspondence with the reachable sets of **M**.

If $\varnothing$ is the reachable set for some string $\omega$, then $\varnothing$ is the reachable set for any string having $\omega$ as a prefix. Thus all transitions from the $\varnothing$ state return to the $\varnothing$ state, and the $\varnothing$ state is a trap state of the accepter.

Example 5.4 suggests that one can always convert a nondeterministic finite-state accepter into a deterministic accepter that recognizes the same language. Let

$$\mathbf{M}_n = (\mathbf{Q}_n, \mathbf{S}, \mathbf{P}_n, \mathbf{I}_n, \mathbf{F}_n)$$

be any finite-state accepter, and suppose that we wish to construct a deterministic accepter

$$\mathbf{M}_d = (\mathbf{Q}_d, \mathbf{S}, \mathbf{P}_d, \mathbf{I}_d, \mathbf{F}_d)$$

such that $\mathbf{L}(\mathbf{M}_d) = \mathbf{L}(\mathbf{M}_n)$. Presenting a string $\omega$ to $\mathbf{M}_n$ may lead it to any one of several states. Let the set of possible states be

$$\mathbf{X}_{[\omega]} = \{q' \in \mathbf{Q}_n \mid q \stackrel{\omega}{\Longrightarrow} q' \text{ for some } q \in \mathbf{I}_n\}$$

The set $\mathbf{X}_{[\omega]}$ contains the *reachable states* of $\mathbf{M}_n$ for the input string $\omega$. If no symbol has been applied to $\mathbf{M}_n$, the machine must be in one of its initial states; hence

$$\mathbf{X}_{[\lambda]} = \mathbf{I}_n$$

For each string $\varphi \cdot s$, we can express $\mathbf{X}_{[\varphi \cdot s]}$ in terms of $\mathbf{X}_{[\varphi]}$: a state $q'$ will be reachable for $\varphi \cdot s$ if and only if

$$q'' \stackrel{s}{\longrightarrow} q'$$

is a transition of $\mathbf{M}_n$ for some $q'' \in \mathbf{X}_{[\varphi]}$. That is,

$$\text{(1)} \qquad \mathbf{X}_{[\varphi \cdot s]} = \{q' \in \mathbf{Q}_n \mid q'' \stackrel{s}{\longrightarrow} q' \text{ for some } q'' \in \mathbf{X}_{[\varphi]}\}$$

Thus $\mathbf{X}_{[\varphi \cdot s]}$ is uniquely determined by the input symbol $s$ and the set $\mathbf{X}_{[\varphi]}$. The number of distinct reachable sets $\mathbf{X}_{[\omega]}$ will be finite because each is a subset of the finite set $\mathbf{Q}_n$. By providing $\mathbf{M}_d$ with a state corresponding to each reachable set and with transitions consistent with equation (1), we obtain a deterministic accepter for $\mathbf{L}(\mathbf{M}_n)$. Since $\mathbf{X}_{[\omega]}$ contains a final state of $\mathbf{M}_n$ if and only if $\omega \in \mathbf{L}(\mathbf{M}_n)$, the final states of $\mathbf{M}_d$ correspond to reachable sets that contain final states of $\mathbf{M}_n$. The details of the construction are as follows:

1. The elements of $\mathbf{Q}_d$ are the subsets of $\mathbf{Q}_n$ reachable for some input string:

$$\mathbf{Q}_d = \{\mathbf{X}_{[\omega]} \mid \omega \in \mathbf{S}^*\}$$

2. The initial state of $\mathbf{M}_d$ is $\mathbf{X}_{[\lambda]} = \mathbf{I}_n$.
3. The accepting states of $\mathbf{M}_d$ are the reachable sets that contain accepting states of $\mathbf{M}_n$:

$$\mathbf{F}_d = \{\mathbf{X} \in \mathbf{Q}_d \mid \mathbf{X} \cap \mathbf{F}_n \neq \varnothing\}$$

4. State $\mathbf{X}'$ is the $s$-successor of state $\mathbf{X}$ in $\mathbf{M}_d$ just if $\mathbf{X}'$ consists precisely of the $s$-successors in $\mathbf{M}_n$ of the members of $\mathbf{X}$:

$$\mathbf{X} \xrightarrow{s} \mathbf{X}' \qquad \text{in } \mathbf{M}_d$$

if and only if

$$\mathbf{X}' = \{q' \mid q \xrightarrow{s} q' \text{ in } \mathbf{M}_n \text{ for some } q \in \mathbf{X}\}$$

**Theorem 5.1:** For each finite-state accepter $\mathbf{M}_n$ one can construct a deterministic finite-state accepter $\mathbf{M}_d$ such that $\mathbf{L}(\mathbf{M}_d) = \mathbf{L}(\mathbf{M}_n)$.

***Proof:*** Let $\mathbf{M}_d$ be the FSA constructed from $\mathbf{M}_n$ by the procedure given above. Clearly, $\mathbf{M}_d$ is deterministic. We must show that $\mathbf{L}(\mathbf{M}_d) = \mathbf{L}(\mathbf{M}_n)$.

A state $\mathbf{X}_{[\omega]}$ of $\mathbf{M}_d$ is accepting if and only if it contains an accepting state of $\mathbf{M}_n$. Since any state in $\mathbf{X}_{[\omega]}$ is reachable for $\omega$, we have

$$\mathbf{X}_{[\omega]} \in \mathbf{F}_d \qquad \text{if and only if } \omega \in \mathbf{L}(\mathbf{M}_n)$$

Thus it is sufficient to show that each string $\omega$ leads $\mathbf{M}_d$ to the state $\mathbf{X}_{[\omega]}$:

$$\mathbf{X}_{[\lambda]} \xRightarrow{\omega} \mathbf{X}_{[\omega]}, \qquad \text{each } \omega \in \mathbf{S}^*$$

We use an induction on the length of $\omega$.

***Basis:*** Certainly $\mathbf{X}_{[\lambda]} \xRightarrow{\lambda} \mathbf{X}_{[\lambda]}$.

***Induction:*** Let $\omega = \varphi \cdot s$, and suppose that

$$\mathbf{X}_{[\lambda]} \xRightarrow{\varphi} \mathbf{X}_{[\varphi]} \tag{2}$$

A state $q'$ is reachable for $\omega$ just if

$$q \xRightarrow{\varphi} q'' \xrightarrow{s} q'$$

for some $q \in \mathbf{X}_{[\lambda]}$ and some state $q''$ reachable for $\varphi$. That is,

$$q' \in \mathbf{X}_{[\omega]} \quad \text{if and only if} \quad q'' \xrightarrow{s} q' \text{ for some } q'' \in \mathbf{X}_{[\varphi]}$$

It follows from construction rule 4 that $\mathbf{M}_d$ has the transition

$$\mathbf{X}_{[\varphi]} \xrightarrow{s} \mathbf{X}_{[\omega]}$$

Using (2), we conclude that

$$\mathbf{X}_{[\lambda]} \overset{\omega}{\Longrightarrow} \mathbf{X}_{[\omega]}$$

Thus, permitting nondeterministic behavior does not increase the language-recognizing ability of finite-state machines.

### 5.1.3 Applications to Machine Design

Nondeterministic accepters are frequently useful in the design of finite-state machines. Two examples will illustrate.

**Example 5.5:** We shall design a deterministic FSA that accepts any string consisting entirely of 0's except for a single occurrence of either the substring 101 or a substring of 1's. [The set of strings satisfying this property is represented by the expression **0*(101 ∪ 11*)0***.] The construction is shown in Figure 5.5. Accepters $\mathbf{M}_1$ and $\mathbf{M}_2$ recognize the sets **101** and **11***, respectively. So that an arbitrary string of 0's may precede or follow either of these sets, we add self-loops to the initial states and to the accepting states to obtain accepters $\mathbf{M}_3$ and $\mathbf{M}_4$. In $\mathbf{M}_4$, a new state G must be included so that a final string of 0's can be accepted only after the last of a string of 1's has been presented. To form an accepter for the union of $\mathbf{L}(\mathbf{M}_3)$ and $\mathbf{L}(\mathbf{M}_4)$, we regard the state diagrams of $\mathbf{M}_3$ and $\mathbf{M}_4$ as jointly constituting a single nondeterministic accepter $\mathbf{M}_5$. The corresponding deterministic machine $\mathbf{M}_6$ is found by starting with the set {A, E} of initial states, and determining what additional state sets must be included to account for all paths in $\mathbf{M}_5$. States BF, CG, D, F, and G are all accepting states in $\mathbf{M}_6$, because they correspond to reachable sets that contain accepting states of $\mathbf{M}_5$.

The construction of an equivalent deterministic accepter can also be carried out using state tables:

**Example 5.6:** Suppose that we wish to construct a deterministic accepter for the set of all binary strings containing, at any position, the substring 0110. One might find it difficult to design the required accepter directly, because prefixes of 0110 may appear in an input

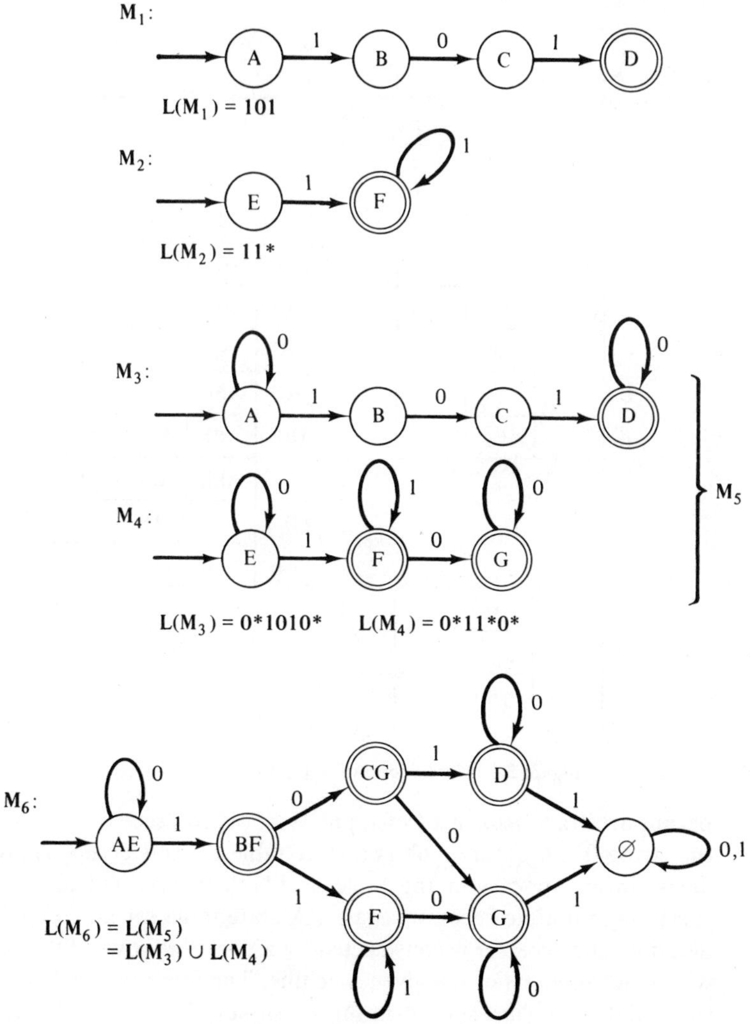


**Figure 5.5.** Construction for Example 5.5.

string with less than four symbols of separation, as in the string 010110. A deterministic accepter must therefore keep track of all possible interpretations of previously presented symbols as initial symbols of the required substring.

Designing a nondeterministic accepter for the language and converting it to a deterministic accepter is an organized way of solving the problem. In Figure 5.6a, the self-loops at states A and E

(a)

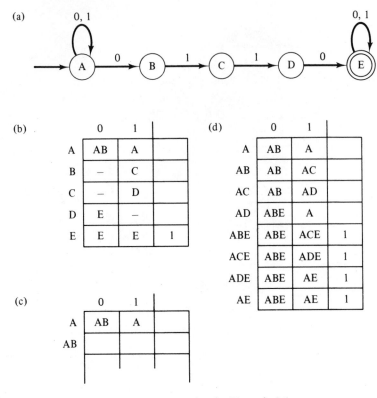

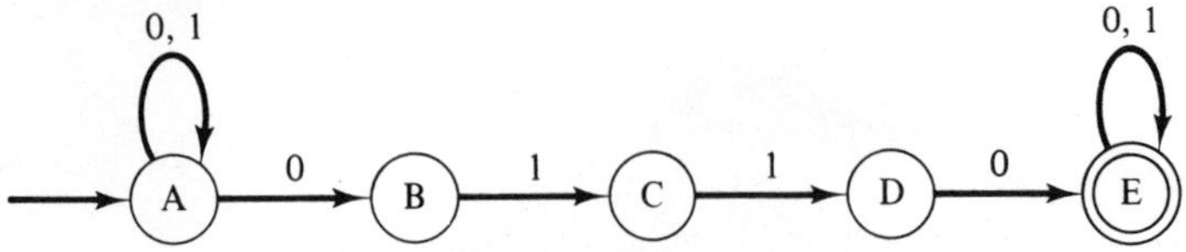


(b)

| | 0 | 1 | |
|---|---|---|---|
| A | AB | A | |
| B | – | C | |
| C | – | D | |
| D | E | – | |
| E | E | E | 1 |

(c)

| | 0 | 1 | |
|---|---|---|---|
| A | AB | A | |
| AB | | | |
| | | | |

(d)

| | 0 | 1 | |
|---|---|---|---|
| A | AB | A | |
| AB | AB | AC | |
| AC | AB | AD | |
| AD | ABE | A | |
| ABE | ABE | ACE | 1 |
| ACE | ABE | ADE | 1 |
| ADE | ABE | AE | 1 |
| AE | ABE | AE | 1 |

**Figure 5.6.** Construction for Example 5.6.

permit arbitrary sequences of input symbols to precede and follow the string 0110. Figure 5.6b is a state table for this accepter. Nondeterminism appears in the table as blank entries and as entries specifying multiple successor states. A state table for an equivalent deterministic accepter is constructed by associating rows of the table with reachable sets of the given machine. The first row is labeled by the initial states (just state A in this example); then the successor set for each combination of row and input symbol is added to the table as a new row. For instance, in the original machine the 0-successors of state A are the states A and B, and thus a row labeled AB is added to the table for the new machine, as shown in Figure 5.6c. The completed table is shown as Figure 5.6d; the final states of the machine are those marked with a 1 in the output column. Note that states ABE, ACE, ADE, and AE are all equivalent: our procedure for constructing a deterministic accepter does not necessarily yield a reduced machine.

## 5.2 Finite-State Accepters and Regular Grammars

The relation between finite-state accepters and regular grammars is established as a correspondence between the sets of strings denoted by the nonterminal letters of a grammar and certain sets of strings associated with states of an accepter. We treat the relationship of right-linear grammars to finite-state accepters explicitly, because these grammars play the more important role in later chapters. An entirely analogous development may be formulated in terms of left-linear grammars.

Given a grammar **G**, we write **L**(**G**, $A$) to mean the set of terminal strings derivable in **G** from the nonterminal letter $A$:

$$\mathbf{L}(\mathbf{G}, A) = \{\omega \in \mathbf{T}^* \mid A \overset{*}{\Longrightarrow} \omega \text{ in } \mathbf{G}\}$$

For any right-linear grammar we shall see how these sets may be identified with certain sets of strings, called *end sets*, associated with the states of a finite-state accepter **M**.

**Definition 5.4:** Let $\mathbf{M} = (\mathbf{Q}, \mathbf{S}, \mathbf{P}, \mathbf{I}, \mathbf{F})$ be an FSA. The *end set* $\mathbf{E}(q)$ of a state $q$ of **M** is the collection of input strings that can lead from $q$ to an accepting state of **M**:

$$\mathbf{E}(q) = \{\omega \in \mathbf{S}^* \mid q \overset{\omega}{\Longrightarrow} q' \text{ for some } q' \in \mathbf{F}\}$$

**Example 5.7:** Consider the finite-state accepter **M** shown in Figure 5.7. The end set **E**(A) is the set of strings that lead **M** from state A

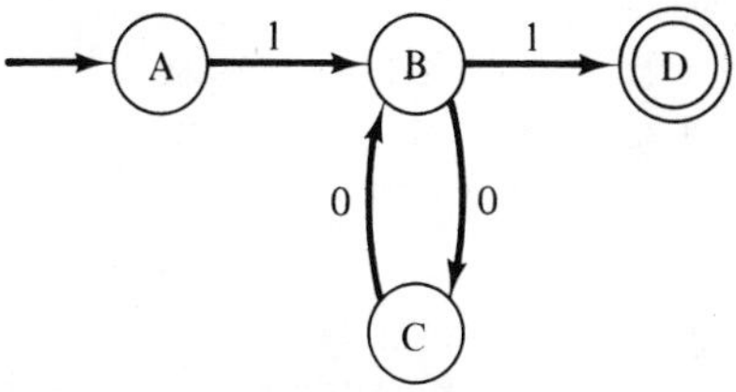


**Figure 5.7.** An accepter.

to the accepting state D. A string in **E**(A) must consist of a 1 followed by some string that leads **M** from state B to state D:

(1) $$\mathbf{E}(\mathrm{A}) = \mathbf{1} \cdot \mathbf{E}(\mathrm{B})$$

Similarly, a string in **E**(C) must be a 0 followed by some string in **E**(B):

(2) $$\mathbf{E}(\mathrm{C}) = \mathbf{0} \cdot \mathbf{E}(\mathrm{B})$$

Finally, a string in **E**(B) can be either a single 1 leading directly to the accepting state D, or a 0 followed by some string in **E**(C):

(3) $$\mathbf{E}(\mathrm{B}) = \mathbf{0} \cdot \mathbf{E}(\mathrm{C}) \cup \mathbf{1}$$

Relations (1), (2), and (3) comprise a system of *set equations* that must be satisfied by the end sets of the accepter **M**.

Note that the end set of state D is $\boldsymbol{\lambda}$, because D is accepting and no transitions exit state D. Thus relation (3) could be written alternatively as

$$(3') \qquad \mathbf{E}(\mathrm{B}) = \mathbf{0} \cdot \mathbf{E}(\mathrm{C}) \cup \mathbf{1} \cdot \mathbf{E}(\mathrm{D})$$

$$(3'') \qquad \mathbf{E}(\mathrm{D}) = \boldsymbol{\lambda}$$

The language recognized by **M** is easily expressed in terms of end sets: it consists of precisely those strings in the end set of **M**'s initial state. That is, $\mathbf{L}(\mathbf{M}) = \mathbf{E}(\mathrm{A})$.

Example 5.7 has shown how a system of set equations may be derived from a finite-state accepter. Before generalizing this example, we introduce some fundamental properties of end sets. It should be clear that the end set $\mathbf{E}(q)$ of an accepting state always contains the empty string. Conversely, if $q$ is not an accepting state, then $\lambda$ is not in $\mathbf{E}(q)$, since at least one input symbol is required to reach another state of **M**. Now suppose that $\omega \in \mathbf{E}(q)$ for nonempty $\omega$. There must be an admissible state sequence for $\omega$ consisting of at least one state transition. If $s$ is the first letter of $\omega$, this state sequence has the form

$$q \xrightarrow{s} q' \overset{\varphi}{\Longrightarrow} q'',$$

where $\omega = s \cdot \varphi$ and $q'' \in \mathbf{F}$. It follows that there is a state $q'$ of **M** such that

$$q \xrightarrow{s} q'$$

is a state transition of **M**, and the string $\varphi$ is in the end set $\mathbf{E}(q')$. The converse is also true. Finally, a string $\omega$ is accepted by **M** if and only if **M** has an admissible state sequence

$$q \overset{\omega}{\Longrightarrow} q'$$

where $q$ and $q'$ are initial and accepting states, respectively. If follows that the language recognized by **M** is the union of the end sets of all initial states of **M**.

**Proposition 5.1:** Let $\mathbf{M} = (\mathbf{Q}, \mathbf{S}, \mathbf{P}, \mathbf{I}, \mathbf{F})$ be an FSA, and let $\mathbf{E}(q)$ be the end set of state $q$. Then

1. $\lambda \in \mathbf{E}(q)$ if and only if $q \in \mathbf{F}$.

2. If $\omega = s\varphi$, then $\omega \in \mathbf{E}(q)$ if and only if $\varphi \in \mathbf{E}(q')$ and $q \xrightarrow{s} q'$ is a transition of **M** for some $q' \in \mathbf{Q}$.

3. $\mathbf{L}(\mathbf{M}) = \bigcup_{q \in \mathbf{I}} \mathbf{E}(q)$.

**Proposition 5.2:** The end sets of a finite-state accepter $\mathbf{M} = (\mathbf{Q}, \mathbf{S}, \mathbf{P}, \mathbf{I}, \mathbf{F})$ satisfy a system of *right-linear set equations*: for each

$q \in \mathbf{Q}$,

$$\mathbf{E}(q) = \bigcup_{q' \in \mathbf{Q}} \mathbf{V}(q, q')\mathbf{E}(q') \cup \mathbf{W}(q)$$

where

$$\mathbf{V}(q, q') = \{s \in \mathbf{S} \mid \mathbf{M} \text{ has } q \xrightarrow{s} q'\}$$

and

$$\mathbf{W}(q) = \begin{cases} \boldsymbol{\lambda} & \text{if } q \in \mathbf{F} \\ \varnothing & \text{otherwise} \end{cases}$$

Each *coefficient set* $\mathbf{V}(q, q')$ contains the input symbols that can take $\mathbf{M}$ from $q$ to $q'$.

Linear set equations are analogous to linear algebraic equations: the set operations union and concatenation are analogous respectively to the arithmetic operations addition and multiplication. (Keep in mind, however, that concatenation is not a commutative operation.) The equations are linear because the end sets, which are the unknowns, make at most one appearance in each term. They are *right* linear because the unknown sets are the right constituent of each term making up the right-hand side. We shall see in Section 5.3 how the system of set equations obtained from a finite-state accepter may be solved to yield regular expressions for the end sets in terms of the coefficient sets of the equations.

In setting up the equation system for an accepter, it helps to note that the end set of a nonaccepting trap state is empty; terms containing such end sets may be deleted from set equations without affecting their solution. Also, if $q$ is an inaccessible state, then the set equation for $\mathbf{E}(q)$ may be omitted from the equation system without affecting the solution for $\mathbf{L}(\mathbf{M})$.

If $\mathbf{M}$ is a finite-state accepter having a transition

$$q \xrightarrow{s} q'$$

then, according to Proposition 5.1, the string $s\varphi$ is in $\mathbf{E}(q)$ whenever $\varphi$ is in $\mathbf{E}(q')$. Thus we may assert that

(1) $$\mathbf{E}(q) \supseteq \mathbf{s} \cdot \mathbf{E}(q')$$

If $\mathbf{G}$ is a right-linear grammar that has a production

$$A \longrightarrow sB$$

then the string $s\varphi$ is denoted by $A$ whenever $\varphi$ is denoted by $B$, and we may assert that

(2) $$\mathbf{L}(\mathbf{G}, A) \supseteq \mathbf{s} \cdot \mathbf{L}(\mathbf{G}, B)$$

The similarity of relations (1) and (2) suggests that, by relating rules of a right-linear grammar to the transitions of an accepter, we may be able to identify the end sets of the accepter with the sets of terminal strings denoted by nonterminal symbols of the grammar.

**Example 5.8:** Consider the grammar

$$\mathbf{G}:\ \Sigma \longrightarrow A \qquad A \longrightarrow 1B \qquad B \longrightarrow 1$$
$$B \longrightarrow 0C$$
$$C \longrightarrow 0B$$

From the $\Sigma$ rule of **G** we find that

$$\mathbf{L}(\Sigma) = \mathbf{L}(A)$$

where, for convenience, we are writing $\mathbf{L}(\mathbf{G}, X)$ as simply $\mathbf{L}(X)$. From the single $A$ rule we have

(1) $$\mathbf{L}(A) = \mathbf{1} \cdot \mathbf{L}(B)$$

and the $C$ rule yields

(2) $$\mathbf{L}(C) = \mathbf{0} \cdot \mathbf{L}(B)$$

The two $B$ rules imply that

(3) $$\mathbf{L}(B) = \mathbf{0} \cdot \mathbf{L}(C) \cup \mathbf{1}$$

Relations (1), (2), and (3) make up a system of right-linear set equations identical to the set equations formulated for the accepter **M** in Example 5.7, except the unknowns here are $\mathbf{L}(A)$, $\mathbf{L}(B)$, and $\mathbf{L}(C)$ instead of $\mathbf{E}(\mathrm{A})$, $\mathbf{E}(\mathrm{B})$ and $\mathbf{E}(\mathrm{C})$. Since any solution of either system is also a solution of the other, and since $\mathbf{L}(\mathbf{M}) = \mathbf{E}(\mathrm{A})$ and $\mathbf{L}(\mathbf{G}) = \mathbf{L}(\mathrm{A})$, the language generated by **G** is exactly the language recognized by **M**.

The equality of the languages defined by **M** and **G** stems from the relationship of the structure of **M** to the productions in **G**:

| In **M** | In **G** |
|---|---|
| $\mathrm{A} \xrightarrow{1} \mathrm{B}$ | $A \longrightarrow 1B$ |
| $\mathrm{B} \xrightarrow{0} \mathrm{C}$ | $B \longrightarrow 0C$ |
| $\mathrm{C} \xrightarrow{0} \mathrm{B}$ | $C \longrightarrow 0B$ |
| $\mathrm{B} \xrightarrow{1} \mathrm{D},\ \mathrm{D} \in \mathbf{F}$ | $B \longrightarrow 1$ |
| $\mathrm{A} \in \mathbf{I}$ | $\Sigma \longrightarrow A$ |

Because of this relationship, there is a one-to-one correspondence between the admissible state sequences of **M** and the derivations of **G**. For each $k \geq 0$, the derivation

$$\Sigma \Longrightarrow A \Longrightarrow 1B \Longrightarrow 10C \Longrightarrow 100B \Longrightarrow \ldots$$
$$\Longrightarrow 1(00)^k B \Longrightarrow 1(00)^k 1$$

corresponds to the accepting state sequence

$$\mathrm{A} \xrightarrow{1} \mathrm{B} \xrightarrow{0} \mathrm{C} \xrightarrow{0} \mathrm{B} \xrightarrow{0} \ldots \xrightarrow{0} \mathrm{B} \xrightarrow{1} \mathrm{D}$$

for the string $1(00)^k1$.

Example 5.8 illustrates the principle used to construct a right-linear grammar for the language recognized by an arbitrary finite-state accepter **M**. The grammar has a nonterminal letter for each state of the accepter:

$$\mathbf{N} = \{N(q) \mid q \in \mathbf{Q}\}$$

The productions of the grammar are obtained from the transitions of **M** so that

$$N(q) \overset{*}{\Longrightarrow} \omega \qquad \text{if and only if} \quad \omega \in \mathbf{E}(q),\ \omega \neq \lambda$$

The rules of the construction are stated in Table 5.1 and are explained in Example 5.9. According to the definition given in Chapter 3, a grammar **G** constructed according to Table 5.1 is not strictly right linear because of

**Table 5.1** Construction of a right-linear grammar from a finite-state accepter

*Given:* An FSA $\mathbf{M} = (\mathbf{Q}, \mathbf{S}, \mathbf{P_M}, \mathbf{I}, \mathbf{F})$ with end sets $\{\mathbf{E}(q) \mid q \in \mathbf{Q}\}$
*Construct:* A right-linear grammar $\mathbf{G} = (\mathbf{N}, \mathbf{S}, \mathbf{P_G}, \Sigma)$ with $\mathbf{N} = \{N(q) \mid q \in \mathbf{Q}\}$ such that $\mathbf{L}(\mathbf{G}, N(q)) = \mathbf{E}(q), q \in \mathbf{Q}$

| Rule | If **M** has | then *G* has | Reason |
|---|---|---|---|
| 1 | $\mathbf{I} \cap \mathbf{F} \neq \varnothing$ | $\Sigma \longrightarrow \lambda$ | $\lambda \in \mathbf{L}(\mathbf{M})$ |
| 2 | $q \in \mathbf{I}$ | $\Sigma \longrightarrow N(q)$ | $\mathbf{E}(q) \subseteq \mathbf{L}(\mathbf{M})$ |
| 3 | $q \overset{s}{\longrightarrow} q', q' \in \mathbf{F}$ | $N(q) \longrightarrow s$ | $s \in \mathbf{E}(q)$ |
| 4 | $q \overset{s}{\longrightarrow} q'$ | $N(q) \longrightarrow sN(q')$ | $\mathbf{E}(q) \supseteq \mathbf{s}\mathbf{E}(q')$ |

productions of the form $\Sigma \longrightarrow N(q)$ resulting from rule 2. However, if we add to **G** the production $\Sigma \longrightarrow \omega$ for each production $N(q) \longrightarrow \omega$ resulting from rules 3 and 4, we can remove the production $\Sigma \longrightarrow N(q)$ without changing the language generated by the grammar. Thus any grammar generated according to Table 5.1 can be transformed, if we so desire, into one that is strictly right linear and that generates the same language.

**Example 5.9:** We shall construct a right-linear grammar **G** from the finite-state accepter **M** shown in Figure 5.8. Let the end sets **E**(A), **E**(B), and **E**(C) of the accepter be written simply as **A**, **B**, and **C**. These sets are related by the right-linear set equations

$$\mathbf{A} = \mathbf{1A} \cup \mathbf{1C}$$

$$\mathbf{B} = \mathbf{0A} \cup \mathbf{1B} \cup \mathbf{1C} \cup \boldsymbol{\lambda}$$

$$\mathbf{C} = \mathbf{1B} \cup \mathbf{0C} \cup \boldsymbol{\lambda}$$

and $\mathbf{L}(\mathbf{M}) = \mathbf{A} \cup \mathbf{B}$.

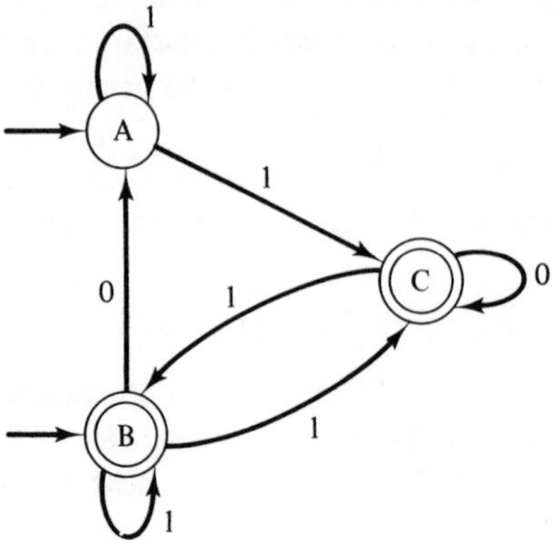


**Figure 5.8.** An accepter.

The nonterminal symbols of **G** are

$$\mathbf{N} = \{A, B, C\}$$

in correspondence with the end sets of **M**. The productions of **G** are obtained using the rules of Table 5.1.

First, since state B is both an initial and final state, **G** has the production $\Sigma \longrightarrow \lambda$ as required by construction rule 1.

Second, **L(M)** is the union of sets **A** and **B**. By construction rule 2, **G** has the productions

$$\Sigma \longrightarrow A \quad \text{and} \quad \Sigma \longrightarrow B$$

Third, **G** has $N(q) \longrightarrow s$ whenever $s \in \mathbf{E}(q)$, by construction rule 3. As noted in Table 5.1,

$$s \in \mathbf{E}(q) \qquad \text{if and only if } \mathbf{M} \text{ has } q \overset{s}{\longrightarrow} q', q' \in \mathbf{F}$$

In the case of state A, **M** has

$$\mathrm{A} \overset{1}{\longrightarrow} \mathrm{C}, \qquad \mathrm{C} \in \mathbf{F}$$

and therefore $1 \in \mathbf{A}$. Accordingly, **G** has the production

$$A \longrightarrow 1$$

Similarly, the transitions

$$\mathrm{B} \overset{1}{\longrightarrow} \mathrm{B} \qquad \mathrm{C} \overset{0}{\longrightarrow} \mathrm{C}$$

$$\mathrm{B} \overset{1}{\longrightarrow} \mathrm{C} \qquad \mathrm{C} \overset{1}{\longrightarrow} \mathrm{B}$$

where B and C are final states, require that **G** have the productions

$$B \longrightarrow 1 \qquad C \longrightarrow 0 \qquad C \longrightarrow 1$$

Next we consider the set equation

$$\mathbf{A} = \mathbf{1A} \cup \mathbf{1C}$$

A nonempty string $\omega$ is in **A** if and only if $\omega = 1\varphi$ and $\varphi$ is in either **A** or **C**. In **G** the corresponding requirement is met by including the productions

$$A \longrightarrow 1A \qquad A \longrightarrow 1C$$

as required by construction rule 4. The remaining two set equations require the productions

$$\begin{array}{ll} B \longrightarrow 0A & C \longrightarrow 1B \\ B \longrightarrow 1B & C \longrightarrow 0C \\ B \longrightarrow 1C & \end{array}$$

by the same reasoning.

Summarizing, the grammar **G** is

$$\begin{array}{lllll} \mathbf{G}: & \textit{rule 1}: & \Sigma \longrightarrow \lambda & \textit{rule 4}: & A \longrightarrow 1A \\ & \textit{rule 2}: & \Sigma \longrightarrow A & & A \longrightarrow 1C \\ & & \Sigma \longrightarrow B & & B \longrightarrow 0A \\ & \textit{rule 3}: & A \longrightarrow 1 & & B \longrightarrow 1B \\ & & B \longrightarrow 1 & & B \longrightarrow 1C \\ & & C \longrightarrow 0 & & C \longrightarrow 1B \\ & & C \longrightarrow 1 & & C \longrightarrow 0C \end{array}$$

The relation between state sequences in **M** and derivations in **G** is illustrated in Figure 5.9. Two accepting state sequences for the

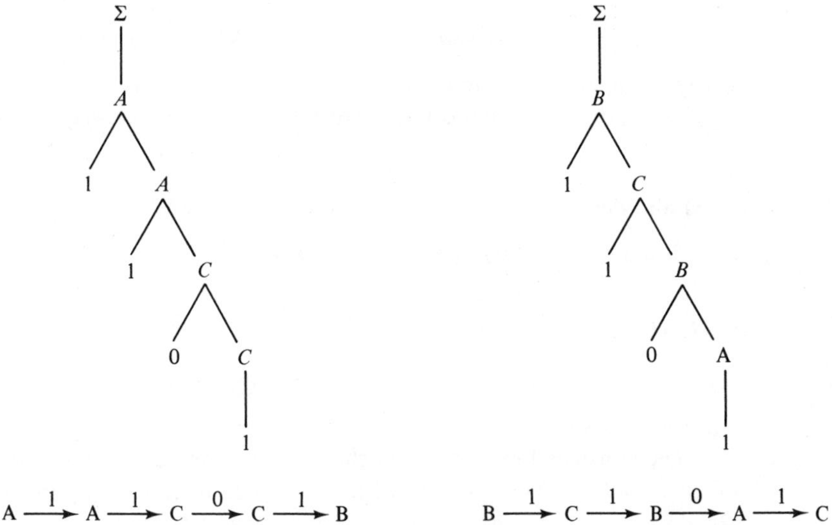


**Figure 5.9.** Relation between derivations of **G** and state sequences of **M**.

string 1101 are shown, together with the corresponding derivations in **G**. The nonterminals of **G** appear in the derivations in the same order as the corresponding states appear in the state sequences. Figure 5.9 shows that **G** is an ambiguous grammar.

Example 5.9 illustrates the one-to-one correspondence between the state sequences of an accepter and the leftmost derivations in the corresponding grammar. In the following proof, this is established as a general property of the construction, and is the basis for our treatment of ambiguity in Section 5.4.

**Theorem 5.2:** For any finite-state accepter **M**, one can construct a right-linear grammar **G** such that $\mathbf{L(G)} = \mathbf{L(M)}$.

***Proof:*** Let $\mathbf{M} = (\mathbf{Q}, \mathbf{S}, \mathbf{P}, \mathbf{I}, \mathbf{F})$ be given, and let $\mathbf{G} = (\mathbf{N}, \mathbf{S}, \mathbf{P}, \Sigma)$ be the right-linear grammar constructed according to Table 5.1. We must show that $\omega \in \mathbf{L(G)}$ if and only if $\omega \in \mathbf{L(M)}$.

We have $\lambda \in \mathbf{L(M)}$ if and only if $\mathbf{I} \cap \mathbf{F} \neq \varnothing$. But, by construction, **G** has the production $\Sigma \longrightarrow \lambda$ if and only if $\mathbf{I} \cap \mathbf{F} \neq \varnothing$; hence $\lambda \in \mathbf{L(G)}$ if and only if $\lambda \in \mathbf{L(M)}$.

The construction rules establish one-to-one correspondences between transitions in **M** and productions in **G**:

| | In **M** | | In **G** |
|---|---|---|---|
| 1. | $q \xrightarrow{s} q'$, | | $N(q) \longrightarrow sN(q')$ |
| 2. | $q \xrightarrow{s} q'$, | $q' \in \mathbf{F}$ | $N(q) \longrightarrow s$ |

It follows by a simple induction that, for each nonempty string $\omega = s_1 s_2 \ldots s_k$, there is a one-to-one corresponce between state sequences

$$q_0 \xrightarrow{s_1} q_1 \xrightarrow{s_2} \cdots \xrightarrow{s_k} q_k, \qquad q_k \in \mathbf{F}$$

in **M** and derivations

$$N(q_0) \Longrightarrow s_1 N(q_1) \Longrightarrow s_1 s_2 N(q_2) \Longrightarrow \cdots$$
$$\Longrightarrow s_1 s_2 \ldots s_{k-1} N(q_{k-1}) \Longrightarrow s_1 s_2 \ldots s_k$$

in **G**. Therefore,

$$(1) \qquad \omega \in \mathbf{E}(q_0) \quad \text{if and only if } N(q_0) \overset{*}{\Longrightarrow} \omega$$

and this holds for each $q_0$ in **Q**.

The construction also establishes a one-to-one correspondence of each end set $\mathbf{E}(q)$, $q \in \mathbf{I}$, with a production $\Sigma \longrightarrow N(q)$ in **G**. Hence

$$\mathbf{L(G)} = \bigcup_{q \in \mathbf{I}} \mathbf{L}(\mathbf{G}, N(q))$$

and since

$$\mathbf{L(M)} = \bigcup_{q \in \mathbf{I}} \mathbf{E}(q)$$

it follows from (1) that $\mathbf{L(M)} = \mathbf{L(G)}$.

**Corollary 5.2.1:** The state sequences in **M** from $q \in \mathbf{I}$ to $q' \in \mathbf{F}$ are in one-to-one correspondence with the derivations of terminal strings from $\Sigma$ in **G**.

**Corollary 5.2.2:** For each $q$, the end set $\mathbf{E}(q)$ of **M** and the nonterminal $N(q)$ in **G** satisfy the relation $\mathbf{L}(\mathbf{G}, N(q)) = \mathbf{E}(q)$.

The construction rules given in Table 5.1 may be reversed to yield an accepter that recognizes the language generated by any right-linear grammar. The rules of the construction are given in Table 5.2 and explained in Example 5.10. For simplicity, we have assumed that each $\Sigma$ rule of **G** is of the form $\Sigma \longrightarrow \lambda$ or $\Sigma \longrightarrow A$.

**Table 5.2** Construction of an FSA from a right-linear grammar

*Given:* A right-linear grammar $\mathbf{G} = (\mathbf{N}, \mathbf{T}, \mathbf{P_G}, \Sigma)$

*Construct:* An FSA $\mathbf{M} = (\mathbf{Q}, \mathbf{T}, \mathbf{P_M}, \mathbf{I}, \{q_F\})$ with $\mathbf{Q} = \{q_A \mid A \in \mathbf{N}\} \cup \{q_F\}$ and end sets $\{\mathbf{E}(q) \mid q \in \mathbf{Q}\}$ such that $\mathbf{L}(\mathbf{G}, A) = \mathbf{E}(q_A)$ for $A \in \mathbf{N} \cup \{\Sigma\}$

| Rule | If **G** has | then **M** has | Reason |
|---|---|---|---|
| 1 | $A \longrightarrow sB$ | $q_A \xrightarrow{s} q_B$ | $\mathbf{L}(\mathbf{G}, A) \supseteq s\mathbf{L}(\mathbf{G}, B)$ |
| 2 | $A \longrightarrow s$ | $q_A \xrightarrow{s} q_F$ | $s \in \mathbf{L}(\mathbf{G}, A)$ |
| 3 | $\Sigma \longrightarrow A$ | $q_A \in \mathbf{I}$ | $\mathbf{L}(\mathbf{G}, A) \subseteq \mathbf{L(G)}$ |
| 4 | $\Sigma \longrightarrow \lambda$ | $q_F \in \mathbf{I}$ | $\lambda \in \mathbf{L(G)}$ |

**Example 5.10:** Consider the language

$$\mathbf{L} = \mathbf{a^*b^*} \cup (\mathbf{ab})^*$$

Using the nonterminal letter $A$ to denote strings in $\mathbf{a^*b^*}$ and the nonterminal letter $C$ to denote strings in $(\mathbf{ab})^*$, the following grammar generates **L**:

$$\mathbf{G}: \quad \begin{array}{l} \Sigma \longrightarrow \lambda \\ \Sigma \longrightarrow A \\ \Sigma \longrightarrow C \end{array} \qquad \left.\begin{array}{l} A \longrightarrow aA \\ A \longrightarrow aB \\ B \longrightarrow bB \\ A \longrightarrow a \\ A \longrightarrow b \\ B \longrightarrow b \end{array}\right\} \mathbf{a^*b^*} - \boldsymbol{\lambda} \qquad \left.\begin{array}{l} C \longrightarrow aD \\ D \longrightarrow bC \\ D \longrightarrow b \end{array}\right\} (\mathbf{ab})^* - \boldsymbol{\lambda}$$

The corresponding accepter **M** (Figure 5.10) will have states A, B, C, D, and $q_F$, and transitions arranged so that the strings denoted by each nonterminal of **G** constitute the end set of the corresponding state in **M**. From the productions $A \longrightarrow aA$ and $A \longrightarrow aB$

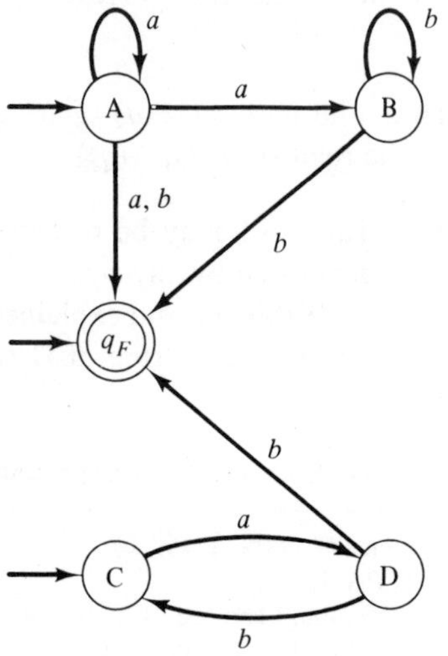


**Figure 5.10.** An accepter.

we see that the end set **A** must include the sets **aA** and **aB**. This is accomplished by including in **M** the transitions

$$\text{A} \xrightarrow{a} \text{A} \quad \text{and} \quad \text{A} \xrightarrow{a} \text{B}$$

as required by rule 1 of Table 5.2. The remaining transitions of **M** are accounted for in a similar way.

Next, the productions

$$A \longrightarrow a \qquad A \longrightarrow b$$

require that the symbols $a$ and $b$ both be in the end set **A**. This is accomplished by including transitions

$$\text{A} \xrightarrow{a} q_F \qquad \text{A} \xrightarrow{b} q_F$$

in **M**, where $q_F$ is the accepting state, as specified by rule 2 of Table 5.2. The remaining transitions into $q_F$ are accounted for in a similar way.

The productions

$$\Sigma \longrightarrow A \qquad \Sigma \longrightarrow C$$

require that **L(M)** contain both end sets **A** and **C**. Therefore, states A and C are made initial states of **M**, as required by rule 3 of Table

5.2. Finally, the production $\Sigma \longrightarrow \lambda$ requires that $q_F$ be an initial state, as specified by rule 4 of Table 5.2.

Example 5.10 illustrates how very naturally a grammar corresponds to a nondeterministic state diagram, and why we have allowed accepters to be nondeterministic. Should we desire, an accepter constructed from a grammar according to Table 5.2 can be converted to a deterministic accepter by the construction of Section 5.1.2. This is often a far simpler procedure than constructing a deterministic accepter directly from a given grammar.

**Theorem 5.3:** For any right-linear grammar **G**, one can construct a finite-state accepter **M** such that **L(M)** = **L(G)**.

***Proof:*** Let **M** be the accepter constructed according to Table 5.2. The argument that **L(M)** = **L(G)** is essentially the same as given in the proof of Theorem 5.2.

Theorems 5.2 and 5.3 assert the equivalence, in terms of the class of languages that they define, of finite-state accepters and right-linear grammars. In Chapter 3 we defined regular grammars to include left-linear grammars as well. That left-linear grammars are equivalent to right-linear grammars, and thus that finite-state accepters are equivalent to regular grammars, is demonstrated quite simply.

Suppose that **G** is a right-linear grammar. Let **G**′ be the left-linear grammar specified by the following construction:

| If **G** has | then **G**′ has |
|---|---|
| $\Sigma \longrightarrow sA$ | $A \longrightarrow s$ |
| $A \longrightarrow sB$ | $B \longrightarrow As$ |
| $A \longrightarrow s$ | $\Sigma \longrightarrow As$ |
| $\Sigma \longrightarrow s$ | $\Sigma \longrightarrow s$ |
| $\Sigma \longrightarrow \lambda$ | $\Sigma \longrightarrow \lambda$ |

This one-to-one correspondence between the productions of **G** and the productions of **G**′ establishes a one-to-one correspondence between derivations in **G** and **G**′ A derivation

$$\Sigma \Longrightarrow s_1A_1 \Longrightarrow s_1s_2A_2 \Longrightarrow \ldots \Longrightarrow s_1s_2 \ldots s_kA_k \Longrightarrow s_1s_2 \ldots s_{k+1}$$

in **G** corresponds to the derivation

$$\Sigma \Longrightarrow A_ks_{k+1} \Longrightarrow A_{k-1}s_ks_{k+1} \Longrightarrow \ldots \Longrightarrow A_1s_2 \ldots s_ks_{k+1} \Longrightarrow s_1s_2 \ldots s_ks_{k+1}$$

in **G**′. Hence **L(G′)** = **L(G)**.

**Example 5.11:** Consider the right-linear grammar

$$\begin{array}{llll} \mathbf{G}: \Sigma \longrightarrow \lambda & (1) & A \longrightarrow aA & (7) \\ \Sigma \longrightarrow aA & (2) & A \longrightarrow aB & (8) \\ \Sigma \longrightarrow aB & (3) & B \longrightarrow bB & (9) \\ \Sigma \longrightarrow bB & (4) & A \longrightarrow a & (10) \\ \Sigma \longrightarrow a & (5) & B \longrightarrow b & (11) \\ \Sigma \longrightarrow b & (6) & & \end{array}$$

for which $\mathbf{L}(\mathbf{G}) = \mathbf{a}^*\mathbf{b}^*$. Following the construction given, a left-linear grammar equivalent to **G** is

$$\begin{array}{llll} \mathbf{G}': \Sigma \longrightarrow \lambda & (1') & A \longrightarrow Aa & (7') \\ A \longrightarrow a & (2') & B \longrightarrow Aa & (8') \\ B \longrightarrow a & (3') & B \longrightarrow Bb & (9') \\ B \longrightarrow b & (4') & \Sigma \longrightarrow Aa & (10') \\ \Sigma \longrightarrow a & (5') & \Sigma \longrightarrow Bb & (11') \\ \Sigma \longrightarrow b & (6') & & \end{array}$$

The derivations of the sentence *aabbb* according to **G** and **G′** are

$$\mathbf{G}: \ \Sigma \Longrightarrow aA \Longrightarrow aaB \Longrightarrow aabB \Longrightarrow aabbB \Longrightarrow aabbb$$
$$\mathbf{G}': \ \Sigma \Longrightarrow Bb \Longrightarrow Bbb \Longrightarrow Bbbb \Longrightarrow Aabbb \Longrightarrow aabbb$$

Left-linear grammars can also be obtained directly from finite-state accepters by a construction similar to that used for right-linear grammars. One defines the *begin set* $\mathbf{B}(q)$ of state $q$ to be the set of strings leading to state $q$ from some initial state

$$\mathbf{B}(q) = \{\omega \mid q' \overset{\omega}{\Longrightarrow} q, q' \in \mathbf{I}\}$$

The left-linear grammar **G** has nonterminals $\{N(q) \mid q \in \mathbf{Q}\}$ and productions chosen so that $\mathbf{L}(\mathbf{G}, N(q)) = \mathbf{B}(q)$. The construction rules, set equations, and other aspects of this approach are analogous to those developed above. They are explored in detail in the Problems.

The principal results developed so far may be summarized by asserting the equivalence of the following statements:

1. The language **L** is recognized by some finite-state accepter.
2. The language **L** is generated by some right-linear grammar.
3. The language **L** is generated by some left-linear grammar.

In addition, we can state some new facts about regular grammars:

1. From a given right-linear grammar, one can always obtain a left-linear grammar that generates the same language, and vice versa.

2. One can always determine whether two regular grammars generate the same language: they generate the same language if and only if their corresponding deterministic accepters are equivalent.

3. One can always determine whether a regular grammar **G** generates any strings at all [that is, whether **L(G)** is empty]: **L(G)** is empty if and only if there is no path from any initial state to any final state in the state diagram of the corresponding accepter.

## 5.3 Regular Expressions and Finite-State Accepters

The state diagram of a finite-state accepter and the productions of a regular grammar provide only indirect descriptions of the structure of regular languages. We would like to be able to express a regular language explicitly in terms of simple sets of strings, and we show in this section that this can always be done. Indeed, the set operations union, concatenation, and closure are sufficient to express any regular language in terms of singleton alphabetic symbols.

### 5.3.1 Regular Expressions

In Chapter 2 we showed informally how the set operations union, concatenation, and closure could be used to form expressions for sets of strings. For example, we might describe a language **L** by the expression $(\mathbf{0} \cup \mathbf{1})^*\mathbf{11}$. (That is, **L** is the collection of strings in $\{0, 1\}^*$ that end in 11.) We distinguish between the string of symbols making up the expression itself and the set of strings the expression describes. The former is a *regular expression*; the latter is a *regular set*. Two distinct regular expressions may describe the same regular set. For example, the expressions

$$\mathbf{1(01)^*} \quad \text{and} \quad \mathbf{(10)^*1}$$

each describe the set containing all strings of alternating 1's and 0's that start and end with a 1.

For the purposes of this section we must be precise about what strings of symbols constitute regular expressions:

> **Definition 5.5:** Let **V** be a finite alphabet. A *regular expression* on **V** is any finite string of symbols from the set
>
> $$\{\mathbf{a} \mid a \in \mathbf{V}\} \cup \{\cup, *, (, ), \boldsymbol{\lambda}, \varnothing\}$$
>
> that may be formed according to the following rules:
>
> 1. $\boldsymbol{\lambda}$ is a regular expression.
> 2. $\varnothing$ is a regular expression.
> 3. If $a \in \mathbf{V}$, then $\mathbf{a}$ is a regular expression.

If $\alpha$ and $\beta$ are regular expressions, then the following are regular expressions:

4. $(\alpha\beta)$.
5. $(\alpha \cup \beta)$.
6. $(\alpha^*)$.

A regular expression *describes* a set according to our usual interpretations of the set operations. The parentheses are generally omitted when it will not cause confusion.

Two regular expressions are *equivalent* if and only if they describe the same set of strings. The reader should be familiar with some simple equivalences for regular expressions. Beyond the usual properties of set union and concatenation, the most important equivalences concern properties of the closure (Kleene star) operation. These are given below, where $\alpha$, $\beta$, and $\gamma$ stand for arbitrary regular expressions:

1. $(\alpha^*)^* = \alpha^*$.
2. $\alpha\alpha^* = \alpha^*\alpha$.
3. $\alpha\alpha^* \cup \lambda = \alpha^*$.
4. $\alpha(\beta \cup \gamma) = \alpha\beta \cup \alpha\gamma$.
5. $\alpha(\beta\alpha)^* = (\alpha\beta)^*\alpha$.
6. $(\alpha \cup \beta)^* = (\alpha^* \cup \beta^*)^*$.
7. $(\alpha \cup \beta)^* = (\alpha^*\beta^*)^*$.
8. $(\alpha \cup \beta)^* = \alpha^*(\beta\alpha^*)^*$.

The validity of each identity follows directly from the properties of union, concatenation, and closure. Verification is left to the reader.

In general, the distributive law does not hold for the closure operation. For example, the statement $(\alpha \cup \beta)^* = \alpha^* \cup \beta^*$ is false because the right-hand side denotes no string in which both $\alpha$ and $\beta$ appear.

Given a regular expression $\gamma$ that describes a set $\mathbf{X}$, it is easy to construct a regular expression $\gamma^R$ that describes the set $\mathbf{X}^R$ containing the reverse of each string in $\mathbf{X}$:

1. If $\gamma$ is $\begin{cases} \boldsymbol{\lambda} \\ \varnothing \\ \mathbf{a},\ a \in \mathbf{V} \end{cases}$ then $\gamma^R$ is $\gamma$.
2. If $\gamma$ is $(\alpha\beta)$, then $\gamma^R$ is $(\beta^R\alpha^R)$.
3. If $\gamma$ is $(\alpha \cup \beta)$, then $\gamma^R$ is $(\alpha^R \cup \beta^R)$.
4. If $\gamma$ is $\alpha^*$, then $\gamma^R$ is $\alpha^{R*}$.

Thus, to construct an expression for the reverse of a regular set, it is only necessary to reverse the order of subexpressions joined by the concatenation operation. For example, if $\alpha$ is

$$\mathbf{01(0^*11 \cup 1^*00)01 = A}$$

then $\alpha^R$ is

$$\mathbf{10(110^* \cup 001^*)10 = A^R}$$

Thus the reverse of every regular set is a regular set.

By reversing the order of subexpressions joined by concatenation in the equivalences given above, we obtain additional equivalences for regular expressions. For instance, from

$$(\alpha \cup \beta)^* = \alpha^*(\beta\alpha^*)^*$$

we conclude that

$$(\alpha \cup \beta)^* = (\alpha^*\beta)^*\alpha^*$$

is also valid.

### 5.3.2 Reduction and Solution of Set Equation Systems

For each finite-state accepter $\mathbf{M} = (\mathbf{Q}, \mathbf{S}, \mathbf{P}, \mathbf{I}, \mathbf{F})$, we may construct a system of right-linear set equations according to Proposition 5.2. If $\mathbf{M}$ has $n$ states $q_1, \ldots, q_n$, the set equations are

$$\mathbf{E}_k = \bigcup_{j=1}^{n} \mathbf{V}_{kj}\mathbf{E}_j \cup \mathbf{W}_k, \qquad k = 1, 2, \ldots, n$$

where

$\mathbf{E}_k$ is the end set for state $q_k$

$\mathbf{V}_{kj} = \{s \in \mathbf{S} \mid q_k \xrightarrow{s} q_j \text{ in } \mathbf{M}\}$

$\mathbf{W}_k = \begin{cases} \boldsymbol{\lambda} & \text{if } q_k \in \mathbf{F} \\ \varnothing & \text{otherwise} \end{cases}$

For some choices of $j$ and $k$, $\mathbf{V}_{kj}$ may be empty, in which case the term $\mathbf{V}_{kj}\mathbf{E}_j$ vanishes.

From Proposition 5.2 we know that the end sets of $\mathbf{M}$ are a solution of the right-linear system. We have yet to establish, however, that these sets are the only such solution. The construction of regular expressions for these solutions and the proof of their uniqueness are the subjects of the following paragraphs. Although in the remainder of this section we deal exclusively with right-linear set equations, our results extend easily to left-linear systems.

The solution of these equation systems resembles the reduction procedure for linear algebraic equations. We manipulate one equation to obtain an expression for an unknown set (say $\mathbf{E}_1$) in terms of the remaining unknown sets. We substitute this expression for every appearance of $\mathbf{E}_1$ in the remaining equations, thereby obtaining a new system having one less equation and one less unknown than the original system. This reduction step is repeated until we obtain an expression for the last unknown (say $\mathbf{E}_n$) in terms of the constant sets $\{\mathbf{V}_{ij}\}$ and $\{\mathbf{W}_k\}$ of the equation system.

To be more specific, we shall exhibit one step in the reduction procedure for the right-linear equation system. Choosing to eliminate $\mathbf{E}_1$, we rewrite the system with the $\mathbf{E}_1$ equation written separately:

$$\mathbf{E}_1 = \mathbf{V}_{11}\mathbf{E}_1 \cup \left(\bigcup_{j=2}^{n} \mathbf{V}_{1j}\mathbf{E}_j\right) \cup \mathbf{W}_1$$

$$\mathbf{E}_k = \mathbf{V}_{k1}\mathbf{E}_1 \cup \left(\bigcup_{j=2}^{n} \mathbf{V}_{kj}\mathbf{E}_j\right) \cup \mathbf{W}_k, \qquad k = 2, \ldots, n$$

First we find a solution for the $\mathbf{E}_1$ equation. The solution is not obvious, because $\mathbf{E}_1$ appears on both sides of the equation. According to the $\mathbf{E}_1$ equation, a string $\omega$ is in $\mathbf{E}_1$ if and only if

1. $\omega \in \bigcup_{j=2}^{n} \mathbf{V}_{1j}\mathbf{E}_j \cup \mathbf{W}_1$

or

2. $\omega = s\varphi, \qquad \text{where } \varphi \in \mathbf{E}_1 \text{ and } s \in \mathbf{V}_{11}$

Figure 5.11a shows how these two conditions may be represented by a *pseudo state graph* in which sets are allowed as labels of transitions. The

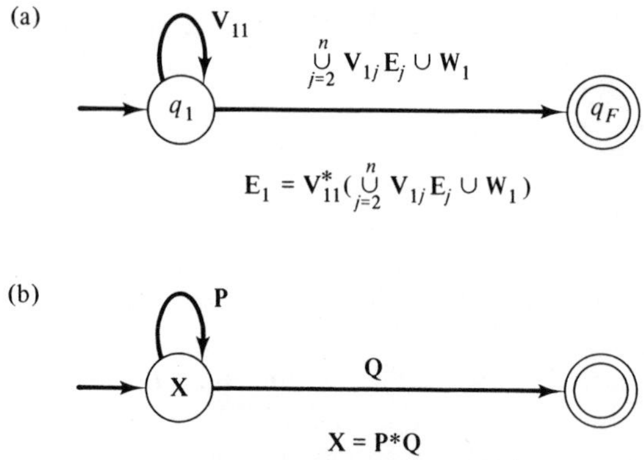


**Figure 5.11.** Solution of a set equation.

structure of this graph is shown abstractly in Figure 5.11b, where

$$\mathbf{Q} = \bigcup_{j=2}^{n} \mathbf{V}_{1j}\mathbf{E}_j \cup \mathbf{W}_1$$

$$\mathbf{P} = \mathbf{V}_{11}$$

$$\mathbf{X} = \mathbf{E}_1$$

Thus the equation has the form

$$\mathbf{X} = \mathbf{P}\mathbf{X} \cup \mathbf{Q}$$

where $\mathbf{X}$ denotes an unknown end set. From the figure it is evident that

$$\mathbf{X} = \mathbf{P}^*\mathbf{Q}$$

is a solution. This fact has been called *Arden's rule*, and the uniqueness of this solution will be shown shortly in the proof of Theorem 5.4. Applying Arden's rule to the $\mathbf{E}_1$ equation, we obtain

$$\mathbf{E}_1 = \mathbf{V}_{11}^*\left(\bigcup_{j=2}^{n} \mathbf{V}_{1j}\mathbf{E}_j \cup \mathbf{W}_1\right)$$

Substituting this expression for $\mathbf{E}_1$ in each of the remaining $n - 1$ equations, we obtain

$$\mathbf{E}_k = \bigcup_{j=2}^{n} (\mathbf{V}_{k1}\mathbf{V}_{11}^*\mathbf{V}_{1j} \cup \mathbf{V}_{kj})\mathbf{E}_j \cup \mathbf{V}_{k1}\mathbf{V}_{11}^*\mathbf{W}_1 \cup \mathbf{W}_k, \qquad k = 2, \ldots, n$$

By assigning

$$\mathbf{V}'_{kj} = \mathbf{V}_{k1}\mathbf{V}_{11}^*\mathbf{V}_{1j} \cup \mathbf{V}_{kj}$$
$$\mathbf{W}'_k = \mathbf{V}_{k1}\mathbf{V}_{11}^*\mathbf{W}_1 \cup \mathbf{W}_k$$

we obtain $n - 1$ right-linear equations in $n - 1$ unknowns

$$\mathbf{E}_k = \bigcup_{j=2}^{n} \mathbf{V}'_{kj}\mathbf{E}_j \cup \mathbf{W}'_k, \qquad k = 2, \ldots, n$$

from which $\mathbf{E}_1$ has been successfully eliminated.

The reduction step has an instructive interpretation in terms of pseudo state graphs. Figure 5.12a represents the original right-linear equation system where state $q_i$ is representative of states with transitions into state $q_1$, and state $q_j$ is representative of states to which there are transitions from state $q_1$. (States $q_i$ and $q_j$ need not be distinct.) A single final state is included with a transition labeled $\mathbf{W}_k$ entering from each node $q_k$ of the graph. Once we have properly accounted for all paths leading to the final state or to state $q_j$ by way of a transition to state $q_1$, state $q_1$ may be eliminated from the graph. Figures 5.12b and c show the transformation of the state graph into a new state graph (without state $q_1$) that represents the reduced system.

The complete solution of the equation system is found through repeated application of the reduction step described above. Let $\mathcal{E}_k$ stand for the right linear system of $n - k$ equations obtained by eliminating unknowns $\mathbf{E}_1, \ldots, \mathbf{E}_k$. Each reduction step transforms system $\mathcal{E}_k$ into $\mathcal{E}_{k+1}$ through the elimination of $\mathbf{E}_{k+1}$. The system $\mathcal{E}_{n-1}$ consists of one equation in the remaining unknown set $\mathbf{E}_n$, and is solved by Arden's rule. The resulting expression for $\mathbf{E}_n$ involves only the operations of union, concatenation, and closure applied to the constant sets (the $\mathbf{V}$'s and $\mathbf{W}$'s), and is therefore a regular expression. For $k = n - 1, \ldots, 1$, we substitute expressions for $\mathbf{E}_{k+1}, \ldots, \mathbf{E}_n$ into the $\mathbf{E}_k$ equation of system $\mathcal{E}_{k-1}$ to obtain a regular expression for the unknown set $\mathbf{E}_k$. In this way we obtain the complete solution of the equation system.

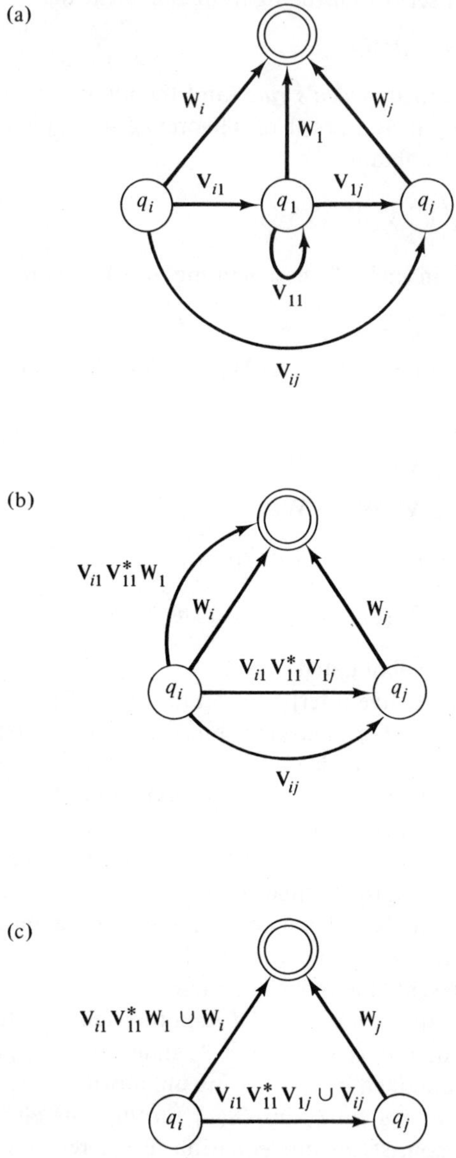


**Figure 5.12.** Transformation of a state graph by an elimination step.

**Example 5.12:** The right-linear equations for the accepter in Figure 5.13a are

$$\mathbf{A} = \mathbf{1A} \cup \mathbf{0B} \cup \boldsymbol{\lambda}$$
$$\mathbf{B} = \mathbf{1B} \cup \mathbf{1C}$$
$$\mathbf{C} = \mathbf{1A} \cup \mathbf{0B} \cup \mathbf{1C}$$

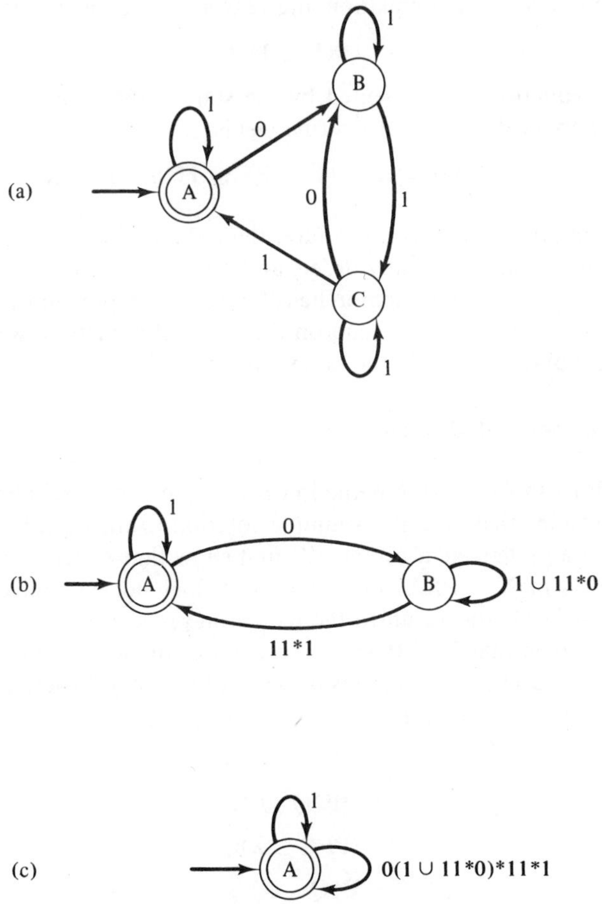


**Figure 5.13.** Accepters for Example 5.12.

Since an expression for $\mathbf{L(M)} = \mathbf{A}$ is desired, we choose to eliminate **C** first, and then **B**. Solving the **C** equation by Arden's rule, we find

$$\mathbf{C} = \mathbf{1^*(1A \cup 0B)}$$

Substituting into the **A** and **B** equations and regrouping terms yields two equations in two unknowns:

$$\mathbf{A} = \mathbf{1A \cup 0B \cup \lambda}$$

$$\mathbf{B} = \mathbf{(1 \cup 11^*0)B \cup 11^*1A}$$

This system corresponds to the graph in Figure 5.13b in which state **C** has been eliminated. Applying Arden's rule to the new **B** equation, we find

$$\mathbf{B} = \mathbf{(1 \cup 11^*0)^*11^*1A}$$

Using this in the **A** equation and regrouping terms, we have

$$\mathbf{A} = (\mathbf{1} \cup \mathbf{0}(\mathbf{1} \cup \mathbf{11^*0})^*\mathbf{11^*1})\mathbf{A} \cup \boldsymbol{\lambda}$$

This equation is represented by the state graph in Figure 5.13c. A final application of Arden's rule yields

$$\mathbf{L(M)} = \mathbf{A} = (\mathbf{1} \cup \mathbf{0}(\mathbf{1} \cup \mathbf{11^*0})^*\mathbf{11^*1})^*\boldsymbol{\lambda}$$

In applying the reduction procedure, the unknown sets of the equation system may be eliminated in any order, and an intelligent choice will often save effort and lead to more comprehensible regular expressions. Although the expressions obtained will depend on the order of reduction, we shall see that they must always describe the same sets.

### 5.3.3 Uniqueness of Solutions

We wish to show that the reduction procedure developed above yields regular expressions that describe a unique solution to the right-linear equation system of a finite-state accepter. We first show that Arden's rule gives a unique solution of $\mathbf{X} = \mathbf{PX} \cup \mathbf{Q}$ whenever **P** does not contain the empty string; then we apply this result to the reduction procedure.

We have noted that $\mathbf{X} = \mathbf{P^*Q}$ is a solution of the set equation $\mathbf{X} = \mathbf{PX} \cup \mathbf{Q}$, where **P** and **Q** are any subsets of $\mathbf{V^*}$, and this may be verified by substituting $\mathbf{P^*Q}$ for **X** on the right side:

$$\begin{aligned} \mathbf{X} &= \mathbf{PX} \cup \mathbf{Q} \\ &= \mathbf{PP^*Q} \cup \mathbf{Q} \\ &= (\mathbf{PP^*} \cup \boldsymbol{\lambda})\mathbf{Q} \\ &= \mathbf{P^*Q} \end{aligned}$$

We have not shown that $\mathbf{P^*Q}$ is the *only* such solution, however, and in general it is not. In particular, if **P** contains the empty string, then $\mathbf{V^*}$ is a solution of the equation regardless of the choice of **P** and **Q**. In Theorem 5.4 we establish the uniqueness of the solution $\mathbf{P^*Q}$ whenever $\lambda$ is not in **P**.

**Theorem 5.4:** Let **P** and **Q** be arbitrary sets of strings on a finite alphabet **V**. Then

$$\mathbf{X} = \mathbf{P^*Q} \text{ is a solution of } \mathbf{X} = \mathbf{PX} \cup \mathbf{Q}$$

and is a unique solution whenever $\lambda \notin \mathbf{P}$.

***Proof:*** We have already shown that $\mathbf{P^*Q}$ is a solution of the equation. We now show that if $\lambda \notin \mathbf{P}$ only one set can satisfy the equation.

Suppose that $\mathbf{X}_1$ and $\mathbf{X}_2$ are distinct solutions to $\mathbf{X} = \mathbf{PX} \cup \mathbf{Q}$, where $\mathbf{P}$ does not contain $\lambda$:

$$\left.\begin{aligned} \mathbf{X}_1 &= \mathbf{PX}_1 \cup \mathbf{Q} \\ \mathbf{X}_2 &= \mathbf{PX}_2 \cup \mathbf{Q} \end{aligned}\right\} \qquad \mathbf{X}_1 \neq \mathbf{X}_2,\ \lambda \notin \mathbf{P}$$

Then $\mathbf{X}_0 = \mathbf{X}_1 \cup \mathbf{X}_2$ is also a solution:

$$\begin{aligned} \mathbf{P}(\mathbf{X}_1 \cup \mathbf{X}_2) \cup \mathbf{Q} &= \mathbf{PX}_1 \cup \mathbf{PX}_2 \cup \mathbf{Q} \\ &= (\mathbf{PX}_1 \cup \mathbf{Q}) \cup (\mathbf{PX}_2 \cup \mathbf{Q}) \\ &= \mathbf{X}_1 \cup \mathbf{X}_2 \end{aligned}$$

Since $\mathbf{X}_1$ and $\mathbf{X}_2$ are distinct, one of $\mathbf{X}_1$ and $\mathbf{X}_2$ must be properly contained in $\mathbf{X}_0$. Suppose that $\mathbf{X}_1 \subset \mathbf{X}_0$, and let $\mathbf{A}$ be the difference

$$\mathbf{A} = \mathbf{X}_0 - \mathbf{X}_1$$

Then

$$\mathbf{A} \neq \varnothing \qquad \mathbf{X}_0 = \mathbf{X}_1 \cup \mathbf{A} \qquad \mathbf{A} \cap \mathbf{X}_1 = \varnothing$$

Since $\mathbf{X}_0$ is a solution, we have

$$\begin{aligned} (\mathbf{X}_1 \cup \mathbf{A}) &= \mathbf{P}(\mathbf{X}_1 \cup \mathbf{A}) \cup \mathbf{Q} \\ &= \mathbf{PA} \cup (\mathbf{PX}_1 \cup \mathbf{Q}) \\ &= \mathbf{PA} \cup \mathbf{X}_1 \end{aligned}$$

Intersecting both sides of the last equation with $\mathbf{A}$ gives

$$(\mathbf{A} \cap \mathbf{X}_1) \cup (\mathbf{A} \cap \mathbf{A}) = (\mathbf{A} \cap \mathbf{PA}) \cup (\mathbf{A} \cap \mathbf{X}_1)$$

Since $\mathbf{A} \cap \mathbf{X}_1 = \varnothing$, this becomes

$$\mathbf{A} = \mathbf{A} \cap \mathbf{PA} \tag{1}$$

Since $\mathbf{A} \neq \varnothing$, there exists a shortest string $\omega_0$ in $\mathbf{A}$. By equation (1), $\omega_0 \in \mathbf{A} \cap \mathbf{PA}$, and therefore $\omega_0 \in \mathbf{PA}$. It follows that

$$\omega_0 = \alpha\beta, \qquad \text{where} \quad \alpha \in \mathbf{P} \quad \text{and} \quad \beta \in \mathbf{A}$$

Since $\lambda \notin \mathbf{P}$ by assumption, $|\alpha| \geq 1$ and therefore $|\beta| < |\omega_0|$. Since $\beta \in \mathbf{A}$, this contradicts the statement that no string in $\mathbf{A}$ is shorter than $\omega_0$. Thus the assumption that $\mathbf{X}_1 \neq \mathbf{X}_2$ leads to a contradiction, and we conclude that all sets that satisfy $\mathbf{X} = \mathbf{PX} \cup \mathbf{Q}$ must be identical. Since $\mathbf{P}^*\mathbf{Q}$ is a solution, it must be unique.

We now apply Theorem 5.4 to show that the reduction procedure developed in the previous paragraphs produces a unique solution to the system of set equations derived from any finite-state accepter, and that this solution consists of the end sets of the accepter.

**Proposition 5.3:** Let $\mathbf{M} = (\mathbf{Q}, \mathbf{S}, \mathbf{P}, \mathbf{I}, \mathbf{F})$ be an FSA with states $\mathbf{Q} = \{q_1, \ldots, q_n\}$ and let

$$\mathbf{V}_{ij} = \{s \in \mathbf{S} \mid q_i \xrightarrow{s} q_j \text{ in } \mathbf{M}\}$$

$$\mathbf{W}_k = \begin{cases} \boldsymbol{\lambda} & \text{if } q_k \in \mathbf{F} \\ \varnothing & \text{otherwise} \end{cases}$$

Then the right-linear system

$$\mathbf{E}_k = \bigcup_{j=1}^{n} \mathbf{V}_{kj}\mathbf{E}_j \cup \mathbf{W}_k, \qquad k = 1, 2, \ldots, n$$

has a unique solution such that

$$\mathbf{L}(\mathbf{M}) = \bigcup_{q_k \in \mathbf{I}} \mathbf{E}_k$$

where $\mathbf{E}_1, \ldots, \mathbf{E}_n$ are the end sets of $\mathbf{M}$.

***Proof:***

*Existence*: The end sets are defined by

$$\mathbf{E}_k = \{\omega \in \mathbf{S}^* \mid q_k \overset{\omega}{\Longrightarrow} q \text{ for some } q \in \mathbf{F}\}$$

From Proposition 5.2, the end sets $\mathbf{E}_1, \ldots, \mathbf{E}_n$ of $\mathbf{M}$ are a solution of the equation system.

*Uniqueness*: Suppose that $\mathbf{E}_1, \ldots, \mathbf{E}_n$ are arbitrary subsets of $\mathbf{S}^*$ that form a solution of the equation system. We shall use Theorem 5.4 to show that each set $\mathbf{E}_k$ is unique.

None of the sets $\mathbf{V}_{ij}$ in the equation system contains $\lambda$. In particular, $\lambda \notin \mathbf{V}_{11}$ in the $\mathbf{E}_1$ equation. Therefore, by Theorem 5.4,

$$\mathbf{E}_1 = \mathbf{V}_{11}^*\left(\bigcup_{j=2}^{n} \mathbf{V}_{j1}\mathbf{E}_j \cup \mathbf{W}_1\right)$$

must be a unique solution of the $\mathbf{E}_1$ equation. Substituting this expression for $\mathbf{E}_1$ into the other equations of the system produces a new system that must be satisfied by $\mathbf{E}_2, \ldots, \mathbf{E}_n$. Again, the coefficients of the sets $\mathbf{E}_2, \ldots, \mathbf{E}_n$ in the system do not contain $\lambda$. Repeating this procedure results, after $n$ steps, in an expression for $\mathbf{E}_n$ in terms of constant sets. From Theorem 5.4, the solutions for the unknowns at each step are unique, and thus the fixed set denoted by this expression is the only possible value of $\mathbf{E}_n$ in any solution to the equation system.

Since the numbering of the states of $\mathbf{M}$ is immaterial, this uniqueness argument applies separately to each set $\mathbf{E}_k$, $k = 1, \ldots, n$. Therefore, the complete solution of the equation system is unique.

Applying the elimination procedure to a right-linear system results in a regular expression for each end set. Since $\mathbf{L}(\mathbf{M})$ is the union of some of the end sets, a regular expression for **L(M)** is easily obtained. We have therefore established the following theorem, which is half of Kleene's important result about finite-state machines.

**Theorem 5.5:** Each finite-state accepter recognizes a language that can be described by some regular expression.

The other half of Kleene's result is the converse of Theorem 5.5: each regular expression describes a set recognized by some finite-state accepter. This is the subject of the next section.

### 5.3.4 Accepters for Regular Sets

We wish to show how a finite-state accepter can be constructed for the set of strings described by an arbitrary regular expression $\alpha$. The synthesis is carried out recursively by combining accepters for subexpressions of $\alpha$. We start with primitive accepters for

1. The empty set $\varnothing$.
2. The set $\boldsymbol{\lambda}$.
3. The set **a**, for each symbol *a* in the appropriate alphabet **V**.

Then, given that accepters $\mathbf{M}_1$ and $\mathbf{M}_2$ recognize arbitrary regular sets $\mathbf{R}_1$ and $\mathbf{R}_2$, we show how $\mathbf{M}_1$ and $\mathbf{M}_2$ can be combined to create an accepter for each of the sets

$$\mathbf{R}_1 \cup \mathbf{R}_2 \qquad \mathbf{R}_1 \cdot \mathbf{R}_2 \qquad \mathbf{R}_1^*$$

For the construction, it will be convenient to assume that each accepter has exactly one initial state with no entering transitions, and exactly one accepting state with no exiting transitions. Example 5.13 demonstrates the difficulties that arise in the construction if this is not the case.

**Example 5.13:** In Figure 5.14a, accepter $\mathbf{M}_1$ recognizes the set $\mathbf{R}_1 =$ **01***, and accepter $\mathbf{M}_2$ recognizes the set $\mathbf{R}_2 =$ **0*10**. To obtain an accepter for $\mathbf{R}_1 \cup \mathbf{R}_2$, it would be convenient to merge the two initial states and to merge the two final states, as in Figure 5.14b. It is obvious from the diagram that this new machine recognizes **0*01*** $\cup$ **0*101***, rather than **01*** $\cup$ **0*10** as intended. Also, if we attempt to find an accepter for $\mathbf{R}_1 \cdot \mathbf{R}_2$ by merging the final state of $\mathbf{M}_1$ with the initial state of $\mathbf{M}_2$, we obtain instead the accepter for **0(0** $\cup$ **1)*10** shown in Figure 5.14c.

In either case, the combined machine recognizes a larger set of strings than desired.

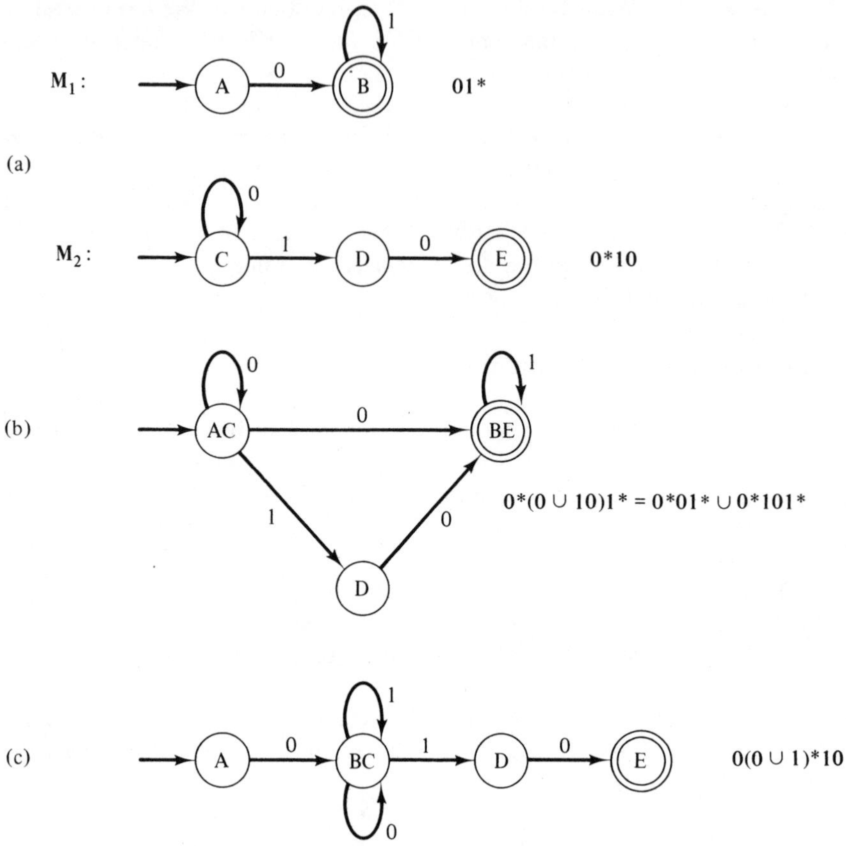


**Figure 5.14.** Undesired path formed by merging accepting and initial states.

The difficulties exposed by Example 5.13 are due to the transition leaving the final state of $\mathbf{M}_1$ and the transition entering the initial state of $\mathbf{M}_2$. These transitions create undesired paths when the state diagrams are combined. If we prohibit such transitions in the accepters used in the construction, complications arise in the case of machines that accept the empty string. A better approach is to use accepters in which *$\lambda$-transitions* are permitted. We digress to study accepters with $\lambda$-transitions, and return to the construction of finite-state accepters from regular expressions in Section 5.3.6.

### 5.3.5 Accepters with Lambda Transitions

A *lambda transition*

$$q \xrightarrow{\lambda} q'$$

in an accepter **M** signifies that **M** may leave state $q$ and enter state $q'$ without the presentation of an input symbol. In an accepter with $\lambda$-transitions, an admissible state sequence for a string may include arbitrarily many such transitions. For example, the machine in Figure 5.15 accepts the string *acb* via the state sequence

$$A \xrightarrow{\lambda} B \xrightarrow{a} C \xrightarrow{c} C \xrightarrow{\lambda} B \xrightarrow{b} C \xrightarrow{\lambda} D$$

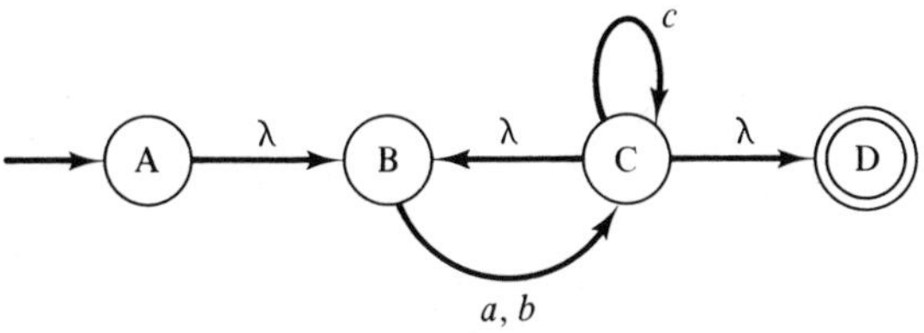


**Figure 5.15.** Accepter with $\lambda$-transtitions.

We define a class of accepters in which $\lambda$-transitions are used to "isolate" single initial and final states.

> **Definition 5.6:** A *$\lambda$-accepter* is a finite-state accepter of the form $\mathbf{M} = (\mathbf{Q}, \mathbf{S}, \mathbf{P}, \mathbf{q}_I, \mathbf{q}_F)$ with $\lambda$-transitions such that
>
> 1. **M** has exactly one initial state, $q_I$, with no transitions entering and only $\lambda$-transitions exiting.
> 2. **M** has exactly one final state, $q_F$, with no transitions exiting and only $\lambda$-transitions entering,
>
> Note that conditions 1 and 2 imply $q_I \neq q_F$.

We must show that the class of $\lambda$-accepters is equivalent to the class of finite-state accepters. To this end, we shall show how to convert any finite-state accepter to a $\lambda$-accepter, and *vice versa*.

The conversion of a finite-state accepter to a $\lambda$-accepter, illustrated in Figure 5.16, is straightforward:

1. Let $\mathbf{M} = (\mathbf{Q}, \mathbf{S}, \mathbf{P}, \mathbf{I}, \mathbf{F})$ be an arbitrary FSA. We wish to construct a $\lambda$-accepter $\mathbf{M}' = (\mathbf{Q}', \mathbf{S}, \mathbf{P}', \mathbf{q}_I, \mathbf{q}_F)$ such that $\mathbf{L}(\mathbf{M}') = \mathbf{L}(\mathbf{M})$. Let

$$\mathbf{Q}' = \mathbf{Q} \cup \{q_F, q_I\}$$

2. The transitions of **M**′ include all the transitions of **M** and the new $\lambda$-transitions

$$q_I \xrightarrow{\lambda} q \qquad \text{for each } q \in \mathbf{I}$$

$$q' \xrightarrow{\lambda} q_F \qquad \text{for each } q' \in \mathbf{F}$$

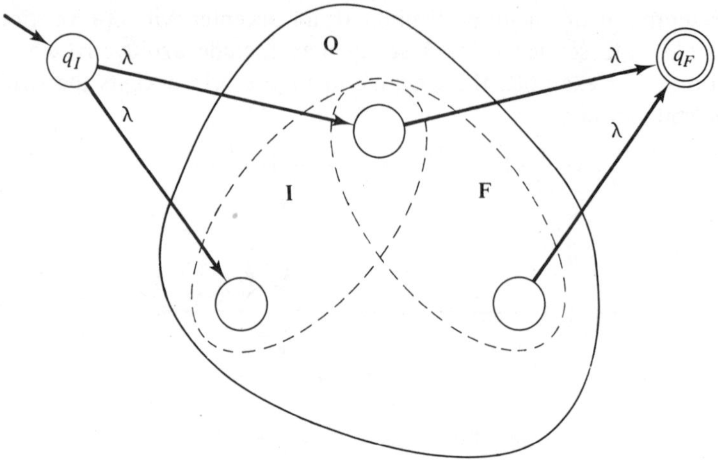


**Figure 5.16.** Construction of a $\lambda$-accepter.

The reader should convince himself that the construction does not alter the language recognized by the accepter.

We must now show that any $\lambda$-accepter **M** can be changed into a finite-state accepter **M**$'$ such that $\mathbf{L}(\mathbf{M}') = \mathbf{L}(\mathbf{M})$. We shall do this in two steps.

First, suppose that **M** has a loop of $\lambda$-transitions

$$q_0 \xrightarrow{\lambda} q_1 \xrightarrow{\lambda} \cdots \xrightarrow{\lambda} q_n \xrightarrow{\lambda} q_0$$

in which $q_0, q_1, \ldots, q_n$ are all distinct states. (Note that by Definition 5.6 no such loop will ever contain the initial state or the final state of the accepter.) Then the end sets of $q_0, q_1, \ldots, q_n$ are identical, because if a state sequence for a string leads from any state of the loop to the final state, then a state sequence for that string leads from *every* state of the loop to the final state. Thus the states in any $\lambda$-loop may be merged into a single state, and this is the first step in the construction of an FSA from a $\lambda$-accepter:

*Step 1:* Suppose that the $\lambda$-accepter $\mathbf{M} = (\mathbf{Q}, \mathbf{S}, \mathbf{P}, \mathbf{q}_I, \mathbf{q}_F)$ contains a loop of $\lambda$-transitions. Let $\mathbf{Q}_\ell \subseteq \mathbf{Q}$ be the states in the loop. Construct the $\lambda$-accepter $\mathbf{M}' = (\mathbf{Q}', \mathbf{S}, \mathbf{P}', \mathbf{q}_I, \mathbf{q}_F)$ without the loop as follows:

1. $\mathbf{Q}' = (\mathbf{Q} - \mathbf{Q}_\ell) \cup \{q_\ell\}$.
2. If **M** has the transition

$$q_1 \xrightarrow{s} q_2, \qquad s \in (\mathbf{S} \cup \{\lambda\})$$

then **M**$'$ has a transition

$$q_1' \xrightarrow{s} q_2'$$

where

$$q_1' = \begin{cases} q_\ell & \text{if } q_1 \in \mathbf{Q}_\ell \\ q_1 & \text{otherwise} \end{cases} \qquad q_2' = \begin{cases} q_\ell & \text{if } q_2 \in \mathbf{Q}_\ell \\ q_2 & \text{otherwise} \end{cases}$$

Repeat the construction until no $\lambda$-loops remain.

We note that, if **M** is an accepter without $\lambda$-loops, a state sequence consisting only of $\lambda$-transitions cannot have repeated appearances of states. For each state $q$, the paths into $q$ consisting only of $\lambda$-transitions constitute a loop-free $\lambda$*-subgraph* of **M** as suggested in Figure 5.17a.

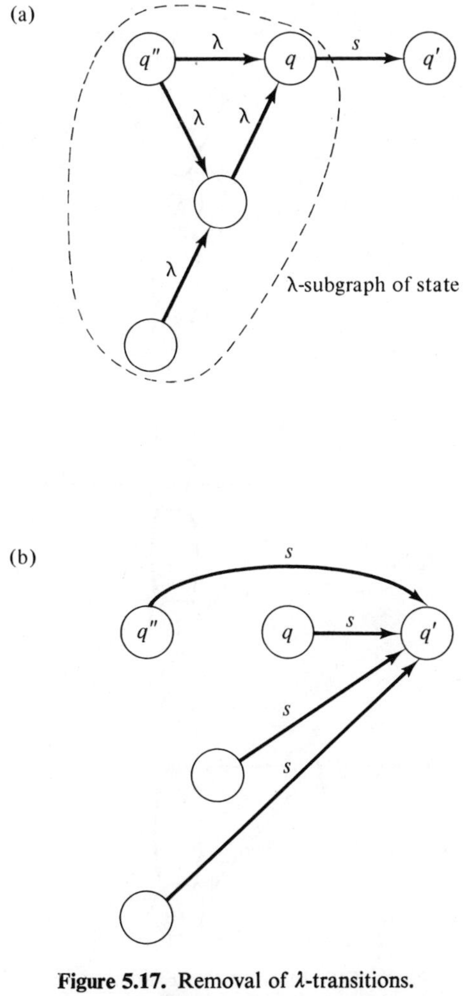


**Figure 5.17.** Removal of $\lambda$-transitions.

A transition

$$q \xrightarrow{s} q'$$

in **M** implies

$$q'' \overset{s}{\Longrightarrow} q'$$

for any state $q''$ in the $\lambda$-subgraph of $q$. Adding the transition

$$q'' \xrightarrow{s} q'$$

to **M** provides a similar path in the accepter that does not contain $\lambda$-transitions. This motivates step 2 of the construction:

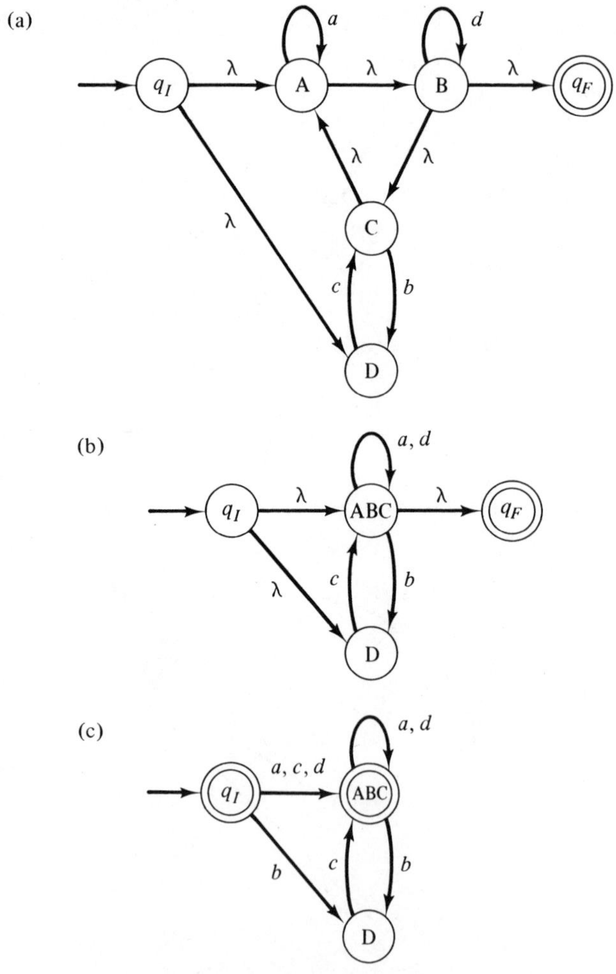


**Figure 5.18.** Machines for Example 5.14.

*Step 2:* Let $\mathbf{M} = (\mathbf{Q}, \mathbf{S}, \mathbf{P}, \mathbf{q}_I, \mathbf{q}_F)$ be a $\lambda$-accepter with no $\lambda$-loops. Construct an FSA $\mathbf{M}' = (\mathbf{Q}', \mathbf{S}, \mathbf{P}', \mathbf{q}_I, \mathbf{F}')$ as follows:

1. $\mathbf{Q}' = \mathbf{Q} - \{q_F\}$.
2. $\mathbf{F}' = \{q \in \mathbf{Q} \mid q \overset{\lambda}{\Longrightarrow} q_F \text{ in } \mathbf{M}\}$.
3. The transitions of $\mathbf{M}'$ are
   a. Each transition $q \xrightarrow{s} q'$ in $\mathbf{M}$ where $s \in \mathbf{S}$.
   b. The transition $q'' \xrightarrow{s} q'$ whenever $\mathbf{M}$ has a state sequence

$$q'' \overset{\lambda}{\Longrightarrow} q \xrightarrow{s} q'.$$

We leave it to the reader to verify that the final $\lambda$-free machine $\mathbf{M}'$ recognizes the same language as the $\lambda$-accepter $\mathbf{M}$.

The result of applying step 2 to the subgraph of Figure 5.17a is illustrated by Figure 5.17b.

**Example 5.14:** Figure 5.18a shows a $\lambda$-accepter with a $\lambda$-loop. Figure 5.18b shows the machine after step 1 of the construction, in which states A, B, and C have been merged to eliminate the loop. The machine obtained after step 2 of the construction is shown in Figure 5.18c.

### 5.3.6 Constructing an Accepter from a Regular Expression

The construction of $\lambda$-accepters for $\mathbf{R}_1 \cup \mathbf{R}_2$, $\mathbf{R}_1 \bullet \mathbf{R}_2$, and $\mathbf{R}_1^*$ from $\lambda$-accepters for $\mathbf{R}_1$ and $\mathbf{R}_2$ is straightforward, as shown in Figure 5.19. A $\lambda$-accepter for $\mathbf{R}_1 \cup \mathbf{R}_2$ is obtained by merging the initial states $q_{I1}$ and $q_{I2}$ and the accepting states $q_{F1}$ and $q_{F2}$. A $\lambda$-accepter for $\mathbf{R}_1 \bullet \mathbf{R}_2$ is obtained by merging the accepting state $q_{F1}$ of $\mathbf{M}_1$ with the initial state $q_{I2}$ of $\mathbf{M}_2$. The initial and final states of the composite accepter are $q_{I1}$ and $q_{F2}$, respectively. A $\lambda$-accepter for $\mathbf{R}_1^*$ is obtained by merging states $q_{I1}$ and $q_{F1}$ of $\mathbf{M}_1$, and then adding new initial and accepting states $q_I$ and $q_F$. (These new states are needed so that the resulting accepter is a $\lambda$-accepter.) The primitive elements for the construction are the $\lambda$-accepters shown in Figure 5.20 for the one-symbol regular expressions.

**Theorem 5.6:** For any regular expression $\alpha$ on an alphabet $\mathbf{V}$, one can construct a finite-state accepter $\mathbf{M}$ such that $\mathbf{L}(\mathbf{M}) = \mathbf{R}$, where $\mathbf{R}$ is the set described by $\alpha$.

***Proof:*** Without loss of generality, we may construct $\mathbf{M}$ as a $\lambda$-accepter. The proof is an induction on the length $|\alpha|$ of the regular expression.

***Basis:*** If $|\alpha| = 1$, then $\alpha$ is either $\varnothing$, $\boldsymbol{\lambda}$, or a symbol in $\mathbf{V}$, and $\mathbf{M}$ is one of the $\lambda$-accepters shown in Figure 5.20.

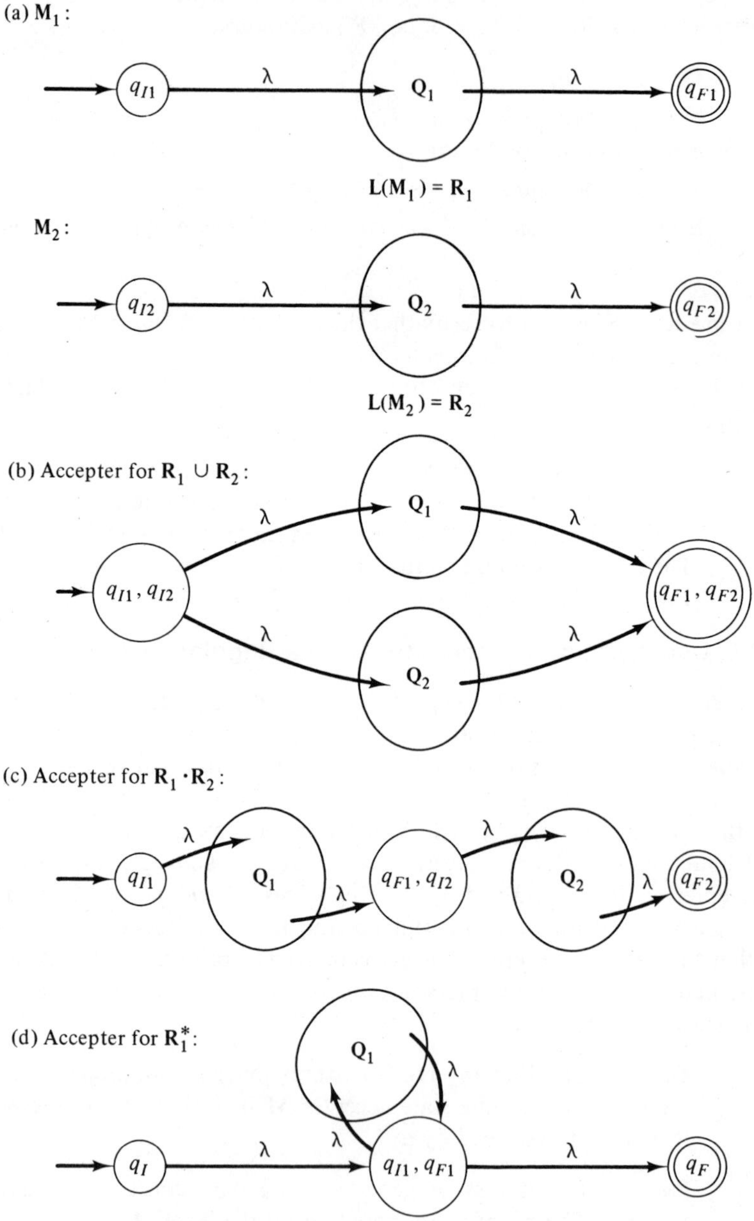


**Figure 5.19.** Recursive construction of $\lambda$-accepters.

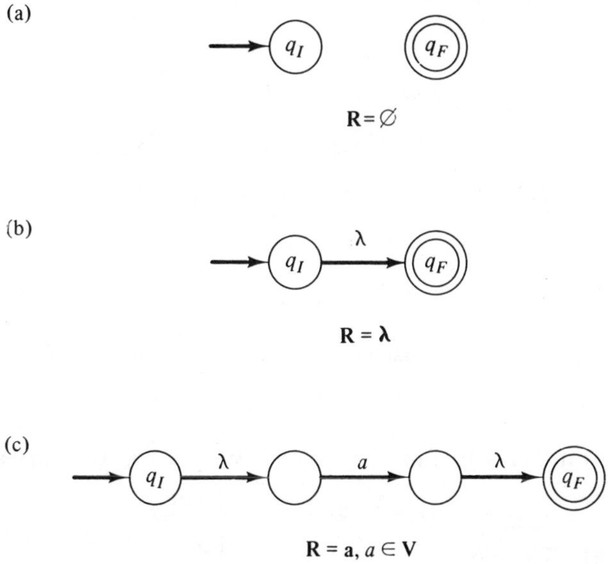


**Figure 5.20.** Lambda-accepters for regular expressions of length 1.

***Induction:*** Assume that whenever $1 \leq |\alpha| < k$ the theorem is true, and let $\alpha$ be any expression such that $|\alpha| = k$. Then one of

1. $\alpha = (\alpha_1 \cup \alpha_2)$.
2. $\alpha = (\alpha_1 \alpha_2)$.
3. $\alpha = \alpha_1^*$.

must hold by Definition 5.5, where $|\alpha_1| < k$ and $|\alpha_2| < k$. By the induction hypothesis, there exist $\lambda$-accepters $\mathbf{M}_1$ and $\mathbf{M}_2$ such that $\mathbf{L}(\mathbf{M}_1)$ is described by $\alpha_1$ and $\mathbf{L}(\mathbf{M}_2)$ is described by $\alpha_2$. We treat the three cases separately.

1. Let **M** be constructed as shown in Figure 5.19a. Then

$$q_I \overset{\omega}{\Longrightarrow} q_F$$

in **M** if and only if

$$q_{I1} \overset{\omega}{\Longrightarrow} q_{F1} \quad \text{or} \quad q_{I2} \overset{\omega}{\Longrightarrow} q_{F2}$$

in $\mathbf{M}_1$ or in $\mathbf{M}_2$, respectively. Hence

$$\mathbf{L}(\mathbf{M}) = \mathbf{L}(\mathbf{M}_1) \cup \mathbf{L}(\mathbf{M}_2)$$

and is described by $\alpha = (\alpha_1 \cup \alpha_2)$.

2. Let **M** be constructed as shown in Figure 5.19b. Then

$$q_I \stackrel{\omega}{\Longrightarrow} q_F$$

in **M** if and only if $\omega = \varphi \cdot \psi$ such that

$$q_{I1} \stackrel{\varphi}{\Longrightarrow} q_{F1} \quad \text{and} \quad q_{I2} \stackrel{\psi}{\Longrightarrow} q_{F2}$$

in $\mathbf{M}_1$ and in $\mathbf{M}_2$, respectively. Hence

$$\mathbf{L(M)} = \mathbf{L(M_1)} \cdot \mathbf{L(M_2)}$$

and is described by $\alpha = \alpha_1\alpha_2$.

3. Let **M** be constructed as shown in Figure 5.19c. Then

$$q_I \stackrel{\omega}{\Longrightarrow} q_F$$

in **M** if and only if $\omega = \lambda$, or $\omega = \varphi_1\varphi_2 \ldots \varphi_n$ for some $n \geq 1$, and

$$q_{I1} \stackrel{\varphi_i}{\Longrightarrow} q_{F1}, \qquad i = 1, 2, \ldots, n$$

in $\mathbf{M}_1$. Therefore,

$$\mathbf{L(M)} = \mathbf{L(M_1)}^*$$

and is described by $\alpha = \alpha_1^*$.

Theorems 5.5 and 5.6 together constitute *Kleene's theorem*: a language is described by a regular expression if and only if it is recognized by some finite-state accepter.

**Example 5.15:** The construction of a finite-state accepter for the regular set ((**b*a** ∪ **ab***)**c**)* is shown in Figure 5.21. In the primitive accepters for **b*a**, **ab***, and **c**, $\lambda$-transitions have been included only where required to isolate an initial or final state. All $\lambda$-transitions introduced in combining the state diagrams have been retained.

**Example 5.16:** To show how a loop of $\lambda$-transitions may arise, consider constructing a state diagram for the regular expression

$$\alpha = ((\mathbf{ab})^*(\mathbf{ac})^* \cup \mathbf{a})^*$$

The construction of a $\lambda$-accepter from $\alpha$ is shown in Figure 5.22. Collapsing the $\lambda$-loop gives the machine $\mathbf{M}_5$, and eliminating the remaining $\lambda$-transitions yields $\mathbf{M}_6$. Accepter $\mathbf{M}_6$ shows that the expression $\alpha$ is equivalent to

$$\beta = (\mathbf{ab} \cup \mathbf{ac} \cup \mathbf{a})^*$$

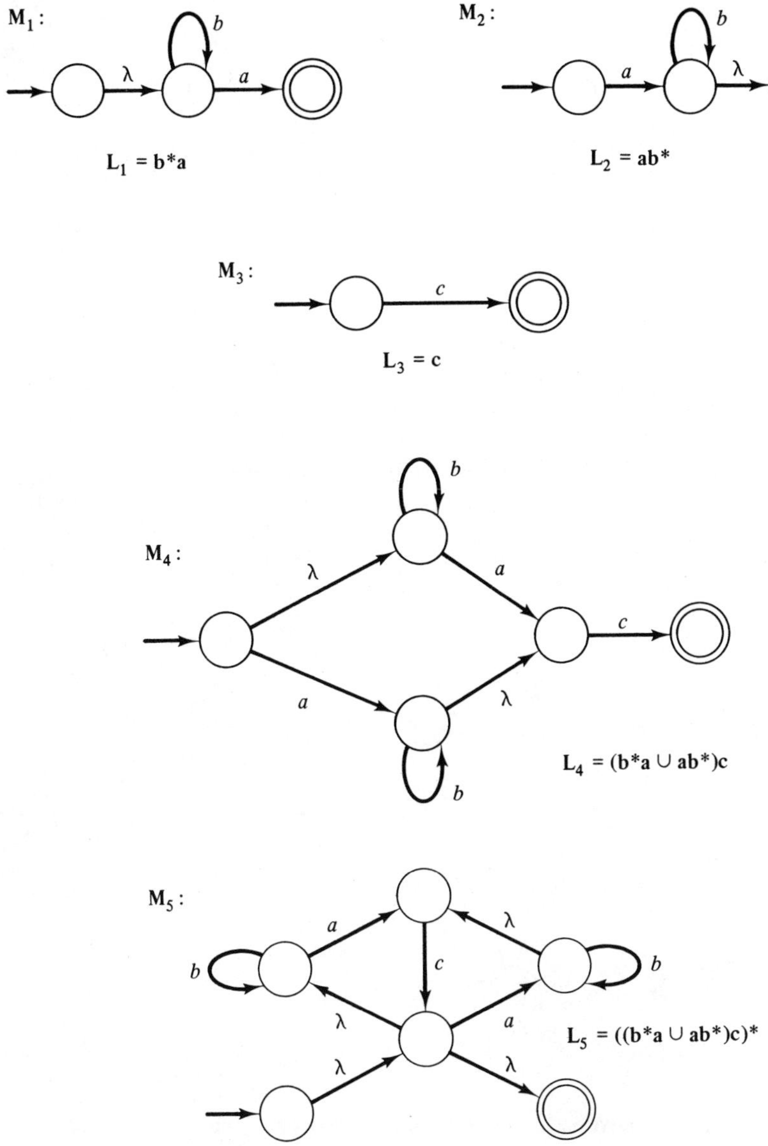


**Figure 5.21.** Construction of an accepter for a regular set.

Example 5.16 suggests that the synthesis and analysis of state diagrams according to Kleene's theorem is a useful way of demonstrating the equivalence of regular expressions.

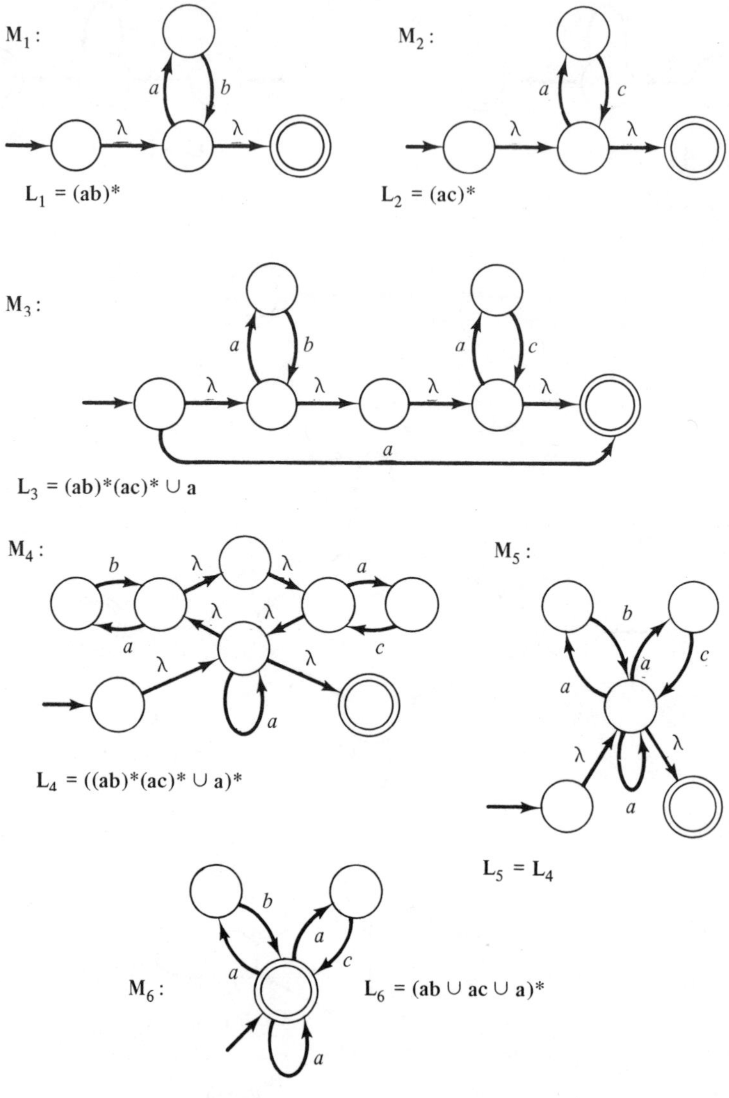


**Figure 5.22.** Construction that creates a $\lambda$-loop.

**Example 5.17:** Figure 5.23 shows the steps involved in proving the equivalence

$$\alpha^*(\beta\alpha^*)^* = (\alpha \cup \beta)^*$$

by means of state diagrams and Kleene's theorem. In Figure 5.23d, the two states are equivalent; hence this state diagram reduces to Figure 5.23e.

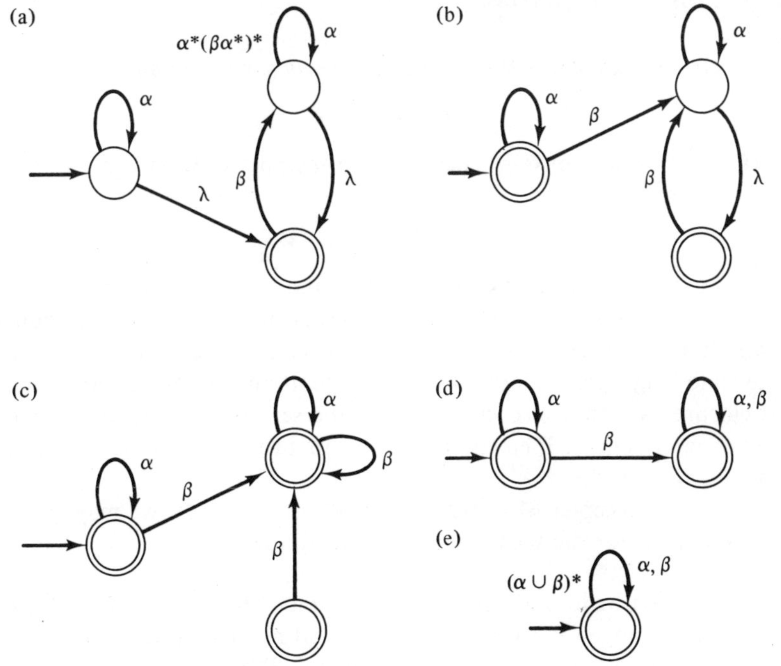


**Figure 5.23.** Proof of an equivalence using Kleene's theorem.

## 5.4 Properties of Finite-State Languages

The developments in this chapter have established the equivalence of three representations for languages. If **L** is a language on some alphabet **V**, these three statements are equivalent:

1. **L** is generated by some regular grammar.
2. **L** is recognized by some finite-state accepter.
3. **L** is described by some regular expression.

Thus we may use the terms *regular set*, *regular language*, and *finite-state language* interchangeably.

If we wish to prove an assertion about finite-state languages, three approaches are always available: we may prove the assertion in terms of (1) the languages generated by right- or left-linear grammars, (2) the sets recognized by finite-state accepters, or (3) the languages described by regular expressions. Frequently, arguments expressed in terms of finite-state machines are the most intuitive and the easiest to understand.

### 5.4.1 Closure Properties

A class of languages $\mathbf{C}$ is *closed under a unary operation*

$$F: \mathbf{C} \longrightarrow \mathbf{C}$$

if $F(\mathbf{L})$ is a member of $\mathbf{C}$ whenever $\mathbf{L}$ is a member of $\mathbf{C}$; it is *closed under a binary operation*

$$G: \mathbf{C} \times \mathbf{C} \longrightarrow \mathbf{C}$$

if $G(\mathbf{L}_1, \mathbf{L}_2)$ is a member of $\mathbf{C}$ whenever $\mathbf{L}_1$ and $\mathbf{L}_2$ are members of $\mathbf{C}$.

Since a finite-state accepter can be constructed for the union or concatenation of any two regular sets, or for the closure of a regular set, the class of finite-state languages is closed under the operations of union, concatenation, and closure. Are they also closed under the set operation of complementation? of intersection? Elementary arguments provide answers to both questions.

Given an accepter $\mathbf{M} = (\mathbf{Q}, \mathbf{S}, \mathbf{P}, \mathbf{I}, \mathbf{F})$ for the set $\mathbf{R}$, we may construct an accepter $\mathbf{M}'$ for the set $\mathbf{R}^c = \mathbf{S}^* - \mathbf{R}$ as follows:

1. Convert $\mathbf{M}$ into a deterministic accepter $\mathbf{M}'' = (\mathbf{Q}'', \mathbf{S}, \mathbf{P}'', \mathbf{I}'', \mathbf{F}'')$.
2. Interchange the roles of accepting and nonaccepting states in $\mathbf{M}''$ to obtain $\mathbf{M}'$; that is $\mathbf{M}' = (\mathbf{Q}'', \mathbf{S}, \mathbf{P}'', \mathbf{I}'', \mathbf{Q}'' - \mathbf{F}'')$.

It is clear that $\mathbf{L}(\mathbf{M}') = \mathbf{L}(\mathbf{M})^c$. (Why is it necessary to perform step 1?) Thus the complement of a regular set is always a regular set.

That the intersection of regular sets is regular follows from the De Morgan law

$$\mathbf{R}_1 \cap \mathbf{R}_2 = (\mathbf{R}_1^c \cup \mathbf{R}_2^c)^c \tag{1}$$

and the closure of regular sets under complementation and union. Given accepters for sets $\mathbf{R}_1$ and $\mathbf{R}_2$, we may construct accepters for sets $\mathbf{R}_1^c$ and $\mathbf{R}_2^c$ as described above, and combine their state diagrams to obtain an accepter $\mathbf{M}$ for $\mathbf{R}_1^c \cup \mathbf{R}_2^c$. We may then construct an accepter $\mathbf{M}'$ for $(\mathbf{L}(\mathbf{M}))^c$, again as described above. From (1), $\mathbf{L}(\mathbf{M}') = \mathbf{R}_1 \cap \mathbf{R}_2$, and thus the finite-state languages are closed under intersection.

It is also instructive to obtain these results directly through the parallel combination of accepters. Let us regard the two accepters $\mathbf{M}_1$ and $\mathbf{M}_2$ in Figure 5.24 as being physically combined to form a machine $\mathbf{M}$. Because we wish to regard $\mathbf{M}_1$ and $\mathbf{M}_2$ as operating independently but on the same input string, they must be deterministic accepters:

$$\mathbf{M}_1 = (\mathbf{Q}_1, \mathbf{S}, \mathbf{P}_1, \mathbf{q}_{I1}, \mathbf{F}_1)$$

$$\mathbf{M}_2 = (\mathbf{Q}_2, \mathbf{S}, \mathbf{P}_2, \mathbf{q}_{I2}, \mathbf{F}_2)$$

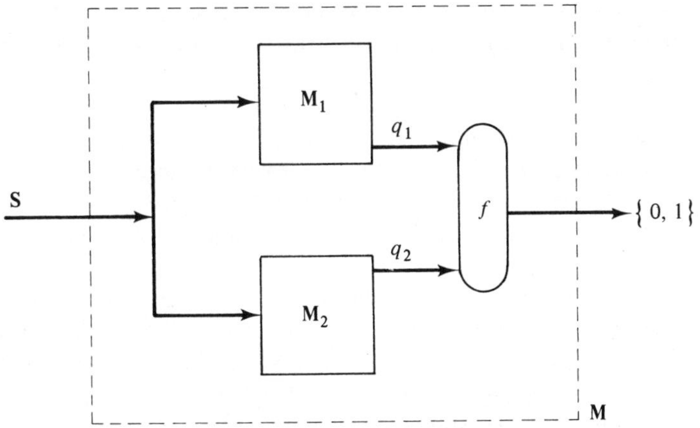


**Figure 5.24.** Parallel combination of deterministic accepters.

Suppose that the combined machine $\mathbf{M}$ accepts strings that leave $\mathbf{M}_1$ and $\mathbf{M}_2$ in combinations of states for which a given function

$$f\colon\ \mathbf{Q}_1 \times \mathbf{Q}_2 \longrightarrow \{0, 1\}$$

has the value 1. The construction of $\mathbf{M}$ is as follows:

1. $\mathbf{Q} = \mathbf{Q}_1 \times \mathbf{Q}_2$.
2. $q_I = (q_{I1}, q_{I2})$.
3. $\mathbf{F} = \{(q_1, q_2) \mid f(q_1, q_2) = 1\}$.
4. $\mathbf{P} = \left\{(q_1, q_2) \xrightarrow{s} (q_1', q_2') \,\middle|\, \begin{matrix} q_1 \xrightarrow{s} q_1' \text{ is in } \mathbf{P}_1 \\ q_2 \xrightarrow{s} q_2' \text{ is in } \mathbf{P}_2 \end{matrix}\right\}$.

As usual,

$$\mathbf{L(M)} = \{\omega \in \mathbf{S}^* \mid q_I \overset{\omega}{\Longrightarrow} q \text{ and } q \in \mathbf{F}\}$$

Particular choices of the function $f$ produce machines for the union, intersection, difference, and complement of the languages $\mathbf{L(M_1)}$ and $\mathbf{L(M_2)}$:

1. *Union*: let $f(q_1, q_2) = 1$ if and only if $(q_1 \in \mathbf{F}_1) \vee (q_2 \in \mathbf{F}_2)$. Then $\mathbf{L(M)} = \mathbf{L(M_1)} \cup \mathbf{L(M_2)}$.
2. *Intersection*: let $f(q_1, q_2) = 1$ if and only if $(q_1 \in \mathbf{F}_1) \wedge (q_2 \in \mathbf{F}_2)$. Then $\mathbf{L(M)} = \mathbf{L(M_1)} \cap \mathbf{L(M_2)}$.
3. *Difference*: let $f(q_1, q_2) = 1$ if and only if $(q_1 \in \mathbf{F}_1) \wedge (q_2 \in \mathbf{Q}_2 - \mathbf{F}_2)$. Then $\mathbf{L(M)} = \mathbf{L(M_1)} - \mathbf{L(M_2)}$.
4. *Complement*: let $f(q_1, q_2) = 1$ if and only if $(q_1 \in \mathbf{Q}_1 - \mathbf{F}_1)$. Then $\mathbf{L(M)} = \mathbf{L(M_1)}^c$.

In the last two cases, the construction breaks down if either $\mathbf{M}_1$ or $\mathbf{M}_2$ is nondeterministic; the reader should be sure to understand just where the construction fails.

> **Example 5.18:** Figure 5.25 shows how two simple accepters for languages $\mathbf{L}_1$ and $\mathbf{L}_2$ may be used to derive accepters for $\mathbf{L}_1 \cup \mathbf{L}_2$, $\mathbf{L}_1 \cap \mathbf{L}_2$, and $\mathbf{L}_1 - \mathbf{L}_2$, according to the choice of accepting states in the state diagram for the parallel combination of the two accepters.

We now know that the class of finite-state languages is closed under the operations of intersection, difference, and complementation, as well as union, concatenation, and closure. Since every finite-state language is also a regular set, the class of finite-state languages is closed under reversal by the arguments of Section 5.3.1. We summarize these facts as a theorem.

> **Theorem 5.7:** The class of finite-state languages is closed under the operations of set union, intersection, complementation, difference, concatenation, closure, and reversal. That is, if $\mathbf{L}_1$ and $\mathbf{L}_2$ are finite-state languages, then so are the following:
>
> 1. $\mathbf{L}_1 \cup \mathbf{L}_2$.
> 2. $\mathbf{L}_1 \cap \mathbf{L}_2$.
> 3. $\mathbf{L}_1^c$.
> 4. $\mathbf{L}_1 - \mathbf{L}_2$.
> 5. $\mathbf{L}_1 \bullet \mathbf{L}_2$.
> 6. $\mathbf{L}_1^*$.
> 7. $\mathbf{L}_1^R$.

It is important to understand the distinction between combining two machines in the manner just described and combining state diagrams as in the proof of Kleene's theorem. The manner of this section amounts to setting two physical, deterministic machines side by side and considering them as one; in the proof of Kleene's theorem, we consider two state diagrams as jointly representing the behavior of one machine. Combining state diagrams in the latter case has no convenient interpretation in terms of physical machines. In particular, the new state set is $\mathbf{Q}_1 \times \mathbf{Q}_2$ when physical machines are combined, but $\mathbf{Q}_1 \cup \mathbf{Q}_2$ when state diagrams are combined. For this reason, the machines that result from these methods are known as *product machines* and *sum machines*, respectively.

There is no simple way to directly combine nondeterministic accepters to obtain accepters for the intersection or difference of two finite-state languages. This is indicative of the difficulties we shall encounter in trying to apply these operations to context-free languages.

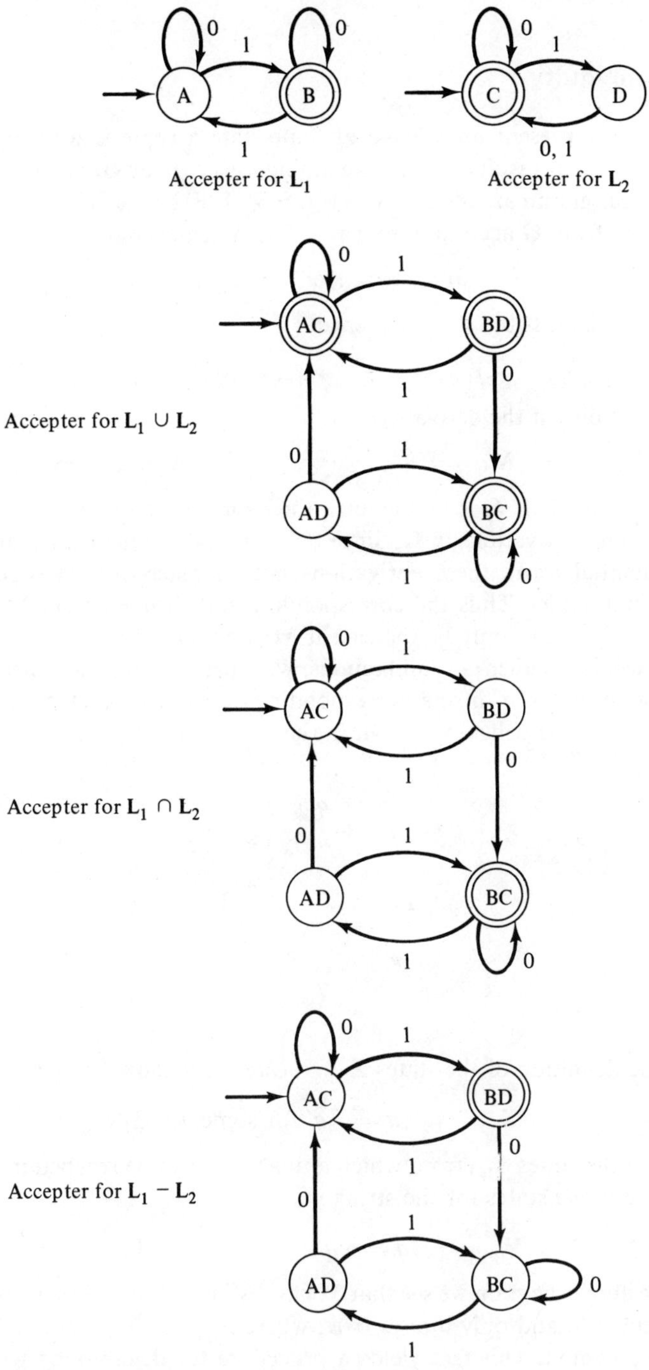


**Figure 5.25.** Machines for Example 5.18.

### 5.4.2 Ambiguity

With our present knowledge of finite-state accepters, we can establish several important results concerning ambiguous regular grammars. Let **G** be a right-linear grammar, and let $\mathbf{M} = (\mathbf{Q}, \mathbf{S}, \mathbf{P}, \mathbf{I}, \mathbf{F})$ be the finite-state accepter constructed from **G** according to Table 5.2. A sentence

$$\omega = s_1 s_2 \ldots s_k, \qquad s_i \in \mathbf{S}$$

will have an admissible state sequence

$$q_0 \xrightarrow{s_1} q_1 \xrightarrow{s_2} \ldots \xrightarrow{s_k} q_k, \qquad q_0 \in \mathbf{I}, q_k \in \mathbf{F}$$

in **M** if and only if the derivation

$$\Sigma \Longrightarrow N(q_0) \Longrightarrow s_1 N(q_1) \Longrightarrow \ldots \Longrightarrow s_1 \ldots s_{k-1} N(q_{k-1}) \Longrightarrow s_1 \ldots s_{k-1} s_k$$

is permitted in **G**. If **G** is ambiguous, then some string $\omega$ will have two (or more) distinct derivations in **G**. Since only one nonterminal ever appears in each sentential form, these derivations must replace distinct sequences of nonterminal letters. Thus the corresponding state sequences in **M** will also be distinct. This can only be the case if **M** is nondeterministic.

To decide whether **G** is ambiguous, we must determine whether there is a pair of states $q$ and $q'$ in the corresponding accepter **M** such that for some string $\omega = \varphi\psi$ the behavior shown in the following diagram is possible:

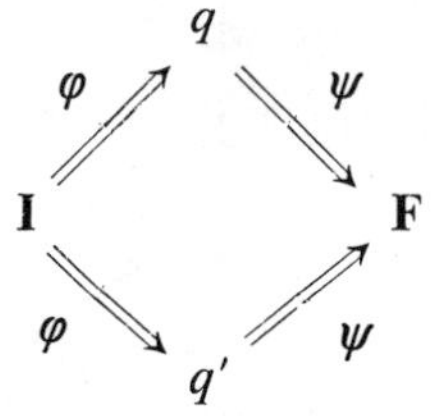


Recall the definition of the states $\mathbf{X}_{[\varphi]}$ *reachable* for the string $\varphi$:

$$\mathbf{X}_{[\varphi]} = \{q' \mid q \overset{\varphi}{\Longrightarrow} q' \text{ for some } q \in \mathbf{I}\}$$

Let us call the states $\mathbf{Y}_{[\psi]}$ from which a final state can be reached in response to $\psi$ the *leavable* states for the string $\psi$:

$$\mathbf{Y}_{[\psi]} = \{q \mid q \overset{\psi}{\Longrightarrow} q' \text{ for some } q' \in \mathbf{F}\}$$

From the above diagram we see that **M** has distinct admissible state sequences for a string $\omega$ if and only if $\omega = \varphi \cdot \psi$, where $\mathbf{X}_{[\varphi]}$ and $\mathbf{Y}_{[\psi]}$ have at least two states in common. This fact yields a procedure for determining whether an arbitrary right-linear grammar **G** is ambiguous and, if so, for finding multiple derivations of some string in **L(G)**:

1. Let **M** be the FSA constructed from **G** using Table 5.2.

2. Construct the tree diagram of reachable sets for **M** starting from $\mathbf{X}_{[\lambda]} = \mathbf{I}$.

3. Construct the tree diagram of leavable sets for **M** starting from $\mathbf{Y}_{[\lambda]} = \mathbf{F}$.

4. The grammar **G** is ambiguous if and only if some set of two or more states appears in both tree diagrams.

5. Each string that labels a path from **I** to **F**, and is incident on the set found in step 4, has ambiguous derivations in **G**.

This procedure will always terminate because the tree diagrams can have no more than $2^n$ nodes for an $n$-state accepter **M**, and only a finite number of comparisons of sets will be required.

**Theorem 5.8:** There is a finite procedure for deciding whether an arbitrary right-linear grammar is ambiguous, and, if so, for finding an ambiguous sentence generated by the grammar.

**Example 5.19:** The right-linear grammar

$$
\begin{array}{lll}
\Sigma \longrightarrow A & A \longrightarrow 1B & C \longrightarrow 0B \\
 & B \longrightarrow 0B & C \longrightarrow 1C \\
 & B \longrightarrow 0C & C \longrightarrow 1
\end{array}
$$

corresponds by Table 5.2 to the accepter in Figure 5.26. The tree of reachable sets and the tree of leavable sets are also shown in the figure. Since the two-element set {B, C} appears in both trees, we conclude that the grammar is ambiguous. In particular, the state sequences

$$\mathrm{A} \xrightarrow{1} \mathrm{B} \xrightarrow{0} \mathrm{B} \xrightarrow{0} \mathrm{B} \xrightarrow{0} \mathrm{C} \xrightarrow{1} \mathrm{D}$$

$$\mathrm{A} \xrightarrow{1} \mathrm{B} \xrightarrow{0} \mathrm{C} \xrightarrow{0} \mathrm{B} \xrightarrow{0} \mathrm{C} \xrightarrow{1} \mathrm{D}$$

correspond to distinct derivations of the string 10001.

A theorem analogous to Theorem 5.8 can be obtained for left-linear grammars, using techniques similar to those of Example 5.11. The details are left as an exercise.

If a regular grammar is ambiguous, we can always find an equivalent grammar that is unambiguous.

**Theorem 5.9:** For any regular grammar **G**, it is possible to construct an unambiguous grammar **G′** such that **L(G′)** = **L(G)**.

***Proof:*** We use Table 5.2 to construct an FSA **M** such that **L(M)** = **L(G)**. We then convert **M** to an equivalent deterministic accepter

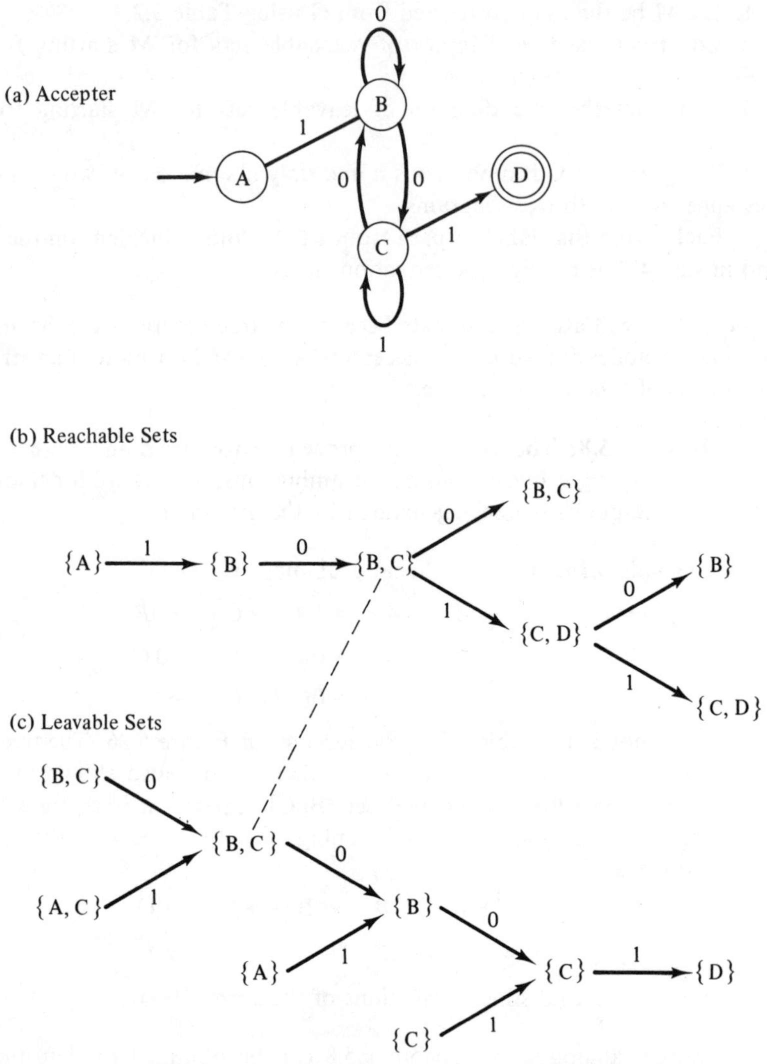


**Figure 5.26.** Finding ambiguity in a regular grammar.

**M′**. Using Table 5.1, we construct a grammar **G′** from **M′** such that **L(G′)** = **L(M′)**. Since **M′** is deterministic, **G′** must be unambiguous.

Theorems 5.8 and 5.9 are of particular interest because their generalizations to wider classes of grammars are not valid. We shall see in Chapter 12, for example, that there is no general procedure to determine whether a given context-free grammar is ambiguous, or to find an ambiguous string even if we know the grammar is ambiguous, or to construct an equivalent unambiguous grammar.

### 5.4.3 Decision Problems

Given a class of objects $\mathfrak{C}$, a predicate

$$p: \quad \mathfrak{C} \longrightarrow \{true, false\}$$

is said to be *decidable* if there is a terminating step-by-step procedure for deciding whether $p(x)$ is true or false for any $x$ in $\mathfrak{C}$. A procedure that produces the correct answer for each member of $\mathfrak{C}$ is an *algorithm* or *effective procedure* for the predicate $p$. The concept of an effective procedure will be studied formally in later chapters of this book; for the present, the informal definition just given will suffice.

Most of the reasonable questions posed about finite-state languages are decidable. From our present knowledge of finite-state machines, we can easily devise algorithms for answering some of these questions.

**Theorem 5.10:** Let $\mathbf{L}_1$ and $\mathbf{L}_2$ be arbitrary finite-state languages, and let $\mathbf{G}$ be an arbitrary regular grammar. Then it is decidable whether

1. $\mathbf{L}_1 = \mathbf{L}_2$.
2. $\mathbf{L}_1 = \varnothing$.
3. $\mathbf{L}_1$ is finite; $\mathbf{L}_1$ is infinite.
4. $\mathbf{L}_1 \cap \mathbf{L}_2 = \varnothing$.
5. $\mathbf{L}_1 \subseteq \mathbf{L}_2$.
6. $\mathbf{G}$ is ambiguous.

***Proof:*** We outline the steps by which each question may be answered.

1. Construct accepters for $\mathbf{L}_1$ and $\mathbf{L}_2$, convert them to deterministic accepters, and test for equivalence.

2. Let $\mathbf{M}_1$ be an accepter for $\mathbf{L}_1$. Then $\mathbf{L}_1 = \varnothing$ if and only if there is no path in $\mathbf{M}_1$ from any initial state to any final state. This is always possible to determine, because in an $n$-state accepter it is only necessary to consider paths of length less than $n$.

3. Let $\mathbf{M}_1$ be an $n$-state accepter for $\mathbf{L}_1$. The reader may verify that $\mathbf{L}(\mathbf{M}_1)$ is infinite if and only if $\mathbf{M}_1$ accepts some string $\omega$ for which $|\omega| \geq n$.

4. Construct an accepter $\mathbf{M}$ for $\mathbf{L}_1 \cap \mathbf{L}_2$ (Theorem 5.7). Then $\mathbf{L}_1 \cap \mathbf{L}_2 = \varnothing$ if and only if $\mathbf{L}(\mathbf{M}) = \varnothing$, which is decidable by (2).

5. $\mathbf{L}_1 \subseteq \mathbf{L}_2$ if and only if $\mathbf{L}_1 \cap \mathbf{L}_2^c = \varnothing$. We need only construct an accepter $\mathbf{M}$ for $\mathbf{L}_1 \cap \mathbf{L}_2^c$ and test whether $\mathbf{L}(\mathbf{M}) = \varnothing$.
6. Theorem 5.8.

In subsequent chapters we shall see that many important questions that are decidable for finite-state languages are undecidable for less restricted classes of languages.

## Notes and References

Nondeterministic finite-state machines were proposed by M. O. Rabin and D. Scott [1959], who demonstrated that this generalization did not increase the capabilities of the machines. Although we have drawn heavily on the properties of nondeterministic machines in this chapter, our major results (summarized in the first paragraph of Section 5.4) were established prior to 1959 in terms of deterministic accepters.

The equivalence of the class of languages accepted by finite-state accepters and that generated by type 3 grammars was demonstrated by Chomsky and Miller [1958]. The relation between these languages and those described by regular expressions was discovered by Kleene [1956]. (His regular expressions differ slightly from ours, and his finite-state accepters were the "nerve nets" of McCulloch and Pitts [1943]; see also Minksy [1967].) McNaughton and Yamada [1960] reaffirmed Kleene's result, and extended it to include regular expressions in which the operations of set intersection and complement were permitted. Brzozowski [1964] described the construction of the characteristic set equations, which we have used in several parts of this chapter.

Most of the closure properties of regular sets described in Theorem 5.7 follow immediately from Kleene's theorem and the relations among the various set operations. The closure of regular languages under reversal was pointed out by Rabin and Scott [1959]; other closure properties (some of which are explored in Problems 5-30 through 5-33) were given by Bar-Hillel, Perles, and Shamir [1961], by Ginsburg and Rose [1963], and by Ginsburg and Spanier [1963]. The decidability result expressed as part 3 of Theorem 5.10 was established by Rabin and Scott [1959].

## Problems

5.1. Design a nondeterministic finite-state accepter that accepts
   a. Any binary string containing an occurrence of one of the substrings 10100, 10110, 010111.
   b. The language $\mathbf{L} = \{10, 101, 110\}^*$.

   In each case, try to construct directly (that is, without recourse to the techniques of Section 5.1.2) an equivalent deterministic accepter.

5.2. Convert each of machines a to c to an equivalent deterministic finite-state accepter. In each case, describe informally the language accepted by the machines.

(a)

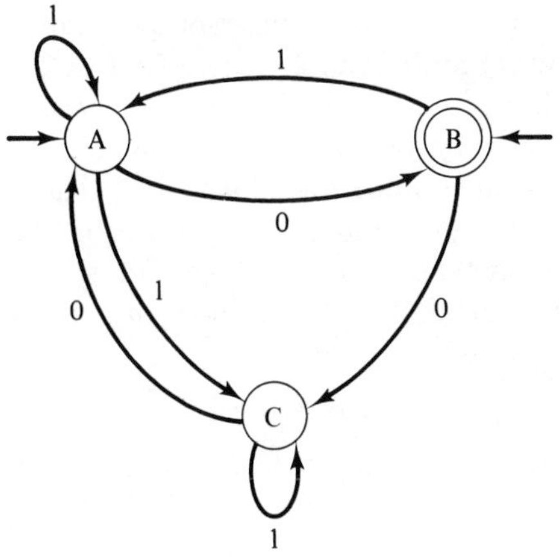


(b)

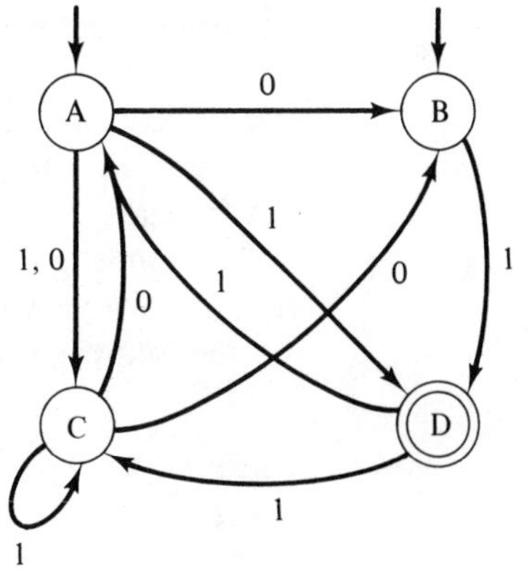


(c)

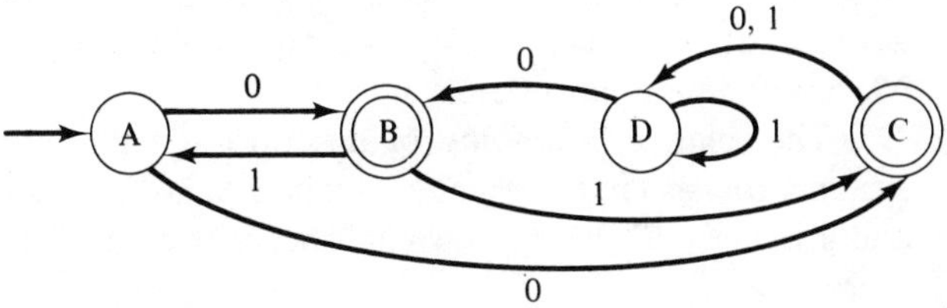


5.3. Let $\mathbf{S} = \{a, b, c, d\}$, and let $\mathbf{L}$ be the language consisting of all strings in $\mathbf{S}^*$ in which at least one of the symbols in $\mathbf{S}$ appears an odd number of times.

a. Design an eight-state nondeterministic FSA for $\mathbf{L}$. Using the techniques of Section 2.5.1, construct an equivalent deterministic accepter and eliminate redundant and nonaccessible states. How many states are in the deterministic machine?

b. Generalize the result of part a. That is, prove that if $\mathbf{S}$ contains $n$ symbols, there exists a $2n$-state nondeterministic accepter for $\mathbf{L}$ and a $2^n$-state deterministic accepter for $\mathbf{L}$.

*c. Prove that if $\mathbf{S}$ has $n$ symbols, no deterministic accepter for $\mathbf{L}$ can have fewer than $2^n$ states. [*Hint:* Show that if $\mathbf{M}$ is a deterministic accepter for $\mathbf{L}$ with fewer than $2^n$ states, there exist input strings $\omega, y$ such that (1) both strings lead $\mathbf{M}$ to the same state, and (2) some symbol in $\mathbf{S}$ occurs in $\omega$ an odd number of times and in $\gamma$ an even number of times. Show that the existence of such strings implies incorrect behavior on the part of **M**.]

***5.4.** Let **M** be an arbitrary $n$-state FSA, and let **M**$'$ be the deterministic FSA constructed from **M** according to the techniques of Section 5.1.2. Since each state of **M**$'$ corresponds to some subset of the states of **M**, the accepter **M**$'$ can contain no more than $2^n$ states. That is, $2^n$ is an upper bound on the number of states in the reduced deterministic accepter equivalent to an arbitrary $n$-state FSA.

Prove that this bound is achievable for all $n > 0$; that is, show that for each $n > 0$ there exists an $n$-state FSA which is equivalent to no deterministic FSA with fewer than $2^n$ states. (*Hint:* For any $n > 0$, let $\mathbf{M}_n$ be an FSA with input alphabet $\{0, 1\}$, state set $\{q_0, q_1, \ldots, q_{n-1}\}$, and the following transitions:

$$q_i \xrightarrow{1} q_{i+1}, \qquad 0 \leq i < n - 1$$

$$q_{n-1} \xrightarrow{1} q_0$$

$$q_i \xrightarrow{0} q_i, \qquad 0 \leq i \leq n - 1$$

$$q_i \xrightarrow{0} q_0, \qquad 0 < i \leq n - 1$$

Show that every subset of $\{q_0, \ldots, q_{n-1}\}$ corresponds to an accessible state in the deterministic accepter constructed from $\mathbf{M}_n$. Show in addition that the deterministic accepter is reduced if the final states of $\mathbf{M}_n$ are chosen appropriately.)

The relative "economy of description" of a number of formal systems for specifying regular languages has been studied by Meyer and Fischer [1971]. The automaton given in the hint was described there.

5.5. From each machine in Problem 5.2, construct a right-linear grammar that generates the language accepted by the machine.

5.6. Let **M** be the following finite-state accepter:

**M:**

| | 0 | 1 | |
|---|---|---|---|
| A | B | C | 1 |
| B | D | E | 0 |
| C | C | A | 1 |
| D | C | E | 0 |
| E | C | E | 0 |

Using the rules in Table 5.1, construct a right-linear grammar **G** such that **L(G)** = **L(M)**. Derive the string 00101 in the grammar and indicate the correspondence of the derivation with **M**'s state sequence for the input 00101.

5.7. Consider the following accepters $\mathbf{M}_1$ and $\mathbf{M}_2$:

$\mathbf{M}_1$:

| | 0 | 1 | |
|---|---|---|---|
| A | A | B | 1 |
| B | C | B | 0 |
| C | B | B | 1 |

$\mathbf{M}_2$:

| | 0 | 1 | |
|---|---|---|---|
| A | A | B | 1 |
| B | C | D | 0 |
| C | B | D | 1 |
| D | C | D | 0 |

Using Table 5.1, construct right-linear grammars for $\mathbf{L}(\mathbf{M}_1)$ and $\mathbf{L}(\mathbf{M}_2)$. Prove that the grammars generate the same language.

**5.8.** Let **M** = (**Q**, **S**, **P**, **I**, **F**) be a finite-state accepter. The *begin set* **B**($q$) of a state $q$ of **M** is the collection of strings that can lead to $q$ from some initial state of **M**:

$$\mathbf{B}(q) = \{\omega \mid q' \xrightarrow{\omega} q,\ q' \in \mathbf{I}\}$$

a. Verify the following assertions:

(1) $\lambda \in \mathbf{B}(q)$ if and only if $q \in \mathbf{I}$.

(2) Suppose that $\omega = \varphi s$. Then $\omega \in \mathbf{B}(q)$ if and only if $\varphi \in \mathbf{B}(q')$ and $q' \xrightarrow{s} q$ is a transition in **M** for some $q' \in \mathbf{Q}$.

(3) $\mathbf{L}(\mathbf{M}) = \bigcup_{q \in \mathbf{F}} \mathbf{B}(q)$.

Compare the assertions with those of Proposition 5.1.

b. A table of rules for constructing a left-linear grammar from a finite-state accepter follows:

*Given:* An FSA **M** = (**Q**, **S**, **P**, **I**, **F**) with begin sets $\{\mathbf{B}(q) \mid q \in \mathbf{Q}\}$
*Construct:* A left-linear grammar **G** = (**N**, **T**, **P**, **Σ**) with $\mathbf{N} = \{N(q) \mid q \in \mathbf{Q}\}$, such that $\mathbf{L}(\mathbf{G}, N(q)) = \mathbf{B}(q)$, $q \in \mathbf{Q}$, and **L(G)** = **L(M)**

| Rule | If **M** has | then **G** has | Reason |
|---|---|---|---|
| 1 | $\mathbf{I} \cap \mathbf{F} = \varnothing$ | $\Sigma \longrightarrow \lambda$ | ? |
| 2 | $q \in \mathbf{F}$ | $\Sigma \longrightarrow N(q)$ | ? |
| 3 | $q \xrightarrow{s} q',\ q \in \mathbf{I}$ | $N(q') \longrightarrow s$ | ? |
| 4 | $q \xrightarrow{s} q'$ | $N(q') \longrightarrow N(q)s$ | ? |

Using the results of part a, provide the justification for each of rules 1 to 4.

c. Using the preceding construction, construct left-linear grammars from the accepters $\mathbf{M}_1$ and $\mathbf{M}_2$ of Problem 5.7. Derive the string 10010 in each grammar, and compare the derivations with the state sequences of the corresponding accepters for input 10010.

5.9. Let **M** be an arbitrary finite-state accepter. Let $\mathbf{G}_R$ be the right-linear grammar obtained from **M** according to the rules of Table 5.1, and let $\mathbf{G}_L$ be the left-linear grammar obtained from **M** according to the rules developed in Problem 5.8. If $\mathbf{G}_R$ is ambiguous, must $\mathbf{G}_L$ be ambiguous? If $\mathbf{G}_L$ is ambiguous, must $\mathbf{G}_R$ be ambiguous?

5.10. Construct a finite-state accepter for **L**(**G**), where **G** is as follows:

a. **G**:

| | |
|---|---|
| $\Sigma \longrightarrow T$ | $S \longrightarrow 1T$ |
| $\Sigma \longrightarrow \lambda$ | $R \longrightarrow 1S$ |
| $P \longrightarrow 0Q$ | $S \longrightarrow 0P$ |
| $P \longrightarrow 1R$ | $T \longrightarrow 0R$ |
| $T \longrightarrow 1P$ | $S \longrightarrow 1$ |
| $R \longrightarrow 0S$ | $Q \longrightarrow 0$ |
| $Q \longrightarrow 1P$ | |
| $Q \longrightarrow 0T$ | |

b. **G**:

| | |
|---|---|
| $\Sigma \longrightarrow A$ | $D \longrightarrow aC$ |
| $A \longrightarrow aB$ | $D \longrightarrow bC$ |
| $A \longrightarrow aC$ | $D \longrightarrow bB$ |
| $A \longrightarrow bC$ | $B \longrightarrow a$ |
| $B \longrightarrow aD$ | $C \longrightarrow a$ |
| $B \longrightarrow bC$ | $D \longrightarrow b$ |
| $B \longrightarrow aA$ | |
| $C \longrightarrow aC$ | |

c. **G**:

| | |
|---|---|
| $\Sigma \longrightarrow aB$ | $D \longrightarrow bC$ |
| $\Sigma \longrightarrow aC$ | $D \longrightarrow bD$ |
| $B \longrightarrow aA$ | $D \longrightarrow aA$ |
| $C \longrightarrow bD$ | $A \longrightarrow cA$ |
| | $A \longrightarrow c$ |

**5.11.** Using the concepts developed in Problem 5.8, establish rules for the construction of a finite-state accepter from an arbitrary left-linear grammar. (Your rules will be analogous to those presented in Table 5.2.) Using these rules, construct a finite-state accepter for the language **L**(**G**), where **G** is the following grammar:

**G**:

| | | | |
|---|---|---|---|
| $\Sigma \longrightarrow D$ | $B \longrightarrow Ab$ | $D \longrightarrow Da$ | $B \longrightarrow Da$ |
| $\Sigma \longrightarrow C$ | $B \longrightarrow Dc$ | $D \longrightarrow Bc$ | $A \longrightarrow a$ |
| $A \longrightarrow Cb$ | $C \longrightarrow Aa$ | $C \longrightarrow Db$ | $D \longrightarrow c$ |
| $A \longrightarrow Ba$ | $C \longrightarrow Bb$ | $B \longrightarrow Aa$ | $C \longrightarrow b$ |

5.12. For each of the following finite-state accepters, construct and solve the corresponding right-linear set equations to obtain a regular expression for the accepted language:

a.

| | 0 | 1 | |
|---|---|---|---|
| A | B | C | 0 |
| B | A | B | 0 |
| C | B | C | 1 |

b.

| | 0 | 1 | |
|---|---|---|---|
| A | B | D | 0 |
| B | C | A | 0 |
| C | A | B | 1 |
| D | D | C | 1 |

c.

| | 0 | 1 | |
|---|---|---|---|
| A | B | E | 0 |
| B | A | C | 1 |
| C | D | B | 1 |
| D | E | A | 0 |
| E | C | D | 0 |

5.13. For each grammar **G** of Problem 5.10, find a regular expression for **L(G)**. (You should be able to construct the systems of set equations from the grammars themselves, rather than from corresponding accepters.)

5.14. Solve the following systems of set equations for the strings in **A**:

a. $\mathbf{A} = \mathbf{0A} \cup \mathbf{0B} \cup \mathbf{1C} \cup \boldsymbol{\lambda}$
$\mathbf{B} = \mathbf{1A} \cup \mathbf{0B}$
$\mathbf{C} = \mathbf{0C} \cup \mathbf{1B}$

b. $\mathbf{A} = \mathbf{0A} \cup \mathbf{1B} \cup \boldsymbol{\lambda}$
$\mathbf{B} = \mathbf{0A} \cup \mathbf{0B} \cup \mathbf{1C}$
$\mathbf{C} = \mathbf{0C} \cup \mathbf{1A}$

In each case, present the state diagram of an accepter corresponding to the system of equations. Use the accepters to decide if the expressions obtained from the systems are equivalent.

**5.15.** Consider the definition of *begin sets* presented at the end of Section 5.2 and again in Problem 5.8.

a. Show that the begin sets of a finite-state accepter satisfy a system of *left-linear* set equations, that is, a system of equations of the form

$$\mathbf{X} = \mathbf{XP} \cup \mathbf{Q}$$

where **P** and **Q** are arbitrary sets. Describe the system in a manner analogous to that of Proposition 5.2.

b. Following the proof of Theorem 5.4, show that $\mathbf{X} = \mathbf{QP}^*$ is a unique solution to the set equation $\mathbf{X} = \mathbf{XP} \cup \mathbf{Q}$ whenever **P** does not contain the empty string.

c. Using the results of parts a and b, construct and solve the system of left-linear set equations corresponding to the accepters shown in Problem 5.2. In each case, provide a regular expression for the accepted language.

**5.16.** Let **M** be a deterministic finite-state accepter with input alphabet **S** and states $\{q_0, \ldots, q_n\}$.

a. Prove that the begin sets $\mathbf{B}(q_0), \ldots, \mathbf{B}(q_n)$ (see Problem 5.8) are a partition of $\mathbf{S}^*$.

b. Prove that the end sets $\mathbf{E}(q_0), \ldots, \mathbf{E}(q_n)$ need not be a partition of $\mathbf{S}^*$. Under what conditions will they be a partition?

c. Must the begin sets be a partition of $\mathbf{S}^*$ if **M** is a nondeterministic accepter?

5.17. Convert each of the following accepters to $\lambda$-accepters:

(a)

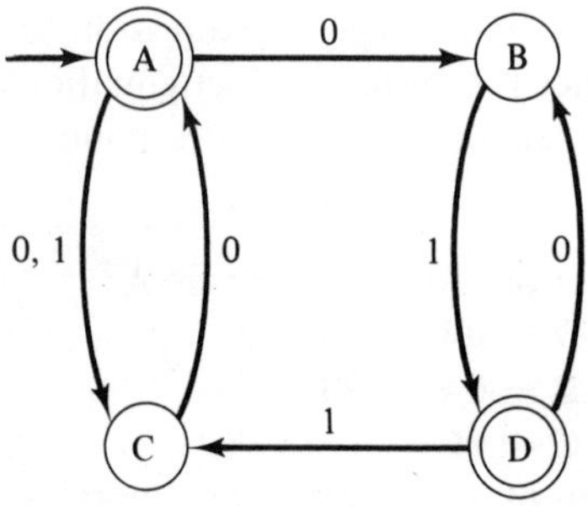


(b)

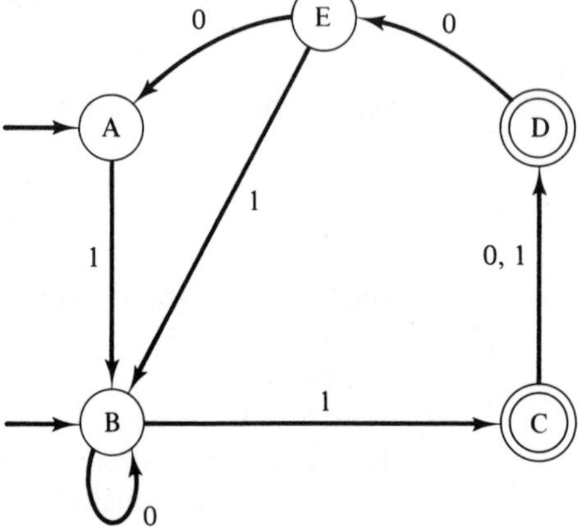


5.18. Convert the following $\lambda$-accepter to an equivalent finite-state accepter:

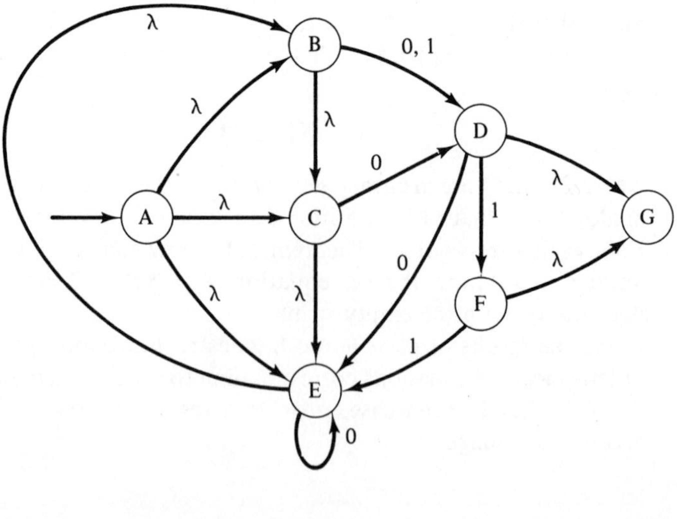

**5.19.** Let **M** be an arbitrary $\lambda$-accepter, and suppose that **M′** is the finite-state accepter without $\lambda$-transitions constructed from **M** in the manner described in Section 5.3.5. Prove that **L(M)** = **L(M′)**.

**5.20.** Let **M** be a $\lambda$-accepter, and let **M′** be a finite-state accepter obtained from **M** according to the construction of Section 5.3.5. Under what conditions on **M** will **M′** be a deterministic accepter?

5.21. Construct $\lambda$-accepters for the following languages **L**:

a. $\mathbf{L} = (\mathbf{00} \cup (\mathbf{10})(\mathbf{101})^* \cup \mathbf{00})^*\mathbf{01}$.

b. $\mathbf{L} = \{00, 010, 1001, 10011, 100111\}^*$.

c. $\mathbf{L} = ((\mathbf{00} \cup \mathbf{11})^* \cup (\mathbf{001} \cup \mathbf{110})^* \cup (\mathbf{0011} \cup \mathbf{1100})^*)^*$.

5.22. Construct a $\lambda$-accepter for the language $\mathbf{L} = (\mathbf{a}^* \cup (\mathbf{ab})^* \cup (\mathbf{abc})^*)^*\mathbf{dc}$. Using the methodology of Section 5.3.5, construct a finite-state accepter for **L**.

5.23. Using Kleene's theorem, prove the following identities:

a. $(\mathbf{00} \cup (\mathbf{00})(\mathbf{11})^*(\mathbf{01} \cup \mathbf{10}))^* = (\mathbf{00} \cup (\mathbf{11})^*\mathbf{10} \cup (\mathbf{11})^*(\mathbf{11})^*\mathbf{01})^*$.

b. $\mathbf{0}^*(\mathbf{11})^*((\mathbf{00})^*\mathbf{0}^*(\mathbf{11})^*)^*\mathbf{0} = \mathbf{0} \cup (\mathbf{0} \cup \mathbf{11} \cup \mathbf{00})(\mathbf{0} \cup \mathbf{11} \cup \mathbf{00})^*$.

5.24. Find a finite-state machine accepting the complement of **L(M)**, where **M** is as follows:

(a)

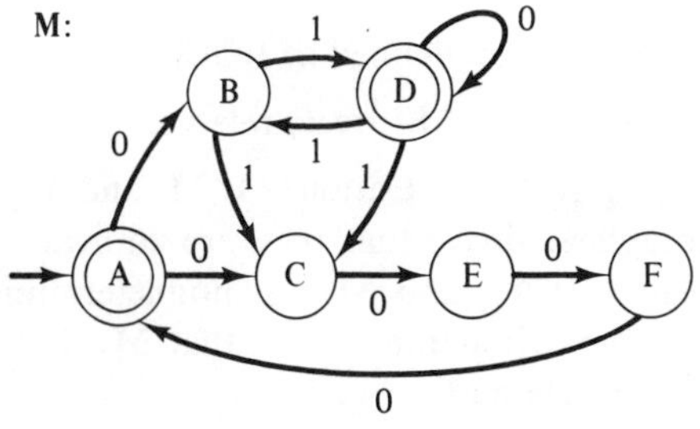


(b)

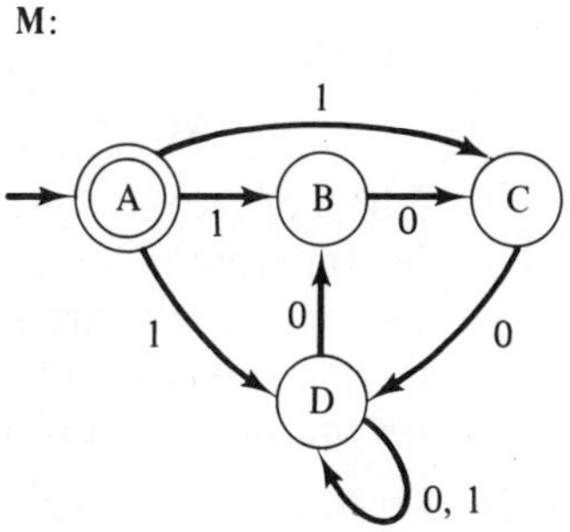


5.25. Using the concept of parallel machine operation, construct a deterministic finite-state accepter for the language $\mathbf{L} = (\mathbf{110}(\mathbf{0} \cup \mathbf{1})^*) \cap ((\mathbf{0} \cup \mathbf{1})^*\mathbf{101})$.

**5.26.** In Section 5.4.1, we showed that particular choices of the function $f$ for the parallel operating accepters of Figure 5.24 produce machines for union, intersection, difference, and complement. If we permit the machines operating in parallel to be nondeterministic accepters, will the indicated choice of $f$ still produce a machine for union? for intersection? for complement? for difference? In each case where the answer is no, will any choice of $f$ produce a machine for the given operation?

**5.27.** Let $\mathbf{M}_1$ and $\mathbf{M}_2$ be finite-state machines with input and output alphabets $\{0, 1\}$, and let $\mathbf{M}$ be the following parallel machine:

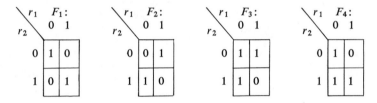

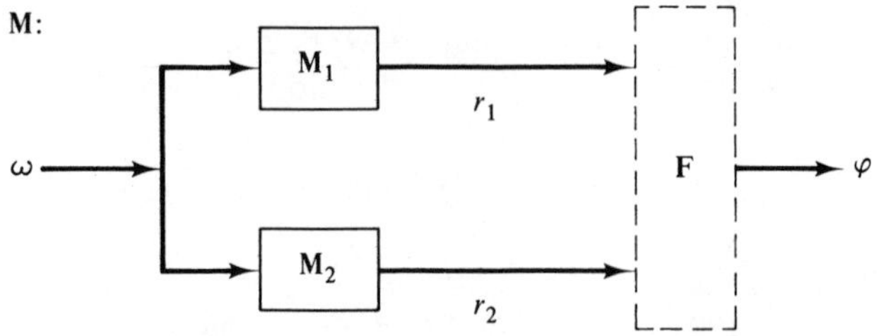


For any Boolean function $F$, we say that $\mathbf{M}_1$ and $\mathbf{M}_2$ are *F-related* if the output from $\mathbf{M}$ is always 1, that is, if $\varphi \in \mathbf{1}^*$ for all $\omega \in \{0, 1\}^*$. Let $F_1$, $F_2$, $F_3$, and $F_4$ be defined as follows:

$F_1$:

| $r_2 \backslash r_1$ | 0 | 1 |
|---|---|---|
| 0 | 1 | 0 |
| 1 | 0 | 1 |

$F_2$:

| $r_2 \backslash r_1$ | 0 | 1 |
|---|---|---|
| 0 | 0 | 1 |
| 1 | 1 | 0 |

$F_3$:

| $r_2 \backslash r_1$ | 0 | 1 |
|---|---|---|
| 0 | 1 | 1 |
| 1 | 1 | 0 |

$F_4$:

| $r_2 \backslash r_1$ | 0 | 1 |
|---|---|---|
| 0 | 1 | 0 |
| 1 | 1 | 1 |

For $i = 1, \ldots, 4$, let $\rho_i$ be the relation defined as follows:

$$\mathbf{M}_1 \rho_i \mathbf{M}_2 \qquad \text{just if } \mathbf{M}_1 \text{ and } \mathbf{M}_2 \text{ are } F_i\text{-related}$$

Which of the relations $\rho_i$ are equivalence relations? If $\mathbf{M}_1$ and $\mathbf{M}_2$ are deterministic finite-state accepters, prove that they are equivalent if and only if they are $F_1$-related. If $\mathbf{M}_1$ and $\mathbf{M}_2$ are nondeterministic accepters, is it possible to define a function $F$ such that $\mathbf{M}_1$ and $\mathbf{M}_2$ are equivalent just if they are $F$-related?

5.28. Let $\mathbf{M}$ be a finite-state accepter for the regular set $\mathbf{X}$, and let $\mathbf{X}^R$ be the reverse of $\mathbf{X}$. Describe a method of obtaining from $\mathbf{M}$ an accepter $\mathbf{M}'$ for $\mathbf{X}^R$. Is the method valid if $\mathbf{M}$ is nondeterministic?

5.29. A *proper prefix* of a string $\omega$ is any string $\varphi$ such that $\omega = \varphi\psi$, $\psi \neq \lambda$. A *proper suffix* of a string $\omega$ is any string $\psi$ such that $\omega = \varphi\psi$, $\varphi \neq \lambda$. Let $\mathbf{R}$ be a regular set.

a. Show that $\mathbf{R}' = \{\omega \mid \omega$ is the proper prefix of some string in $\mathbf{R}\}$ is regular.
b. Show that $\mathbf{R}'' = \{\omega \mid \omega$ is the proper suffix of some string in $\mathbf{R}\}$ is regular.
c. Suppose that we define $\mathbf{R}'''$ to be the set $\{\omega \mid \omega = \varphi\psi$, where $\varphi$ is the proper prefix of some string $\alpha \in \mathbf{R}$, and $\psi$ is the proper suffix of some string $\beta \in \mathbf{R}\}$. Is $\mathbf{R}'''$ a regular set?

**5.30.** Let **R** be a regular set and define

$$Min\,(\mathbf{R}) = \{\omega \text{ in } \mathbf{R} \mid \text{no string in } \mathbf{R} \text{ is a proper prefix of } \omega \text{ (see Problem 5.29)}\}$$

$$Max\,(\mathbf{R}) = \{\omega \text{ in } \mathbf{R} \mid \text{no string in } \mathbf{R} \text{ is a proper suffix of } \omega\}$$

a. Find *Min* (**R**) and *Max* (**R**) for $\mathbf{R} = \mathbf{10^*}$; for $\mathbf{R} = (\mathbf{0} \cup \mathbf{1})^*\mathbf{10}$.
b. Show that both *Min* (**R**) and *Max* (**R**) are regular for *any* regular set **R**.

**5.31.** Let $\mathbf{R} \subseteq \mathbf{V}^*$ be a regular set on some alphabet **V**, and let $\alpha$ be a fixed string in $\mathbf{V}^*$. Define *the quotient of* **R** *with respect to* $\alpha$ to be the set $\mathbf{R}/\alpha = \{\beta \mid \beta\alpha \text{ is in } \mathbf{R}\}$. Prove that $\mathbf{R}/\alpha$ is regular. (*Hint:* Consider tracing paths for $\alpha$ back from the final states of an accepter for **R**.)

**5.32.** Let $\mathbf{R} \subseteq \mathbf{V}^*$ be a regular set on some alphabet **V**, and let $\alpha$ be a fixed string in $\mathbf{V}^*$. Define the *derivative of* **R** *with respect to* $\alpha$ to be the set $\mathbf{R}_\alpha = \{\beta \mid \alpha\beta \text{ is in } \mathbf{R}\}$. Prove that $\mathbf{R}_\alpha$ is regular. Given that there exists an $n$-state accepter for **R**, how many distinct derivatives can **R** possess? (*Hint:* Consider adding $\lambda$-transitions to an accepter for **R**.)

**5.33.** Theorem 5.7 states that the family $\mathcal{R}$ of regular sets on a given alphabet **V** is closed under the operations of set union, concatenation, and closure. In addition, we know that $\mathcal{R}$ contains all finite sets in $\mathbf{V}^*$, since each such set is accepted by some finite-state accepter. Show that if $\mathcal{S}$ is any family of sets in $\mathbf{V}^*$ that contains the finite sets and is closed under the operations of set union, concatenation, and closure, then $\mathcal{S}$ contains $\mathcal{R}$. (That is, $\mathcal{R}$ is the *smallest* family of sets in $\mathbf{V}^*$ that is closed under these operations and contains the finite sets.)

5.34. Which of the grammars of Problem 5.10 are ambiguous? For each ambiguous grammar, exhibit multiple derivations of some string generated by the grammar. Convert each ambiguous grammar to an unambiguous grammar generating the same language.

***5.35.** We say that a grammar **G** is *minimal* if no grammar for **L(G)** contains fewer productions than **G**. Let **G** be a right-linear grammar generating a regular set **R**, and suppose that **G** has $n$ productions. What is the maximum number of productions in a minimal unambiguous grammar for **L(G)**? (*Hint:* See Problem 5.4.)

**5.36.** Prove the assertion in part 3 of the proof of Theorem 5.10: an $n$-state FSA **M** accepts infinitely many strings just if **M** accepts a string of length at least $n$.

**5.37.** A word $\omega$ is a *palindrome* if it is its own reverse (that is, if $\omega = \omega^R$); a language is a *palindrome language* just if each of its elements is a palindrome. (See Problem 3.3.) Define a decision procedure for deciding whether a finite-state accepter accepts a palindrome language. In terms of their accepters, how might such languages be characterized?

***5.38.** Let **G** and **G**′ be right-linear grammars. We say that **G**′ is a *reduction* of **G** if **L**(**G**′) = **L**(**G**), and **G**′ has fewer productions than **G**, or **G**′ has the same number of productions as **G** but has fewer nonterminal symbols. We say that a right-linear grammar is *choice free* if, during any derivation permitted by the grammar, only one production is applicable at any but the first step of the derivation. We say that a grammar **G** is *irreducible* if it is choice free and there is no choice-free reduction of **G**.

a. Give a procedure for determining whether a given right-linear grammar is choice free.
b. Give a procedure for determining whether a given right-linear grammar is irreducible.
c. Show how to construct from a given right-linear grammar **G** an irreducible right-linear grammar **G**′ such that **L**(**G**′) = **L**(**G**). (*Hint:* Consider the interpretations of reduced and choice free in terms of a finite-state accepter corresponding to **G**.)

# 6

# *Limitations of Finite Automata*

We have remarked several times in earlier chapters that there are classes of computations beyond the capability of finite-state machines. To appreciate the importance of more powerful classes of automata, the reader must understand the limitations of finite-state automata. This chapter characterizes these limitations and provides examples of tasks that cannot be performed by finite-state machines.

We measure the "power" of a class of automata in terms of its ability to solve *decision problems*. The following are examples of problems that might be presented to an automaton:

1. Is the string $\omega \in (\mathbf{0} \cup \mathbf{1})^*$ of even parity?
2. Does $\omega \in (\mathbf{0} \cup \mathbf{1})^*$ contain more ones than zeros?
3. Is the integer $x$ a perfect square?
4. What is the sum of integers $x$ and $y$?
5. What is the product of integers $x$ and $y$?

Problems 1, 2, and 3 are examples of the general *set membership problem*:

6. Is the string $\omega$ a member of the set $\mathbf{A}$?

We can also express problems 4 and 5 as membership problems. For example, problem 4 can be expressed as follows:

7. Is the string $(x, y, z)$ a member of the set $\mathbf{A} = \{(x, y, z) | z = x + y\}$?

Similarly, problem 5 can be expressed:

8. Is the string $(x, y, z)$ a member of the set $\mathbf{A} = \{(x, y, z) | z = xy\}$?

We specify an *instance* of one of these problems by fixing the values of the variable letters $x, y, z$, or $\omega$. We say that an automaton **M** *solves* an instance of problem $\mathcal{P}$ if, when presented with the values specifying the instance, **M** provides the correct answer in a finite number of steps. The answer may be a *yes–no* decision, or it may be a string of symbols functionally related to the variables of the problem.

Decision problems provide us with a means of comparing the relative power of various classes of automata: *A class of automata* $\mathfrak{M}$ *is* sufficiently powerful *for a problem* $\mathcal{P}$ *if there is a particular machine in* $\mathfrak{M}$ *that solves all instances of* $\mathcal{P}$. We know, for example, that the class of finite-state accepters is sufficiently powerful for the parity problem, since the set of all strings of even parity is regular. Whether the other problems listed can be solved by finite-state devices will be settled in the remainder of this chapter and in the Problems.

Each machine in a class $\mathfrak{M}$ of automata can be described by some string of symbols on a finite alphabet **A**. (For finite-state accepters, a corresponding regular expression will do. For more powerful automata, other finite description schemes will be developed.) The descriptions of the members of $\mathfrak{M}$ constitute a subset of $\mathbf{A}^*$, and $\mathfrak{M}$ is therefore a countable set. Thus the class of membership problems that may be solved by the members of $\mathfrak{M}$ is countable. We have already noted in Chapter 2 that the class of all languages on an alphabet **V**, being the power set of $\mathbf{V}^*$, is uncountable. We are therefore assured that for each class of automata there exist membership problems beyond the power of that class.

The limitations on the problem-solving power of finite-state machines stem from their inability to count arbitrarily large numbers of events. Put another way, a finite-state machine is capable of sorting stimuli into only a fixed, finite number of classes—its memory is bounded. Any problem that requires the sorting of stimuli into an arbitrarily large number of classes is beyond the capabilities of finite-state devices. These limitations are explored in the following sections, regarding the machines first as accepters, then as generators, and finally as transducers.

## 6.1 Limitations of Finite-State Accepters

There are several ways to demonstrate that a given language is not finite state. We may show that

1. There is no finite state accepter for the language; or
2. There is no regular grammar for the language; or
3. There is no regular expression for the language.

Once any one of these statements has been demonstrated, the truth of the other two follows from the results of Chapter 5. In many cases, the most intuitive and easily understood approach uses finite-state accepters. Accordingly, a demonstration that a language **L** is not finite state usually follows this outline:

1. Assume that there exists a finite-state accepter **M** for **L**.
2. Show that because **M** is finite state, **M** must accept certain strings that are not in **L** or must fail to accept certain strings that are in **L**.
3. From this contradiction, conclude that **L** cannot be a finite-state language.

### 6.1.1 A Simple Nonregular Language

Consider the simple matching language

$$\mathbf{L}_m = \{a^k b^k \mid k \geq 1\}$$

whose sentences are the nonempty strings in **a*b*** having equal numbers of $a$'s and $b$'s. This language is generated by the context-free grammar

$$\mathbf{G}\colon\ \Sigma \longrightarrow S \qquad S \longrightarrow aSb$$
$$S \longrightarrow ab$$

The grammar **G** is neither left nor right linear, but this does not imply that *all* grammars for $\mathbf{L}_m$ are nonregular. To show that $\mathbf{L}_m$ is not a regular language we follow the outline given above.

Intuitively, any automaton that recognizes $\mathbf{L}_m$ must be capable of counting an arbitrarily large number of $a$'s for comparison with the number of $b$'s subsequently presented. A finite-state machine, however, can count only as high as the number of its internal states, which is fixed. We therefore expect an alleged finite-state accepter for $\mathbf{L}_m$ to behave improperly when the number of $a$'s exceeds the number of internal states. These ideas are made precise in the following argument.

For the sake of a contradiction, suppose that **M** is a deterministic $n$-state accepter that recognizes $\mathbf{L}_m$. (From Theorem 5.1, there is no difference in the computing power of deterministic and nondeterministic FSA's.) The behavior of **M** is illustrated in Figure 6.1, and is described by the state sequence

$$q_0 \xrightarrow{a} q_1 \xrightarrow{a} \cdots \xrightarrow{a} q_r \xrightarrow{b} q_{r+1} \xrightarrow{b} \cdots \xrightarrow{b} q_{2r}$$

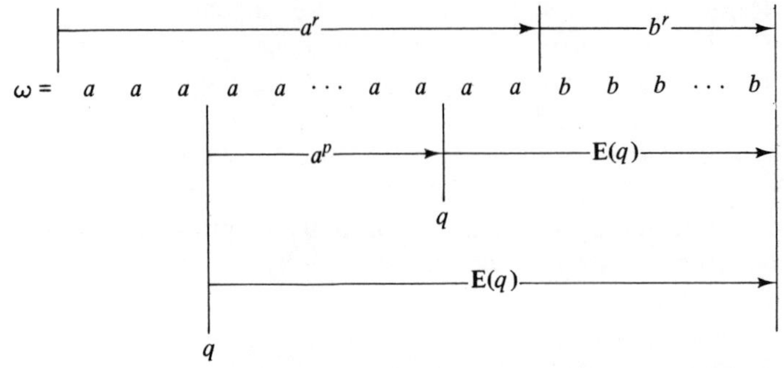


**Figure 6.1.** Illustration for the proof that $\mathbf{L}_m$ is not finite state.

where $q_0 = q_I$ and $q_{2r} \in \mathbf{F}$. If $r \geq n$, some state in the sequence $q_0, q_1, \ldots, q_r$ must repeat; that is, $q_i = q_j = q$ for some $i, j$ with $0 \leq i < j \leq r$. Thus, for the nonzero integer $p = j - i$, the string $a^p$ returns $\mathbf{M}$ to state $q$:

$$q \overset{a^p}{\Longrightarrow} q$$

But then the end set $\mathbf{E}(q)$ satisfies

$$\mathbf{E}(q) \supseteq (\mathbf{a}^p)^*\mathbf{E}(q)$$

and $\mathbf{M}$ accepts all strings in the set

$$\mathbf{a}^{r-p}(\mathbf{a}^p)^*\mathbf{b}^r$$

only one of which is in $\mathbf{L}_m$. Assuming that $\mathbf{M}$ recognizes $\mathbf{L}_m$ has led to a contradiction; therefore, $\mathbf{L}_m$ is not a finite-state language.

Generalizing the idea used above yields an important structure theorem for regular sets.

### 6.1.2 Finite-State Language Theorem

In many cases the following theorem will allow one to conclude that a given language is not a regular set.

> **Theorem 6.1 (Finite-State Language Theorem):** Let $\mathbf{L}$ be a regular set, and suppose that there is an integer $p \geq 0$ such that
>
> $$\mathbf{X} = \{\alpha_1(\alpha_2)^k\alpha_3(\alpha_4)^k\alpha_5 \mid k \geq p\}$$
>
> is contained in $\mathbf{L}$, where $\alpha_1, \ldots, \alpha_5$ are strings with $\alpha_2$ and $\alpha_4$ nonempty. Then there exist strings $\beta_1, \ldots, \beta_5$ such that
>
> $$\mathbf{Y} = \beta_1(\beta_2)^*\beta_3(\beta_4)^*\beta_5$$
>
> is a subset of $\mathbf{L}$, and
>
> $$\beta_1 \in \alpha_1\alpha_2^*$$
> $$\beta_2 \in \alpha_2^* - \boldsymbol{\lambda}$$

$$\beta_3 \in \alpha_2^*\alpha_3\alpha_4^*$$
$$\beta_4 \in \alpha_4^* - \lambda$$
$$\beta_5 \in \alpha_4^*\alpha_5$$

Theorem 6.1 states that a finite-state language containing arbitrarily many strings that have matched repetitions of some pair of substrings ($\alpha_2$ and $\alpha_4$) must also contain arbitrarily many strings in which these substrings are not paired one for one.

***Proof of Theorem 6.1*** (*refer to Figure 6.2.*): Let **M** be an $n$-state deterministic finite-state accepter that recognizes **L**. Suppose that **L**

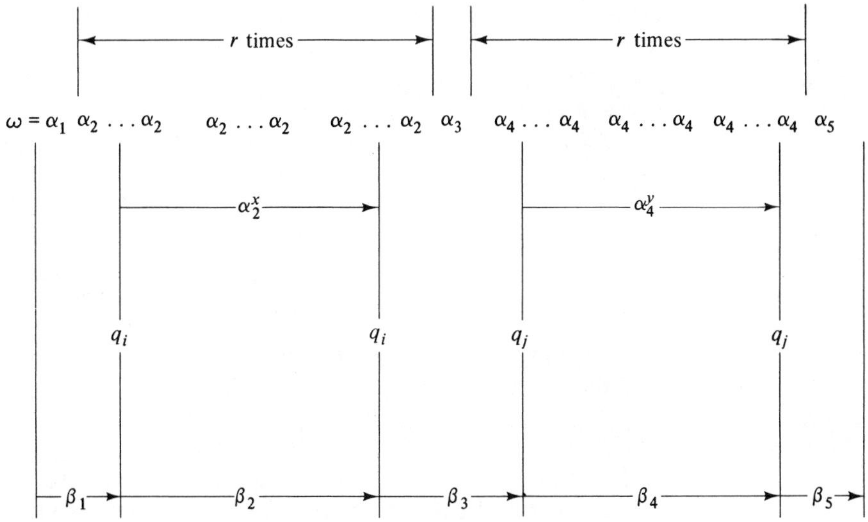


**Figure 6.2.** Illustration for the proof of Theorem 6.1.

contains the set **X** as in the theorem statement. Choose an integer $r \geq \max(n, p)$. The behavior of **M** in response to the string $\omega = \alpha_1(\alpha_2)^r\alpha_3(\alpha_4)^r\alpha_5$ in **X** is described by the state sequence

$$q_0 \overset{\alpha_1}{\Longrightarrow} q_1 \overset{\alpha_2}{\Longrightarrow} \cdots \overset{\alpha_2}{\Longrightarrow} q_{r+1} \overset{\alpha_3}{\Longrightarrow} q_{r+2} \overset{\alpha_4}{\Longrightarrow} \cdots \overset{\alpha_4}{\Longrightarrow} q_{2r+2} \overset{\alpha_5}{\Longrightarrow} q_{2r+3}$$

where $q_0 = q_I$ and $q_{2r+3} \in \mathbf{F}$. Since $r \geq n$, some state, say $q_i$, must repeat in the sequence $q_1, \ldots, q_{r+1}$. Similarly, some state, say $q_j$, must repeat in the sequence $q_{r+2}, \ldots, q_{2r+2}$. Thus there exist integers $x > 0$ and $y > 0$ such that

$$q_i \overset{\alpha_2^x}{\Longrightarrow} q_i \quad \text{and} \quad q_j \overset{\alpha_4^y}{\Longrightarrow} q_j$$

as shown in Figure 6.2. With $\beta_1, \ldots, \beta_5$ as shown in the figure, we have

$$\mathbf{E}(q_i) \supseteq (\beta_2)^* \mathbf{E}(q_i)$$
$$\mathbf{E}(q_j) \supseteq (\beta_4)^* \mathbf{E}(q_j)$$

and therefore

$$\mathbf{Y} = \beta_1(\beta_2)^*\beta_3(\beta_4)^*\beta_5 \subseteq \mathbf{L}$$

A few examples of the application of Theorem 6.1 to familiar sets follow. Additional applications are covered in the Problems.

**Example 6.1 (Parenthesis Language):** The language $\mathbf{L}_p$ contains all well-formed strings of left and right parentheses. This set can be defined recursively by the following three rules:

1. The string ( ) is in $\mathbf{L}_p$.
2. If $\omega$ is in $\mathbf{L}_p$, then $(\omega)$ is in $\mathbf{L}_p$.
3. If $\omega$, $\varphi$ are in $\mathbf{L}_p$, then $\omega\varphi$ is in $\mathbf{L}_p$.

A grammar that generates $\mathbf{L}_p$ is

$$\mathbf{G}_p\colon\ \Sigma \longrightarrow S \qquad S \longrightarrow SS$$
$$S \longrightarrow (S)$$
$$S \longrightarrow ()$$

and so $\mathbf{L}_p$ is a context-free language. To show that $\mathbf{L}_p$ is nonregular, we note that the nonregular set

$$\mathbf{X} = \{(^k)^k \mid k \geq 1\}$$

is contained in $\mathbf{L}_p$. Although $\mathbf{X}$ is not finite state, we cannot immediately conclude that $\mathbf{L}_p$ is not finite state. (Why?) If we assume that $\mathbf{L}_p$ is regular, then by Theorem 6.1 there exist integers $u, v, w, x, y, z$ (with $v \neq 0$, $y \neq 0$) such that

$$\mathbf{Y} = (^u((^v)^*(^w)^x()^y)^*)^z \subseteq \mathbf{L}_p$$

But not every string in $\mathbf{Y}$ has equal numbers of left and right parentheses; thus $\mathbf{Y} \nsubseteq \mathbf{L}_p$. This contradiction establishes that $\mathbf{L}_p$ is not regular.

**Example 6.2 (Mirror-Image Language):** Let $\omega^R$ be the reverse of $\omega$, and consider the *mirror-image* language

$$\mathbf{L}_{mi} = \{\omega\omega^R \mid \omega \in (\mathbf{a} \cup \mathbf{b})^*\}$$

Let $\mathbf{X} \subseteq \mathbf{L}_{mi}$ be the set

$$\mathbf{X} = \{(ab)^k(ba)^k \mid k \geq 1\}$$

If $\mathbf{L}_{mi}$ is a finite-state language, there must exist integers $u, v, w, x, y, z$ (where $v \neq 0$, and $y \neq 0$) such that

$$\mathbf{Y} = (\mathbf{ab})^u((\mathbf{ab})^v)^*(\mathbf{ab})^w(\mathbf{ba})^x((\mathbf{ba})^y)^*(\mathbf{ba})^z$$

is contained in $\mathbf{L}_{mi}$. Since there are members of $\mathbf{Y}$ that are not mirror-image strings, $\mathbf{L}_{mi}$ is nonregular.

A final example shows how closure properties of regular sets can be used to demonstrate that a set is nonregular.

**Example 6.3:** Consider the language $\mathbf{L}_1 = \{a^n b^m \mid n \geq m \geq 1\}$, and assume that $\mathbf{L}_1$ is regular. Since regular sets are closed under reversal, the reverse of $\mathbf{L}_1$

$$\mathbf{L}_1^R = \{b^m a^n \mid n \geq m \geq 1\}$$

must be regular, as must the language

$$\mathbf{L}_2 = \{a^m b^n \mid n \geq m \geq 1\}$$

by symmetry. Also, $\mathbf{L} = \mathbf{L}_1 \cap \mathbf{L}_2$ must be regular, since regular sets are closed under intersection. But $\mathbf{L}$ is the matching language $\mathbf{L}_m = \{a^k b^k \mid k \geq 1\}$, which we know is not regular. Thus we conclude that $\mathbf{L}_1$ is not regular.

## 6.2 Limitations of Finite-State Generators

By regarding transitions as labeled with output symbols rather than input symbols, the state diagram of a finite-state accepter becomes the state diagram of a generator of strings.

**Definition 6.1:** A *finite-state generator* (FSG) is a five-tuple

$$\mathbf{M} = (\mathbf{Q}, \mathbf{R}, \mathbf{P}, \mathbf{I}, \mathbf{F})$$

where $\mathbf{Q}$ is a finite set of states including initial states $\mathbf{I}$ and final states $\mathbf{F}$, $\mathbf{R}$ is a finite output alphabet, and $\mathbf{P}$ is a relation in $\mathbf{Q} \times \mathbf{R} \times \mathbf{Q}$. Whenever $(q, r, q')$ is in $\mathbf{P}$, we say $\mathbf{M}$ has the transition

$$q \xrightarrow{r} q'$$

The string $\varphi \in \mathbf{R}^*$ is *generated* by $\mathbf{M}$ if and only if there are states $q \in \mathbf{I}$ and $q' \in \mathbf{F}$ such that $q \overset{\varphi}{\Longrightarrow} q'$. The *language* generated by $\mathbf{M}$ is the set $\mathbf{L}(\mathbf{M}) = \{\varphi \in \mathbf{R}^* \mid \mathbf{M} \text{ generates } \varphi\}$.

If $\mathbf{M}$ has a single initial state and exactly one transition exiting each state, $\mathbf{M}$ is a *deterministic* FSG.

We may think of a finite-state generator as making arbitrary transitions between states, emitting as it moves the symbols labeling the transitions in its state diagram. When a final state is entered, the sequence of emitted symbols is identified as a string of the generated language. In illustration, Figure 6.3 is a generator of the set $(\mathbf{10} \cup \mathbf{01})^*$. A finite-state generator is deterministic only when there is a single transition from each state. Thus a state diagram (in particular, Figure 6.3) can describe a machine that is a deterministic accepter, but a nondeterministic generator. In Section 6.4, we shall see that the state diagrams of reduced, deterministic generators have a unique and simple form.

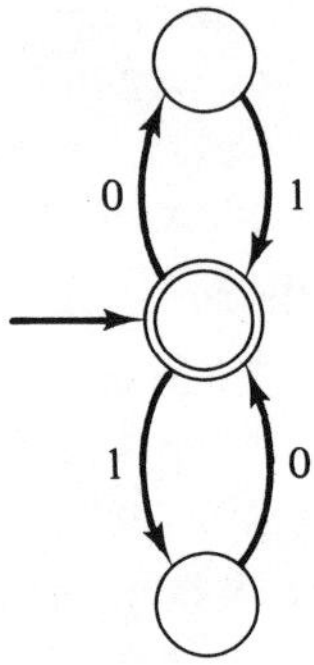


**Figure 6.3.** Finite-state generator for $(\mathbf{01} \cup \mathbf{10})^*$.

Since the strings emitted by a finite-state generator are exactly the strings accepted by the corresponding accepter, we have immediately the following result:

> **Theorem 6.2:** A language is regular if and only if it is generated by some (nondeterministic) finite-state generator.

By Theorem 6.2, the limitations of finite-state accepters discussed in the previous section apply without qualification to finite-state generators.

## 6.3 Limitations of Finite-State Transducers

The concept of the finite-state generator is useful for obtaining an interesting result on the processing of languages by *finite-state transducers* (that is, transition-assigned finite-state machines). In later chapters, additional results on the transduction of languages will be discussed.

> **Definition 6.2:** Let $\mathbf{M} = (\mathbf{Q}, \mathbf{S}, \mathbf{R}, f, g, q_I)$ be a deterministic finite-state transducer. If $\mathbf{X}$ is any collection of input strings, the *transduction* of $\mathbf{X}$ by $\mathbf{M}$ is
>
> $$\mathbf{Y} = \{\varphi \in \mathbf{R}^* \mid \varphi \text{ is the response of } \mathbf{M} \text{ to some stimulus } \omega \in \mathbf{X}\}$$

Thus **M** may be regarded as a mapping of input languages into output languages:

$$\mathbf{M}: \ \mathcal{P}(\mathbf{S}^*) \longrightarrow \mathcal{P}(\mathbf{R}^*)$$

This is called the *transducer mapping* of **M**, and is defined by

$$\mathbf{M}(\mathbf{X}) = \text{transduction of } \mathbf{X} \text{ by } \mathbf{M}, \text{ for each } \mathbf{X} \subseteq \mathbf{S}^*$$

Consider the transduction of a regular language **X** by a finite-state transducer $\mathbf{M}_t$. As shown in Figure 6.4, we may consider the language **X** to be generated by a finite-state generator $\mathbf{M}_g$, whose output sequences become input sequences to the transducer. The cascade combination of $\mathbf{M}_g$ and $\mathbf{M}_t$ is a finite-state generator **M** that generates the set **Y**. The state set of **M** is the Cartesian product of the state sets of $\mathbf{M}_g$ and $\mathbf{M}_t$, and each transition of **M** represents a transition of $\mathbf{M}_g$ generating a symbol that in turn causes a transition in $\mathbf{M}_t$. This construction is the basis for showing that transductions of regular sets are regular.

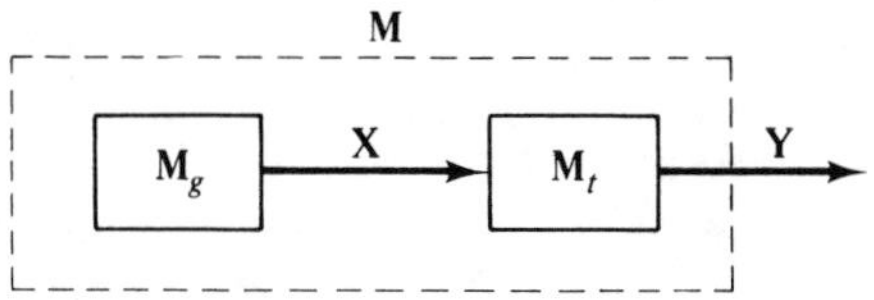


**Figure 6.4.** Transduction of a regular set by a finite-state machine.

**Theorem 6.3:** The transduction of a regular set by a finite-state transducer is a regular set. That is, the class of regular sets on a given alphabet is closed under finite-state transducer mappings.

***Proof:*** Let $\mathbf{M}_t = (\mathbf{Q}_t, \mathbf{S}, \mathbf{R}, f_t, g_t, q_I)$ be a finite-state transducer, and let $\mathbf{X} \subseteq \mathbf{S}^*$ be a regular set. By Theorem 6.2, there is an FSG $\mathbf{M}_g = (\mathbf{Q}_g, \mathbf{S}, \mathbf{P}_g, \mathbf{I}_g, \mathbf{F}_g)$ such that $\mathbf{L}(\mathbf{M}_g) = \mathbf{X}$. Define a new FSG $\mathbf{M} = (\mathbf{Q}, \mathbf{R}, \mathbf{P}, \mathbf{I}, \mathbf{F})$ where

$$\mathbf{Q} = \mathbf{Q}_g \times \mathbf{Q}_t$$
$$\mathbf{I} = \mathbf{I}_g \times \{q_I\}$$
$$\mathbf{F} = \mathbf{F}_g \times \mathbf{Q}_t$$

and

$$(p, q) \xrightarrow{r} (p', q')$$

is a transition in **M** if and only if for some symbol $s$, $\mathbf{M}_g$ has the transition

$$p \xrightarrow{s} p'$$

and $\mathbf{M}_t$ has the transition

$$q \xrightarrow{s/r} q'$$

Now, $\varphi \in \mathbf{M}_t(\mathbf{X})$ if and only if $\mathbf{M}_t$ has

$$q_0 \overset{\omega/\varphi}{\Longrightarrow} q_k$$

for some $\omega \in \mathbf{X}$, where $q_0 = q_I$ and $|\omega| = |\varphi| = k$. Also, $\omega \in \mathbf{X}$ if and only if $\mathbf{M}_g$ has

$$p_0 \overset{\omega}{\Longrightarrow} p_k$$

for some $p_0 \in \mathbf{I}_g$, $p_k \in \mathbf{F}_g$. But the construction guarantees that $q_0 \overset{\omega/\varphi}{\Longrightarrow} q_k$ in $\mathbf{M}_t$ and $p_0 \overset{\omega}{\Longrightarrow} p_k$ in $\mathbf{M}_g$ if and only if $\mathbf{M}$ has

$$(p_0, q_0) \overset{\varphi}{\Longrightarrow} (p_k, q_k)$$

with $(p_0, q_0) \in \mathbf{I}$ and $(p_k, q_k) \in \mathbf{F}$. Since $\mathbf{Y}$ is generated by $\mathbf{M}$, Theorem 6.2 shows that $\mathbf{Y}$ is regular.

**Example 6.4:** In Figure 6.5, $\mathbf{M}_g$ generates the set $\mathbf{X} = (\mathbf{00^*1})^*$ and $\mathbf{M}_t$ is the parity machine. Combining $\mathbf{M}_g$ and $\mathbf{M}_t$ according to the

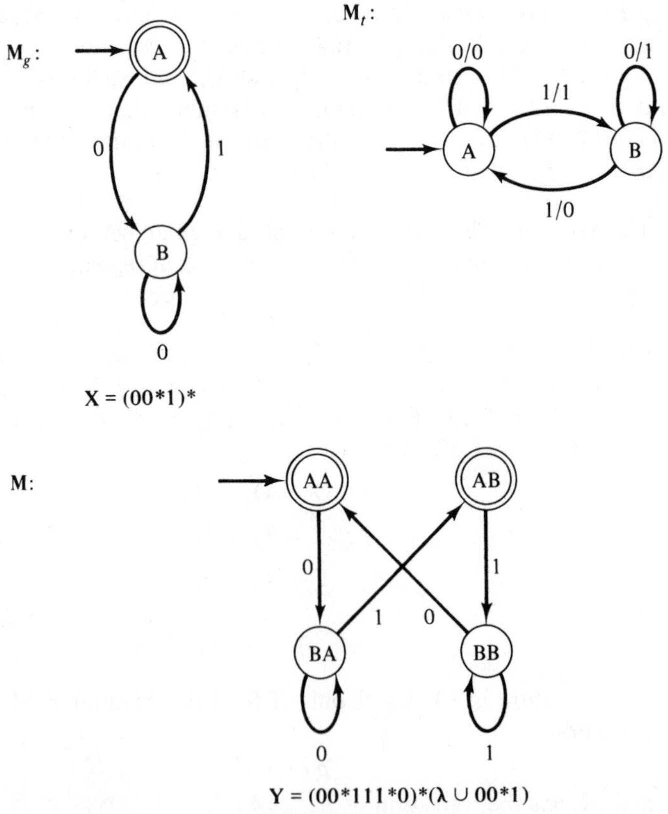


**Figure 6.5.** Generator for the transduction of a regular set.

construction of Figure 6.4 yields the finite-state generator $\mathbf{M}_t$ from which we find that the transduction of $\mathbf{X}$ by $\mathbf{M}_t$ is

$$\mathbf{Y} = (\mathbf{00^*111^*0})^*(\boldsymbol{\lambda} \cup \mathbf{00^*1})$$

The definition of transducer mapping (Definition 6.2) was stated for deterministic transducers. It is extended trivially to nondeterministic transducers if we define a response to an input $\omega$ to be any string $\varphi$ such that

$$q \overset{\omega/\varphi}{\Longrightarrow} q', \qquad q \text{ an initial state}$$

(In particular, the response to $\omega$ need not be unique.) The property that the transduction of a regular set is regular holds also for nondeterministic transducers; the reader may verify that the proof of Theorem 6.3 remains valid.

## 6.4 Ultimately Periodic Behavior

In some cases, it is possible to obtain important results about the power of a class of automata by considering how the automata react to very simple stimuli. In this section, we consider the behavior of finite-state devices for simple stimuli, and obtain results that will enable us to characterize the arithmetic capabilities of such machines.

An example of a very simple stimulus is the *constant input*

$$aa \ldots a \ldots$$

for some given input symbol $a$. A generalization of the constant input is the *periodic input*

$$\rho\rho \ldots \rho \ldots, \qquad \rho \neq \lambda$$

where $\rho$ is a given input string called the *period.* A further generalization is the *ultimately periodic* input

$$\tau\rho\rho \ldots \rho \ldots, \qquad \rho \neq \lambda$$

where $\tau$ and $\rho$ are given input strings called the *transient* and *period*, respectively.

We shall show that the response of a deterministic transducer to an ultimately periodic input must be ultimately periodic. The proof of the result is analogous to the proof of Theorem 6.3: we construct a generator for the ultimately periodic input, form the cascade combination of the generator and the given transducer, and demonstrate that the resulting machine is a generator for an ultimately periodic output. To do this, we first show that ultimately periodic strings are precisely the strings generated by deterministic finite-state generators.

Since each state of a deterministic finite-state generator has a single successor, its state diagram must have the form shown in Figure 6.6, as-

M:

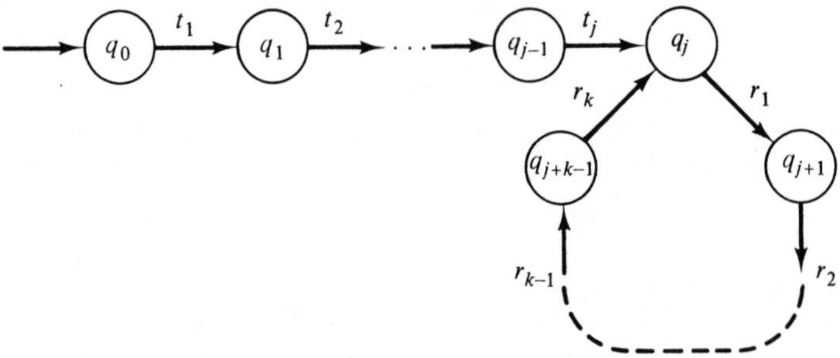


**Figure 6.6.** State diagram of a deterministic generator.

suming inaccessible states have been omitted. The only possible state sequences of **M** are the initial subsequences of

$$q_0 \overset{\tau}{\Longrightarrow} q_j \overset{\rho}{\Longrightarrow} q_j \overset{\rho}{\Longrightarrow} q_j \overset{\rho}{\Longrightarrow} \ldots, \qquad j \geq 0$$

where $\tau = t_1 \ldots t_j$ and $\rho = r_1 \ldots r_k$. Since not all states of **M** need be final states, only certain prefixes of the ultimately periodic string $\tau\rho\rho\rho \ldots$ can be valid outputs of **M**. These valid outputs constitute an *ultimately periodic language*.

**Definition 6.3:** Let $\tau$ and $\rho$ be strings on some alphabet **V** with $\rho \neq \lambda$. Suppose that

$$\mathbf{L} = \mathbf{T} \cup \tau\rho^*\mathbf{P}$$

where **T** is a finite set of proper prefixes of $\tau$

$$\mathbf{T} = \{\tau_1, \ldots, \tau_l\}$$

and **P** is a finite set of proper prefixes of $\rho$

$$\mathbf{P} = \{\rho_1, \ldots, \rho_m\}$$

Then **L** is an *ultimately periodic language*. String $\tau$ is the *transient* of **L**, and string $\rho$ is the *period.* If there are no shorter strings $\tau$ and $\rho$ (with $\rho$ nonempty) such that **L** can be expressed in the form $\mathbf{L} = \mathbf{T} \cup \tau\rho^*\mathbf{P}$, then $\tau$ and $\rho$ are known respectively as the *basic transient* and the *basic period* of **L**.

It should be obvious that any ultimately periodic language is a regular set.

**Theorem 6.4:** (1) Let **M** be an $n$-state deterministic FSG. Then **M** generates an ultimately periodic language $\mathbf{L(M)} = \mathbf{T} \cup \tau\rho^*\mathbf{P}$, where $|\tau| + |\rho| \leq n$. (2) Conversely, each ultimately periodic language $\mathbf{L} = \mathbf{T} \cup \tau\rho^*\mathbf{P}$ is generated by some deterministic FSG with no more than $|\tau\rho|$ states; moreover, if $\tau$ and $\rho$ are respectively the basic transient and basic period of $\mathbf{L}$, then no deterministic generator for $\mathbf{L}$ has fewer than $|\tau\rho|$ states.

***Proof:*** (1) Let $\mathbf{M} = (\mathbf{Q}, \mathbf{R}, \mathbf{P}, \{q_0\}, \mathbf{F})$ be an $n$-state deterministic generator. The state diagram of $\mathbf{M}$ has the form shown in Figure 6.6, where only the accessible states are shown. Let

$$\mathbf{J} = \{q_0, \ldots, q_{j-1}\}, \qquad j \geq 0$$

be the $j$ nonrecurring states and

$$\mathbf{K} = \{q_j, \ldots, q_{j+k-1}\}, \qquad j \geq 0, k > 0$$

be the $k$ recurring states. Note that $j + k \leq n$. Choose the shortest string $\tau$ and the shortest nonempty string $\rho$ such that

$$q_0 \overset{\tau}{\Longrightarrow} q_j \quad \text{and} \quad q_j \overset{\rho}{\Longrightarrow} q_j$$

Let

$$\mathbf{T} = \{\varphi \mid q_0 \overset{\varphi}{\Longrightarrow} q, q \in \mathbf{J} \cap \mathbf{F}\}$$

$$\mathbf{P} = \{\varphi \mid |\varphi| < k \text{ and } q_j \overset{\varphi}{\Longrightarrow} q, q \in \mathbf{K} \cap \mathbf{F}\}$$

Then

$$\mathbf{L}(\mathbf{M}) = \mathbf{T} \cup \tau\rho^*\mathbf{P}$$

and we have $|\tau| + |\rho| = j + k \leq n$.

(2) Let $\mathbf{L}$ be an ultimately periodic language

$$\mathbf{L} = \mathbf{T} \cup \tau\rho^*\mathbf{P}$$

where $\tau = t_1 t_2 \ldots t_j$
$\rho = r_1 r_2 \ldots r_k$
$\mathbf{T} = \{\tau_1, \ldots, \tau_l\}$, $\tau_i$ a proper prefix of $\tau$
$\mathbf{P} = \{\rho_1, \ldots, \rho_m\}$, $\rho_i$ a proper prefix of $\rho$

Let $\mathbf{M}$ have states and transitions as shown in Figure 6.6. The final states of $\mathbf{M}$ are the union of

$$\{q \mid q_0 \overset{\tau_i}{\Longrightarrow} q \text{ for some } \tau_i \in \mathbf{T}\}$$

and

$$\{q \mid q_j \overset{\rho_i}{\Longrightarrow} q \text{ for some } \rho_i \in \mathbf{P}\}$$

The reader may verify that $\mathbf{M}$ generates the language $\mathbf{L}$. Also, we note that $\mathbf{M}$ has $j + k = |\tau\rho|$ states. If $\tau$ and $\rho$ are the basic transient and basic period of $\mathbf{L}$, no deterministic generator for $\mathbf{L}$ can have fewer than $|\tau\rho|$ states, since we could otherwise obtain a shorter transient or shorter period using the construction in part 1 of the proof.

We now investigate what happens when a periodic input is presented to a deterministic finite-state transducer. We use the construction of Figure 6.4 to show that the response of such a transducer to an ultimately periodic input must be ultimately periodic.

**Theorem 6.5:** Let $\mathbf{X} \subseteq \mathbf{S}^*$ be an ultimately periodic language, and let $\mathbf{M}_t$ be a deterministic finite-state transducer with input alphabet $\mathbf{S}$. Then the transduction of $\mathbf{X}$ by $\mathbf{M}_t$ is an ultimately periodic language $\mathbf{Y}$. Furthermore, if $\tau$ and $\rho$ are the basic transient and basic period of the input $\mathbf{X}$, and $\alpha$ and $\beta$ are the basic transient and basic period of the output $\mathbf{Y}$, then

$$|\alpha\beta| \leq |\tau| + n_t|\rho|$$

where $n_t$ is the number of states in $\mathbf{M}_t$.

***Proof:*** By Theorem 6.4, $\mathbf{X}$ is generated by some deterministic finite-state generator $\mathbf{M}_g$. From the construction used in the proof of Theorem 6.2 (shown in Figure 6.4), the cascade combination of $\mathbf{M}_g$ and $\mathbf{M}_t$ is a finite-state generator $\mathbf{M}$ that generates $\mathbf{Y}$. Let $(p, q)$ be any state in $\mathbf{M}$. Since $\mathbf{M}_g$ is a deterministic generator, there is a single transition

$$p \xrightarrow{s} p'$$

leaving state $p$ in $\mathbf{M}_g$. Since $\mathbf{M}_t$ is a deterministic transducer, state $q$ has a single $s$-successor in $\mathbf{M}_t$; that is, there is a single transition

$$q \xrightarrow{s/r} q'$$

in $\mathbf{M}_t$ for state $q$ and symbol $s$. Thus there is a single transition

$$(p, q) \xrightarrow{r} (p', q')$$

leaving state $(p, q)$ in $\mathbf{M}$, and $\mathbf{M}$ is a deterministic generator. By Theorem 6.4, $\mathbf{Y}$ is ultimately periodic.

Now, suppose that the response of $\mathbf{M}_t$ to $\tau$ is $\alpha_1$. The remainder of $\mathbf{M}_t$'s response is a response to the stimulus produced by $\mathbf{M}_g$ once it has entered its cycle of recurring states. Since $\rho$ is the basic period of $\mathbf{L}(\mathbf{M}_g)$, this cycle contains $m = |\rho|$ states. Thus the cascade combination of $\mathbf{M}_t$ and the cyclic portion of $\mathbf{M}_g$ has $n_t m$ states, and this combination must generate an ultimately periodic language with some basic transient $\alpha_2$ and some basic period $\beta$. The complete response of $\mathbf{M}_t$ to the output of $\mathbf{M}_g$ is therefore an ultimately periodic language $\mathbf{Y}$ with basic transient $\alpha = \alpha_1\alpha_2$ and basic period $\beta$. From Theorem 6.4, we have

$$|\alpha_2\beta| \leq n_t m = n_t|\rho|$$

Since $\alpha_1$ is the response of $\mathbf{M}_t$ to $\tau$, we have $|\alpha_1| = |\tau|$. Thus

$$|\alpha\beta| = |\alpha_1| + |\alpha_2\beta| \leq |\tau| + n_t|\rho|$$

If, in the proof of Theorem 6.5, we take $\mathbf{M}_g$ to be a one-state generator for the language $\mathbf{a}^*$ (in which case $\rho = a$ and $\tau = \lambda$), we have shown that presenting a constant input to an $n$-state machine always produces an ultimately periodic output for which $|\alpha\beta| \leq n$. Thus an $n$-state deterministic transducer, when driven by constant input, is equivalent to some $n$-state deterministic generator.

**Example 6.5:** In Figure 6.7, $\mathbf{M}_g$ generates the ultimately periodic language

$$\mathbf{X} = \boldsymbol{\lambda} \cup \mathbf{a(bc)^*b}$$

with basic transient $\tau = a$ and basic period $\rho = bc$. The output symbols of $\mathbf{M}_g$ are presented in succession to a three-state transducer $\mathbf{M}_t$. The combination of $\mathbf{M}_g$ and $\mathbf{M}_t$ is equivalent, by the construction of Theorem 6.2, to the finite-state generator $\mathbf{M}$. The transduction of $\mathbf{X}$ by $\mathbf{M}_t$ is therefore the ultimately periodic language

$$\mathbf{Y} = (\boldsymbol{\lambda} \cup \mathbf{00}) \cup \mathbf{000(0001)^*(0 \cup 000)}$$

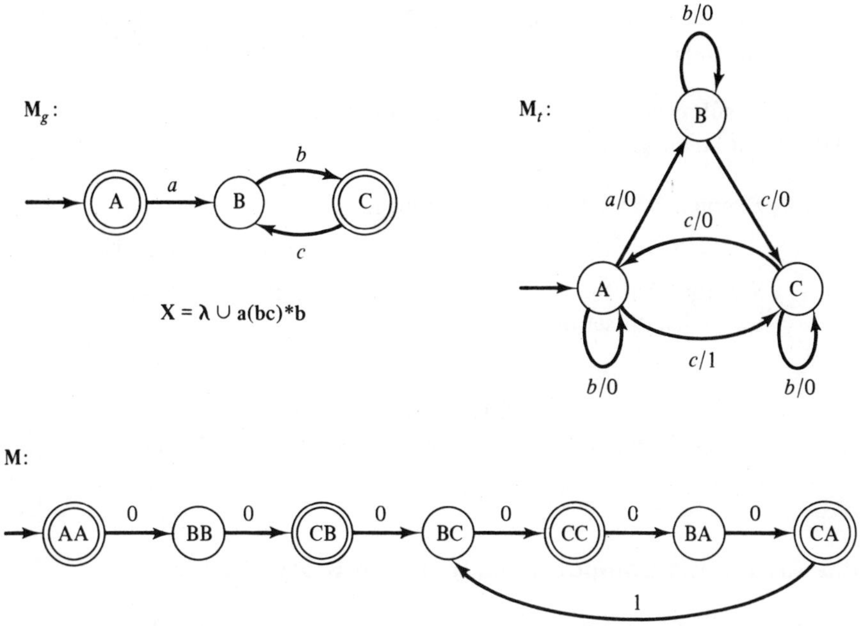


Y = (λ ∪ 00) ∪ 000(0001)*(0 ∪ 000)

**Figure 6.7.** Transduction of an ultimately periodic set.

with basic transient $\alpha = 000$ and basic period $\beta = 0001$. We see that the bound specified by Theorem 6.4 is achieved:

$$\underset{\alpha}{|000|} + \underset{\beta}{|0001|} = \underset{\tau}{|a|} + \underset{n_t}{3}\,\underset{p}{|bc|}$$

**Example 6.6:** Suppose that the regular set **X** in **S*** is the input language of the one-state transducer $\mathbf{M}_t$ in Figure 6.8. The transduction

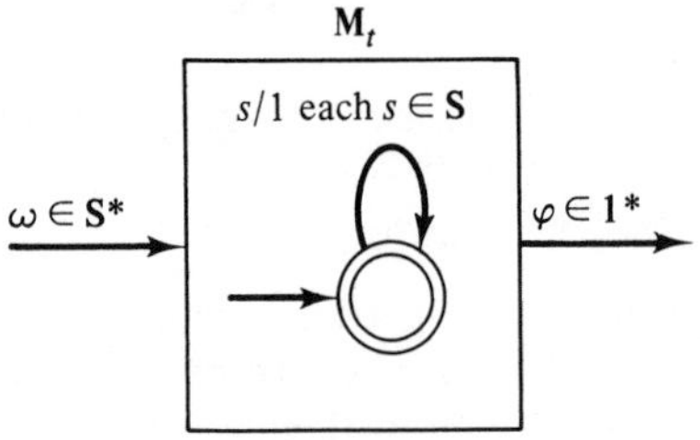


**Figure 6.8.** Transducer for the length set of a language.

of a string $\omega \in \mathbf{X}$ is $\varphi = 1^{|\omega|}$ and is called the *length string* of $\omega$. If $\mathbf{M}_g$ is a finite-state generator of **X**, then the cascade combination of $\mathbf{M}_g$ and $\mathbf{M}_t$ is a generator **M** of the *length set* $\mathbf{Y} = \mathbf{M}_t(\mathbf{X})$. Because **M** has the singleton output alphabet $\{1\}$, there is an equivalent deterministic generator of **Y**, and **Y** must be an ultimately periodic language. Thus the length set of any regular set is ultimately periodic.

The result established in Example 6.6 is quite useful for demonstrating that certain languages are nonregular.

**Example 6.7:** Consider the language

$$\mathbf{L} = \{a^{n-1}ba^{n-2}b^2 \ldots a^{n-i}b^i \ldots a^2b^{n-2}ab^{n-1}b^n \,|\, n \geq 1\}$$

We note that the length of each string in **L** is a perfect square; that is, the length set of **L** is the language

$$\mathbf{Y} = \{1^{n^2} \,|\, n \geq 1\}$$

Since the difference of successive perfect squares grows without bound, **Y** cannot be ultimately periodic and thus **L** cannot be regular.

## 6.5 Arithmetic Computations by Finite-State Machines

The finite-state machine is a satisfactory model for many of the functional components of computers. For this reason, we conclude this chapter with a brief examination of the arithmetic capabilities of such machines.

Consider the device **M** in Figure 6.9. Suppose that the input strings and output strings of **M** are on the alphabet $\mathbf{B} = \{0, 1, \ldots, b-1\}$, for some integer $b > 1$. We may consider the device as performing an arithmetic

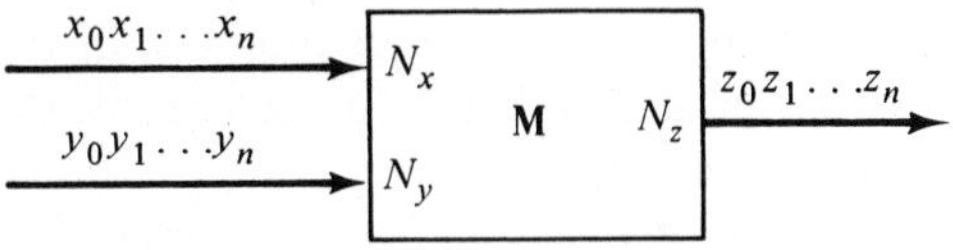


**Figure 6.9.** Finite-state arithmetic device.

computation on each pair of input strings, the output string representing the result of the computation. That is, we may consider the strings as representing integers in the base $b$ number system:

$$N_x = \sum_{i=0}^{n} x_i b^i, \qquad x_i \in \{0, 1, \ldots, b-1\}$$

$$N_y = \sum_{i=0}^{n} y_i b^i, \qquad y_i \in \{0, 1, \ldots, b-1\}$$

$$N_z = \sum_{i=0}^{n} z_i b^i, \qquad z_i \in \{0, 1, \ldots, b-1\}$$

where $N_z$ is the result of **M**'s computation on $N_x$ and $N_y$.

So that we may consider **M** a finite-state transducer, we regard the symbols representing $N_x$ and $N_y$ as being presented to **M** in pairs: at any time $t > 0$, the input symbol to **M** is the pair $(x_t, y_t)$. Thus, if **M** performs computations in the base $b$ number system, the output alphabet of **M** is the set $\mathbf{B} = \{0, 1, \ldots, b-1\}$, while the input alphabet is the set $\mathbf{B} \times \mathbf{B}$. Also, to ensure that the input string of **M** is the same length as its output string, we append 0's to the representations of $N_x$, $N_y$, and $N_z$ as needed to ensure that the three representations contain a like number of symbols. (Since the appended 0's are the highest-order digits in the representations, the integers $N_x$, $N_y$, and $N_z$ are unchanged.)

An adding device for two binary numbers is shown in Figure 6.10. At time $t$, $\mathbf{M}_a$ computes $(x_t + y_t + c_{t-1})$, where $c_{t-1}$ is the carry from the ad-

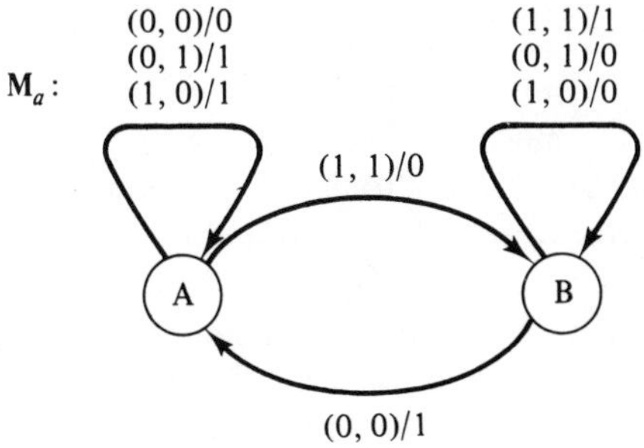


**Figure 6.10.** State diagram of an adding device.

dition at time $t - 1$. State A represents $c_{t-1} = 0$, and state B represents $c_{t-1} = 1$. The reader should convince himself that the output sequence $z_0 z_1 \ldots z_t z_{t+1}$ is indeed the binary sum of $x_0 x_1 \ldots x_t 0$ and $y_0 y_1 \ldots y_t 0$.

Since multiplication can be performed by repeated addition, one might suppose that multiplication is within the capabilities of finite-state devices. Interestingly, this is not the case; a demonstration of this fact follows readily from the results of the preceding section.

Suppose that **M** is a finite-state device that multiplies arbitrary base $b$ integers $N_x$ and $N_y$, for some $b > 1$. Let **M** be as shown in Figure 6.9, and let $k$ be the number of states in **M**. The input symbols presented to **M** are successive pairs from the sequences $x_0 x_1 \ldots x_n$ and $y_0 y_1 \ldots y_n$, and the corresponding output is the sequence $z_0 z_1 \ldots z_n$, where

$$\sum_{i=0}^{n} z_i b^i = \left(\sum_{i=0}^{n} x_i b^i\right)\left(\sum_{i=0}^{n} y_i b^i\right)$$

Consider requiring **M** to multiply the number $b^m$ by itself, for some $m > k$. If we represent $b^m$ as $0^m 1 0^m$, the input sequence of **M** will be $(0, 0)^m(1, 1)(0, 0)^m$ and the output sequence must be $0^{2m}1$. Let $q$ be the state of **M** after the sequence $(0, 0)^m(1, 1)$ has been presented. According to Theorem 6.4, the subsequent response of **M** to the input sequence $(0, 0)^m$ must be a prefix of an ultimately periodic string $\tau\rho\rho\rho \ldots$, where $|\tau| + |\rho| \leq k < m$. But the first $m$ symbols in this response must be 0's; thus both $\tau$ and $\rho$ must be strings of 0's, and **M** cannot produce the required 1 as its last output symbol.

Using arguments similar to that above, one can show that many other arithmetic operations are beyond the capability of finite-state machines. (Several such operations are considered in the Problems.) The limitations represented by these results are not serious in actual practice, however: since all computers impose limitations on the lengths of representations of numbers, all these operations can be performed by finite-state devices when restricted to the class of representable numbers. Although the number of states required for some operations might be quite large, states are inexpensive in computer hardware, and it is generally possible to include enough states to perform most computations with acceptable precision.

## Notes and References

The limitations of the finite-state machine have been recognized ever since the machine model was developed, and the authors who have demonstrated such limitations are too numerous to list here. However, in many cases (for example, Ritchie [1963], Minsky and Papert [1966], and Hartmanis and Shank [1968]) these demonstrations have been based on number theoretic arguments, rather than arguments based directly on the behavioral properties of finite automata. In this chapter, we have attempted to characterize the properties of such automata that imply these limitations.

The major result in this chapter, the finite-state language theorem, is a slight modification of the "pumping lemma" for finite-state languages proved by Rabin and Scott [1959]. We have expressed the result in such a way as to be most useful in demonstrating the nonregularity of languages, and also to resemble closely a similar theorem for context-free languages considered in Chapter 9.

Our discussion of the arithmetic capabilities of finite-state devices follows closely the treatment of this topic in Minsky [1967]. In particular, Minsky demonstrates the inability of finite-state devices to perform multiplication, and our proof is virtually identical to his.

## Problems

6.1. Show that each of the following sets is nonregular:
 a. $\{a^k b^{3k} \mid k \geq 1\}$.
 b. $\{\omega c \omega \mid \omega \in \{0, 1\}^*\}$.

6.2. For each of the following languages, design a finite-state accepter for the language or prove that it is nonregular:
 a. $\{a^k c a^{k'} c a^{k''} \mid k'' = k + k'\}$.
 b. $\{a^k c a^{k'} c a^{k''} \mid k'' = (k \bmod 3 + k' \bmod 2) \bmod 3\}$.
 c. $\{a_1 \ldots a_n \mid a_1 \ldots a_{n/2} = a_{n/2+1} \ldots a_n,\ n$ an even integer$\}$.
 d. $\{\omega \in \{0, 1\}^* \mid N_0(\omega) - N_1(\omega)$ is a positive even integer$\}$, where $N_0(\omega)$ and $N_1(\omega)$ denote the number of occurrences in $\omega$ of the symbols 0 and 1, respectively.

6.3. Prove that the language $\mathbf{L} = \{a^p \mid p$ a prime number$\}$ is nonregular.

6.4. Let $\mathbf{X}$ and $\mathbf{Y}$ be regular sets on an alphabet $\mathbf{V}$. Which of the following languages, if any, are necessarily regular?
 a. $\{\omega \mid \omega \in \mathbf{X}$ and $\omega^R \in \mathbf{Y}\}$.
 b. $\{\omega \mid \omega \in \mathbf{X}$ and $\omega^R \notin \mathbf{Y}\}$.
 c. $\{\omega \mid \omega \in \mathbf{X}$ and $\omega^R = \omega\}$.

6.5. Consider the language

$$\mathbf{L} = \{\mathbf{P}0^n\mathbf{Q}1^n\mathbf{R} \mid n \geq 1\}$$

where $\mathbf{P}$, $\mathbf{Q}$, and $\mathbf{R}$ are nonempty sets on some alphabet $\mathbf{V}$. Is there any choice of $\mathbf{P}$, $\mathbf{Q}$, and $\mathbf{R}$ for which $\mathbf{L}$ is regular?

**6.6.** Let $\mathbf{L}_1$, $\mathbf{L}_2$, and $\mathbf{L}_3$ be languages satisfying the relation $\mathbf{L}_1 \subset \mathbf{L}_2 \subset \mathbf{L}_3$.
 a. Find infinite sets $\mathbf{L}_1$, $\mathbf{L}_2$, $\mathbf{L}_3$ as above such that $\mathbf{L}_1$ and $\mathbf{L}_3$ are nonregular and $\mathbf{L}_2$ is regular.
 b. Find infinite sets $\mathbf{L}_1$, $\mathbf{L}_2$, $\mathbf{L}_3$ as above such that $\mathbf{L}_1$ and $\mathbf{L}_3$ are regular and $\mathbf{L}_2$ is nonregular.
 c. Suppose it is known that $\mathbf{L} \subset \mathbf{L}'$ for languages $\mathbf{L}$ and $\mathbf{L}'$, and that $\mathbf{L}$ is of class $i$, $i \in \{0, 1, 2, 3\}$. What can be concluded about the class

of $\mathbf{L}'$? Suppose it is known that $\mathbf{L}'$ is of class $i, i \in \{0, 1, 2, 3\}$. What can be concluded about the class of $\mathbf{L}$?

**6.7.** Let $\mathbf{A}$ and $\mathbf{B}$ be nonregular sets. Which of the following sets may be regular?

a. $\mathbf{A} - \mathbf{B}$.
b. $\mathbf{A} \cup \mathbf{B}$.
c. $\mathbf{A} \cdot \mathbf{B}$.

6.8. Design finite-state generators for the following languages:

a. $\{0, 1\}^*$.
b. $(\mathbf{0} \cup \mathbf{1^*01} \cup \mathbf{0^*11})^*\mathbf{0}$.
c. $(\mathbf{1} \cup \mathbf{101} \cup \mathbf{1010(10001)^*(10} \cup \mathbf{1000))1}$.
d. $(\mathbf{11})^*\mathbf{11}(\mathbf{1} \cup \mathbf{1^*111})^*$.

For which of the languages do there exist deterministic generators?

**6.9.** Let $\mathbf{R} \subseteq \mathbf{a}^*$ be a regular set. Prove there exists a deterministic finite-state generator for $\mathbf{R}$.

6.10. For each of the following sets $\mathbf{X}$, find a regular expression for the transduction of $\mathbf{X}$ by $\mathbf{M}$, where $\mathbf{M}$ is the following transducer:

$\mathbf{M}$:

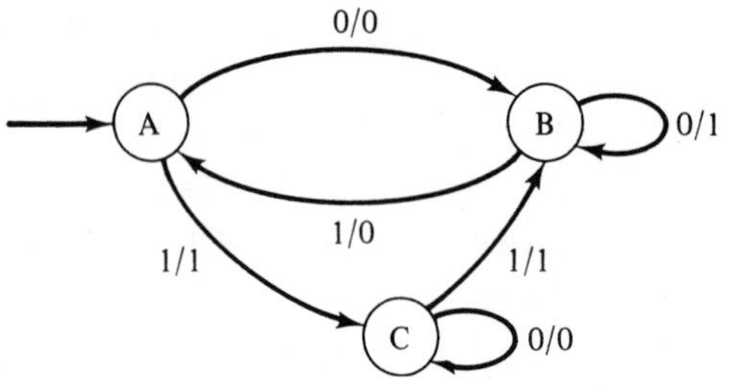


a. $\mathbf{X} = (\mathbf{0} \cup \mathbf{1^*0})^*\mathbf{1} \cup \mathbf{0}$.
b. $\mathbf{X} = \mathbf{01}\{0, 1\}^* \cap \{0, 1\}^*\mathbf{0}$.
c. $\mathbf{X} = (\mathbf{0101}\{0, 1\}^*)^c$.

6.11. Let $\mathbf{M}_1$ be the generators and $\mathbf{M}_2$ the transducers shown. Construct a finite-state generator for the transduction by $\mathbf{M}_2$ of $\mathbf{L}(\mathbf{M}_1)$:

a.

$\mathbf{M}_1$:

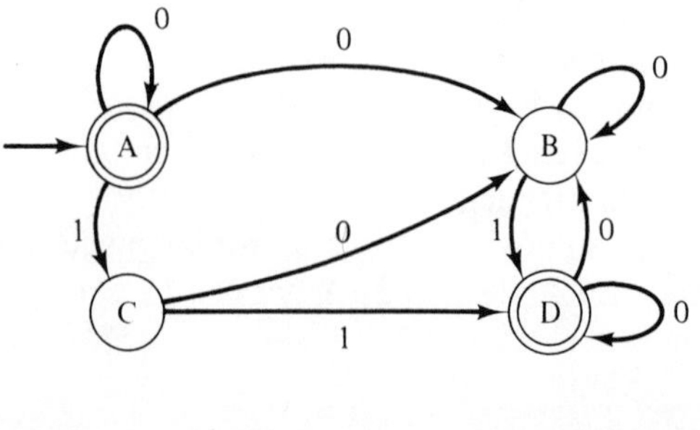

**M**$_2$:

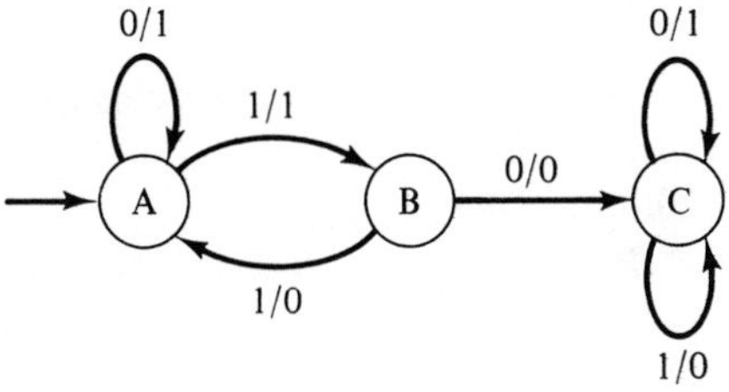


b.

**M**$_1$:

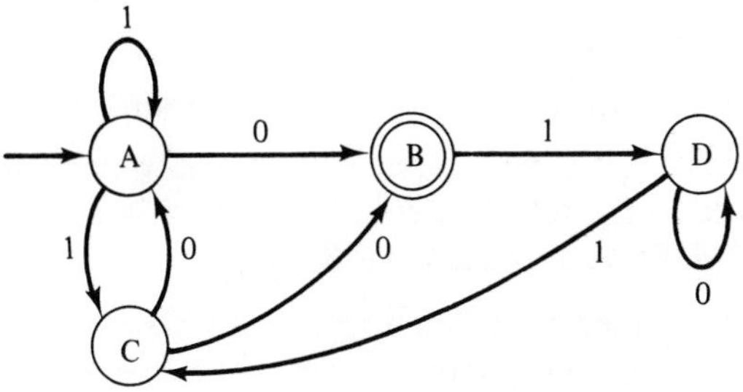


**M**$_2$:

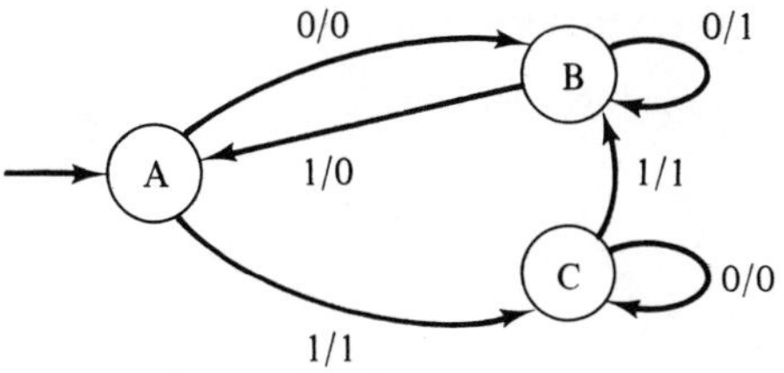


6.12. Let **M** be the transducer shown:

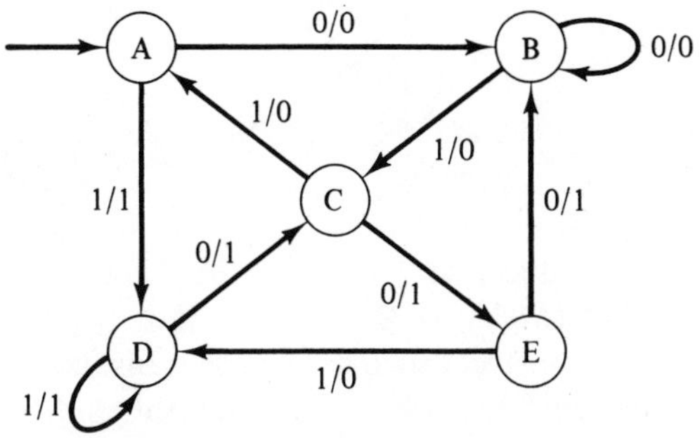


Describe the response of **M** to each of the following ultimately periodic inputs:

a. 1111111111 . . . 1 . . . .

b. 0000000000 . . . 0 . . . .

c. **1001(101)***.

d. $\mathbf{1 \cup 11(00)^*(0 \cup \lambda)}$.

**6.13.** We define a *nondeterministic finite-state transducer* to be a five-tuple $\mathbf{M} = (\mathbf{Q}, \mathbf{S}, \mathbf{R}, r, \mathbf{I})$, where

$\mathbf{Q}$ is a finite set of *states*, including *initial states* $\mathbf{I}$

$\mathbf{S}$ is a finite *input alphabet*

$\mathbf{R}$ is a finite *output alphabet*

$r \subseteq \mathbf{Q} \times \mathbf{S} \times \mathbf{R} \times \mathbf{Q}$ is a *transition relation*.

Whenever $(q, s, t, q')$ is in $r$, $\mathbf{M}$ has the transition $q \xrightarrow{s/t} q'$.

If $\omega$ is any string in $\mathbf{S}^*$, a *response* of $\mathbf{M}$ to $\omega$ is any string $\varphi$ in $\mathbf{R}^*$ such that $q \overset{\omega/\varphi}{\Longrightarrow} q'$ in $\mathbf{M}$, for some initial state $q$. For any set $\mathbf{X} \subseteq \mathbf{R}^*$, the *transduction* of $\mathbf{X}$ by $\mathbf{M}$ is the set

$$\mathbf{M}(\mathbf{X}) = \{\varphi \mid \varphi \text{ is a response of } \mathbf{M} \text{ to some string } \omega \text{ in } \mathbf{X}\}$$

Prove that if $\mathbf{X}$ is a regular set and $\mathbf{M}$ is any nondeterministic finite-state transducer, $\mathbf{M}(\mathbf{X})$ is a regular set. If $\mathbf{X}$ is an ultimately periodic set, need $\mathbf{M}(\mathbf{X})$ be ultimately periodic?

**6.14.** a. Show that there exists a nonregular set $\mathbf{X}$ such that $\mathbf{M}(\mathbf{X})$ is regular for some deterministic finite-state transducer $\mathbf{M}$.

b. Show that there exists a nonregular set $\mathbf{X}$ such that $\mathbf{M}(\mathbf{X})$ is nonregular for every deterministic finite-state transducer $\mathbf{M}$.

**6.15.** Let $\mathbf{M}$ be the transducer shown:

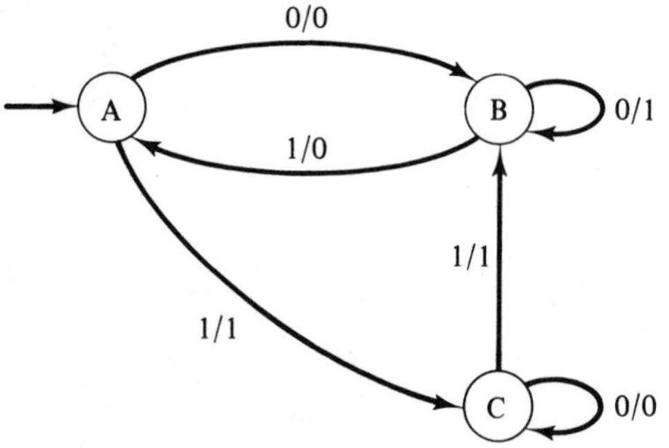


Construct a transducer $\mathbf{M}^{-1}$ such that $\mathbf{M}^{-1}$ is the "inverse" of $\mathbf{M}$, that is, such that $\mathbf{M}^{-1}(\mathbf{M}(\mathbf{X})) = \mathbf{X}$ for all sets $\mathbf{X} \subseteq \{0, 1\}^*$. Is it possible, for arbitrary $\mathbf{M}$, to construct such an inverse transducer? If so, describe in detail the construction; otherwise, establish conditions on $\mathbf{M}$ for the existence of an inverse transducer.

**6.16.** Let $\mathbf{R}$ be a regular language, and let $\omega_1, \omega_2, \ldots, \omega_i, \ldots$ be an enumeration of the elements of $\mathbf{R}$ such that $|\omega_i| \geq |\omega_{i-1}|$ for all $i > 0$. Prove that there exists a constant $c$ such that $|\omega_i| - |\omega_{i-1}| < c$ for all $i > 0$. If such a constant exists for a language $\mathbf{X}$, may we conclude that $\mathbf{X}$ is regular?

6.17. Let $n$ and $m$ be arbitrary integers in the base $b$ system, for any $b > 0$. Show whether there does or does not exist a finite-state device that computes, in the sense of Section 6.5, the function $f$, where $f$ is defined as follows:

a. $f(k) = kb^n$, $k$ any input integer $\geq 0$.
b. $f(k) = km$, $k$ any input integer $\geq 0$.
c. $f(k) = kmb^n$, $k$ any input integer $\geq 0$.
d. $f(k, i) = k^i$, $k$ and $i$ arbitrary input integers $\geq 0$.
e. $f(k) = k^n$, $k$ an arbitrary input integer $\geq 0$.

6.18. We have seen that there exists a finite-state device that performs addition in the base 2 system. Show that, if we adopt suitable conventions regarding signs, there exists a finite-state device that performs subtraction in the base 2 system. Does any finite-state device exist that computes "monus" in the base 2 system? (*Monus* is the operation $\dot{-}$ defined as

$$k \dot{-} n = \begin{cases} k - n & \text{if } k \geq n \\ 0 & \text{otherwise} \end{cases}$$

where $k$ and $n$ are arbitrary positive integers.)

# 7

# Tape Automata

If we wish to model computational processes beyond the capabilities of finite-state machines, we require abstract machines that may assume arbitrarily many distinct configurations—machines with *unbounded memory*. So far we have represented an abstract machine by a graph having nodes in one-to-one correspondence with machine configurations. However, when the number of configurations must be unbounded, a graph representation is no longer suitable since it fails to provide a finite description of the machine. If we desire finite descriptions of machines having unlimited numbers of configurations, we must modify our conception of abstract machines.

All automata are considered to perform one step at a time, such as the absorption of an input symbol or the emission of an output symbol, as they proceed through a sequence of configurations. After a finite time, such a machine can have performed only a finite number of steps, and can have entered only a finite number of distinct configurations, even though infinitely many configurations of the machine are possible. The significance of unbounded memory is not that successful operation of the automaton may require storage of an infinite amount of information, but that no bound on the memory required during operation can be fixed as part of the machine's specification.

In illustration, consider the problem of computing the square of an arbitrary integer in binary notation. In Chapter 6 we saw that this problem requires unbounded memory; that is, for each integer $n$ we can find some other integer whose square cannot be computed by any machine limited to $n$

distinct configurations. Any machine capable of squaring an arbitrary integer must have an infinity of possible configurations, even though only finitely many of them will be assumed during any particular computation.

When we compute the square of an integer using pencil and paper, we store intermediate results as lines of symbols written on the paper. Assuming that a definite amount of space is occupied by each written symbol, the squaring of larger integers requires larger amounts of paper. Indeed, for any given sheet of paper, there is an integer sufficiently large that the paper cannot contain the calculation of its square.

By analogy with computations on paper, we consider a class of abstract machines that can print and read symbols on a storage medium of unlimited extent. A two-dimensional sheet of paper is a convenience rather than a necessity, since a strip of paper, a *tape*, just wide enough to accommodate one symbol can be marked off into successive segments that represent the lines of a computation. Correspondingly, the simplest abstract machine with unbounded memory is one that uses an unbounded tape for its storage medium; its access mechanism can read or print one tape square at a time, and can move only to adjacent squares in a single step. In later chapters we shall see that this simple model has universal computing power.

## 7.1 Automata with Tapes

Figure 7.1 illustrates the general form of a *tape automaton*. The automaton has a *control unit* (a finite-state device), a *storage tape* that can be inscribed with symbols from a *tape alphabet*, and a movable *head* that can read and write symbols on the storage tape. In general, a tape automaton may carry out steps that manipulate information on its storage tape between

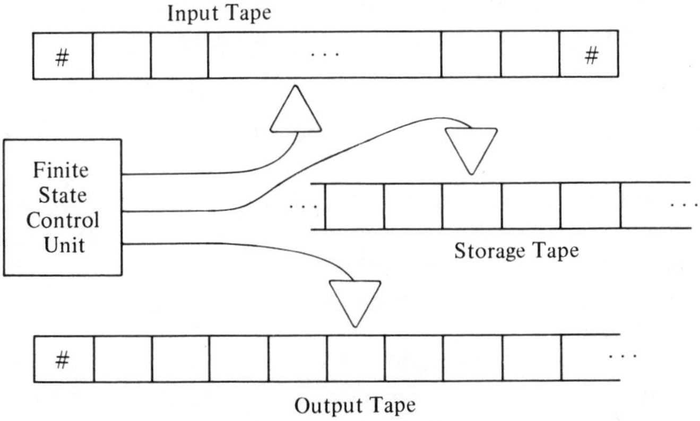


**Figure 7.1.** General form of tape automaton.

moments at which it examines input symbols. For such an automaton, it is not convenient to assume that input symbols "arrive" at successive moments in time. Instead, we equip the automaton with an *input tape* on which we inscribe the entire sequence of input symbols, and permit the automaton to examine these symbols when and if it requires. Similarly, we equip the automaton with an *output tape* and permit it to write its output symbols in successive squares of the tape. In general, the automaton may read from but not write on its input tape; it may write on but not read from its output tape; and it may read from and write on its storage tape.

Each tape is a storage medium consisting of a sequence of squares (Figure 7.2). We imagine that a tape is oriented horizontally, and that it

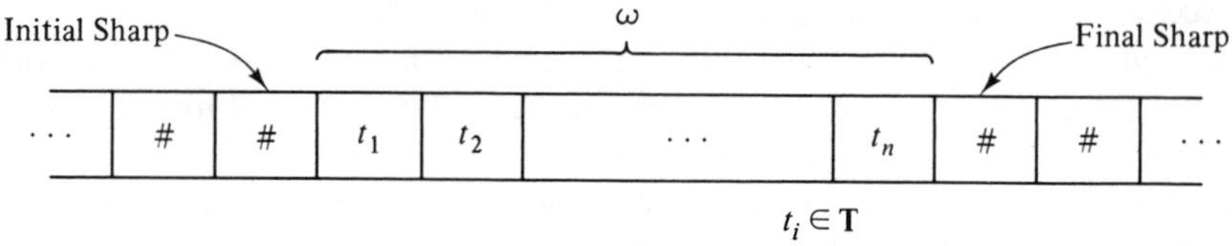


**Figure 7.2.** Tape containing the string $\omega$.

extends indefinitely to the left and to the right. At any time, all but a finite sequence of adjacent squares are inscribed with the symbol *sharp* (#) which signifies a blank square. The sequence of symbols written in the nonblank region of a tape is the *string contained* by the tape. Figure 7.2 shows a tape containing the string $\omega = t_1 t_2 \ldots t_n$, the symbols $t_i$ being elements of a tape alphabet **T**. The sharp bounding $\omega$ on the left is known as the *initial sharp*; the sharp bounding $\omega$ on the right is known as the *final sharp*. The initial sharp and final sharp are end markers used by an automaton to detect that it is no longer scanning within the region occupied by the string $\omega$. For this reason, the sharp is not an element of the automaton's tape alphabet.

Each step in the operation of a tape automaton consists of three actions:

1. The movement of a given head one square to the left or to the right along its tape.
2. The reading of the symbol found in the new square, or the writing of a specified symbol in the new square. (A symbol written replaces any symbol previously written in the square.)
3. The transition of the control unit to a new state.

It might appear that our restriction of head motion to one square in each step is unduly severe. However, this restriction results in no loss of generality, since a move of $n$ squares can be accomplished by $n$ successive moves of one square, and is therefore within the capability of a finite-state control.

So that the description of a tape automaton may be readily understood, the behavior of the control unit will be specified by a *program of instructions*. Each instruction is written in the form

$$q] \textbf{ move } (t, q')$$

where $q$ and $q'$ are states of the control unit (*internal states*), **move** stands for one of several commands that specifies the tape affected and the type of move, and $t$ is a symbol in the appropriate tape alphabet. State $q$ is called the *label* of the instruction, and state $q'$ is the *successor state* of the instruction.

A *step* in a computation by a tape automaton is the execution of an instruction labeled by the current state of the control unit. The execution of an instruction places the automaton in a new configuration in which the following occur:

1. One tape head is a square to the left or to the right of its previous position.
2. A symbol may have been written in the square at which the tape head is now positioned (in which case the instruction is a form of *write* instruction).
3. The control has entered a state $q'$, where $q'$ may depend on a symbol read from the square at which the tape head is now positioned (in which case the instruction is a form of *read* instruction).

Various types of tape automata utilize various types of instructions; the specific forms of these instructions are described as they are encountered in our discussions of the automata.

The automaton shown in Figure 7.1 is a transducer. If we remove its output tape and designate certain states of its control as accepting states, it becomes an accepter. Similarly, if we remove its input tape, the machine becomes a generator. In fact, we can define a number of classes of tape automata in terms of their structural and behavioral characteristic:

I. Structural Characteristics
  A. Function of machine:
    1. Transducer (input and output tapes).
    2. Accepter (no output tape).
    3. Generator (no input tape).
  B. Presence or absence of a storage tape.
  C. Number of symbols in the storage tape alphabet.
II. Behavioral Characteristics
  A. Type of operation:
    1. Deterministic.
    2. Nondeterministic.
  B. Motion of input tape head:
    1. One way (left to right).

   2. Two way (arbitrary motion).

C. Storage tape access restrictions:
   1. Last in, first out (pushdown storage).
   2. Arbitrary access within a region whose length is bounded linearly by that of its input.
   3. Unrestricted access.

For each of the four classes of grammars introduced in Chapter 3, we can describe a class of one-way tape automata that has equivalent language defining ability; these equivalences are given in Table 7.1. Two of these

**Table 7.1** Equivalences of tape accepters and formal grammars

| Type of Grammar | Type of Accepter | Characteristics |
|---|---|---|
| 3 (regular) | Finite state | No storage tape |
| 2 (context free) | Pushdown | One pushdown storage tape<br>Nondeterministic operation |
| 1 (context sensitive) | Linear bounded | One linear-bounded storage tape<br>Nondeterministic operation |
| 0 | Turing machine | One arbitrarily accessed storage tape |

equivalences, that of context-free grammars and pushdown automata, and that of type 0 languages and Turing machines, are the topics of later chapters. In the remaining sections of this chapter, we show that two important generalizations of the finite-state accepter result in no increased language-defining ability. These are the *generalized sequential machine* (a one-way, nondeterministic tape transducer with no storage tape) and the *two-way accepter* (a two-way, deterministic tape accepter with no storage tape).

## 7.2 Generalized Sequential Machines

For a finite-state machine as defined in Chapter 4, each transition of the machine is accompanied by the absorption of a symbol of its stimulus and the generation of a symbol of its response. Consider now a tape transducer with one-way input tape motion and no storage tape (Figure 7.3). In response to reading a symbol from its input tape, this automaton may print zero or more symbols on its output tape. Such automata, called *generalized sequential machines*, have important properties in language transduction. We introduce tape automata by studying the generalized transduction of regular sets. Transduction of context-free languages by these machines is taken up in Chapter 8.

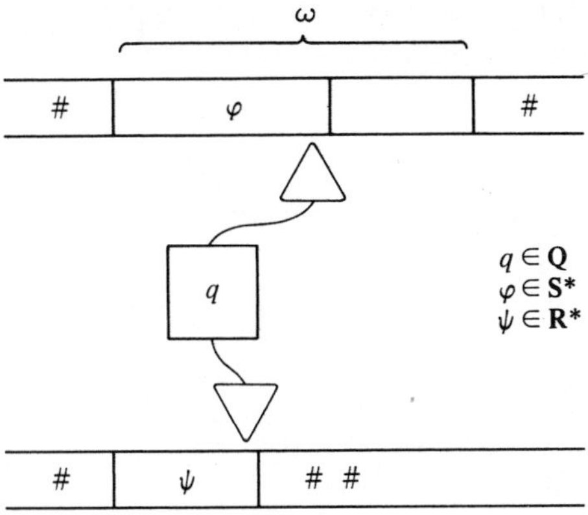


**Figure 7.3.** Sequential transducer in configuration $(q, \varphi, \psi)$.

**Definition 7.1:** *A generalized sequential transducer* (GST) is a six-tuple

$$\mathbf{M} = (\mathbf{Q}, \mathbf{S}, \mathbf{R}, \mathbf{P}, \mathbf{I}, \mathbf{F})$$

where

**Q** is a finite set of internal states, including initial states **I** and final states **F**
**S** is a finite input alphabet
**R** is a finite output alphabet
**P** is a program

The *program* **P** is a finite set of *instructions* of two types:

$$\begin{matrix} q]\ \textbf{scan}\ (s, q') \\ q]\ \textbf{print}\ (r, q') \end{matrix} \quad \begin{cases} q, q' \in \mathbf{Q} \\ s \in \mathbf{S} \\ r \in \mathbf{R} \end{cases}$$

Each state of **M** is either a scan state or a print state and must label instructions of only one type.

To specify the complete behavior of a GST during a computation, it is not sufficient to specify the state of the transducer's control at each step; we must also specify the symbols scanned or written at each step. At each moment, the *total state* of a sequential transducer comprises the following:

1. The state of its control unit.
2. The string of symbols scanned from its input tape.
3. The string of symbols written on its output tape.

The total state of a sequential transducer is called a *configuration* and is an element of the set $\mathbf{Q} \times \mathbf{S}^* \times \mathbf{R}^*$. Figure 7.3 shows the configuration $(q, \varphi, \psi)$: the control unit of the automaton is in state $q$, the string $\varphi$ of input symbols has been scanned from its input tape, and the string $\psi$ of output symbols has been written on its output tape. The new configuration resulting from the execution of a scan or print instruction by the automaton is shown in Figure 7.4.

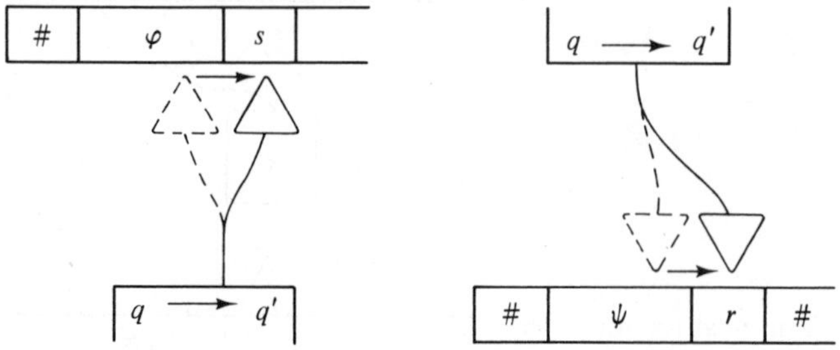


(a) scan (b) print

**Figure 7.4.** Moves of a sequential transducer.

**Definition 7.2:** Let **M** be a GST with program **P** and suppose that the string $\omega \in \mathbf{S}^*$ is written on its input tape. Instructions in the program **P** are *applicable* in configurations of **M** according to the following rules:

1. An instruction $q]$ **scan** $(s, q')$ applies in a configuration $(q, \varphi, \psi)$ just if $\varphi s$ is a prefix of the input string $\omega$. In executing a scan instruction, **M** moves its input head one square to the right, observes the symbol $s$ written therein, and enters state $q'$. We indicate how a scan move changes the configuration of **M** by writing

$$(q, \varphi, \psi) \xrightarrow{s} (q', \varphi s, \psi)$$

2. An instruction $q]$ **print** $(r, q')$ applies in any configuration of **M**. In executing a print instruction, **M** moves its output head one square to the right, prints the symbol $r$, and enters state $q'$. We represent a print move by writing

$$(q, \varphi, \psi) \xrightarrow{P} (q', \varphi, \psi r)$$

Whenever **M** has a sequence of moves

$$(q_0, \varphi_0, \psi_0) \longrightarrow (q_1, \varphi_1, \psi_1) \longrightarrow \dots \longrightarrow (q_k, \varphi_k, \psi_k)$$

(where each move is either a print or a scan move), we write

$$(q_0, \varphi_0, \psi_0) \Longrightarrow (q_k, \varphi_k, \psi_k)$$

Since several scan or several print instructions may be applicable in a given configuration, a sequential transducer is a nondeterministic automaton. A GST is *deterministic* if no more than one instruction is applicable in any of its configurations.

A sequential transducer begins operation from a configuration in which its input and output heads are positioned at the initial sharps of their respective tapes. If there is a sequence of moves that permits the machine to reach a final state, the string printed on the output tape is a *response* of the machine to the scanned string of input symbols. Since the operation of a sequential transducer may be nondeterministic, its response to a stimulus is not necessarily unique.

**Definition 7.3:** Suppose that **M** is a GST with initial states **I** and final states **F**. An *initial* configuration of **M** is a configuration of the form $(q, \lambda, \lambda)$, where $q \in \mathbf{I}$ is any initial state. A *final* configuration of **M** is a configuration of the form $(q', \varphi, \psi)$, where $q' \in \mathbf{F}$ is any final state. If

$$(q, \lambda, \lambda) \Longrightarrow (q', \varphi, \psi), \qquad q \in \mathbf{I}, \quad q' \in \mathbf{F}$$

is a move sequence of **M**, we say that $\psi$ is a *response* of **M** to the *stimulus* $\varphi$. If **X** is a subset of $\mathbf{S}^*$, then

$$\mathbf{Y} = \{\psi \in \mathbf{R}^* \mid \psi \text{ is a response of } \mathbf{M} \text{ to some } \varphi \in \mathbf{X}\}$$

is the *transduction* of **X** by **M**, and we write $\mathbf{Y} = \mathbf{M}(\mathbf{X})$. Conversely, if **Y** is a subset of $\mathbf{R}^*$, then

$$\mathbf{X} = \{\varphi \in \mathbf{S}^* \mid \psi \in \mathbf{Y} \text{ is a response of } \mathbf{M} \text{ to } \varphi\}$$

is the *inverse transduction* of **Y** by **M**, and we write $\mathbf{X} = \mathbf{M}^{-1}(\mathbf{Y})$.

In specific examples of tape automata, it is usually easier to understand a state graph than a program. State graphs for the control units of sequential transducers are drawn according to the conventions illustrated in Figure 7.5:

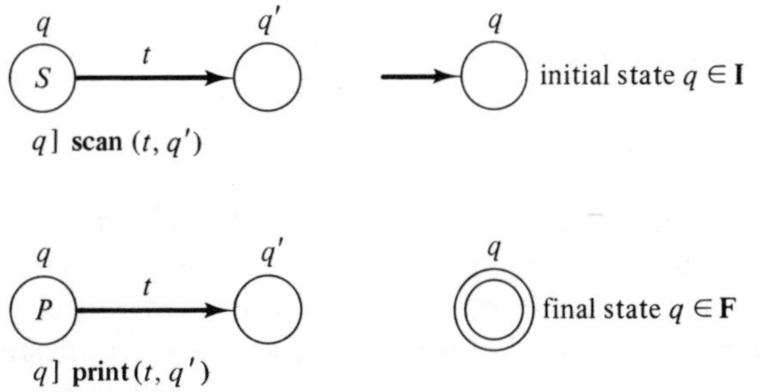


**Figure 7.5.** State diagram conventions for tape automata.

1. Each control state is represented by a circle. A letter inside the circle indicates the type of instructions labeled by the state; we use the letter $S$ for scan instructions, the letter $P$ for print instructions. If labels are needed to refer to states, numbers are used and written adjacent to the circles.

2. Each instruction

$$q]\ \textbf{scan}\ (t, q')$$

or

$$q]\ \textbf{print}\ (t, q')$$

is represented by an arc directed from state $q$ to state $q'$, and labeled with the symbol $t$.

3. The initial and final states are indicated as for finite-state accepters.

**Example 7.1:** Figure 7.6 shows the program and state diagram of a sequential transducer. For convenience, instructions labeled by the

(a) State Diagram

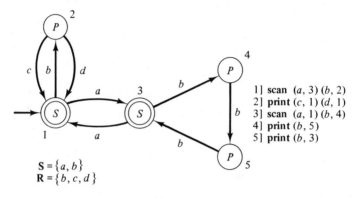

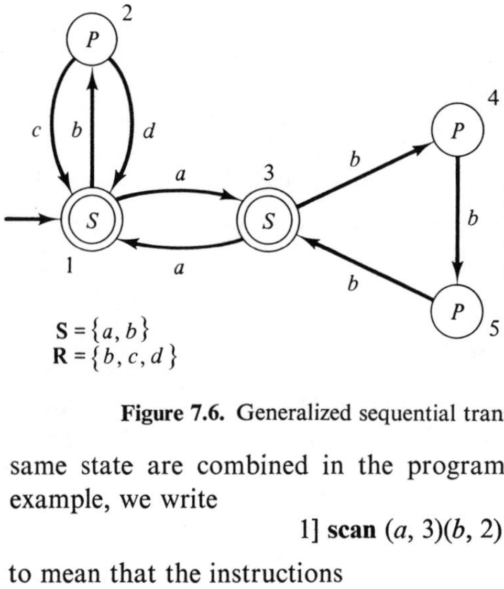


(b) Program

1] **scan** $(a, 3)\ (b, 2)$
2] **print** $(c, 1)\ (d, 1)$
3] **scan** $(a, 1)\ (b, 4)$
4] **print** $(b, 5)$
5] **print** $(b, 3)$

**Figure 7.6.** Generalized sequential transducer.

same state are combined in the program of the transducer. For example, we write

$$1]\ \textbf{scan}\ (a, 3)(b, 2)$$

to mean that the instructions

$$1]\ \textbf{scan}\ (a, 3)$$

$$1]\ \textbf{scan}\ (b, 2)$$

are both in the program of the machine. The machine is in one of two modes, indicating whether it has scanned an even or odd number of $a$'s. If the number of $a$'s is even, a scanned $b$ results in a symbol $c$ or $d$ in the response; otherwise, a scanned $b$ is translated into a pair of $b$'s. The operation of the transducer is illustrated by the move sequence

$$(1, \lambda, \lambda) \xrightarrow{S} (2, b, \lambda) \xrightarrow{P} (1, b, c) \xrightarrow{S} (3, ba, c)$$
$$\xrightarrow{S} (4, bab, c) \xrightarrow{P} (5, bab, cb) \xrightarrow{P} (3, bab, cbb)$$

which shows that $cbb$ is one response of the machine to the stimulus $bab$.

In Chapter 6 we demonstrated that the transduction of a regular set by a finite-state transducer is always a regular set. A construction similar to the one used there can be applied to generalized sequential transducers.

Given a finite-state generator

$$\mathbf{M}_g = (\mathbf{Q}_g, \mathbf{S}, \mathbf{P}_g, \mathbf{I}_g, \mathbf{F}_g)$$

and a generalized transducer

$$\mathbf{M}_t = (\mathbf{Q}_t, \mathbf{S}, \mathbf{R}, \mathbf{P}_t, \mathbf{I}_t, \mathbf{F}_t)$$

we can construct a new finite-state generator

$$\mathbf{M} = (\mathbf{Q}, \mathbf{R}, \mathbf{P}, \mathbf{I}, \mathbf{F})$$

that generates the transduction of $\mathbf{L}(\mathbf{M}_g)$ by $\mathbf{M}_t$. The transitions of $\mathbf{M}$ are specified in Table 7.2. (The $\lambda$-transitions resulting from the construction may

**Table 7.2** Construction of a generator for the transduction of a regular set

*Given:* $\mathbf{M}_g = (\mathbf{Q}_g, \mathbf{S}, \mathbf{P}_g, \mathbf{I}_g, \mathbf{F}_g)$, an FSG
$\mathbf{M}_t = (\mathbf{Q}_t, \mathbf{S}, \mathbf{R}, \mathbf{P}_t, \mathbf{I}_t, \mathbf{F}_t)$, a GST

*To construct:* $\mathbf{M} = (\mathbf{Q}, \mathbf{R}, \mathbf{P}, \mathbf{I}, \mathbf{F})$, an FSG such that $\mathbf{L}(\mathbf{M}) = \mathbf{M}_t(\mathbf{L}(\mathbf{M}_g))$

*Let:* $\mathbf{Q} = \mathbf{Q}_g \times \mathbf{Q}_t$ $\quad \mathbf{I} = \mathbf{I}_g \times \mathbf{I}_t$ $\quad \mathbf{F} = \mathbf{F}_g \times \mathbf{F}_t$

| If $\mathbf{M}_g$ has | and $\mathbf{M}_t$ has | then $\mathbf{M}$ has |
|---|---|---|
| $q \xrightarrow{s} q'$ | $p]$ **scan** $(s, p')$ | $(q, p) \xrightarrow{\lambda} (q', p')$ |
| $q \in \mathbf{Q}_g$ | $p]$ **print** $(r, p')$ | $(q, p) \xrightarrow{r} (q, p')$ |

be eliminated from $\mathbf{M}$ by the methods of Chapter 5.) Thus we have the following result:

**Theorem 7.1:** The class of regular sets is closed under transduction by a generalized sequential machine.

***Proof:*** The proof is analogous to that of Theorem 6.3 and is omitted.

Note that although sequential transducers can map regular sets only into other regular sets, they can still perform transductions impossible for finite-state transducers. In particular, a finite-state transducer must transduce each input string into an output string of the same length, whereas a GST may transduce an input string into one which is shorter or longer than the input.

**Example 7.2:** Figure 7.7 shows the construction of a finite-state generator for $\mathbf{M}_t((\mathbf{ab})^*)$, where $\mathbf{M}_t$ is the sequential transducer of Figure 7.6.

(a) $M_g$:

$L(M_g) = (ab)*$

(b) $M_t$:

(c) M:

$L(M) = M_t((ab)*) = (bb(c \cup d))*(\lambda \cup bb)$

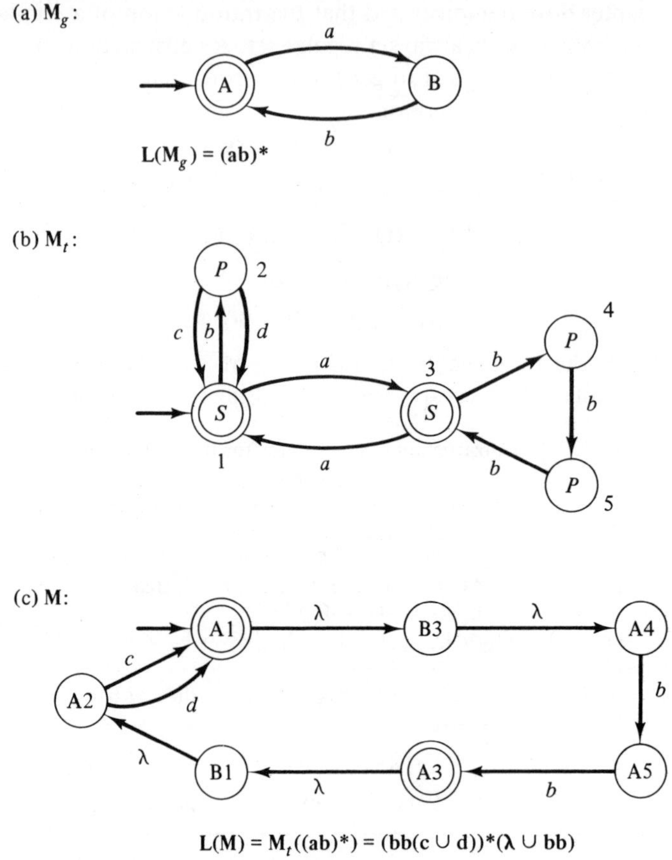

**Figure 7.7.** Generalized transduction of a regular set.

**Table 7.3** Construction of an accepter for the inverse transduction of a regular set

---

*Given:*   $M_a = (Q_a, R, P_a, I_a, F_a)$ an FSA
     $M_t = (Q_t, S, R, P_t, I_t, F_t)$ a GST
*To construct:*   $M = (Q, S, P, I, F)$ an FSA
     such that $L(M) = M_t^{-1}(L(M_a))$
*Let:*   $Q = Q_a \times Q_t$     $I = I_a \times I_t$     $F = F_a \times F_t$

---

| If $M_a$ has | and $M_t$ has | then $M$ has |
|---|---|---|
| $q \xrightarrow{r} q'$ | $p]$ **print** $(r, p')$ | $(q, p) \xrightarrow{\lambda} (q', p')$ |
| $q \in Q_a$ | $p]$ **scan** $(s, p')$ | $(q, p) \xrightarrow{s} (q, p')$ |

---

Suppose now that the output of a sequential transducer $\mathbf{M}_t$ is fed to some finite-state accepter $\mathbf{M}_a$. The cascade combination of $\mathbf{M}_t$ and $\mathbf{M}_a$ will be an accepter for those strings that can be transduced by $\mathbf{M}_t$ into members of $\mathbf{L}(\mathbf{M}_a)$. That is, it will be an accepter for the inverse transduction $\mathbf{M}_t^{-1}(\mathbf{L}(\mathbf{M}_a))$ of the language recognized by $\mathbf{M}_a$.

Table 7.3 gives the rules for constructing, from a generalized sequential transducer $\mathbf{M}_t$ and a finite-state accepter $\mathbf{M}_a$, a finite-state accepter $\mathbf{M}$ such that $\mathbf{L}(\mathbf{M}) = \mathbf{M}_t^{-1}(\mathbf{L}(\mathbf{M}_a))$. Again, the proof of the construction is similar to the proof of Theorem 6.3 and is left to the reader.

**Theorem 7.2:** The class of regular sets is closed under inverse transduction by a generalized sequential machine.

**Example 7.3:** Figure 7.8 illustrates the construction of a finite-state accepter for the inverse transduction by $\mathbf{M}_t$ of the language $\mathbf{L} = (\mathbf{bb}(\mathbf{c} \cup \mathbf{d}))^*(\boldsymbol{\lambda} \cup \mathbf{bb})$, where $\mathbf{M}_t$ is the transducer considered in Example 7.2. In that example, we showed that $\mathbf{L}$ is the transduction by $\mathbf{M}_t$ of the set $(\mathbf{ab})^*$. Yet we note that the inverse transduction of $\mathbf{L}$ by $\mathbf{M}_t$ is the set $(\mathbf{a}(\mathbf{a} \cup \mathbf{b}))^* \cup \boldsymbol{\lambda}$, rather than the set $(\mathbf{ab})^*$. Why?

If the program of a sequential transducer contains only scan instructions, it is a *sequential accepter*. The transduction of any set by a sequential accepter is either the regular set $\{\lambda\}$, or the empty set $\varnothing$ if no input leads to an accepting state. Therefore, the set of input strings for which a sequential accepter has a move sequence leading to a final state is, by Theorem 7.2, a regular set. Similarly, a sequential transducer with only print instructions is a sequential generator, and generates only regular sets. Since it should be clear that any finite-state accepter or generator may be simulated by a sequential tape accepter or generator, the class of languages definable by one-way tape automata having no storage tape is precisely the regular sets.

## 7.3 Two-Way Accepters

Our study of two-way accepters in this section serves two purposes. First, it shows that tape automata without storage tapes are no more capable as language recognizers than finite-state accepters, and thus that storage tapes are essential if the limitations of finite-state devices are to be overcome by tape automata. Second, our study illustrates an inverse relation between the complexity of processing and the time required for the completion of a computation. Whereas a finite-state accepter completes its analysis of an $n$-symbol input string in exactly $n$ steps, we find that a two-way accepter may require considerably fewer internal states but may take considerably more computation time.

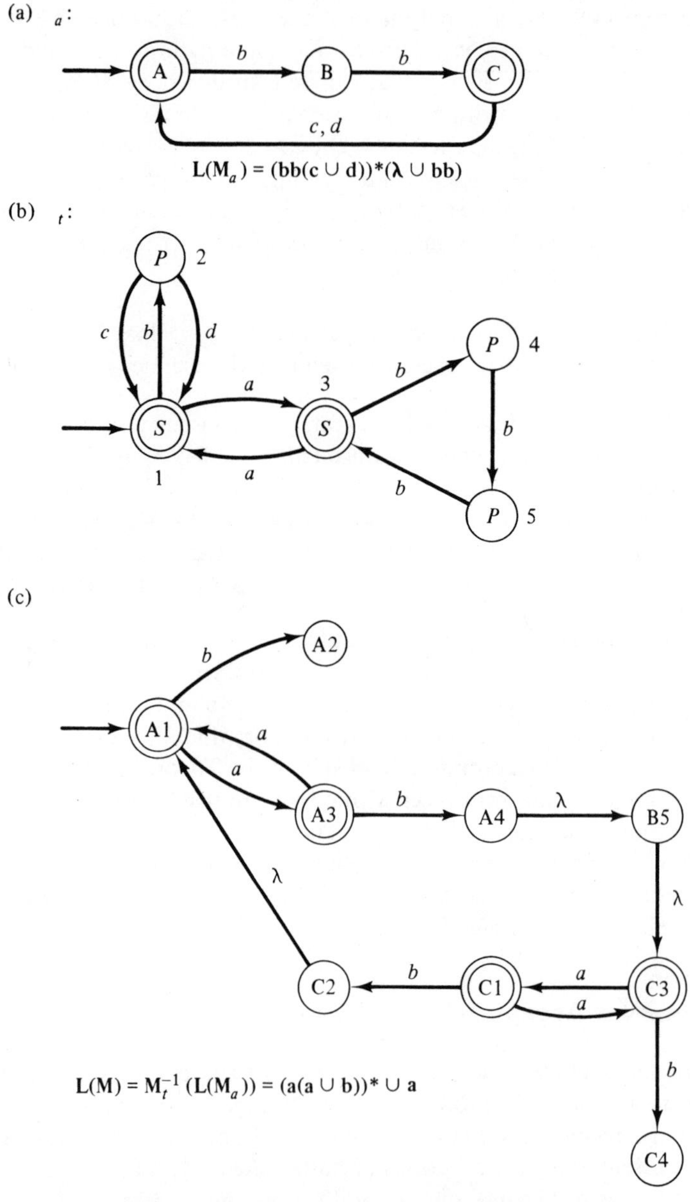


**Figure 7.8.** Inverse transduction of a regular set.

### 7.3.1 Definitions

As shown in Figure 7.9, a two-way accepter consists of a finite-state control unit and a head capable of moving, one square at a time, in either direction along an input tape.

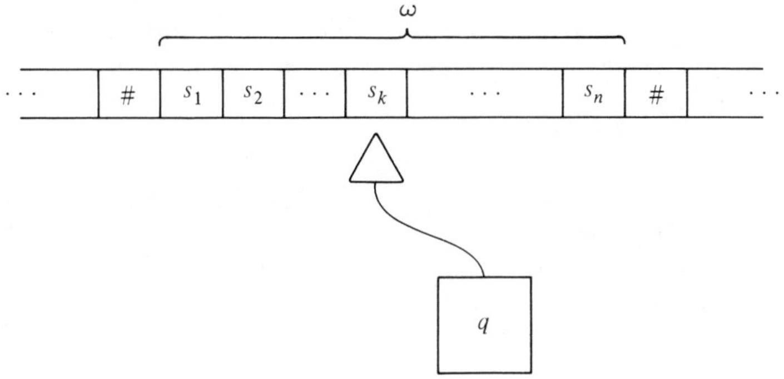


**Figure 7.9.** Two-way accepter.

**Definition 7.4:** A *two-way accepter* (TWA) is a five-tuple

$$\mathbf{M} = (\mathbf{Q}, \mathbf{S}, \mathbf{P}, \mathbf{I}, \mathbf{F})$$

where

**Q** is a finite set of internal states, including initial states **I** and final states **F**
**S** is a finite input alphabet
**P** is a program

Each instruction in the program **P** is of the form

$$q]\ \textbf{left}\ (s, q') \quad \text{or} \quad q]\ \textbf{right}\ (s, q') \qquad \text{where} \begin{cases} q, q' \in \mathbf{Q} \\ s \in \mathbf{S} \cup \{\#\} \end{cases}$$

Each state of **M** labels no more than one type of instruction, and is called a left state if it labels leftward instructions and a right state if it labels rightward instructions.

Since a two-way accepter may scan the same input symbol many times, we must define its configuration in terms of its input head location rather than by its sequence of scanned input symbols. As shown in Figure 7.9, a two-way accepter in configuration $(q, k)$, where $k \geq 0$, is in control state $q$ with its head positioned at the $k$th symbol of its input tape. The accepter begins operation with its head positioned at the initial sharp; during its sequence of moves, its head may make arbitrary excursions back and forth along the tape. If it reaches a final internal state, the machine accepts its input string. Note that such an accepter need not scan all its input symbols to accept a string.

**Definition 7.5:** Let **M** be a TWA with an input string $\omega$ written on its tape. Instructions in its program are applicable in configurations of **M** as follows:

1. An instruction $q]$ **right** $(s, q')$ applies in a configuration $(q, k)$ just if the $k + 1$st tape square contains $s$. Execution of a right instruction moves the head one square to the right and places the control in state $q'$. We represent such a move by

$$(q, k) \xrightarrow{R} (q', k + 1)$$

2. An instruction $q]$ **left** $(s, q')$ applies in a configuration $(q, k)$, $k \geq 1$, just if the $k - 1$st tape square contains $s$. Execution of this instruction moves the head one square to the left and places the control unit in state $q'$. We represent the move by

$$(q, k) \xrightarrow{L} (q', k - 1)$$

If **M** has a sequence of moves

$$(q, 0) \Longrightarrow (q', k), \qquad q \in \mathbf{I}, \quad q' \in \mathbf{F}, \quad k \geq 0$$

then the string $\omega$ is *accepted* by **M**. A TWA is *deterministic* if at most one instruction is applicable in each configuration. If no instruction is applicable in a given configuration, the configuration is *dead* and the machine halts.

In the examples, problems, and discussions of this chapter, two-way accepters are assumed deterministic.† Under this assumption, there are three ways in which an input string may be rejected by an accepter:

1. The accepter reaches a dead configuration $(q, k)$, where $q$ is not a final state.
2. The accepter loops; that is, it repeats a cycle of moves indefinitely without reaching a final state.
3. The accepter scans indefinitely to the right along its tape without entering a final state.

### 7.3.2 Examples

The following examples illustrate how dividing the analysis of an input string into stages, each conducted during a single pass along the tape, can result in a surprising economy of states.

**Example 7.4:** Let $N_s(\omega)$ denote the number of occurrences of the symbol $s$ in the string $\omega$. We shall construct a TWA **M** that accepts a string $\omega$ in $(\mathbf{a} \cup \mathbf{b})^*$ just if $\omega$ has both of the following properties:

P1. $N_a(\omega) \bmod 2 = 0$.
P2. $N_b(\omega) \bmod 3 = 0$.

†This assumption implies no loss of generality, since nondeterministic behavior does not increase the language-defining ability of two-way accepters. See Problem 7.16.

A program and a state diagram for **M** are shown in Figure 7.10. The automaton makes two left-to-right passes over the input tape: the first pass checks property P1; the second pass checks property P2.

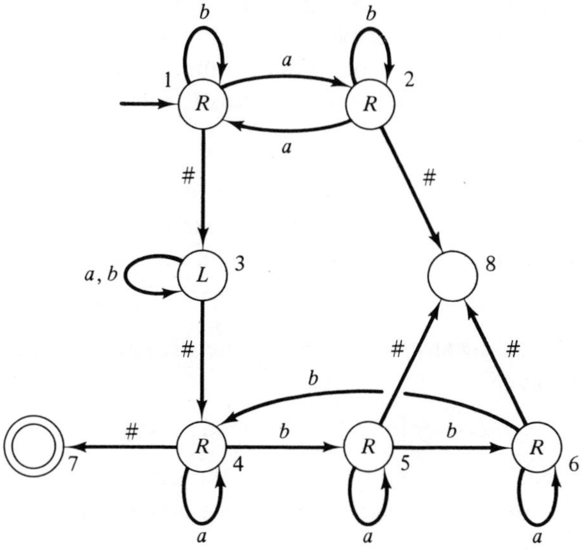


(a) State Diagram

1] **right** $(a, 2)\ (b, 1)\ (\#, 3)$
2] **right** $(a, 1)\ (b, 2)\ (\#, 8)$
3] **left** $(a, 3)\ (b, 3)\ (\#, 4)$
4] **right** $(a, 4)\ (b, 5)\ (\#, 7)$
5] **right** $(a, 5)\ (b, 6)\ (\#, 8)$
6] **right** $(a, 6)\ (b, 4)\ (\#, 8)$

(b) Program

**Figure 7.10.** Simple two-way accepter.

**Example 7.5:** Now suppose that the properties in Example 7.4 are changed as follows:

P1. $N_a(\omega) \bmod m = 0$.
P2. $N_b(\omega) \bmod n = 0$.

Let the language **L**$(m, n)$ consist of the strings in $(\mathbf{a} \cup \mathbf{b})^*$ that satisfy both P1 and P2. We are interested in how the control-state complexity and the speed of a two-way accepter for $\mathbf{L}(m, n)$ compare with those of an equivalent finite-state accepter.

A finite-state accepter for $\mathbf{L}(m, n)$ must maintain independent counts of $N_a$ mod $m$ and $N_b$ mod $n$ as successive input symbols are presented; thus at least $mn$ states are required. Yet a two-way accepter for $\mathbf{L}(m, n)$ can be constructed with only $m + n + 3$ states, by generalizing the principle illustrated by Example 7.4. The penalty for fewer states is increased running time: to process $\omega$ the two-way accepter performs $3|\omega|$ steps, whereas the finite-state accepter performs only $\omega$ steps.

Example 7.5 shows that a finite-state equivalent of a given two-way accepter may require more states. The next example illustrates this point even more dramatically. In Chapter 6, we found that the matching language

$$\mathbf{L}_m = \{a^k b^k \mid k \geq 1\}$$

cannot be recognized by any finite-state accepter. However, for each positive integer $r$, the language

$$\mathbf{L}(r) = \{a^x b^y \,\big|\, |x - y| \bmod r = 0\}$$

can be recognized by an FSA with $2r$ states. We shall show that for certain values of $r$, $\mathbf{L}(r)$ can be recognized by a two-way accepter having many fewer than $2r$ states.

**Example 7.6:** We shall design a two-way accepter $\mathbf{M}$ that recognizes $\mathbf{L}(r)$ for certain large values of $r$. Let $p_1, p_2, \ldots, p_n$ be the first $n$ prime numbers. The program of $\mathbf{M}$ will consist of $n$ routines $\mathbf{M}(p_1)$, $\mathbf{M}(p_2), \ldots, \mathbf{M}(p_n)$, where each routine performs two operations:

1. A left-to-right pass in which $N_a(\omega)$ mod $p_i$ is tested for equality with $N_b(\omega)$ mod $p_i$. (This pass also checks that $\omega$ is a string of $a$'s followed by a string of $b$'s.)
2. A right-to-left pass that returns the head to the initial sharp.

Figure 7.11 specifies the routines $\mathbf{M}(p_i)$ and shows how they are to be coupled together to form the state diagram of $\mathbf{M}$.

What language does $\mathbf{M}$ recognize? Clearly, each string accepted by $\mathbf{M}$ is of the form $a^x b^y$, where

$$x \bmod p_i = y \bmod p_i, \qquad i = 1, 2, \ldots, n$$

That is, both $x$ and $y$ yield the same remainder when divided by $p_i$:

$$\left.\begin{aligned} x &= u_i p_i + r_i \\ y &= v_i p_i + r_i \end{aligned}\right\} \; i = 1, 2, \ldots, n$$

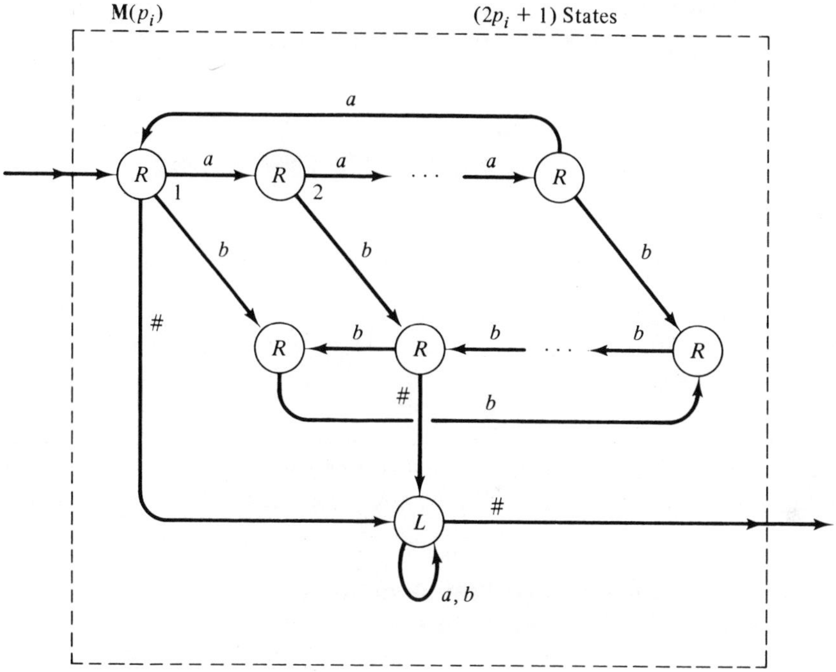


(a) Structure of M($p_i$)

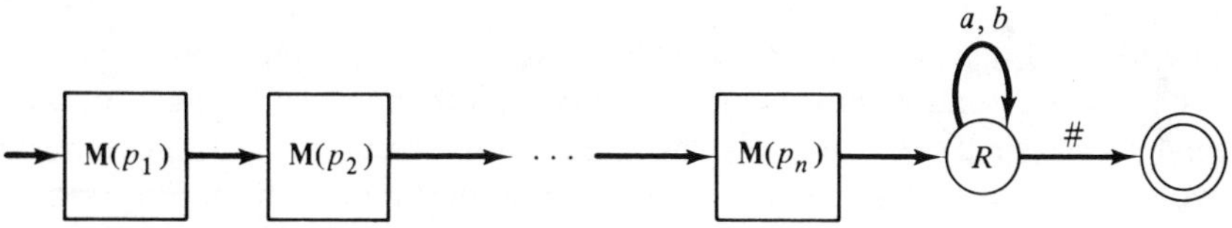


(b) Structure of **M**

**Figure 7.11.** Construction of a two-way accepter for **L**($r$).

Taking the difference of these two equations, we find that

$$x - y = (u_i - v_i)p_i, \qquad i = 1, 2, \ldots, n$$

Since the integer $(u_i - v_i)p_i$ is divisible by $p_i$, the equal integer $x - y$ must also be divisible by $p_i$. This being true for each of the prime numbers $p_1, \ldots, p_n$, the integer $x - y$ must be an integral multiple of the product of the primes:

$$x - y = c(p_1 p_2 \ldots p_n)$$

Thus

$$\mathbf{L(M)} = \{a^x b^y \,\big|\, |x - y| \bmod r = 0\} = \mathbf{L}(r)$$

where $r = p_1 p_2 \ldots p_n$.

Now the first seven prime numbers are 2, 3, 5, 7, 11, 13, and 17. For $n = 7$, the two-way accepter in Figure 7.11 has

$$\sum_{i=1}^{7} (2p_i + 1) + 1 = 124$$

states, whereas a finite-state accepter for the same language $\mathbf{L}(r)$ would require at least

$$2r = 2(2 \times 3 \times 5 \times 7 \times 11 \times 13 \times 17) = 1{,}021{,}020$$

states!

These examples show that significant state savings may be realized by defining certain regular sets in terms of two-way accepters. In the Problems, we consider exactly how great this economy can be.

### 7.3.3 Equivalence of Two-Way Accepters and Finite-State Accepters

To construct an equivalent finite-state accepter from any given deterministic two-way accepter, it is convenient to assume that the two-way accepter always halts with its head positioned at the final sharp; a two-way accepter that behaves in this manner is said to be in *standard form.* (The accepter of Figure 7.10 is in standard form, but the accepter of Figure 7.11 is not; it may halt at any point along its tape if the input string is not accepted.) We shall show that it is possible to convert an arbitrary deterministic two-way accepter **M** to an equivalent accepter in standard form. For simplicity, we assume that the TWA never scans right of its final sharp or left of its initial sharp. (This assumption implies no loss of generality. In fact, it is quite easy to show that any deterministic TWA can be modified to obtain an equivalent machine that never scans outside the region delimited by its initial and final sharps; the details are explored in the Problems.)

Let $\mathbf{Q}$ be the states of **M**, and let $\mathbf{Q}_L \subseteq \mathbf{Q}$ and $\mathbf{Q}_R \subseteq \mathbf{Q}$ be the sets of states that label left instructions and right instructions, respectively. (For convenience, a state that labels no instructions will be thought of as a left state. Thus $\mathbf{Q} = \mathbf{Q}_L \cup \mathbf{Q}_R$ and $\mathbf{Q}_L \cap \mathbf{Q}_R = \varnothing$.) The construction of an equivalent two-way accepter in standard form is illustrated in Figure 7.12. As shown, we add two routines to **M** that cause the tape head to move right until the final sharp is scanned. The *accept routine* is entered whenever **M** would otherwise have entered an accepting state. The *reject routine* is entered whenever **M** would otherwise have entered a dead or looping configuration.

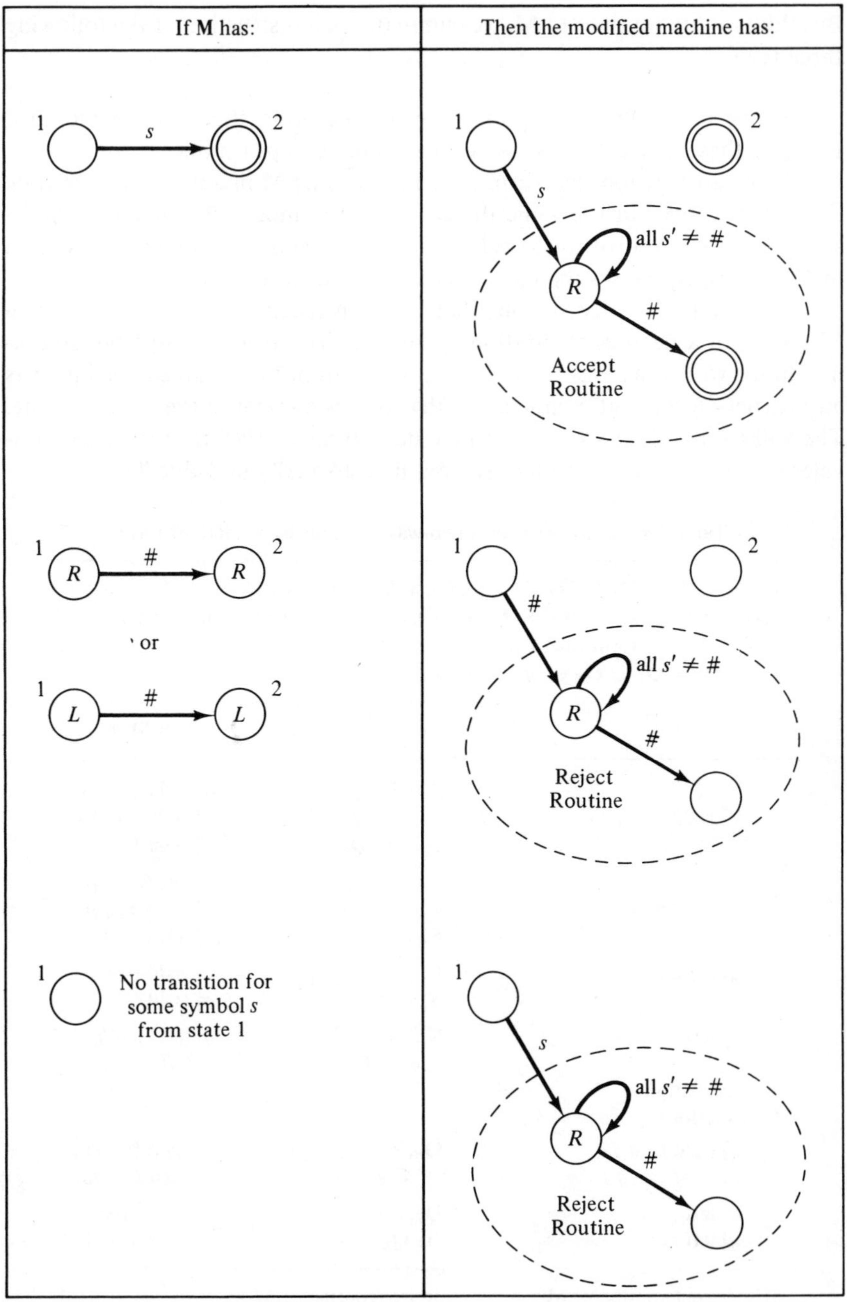


**Figure 7.12.** Converting a two-way accepter into standard form.

By adding these routines to **M**, we eliminate each instruction of the following three types:

1. An instruction that puts **M** in an accepting state. In the modified machine these instructions pass control to the accept routine.
2. An instruction that scans a sharp and puts **M** in a nonaccepting state that labels moves in the same direction. In the modified machine such instructions pass control to the reject routine, since their attempted execution in **M** necessarily causes the machine to enter a dead configuration.
3. A "missing" instruction; that is, an instruction whose absence from **M** results in a dead configuration. Whenever **M** has a state–symbol combination for which there is no applicable instruction, the modified machine has an instruction for that combination that passes control to the reject routine.

The rules for modifying an arbitrary deterministic TWA to obtain an equivalent standard-form accepter are presented formally in Table 7.4.

**Table 7.4** Conversion of a two-way accepter into standard form

*Given:* $\mathbf{M} = (\mathbf{Q}_L \cup \mathbf{Q}_R, \mathbf{S}, \mathbf{P}, \mathbf{q}_I, \mathbf{F})$, a deterministic TWA
*To construct:* $\mathbf{M}' = (\mathbf{Q}', \mathbf{S}, \mathbf{P}', \mathbf{q}_I, \mathbf{q}'_A)$, a deterministic TWA in standard form such that $\mathbf{L}(\mathbf{M}) = \mathbf{L}(\mathbf{M}')$
*Let:* $\mathbf{Q}' = \mathbf{Q}_L \cup \mathbf{Q}_R \cup \{q_A, q'_A, q_B, q'_B\}$

| If **M** has | and | then **M′** has |
|---|---|---|
| $q]$ **right** $(\#, q')$ | $q' \in \mathbf{F}$ | $q]$ **right** $(\#, q'_A)$ |
| | $q' \notin \mathbf{F}, q' \in \mathbf{Q}_L$ | $q]$ **right** $(\#, q')$ |
| | $q' \notin \mathbf{F}, q' \in \mathbf{Q}_R$ | $q]$ **right** $(\#, q'_B)$ |
| $q]$ **left** $(\#, q')$ | $q' \in \mathbf{F}$ | $q]$ **left** $(\#, q_A)$ |
| | $q' \notin \mathbf{F}, q' \in \mathbf{Q}_L$ | $q]$ **left** $(\#, q_B)$ |
| | $q' \notin \mathbf{F}, q' \in \mathbf{Q}_R$ | $q]$ **left** $(\#, q')$ |
| $q]$ **right** $(s, q')$ | $s \in \mathbf{S}, q' \in \mathbf{F}$ | $q]$ **right** $(s, q_A)$ |
| | $s \in \mathbf{S}, q' \notin \mathbf{F}$ | $q]$ **right** $(s, q')$ |
| $q]$ **left** $(s, q')$ | $s \in \mathbf{S}, q' \in \mathbf{F}$ | $q]$ **left** $(s, q_A)$ |
| | $s \in \mathbf{S}, q' \notin \mathbf{F}$ | $q]$ **left** $(s, q')$ |
| No instruction of the form: | | |
| $q]$ **right** $(s, q')$ | $q \in \mathbf{Q}_R, s \in \mathbf{S}$ | $q]$ **right** $(s, q_B)$ |
| $q]$ **right** $(\#, q')$ | $q \in \mathbf{Q}_R$ | $q]$ **right** $(\#, q'_B)$ |
| $q]$ **left** $(s, q')$ | $q \in \mathbf{Q}_L, s \in \mathbf{S}$ | $q]$ **left** $(s, q_B)$ |
| $q]$ **left** $(\#, q')$ | $q \in \mathbf{Q}_L$ | $q]$ **left** $(\#, q_B)$ |

Accept routine of **M′**:
$q_A]$ **right** $(s, q_A)$, $s \in \mathbf{S}$
$q_A]$ **right** $(\#, q'_A)$

Reject routine of **M′**:
$q_B]$ **right** $(s, q_B)$, $s \in \mathbf{S}$
$q_B]$ **right** $(\#, q'_B)$

Now let $\mathbf{M} = (\mathbf{Q}, \mathbf{S}, \mathbf{P}, \mathbf{I}, \mathbf{F})$ be a deterministic two-way accepter in standard form. In analyzing an input string $\omega$, $\mathbf{M}$ may make arbitrary excursions up and down its tape (Figure 7.13). However, for any prefix $\alpha$ of $\omega$, the states of $\mathbf{M}$ can record only a bounded number of "different facts" about $\alpha$, since $\mathbf{M}$ has a finite-state control unit. This observation is essential in our construction.

As before, let $\mathbf{Q}_L$ and $\mathbf{Q}_R$ be the disjoint sets of states that label left and right instructions of $\mathbf{M}$, respectively. Figure 7.14 shows $\mathbf{M}$ during its analysis of an input string. The control unit is in state $q$, and the letter $s$ has just been

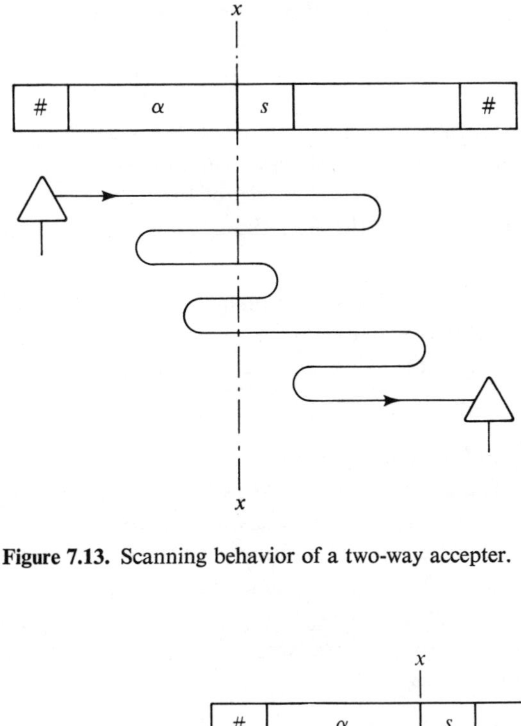


**Figure 7.13.** Scanning behavior of a two-way accepter.

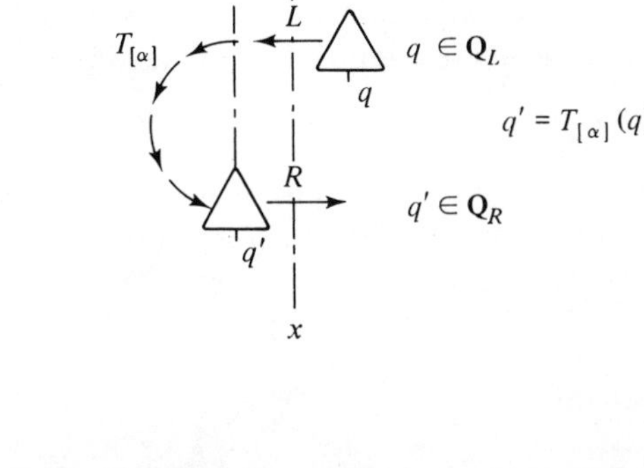


**Figure 7.14.** Definition of the transformation $T_{[\alpha]}$.

scanned. If $q \in \mathbf{Q}_L$, $\mathbf{M}$ will move left, crossing the boundary $xx$ in the figure, and its subsequent behavior will follow one of two courses:

1. $\mathbf{M}$ will eventually recross the boundary $xx$ by executing a right instruction labeled by some state $q' \in \mathbf{Q}_R$.
2. $\mathbf{M}$ will continue running forever without recrossing boundary $xx$.

Note that no other possibilities exist because $\mathbf{M}$, being in standard form, halts only at its final sharp.

The behavior of $\mathbf{M}$ while scanning to the left of boundary $xx$ is completely determined by the state $q$, the string $\alpha$ lying to the left of the boundary, and the program of $\mathbf{M}$. Thus, given the program, we may associate a transformation

$$T_\alpha : \mathbf{Q}_L \longrightarrow \mathbf{Q}_R \cup \{\Delta\}$$

with each string $\alpha$ in $\mathbf{S}^*$, where $\Delta$ signifies "no state." If $\mathbf{M}$ executes a left instruction labeled $q$ and never recrosses the boundary, we define $T_\alpha(q) = \Delta$; otherwise, we define $T_\alpha(q)$ to be the label of the right instruction by which $\mathbf{M}$ recrosses the boundary for the first time. Thus, if $\alpha$ is a string of $k$ input symbols,

$$T_\alpha(q) = \begin{cases} q' & \text{if } \mathbf{M} \text{ has a move sequence } (q, k+1) \Longrightarrow (q', k)\text{, where} \\ & q' \text{ is the first right state entered by } \mathbf{M} \text{ during the} \\ & \text{sequence while at tape position } k \\ \Delta & \text{otherwise} \end{cases}$$

This definition is illustrated by Figure 7.14.

Since there is an infinity of strings in $\mathbf{S}^*$, one might conclude that there is an infinity of distinct transformations for a given machine. But this is not so. Each transformation maps the finite set $\mathbf{Q}_L$ into the finite set $\mathbf{Q}_R \cup \{\Delta\}$. If the control unit of $\mathbf{M}$ has $m$ left states and $n$ right states, the number of distinct functions from $\mathbf{Q}_L$ to $\mathbf{Q}_R \cup \{\Delta\}$ is $(n + 1)^m$, and thus there can be no more than $(n + 1)^m$ distinct transformations for $\mathbf{M}$. Let $\mathfrak{T}$ be the collection of these transformations:

$$\mathfrak{T} = \{T \mid T: \mathbf{Q}_L \longrightarrow \mathbf{Q}_R \cup \{\Delta\}\}$$

The association of a member of $\mathfrak{T}$ with each string in $\mathbf{S}^*$ defines an equivalence relation of finite index on $\mathbf{S}^*$:

$$\omega \sim \varphi \qquad \text{if and only if } T_\omega = T_\varphi$$

Let $[\alpha]$ denote the equivalence class of the string $\alpha$. We use the notation $T_{[\alpha]}$ to represent the transformation in $\mathfrak{T}$ that applies for each string in the equivalence class $[\alpha]$. The transformation $T_{[\alpha]}$ represents the total "knowledge" $\mathbf{M}$ has concerning the string to the left of the boundary in Figure 7.14.

Our approach to constructing an FSA $\mathbf{M}'$ equivalent to $\mathbf{M}$ is to provide $\mathbf{M}'$ with sufficient states to keep track of the transformation associated by $\mathbf{M}$ with its current input string, as the string is extended by successive input symbols. For each symbol $s$ presented to $\mathbf{M}'$, the finite-state accepter makes a transition from a state representing $T_{[\alpha]}$ to one representing $T_{[\alpha s]}$, where $\alpha$ is the string of symbols previously presented to the machine.

The relation between $T_{[\alpha s]}$ and $T_{[\alpha]}$ is shown in Figure 7.15. Suppose that $q \in \mathbf{Q}_L$ and $\mathbf{M}$ has the instruction

$$q]\ \textbf{left}\ (s, q_1)$$

Then if $q_1 \in \mathbf{Q}_L$ and $T_{[\alpha]}(q_1) = q'_1$, $\mathbf{M}$ recrosses the boundary $xx$ by executing an instruction

$$q'_1]\ \textbf{right}\ (s, q_2)$$

If $q_2$ is in $\mathbf{Q}_L$ and $T_{[\alpha]}(q_2) = q'_2$, the same pattern will repeat. This continues until a state $q_k$ is reached for which one of three conditions holds:

1. Some state is repeated in the sequence $q_1, q_2, \ldots, q_k$; in this case $\mathbf{M}$ is in a loop.
2. $T_{[\alpha]}(q_k) = \Delta$; that is, $\mathbf{M}$ moves left again and never recrosses the boundary $xx$.
3. $q_k \in \mathbf{Q}_R$.

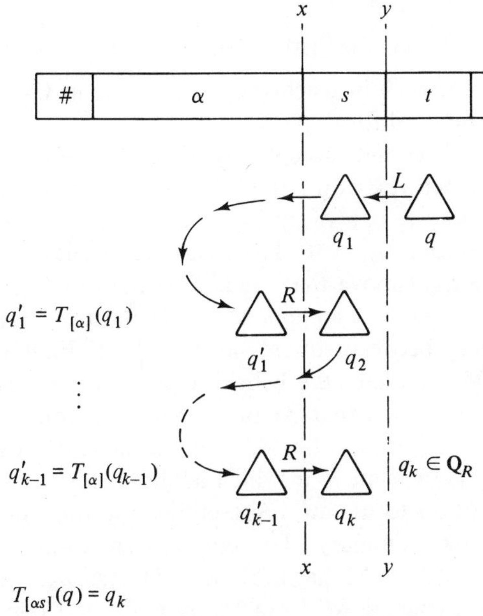


**Figure 7.15.** Formation of $T_{[\alpha s]}$ from $T_{[\alpha]}$.

In the first two cases $T_{[\alpha s]}(q) = \Delta$. In the third case, **M** will recross the boundary $yy$ by executing an instruction

$$q_k] \textbf{ right } (t, q')$$

and therefore $T_{[\alpha s]}(q) = q_k$. In summary:

$$T_{[\alpha s]}(q) = \begin{cases} q_k \begin{cases} \text{if } \mathbf{M} \text{ has instructions} \\ \qquad q] \textbf{ left } (s, q_1) \\ \qquad q_1'] \textbf{ right } (s, q_2) \\ \qquad \quad \vdots \\ \qquad q_{k-1}'] \textbf{ right } (s, q_k) \\ \text{such that} \\ q_1, \ldots, q_k \text{ are distinct} \\ \left.\begin{array}{l} q_i \in \mathbf{Q}_L \\ T_{[\alpha]}(q_i) = q_i' \end{array}\right\} i = 1, \ldots, k-1 \\ q_k \in \mathbf{Q}_R \end{cases} \\ \Delta \quad \text{otherwise} \end{cases}$$

The transformation $T_{[\lambda]}$ that applies to the boundary adjacent to the initial sharp maps each left state of **M** into the right state that **M** assumes upon scanning the initial sharp:

$$T_{[\lambda]}(q) = q' \quad \text{where } \mathbf{M} \text{ has the instruction } q] \textbf{ left } (\#, q') \text{ with } q' \text{ in } \mathbf{Q}_R$$

There will be exactly one such instruction for each state in $\mathbf{Q}_L$ because **M** is deterministic and in standard form.

The construction of the finite accepter **M**′ that simulates the behavior of the given two-way accepter **M** is now straightforward. After **M**′ has processed the $k$ symbols forming a prefix $\alpha$ of an input string, its state will be a pair $(q, T_{[\alpha]})$, where $q \in \mathbf{Q}_R$ and $T_{[\alpha]} \in \mathfrak{T}$. The first component $q$ is the state in which **M** executes the right move that reads the symbol $s$ in square $k + 1$ for the first time. The second component $T_{[\alpha]}$ is the transformation that applies to the boundary between squares $k$ and $k + 1$. Figure 7.16 shows how a transition of **M**′ simulates the behavior of **M** [the transition shown models the sequence of moves that **M** makes starting from configuration $(q, k)$ and ending in configuration $(q', k + 1)$]: machine **M**′ uses transformation $T_{[\alpha]}$ to determine the state $q'$ in which **M** first reads the input symbol $s$, then makes a transition to a state representing the transformation $T_{[\alpha s]}$ that applies to the new boundary. To represent situations in which **M** never does cross the boundary, **M**′ has the additional state $q_\Delta$, which is a trap state. The rules for constructing **M**′ from **M** are given in Table 7.5 and are explained in detail below:

**Table 7.5** Construction of a finite-state accepter from a two-way accepter

| | |
|---|---|
| *Given:* the two-way accepter<br>$\mathbf{M} = (\mathbf{Q}, \mathbf{S}, \mathbf{P}, \mathbf{q}_I, \mathbf{F})$<br>with $\mathbf{Q} = \mathbf{Q}_L \cup \mathbf{Q}_R$ | *Construct:* the finite-state accepter<br>$\mathbf{M}' = (\mathbf{Q}', \mathbf{S}, \mathbf{P}', \mathbf{q}'_I, \mathbf{F}')$,<br>where $\mathbf{Q}' = (\mathbf{Q}_R \times \mathfrak{T}) \cup \{q_\Delta\}$,<br>$\mathfrak{T} = \{T: \mathbf{Q}_L \longrightarrow \mathbf{Q}_R \cup \{\Delta\}\}$,<br>$q'_I = (q_I, T_{[\lambda]})$ |
| *Let:* $T_{[\alpha]}$ be any transformation in $\mathfrak{T}$ | |

| If **M** has | then **M**′ has |
|---|---|
| $q]$ **right** $(s, q_0)$, $q_0 \in \mathbf{Q}_R$ | $(q, T_{[\alpha]}) \xrightarrow{s} (q_0, T_{[\alpha s]})$ |
| $q]$ **right** $(s, q_0)$, $q_0 \in \mathbf{Q}_L$<br>and $q'_0]$ **right** $(s, q_1)$, $q'_0 = T_{[\alpha]}(q_0)$<br>$q'_1]$ **right** $(s, q_2)$, $q'_1 = T_{[\alpha]}(q_1)$<br>.<br>.<br>.<br>$q'_{k-1}]$ **right** $(s, q_k)$, $q'_{k-1} = T_{[\alpha]}(q_{k-1})$<br>where $q_0, \ldots, q_{k-1}$ are distinct states in $\mathbf{Q}_L$ and $q_k \in \mathbf{Q}_R$ | $(q, T_{[\alpha]}) \xrightarrow{s} (q_k, T_{[\alpha s]})$ |
| $q]$ **right** $(s, q_0)$, $q_0 \in \mathbf{Q}_L$<br>and there is no sequence of states $q_0, q_1, \ldots, q_k$ as above | $(q, T_{[\alpha]}) \xrightarrow{s} q_\Delta$<br>$q_\Delta \xrightarrow{s} q_\Delta$, each $s \in \mathbf{S}$ |
| $q_0]$ **right** $(\#, q_1)$<br>$q'_1]$ **right** $(\#, q_2)$, $q'_1 = T_{[\alpha]}(q_1)$<br>.<br>.<br>.<br>$q'_{k-1}]$ **right** $(\#, q_k)$, $q'_{k-1} = T_{[\alpha]}(q_{k-1})$<br>where $q_1, \ldots, q_{k-1}$ are in $\mathbf{Q}_L$ and $q_k \in \mathbf{F}$ | $(q_0, T_{[\alpha]}) \in \mathbf{F}'$ |

The accepter **M** scans an input symbol $s$ for the first time by executing a right instruction

$$q]\ \mathbf{right}\ (s, q_0)$$

If $q_0$ is a right-moving state, the corresponding transition of **M**′ updates the transformation $T_{[\alpha]}$ to obtain the transformation $T_{[\alpha s]}$ that applies to the new boundary. If $q$ is a left-moving state, the transition in **M**′ is determined by using $T_{[\alpha]}$ to find the state $q_k$ from which **M** first scans the next input symbol. A state $(q_0, T_{[\alpha]})$ is a final state of **M** just if $q_0$ is the label of a right instruction

$$q_0]\ \mathbf{right}\ (\#, q_1)$$

and either $q_1$ is a final state of **M** or a series of excursions to the left leads **M** to a final state, as shown in Figure 7.17.

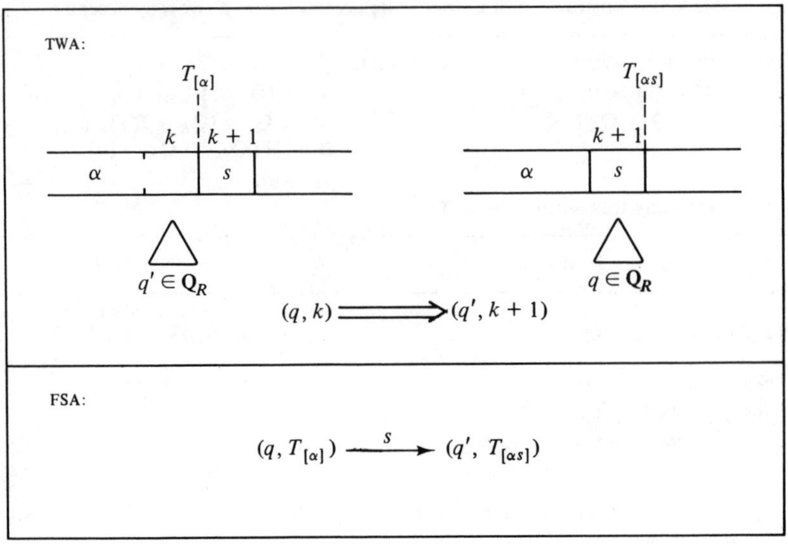


**Figure 7.16.** Simulation of a two-way accepter by a finite-state accepter.

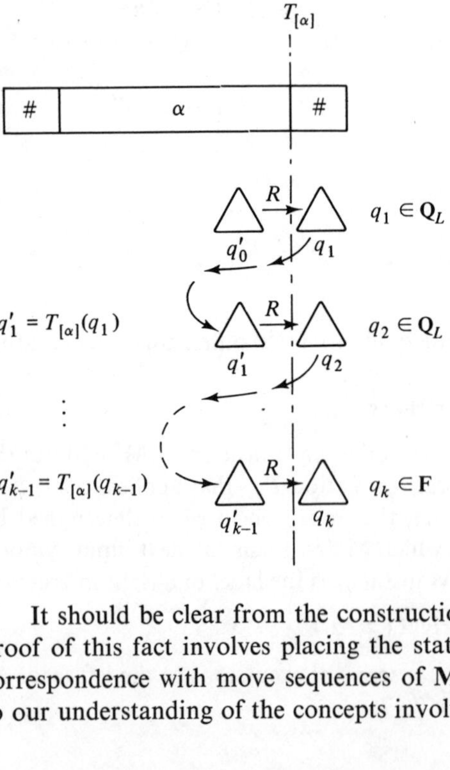


**Figure 7.17.** Determination of final states.

It should be clear from the construction that $\mathbf{L}(\mathbf{M}') = \mathbf{L}(\mathbf{M})$. A formal proof of this fact involves placing the state sequences of $\mathbf{M}'$ in one-to-one correspondence with move sequences of $\mathbf{M}$; writing it out would add little to our understanding of the concepts involved.

**Theorem 7.3:** From any deterministic two-way accepter **M**, one can construct a finite-state accepter **M**$'$ such that **L**(**M**$'$) = **L**(**M**).

**Example 7.7:** The two-way accepter **M** shown in Figure 7.18a is in standard form and has one left-moving state and two right-moving states:

$$\mathbf{Q}_L = \{2\} \qquad \mathbf{Q}_R = \{1, 3\}$$

Therefore, each transformation $T_{[\alpha]}$ has the form

$$T: \{2\} \longrightarrow \{1, 3, \Delta\}$$

(a) Two-way accepter **M**:

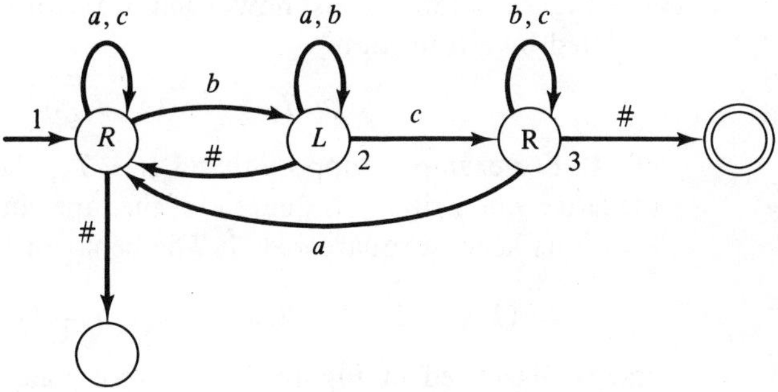


(b) $T_{[\alpha s]}$ in terms of $T_{[\alpha]}$ and $s$

| $T_{[\alpha]}$ \ $s$ | $a$ | $b$ | $c$ |
|---|---|---|---|
| $T_{21}$ | $T_{21}$ | $T_{2\Delta}$ | $T_{23}$ |
| $T_{23}$ | $T_{21}$ | $T_{23}$ | $T_{23}$ |
| $T_{2\Delta}$ | $T_{2\Delta}$ | $T_{2\Delta}$ | $T_{23}$ |

(c) Determination of $T_{[\alpha a]}$ for $T_{[\alpha]} = T_{21}$

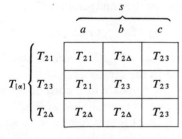

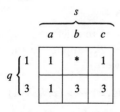

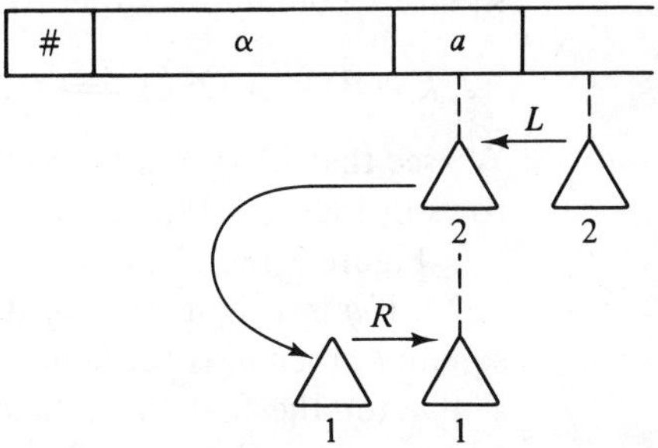


(d) $q'$ in terms of $T_{[\alpha]}$, $q$ and $s$
For each $T_{[\alpha]}$:

| $q$ \ $s$ | $a$ | $b$ | $c$ |
|---|---|---|---|
| 1 | 1 | * | 1 |
| 3 | 1 | 3 | 3 |

*If $q = 1$ and $s = b$, $q'$ in terms of $T_{[\alpha]}$ is:

| $T_{[\alpha]}$ | $q'$ |
|---|---|
| $T_{21}$ | $q_\Delta$ |
| $T_{23}$ | 3 |
| $T_{2\Delta}$ | $q_\Delta$ |

**Figure 7.18.** Analysis of a two-way accepter for the construction of an equivalent finite-state accepter.

and the collection of possible transformations is

$$\mathfrak{T} = \{(2, 1), (2, 3), (2, \Delta)\}$$

Let us abbreviate the three transformations by

$$T_{21} = \{(2, 1)\} \qquad T_{23} = \{(2, 3)\} \qquad T_{2\Delta} = \{(2, \Delta)\}$$

The only instruction of **M** that scans a sharp by a left move is

2] **left** (#, 1)

Hence $T_{[\lambda]} = T_{21}$.

Figure 7.18b shows how each transformation $T_{[\alpha]}$ must be updated by a transition

$$(q, T_{[\alpha]}) \xrightarrow{s} (q', T_{[\alpha s]})$$

of **M**′. For example, suppose that $T_{[\alpha]} = T_{21}$. To determine $T_{[\alpha a]}$, let the letter $a$ be written in square $k$ of the tape, and let **M** start in state 2 with its head at square $k + 1$. The behavior that follows is

$$(2, k + 1) \xrightarrow{L} (2, k) \xRightarrow{T_{21}} (1, k - 1) \xrightarrow{R} (1, k)$$

and is illustrated in Figure 7.18c. Since state 1 is a right-moving state, we conclude that $T_{[\alpha a]}(2) = 1$, and therefore $T_{[\alpha a]} = T_{21}$. By a similar analysis we find that $T_{[\alpha c]} = T_{23}$. To determine $T_{[\alpha b]}$, let square $k$ contain $b$ and let **M** start in the configuration $(2, k + 1)$:

$$(2, k + 1) \xrightarrow{L} (2, k) \xRightarrow{T_{21}} (1, k - 1) \xrightarrow{R} (2, k) \xRightarrow{T_{21}} (1, k - 1) \ldots$$

We see that **M** is in a loop; thus $T_{[\alpha b]} = T_{2\Delta}$. The second and third rows in Figure 7.18b are obtained in the same way.

Figure 7.18d shows how **M**′ must update its record of the state of **M**. If $q$ is a right-moving state and **M** is positioned at symbol $s$ in square $k$, then $q'$ is the state in which **M** moves right to scan square $k + 1$ for the first time. In our example, $q'$ depends on $T_{[\alpha]}$ only when $q = 1$ and $s = b$. This is because

1] **right** ($b$, 2)

is the only right instruction that puts **M** in a left-moving state. If $b$ is written in square $k + 1$, and $T_{[\alpha]} = T_{21}$ applies to the boundary between squares $k$ and $k + 1$, we have

$$(1, k) \xrightarrow{R} (2, k + 1) \xRightarrow{T_{21}} (1, k) \xrightarrow{R} (2, k + 1)$$

Since **M** is in a loop, the new state of **M**′ is $q_\Delta$. The cases in which $T_{[\alpha]}$ is $T_{23}$ or $T_{2\Delta}$ are handled similarly.

The finite-state accepter corresponding to **M** is shown in Figure 7.19. The reader may check that **L(M)** = **L(M′)**.

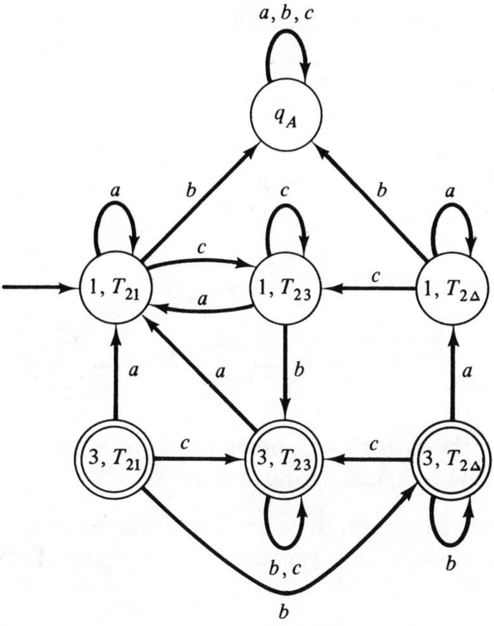


**Figure 7.19.** Finite-state accepter equivalent to a two-way accepter.

## Notes and References

The first description of a tape automaton was presented by A. M. Turing in 1936.

Since Turing's work, a wide variety of tape automata has been studied, including the sequential machines and two-way accepters of this chapter, the pushdown automata of Chapter 8, the "linear-bounded" automata of Myhill [1960] and Kuroda [1964], the "stack" automata of Ginsburg, Greibach, and Harrison [1967], and many variations of the Turing machine, several of which are described in Chapter 11.

The generalized sequential machine has been studied by Ginsburg and Rose [1963], who demonstrated the closure of regular languages under transduction and inverse transduction by such machines. Similar results for other classes of languages have been shown by Ginsburg and Rose [1963], Ginsburg and Greibach [1967], and Greibach and Hopcroft [1967].

Two-way accepters have been studied by Rabin and Scott [1959] and Shepherdson [1959]. The fact that these automata accept only regular languages was demonstrated in both papers. Our proof of this result is essentially that found in the latter work.

## Problems

7.1. Consider the following GST $\mathbf{M}_t$:

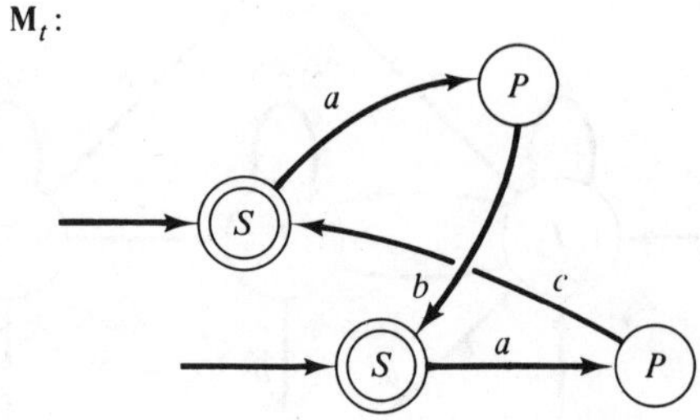


What are the possible responses of $\mathbf{M}_t$ to input *aaaa*? To input $a^n$, $n \geq 0$? Find a regular expression for $\mathbf{M}_t(\mathbf{a}^*)$.

7.2. For the GST $\mathbf{M}_t$ shown, for each finite-state generator $\mathbf{M}_i$, $i = 1, 2, 3$, construct a finite-state generator $\mathbf{M}$ such that $\mathbf{L}(\mathbf{M}) = \mathbf{M}_t(\mathbf{L}(\mathbf{M}_i))$.

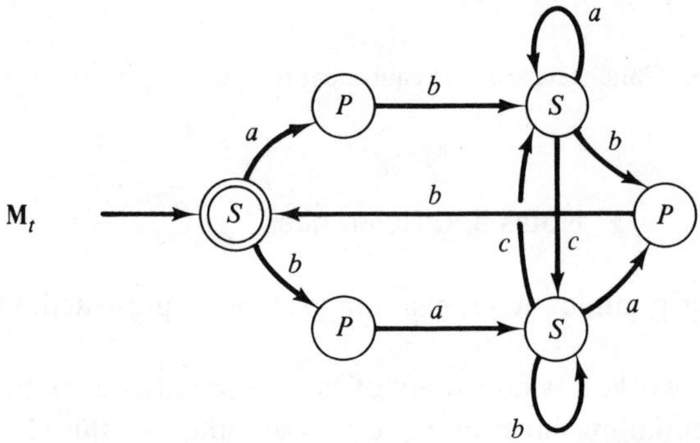


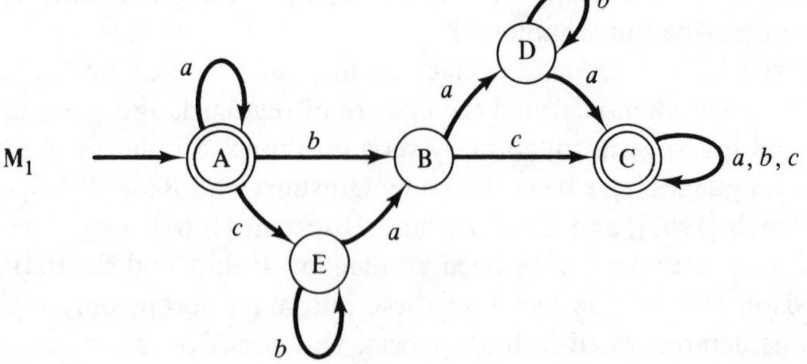

M$_2$

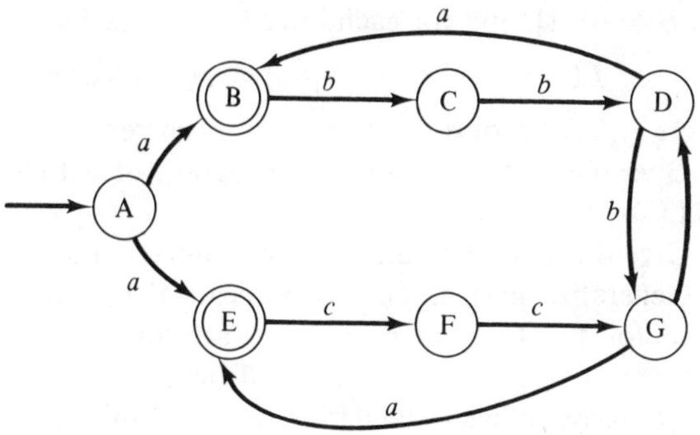


M$_3$

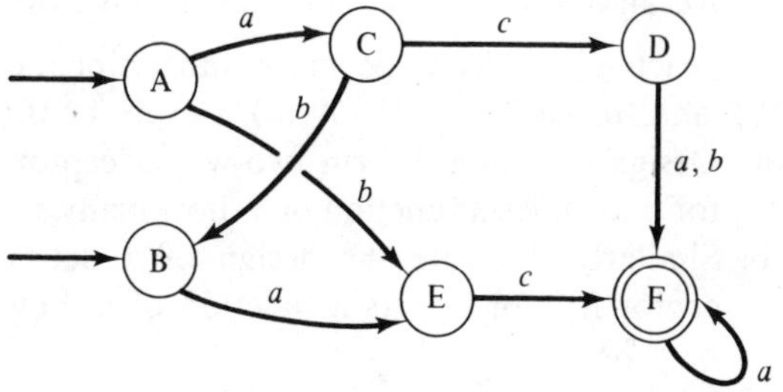


**7.3.** Let $\mathbf{M}_t$ be an arbitrary GST. We have noted (Example 7.3) that it need not be the case that $\mathbf{L} = \mathbf{M}_t^{-1}(\mathbf{M}_t(\mathbf{L}))$. Under what conditions on $\mathbf{M}_t$ is it true that $\mathbf{L} = \mathbf{M}_t^{-1}(\mathbf{M}_t(\mathbf{L}))$?

7.4. Find a generalized sequential transducer $\mathbf{M}_t$ such that
a. $\mathbf{M}_t(a^n) = \{a^i \mid n \leq i \leq 2n\}$.
b. $\mathbf{M}_t(a^n b^m) = \{a^i b^j \mid i < n, j > m\}$.

7.5. Prove that there is no GST $\mathbf{M}_t$ such that, for all $i \geq 0$,

$$\mathbf{M}_t(a^i) = \begin{cases} 1 & \text{if } i \text{ is prime} \\ 0 & \text{if } i \text{ is not prime} \end{cases}$$

***7.6.** a. Let $\mathbf{M}_t$ be a GST and let $\mathbf{G}$ be a context-free grammar. Prove that $\mathbf{M}_t(\mathbf{L}(\mathbf{G}))$ is context free. [*Hint:* Consider the construction of a context-free grammar for $\mathbf{M}_t(\mathbf{L}(\mathbf{G}))$.]
b. For an arbitrary language $\mathbf{L}$, we define *Init* ($\mathbf{L}$) to be the set of nonempty prefixes of strings in $\mathbf{L}$. That is,

$$\textit{Init}\ (\mathbf{L}) = \{\alpha \neq \lambda \mid \alpha\beta \text{ is in } \mathbf{L} \text{ for some string } \beta\}$$

Use the result of part a to prove that $\mathbf{L}$ is context free only if *Init* ($\mathbf{L}$) is context free.

7.7. Let $\mathbf{S} = \{0, 1\}$, and for each integer $r \geq 0$ define

$$\mathbf{L}(r) = \{\omega \text{ in } \mathbf{S}^* \mid (N_1(\omega) \leq r) \wedge (N_0(\omega) > N_1(\omega))\}$$

where $N_s(\omega)$ denotes the number of occurrences of symbol $s$ in $\omega$.

a. Give the state diagram and program of a two-way acceptor for $\mathbf{L}(3)$.

b. Give the state diagram of a deterministic FSA for $\mathbf{L}(3)$.

c. Generalize part a. That is, indicate the design of a two-way acceptor for $\mathbf{L}(r)$ where $r$ is an arbitrary integer greater than 0. Show that $2r + 1$ states are sufficient.

d. Similarly, indicate the design of a deterministic FSA for $\mathbf{L}(r)$. Show that at least $r^2$ states are necessary.

e. Prove that there exists no two-way accepter for $\mathbf{L}(\infty)$. (*Hint:* Recall that TWA's are finite-state and use the methods of Chapter 6.)

7.8. For each $n > 0$, let $\mathbf{V}_n$ be an $n$-symbol alphabet, and let $\mathbf{L}_n = \{\alpha \mid \alpha \in \mathbf{V}_n^*$ and for each $x \in \mathbf{V}_n$, $N_x(\alpha)$ is even (or 0)$\}$. (See Problem 7.7).

a. Design a standard-form two-way acceptor $\mathbf{M}_n$ that recognizes $\mathbf{L}_n$ for $n > 0$. As a function of $n$, how many states will $\mathbf{M}_n$ have?

b. Similarly, indicate the design of a deterministic finite-state acceptor $\mathbf{M}_n'$ for $\mathbf{L}_n$. As a function of $n$, how many states must $\mathbf{M}_n'$ have?

7.9. Let $\mathbf{S} = \{a, b, c\}$, and let integers $n_a, n_b, n_c \geq 0$ be given. A word $\omega$ in $\mathbf{S}^*$ is an element of $\mathbf{L}(n_a, n_b, n_c)$ if and only if

1. $N_a(\omega) \geq n_a$.

2. Each occurrence of $a$ in $\omega$ is followed by $n_b$ occurrences of $b$ and $n_c$ occurrences of $c$ (in any order), before the next occurrence of $a$.

a. Give the state diagram and the program of a TWA $\mathbf{M}_t$ that recognizes $\mathbf{L}(3, 3, 2)$.

b. Design a deterministic FSA $\mathbf{M}_f$ that recognizes $\mathbf{L}(3, 3, 2)$.

c. Indicate the design of $\mathbf{M}_t$ and $\mathbf{M}_f$ for arbitrary integers $n_a, n_b, n_c$. Show that the FSA needs a number of states proportional to the product of $n_a$, $n_b$, and $n_c$, while the TWA needs a number of states proportional to their sum.

7.10. Consider the following program of a two-way accepter $\mathbf{M}$:

1] **right** $(a, 2), (b, 1), (\#, 3)$

2] **right** $(a, 1), (b, 2)$

3] **left** $(a, 3), (b, 4), (\#, 5)$

4] **left** $(a, 4), (b, 3)$

5] **right** $(a, 5), (b, 5)$

The initial and final states are 1 and 5, respectively.

a. Describe **L(M)**.

b. Construct a minimum state FSA equivalent to **M**.

**7.11.** Let **M** be an arbitrary two-way accepter. Describe a procedure for modifying **M** so that it accepts the same language without ever scanning right of the final sharp or left of the initial sharp. (*Hint:* Suppose that **M** scans to the right of the final sharp. **M**'s subsequent behavior must be one of the following:

1. It enters a final state while scanning to the right of the final sharp.
2. It scans forever to the right of the final sharp without entering a final state.
3. It eventually executes a left move that causes it to scan the final sharp.

Show how to determine which of these behaviors is exhibited by **M** if it scans to the right of the final sharp in a given state $q$; then describe how to modify its program so that **M** simulates the appropriate behavior without scanning to the right of the final sharp.)

**7.12.** Let **M** be an $n$-state TWA in standard form, and let **M**$'$ be the finite-state accepter constructed from **M** according to the methods of Section 7.3.3. Prove that **M**$'$ will have no more than $(n + 1)^{(n+1)}$ states. (Thus this function bounds the "state economy" achievable through the use of two-way accepters in place of finite-state accepters.) Show further that such economy is roughly achievable by considering the language

$$\mathbf{L}(r) = \{0^{i_1}10^{i_2}1 \ldots 10^{i_r}c0^k10^{i_k} \mid 1 \leq k \leq r, 1 \leq i_j \leq r \text{ for } j = 1, \ldots, r\}$$

Specifically, show that for each $r$ there exists a TWA recognizing **L**$(r)$ with a number of states proportional to $r$, whereas no finite-state accepter for **L**$(r)$ can have fewer than $r^r$ states. (This example was described by Meyer and Fischer [1972].)

***7.13.** Suppose that a TWA **M** is in state $q$ and is positioned at symbol $s$ in a prefix string $\alpha s$, where $|\alpha| = k$. [Thus **M** is in configuration $(q, k + 1)$.] Suppose further that $q$ labels a left instruction.

a. Assuming that **M**'s state is known after each move, how many moves must we observe in order to determine $T_{\alpha s}(q)$?

b. What is the minimum number of moves that must be observed to conclude that $T_{\alpha s}(q) = \Delta$?

**7.14.** Let **M** be a TWA with $n$ states. Describe an algorithm for deciding whether or not **M** halts on an arbitrary input tape. Show that, if we modify the definition of two-way accepter to permit states to label both left and right instructions, it is still possible to specify such an algorithm.

**7.15.** Let **M** be an $n$-state TWA. For an arbitrary integer $k \geq 1$ and an arbitrary input tape of length at least $k$, describe an algorithm for deciding whether or not **M** ever scans the $k$th symbol of its input.

**7.16.** Show that if **M** is a nondeterministic two-way accepter, **M** accepts a regular language. (*Hint:* Rather than constructing a procedure for converting **M** into a deterministic automaton, consider how the construction of Section 7.3.3 must be modified to apply to nondeterministic TWA's.)

**7.17.** The two diagrams show automata made by combining two-way accepters $\mathbf{M}_1$ and $\mathbf{M}_2$. In $\mathbf{M}_a$, the two accepters move over the input tape independently, and the tape is accepted by $\mathbf{M}_a$ if and only if $\mathbf{M}_1$ and $\mathbf{M}_2$ each halt in an accepting state. In $\mathbf{M}_b$, $\mathbf{M}_2$ moves only at those moments that $\mathbf{M}_1$ enters an accepting state, and the tape is accepted just if $\mathbf{M}_2$ halts in an accepting state. (We can think of $\mathbf{M}_1$ as emitting signals that trigger moves of $\mathbf{M}_2$.)

$\mathbf{M}_a$:

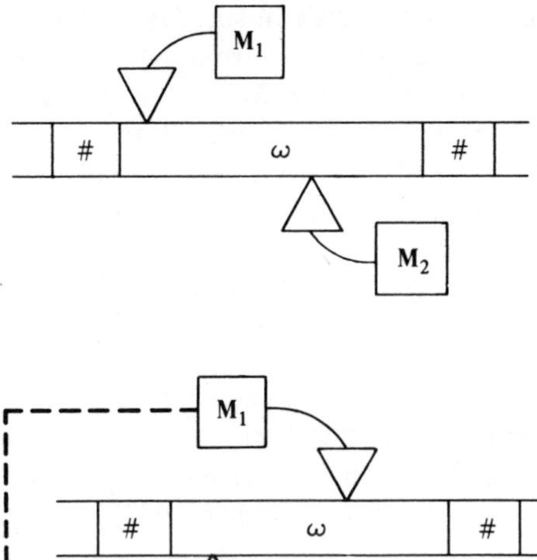


$\mathbf{M}_b$:

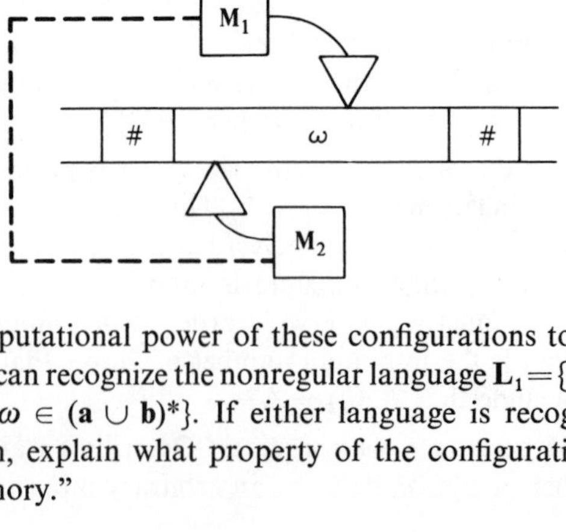


Study the computational power of these configurations to determine whether either can recognize the nonregular language $\mathbf{L}_1 = \{a^n b^n \mid n \geq 1\}$ or $\mathbf{L}_2 = \{\omega\omega \mid \omega \in (\mathbf{a} \cup \mathbf{b})^*\}$. If either language is recognizable by a configuration, explain what property of the configuration violates "bounded memory."

# 8

# *Pushdown Automata*

Pushdown automata form the most important class of automata between finite-state machines and Turing machines. Their operation relates intimately to many computing processes, especially the analysis and translation of artificial languages.

This chapter is concerned primarily with pushdown accepters and their relation to context-free grammars. As shown in Figure 8.1, a pushdown accepter comprises a finite-state control, a semiinfinite input tape, and a semiinfinite storage tape. The machine is not allowed to move its input head to the left; thus it must examine the symbols on its input tape strictly in the order in which they were written on the tape. The machine starts with the storage tape entirely blank (inscribed with $\#$ in every square). It prints a symbol on the storage tape each time it moves the storage head to the right, and it reads a symbol from the storage tape each time it moves the storage head to the left. Any information written to the right of the head is irretrievable, because it will be overwritten when the head again moves right.

Because the storage tape string, which may be arbitrarily long, can affect the behavior of the automaton, a pushdown accepter has unbounded memory. However, the information most recently written into the memory must be the first to be retrieved. This form of limited-access storage mechanism, common in computer practice, is known as a *pushdown stack* because it implements a "last-in, first-out" retrieval rule. (This term is reputed to originate from the spring-loaded plate storage wells found in cafeterias, from which the top plate must be removed to gain access to those below.)

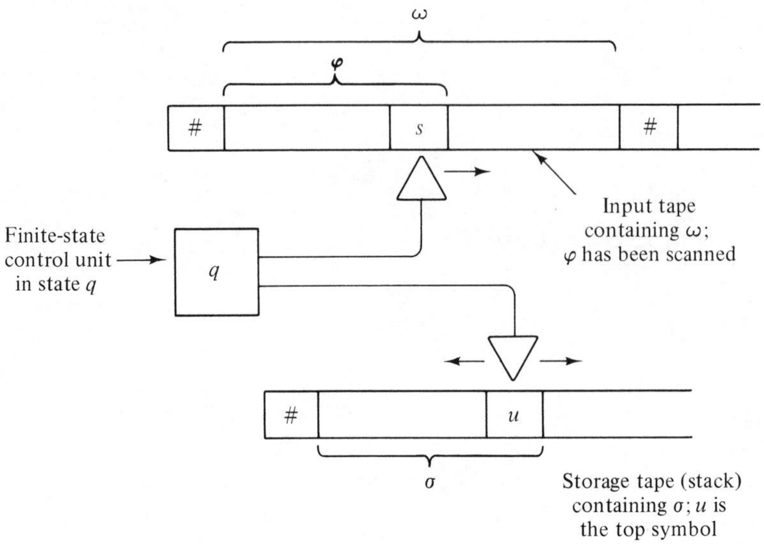


**Figure 8.1.** Pushdown accepter in configuration $(q, \varphi, \sigma)$.

This restricted form of unbounded memory results in a language-defining ability intermediate between that of finite-state machines and Turing machines. The application of the pushdown storage principle to the analysis of the sentences generated by context-free languages is studied in Section 8.3.

## 8.1 Pushdown Accepters: Definitions and Examples

### 8.1.1 Definitions

**Definition 8.1:** A *pushdown accepter* (PDA) is a six-tuple

$$\mathbf{M} = (\mathbf{Q}, \mathbf{S}, \mathbf{U}, \mathbf{P}, \mathbf{I}, \mathbf{F})$$

in which

- $\mathbf{Q}$ is a finite set of control states
- $\mathbf{S}$ is a finite input alphabet
- $\mathbf{U}$ is a finite stack alphabet
- $\mathbf{P}$ is the program of $\mathbf{M}$
- $\mathbf{I} \subseteq \mathbf{Q}$ is a set of initial states
- $\mathbf{F} \subseteq \mathbf{Q}$ is a set of final or accepting states

The program $\mathbf{P}$ is a finite sequence of instructions, each taking one of the forms

$$\begin{matrix} q] \textbf{ scan } (s, q') \\ q] \textbf{ write } (u, q') \\ q] \textbf{ read } (u, q') \end{matrix} \quad \begin{cases} q, q' \in \mathbf{Q} \\ s \in \mathbf{S} \\ u \in \mathbf{U} \end{cases}$$

In each case, the state $q$ is the *label* of the instruction, and the state $q'$ is the *successor state*. Each state in **Q** labels at most one type of instruction, read, write, or scan.

If $q$ is any state, $\varphi$ any string in $\mathbf{S}^*$, and $\sigma$ any string in $\mathbf{U}^*$, then $(q, \varphi, \sigma)$ is a *configuration* of **M**. The string $\sigma$ is usually called the *stack*, and the symbol under the stack head the *top stack symbol.*

A configuration $(q, \varphi, \sigma)$ is a complete description of the total state of a pushdown accepter at some point in its analysis of an input tape. It is interpreted as shown in Figure 8.1: the control unit is in state $q$; the prefix $\varphi$ of the entire input string $\omega$ has been scanned, and the input head is positioned at the last symbol of $\varphi$; the stack $\sigma$ is the contents of the storage tape, and the stack head is positioned at the last symbol of $\sigma$.

Definition 8.2 specifies how the execution of instructions by a pushdown accepter takes it from one configuration to another. (The definition is illustrated by Figure 8.2.) The scan instructions read successive symbols from the input tape, write instructions load symbols into the stack, and read instructions retrieve symbols from the stack.

**Definition 8.2:** Let **M** be a pushdown accepter with program **P**, and suppose that the string $\omega \in \mathbf{S}^*$ is written on the input tape. Instructions of **M**'s program are *applicable* in configurations according to the following rules:

1. An instruction $q]$ **scan** $(s, q')$ applies in a configuration $(q, \varphi, \sigma)$ if $\varphi s$ is a prefix of $\omega$. In executing this instruction, **M** moves its input head one square to the right, observes the symbol $s$ inscribed therein, and enters state $q'$. We represent a scan move by the notation

$$(q, \varphi, \sigma) \xrightarrow{s} (q', \varphi s, \sigma)$$

2. An instruction $q]$ **write** $(u, q')$ applies in any configuration $(q, \varphi, \sigma)$. In executing this instruction, **M** moves the stack head one square to the right, prints the symbol $u$ therein, and enters state $q'$. We represent a write move by the notation

$$(q, \varphi, \sigma) \xrightarrow{w} (q', \varphi, \sigma u)$$

3. An instruction $q]$ **read** $(u, q')$ applies in any configuration $(q, \varphi, \sigma)$ in which $\sigma = \sigma' u$. In executing this instruction, **M** observes the symbol $u$ under the stack head, moves the stack head one square to

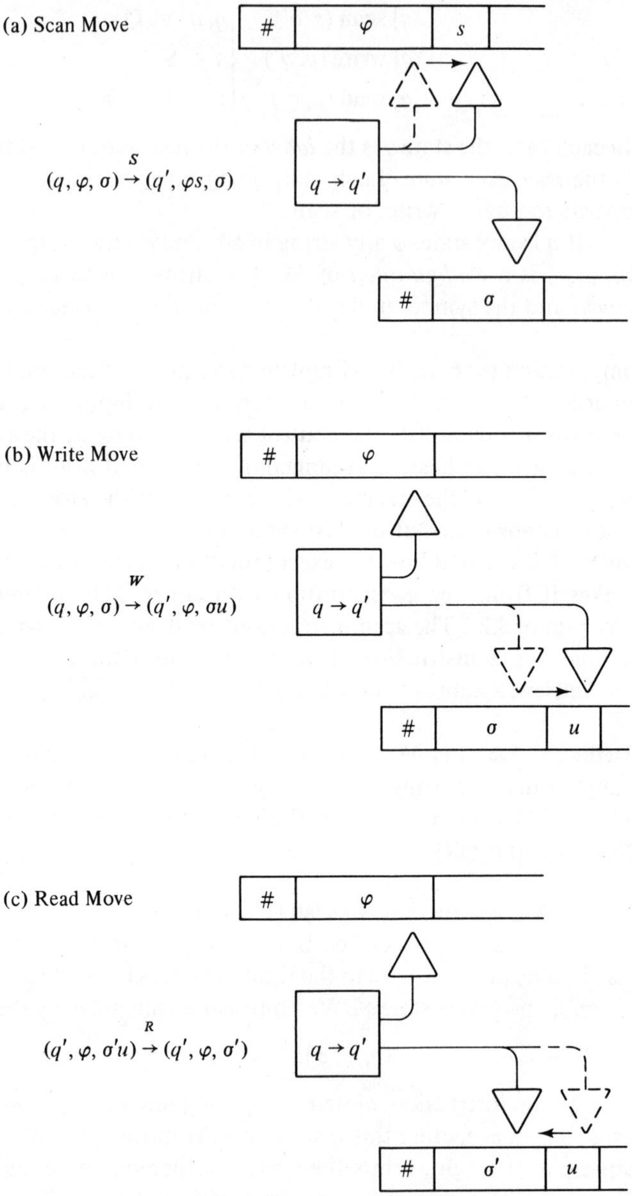


**Figure 8.2.** Moves of a pushdown accepter.

the left, and enters state $q'$. We represent a read move by the notation

$$(q, \varphi, \sigma' u) \xrightarrow{R} (q', \varphi, \sigma')$$

If **M** has a move sequence

$$(q_0, \varphi_0, \sigma_0) \longrightarrow (q_1, \varphi_1, \sigma_1) \ldots \longrightarrow (q_k, \varphi_k, \sigma_k)$$

(where each move is a scan, read, or write move), we write

$$(q_0, \varphi_0, \sigma_0) \Longrightarrow (q_k, \varphi_k, \sigma_k)$$

A pushdown accepter begins operation with the control in an initial state and the heads positioned at the initial sharps of their tapes, as shown in Figure 8.3a. The machine passes through a sequence of configurations, each resulting from the execution of an instruction applicable in the preceding configuration. Operation continues until a configuration is reached in which there is no applicable instruction. If at any point all symbols of some input string $\varphi$ have been scanned, the stack is empty, and the control unit is in a

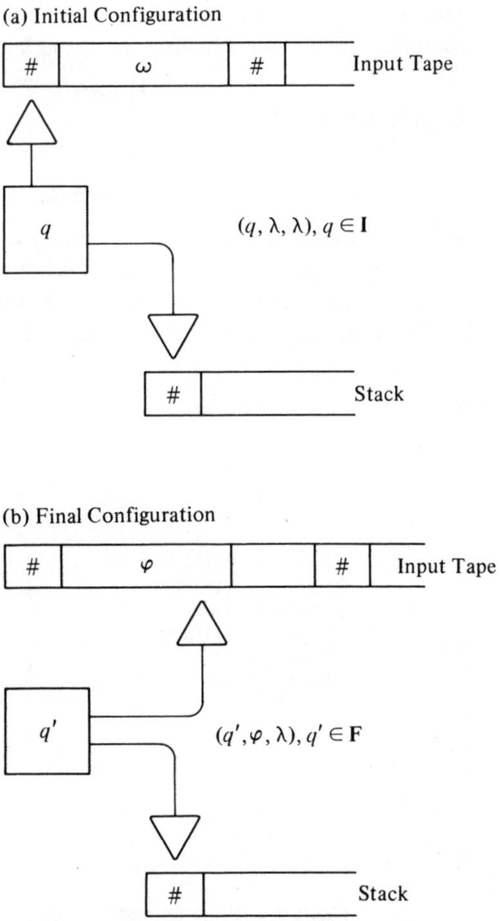


**Figure 8.3.** Initial and accepting configurations of a pushdown accepter.

final state, the string $\varphi$ is accepted by **M**. The accepting configuration is shown in Figure 8.3b.

> **Definition 8.3:** An *initial configuration* of a pushdown accepter **M** is any configuration $(q, \lambda, \lambda)$ in which $q$ is an initial state of **M**. A *final configuration* of **M** is any configuration $(q', \varphi, \lambda)$, where $q'$ is a final state of **M** and $\varphi$ is a prefix of the string written on **M**'s input tape. The string $\varphi$ is *accepted* by **M** just if **M** has a move sequence
>
> $$(q, \lambda, \lambda) \Longrightarrow (q', \varphi, \lambda), \qquad q \in \mathbf{I}, q' \in \mathbf{F}$$
>
> The *language recognized* by **M** is the set of accepted strings.

## 8.1.2 Examples: Mirror-Image Languages

Figure 8.4a shows the program of a pushdown accepter $\mathbf{M}_{cm}$ with alphabets $\mathbf{S} = \{a, b, c\}$ and $\mathbf{U} = \{a, b\}$. As with other tape automata, we have combined instructions having the same label. For example

1] **scan** $(a, 2)(b, 3)$

is equivalent to

1] **scan** $(a, 2)$

1] **scan** $(b, 3)$

State 1 will by convention be the initial state, unless we specify otherwise.

A state diagram (for example, Figure 8.4b) assists in understanding a machine's operation. The nodes of the state diagram represent states of the control unit, and each node is inscribed with $S$, $R$, or $W$ according to the

(a) Program of $\mathbf{M}_{cm}$

```
1] scan  (a, 2) (b, 3) (c, 4)
2] write (a, 1)
3] write (b, 1)
4] scan  (a, 5) (b, 6)
5] read  (a, 4)
6] read  (b, 4)
```

(b) State Diagram of $\mathbf{M}_{cm}$

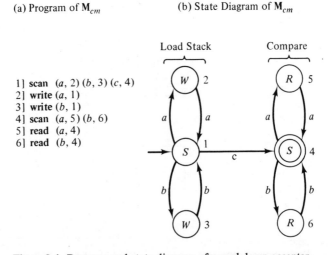

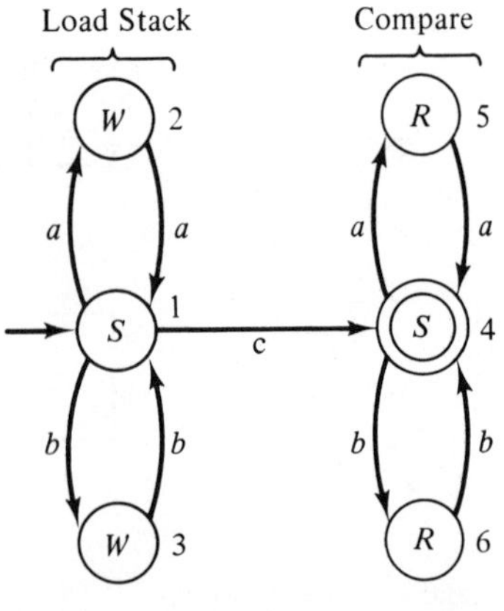


**Figure 8.4.** Program and state diagram of a pushdown accepter.

type of instruction labeled by the state. The initial states and the accepting states are identified in the same manner as for finite-state automata.

A study of either the program or the state diagram of the automaton reveals that at most one instruction is applicable to any configuration of $\mathbf{M}_{cm}$; thus the behavior of the machine is uniquely determined by its input string $\omega$. The machine begins operation in state 1 and passes through two stages: in the *load stack* stage it copies into the stack the portion of $\omega$ up to the symbol $c$; in the *compare* stage it matches the stack symbols against the remaining symbols of the input.

If the portion of $\omega$ following the letter $c$ is exactly the reverse of the string loaded into the stack, **M** will empty the storage tape immediately after scanning the final letter of $\omega$, leaving $\mathbf{M}_{cm}$ in the accepting configuration $(4, \omega, \lambda)$. Thus $\mathbf{M}_{cm}$ accepts each string $\omega = \varphi c \varphi^R$, where $\varphi \in (\mathbf{a} \cup \mathbf{b})^*$. For example, the move sequence by which $\mathbf{M}_{cm}$ accepts $\omega = abcba$ is

$$\begin{aligned}(1, \lambda, \lambda) &\xrightarrow{S} (2, a, \lambda) \xrightarrow{W} (1, a, a)\\ &\xrightarrow{S} (3, ab, a) \xrightarrow{W} (1, ab, ab)\\ &\xrightarrow{S} (4, abc, ab)\\ &\xrightarrow{S} (6, abcb, ab) \xrightarrow{R} (4, abcb, a)\\ &\xrightarrow{S} (5, abcba, a) \xrightarrow{R} (4, abcba, \lambda) \quad \text{[accept]}\end{aligned}$$

If a letter scanned by $\mathbf{M}_{cm}$ in state 4 does not match the last letter of the stack, or if symbols remain in the stack after all of $\omega$ has been scanned, $\mathbf{M}_{cm}$ will stop with a nonempty stack and reject the input. The rejection of $\omega = abca$ is illustrated by the move sequence

$$\begin{aligned}(1, \lambda, \lambda) &\xrightarrow{S} (2, a, \lambda) \xrightarrow{W} (1, a, a)\\ &\xrightarrow{S} (3, ab, a) \xrightarrow{W} (1, ab, ab)\\ &\xrightarrow{S} (4, abc, ab)\\ &\xrightarrow{S} (5, abca, ab) \quad \text{[stop and reject]}\end{aligned}$$

We conclude that the language recognized by $\mathbf{M}_{cm}$ is

$$\mathbf{L}_{cm} = \{\varphi c \varphi^R \mid \varphi \in (\mathbf{a} \cup \mathbf{b})^*\}$$

This language is known as the *mirror-image language with center marker*, or the *center-marked palindrome language*. It is generated by the context-free grammar

$$\begin{aligned}\mathbf{G}_{cm}\colon\quad \Sigma &\longrightarrow S\\ S &\longrightarrow aSa\\ S &\longrightarrow bSb\\ S &\longrightarrow c\end{aligned}$$

(Later in this chapter, we show that a context-free grammar can be found for *any* language recognized by a pushdown accepter. In fact, we shall establish the equivalence of the class of context-free languages and the class of languages recognized by these accepters.)

The pushdown accepter $\mathbf{M}_{cm}$ is *deterministic* because there is never a choice of move for any configuration. A slight modification of the language $\mathbf{L}_{cm}$ requires a nondeterministic pushdown accepter. Consider the language

$$\mathbf{L}_{mi} = \{\varphi\varphi^R \mid \varphi \in (\mathbf{a} \cup \mathbf{b})^*\}$$

which is known simply as the *mirror-image language*. Unlike the language $\mathbf{L}_{cm}$, there is no special symbol in sentenecs of $\mathbf{L}_{mi}$ to indicate when a pushdown accepter should switch from a load-stack mode to a compare mode. Does there exist a pushdown accepter for $\mathbf{L}_{mi}$? Indeed there does. In fact, it is quite easy to modify $\mathbf{M}_{cm}$ to obtain an automaton with an accepting move sequence for each string of $\mathbf{L}_{mi}$. Instead of waiting for a symbol $c$ to be scanned, we allow the machine $\mathbf{M}_{mi}$ (Figure 8.5) to switch to its compare mode whenever it writes a scanned symbol into its stack. Such behavior must be permitted because there is no way for the machine to determine when it has scanned the first half of a mirror-image string: we must permit the machine to "guess" after each symbol scanned whether it should or should not switch to compare mode.

The possible move sequences of $\mathbf{M}_{mi}$ for the input string *aabbaa* are shown in Figure 8.6. Accepting configurations are reached for strings *aa* and *aabbaa* by unique sequences of moves; all other sequences terminate in rejecting configurations.

The need for $\mathbf{M}_{mi}$ to nondeterministically change mode during its operation suggests the possibility of a fundamental difference in the language-

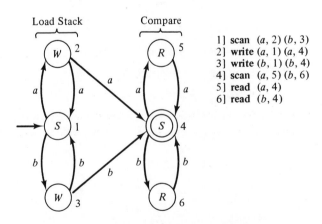

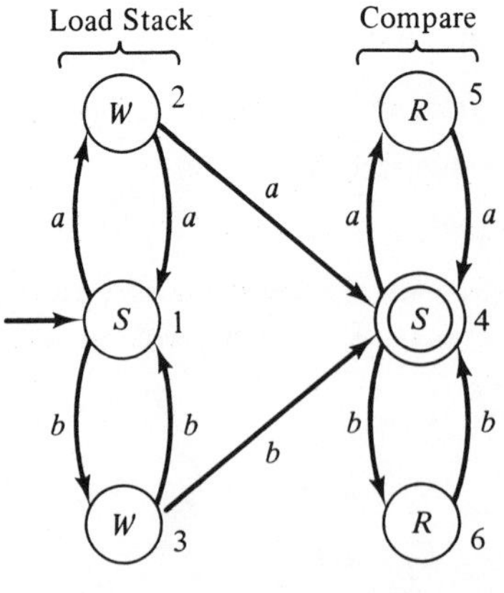


1] **scan** $(a, 2)\,(b, 3)$
2] **write** $(a, 1)\,(a, 4)$
3] **write** $(b, 1)\,(b, 4)$
4] **scan** $(a, 5)\,(b, 6)$
5] **read** $(a, 4)$
6] **read** $(b, 4)$

**Figure 8.5.** Nondeterministic pushdown accepter.

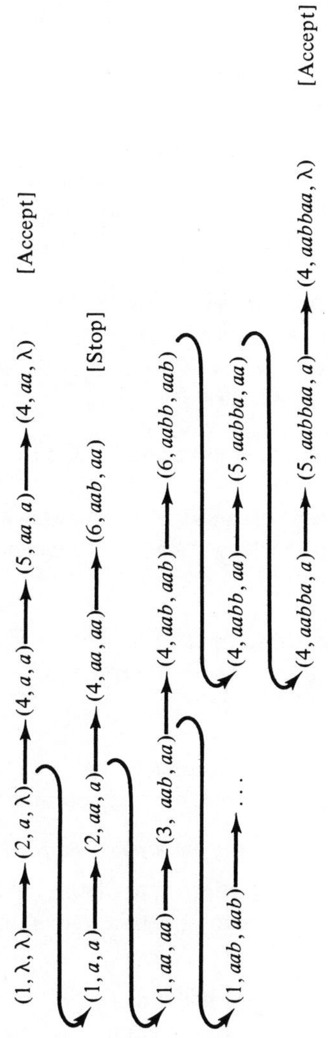


**Figure 8.6.** Nondeterministic behavior of a pushdown accepter.

defining abilities of deterministic and nondeterministic pushdown automata. We shall see in Section 8.6 that this is indeed the case.

## 8.2 Proper and Loop-Free Accepters

To facilitate proving the important theorems about pushdown accepters, it is convenient to restrict our attention to a "well-behaved" subclass of the accepters whose language-recognizing ability is equivalent to that of the full class of pushdown accepters.

We begin with a subclass called the *proper* PDA's. To demonstrate that no generality is lost in considering only these accepters, we develop a construction by means of which any PDA can be transformed into an equivalent proper PDA.

### 8.2.1 Proper Pushdown Accepters

Our definition of pushdown accepter disallows certain kinds of anomalous or unproductive behavior. In particular,

1. A pushdown accepter cannot scan beyond the end of the string on its input tape because it can make no move in which a sharp is scanned.
2. A pushdown accepter cannot move its stack head left of the first square of the storage tape because it can make no move in which a sharp is read from the stack.

However, two other types of unproductive behavior may lead to difficulties in analyzing properties of pushdown accepters. One is the occurrence of a read move immediately after a write move; the other is the unending repetition (that is, a loop) of write moves.

Suppose that a pushdown accepter **M** has a move sequence in which a write move is followed by a read move, with no intervening scan moves:

$$\ldots (q, \varphi, \sigma) \xrightarrow{W} (q', \varphi, \sigma u) \xrightarrow{R} (q'', \varphi, \sigma) \ldots$$

This pair of moves has no net effect apart from switching the control unit from state $q$ to state $q''$. Such inconsequential move sequences can occur only if **M** has a write instruction

$$q] \textbf{ write } (u, q')$$

for which the successor state $q'$ is the label of a read instruction.

> **Definition 8.4:** In the program of a pushdown accepter **M**, a write instruction
>
> $$q] \textbf{ write } (u, q')$$

is *improper* if $q'$ is the label of any read instruction. A pushdown accepter is *proper* if its program contains no improper instructions.

Improper instructions are readily identified in the state diagram of a pushdown accepter, and can always be eliminated without altering the language recognized. In particular, if **M** is any PDA, a proper pushdown accepter **M**$'$ may be constructed from **M** by adding and deleting instructions as follows:

*Step 1:* Let $q$ and $q'$ be any pair of states for which **M** has a move sequence

$$(q, \varphi, \sigma) \overset{k \text{ write moves}}{\Longrightarrow} (q'', \varphi, \sigma\tau) \overset{k \text{ read moves}}{\Longrightarrow} (q', \varphi, \sigma)$$

consisting of $k$ write moves followed by $k$ read moves, for some $k \geq 1$. Whenever

$p]$ **move** (-, $q$)

is an instruction in **M**, we add the instruction

$p]$ **move** (-, $q'$)

If state $q$ is an initial state in **M**, we make $q'$ an initial state in **M**$'$.

Step 1 must be performed for each pair of states $q$ and $q'$ for which **M** has a move sequence as above.

*Step 2:* Delete each improper instruction. The instructions that remain form the program of **M**$'$.

**Proposition 8.1:** Let **M** be any pushdown accepter. One can construct a proper pushdown accepter **M**$'$ such that **L(M**$'$**)** = **L(M)**.

***Proof:*** Let **M**$'$ be the proper PDA constructed as above. We must show that $\omega \in$ **L(M**$'$**)** if and only if $\omega \in$ **L(M)**. Suppose that

(1) $$(q_0, \lambda, \lambda) \Longrightarrow (q_k, \omega, \lambda)$$

is a move sequence by which **M** accepts some string $\omega$. If this sequence contains improper moves, we remove them in succession to obtain an accepting move sequence of **M**$'$ for $\omega$. Let

(2) $$(q, \varphi, \sigma) \Longrightarrow (q'', \varphi, \sigma\tau) \Longrightarrow (q', \varphi, \sigma)$$

be the longest subsequence of (1) consisting of $k$ write moves followed by $k$ read moves, $k \geq 1$, that contains the first improper move. At least one of the following two statements must be true:

1. Either $q$ is the first state of sequence (1) (that is, $q = q_0$), or the move preceding subsequence (2) is not a write move.

2. Either $q'$ is the last state of sequence (1) (that is, $q' = q_k$), or the move following subsequence (2) is not a read move.

If $q$ is the first state of sequence (1), then $q$ is an initial state of **M**, and $q'$ is by construction an initial state of **M**′. Therefore, the subsequence

$$(q', \lambda, \lambda) \Longrightarrow (q_k, \omega, \lambda)$$

is an accepting move sequence for $\omega$ that does not contain the improper move.

If $q$ is not the first state of sequence (1), the instruction

$$p] \ \textbf{move} \ (\text{-}, q)$$

executed just before subsequence (2) cannot be improper, and **M**′ has by construction the instruction

$$p] \ \textbf{move} \ (\text{-}, q')$$

Therefore, $\omega$ is accepted by the new sequence

$$(q_0, \lambda, \lambda) \Longrightarrow (p, \text{-}, \text{-}) \longrightarrow (q', \varphi, \sigma) \Longrightarrow (q_k, \omega, \lambda)$$

that does not contain the improper move.

Repeating the argument for each remaining improper move yields an accepting move sequence of **M**′ for $\omega$; thus $\omega \in$ **L(M′)** if $\omega \in$ **L(M)**. We leave it to the reader to show that $\omega \in$ **L(M′)** *only* if $\omega \in$ **L(M)**.

**Example 8.1:** Figure 8.7a shows a PDA that writes a string from the set **(b*ba)*** into its stack, and then uses it to control its scanning of an input string in **(x ∪ y)***. The instruction

$$2] \ \textbf{write} \ (a, 5)$$

is improper since state 5 labels a read instruction:

$$5] \ \textbf{read} \ (a, 4)$$

This accepter has, for instance, the inconsequential move sequences

$$(2, \lambda, \lambda) \xrightarrow{W} (5, \lambda, a) \xrightarrow{R} (4, \lambda, \lambda)$$

and

$$(1, \lambda, \lambda) \xrightarrow{W} (2, \lambda, b) \xrightarrow{W} (5, \lambda, ba)$$
$$\xrightarrow{R} (4, \lambda, b) \xrightarrow{R} (3, \lambda, \lambda)$$

Therefore, to obtain an equivalent proper accepter **M**′, each instruction in **M** having state 1 or state 2 as a successor state is duplicated with state 3 or state 4 as the successor state, respectively. Similarly,

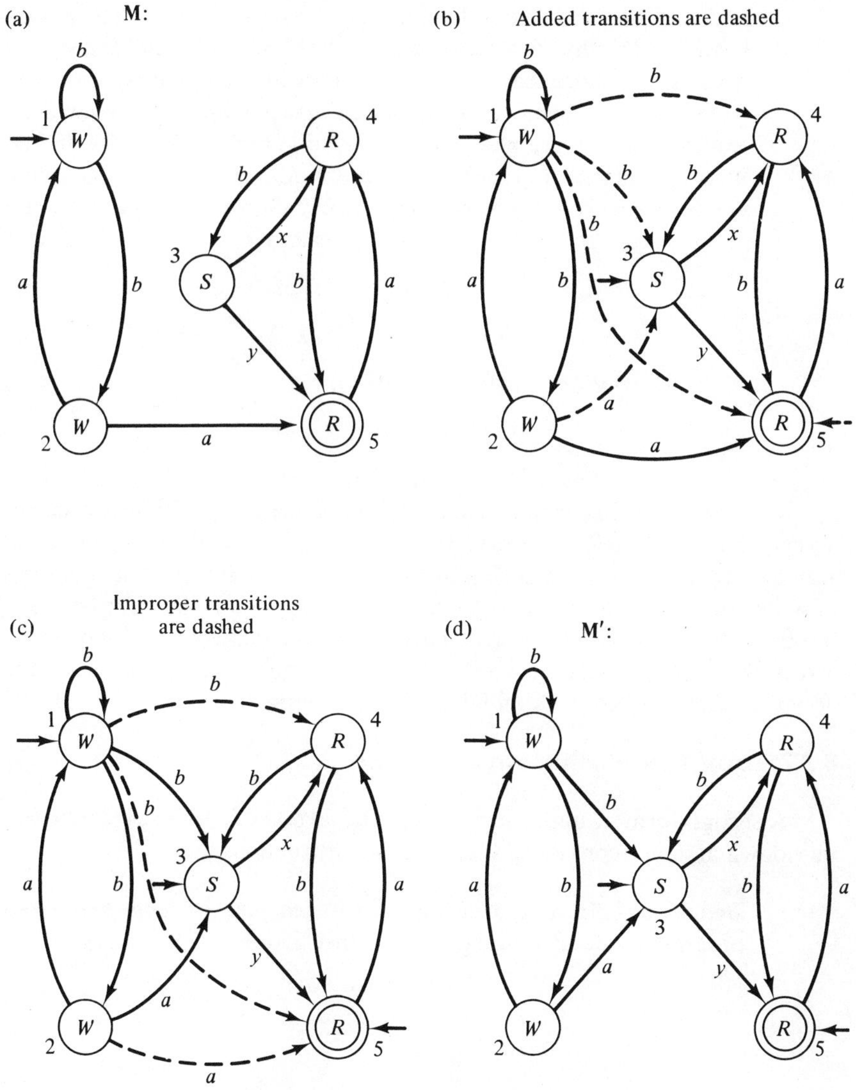


**Figure 8.7.** Conversion of a pushdown accepter to proper form.

**M** has the move sequence

$$(1, \lambda, \lambda) \xrightarrow{W} (2, \lambda, b) \xrightarrow{W} (1, \lambda, ba)$$
$$\xrightarrow{W} (2, \lambda, bab) \xrightarrow{W} (5, \lambda, baba) \xrightarrow{R} (4, \lambda, bab)$$
$$\xrightarrow{R} (5, \lambda, ba) \xrightarrow{R} (4, \lambda, b) \xrightarrow{R} (5, \lambda, \lambda)$$

and thus any instruction having state 1 as a successor state is duplicated with state 5 as a successor state. States 3 and 5 are now initial states, since they may be reached by inconsequential sequences from state 1. Figure 8.7b shows by dashed lines the transitions resulting from these new instructions; Figure 8.7c shows by dashed lines the improper transitions in the modified machine. These are deleted to yield the proper accepter **M**′ shown in Figure 8.7d. By Proposition 8.1, **L**(**M**′) = **L**(**M**). For example, the move sequence

$$(1, \lambda, \lambda) \xrightarrow{W} (2, \lambda, b) \xrightarrow{W} (5, \lambda, ba)$$
$$\xrightarrow{R} (4, \lambda, b) \xrightarrow{R} (3, \lambda, \lambda) \xrightarrow{S} (5, y, \lambda)$$

by which **M** accepts $y$ becomes simply

$$(3, \lambda, \lambda) \xrightarrow{S} (5, y, \lambda)$$

in **M**′.

It is worth taking explicit note of how a proper pushdown accepter accepts the empty string. In any PDA, a sequence accepting $\lambda$ must contain no scan moves. Moreover, any such move sequence must contain equal numbers of write and read moves, and at least one write move must precede any read moves. In a proper accepter a write move cannot be immediately followed by a read move, thus $\lambda$ can be accepted only with no moves at all: a proper accepter accepts $\lambda$ just if its initial state is accepting.

### 8.2.2 Loop-Free Pushdown Accepters

A second form of unproductive behavior is possible if the program of a pushdown accepter contains a loop of write instructions.

**Definition 8.5:** A proper pushdown accepter is *loop free* if its program contains no loop of write instructions

$$q_1] \ \textbf{write}\ (u_1, q_2)$$
$$q_2] \ \textbf{write}\ (u_2, q_3)$$
$$\vdots$$
$$q_n] \ \textbf{write}\ (u_n, q_1)$$

Suppose that a deterministic pushdown accepter **M** has a loop of write instructions in its program. Should **M** perform any instruction of the loop, it would thereafter print the symbols $u_1, u_2, \ldots, u_n$ in endless repetition. Since the states $q_1, q_2, \ldots, q_n$ of the loop cannot appear in any configuration of an accepting move sequence, the loop may be discarded from the program of **M** without altering the language defined by **M**.

**Proposition 8.2:** For any deterministic pushdown accepter **M**, one can construct a loop-free pushdown accepter **M′** such that **L(M′)** = **L(M)**.

Proposition 8.2 is valid for nondeterministic accepters also, although a direct proof of this fact is complicated. An indirect proof, however, follows from the correspondence between pushdown accepters and context-free languages developed in Sections 8.3 and 8.4. We shall show that a loop-free accepter can be constructed for any context-free language; we then show that a context-free grammar can be found for the language defined by any pushdown accepter, loop free or not.

## 8.3 Pushdown Accepters for Context-Free Languages

### 8.3.1 Syntax Analysis

Translators of artificial languages (compilers of programs, for example) use several stages of processing. When the valid sentences of the language are specified by a phrase-structure grammar, the first stage of the translation process constructs a derivation tree for a given sentence. When a given sentence is unambiguous, the unique derivation tree assigns a syntactic type to each of its phrases; the nesting of phrase types in the derivation is used by the translator to assign meaning to the sentence. Constructing a derivation tree for a sentence according to a specific grammar is known as *syntax analysis.*

Consider the grammar $\mathbf{G}_E$, which is a portion of the grammar for the Algol assignment statement used as an example in Chapter 3:

$$
\begin{array}{lll}
\mathbf{G}_E: & E \longrightarrow A & \\
& E \longrightarrow \textbf{if } B \textbf{ then } A \textbf{ else } E & \\
& B \longrightarrow A = A & T \longrightarrow x \\
& A \longrightarrow T & T \longrightarrow y \\
& A \longrightarrow T + A & T \longrightarrow z
\end{array}
$$

Let us consider how one could methodically construct a derivation tree for the sentence

$$\textbf{if } x = y \textbf{ then } z \textbf{ else } x + y$$

considered as a phrase of syntactic type $E$. Our procedure traces each possible chain of leftmost derivation steps permitted by the grammar, and is illustrated in Figure 8.8 (where the letters $i$, $t$, and $e$ are shorthand for the terminal symbols **if**, **then**, and **else**).

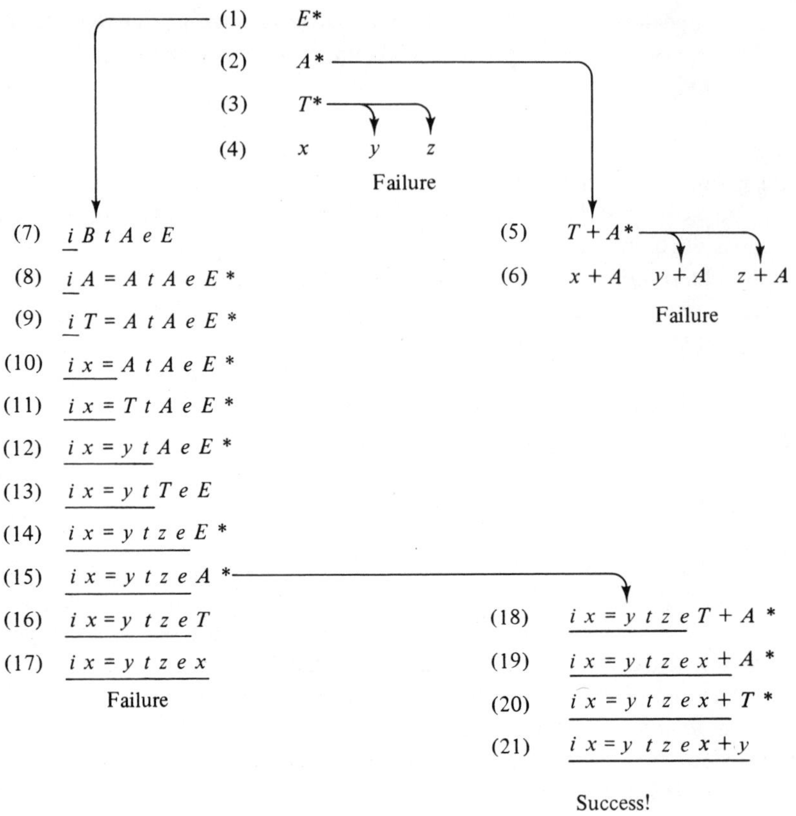


**Figure 8.8.** Top-down syntax analysis.

Each chain of derivation steps starts from the sentential form $E$. We scan the grammar for a production with $E$ as its lefthand side and find the candidates

$$E \longrightarrow A$$

$$E \longrightarrow i\,B\,t\,A\,e\,E$$

Let us determine the consequences of applying $E \longrightarrow A$, remembering (by the *) that there is an alternative production that might be tried at this point. Applying the production, we obtain line (2), and again there are two possible rules that may be used:

$$A \longrightarrow T$$

$$A \longrightarrow T + A$$

Trying $A \longrightarrow T$ [yielding line (3)], we find that $T$ may be replaced by terminal letters $x$, $y$, or $z$ [line (4)], none of which matches the first letter of the given sentence. We backtrack to line (2) and try the alternative $A$ rule, yielding line (5). Once again, all the possibilities fail at line (6). We must now backtrack all the way to line (1), since we have exhausted all the possible $A$ rules. The remaining $E$ rule gives line (7). The first symbol of line (7) matches the first symbol of the given sentence, and is therefore underlined.

Now the leftmost nonterminal of line (7) is $B$, and there is one $B$ rule, so line (8) is obtained immediately. In line (8) we try the first $A$ rule to obtain line (9), and again mark this point with * to indicate that an alternative rule can be applied. We continue in this fashion through line (17), marking each line where there is an alternative by *, and underlining the portion of the sentential form that thus far matches the given sentence. At line (17) we discover that

$$i\, x = y\, t\, z\, e\, x$$

is a phrase of type $E$. This is yet a failure, however, as the last two symbols of the given sentence have not been matched. We must backtrack to line (15) where the most recent choice was made, and apply the other $A$ rule. This yields line (18), which leads to a success at line (21). The successful chain of derivation steps specifies the tree diagram given in Figure 8.9.

This method of syntax analysis is called a *top-down* procedure because the derivation tree for a sentence is assembled starting from the root node at the top of the tree and working down toward the leaves. There are also

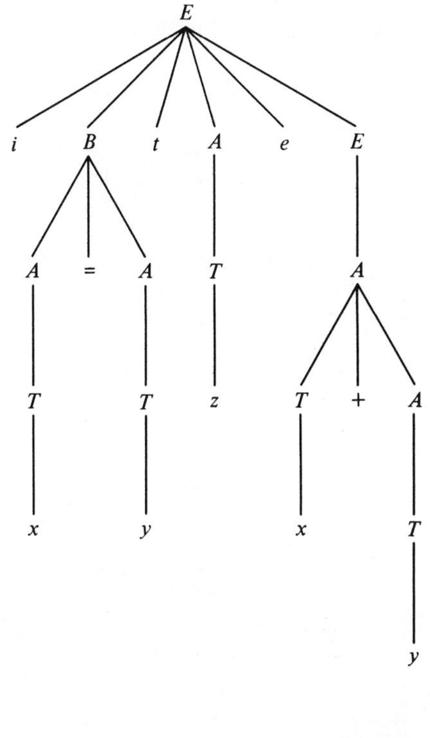


**Figure 8.9.** Derivation tree obtained from syntactic analysis.

*bottom-up* procedures, which assemble the derivation tree from the leaf nodes back up toward the root. Either approach can be made more efficient through elaborations that avoid investigating alternatives that can easily be ruled out. These methods are studied further in Chapter 10.

### 8.3.2 Construction of Pushdown Syntax Analyzers

It is easy to design a pushdown accepter that carries out the operation of top-down syntax analysis. Let $\mathbf{G} = (\mathbf{N}, \mathbf{T}, \mathbf{P}, \Sigma)$ be an arbitrary context-free grammar. We show how to construct a pushdown accepter $\mathbf{M}$ that "derives" any string in $\mathbf{L}(\mathbf{G})$. Suppose that

$$\Sigma \Longrightarrow \varphi_1 A_1 \beta_1 \Longrightarrow \ldots \Longrightarrow \varphi_k A_k \beta_k \Longrightarrow \omega$$

is a leftmost derivation of $\omega$ where

$$\left.\begin{array}{l} \varphi_i \in \mathbf{T}^* \\ A_i \in \mathbf{N} \\ \beta_i \in (\mathbf{N} \cup \mathbf{T})^* \end{array}\right\} i = 1, \ldots, k$$

The sentential forms in such a derivation are represented by configurations of $\mathbf{M}$, as shown in Figure 8.10. Specifically, a sentential form

$$\varphi_i A_i \beta_i$$

is represented by a configuration

$$(q_R, \varphi_i, \beta_i^R A_i)$$

in which the string of input symbols scanned so far is $\varphi_i$, the stack contents is the reverse of $A_i\beta_i$, and $q_R$ is a special state of $\mathbf{M}$.

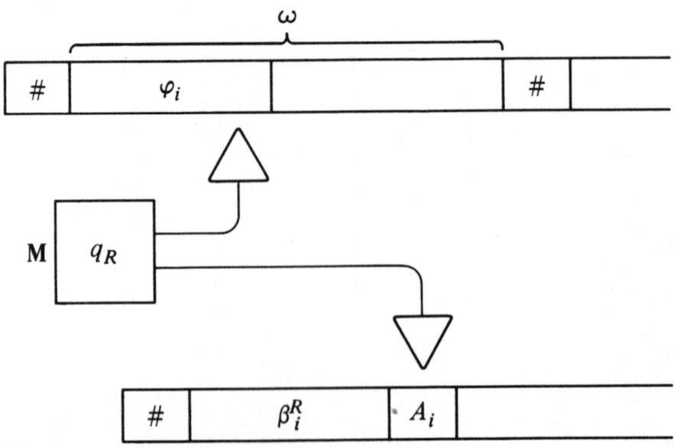


**Figure 8.10.** Representation of a sentential form $\varphi_i A_i \beta_i$ in a pushdown accepter.

The behavior of **M** when presented with an input tape containing some string $\omega$ in **L(G)** will be to assume in succession the configurations corresponding to the sentential forms of any leftmost derivation of $\omega$:

$$(q_I, \lambda, \lambda) \Longrightarrow (q_R, \lambda, \Sigma) \Longrightarrow (q_R, \varphi_1, \beta_1^R A_1) \dots$$
$$\Longrightarrow (q_R, \varphi_k, \beta_k^R A_k) \Longrightarrow (q_R, \omega, \lambda)$$

We must provide the accepter with a program of instructions that carries out each move sequence

$$(q_R, \varphi_i, \beta_i^R A_i) \Longrightarrow (q_R, \varphi_{i+1}, \beta_{i+1}^R A_{i+1})$$

corresponding to a derivation step in the grammar **G**. Whenever there are alternative productions applicable to a sentential form, the accepter must have a corresponding set of alternative moves. Thus **M** must in general be a nondeterministic automaton.

The program for **M** is realized with the two basic operations *expansion* and *matching*. Expansion corresponds to applying a production $A_i \longrightarrow \psi$ to the sentential form $\varphi_i A_i \beta_i$. Matching determines whether the terminal symbols beginning $\psi$ can be matched with the next symbols on the input tape. The top symbol of the stack determines which of these two operations occurs; a nonterminal letter indicates expansion, a terminal letter indicates matching. The state $q_R$ is used to read the top stack symbol.

1. *Expansion:* Replace the nonterminal letter $A$ at the top of the stack by $\psi^R$, the reverse of the righthand side of some production $A \longrightarrow \psi$ in **G**. Return to state $q_R$.

This is illustrated by Figure 8.11a. Expansion according to the rule $A \longrightarrow \psi$ is implemented by the instructions

$$q_R]\ \mathbf{read}\ (A, q_A)$$
$$q_A]\ \mathbf{write}\ (\psi^R, q_R)$$

We have used here a *generalized write instruction* as an obvious abbreviation for a sequence of write moves that appends the fixed string $\psi^R$ to the stack.

2. *Matching:* If the top stack symbol is a terminal letter $t$, scan the next letter $s$ on the input tape. If $s = t$, matching is successful and may continue. Otherwise, matching fails and operation ceases.

Matching is illustrated in Figure 8.11b, and is implemented by the instructions

$$\left.\begin{array}{l} q_R]\ \mathbf{read}\ (t, q_t) \\ q_t]\ \mathbf{scan}\ (t, q_R) \end{array}\right\}\ \text{each } t \in \mathbf{T}$$

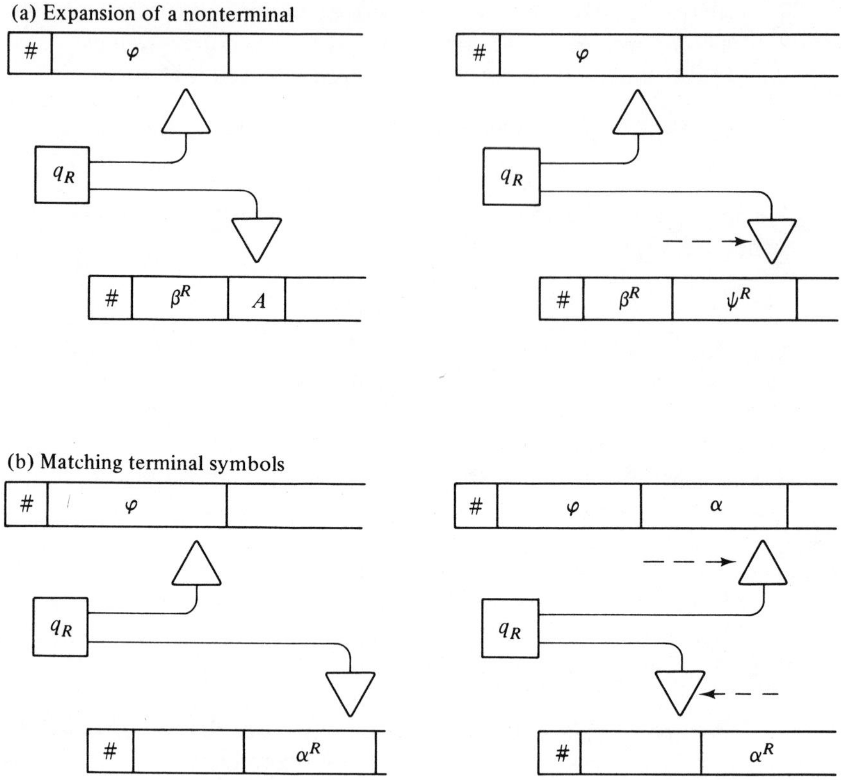


**Figure 8.11.** Basic operations of a pushdown analyzer.

The recognizer for **L(G)** is completed by adding the initial instruction

$$q_I] \textbf{ write } (\Sigma, q_R)$$

which initializes the stack with the sentential form Σ. The initial and final states of **M** are

$$\mathbf{I} = \{q_I\}$$
$$\mathbf{F} = \{q_R\}$$

We must include $q_I$ in **F** if $\Sigma \longrightarrow \lambda$ is a production of **G**. These rules of construction are summarized in Table 8.1, and the general form of **M** is pictured in Figure 8.12. Applying this construction to the grammar $\mathbf{G}_E$ of Section 8.3.1, we obtain the pushdown program given in Table 8.2.

Note that the rules of Table 8.1 do not produce a proper pushdown accepter, because the accepter executes a read move immediately after the last write move in the expansion of a nonterminal letter. Proposition 8.1 assures us that we may remove the improper moves.

**Table 8.1** Construction of a pushdown analyzer

*Given:* A context-free grammar $\mathbf{G} = (\mathbf{N}, \mathbf{T}, \mathbf{P}, \Sigma)$
*To construct:* A pushdown accepter $\mathbf{M} = (\mathbf{Q}, \mathbf{T}, \mathbf{U}, \mathbf{P}, \mathbf{I}, \mathbf{F})$ such that $\mathbf{L}(\mathbf{M}) = \mathbf{L}(\mathbf{G})$
*Let:* $\mathbf{U} = \mathbf{N} \cup \mathbf{T} \cup \{\Sigma\}$
$\mathbf{Q} = \{q_I, q_R\} \cup \{q_x \mid x \in \mathbf{U}\}$
$\mathbf{I} = \{q_I\}$ $\quad q_R \in \mathbf{F}$
The instructions of **M** are:

| | |
|---|---|
| To initialize: | $q_I]$ **write** $(\Sigma, q_R)$ |
| To expand:<br>For each production<br>$A \longrightarrow \psi$ in **G**, where<br>$A \in \mathbf{N} \cup \{\Sigma\}$ and<br>$\psi \in (\mathbf{N} \cup \mathbf{T})^* - \lambda$ | $q_R]$ **read** $(A, q_A)$<br>$q_A]$ **write** $(\psi^R, q_R)$ |
| To match:<br>For each symbol $t \in \mathbf{T}$ | $q_R]$ **read** $(t, q_t)$<br>$q_t]$ **scan** $(t, q_R)$ |
| To accept $\lambda$:<br>If **G** has $\Sigma \longrightarrow \lambda$ | $q_I \in \mathbf{F}$ |

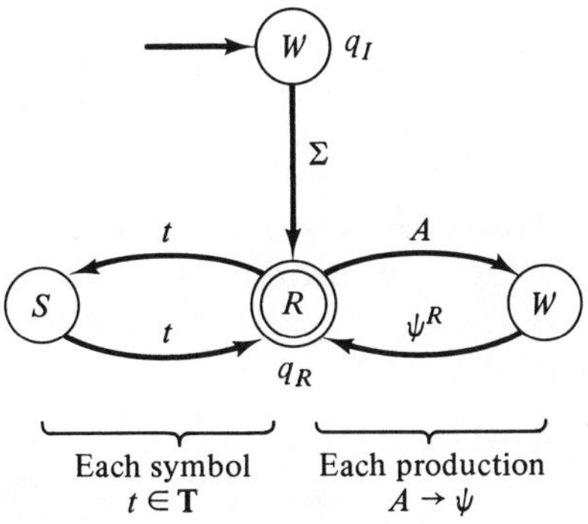


**Figure 8.12.** General form of a top-down pushdown analyzer.

### 8.3.3 Proof of the Construction

We present the proof that the construction of Table 8.1 can be used to obtain a pushdown accepter for the language generated by any context-free grammar.

**Theorem 8.1:** For any context-free grammar **G**, one can construct a pushdown accepter **M** such that $\mathbf{L}(\mathbf{M}) = \mathbf{L}(\mathbf{G})$. Moreover, the accepting move sequences in **M** are in one-to-one correspondence with leftmost derivations in **G**.

**Table 8.2** Construction of a pushdown accepter for $\mathbf{L}(\mathbf{G}_E)$

| | |
|---|---|
| $\mathbf{G}_E$: $E \longrightarrow A$ | $B \longrightarrow A = A$ |
| $E \longrightarrow iBtAeE$ | $T \longrightarrow x$ |
| $A \longrightarrow T$ | $T \longrightarrow y$ |
| $A \longrightarrow T + A$ | $T \longrightarrow z$ |
| Instructions of $\mathbf{M}_E$: | |
| To initialize: | $q_I]$ **write** $(\Sigma, q_R)$ |
| To expand: | $q_R]$ **read** $(E, q_E)(A, q_A)(B, q_B)(T, q_T)$ |
| | $q_E]$ **write** $(A, q_R)$ |
| | $q_E]$ **write** $(EeAtBi, q_R)$ |
| | $q_A]$ **write** $(T, q_R)$ |
| | $q_A]$ **write** $(A + T, q_R)$ |
| | $q_B]$ **write** $(A = A, q_R)$ |
| | $q_T]$ **write** $(x, q_R)(y, q_R)(z, q_R)$ |
| To match: | $q_R]$ **read** $(i, q_i)(t, q_t)(e, q_e)$ |
| | $q_R]$ **read** $(+, q_+)(=, q_=)$ |
| | $q_R]$ **read** $(x, q_x)(y, q_y)(z, q_z)$ |
| | $q_i]$ **scan** $(i, q_R)$ |
| | $q_t]$ **scan** $(t, q_R)$ |
| | $q_e]$ **scan** $(e, q_R)$ |
| | $q_+]$ **scan** $(+, q_R)$ |
| | $q_=]$ **scan** $(=, q_R)$ |
| | $q_x]$ **scan** $(x, q_R)$ |
| | $q_y]$ **scan** $(y, q_R)$ |
| | $q_z]$ **scan** $(z, q_R)$ |

***Proof:*** Let $\mathbf{G}$ be a context-free grammar, and let $\mathbf{M}$ be the pushdown accepter formed from $\mathbf{G}$ according to Table 8.1. Let $\omega_0 = \Sigma$, and let $\omega_i$, $i = 1, 2, \ldots, k$, be a sequence of strings

$$\omega_i = \varphi_i A_i \beta_i$$

in which

$$\varphi_i \in \mathbf{T}^* \qquad A_i \in \mathbf{N} \qquad \beta_i \in (\mathbf{N} \cup \mathbf{T})^*$$

Thus, in each string $\omega_i$, $A_i$ is the leftmost nonterminal symbol. We shall show that

$$\Sigma \Longrightarrow \omega_1 \Longrightarrow \omega_2 \Longrightarrow \ldots \Longrightarrow \omega_k \Longrightarrow \omega$$

is a leftmost derivation of $\omega$ in $\mathbf{G}$ if and only if

$$\begin{aligned}(q_R, \lambda, \Sigma) &\Longrightarrow (q_R, \varphi_1, \beta_1^R A_1)\\ &\Longrightarrow (q_R, \varphi_2, \beta_2^R A_2)\\ &\quad\vdots\\ &\Longrightarrow (q_R, \varphi_k, \beta_k^R A_k)\\ &\Longrightarrow (q_R, \omega, \lambda)\end{aligned}$$

is a move sequence of **M**. Since

$$(q_I, \lambda, \lambda) \xrightarrow{w} (q_R, \lambda, \Sigma)$$

is the only possible initial move of **M**, and since $q_R$ is a final state, this result will verify that $\omega \in \mathbf{L(G)}$ if and only if $\omega \in \mathbf{L(M)}$. Moreover, the relation of the sentential form $\varphi A \beta$ to the configuration $(q_R, \varphi, \beta^R A)$ provides the required one-to-one correspondence between derivations in **G** and move sequences of **M**.

The assertion follows by induction from these two propositions:

1. Grammar **G** permits the leftmost derivation step

$$\varphi A \beta \Longrightarrow \varphi' A' \beta'$$

if and only if

$$(q_R, \varphi, \beta^R A) \Longrightarrow (q_R, \varphi' \beta'^R A')$$

is a move sequence of **M** containing exactly one generalized write move.

2. Grammar **G** permits the derivation step

$$\varphi A \beta \Longrightarrow \omega$$

if and only if

$$(q_R, \varphi, \beta^R A) \Longrightarrow (q_R, \omega, \lambda)$$

is a move sequence containing exactly one generalized write move. We give below a detailed argument for the first of these propositions; the argument for the second is similar and is left as an exercise for the reader.

*Only if:* If

$$\varphi A \beta \Longrightarrow \varphi' A' \beta'$$

then **G** has a production $A \longrightarrow \psi$ such that

$$\varphi' A' \beta' = \varphi \psi \beta$$

According to Table 8.1, **M** has read and write instructions such that

$$(q_R, \varphi, \beta^R A) \qquad q_R] \ \textbf{read}\ (A, q_A)$$

$$(q_A, \varphi, \beta^R) \qquad q_A] \ \textbf{write}\ (\psi^R, q_R)$$

$$(q_R, \varphi, \beta^R \psi^R)$$

are moves of **M**. Thus

$$(q_R, \varphi, \beta^R A) \Longrightarrow (q_R, \varphi, \beta^R \psi^R)$$

The string $\psi \beta$ contains, by assumption, the leftmost nonterminal $A'$. That is,

$$\psi \beta = \varphi'' A' \beta'$$

where $\varphi'' \in \mathbf{T}^*$ and $\beta' \in (\mathbf{N} \cup \mathbf{T})^*$. Suppose that

$$\varphi'' = s_1 s_2 \ldots s_m$$

By construction, **M** has read and scan instructions that permit the moves

$$\begin{array}{ll}
(q_R, \varphi, \beta'^R A' s_m \ldots s_2 s_1) & \\
 & q_R] \ \mathbf{read}\ (s_1 q_{s_1}) \\
(q_{s_1}, \varphi, \beta'^R A' s_m \ldots s_2) & \\
 & q_{s_1}] \ \mathbf{scan}\ (s_1, q_R) \\
(q_R, \varphi s_1, \beta'^R A' s_m \ldots s_2) & \vdots \\
\vdots & q_R] \ \mathbf{read}\ (s_m, q_{s_m}) \\
(q_{s_m}, \varphi s_1 s_2 \ldots s_{m-1}, \beta'^R A' s_m) & \\
 & q_{s_m}] \ \mathbf{scan}\ (s_m, q_R) \\
(q_R, \varphi s_1 s_2 \ldots s_m, \beta'^R A') &
\end{array}$$

Thus

$$(q_R, \varphi, \beta'^R A' \varphi''^R) \Longrightarrow (q_R, \varphi', \beta'^R A')$$

where $\varphi' = \varphi\varphi''$.

*If:* Suppose that

$$(q_R, \varphi, \beta^R A) \Longrightarrow (q_R, \varphi', \beta'^R A')$$

is a move sequence of **M** containing just one generalized write move. Because the top symbol in the stack is a nonterminal, the first moves of the sequence must be a read followed by a generalized write:

$$\begin{array}{ll}
(q_R, \varphi, \beta^R A) & \\
 & q_R] \ \mathbf{read}\ (A, q_A) \\
(q_A, \varphi, \beta^R) & \\
 & q_A] \ \mathbf{write}\ (\psi^R, q_R) \\
(q_R, \varphi, \beta^R \psi^R) &
\end{array}$$

where $A \longrightarrow \psi$ is a production of **G**. The remaining moves can only be read and scan moves that match successive terminal letters in $\psi\beta$ with letters on the input tape:

$$(q_R, \varphi, \beta^R \psi^R) \Longrightarrow (q_R, \varphi', \beta'^R A')$$

Hence

$$\varphi\psi\beta = \varphi' A' \beta'$$

and, because $A \longrightarrow \psi$ is in **G**, we have

$$\varphi A \beta \Longrightarrow \varphi' A' \beta'$$

permitted by **G**.

To complete the proof that $\mathbf{L(M)} = \mathbf{L(G)}$, it is necessary to show that $\lambda \in \mathbf{L(M)}$ if and only if $\lambda \in \mathbf{L(G)}$. From Table 8.1, it is clear that $\lambda \in \mathbf{L(G)}$

implies that $\lambda \in \mathbf{L}(\mathbf{M})$, for $q_I$ is a final state of **M** just if $\Sigma \longrightarrow \lambda$ is a production of **G**. It is not obvious, however, that **M** accepts $\lambda$ only if $q_I$ is a final state, because **M** is not a proper pushdown accepter. We leave it to the reader to show that this is nevertheless the case.

## 8.4 Context-Free Grammars from Pushdown Accepters

### 8.4.1 Traverse Sets

Suppose that **M** is a pushdown accepter constructed from a context-free grammar **G** according to Table 8.1. Figure 8.13 illustrates the behavior of **M** from the moment it writes a nonterminal letter $A$ in position $k$ of the stack until the moment at which it reads from that position for the first time. During this interval the form of the move sequence performed by **M** is

$$(q, \varphi, \sigma) \Longrightarrow (q', \varphi\omega, \sigma)$$

where $\sigma$ is the initial contents of the stack and state $q$ labels a write instruction that appends the nonterminal $A$ to the stack. Such a move sequence, in which the stack head returns to an initial position without moving left of that position, is called a *traverse*, and the string $\omega$ over which the input head has advanced is called the *string observed by the traverse*. Now, according to

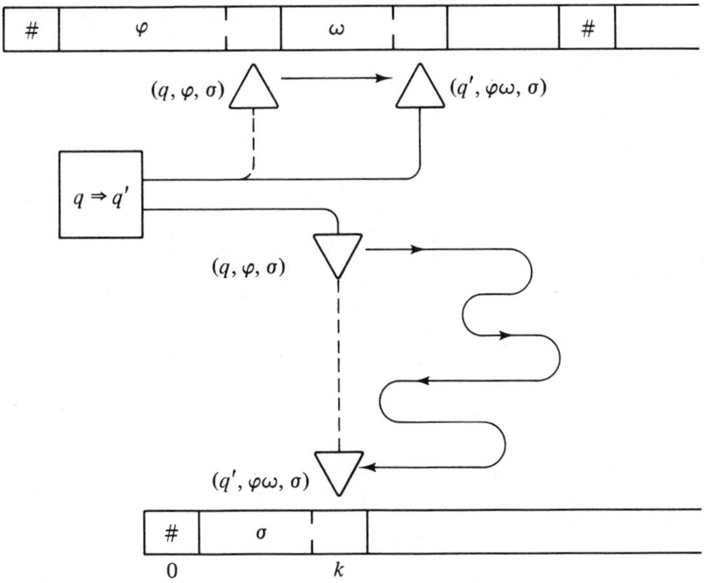


**Figure 8.13.** A traverse that observes the string $\omega$.

Theorem 8.1, the move sequence given above corresponds uniquely to a derivation

$$\varphi A \sigma^R \overset{*}{\Longrightarrow} \varphi \omega \sigma^R$$

in the grammar **G**. That is, the terminal string $\omega$ is derivable from the nonterminal letter $A$,

$$A \overset{*}{\Longrightarrow} \omega$$

in **G**. This suggests that in general the string observed by a traverse of a pushdown accepter is derivable from a nonterminal letter in a corresponding grammar. The construction for obtaining a grammar from a given PDA is based on this idea. Just as the notion of "end set" helped in the construction of right-linear grammars from finite-state accepters (Chapter 5), so the corresponding notion of "traverse set" permits the construction of a context-free grammar from any pushdown accepter by associating nonterminals with these sets.

**Definition 8.6:** Let $\mathbf{M} = (\mathbf{Q}, \mathbf{S}, \mathbf{U}, \mathbf{P}, \mathbf{I}, \mathbf{F})$ be a proper pushdown accepter. A move sequence of **M**

$$(q, \varphi, \sigma) \Longrightarrow (q', \varphi', \sigma')$$

is called a *traverse of* $\omega$ *from state* $q$ *to state* $q'$ provided

1. $\sigma = \sigma'$.
2. $\varphi\omega = \varphi'$.
3. Each configuration $(q_i, \varphi_i, \sigma_i)$ occurring within the move sequence satisfies $|\sigma_i| \geq |\sigma|$.

In such a case, we say that $\omega$ is the string *observed* by the traverse. To indicate that a move sequence is a traverse, we write

$$(q, \varphi, \sigma) \overset{T}{\Longrightarrow} (q', \varphi\omega, \sigma)$$

The *traverse set* $\mathbf{T}(q, q')$ is the set of all strings observed by traverses from $q$ to $q'$:

$$\mathbf{T}(q, q') = \left\{ \omega \in \mathbf{S}^* \,\middle|\, \begin{array}{l} (q, \varphi, \sigma) \overset{T}{\Longrightarrow} (q', \varphi\omega, \sigma) \\ \text{for some } \varphi \in \mathbf{S}^* \text{ and some } \sigma \in \mathbf{U}^* \end{array} \right\}$$

A traverse comprising no moves

$$(q, \varphi, \sigma) \overset{T}{\Longrightarrow} (q, \varphi, \sigma)$$

observes the empty string and is called a *trivial traverse*. Thus $\lambda \in \mathbf{T}(q, q)$ for each $q \in \mathbf{Q}$.

This definition is illustrated by Figure 8.13. As the input head scans the symbols of $\omega$, the stack head makes arbitrary excursions on the storage tape, but never moves left of the position at which it starts and finishes the traverse.

**Example 8.2:** Consider the *double parenthesis language* $\mathbf{L}_{dp}$ comprising all well-formed strings over two kinds of bracketing symbols. The language has the following recursive definition:

1. ( ) and [ ] are in $\mathbf{L}_{dp}$.
2. If $\omega$ is in $\mathbf{L}_{dp}$, then so are $(\omega)$ and $[\omega]$.
3. If $\omega$ and $\varphi$ are in $\mathbf{L}_{dp}$, then so is $\omega\varphi$.

$\mathbf{L}_{dp}$ contains, for example, the string [( )]( ). A pushdown accepter for the language is shown in Figure 8.14. The traverse by which it accepts [( )]( ) is

$$
\begin{aligned}
(1, \lambda, \lambda) &\longrightarrow (3, [, \lambda) \longrightarrow (1, [, b) \\
&\longrightarrow (2, [(, b) \longrightarrow (1, [(, ba) \\
&\longrightarrow (4, [(\ ), ba) \longrightarrow (1, [(\ ), b) \\
&\longrightarrow (5, [(\ )], b) \longrightarrow (1, [(\ )], \lambda) \\
&\longrightarrow (2, [(\ )](, \lambda) \longrightarrow (1, [(\ )](, a) \\
&\longrightarrow (4, [(\ )](\ ), a) \longrightarrow (1, [(\ )](\ ), \lambda)
\end{aligned}
$$

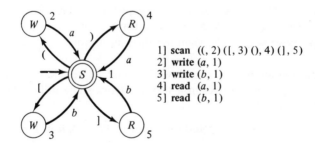

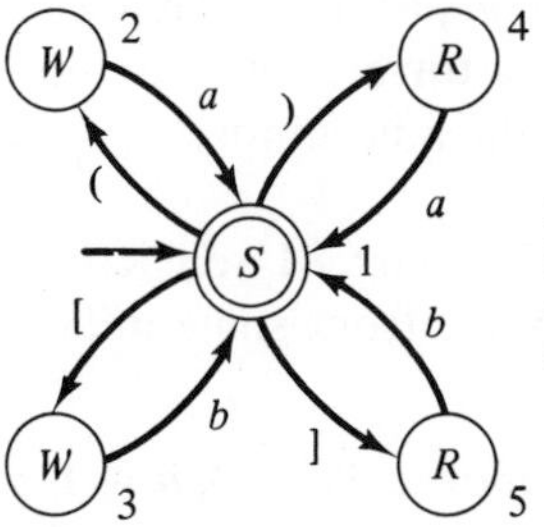


1] **scan** ((, 2) ([, 3) (), 4) (], 5)
2] **write** ($a$, 1)
3] **write** ($b$, 1)
4] **read** ($a$, 1)
5] **read** ($b$, 1)

**Figure 8.14.** Pushdown accepter for the double parenthesis language.

Therefore, we write

$$(1, \lambda, \lambda) \overset{T}{\Longrightarrow} (1, [(\ )](\ ), \lambda)$$

This traverse contains subsequences of moves that are also traverses:

$$(1, \lambda, \lambda) \overset{T}{\Longrightarrow} (1, [(\ )], \lambda)$$

$$(1, [(\ )], \lambda) \overset{T}{\Longrightarrow} (1, [(\ )](\ ), \lambda)$$

$$(1, [, b) \overset{T}{\Longrightarrow} (1, [(\ ), b)$$

Thus $\mathbf{T}(1, 1)$ contains the strings [( )]( ), [( )], and ( ), as well as $\lambda$. We also have

$$(1, \lambda, \lambda) \overset{T}{\Longrightarrow} (3, [, \lambda)$$

Hence [ is in $\mathbf{T}(1, 3)$. Finally, we have

$$(1, [(, ba) \overset{T}{\Longrightarrow} (4, [(\ ), ba)$$

Hence ( ) is in $\mathbf{T}(1, 4)$.

### 8.4.2 Properties of Traverse Sets

From Figure 8.13 it is clear that the choices of the initially scanned string $\varphi$ and the initial stack contents $\sigma$ are arbitrary in a traverse:

> **Proposition 8.3:** If
>
> $$(q, \varphi, \sigma) \overset{T}{\Longrightarrow} (q', \varphi\omega, \sigma)$$
>
> is a traverse of $\omega$ for some $\varphi$ in $\mathbf{S}^*$ and some $\sigma$ in $\mathbf{U}^*$, then it is a traverse of $\omega$ for any $\varphi$ in $\mathbf{S}^*$ and any $\sigma$ in $\mathbf{U}^*$.

If, for some traverse of $\omega$, the strings $\varphi$ and $\sigma$ are each empty, we have

$$(q, \lambda, \lambda) \overset{T}{\Longrightarrow} (q', \omega, \lambda)$$

which is an accepting move sequence for $\omega$ just if $q \in \mathbf{I}$ and $q' \in \mathbf{F}$. Also, any accepting move sequence for $\omega$ must be a traverse of $\omega$, because no left move of the stack head is possible when the stack is empty.

> **Proposition 8.4:** A pushdown accepter $\mathbf{M}$ accepts a string $\omega$ if and only if it observes $\omega$ in a traverse from some initial state to some final state:
>
> $$\omega \in \mathbf{L}(\mathbf{M}) \qquad \text{if and only if } \omega \in \mathbf{T}(q, q'),\ q \in \mathbf{I},\ q' \in \mathbf{F}$$
>
> Thus the language recognized by $\mathbf{M}$ is
>
> $$\mathbf{L}(\mathbf{M}) = \bigcup_{\substack{q \in \mathbf{I} \\ q' \in \mathbf{F}}} \mathbf{T}(q, q')$$

Consider now a traverse by $\mathbf{M}$ of the empty string $\lambda$. Any such traverse must contain no scan moves, and therefore consists entirely of read and write moves. Since a traverse must return the stack head to its starting position, the read and write moves must be equinumerous. Furthermore, the first move of such a traverse must be a write, since a read would move the stack head left of its initial position. Consequently, it is impossible to complete the traverse without somewhere having a read move immediately following a write move. Since this is ruled out when $\mathbf{M}$ is a proper accepter, we have

**Proposition 8.5:** Let **M** be a proper pushdown accepter. The only traverses of $\lambda$ by **M** are the trivial traverses

$$(q, \varphi, \sigma) \overset{T}{\Longrightarrow} (q, \varphi, \sigma) \qquad \begin{cases} q \in \mathbf{Q} \\ \varphi \in \mathbf{S}^* \\ \sigma \in \mathbf{U}^* \end{cases}$$

That is,

$$\lambda \in \mathbf{T}(q, q') \qquad \text{if and only if } q = q'$$

Thus each nontrivial traverse by a proper pushdown accepter must contain at least one scan move.

### 8.4.3 Construction of a Grammar

In constructing a formal grammar from a pushdown accepter, we wish to associate a nonterminal letter $N(q, q')$ with certain traverse sets $\mathbf{T}(q, q')$ of the automaton, in analogy with our use of end sets in Chapter 5 for the analysis of finite-state accepters. Each nonterminal letter will denote exactly those strings that are members of the corresponding traverse set. To obtain grammatical productions, we must relate membership of a string in a traverse set to the membership of its substrings in other traverse sets. Some additional terminology will be helpful in developing these relations:

**Definition 8.7:** In a traverse

$$(q, \varphi, \sigma) \overset{T}{\Longrightarrow} (q', \varphi\omega, \sigma)$$

by a pushdown accepter, let $\sigma$ be the initial and final contents of the stack. A write move in the traverse is called a *base write move* if it is performed from a configuration in which the stack contents are $\sigma$; a read move is called a *base read move* if it leaves the stack containing $\sigma$. A base write move and a base read move form a *matched pair* if the write move precedes the read move, and no other base write or read moves intervene.

In a matched pair of base moves, the read move fetches the symbol placed on the stack by the write move.

**Example 8.3:** In Example 8.2, the traverse

$$(1, \lambda, \lambda) \overset{T}{\Longrightarrow} (1, [(\ )](\ ), \lambda)$$

consists of this sequence of move types:

$$S\ W\ S\ W\ S\ R\ S\ R\ S\ W\ S\ R$$

There are two matched pairs in this traverse, indicated by the solid lines. The move sequence within the first matched pair is the traverse

$$(1, [, b) \xrightarrow{T} (1, [(\ ), b)$$

which itself contains a matched pair, indicated by the dashed line.

In Example 8.3, each base read move in a traverse is matched by a base write move in the same traverse. Indeed, this must always be the case. To return the stack head to its position at the beginning of a traverse, an accepter must read all the symbols written in its stack since the start of the traverse. If a symbol has been written by a base write move of the traverse, the move that reads the symbol must be the following base read move; similarly, any symbol read by a base read move of the traverse must have been written by the preceding base write move. Thus we have the following:

**Proposition 8.6:** A traverse that contains a base read (write) move also contains a matching base write (read) move.

We are now prepared for the basic result that relates membership of a string in a traverse set to membership of simpler strings in other traverse sets. Proposition 8.7 expresses formally the observation that a traverse must have one of four mutually exclusive forms. Figure 8.15 should help the reader interpret the statements in the proposition.

**Proposition 8.7:** Let **M** be a proper pushdown accepter and suppose that

$$(q, \varphi, \sigma) \xrightarrow{T} (q', \varphi\omega, \sigma)$$

is a traverse of $\omega$ by **M**; that is, $\omega \in \mathbf{T}(q. q')$. Then exactly one of the following statements is true:

1. The traverse consists of a single scan move:

$$(q, \varphi, \sigma) \xrightarrow{S} (q', \varphi s, \sigma)$$

and $\omega = s$.

2. The traverse has more than one move, and the final move is a scan:

$$(q, \varphi, \sigma) \xrightarrow{T} (q'', \varphi\psi, \sigma)$$
$$\xrightarrow{S} (q', \varphi\psi s, \sigma)$$

where $\omega = \psi s$ and $\psi \in \mathbf{T}(q, q'')$.

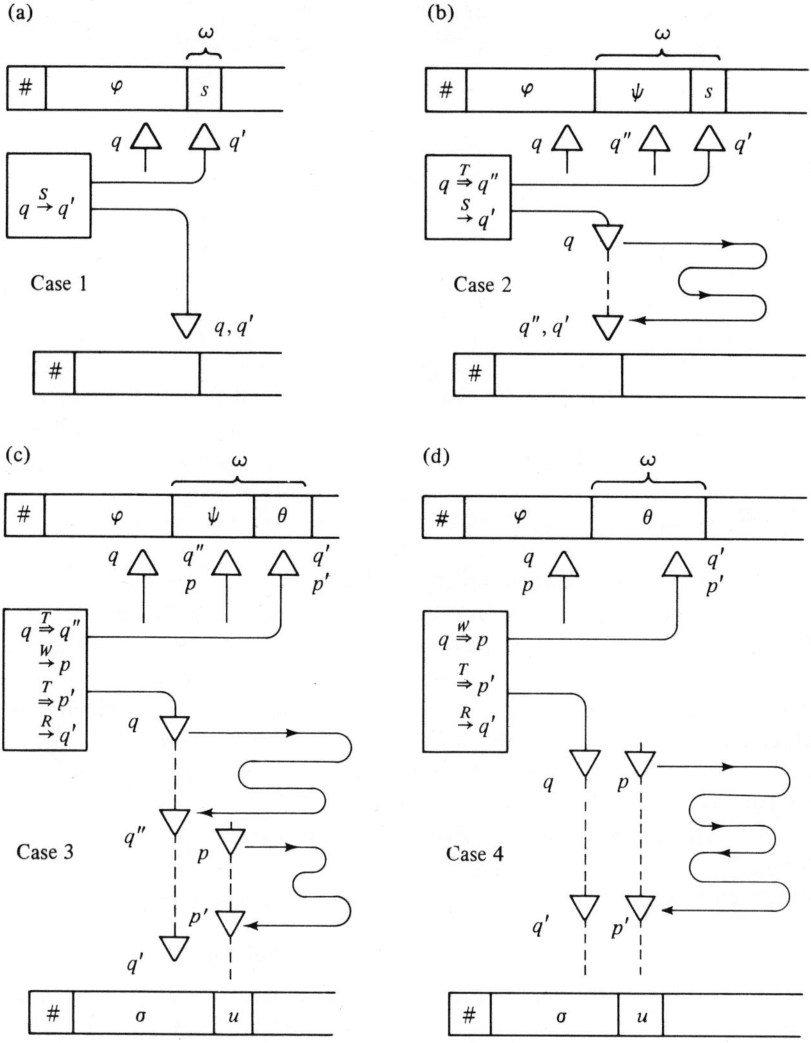


**Figure 8.15.** The four forms of a traverse that observes $\omega$.

3. The traverse has more than one move, the final move is a read, and the matching write is not the first move:

$$
\begin{aligned}
(q, \varphi, \sigma) &\xRightarrow{T} (q'', \varphi\psi, \sigma) \\
&\xrightarrow{W} (p, \varphi\psi, \sigma u) \xRightarrow{T} (p', \varphi\psi\theta, \sigma u) \\
&\xrightarrow{R} (q', \varphi\psi\theta, \sigma)
\end{aligned}
$$

where $\omega = \psi\theta$, $\psi \in \mathbf{T}(q. q'')$, and $\theta \in \mathbf{T}(p, p')$.

4. The traverse has more than one move, the final move is a read, and the matching write is the first move of the traverse:

$$(q, \varphi, \sigma) \xrightarrow{W} (p, \varphi, \sigma u) \overset{T}{\Longrightarrow} (p', \varphi\theta, \sigma u)$$
$$\xrightarrow{R} (q', \varphi\theta, \sigma)$$

where $\omega = \theta$ and $\theta \in \mathbf{T}(p, p')$.

***Proof:*** Clearly, the four statements are mutually exclusive. We claim that all possible cases are covered. If a traverse in a proper pushdown accepter consists of one move, that move must be a scan. If a traverse has more than one move, the final move must be either a scan or a read. If it is a read, it is a base read, and the matching base write either is or is not the first move of the traverse. In statements 2 and 3 the initial moves are by definition traverses of $\psi$; in statements 3 and 4 the move sequences between the matched pairs must be traverses of $\theta$ because they contain no base moves of the enclosing traverse.

In studying finite-state accepters, we found that two grammar constructions arise naturally from the properties of state diagrams. The construction of right-linear grammars is based on move sequences that connect a specified state to some final state. Similarly, the construction of left-linear grammars is based on move sequences that connect any initial state to a specified state. Either method can be generalized and applied to the construction of grammars from pushdown accepters. Our approach is analogous to the latter construction.

The principle by which we relate grammars to accepters is the same as in Chapter 5. We obtain the productions of a grammar **G** from the program of a pushdown accepter **M** in such a way that for any string $\omega$ in $\mathbf{S}^*$:

$$\omega \in \mathbf{T}(q, q') \text{ in } \mathbf{M} \qquad \text{if and only if} \qquad N(q, q') \overset{*}{\Longrightarrow} \omega \text{ in } \mathbf{G}$$

where $\mathbf{T}(q, q')$ is a traverse set and $N(q, q')$ is a corresponding nonterminal symbol.

Each of the four possible traverse types in Proposition 8.7 results from certain specific instructions in the program of **M**: each specifies relations among traverse sets corresponding to relations among the sets of strings derivable from the nonterminal letters of grammar **G**. These relations are shown in Figure 8.16.

Now we ask: With which pairs of states $(q, q')$ must we associate nonterminal letters $N(q, q')$ of **G**? Since each $N(q, q')$ is associated with a traverse, we need to identify the set **B** of states on which traverses may begin. The traverse sets relevant to the construction of a grammar are then

$$\{\mathbf{T}(q, q') \mid q \in \mathbf{B}, q' \in \mathbf{Q}\}$$

(1) $(q, \varphi, \sigma) \xrightarrow{S} (q', \varphi s, \sigma)$

$N(q, q') \Longrightarrow s$

(2) $\underbrace{(q, \varphi, \sigma) \overset{T}{\Longrightarrow} (q'', \varphi\psi, \sigma)}_{N(q, q'') \overset{*}{\Longrightarrow} \psi} \xrightarrow{S} (q', \varphi\psi s, \sigma)$

$N(q, q') \Longrightarrow N(q, q'')s$

(3) $\underbrace{(q, \varphi, \sigma) \overset{T}{\Longrightarrow} (q'', \varphi\psi, \sigma)}_{N(q, q'') \overset{*}{\Longrightarrow} \psi} \xrightarrow{W} \underbrace{(p, \varphi\psi, \sigma u) \overset{T}{\Longrightarrow} (p', \varphi\psi\theta, \sigma u)}_{N(p, p') \overset{*}{\Longrightarrow} \theta} \xrightarrow{R} (q', \varphi\psi\theta, \sigma)$

$N(q, q') \Longrightarrow N(q, q'')N(p, p')$

(4) $(q, \varphi, \sigma) \xrightarrow{W} \underbrace{(p, \varphi, \sigma u) \overset{T}{\Longrightarrow} (p', \varphi\theta, \sigma u)}_{N(p, p') \overset{*}{\Longrightarrow} \theta} \xrightarrow{R} (q', \varphi\theta, \sigma)$

$N(q, q') \Longrightarrow N(p, p')$

**Figure 8.16.** Relations among traverse types and derivation steps.

From Proposition 8.4 we know that a traverse by which a string is accepted always starts from an initial state of **M**. Furthermore, Figure 8.16 shows that, when a traverse is decomposed into simpler traverses according to Proposition 8.7, each simpler traverse either starts from the same first state as the enclosing traverse, or starts at the successor state of a write move. Accordingly, the set **B** is

$$\mathbf{B} = \mathbf{I} \cup \left\{ q' \,\middle|\, \begin{array}{l} q] \textbf{ write } (u, q') \text{ is an instruction in } \mathbf{M} \\ \text{for some } q \in \mathbf{Q} \text{ and some } u \in \mathbf{U} \end{array} \right\}$$

The set of nonterminal symbols of **G** is

$$\mathbf{N} = \{N(q, q') \mid q \in \mathbf{B},\, q' \in \mathbf{Q}\}$$

From Proposition 8.7 and Figure 8.16, we deduce the following construction rules for the grammar **G**:

*Rule 1:* Suppose that **M** has the instruction

$$q] \textbf{ scan } (s, q'), \qquad q \in \mathbf{B}$$

Then $s \in \mathbf{T}(q, q')$, and **G** has the production

$$N(q, q') \longrightarrow s$$

*Rule 2:* Suppose that **M** has the instruction

$$q''] \textbf{ scan } (s, q')$$

Then if $\psi$ is a string in $\mathbf{T}(q, q'')$, it follows that $\psi s$ is in $\mathbf{T}(q, q')$. This is expressed by the production

$$N(q, q') \longrightarrow N(q, q'')s$$

in **G**.

*Rule 3:* Suppose that **M** has instructions

$$q''] \textbf{ write } (u, p)$$
$$p'] \textbf{ read } (u, q')$$

If $\psi$ and $\theta$ are nonempty strings in $\mathbf{T}(q, q'')$ and $\mathbf{T}(p, p')$, then $\omega = \psi\theta$ is a string in $\mathbf{T}(q, q')$. This is expressed by the production

$$N(q, q') \longrightarrow N(q, q'')N(p, p')$$

*Rule 4:* Suppose that **M** has instructions

$$q] \textbf{ write } (u, p), \qquad q \in \mathbf{B}$$
$$p'] \textbf{ read } (u, q')$$

Then any string in $\mathbf{T}(p, p')$ is also in $\mathbf{T}(q, q')$, as expressed by the production

$$N(q, q') \longrightarrow N(p, p')$$

in **G**.

The construction rules are summarized in Table 8.3. Rule 5 relates traverses between initial and final states in **M** to strings derivable from $\Sigma$ in

**Table 8.3** Construction of a context-free grammar from a pushdown accepter

*Given:* A proper pushdown accepter $\mathbf{M} = (\mathbf{Q}, \mathbf{S}, \mathbf{U}, \mathbf{P}, \mathbf{I}, \mathbf{F})$
*To construct:* The context-free grammar $\mathbf{G} = (\mathbf{N}, \mathbf{S}, \mathbf{P}, \Sigma)$ such that $\mathbf{L}(\mathbf{G}) = \mathbf{L}(\mathbf{M})$

*Let:* $\mathbf{B} = \mathbf{I} \cup \left\{ q' \,\middle|\, \begin{array}{l} q] \textbf{ write } (u, q') \text{ is in } \mathbf{M} \text{ for} \\ \text{some } q \in \mathbf{Q} \text{ and some } u \in \mathbf{U} \end{array} \right\}$

$\mathbf{N} = \{N(q, q') \mid q \in \mathbf{B}, q' \in \mathbf{Q}\}$

The productions of **G** are as follows:

| Rule | If **M** has | then **G** has |
|---|---|---|
| 1 | $q]$ **scan** $(s, q')$<br>$q \in \mathbf{B}$ | $N(q, q') \longrightarrow s$ |
| 2 | $q'']$ **scan** $(s, q')$<br>$q \in \mathbf{B}$ | $N(q, q') \longrightarrow N(q, q'')s$ |
| 3 | $q'']$ **write** $(u, p)$<br>$p']$ **read** $(u, q')$<br>$q \in \mathbf{B}$ | $N(q, q') \longrightarrow N(q, q'')N(p, p')$ |
| 4 | $q]$ **write** $(u, p)$<br>$p']$ **read** $(u, q')$<br>$q \in \mathbf{B}$ | $N(q, q') \longrightarrow N(p, p')$ |
| 5 | $q \in \mathbf{I}, q' \in \mathbf{F}$ | $\Sigma \longrightarrow N(q, q')$ |
| 6 | $\mathbf{I} \cap \mathbf{F} \neq \varnothing$ | $\Sigma \longrightarrow \lambda$ |

**G**, and follows directly from Proposition 8.4; rule 6 provides that **G** generates $\lambda$ just if $\lambda$ is accepted by **M**.

A context-free grammar may also be obtained from a pushdown accepter by a procedure analogous to the use of end sets in Chapter 5. The traverse sets of interest are those in which the terminal state is in the set

$$\mathbf{E} = \mathbf{F} \cup \left\{ q \,\middle|\, \begin{array}{l} q] \textbf{ read } (u, q') \text{ is an instruction in } \mathbf{M} \\ \text{for some } q' \in \mathbf{Q} \text{ and some } u \in \mathbf{U} \end{array} \right\}$$

The nonterminal symbols of the grammar denote the strings of these traverse sets. The details of the construction are left to the Problems.

### 8.4.4 Examples of the Construction

Before proving that the construction of Table 8.3 ensures $\mathbf{L(G)} = \mathbf{L(M)}$, we consider two examples.

**Example 8.4:** Let us construct a grammar from the pushdown accepter $\mathbf{M}_{dp}$ that recognizes the double parenthesis language $\mathbf{L}_{dp}$. (This machine, presented in Example 8.2, is redrawn in Figure 8.17.)

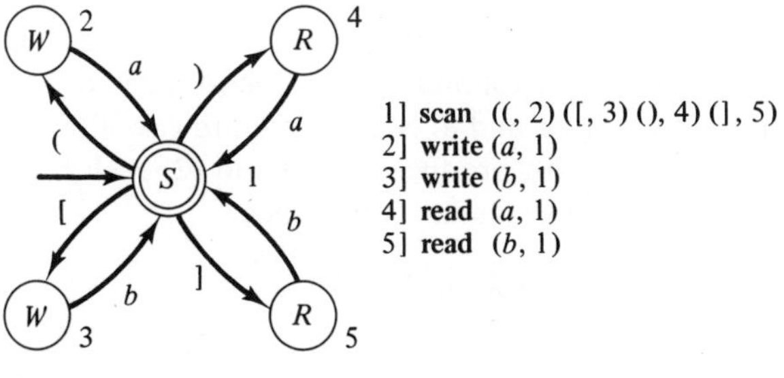
W
2
R
4
a
)
a
(
S
1
[
b
]
b
W
3
R
5
1] scan ((, 2) ([, 3) (), 4) (], 5)
2] write (a, 1)
3] write (b, 1)
4] read (a, 1)
5] read (b, 1)

**Figure 8.17.** Pushdown accepter for the double parenthesis language.

State 1 is the only initial state and is also the successor state of both write instructions. Thus $\mathbf{B} = \{1\}$, and the traverse sets of interest are $\mathbf{T}(1, 1)$, $\mathbf{T}(1, 2)$, $\mathbf{T}(1, 3)$, $\mathbf{T}(1, 4)$, and $\mathbf{T}(1, 5)$. Since state 1 of $\mathbf{M}_{dp}$ is also its only final state, we have $\mathbf{L}(\mathbf{M}_{dp}) = \mathbf{T}(1, 1)$. For convenience, we shall use single capitals for nonterminals as follows:

$$N(1, 1)\colon S \qquad N(1, 2)\colon A \qquad N(1, 4)\colon C$$
$$N(1, 3)\colon B \qquad N(1, 5)\colon D$$

The productions resulting from the application of each rule of Table 8.3 are as follows:

*Rule 1:* $A \longrightarrow ($ $\qquad C \longrightarrow )$
$B \longrightarrow [$ $\qquad D \longrightarrow ]$

*Rule 2:* $A \longrightarrow S($ $\quad C \longrightarrow S)$

$B \longrightarrow S[$ $\quad D \longrightarrow S]$

In applying rule 2, note that productions result only when $q = q' = 1$.

*Rule 3:*
(1) $S \longrightarrow AC$
(2) $S \longrightarrow BD$
Productions (1) and (2) result from taking $p' = 4$ and $p' = 5$, respectively.

*Rule 4:* [None].

*Rule 5:* $\Sigma \longrightarrow S$.

*Rule 6:* $\Sigma \longrightarrow \lambda$.

The relationship of a derivation in this grammar to a move sequence of $\mathbf{M}_{dp}$ is illustrated for the string [( )]( ) by Figure 8.18.

The grammar above can be put into a more readily understood form: we substitute for nonterminals $A$, $B$, $C$, and $D$ in productions (1) and (2) the corresponding right-hand sides of the productions obtained by rules 1 and 2. Since there are two alternatives for each of the nonterminals, productions (1) and (2) each become four productions, and the grammar $\mathbf{G}$ becomes

$$\begin{array}{lll} \Sigma \longrightarrow \lambda & S \longrightarrow (\,) & S \longrightarrow [\,] \\ \Sigma \longrightarrow S & S \longrightarrow S(\,) & S \longrightarrow S[\,] \\ & S \longrightarrow (S) & S \longrightarrow [S] \\ & S \longrightarrow S(S) & S \longrightarrow S[S] \end{array}$$

This is not the simplest grammar for $\mathbf{L}_{dp}$, for the grammar

$$\begin{array}{lll} \Sigma \longrightarrow \lambda & S \longrightarrow (S) & S \longrightarrow [S] \\ \Sigma \longrightarrow S & S \longrightarrow (\,) & S \longrightarrow [\,] \\ S \longrightarrow SS & & \end{array}$$

also generates $\mathbf{L}_{dp}$. However, this simple grammar is ambiguous, whereas, as we shall see, the grammar obtained from Table 8.3 is guaranteed to be unambiguous because $\mathbf{M}_{dp}$ operates deterministically.

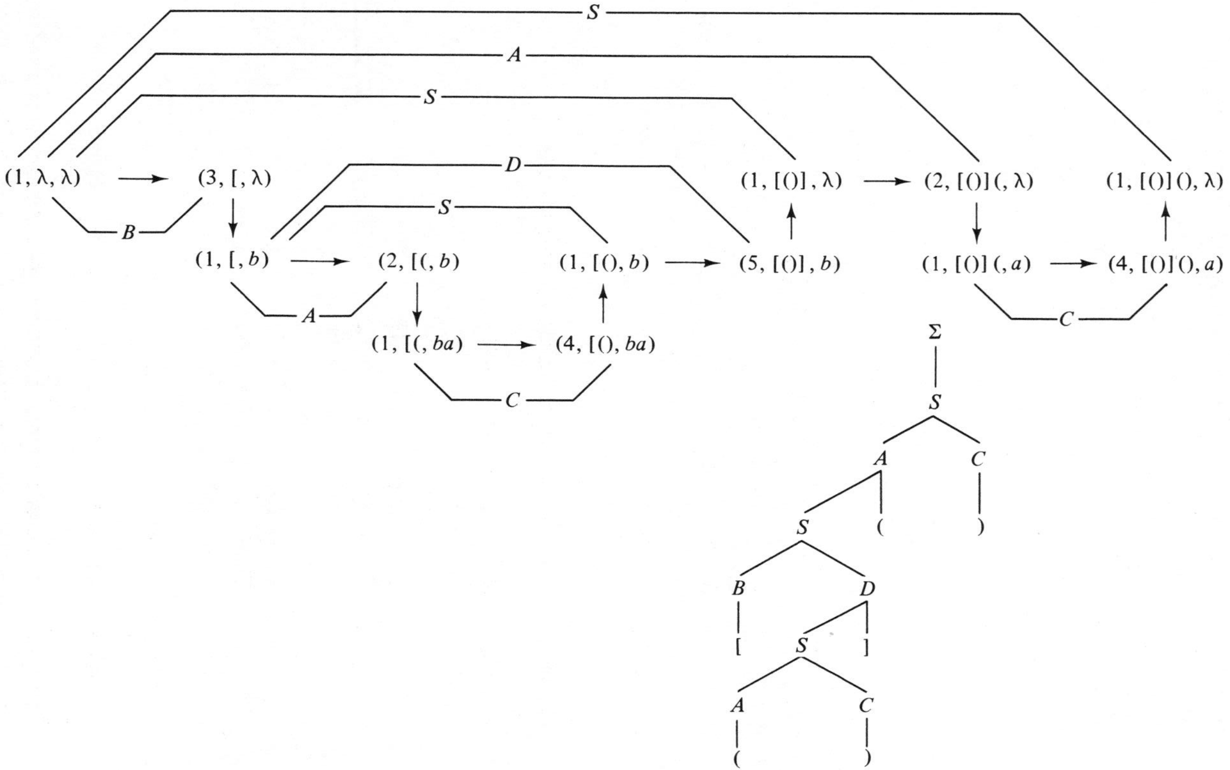


Figure 8.18. Move sequence for the parenthesis string [( )]( ).

**Example 8.5:** For the palindrome accepter $\mathbf{M}_{mi}$ of Figure 8.19, the set $\mathbf{B}$ has two elements: $\mathbf{B} = \{1, 4\}$. We associate nonterminal letters with traverse sets of $\mathbf{M}_{mi}$ as follows:

| | | | |
|---|---|---|---|
| $\mathbf{T}(1, 1)$: $A$ | $\mathbf{T}(1, 4)$: $S$ | $\mathbf{T}(4, 1)$: $F$ | $\mathbf{T}(4, 4)$: $I$ |
| $\mathbf{T}(1, 2)$: $B$ | $\mathbf{T}(1, 5)$: $D$ | $\mathbf{T}(4, 2)$: $G$ | $\mathbf{T}(4, 5)$: $J$ |
| $\mathbf{T}(1, 3)$: $C$ | $\mathbf{T}(1, 6)$: $E$ | $\mathbf{T}(4, 3)$: $H$ | $\mathbf{T}(4, 6)$: $K$ |

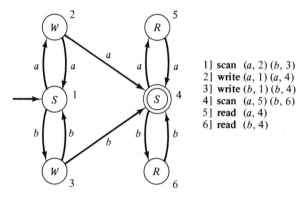

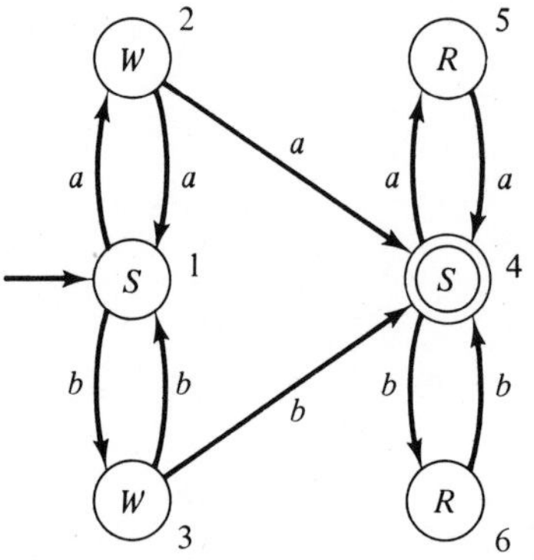


1] **scan** $(a, 2)\,(b, 3)$
2] **write** $(a, 1)\,(a, 4)$
3] **write** $(b, 1)\,(b, 4)$
4] **scan** $(a, 5)\,(b, 6)$
5] **read** $(a, 4)$
6] **read** $(b, 4)$

**Figure 8.19.** Palindrome accepter $\mathbf{M}_{mi}$.

The grammar $\mathbf{G}$ obtained from Table 8.3 is as follows:

*Rule 1:* $B \longrightarrow a \qquad C \longrightarrow b$
$J \longrightarrow a \qquad K \longrightarrow b$

*Rule 2:* $B \longrightarrow Aa \qquad C \longrightarrow Ab \qquad D \longrightarrow Sa$
$E \longrightarrow Sb \qquad G \longrightarrow Fa \qquad H \longrightarrow Fb$
$J \longrightarrow Ia \qquad K \longrightarrow Ib$

*Rule 3:* $S \longrightarrow BD \qquad S \longrightarrow BJ \qquad S \longrightarrow CK$
$S \longrightarrow CE \qquad I \longrightarrow GJ \qquad I \longrightarrow GD$
$I \longrightarrow HK \qquad I \longrightarrow HE$

*Rule 4:* [none].

*Rule 5:* $\Sigma \longrightarrow S$.

This grammar contains many productions that cannot be used in deriving a terminal string according to $\mathbf{G}$. For example, the nonterminals $A$ and $F$ can never be eliminated from a sentential form because there are no productions in which these symbols appear as the left-hand side. Thus no terminal string can ever be derived from a sentential form in which either $A$ or $F$ appears, and productions containing these symbols can be eliminated from the grammar. Similarly, nonterminals $G$ and $H$ can be eliminated from a sentential form only by productions that introduce the nonterminal $F$; therefore, productions containing $G$ or $H$ can also be eliminated from the grammar. Once these productions have been eliminated, no $I$ rules remain in the grammar and the productions

$$J \longrightarrow Ia$$

$$K \longrightarrow Ib$$

introduced by rule 2 can be eliminated. The resulting grammar contains the productions

$$\begin{array}{lll} \Sigma \longrightarrow S & S \longrightarrow BD & D \longrightarrow Sa \\ & S \longrightarrow BJ & E \longrightarrow Sb \\ & S \longrightarrow CK & B \longrightarrow a \\ & S \longrightarrow CE & C \longrightarrow b \\ & & J \longrightarrow a \\ & & K \longrightarrow b \end{array}$$

which, after substituting for $B$, $C$, $D$, $E$, $K$, and $J$, becomes the simpler grammar

$$\begin{array}{lll} \Sigma \longrightarrow S & S \longrightarrow aSa & S \longrightarrow bb \\ & S \longrightarrow aa & S \longrightarrow bSb \end{array}$$

Figure 8.20 shows the relation between a traverse of the string *aabbaa* by $\mathbf{M}_{mi}$ and its derivation in **G**.

### 8.4.5 Proof of the Construction

The correspondence between move sequences and derivations illustrated in the preceding examples holds for any grammar constructed according to the rules of Table 8.3. This correspondence is the foundation of our proof that the construction rules are an effective procedure for obtaining a context-free grammar for the language recognized by any pushdown accepter.

**Theorem 8.2:** For any pushdown accepter **M**, one can construct a context-free grammar **G** such that **L(G)** = **L(M)**.

***Proof:*** Without loss of generality we may assume that **M** is a proper pushdown accepter. Let **G** be the context-free grammar obtained from **M** by use of Table 8.3. The proof proceeds as follows: first, we show how to construct a derivation $N(q, q') \overset{*}{\Longrightarrow} \omega$ from any traverse

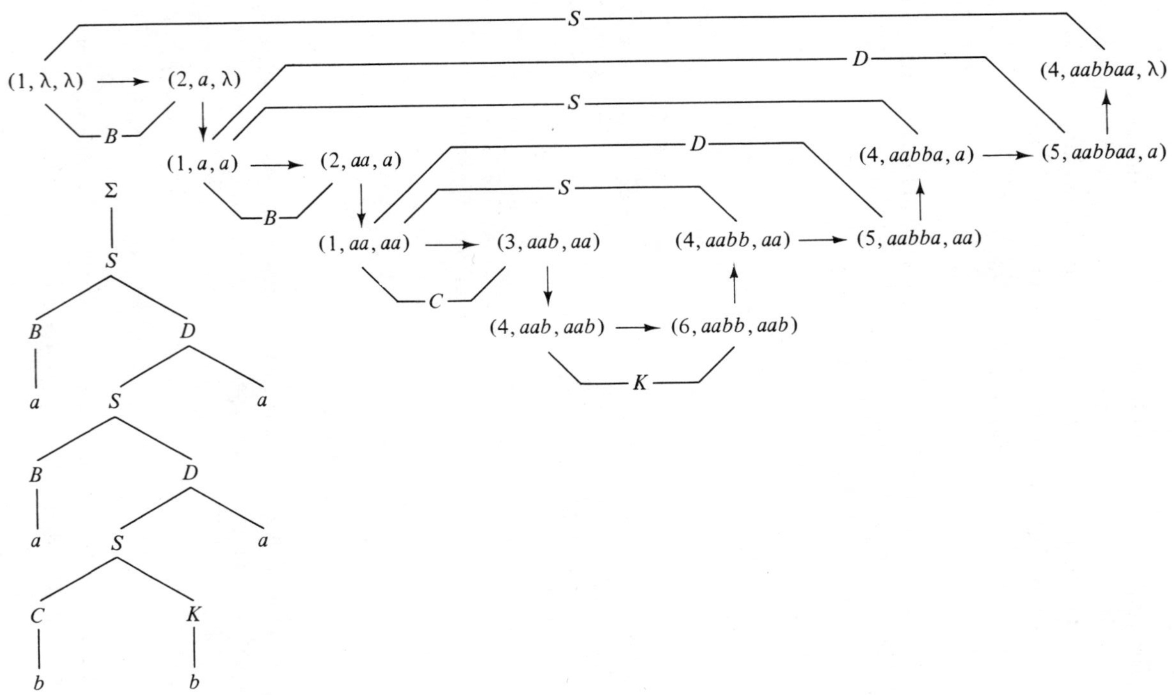


Figure 8.20. Move sequence for the palindrome *aabbaa*.

of $\omega$ from state $q$ to state $q'$; then we show how to construct a traverse of $\omega$ from state $q$ to state $q'$ from any derivation $N(q, q') \overset{*}{\Longrightarrow} \omega$; we conclude from this that $\mathbf{L(M)} = \mathbf{L(G)}$.

For the first part of the proof, suppose that

$$(1) \qquad (q, \varphi, \sigma) \overset{T}{\Longrightarrow} (q', \varphi\omega, \sigma), \qquad q \in \mathbf{B}$$

is a traverse of $\omega$ by **M**. The construction of the corresponding derivation is by induction on the number of moves in the traverse.

***Basis:*** If the traverse of $\omega$ consists of just one move, it must be a scan

$$(q, \varphi, \sigma) \overset{s}{\longrightarrow} (q', \varphi s, \sigma)$$

where $\omega = s$, and thus **M** has the instruction

$$q] \ \textbf{scan} \ (s, q')$$

By Table 8.3, **G** has the production

$$N(q, q') \longrightarrow s$$

and the derivation $N(q, q') \overset{*}{\Longrightarrow} \omega$ consists of one step.

***Induction:*** For some $n \geq 1$, assume that a derivation $N(p, p') \overset{*}{\Longrightarrow} \psi$ can be constructed for any string $\psi$ observed in a traverse from state $p$ to state $p'$, whenever the traverse contains $n$ or fewer moves. Suppose that the traverse ($i$) contains $n + 1$ moves. There are two mutually exclusive possibilities, according as the last move of the traverse is a scan or a read:

*Case 1:* The last move is a scan:

$$(2) \qquad (q, \varphi, \sigma) \overset{T}{\Longrightarrow} (q'', \varphi\psi, \sigma)$$
$$\overset{s}{\longrightarrow} (q', \varphi\psi s, \sigma)$$

for some $q'' \in \mathbf{Q}$ such that $\omega = \psi s$. Then **M** has the instruction

$$q''] \ \textbf{scan} \ (s, q')$$

and rule 2 in Table 8.3 shows that **G** has the production

$$N(q, q') \longrightarrow N(q, q'')s$$

Since the first $n$ moves of (2) constitute a traverse of $\psi$, the induction hypothesis ensures that a derivation $N(q, q'') \overset{*}{\Longrightarrow} \psi$ can be constructed, and

$$N(q, q') \Longrightarrow N(q, q'')s$$
$$N(q, q'') \overset{*}{\Longrightarrow} \psi$$

forms a derivation of $\psi s = \omega$.

*Case 2:* The last move is a read:

$$(q, \varphi, \sigma) \Longrightarrow (p', \varphi\omega, \sigma u)$$
$$\xrightarrow{R} (q', \varphi\omega, \sigma)$$

for some $p' \in \mathbf{Q}$ and some $u \in \mathbf{U}$. By Proposition 8.7, this read move must be matched by the last base write move of the traverse:

$$(3) \quad \begin{aligned} (q, \varphi, \sigma) &\overset{T}{\Longrightarrow} (q'', \varphi\psi, \sigma) \\ &\xrightarrow{W} (p, \varphi\psi, \sigma u) \\ &\overset{T}{\Longrightarrow} (p', \varphi\psi\theta, \sigma u) \\ &\xrightarrow{R} (q', \varphi\psi\theta, \sigma) \end{aligned}$$

where $\omega = \psi\theta$. In this case, **M** has the instruction

$$q''] \textbf{ write } (u, p)$$

so $p \in \mathbf{B}$. The move sequence (3) contains two traverses, neither of which can be longer than $n$ moves:

$$(4) \quad (q, \varphi, \sigma) \overset{T}{\Longrightarrow} (q'', \varphi\psi, \sigma)$$

$$(5) \quad (p, \varphi\psi, \sigma u) \overset{T}{\Longrightarrow} (p', \varphi\psi\theta, \sigma u)$$

The second of these must contain at least one scan move if **M** is proper, and is therefore nontrivial. The first traverse will be trivial if and only if the write move is the first move of sequence 3.

Suppose that (4) is trivial. Then $q'' = q$ and $\psi = \lambda$. Rule 4 of Table 8.3 requires that **G** have the production

$$N(q, q') \longrightarrow N(p, p')$$

Applying the induction hypothesis to (5), a derivation $N(p, p') \overset{*}{\Longrightarrow} \theta$ can be constructed and

$$N(q, q') \Longrightarrow N(p', p') \overset{*}{\Longrightarrow} \theta$$

is a derivation in **G** of $\theta = \omega$.

Suppose that (4) is nontrivial. Rule 3 of Table 8.3 requires that **G** have the production

$$N(q, q') \longrightarrow N(q, q'')N(p, p')$$

The induction hypothesis ensures that derivations $N(q, q'') \overset{*}{\Longrightarrow} \psi$ and $N(p, p') \overset{*}{\Longrightarrow} \theta$ may be constructed in **G**; thus

$$N(q, q') \Longrightarrow N(q, q'')N(p, p') \quad \text{and} \quad \begin{cases} N(q, q'') \overset{*}{\Longrightarrow} \psi \\ N(p, p') \overset{*}{\Longrightarrow} \theta \end{cases}$$

form a derivation of $\psi\theta = \omega$.

For the second part of the proof, suppose that $N(q, q') \stackrel{*}{\Longrightarrow} \omega$ is a derivation of $\omega$ according to **G**, where $q \in \mathbf{B}$. The construction of the corresponding traverse of $\omega$ by **M** is by induction on the number of steps in the derivation.

***Basis:*** If the derivation of $\omega$ consists of one step, it must be an application of

$$N(q, q') \longrightarrow s, \qquad q \in \mathbf{B}, q' \in \mathbf{Q}$$

where $\omega = s$. From Table 8.3, **M** must have the instruction

$$q]\ \mathbf{scan}\ (s, q')$$

and

$$(q, \varphi, \sigma) \stackrel{s}{\longrightarrow} (q', \varphi s, \sigma)$$

is a traverse of $\omega$.

***Induction:*** For some $n \geq 1$, assume that if $\psi$ is derived from $N(p, p')$ in $n$ or fewer steps, then $\psi$ is observed by **M** in a traverse from state $p$ to state $p'$. Suppose that $\omega$ is derived from $N(q, q')$ in $n + 1$ steps. The first production applied cannot be of the form $N(q, q') \longrightarrow s$, for no production could be subsequently applied. Therefore, the first derivation step must be an application of a production having one of the remaining three formats in Table 8.3:

1. $N(q, q') \longrightarrow N(q, q'')s$, where $\omega = \psi s$ for some $\psi$ such that $N(q, q'') \stackrel{*}{\Longrightarrow} \psi$.
2. $N(q, q') \longrightarrow N(q, q'')N(p, p')$, where $\omega = \psi\theta$ such that $N(q, q'') \stackrel{*}{\Longrightarrow} \psi$ and $N(p, p') \stackrel{*}{\Longrightarrow} \theta$.
3. $N(q, q') \longrightarrow N(p, p')$, where $\omega = \theta$ and $N(p, p') \stackrel{*}{\Longrightarrow} \theta$.

*Case 1:* If $N(q, q') \longrightarrow N(q, q'')s$ is a production of **G**, then **M** must have the instruction

$$q'']\ \mathbf{scan}\ (s, q')$$

Since the derivation $N(q, q'') \stackrel{*}{\Longrightarrow} \psi$ has $n$ steps, the induction hypothesis ensures that a traverse of $\psi$ by **M** may be constructed. Thus

$$(q, \varphi, \sigma) \stackrel{T}{\Longrightarrow} (q'', \varphi\psi, \sigma) \stackrel{s}{\longrightarrow} (q', \varphi\psi s, \sigma)$$

is a traverse of $\psi s = \omega$ from state $q$ to state $q'$.

*Case 2:* If $N(q, q') \longrightarrow N(q, q'')N(p, p')$ is a production of **G**, then **M** must have instructions

$$q'']\ \mathbf{write}\ (u, p) \qquad p']\ \mathbf{read}\ (u, q')$$

for some stack symbol $u$. Neither of the derivations $N(q, q'') \overset{*}{\Longrightarrow} \psi$ and $N(p, p') \overset{*}{\Longrightarrow} \theta$ may have more than $n$ steps; hence traverses may be constructed for $\psi$ between states $q$ and $q''$, and for $\theta$ between states $p$ and $p'$. Then

$$\begin{aligned}(q, \varphi, \sigma) &\overset{T}{\Longrightarrow} (q'', \varphi\psi, \sigma) \overset{W}{\longrightarrow} (p, \varphi\psi, \sigma u)\\ &\overset{T}{\Longrightarrow} (p', \varphi\psi\theta, \sigma u) \overset{R}{\longrightarrow} (q', \varphi\psi\theta, \sigma)\end{aligned}$$

is a traverse of $\psi\theta = \omega$ from state $q$ to state $q'$.

*Case 3:* If $N(q, q') \longrightarrow N(p, p')$ is a production of **G**, the argument for case $b$ applies with $q'' = q$ and $\psi = \lambda$. Thus

$$\begin{aligned}(q, \varphi, \sigma) &\overset{W}{\longrightarrow} (p, \varphi, \sigma u)\\ &\overset{T}{\Longrightarrow} (p', \varphi\theta, \sigma u) \overset{R}{\longrightarrow} (q', \varphi\theta, \sigma)\end{aligned}$$

is the required traverse of $\omega$.

We have shown that for any states $q \in \mathbf{B}$ and $q' \in \mathbf{Q}$

$$\omega \in \mathbf{T}(q, q') \qquad \text{if and only if } N(q, q') \overset{*}{\Longrightarrow} \omega$$

Consequently,

$$\begin{aligned}\mathbf{L}(\mathbf{M}) &= \{\omega \in \mathbf{S}^* \mid \omega \in \mathbf{T}(q, q'), q \in \mathbf{I}, q' \in \mathbf{F}\}\\ &= \{\omega \in \mathbf{S}^* \mid N(q, q') \overset{*}{\Longrightarrow} \omega, q \in \mathbf{I}, q' \in \mathbf{F}\}\end{aligned}$$

Since $\Sigma \longrightarrow N(q, q')$ is a production of **G** if and only if $q \in \mathbf{I}$ and $q' \in \mathbf{F}$, we have

$$\begin{aligned}\mathbf{L}(\mathbf{M}) &= \{\omega \in \mathbf{S}^* \mid \Sigma \overset{*}{\Longrightarrow} \omega\}\\ &= \mathbf{L}(\mathbf{G})\end{aligned}$$

The correspondence between derivation trees (leftmost derivations) and traverses established by the construction of this proof is summarized in Table 8.4. The construction is reversible; that is, if we construct a derivation from a traverse and then construct a traverse from the derivation, we always obtain the original traverse. Thus we have the following:

**Corollary 8.3:** If **M** is a proper pushdown accepter and **G** is the grammar obtained from **M** by the rules of Table 8.3, then for each $\omega \in \mathbf{S}^*$ the traverses by which **M** accepts $\omega$ correspond one-to-one with terminal leftmost derivations of $\omega$ in **G**.

This result will be cited in the study of ambiguity in context-free grammars in Section 8.8.

**Table 8.4** Correspondence between traverse constructions and derivation steps

| Traverse Construction | Derivation Step |
|---|---|
| 1. One scan move: $(q, \varphi, \sigma) \xrightarrow{S} (q', \varphi s, \sigma)$ | $N(q, q') \Longrightarrow s$ |
| 2. Last move is scan: $(q, \varphi, \sigma) \overset{T}{\Longrightarrow} (q'', \varphi\psi, \sigma) \xrightarrow{S} (q', \varphi\psi s, \sigma)$ | $N(q, q') \Longrightarrow N(q, q'')s$, where $N(q, q'') \overset{*}{\Longrightarrow} \psi$ |
| 3. Last move is read; the matching write is not the first move: $(q, \varphi, \sigma) \overset{T}{\Longrightarrow} (q'', \varphi\psi, \sigma) \xrightarrow{W} (p, \varphi\psi, \sigma u) \overset{T}{\Longrightarrow} (p', \varphi\psi\theta, \sigma u) \xrightarrow{R} (q', \varphi\psi\theta, \sigma)$ | $N(q, q') \Longrightarrow N(q, q'')N(p, p')$, where $N(q, q'') \overset{*}{\Longrightarrow} \psi$, $N(p, p') \overset{*}{\Longrightarrow} \theta$ |
| 4. Last move is a read; the matching write is the first move: $(q, \varphi, \sigma) \xrightarrow{W} (p, \varphi, \sigma u) \overset{T}{\Longrightarrow} (p', \varphi\theta, \sigma u) \xrightarrow{R} (q', \varphi\theta, \sigma)$ | $N(q, q') \Longrightarrow N(p, p')$ where $N(p, p') \overset{*}{\Longrightarrow} \theta$ |

## 8.5 Closure Properties of Context-Free Languages

Having shown that pushdown accepters and context-free grammars have equivalent language-defining ability, we may use the automata as a tool for investigating the closure properties of this important class of languages. We shall see that, with two notable exceptions, they have closure properties similar to those of the regular languages.

We begin our study by demonstrating that the context-free languages are closed under intersection with a regular set and transduction by a generalized sequential machine. The principle of the two constructions, illustrated in Figures 8.21 and 8.22, are analogous to the constructions used in obtaining the corresponding results (Theorems 5.7 and 7.1) for finite-state languages.

We study first the intersection of a context-free language $\mathbf{L}$ with a regular set $\mathbf{R}$. Suppose that

$$\mathbf{M}_f = (\mathbf{Q}_f, \mathbf{T}, \mathbf{P}_f, \mathbf{I}_f, \mathbf{F}_f)$$

is a finite-state accepter for $\mathbf{R}$, and that

$$\mathbf{M}_p = (\mathbf{Q}_p, \mathbf{T}, \mathbf{U}, \mathbf{P}_p, \mathbf{I}_p, \mathbf{F}_p)$$

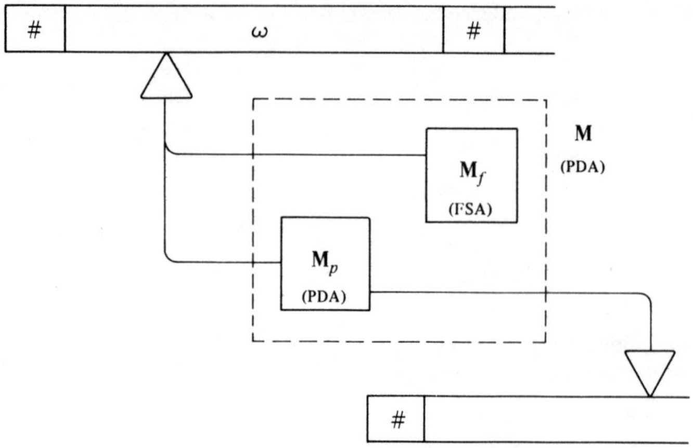


**Figure 8.21.** The intersection of a regular set and a context-free language.

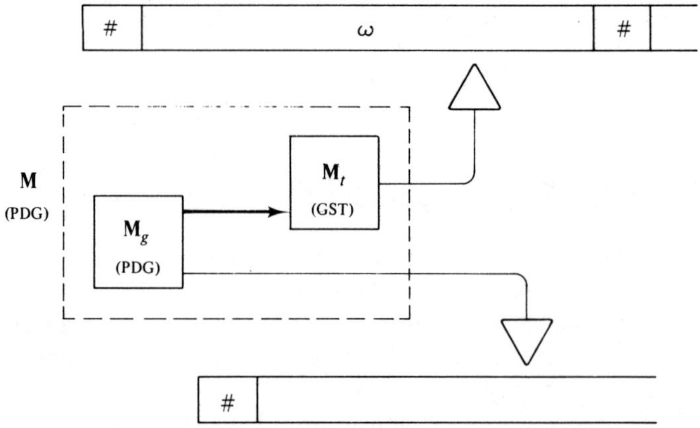


**Figure 8.22.** Transduction of a context-free language.

is a pushdown accepter for **L**. If we combine these automata as shown in Figure 8.21, we obtain a pushdown accepter

$$\mathbf{M} = (\mathbf{Q}, \mathbf{T}, \mathbf{U}, \mathbf{P}, \mathbf{I}, \mathbf{F}), \qquad \mathbf{Q} = \mathbf{Q}_p \times \mathbf{Q}_f,$$
$$\mathbf{I} = \mathbf{I}_p \times \mathbf{I}_f, \qquad \mathbf{F} = \mathbf{F}_p \times \mathbf{F}_f$$

that recognizes $\mathbf{L} \cap \mathbf{R}$. The program for **M** is specified in Table 8.5, and we assert that **M** has an accepting move sequence for $\omega$

$$((q, p), \lambda, \lambda) \overset{T}{\Longrightarrow} ((q', p'), \omega, \lambda), \qquad (q, p) \in \mathbf{I}, (q', p') \in \mathbf{F}$$

**Table 8.5** Program specification of a pushdown accepter for $\mathbf{L}(\mathbf{M}_p) \cap \mathbf{L}(\mathbf{M}_f)$

| If $\mathbf{M}_p$ has | and $\mathbf{M}_f$ has | then $\mathbf{M}$ has |
|---|---|---|
| $q]$ **scan** $(s, q')$ | $p \xrightarrow{s} p'$ | $(q, p)]$ **scan** $(s, (q', p'))$ |
| $q]$ **write** $(u, q')$ | $p \in \mathbf{Q}_f$ | $(q, p)]$ **write** $(u, (q', p))$ |
| $q]$ **read** $(u, q')$ | $p \in \mathbf{Q}_f$ | $(q, p)]$ **read** $(u, (q', p))$ |

if and only if

$$(q, \lambda, \lambda) \overset{T}{\Longrightarrow} (q', \omega, \lambda)$$

in $\mathbf{M}_p$ and

$$p \overset{\omega}{\Longrightarrow} p'$$

in $\mathbf{M}_f$. The details are left to the reader.

Since the complement of a regular set is regular, and $\mathbf{L} - \mathbf{R} = \mathbf{L} \cap \mathbf{R}^c$, this construction also shows that $\mathbf{L} - \mathbf{R}$ is always a context-free language. That is, the class of context-free languages is closed under difference with a regular set.

To study the finite-state transduction of a context-free language, it is useful to think in terms of pushdown automata that *generate* context-free languages. A *pushdown generator* (PDG) is a pushdown accepter in which we consider the input tape to be an output tape, and replace each scan move

$$q] \ \textbf{scan} \ (s, q')$$

with a *print* move

$$q] \ \textbf{print} \ (s, q')$$

that prints the symbol $s$ on the output tape. Clearly, a pushdown generator *generates* a string $\omega$ (that is, prints $\omega$ on its output tape) by a traverse

$$(q, \lambda, \lambda) \overset{T}{\Longrightarrow} (q', \omega, \lambda)$$

if and only if the machine, acting as an accepter, accepts $\omega$ by the same sequence of moves.

In Figure 8.22, the pushdown generator

$$\mathbf{M}_g = (\mathbf{Q}_g, \mathbf{S}, \mathbf{U}, \mathbf{P}_g, \mathbf{I}_g, \mathbf{F}_g)$$

generates strings in $\mathbf{L}$ that are processed by the generalized sequential transducer

$$\mathbf{M}_t = (\mathbf{Q}_t, \mathbf{S}, \mathbf{R}, \mathbf{P}_t, \mathbf{I}_t, \mathbf{F}_t)$$

The cascade combination of $\mathbf{M}_g$ and $\mathbf{M}_t$ is a new pushdown generator

$$\mathbf{M} = (\mathbf{Q}, \mathbf{R}, \mathbf{U}, \mathbf{P}, \mathbf{I}, \mathbf{F}), \qquad \mathbf{Q} = \mathbf{Q}_g \times \mathbf{Q}_t,$$

$$\mathbf{I} = \mathbf{I}_g \times \mathbf{I}_t, \qquad \mathbf{F} = \mathbf{F}_g \times \mathbf{F}_t$$

that generates just those strings in $\mathbf{R}^*$ that are transductions by $\mathbf{M}_t$ of strings in $\mathbf{L}$. That is, $\mathbf{M}$ generates $\varphi$ by a traverse

$$((q, p), \lambda, \lambda) \overset{T}{\Longrightarrow} ((q', p'), \varphi, \lambda), \qquad (q, p) \in \mathbf{I}, (q', p') \in \mathbf{F}$$

if and only if $\mathbf{M}_g$ generates some string $\omega$ by the traverse

$$(q, \lambda, \lambda) \overset{T}{\Longrightarrow} (q', \omega, \lambda)$$

and $\varphi$ is the transduction of $\omega$ by $\mathbf{M}_t$:

$$p \overset{\omega/\varphi}{\Longrightarrow} p'$$

Again, the details of this argument are left to the reader. The program of $\mathbf{M}$ is specified by Table 8.6, and makes use of the additional instruction

$$q]\ \textbf{null}\ (q')$$

which puts the control unit of a pushdown automaton in state $q'$ without moving either tape head. The null instructions are analogous to $\lambda$-transitions in finite-state automata and may be replaced with the pair of instructions

$$q]\ \textbf{write}\ (u, q'')$$

$$q'']\ \textbf{read}\ (u, q')$$

where $q''$ is a new auxiliary state and $u$ is an arbitrary stack symbol; the improper moves may then be eliminated by the method described in Section 8.2.

**Table 8.6** Program specification of a pushdown generator for the transduction of $\mathbf{L}(\mathbf{M}_g)$ by $\mathbf{M}_t$

| If $\mathbf{M}_g$ has | and $\mathbf{M}_t$ has | then $\mathbf{M}$ has |
|---|---|---|
| $q]$ **write** $(u, q')$ | $p \in \mathbf{Q}_t$ | $(q, p)]$ **write** $(u, (q', p))$ |
| $q]$ **read** $(u, q')$ | $p \in \mathbf{Q}_t$ | $(q, p)]$ **read** $(u, (q', p))$ |
| $q]$ **print** $(s, q')$ | $p]$ **scan** $(s, p')$ | $(q, p)]$ **null** $(q', p')$ |
| $q \in \mathbf{Q}_g$ | $p]$ **print** $(r, p')$ | $(q, p)]$ **print** $(r, (q, p'))$ |

The closure of the class of context-free languages under the set operations of union, concatenation, and reversal is easily shown by arguments involving context-free grammars. For example, let

$$\mathbf{G}_1 = (\mathbf{T}, \mathbf{N}_1, \mathbf{P}_1, \Sigma_1)$$

$$\mathbf{G}_2 = (\mathbf{T}, \mathbf{N}_2, \mathbf{P}_2, \Sigma_2)$$

be context-free grammars having the same terminal alphabet $\mathbf{T}$, but with disjoint sets of nonterminals ($\mathbf{N}_1 \cap \mathbf{N}_2 = \varnothing$). Then a grammar for the language

$$\mathbf{L} = \mathbf{L}(\mathbf{G}_1) \cdot \mathbf{L}(\mathbf{G}_2)$$

may be obtained by using new nonterminal letters $A_1$ and $A_2$ in place of $\Sigma_1$ and $\Sigma_2$, and adding the production

$$\Sigma \longrightarrow A_1 A_2$$

to the union of $\mathbf{P}_1$ and $\mathbf{P}_2$. For completeness, we include the production $\Sigma \longrightarrow \lambda$ just if $\mathbf{G}_1$ has $\Sigma_1 \longrightarrow \lambda$ and $\mathbf{G}_2$ has $\Sigma_2 \longrightarrow \lambda$.

That the context-free languages are not closed under the operations of intersection and complement is established by counterexample. On this and several later occasions we make use of the fact that the *double matching language*

$$\mathbf{L}_{dm} = \{a^k b^k c^k \mid k \geq 0\}$$

is not context free. (A formal demonstration of this fact involves an intricate argument and is left to Chapter 9, where additional properties of context-free languages may be applied. Intuitively, the inability of pushdown accepters to recognize $\mathbf{L}_{dm}$ stems from their inability to store the count of $a$'s scanned in a string so that it can be used to check both the number of $b$'s and the number of $c$'s subsequently scanned.) Unlike $\mathbf{L}_{dm}$, the languages

$$\mathbf{L}_1 = \{a^n b^n c^m \mid m, n \geq 0\}$$

and

$$\mathbf{L}_2 = \{a^m b^n c^n \mid m, n \geq 0\}$$

are both context free, since $\mathbf{L}_1$ is the concatenation of the simple matching language $\mathbf{L}_m = \{a^k b^k \mid k \geq 0\}$ and the regular set $\mathbf{c}^*$, and $\mathbf{L}_2$ is the concatenation of the regular set $\mathbf{a}^*$ and the matching language $\mathbf{L}'_m = \{b^k c^k \mid k \geq 0\}$. The intersection of $\mathbf{L}_1$ and $\mathbf{L}_2$ is

$$\mathbf{L}_1 \cap \mathbf{L}_2 = \{a^n b^n c^n \mid n \geq 0\} = \mathbf{L}_{dm}$$

and is not context free. Thus the class of context-free languages is not closed under intersection.

Now, if the complement of a context-free language were always context free, we could demonstrate closure under intersection by using the De Morgan relation

$$\mathbf{L}_1 \cap \mathbf{L}_2 = (\mathbf{L}_1^c \cup \mathbf{L}_2^c)^c$$

Since we have just seen that the context-free languages are not closed under intersection, we conclude that they are not closed under complement with respect to their terminal alphabet.

The following theorem summarizes the closure properties of the context-free languages. The properties for which arguments have not been provided are explored in the Problems.

**Theorem 8.4:** The class of context-free languages on a terminal alphabet $\mathbf{T}$ is closed under the operations union, concatenation, closure, reversal, transduction by a generalized sequential machine, and intersection and difference with a regular set. That is, if $\mathbf{L}_1$ and

$\mathbf{L}_2$ are context-free languages, $\mathbf{R}$ is a regular set, and $\mathbf{M}$ is a generalized sequential transducer, then

$$\begin{array}{ll} \mathbf{L}_1 \cup \mathbf{L}_2 & \mathbf{M}(\mathbf{L}_1) \\ \mathbf{L}_1 \cdot \mathbf{L}_2 & \mathbf{L}_1 \cap \mathbf{R} \\ \mathbf{L}_1^* & \mathbf{L}_1 - \mathbf{R} \\ \mathbf{L}_1^R & \end{array}$$

are all context free. However,

$$\mathbf{L}_1 \cap \mathbf{L}_2 \quad \text{and} \quad \mathbf{L}_1^c = \mathbf{T}^* - \mathbf{L}_1$$

need not be context free.

## 8.6 Deterministic Pushdown Accepters

Since they are closely related to classes of practical languages and to the methods of syntax analysis studied in Chapter 10, deterministic pushdown accepters are an important subclass of pushdown automata. For the present, our goals are to understand some basic properties of deterministic pushdown automata and to compare their capabilities with those of the pushdown automata studied thus far.

**Definition 8.8:** A *deterministic pushdown accepter* (DPDA) is a pushdown accepter

$$\mathbf{M} = (\mathbf{Q}, \mathbf{S}, \mathbf{U}, \mathbf{P}, \mathbf{q}_I, \mathbf{F})$$

with a single initial state $q_I$, and a program in which no more than one instruction is applicable in a given configuration.

In studying these automata, we wish to distinguish between limitations deriving from deterministic behavior and those arising from our choice of conventions defining acceptance of an input string. We shall define an input string as being accepted by a deterministic pushdown accepter if the machine reaches a final state after scanning the string, regardless of the contents of its stack. The following example illustrates why requiring a deterministic pushdown accepter to accept strings with an empty stack is too strict. Consider the language

$$\mathbf{L} = \mathbf{a}^* \cup \{a^k b^k \mid k \geq 1\}$$

formed by adding to the simple matching language the set of all strings of $a$'s. If acceptance is defined by the machine's reaching a final state, without regard to the contents of the stack, then the deterministic accepter in Figure 8.23 recognizes $\mathbf{L}$. (The accepter's stack is initialized with an *end marker*, the letter

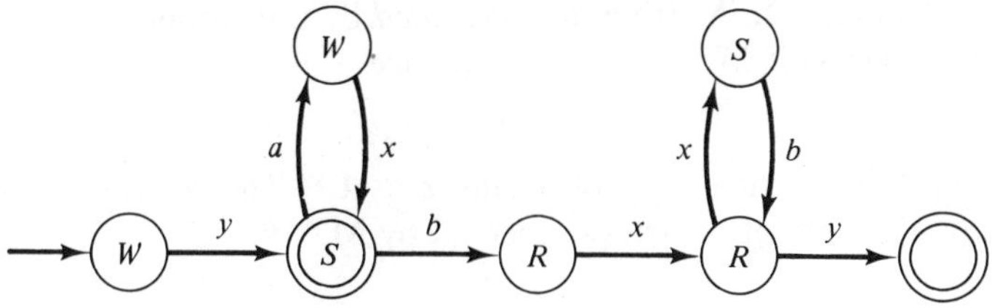


**Figure 8.23.** Deterministic PDA for $\mathbf{a}^* \cup \{a^k b^k \mid k \geq 1\}$.

$y$, so that if any $b$ appears in the input string, the machine can check that each previously scanned $a$ is matched by a scanned $b$.) However, the following argument shows that no deterministic pushdown accepter can recognize $\mathbf{L}$ when an empty stack is a condition of acceptance.

If a deterministic pushdown accepter accepts both a string $\omega$ and a proper prefix of $\omega$, then the accepting move sequence for the prefix must be an initial subsequence of the move sequence for $\omega$. Suppose that $\mathbf{M}$ is an $n$-state deterministic pushdown accepter that accepts each string $\omega$ of $\mathbf{L}$ by a traverse

$$(q_I, \lambda, \lambda) \overset{T}{\Longrightarrow} (q', \omega, \lambda), \qquad q' \in \mathbf{F}$$

Then for any $p \geq n$, the behavior of $\mathbf{M}$ for $\omega = a^p b^p$ is

$$(q_I, \lambda, \lambda) \overset{T}{\Longrightarrow} (q_1, a, \lambda) \overset{T}{\Longrightarrow} \dots$$
$$\overset{T}{\Longrightarrow} (q_p, a^p, \lambda) \overset{T}{\Longrightarrow} (q', a^p b^p, \lambda)$$

in which $(q_i, a^i, \lambda)$ denotes the configuration by which $\mathbf{M}$ accepts the string $a^i$. Among the first $p + 1$ configurations of this sequence, some state must repeat. Suppose, therefore, that $q_i = q_j = q$, for some $j > i$. That is, suppose that

$$(q_I, \lambda, \lambda) \overset{T}{\Longrightarrow} (q, a^i, \lambda)$$
$$\overset{T}{\Longrightarrow} (q, a^j, \lambda) \overset{T}{\Longrightarrow} (q_p, a^p, \lambda)$$
$$\overset{T}{\Longrightarrow} \dots \overset{T}{\Longrightarrow} (q', a^p b^p, \lambda)$$

is a move sequence of $\mathbf{M}$. Then we must also have

$$(q_I, \lambda, \lambda) \overset{T}{\Longrightarrow} (q, a^i, \lambda) \overset{T}{\Longrightarrow} (q_p, a^{p-(j-i)}, \lambda)$$
$$\overset{T}{\Longrightarrow} \dots \overset{T}{\Longrightarrow} (q', a^{p-(j-i)} b^p, \lambda)$$

Thus $\mathbf{M}$ accepts the string $a^{p-(j-i)} b^p$, which is not in $\mathbf{L}$.

This example shows that requiring an empty stack as a condition of acceptance limits the language-defining capabilities of deterministic pushdown automata. Consequently, we adopt for the automata the more general notion of acceptance by final state.

**Definition 8.9:** A string $\omega$ is *accepted* by a deterministic pushdown accepter **M** if **M** has a move sequence

$$(q_I, \lambda, \lambda) \Longrightarrow (q', \omega, \sigma)$$

where $q'$ is a final state of **M** and $\sigma \in \mathbf{U}^*$. The *language recognized* by **M** is the set of strings accepted by **M**.

The reader may wonder whether the empty stack requirement also limits the language-recognizing capabilities of nondeterministic pushdown accepters In particular, if we define acceptance as in Definition 8.9, is it possible that (nondeterministic) PDA's can accept languages that are not context free? The answer is no. In fact, it is straightforward to convert *any* such PDA **M** into a (possibly) nondeterministic accepter **M′** that accepts the same set of strings with an empty stack. We merely add to **M** the instructions

$$q]\ \textbf{read}\ (u, q_A), \qquad \text{each } u \in \mathbf{U}$$

for each final state $q$ of **M**, and the instructions

$$q_A]\ \textbf{read}\ (u, q_A), \qquad \text{each } u \in \mathbf{U}$$

where $q_A$ is a new final state of **M′**. These instructions empty the stack following any accepting move sequence of **M**. For example, Figure 8.24 shows the machine of Figure 8.23 modified to empty its stack.

Using the modification described above, we can obtain from any deterministic pushdown accepter an equivalent pushdown accepter that accepts with an empty stack (although the modified machine need not be deterministic). Thus the class of languages defined by deterministic pushdown accepters is at best a subclass of the context-free languages.

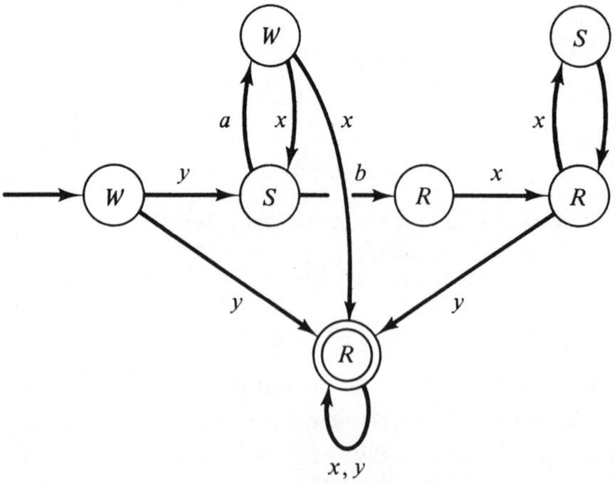


**Figure 8.24.** Stack emptying accepter for **a*** $\cup \{a^k b^k \mid k \geq 1\}$.

**Definition 8.10:** A context-free language is called *deterministic* if it is recognized by some deterministic pushdown accepter (DPDA).

**Example 8.6:** The simple matching language $\mathbf{L}_m$, the parenthesis language $\mathbf{L}_p$, and the double parenthesis language $\mathbf{L}_{dp}$ are all deterministic languages. The accepters we have constructed for these languages may be arranged to accept strings in the manner required by Definition 8.9, by having the accepter initialize the stack with an unused stack letter and halt in a final state when this symbol is read. For example, a DPDA for $\mathbf{L}_p$ is shown in Figure 8.25.

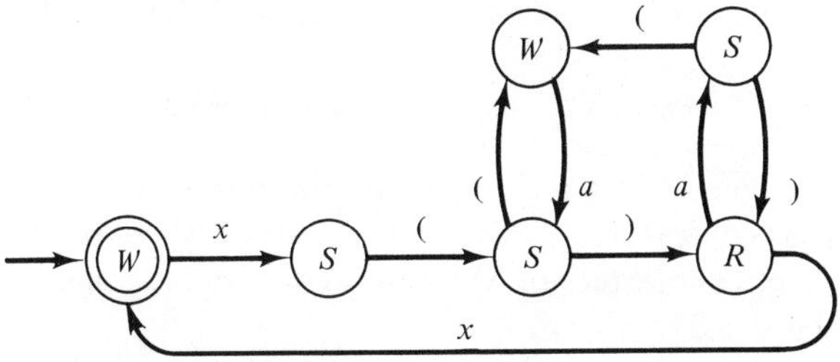


**Figure 8.25.** Deterministic accepter for the parenthesis language.

**Example 8.7:** Every regular language is deterministic since each is recognized by some deterministic finite-state accepter, which is trivially a deterministic pushdown accepter.

Is the class of deterministic languages a proper subclass of the context-free languages? In the first part of this chapter (Section 8.1.2), we found a strong affirmative suggestion in the mirror-image language. For a precise demonstration of this fact, we use the nondeterministic language

$$\mathbf{L}_{nd} = \{a^k b^k \mid k \geq 1\} \cup \{a^k b^{2k} \mid k \geq 1\}$$

which will also be of use in our study of the closure properties of the deterministic languages. Each string in $\mathbf{L}_{nd}$ has the form

$$a^k b^m, \quad m = k \quad \text{or} \quad m = 2k$$

A nondeterministic pushdown accepter for $\mathbf{L}_{nd}$ is shown in Figure 8.26. Intuitively, a deterministic accepter must fail to recognize the language because, having just scanned all the $a$'s, it has no basis for deciding whether to match them against $b$'s individually or in pairs. (The nondeterministic accepter does not have to make this decision; it is capable of pursuing either alternative.)

**Theorem 8.5:** The deterministic context-free languages are a proper subclass of all context-free languages. In particular, the language $\mathbf{L}_{nd} = \{a^k b^m \mid m = k \text{ or } m = 2k,\ k \geq 1\}$ is context free but not deterministic.

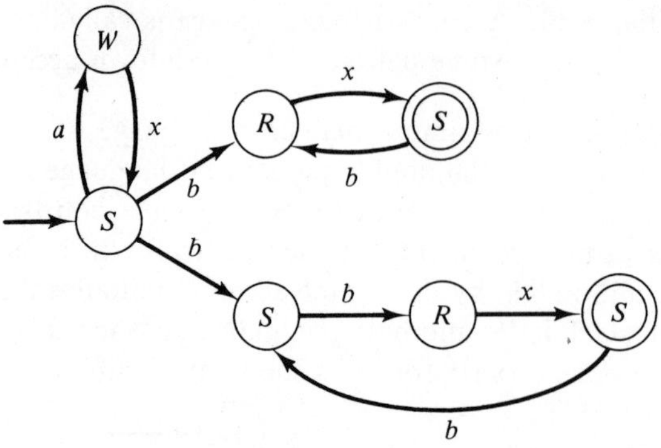


**Figure 8.26.** Pushdown accepter for $\mathbf{L}_{nd}$.

***Proof:*** Since $\mathbf{L}_{nd}$ is recognized by the PDA in Figure 8.26, the language is context free. Now suppose that $\mathbf{M}$ is a DPDA that recognizes $\mathbf{L}_{nd}$. From two copies of $\mathbf{M}$ we may construct the DPDA $\mathbf{M}'$ suggested in Figure 8.27:

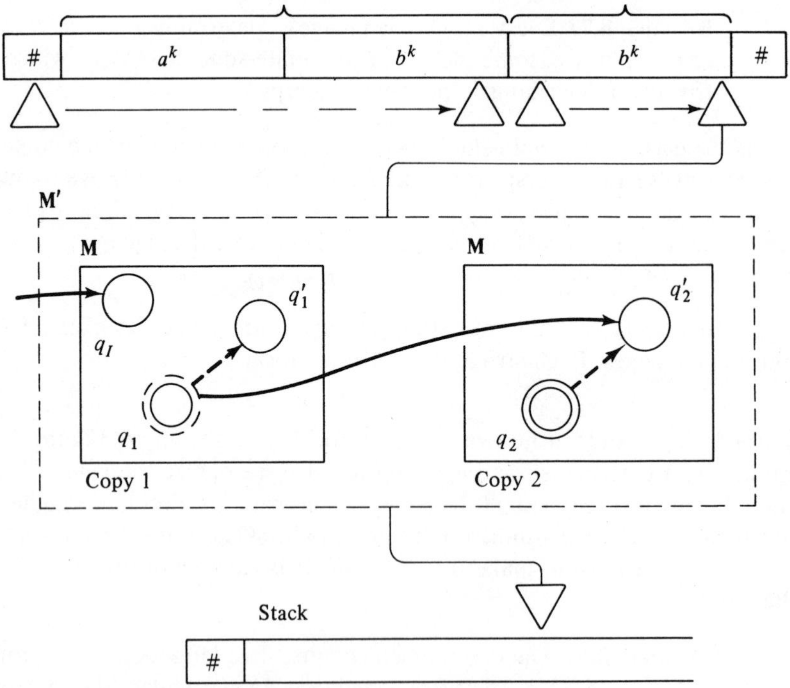


**Figure 8.27.** Demonstration that $\mathbf{L}_{nd} = \{a^k b^m \mid m = k \text{ or } m = 2k, k \geq 1\}$ is not deterministic.

1. The stack and stack head are shared by both copies of **M**.
2. The initial state of **M**′ is the initial state of copy 1 of **M**.
3. The final states of **M**′ are the final states of copy 2 of **M**.

We arrange the program of **M**′ to "transfer control" from copy 1 of **M** to copy 2 of **M** immediately after any move that places copy 1 in a final state:

4. Each instruction labeled by a final state in **M**

$$q] \textbf{ move } (x, q'), \qquad q \in \mathbf{F}$$

becomes the instruction

$$q_1] \textbf{ move } (x, q_2')$$

in **M**′, where $q_1$ is the instance of $q$ in copy 1 of **M**, and $q_2'$ is the instance of $q'$ in copy 2.

5. All other instructions are retained in both copies of **M**. If **M** has

$$q] \textbf{ move } (x, q'), \qquad q \notin \mathbf{F}$$

then **M**′ has both

$$q_1] \textbf{ move } (x, q_1') \quad \text{and} \quad q_2] \textbf{ move } (x, q_2')$$

By construction, **M**′ is deterministic if **M** is. We claim that $\mathbf{L}(\mathbf{M}') = \{a^k b^{2k} \mid k \geq 1\}$. To see this, note that each string $\omega = a^k b^k$ leads **M**′ to a final state of copy 1, which cannot be a final state of **M**′; thus no such string $\omega$ is accepted by **M**′. However, **M**′ accepts each string $a^k b^{2k} = a^k b^k b^k$ by the move sequence

$$\underbrace{(q_I, \lambda, \lambda) \Longrightarrow (q_1', a^k b^k, \sigma_1)}_{\text{in copy 1}} \underbrace{\Longrightarrow (q_2', a^k b^k b^k, \sigma_2)}_{\text{in copy 2}}, \qquad q_2' \in \mathbf{F}'$$

which transfers control into copy 2 immediately after the move sequence for $a^k b^k$.

Now, if we convert **M**′ to **M**″ by changing each scan move in copy 2 of **M**

$$q_2] \textbf{ scan } (b, q_2')$$

to

$$q_2] \textbf{ scan } (c, q_2')$$

then the accepting move sequence for $a^k b^k b^k$ in **M**′ becomes an accepting move sequence for $a^k b^k c^k$ in **M**″. Thus **M**″ is a DPDA that recognizes

$$\mathbf{L}_{dm} = \{a^k b^k c^k \mid k \geq 1\}$$

which is not context free. This contradiction establishes the theorem.

A demonstration that the mirror-image language $\mathbf{L}_{mi}$ is not deterministic is taken up in the Problems.

As in the case of (nondeterministic) pushdown accepters, it is no restriction to require that a deterministic pushdown accepter be proper and loop free. In fact, it is much easier to prove these facts for the deterministic automata. (The reader should consider why this is so.)

### 8.6.1 Closure Properties of Deterministic Context-Free Languages

The closure properties of the deterministic context-free languages differ significantly from those of the complete class of context-free languages. One surprising result is that the complement of any deterministic language is always a deterministic language. In establishing this result, we make use of the idea of interchanging the roles of final and nonfinal states in a pushdown accepter for an arbitrary deterministic language. Constructing the appropriate deterministic accepter is not simple, however, and we defer the details to Section 8.6.2.

The construction shown in Figure 8.21 to demonstrate the closure of the context-free languages under intersection with a regular set also applies to deterministic languages: If $\mathbf{M}_p$ is a deterministic pushdown accepter for $\mathbf{L}$, and $\mathbf{M}_f$ is a deterministic finite-state accepter for $\mathbf{R}$, then $\mathbf{M}$ is a deterministic pushdown accepter for $\mathbf{L} \cap \mathbf{R}$.

The construction of Figure 8.22 to demonstrate closure under finite-state transduction does not carry over to deterministic languages, even if we restrict attention to deterministic finite-state transducers. For example, the language

$$\mathbf{L} = \{a^k b^k \mid k \geq 1\} \cup \{a^k c^{2k} \mid k \geq 1\}$$

is deterministic, but the transduction of $\mathbf{L}$ by a machine that translates $c$'s into $b$'s is the nondeterministic language $\mathbf{L}_{nd}$. Thus the deterministic context-free languages are not a closed class under transduction by finite-state machines.

To determine the closure of these languages under other elementary set operations, we use the facts that

$$\mathbf{L}_1 = \{a^k b^k \mid k \geq 1\} \qquad \mathbf{L}_2 = \{a^k b^{2k} \mid k \geq 1\}$$

$$\mathbf{L}_1 \cup \mathbf{c} \cdot \mathbf{L}_2 \qquad \mathbf{L}_1^R \cup \mathbf{c} \cdot \mathbf{L}_2^R$$

are deterministic languages, whereas the languages

$$\mathbf{L}_{nd} = \mathbf{L}_1 \cup \mathbf{L}_2$$

$$\mathbf{L}_1 \cup \mathbf{L}_2 \cdot \mathbf{c} \qquad \mathbf{c} \cdot \mathbf{L}_{nd}$$

are not deterministic. Since $\mathbf{L}_{nd}$ is the union of deterministic languages, but is not in itself deterministic, closure does not hold for union. Similarly, the language

$$\mathbf{L}_1^R \cup \mathbf{c} \cdot \mathbf{L}_2^R = \{b^k a^k \cup cb^{2k}a^k \mid k \geq 1\}$$

is deterministic, but its reverse

$$\mathbf{L}_1 \cup \mathbf{L}_2 \cdot \mathbf{c}$$

is not. Were the concatenation of sets

$$\mathbf{L}_4 = (\mathbf{c} \cup \boldsymbol{\lambda}) \cdot (\mathbf{L}_1 \cup \mathbf{c} \cdot \mathbf{L}_2)$$

deterministic, its intersection with any regular set would be deterministic. But the intersection of $\mathbf{L}_4$ and the regular set $\mathbf{ca^*b^*}$ is

$$\mathbf{L}_4 \cap \mathbf{ca^*b^*} = \mathbf{c} \cdot \mathbf{L}_{nd}$$

which is not deterministic. Finally,

$$\mathbf{L}_5 = \mathbf{c} \cup \mathbf{L}_1 \cup \mathbf{c} \cdot \mathbf{L}_2$$

is a deterministic language. If its closure $\mathbf{L}_5^*$ were deterministic, then

$$\mathbf{L}_5^* \cap \mathbf{ca^*b^*} = \mathbf{c} \cdot \mathbf{L}_1 \cup \mathbf{c} \cdot \mathbf{L}_2 = \mathbf{c} \cdot \mathbf{L}_{nd}$$

would also be deterministic, which it is not.

In summary, we have the following:

**Theorem 8.6:** The class of deterministic context-free languages on a terminal alphabet $\mathbf{T}$ is closed under the operations complement, intersection with a regular set, and difference with a regular set. It is not closed under the operations union, intersection, concatenation, reversal, set closure, or (deterministic) transduction by a finite-state machine. That is, if $\mathbf{L}_1$ and $\mathbf{L}_2$ are deterministic context-free languages, $\mathbf{R}$ is a regular set, and $\mathbf{M}$ is a finite-state transducer, then

$$\mathbf{L}_1^c = \mathbf{T}^* - \mathbf{L}_1 \qquad \mathbf{L}_1 \cap \mathbf{R} \qquad \mathbf{L}_1 - \mathbf{R}$$

are deterministic context-free languages, whereas

$$\mathbf{L}_1 \cup \mathbf{L}_2 \qquad \mathbf{L}_1 \cdot \mathbf{L}_2 \qquad \mathbf{L}_1^R$$

$$\mathbf{L}_1 \cap \mathbf{L}_2 \qquad \mathbf{L}_1^* \qquad \mathbf{M}(\mathbf{L}_1)$$

need not be deterministic languages.

### 8.6.2 Complements of Deterministic Languages

Let $\mathbf{M}$ be a deterministic pushdown accepter for the language $\mathbf{L}$. We wish to design a deterministic pushdown accepter $\mathbf{M}_c$ that reaches a final state just for each string not in $\mathbf{L}$ [that is, such that $\mathbf{L}(\mathbf{M}_c) = \mathbf{L}^c$]. By analogy with deterministic finite-state accepters, we would like to interchange the final and nonfinal states of $\mathbf{M}$ to obtain $\mathbf{M}_c$. But we encounter an immediate difficulty in applying this idea, for $\mathbf{M}$ may not have move sequences for every string in $\mathbf{S}^*$; some strings may lead $\mathbf{M}$ to *dead configurations*, from which the accepter has no applicable instruction. Let $\mathbf{Y}$ be the set of strings that are observed by no move sequence of $\mathbf{M}$, and let $\mathbf{M}'$ be the machine obtained from $\mathbf{M}$ by interchanging final and nonfinal states. Since $\mathbf{M}'$ cannot have a move sequence for any string in $\mathbf{Y}$, $\mathbf{M}'$ does not recognize the complement of $\mathbf{L}(\mathbf{M})$.

A dead configuration $(q, \varphi, \sigma)$ of an accepter can arise in two ways:

1. *Attempt to read an empty stack:* $q$ labels a read instruction and $\sigma = \lambda$.
2. *Effect of an incomplete program:*
   a. $q$ labels a scan instruction with no specified successor state for the next input symbol.
   b. $q$ labels a read instruction with no specified successor state for the top stack symbol.
   c. $q$ labels no instruction.

We may modify a deterministic pushdown accepter $\mathbf{M}$ so that dead configurations cannot occur for any input string. To prevent $\mathbf{M}$ from attempting to read an empty stack, we enlarge the stack alphabet to include a new letter $x$ that will mark the bottom of the stack. We add to $\mathbf{M}$ a new initial state $q_I'$ and the stack initializing instruction

$$q_I'] \ \mathbf{write}\ (x, q_I)$$

Then, for each read instruction

$$q] \ \mathbf{read}\ (u, q')$$

we add the instruction

$$q] \ \mathbf{read}\ (x, q_R)$$

where $q_R$ is a new (nonfinal) auxiliary state. With these changes, $\mathbf{M}$ has an incomplete program, but will never try to read the stack when it is empty.

To provide $\mathbf{M}$ with a *complete* program, we add the instructions

$$q_R] \ \mathbf{scan}\ (s, q_R), \qquad \text{each } s \in \mathbf{S}$$

that cause $\mathbf{M}$ to scan any remaining input symbols in the nonfinal state $q_R$. We also add, as needed, new instructions

$$q] \ \mathbf{read}\ (u, q_R) \quad \text{or} \quad q] \ \mathbf{scan}\ (s, q_R)$$

to ensure that each read or scan state of $\mathbf{M}$ has a successor state for each stack or input symbol, thereby eliminating dead configurations. The reader should convince himself that these changes to the program do not alter the language recognized by $\mathbf{M}$.

The absence of dead configurations in a deterministic accepter $\mathbf{M}$ is not enough to guarantee a move sequence for each input string in $\mathbf{S}^*$, for the machine may enter an endless loop of write and read instructions. However, if **M** is proper and loop free according to Definitions 8.4 and 8.5, endless loops cannot occur. Hence, making the above changes to a deterministic accepter that is proper and loop free will yield a deterministic accepter that has a move sequence for each possible input string.

> **Definition 8.11:** A deterministic pushdown accepter **M** is *complete* if each string $\omega \in \mathbf{S}^*$ is observed by a move sequence starting from the initial configuration $(q_I, \lambda, \lambda)$.

If the methods of Section 8.2 are used to remove improper moves and loops of write instructions from a deterministic pushdown accepter, the resultant accepter will be deterministic. Thus it follows that a complete deterministic accepter can be found for any deterministic language.

> **Proposition 8.8:** Each deterministic context-free language is recognized by some complete deterministic pushdown accepter.

> **Example 8.8:** A complete DPDA for $\mathbf{L} = \mathbf{a}^* \cup \{a^k b^k \mid k \geq 1\}$ is shown in Figure 8.28. Since the DPDA of Figure 8.23 already uses $y$ as a marker for the bottom of the stack, the empty stack modification is not required.

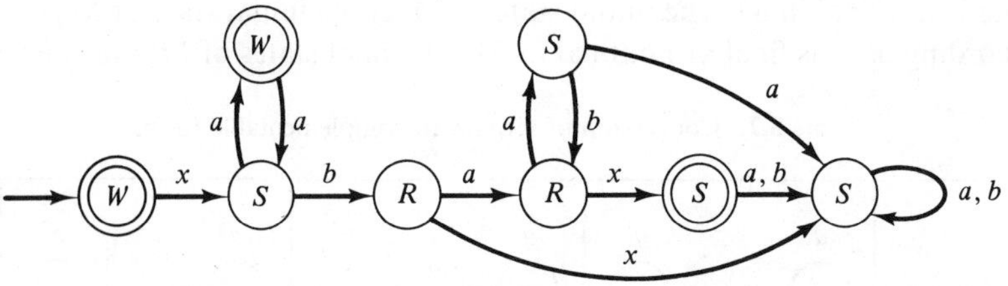


**Figure 8.28.** Complete DPDA for $\mathbf{a}^* \cup \{a^k b^k \mid k \geq 1\}$.

The remaining problem in obtaining a deterministic accepter for the complement of an arbitrary deterministic language is this: between executing two scan moves, a complete accepter **M** may pass through a sequence of states

$$\ldots \longrightarrow (q_{p-1}, \varphi, \sigma_{p-1}) \xrightarrow{s} (q_p, \varphi s, \sigma_p) \longrightarrow \ldots$$
$$\longrightarrow (q_r, \varphi s, \sigma_r) \xrightarrow{s} (q_{r+1}, \varphi st, \sigma_{r+1}) \longrightarrow \ldots$$

some of which are final and some of which are not. The string $\varphi s$ will be accepted by **M** if any of the states $q_p, \ldots, q_r$ is a final state of **M**. If **M′** is the accepter obtained from **M** by interchanging final and nonfinal states, it is likely that some strings would be accepted by both **M** and **M′**. Specifically, if $q_p$ is a final state of **M** and $q_r$ is not, then **M** will accept the string $\varphi s$ by the move sequence

$$(q_I, \lambda, \lambda) \Longrightarrow (q_p, \varphi s, \sigma_p)$$

and **M**′ will accept $\varphi s$ by the move sequence

$$(q_I, \lambda, \lambda) \Longrightarrow (q_r, \varphi s, \sigma_r)$$

Therefore, **M**′ cannot be the desired recognizer for $\mathbf{L}^c(\mathbf{M})$.

This problem is resolved by modifying **M** so that each final state is the label of some scan instruction.

> **Definition 8.12:** Let **M** be a complete DPDA, and let $\mathbf{Q}_s$ be the set of states of **M** that label scan instructions. If each final state of **M** is a member of $\mathbf{Q}_s$, then **M** is in *complementable form.*

To put a complete deterministic pushdown accepter into complementable form, let **M**′ consist of two copies of **M**, called $\mathbf{M}_1$ and $\mathbf{M}_2$. We want **M**′ to have the same behavior as **M** except that control will be in $\mathbf{M}_1$ or $\mathbf{M}_2$, according as a final state of **M** has or has not been visited since the last scan move. The program for **M**′ is specified by Table 8.7. Each instruction whose successor state is final in **M** transfers control to the corresponding state in copy $\mathbf{M}_2$. Control reverts to copy $\mathbf{M}_1$ at the next scan move whose successor state is not final in **M**. The initial state of **M**′ is the initial state of $\mathbf{M}_2$ or $\mathbf{M}_1$, according as $q_I$ is final or nonfinal in **M**. The final states of **M**′ are the states

**Table 8.7** Conversion of a DPDA to complementable form.

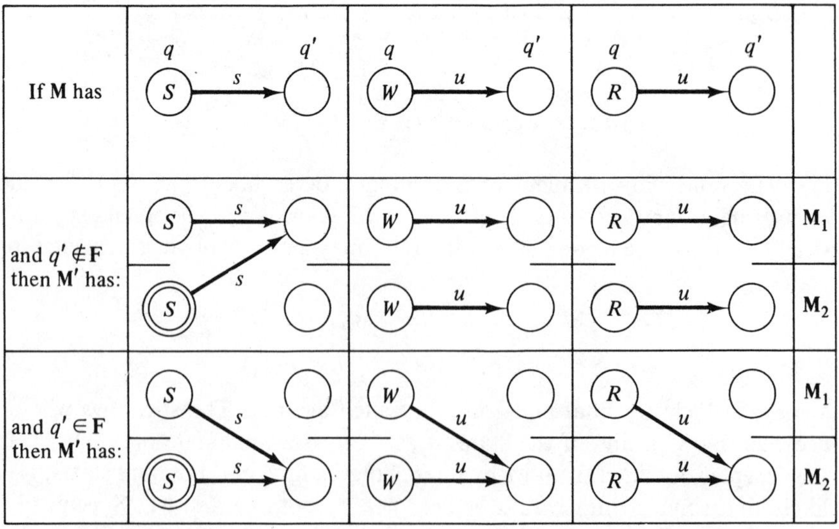

of $\mathbf{M}_2$ that label scan instructions. The reader may verify that $\mathbf{M}'$ is a deterministic accepter in complementable form that recognizes $\mathbf{L}(\mathbf{M})$.

Now suppose that $\mathbf{M}$ is a deterministic pushdown accepter in complementable form. Because $\mathbf{M}$ is complete, each string $\omega$ in $\mathbf{S}^*$ is observed by a *unique* move sequence that terminates at a state in $\mathbf{Q}_s$:

$$(q_I, \lambda, \lambda) \Longrightarrow (q', \omega, \sigma), \qquad q' \in \mathbf{Q}_s$$

If we take $\mathbf{M}_c$ to be $\mathbf{M}$ with final states

$$\mathbf{F}_c = \mathbf{Q}_s - \mathbf{F}$$

then $\mathbf{M}_c$ is a complementable deterministic accepter for just the strings rejected by $\mathbf{M}$. Thus we have the following:

**Proposition 8.9:** Let $\mathbf{L}$ be a context-free language. Then $\mathbf{L}$ is deterministic if and only if $\mathbf{L}^c$ is deterministic.

**Example 8.9:** The application of Table 8.7 to the complete DPDA of Figure 8.28 is shown in Figure 8.29a. Omitting the inaccessible states, we obtain the complementable DPDA shown in Figure 8.29b. Interchanging the final and nonfinal scanning states in this machine yields the DPDA for $(\mathbf{a}^* \cup \{a^k b^k \mid k \geq 1\})^c$ shown in Figure 8.29c.

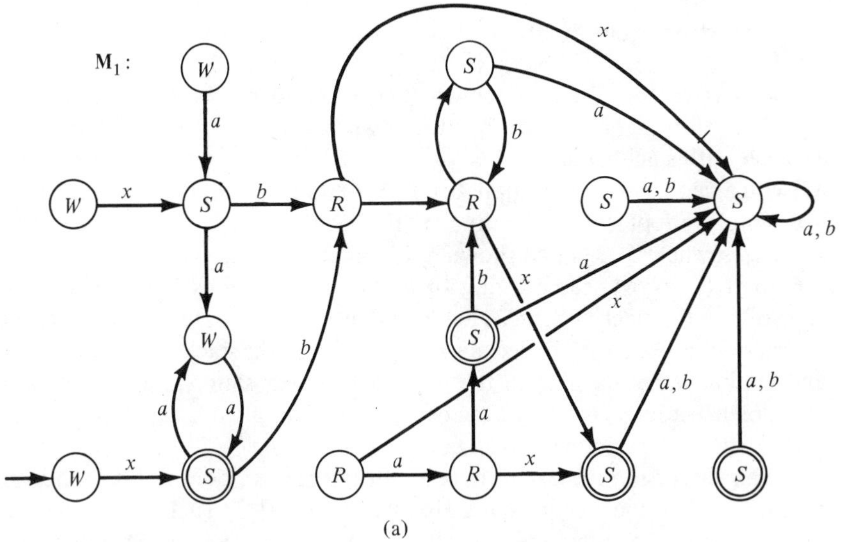


**Figure 8.29.** Construction of a DPDA for the complement of a deterministic language.

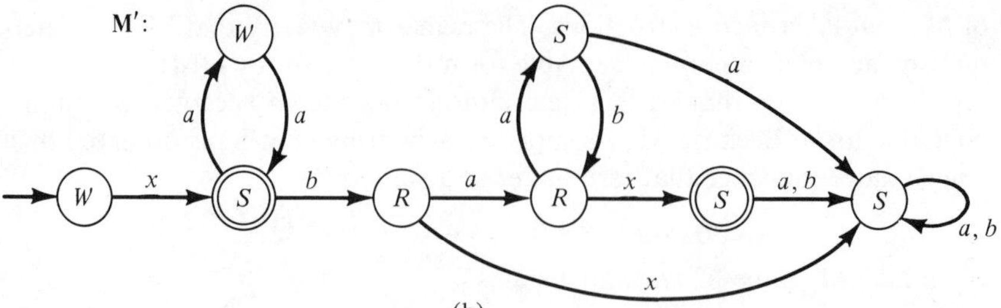


(b)

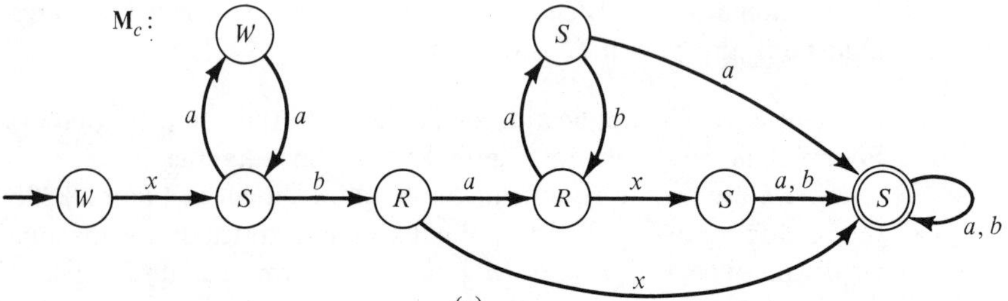


(c)

**Figure 8-29.** (*Continued*)

## 8.7 Counting Accepters

It is interesting to consider whether a bound on the size of the stack alphabet limits the capability of pushdown accepters. If **M** is a pushdown accepter with stack alphabet $\mathbf{U} = \{u_1, \ldots, u_n\}$, it is easy to obtain a machine **M′** with a two-symbol stack alphabet {0, 1} that recognizes the same language. We simply adopt some encoding of the symbols in **U** as *m*-digit binary sequences, where $2^m \geq n$. As shown in Figure 8.30, whenever **M** has an instruction **write** $(u, q)$, **M′** has a string of *m* write instructions that appends the code of *u* to the stack. Where **M** has a read instruction, an *m*-level tree of read instructions is used in **M′** to decode *m* symbols from the stack (in reverse order) and to direct the machine to the appropriate next state. Thus the class of pushdown accepters with two stack symbols has all the capability of the general class of pushdown accepters.

This discussion reveals nothing about the relative power of a pushdown accepter with a one-symbol stack alphabet $\mathbf{U} = \{\Delta\}$. In such an automaton, the content of the storage tape is always $\Delta^k$ for some $k \geq 1$. Therefore, the information contained in the storage tape is completely determined by the integer *k* specifying the distance of the stack head from the origin of the

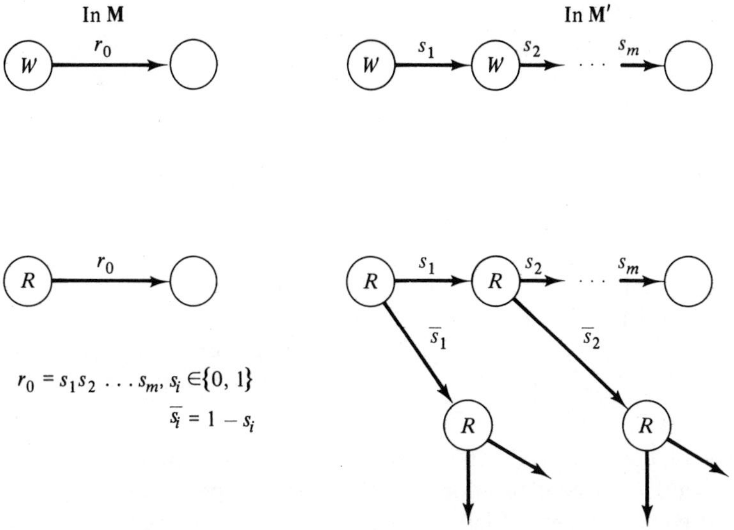


**Figure 8.30.** Conversion to two stack symbols.

storage tape. Since write and read instructions have the effect of incrementing or decrementing this integer by one, pushdown accepters with just one stack symbol are known as *counting accepters*.

**Definition 8.13:** A *counting accepter* is a pushdown accepter

$$\mathbf{M} = (\mathbf{Q}, \mathbf{S}, \{\Delta\}, \mathbf{P}, \mathbf{I}, \mathbf{F})$$

with a one-symbol stack alphabet. A configuration

$$(q, \varphi, \Delta^k)$$

of a counting accepter is abbreviated to

$$(q, \varphi, k)$$

and $k$ is called the *count*. Instead of

**write** $(\Delta, q)$ and **read** $(\Delta, q)$

we write simply

**up** $(q)$ and **down** $(q)$

**Example 8.10:** Figure 8.31 shows a counting accepter $\mathbf{M}_p$ with input alphabet {(,)}. This machine adds one to its count for each left parenthesis scanned, and subtracts one for each right parenthesis. If $\ell(\varphi)$ and $r(\varphi)$ are, respectively, the numbers of left and right parentheses in the string $\varphi$, the configuration of $\mathbf{M}_p$ after scanning $\varphi$ will be $(1, \varphi, \ell(\varphi) - r(\varphi))$. Thus $\mathbf{M}_p$ uses its storage tape to keep account

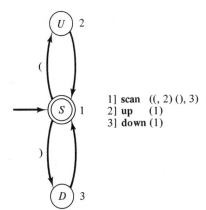

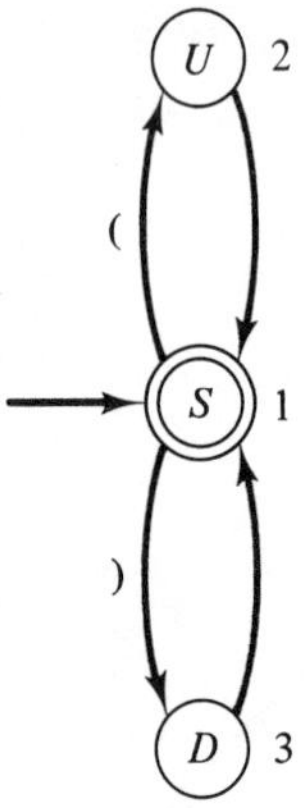


1] **scan** ((, 2) (), 3)
2] **up** (1)
3] **down** (1)

**Figure 8.31.** Counting accepter for the parenthesis language.

of the excess of left parentheses over right parentheses. Since the accepting configuration is $(1, \varphi, 0)$, $\mathbf{M}_p$ accepts only strings that have equal numbers of left and right parentheses. Moreover, no prefix $\varphi$ of an accepted string may have $\ell(\varphi) < r(\varphi)$, because no configuration of a counting accepter may have a negative count. From these facts, the reader may convince himself that $\mathbf{M}_p$ recognizes exactly the language $\mathbf{L}_p$ of well-formed parenthesis strings introduced in Chapter 3. An accepting move sequence for the string (( )( )) is

$$(1, \lambda, 0) \xrightarrow{S} (2, (, 0) \xrightarrow{U} (1, (, 1)$$
$$\xrightarrow{S} (2, ((, 1) \xrightarrow{U} (1, ((, 2)$$
$$\xrightarrow{S} (3, ((\ ), 2) \xrightarrow{D} (1, ((\ ), 1)$$
$$\xrightarrow{S} (2, ((\ )(, 1) \xrightarrow{U} (1, ((\ )(, 2)$$
$$\xrightarrow{S} (3, ((\ )(\ ), 2) \xrightarrow{D} (1, ((\ )(\ ), 1)$$
$$\xrightarrow{S} (3, ((\ )(\ )), 1) \xrightarrow{D} (1, ((\ )(\ )), 0) \quad \text{[accept]}$$

Since the class of counting accepters is sufficiently powerful to recognize the parenthesis language, the counting accepters are more powerful than the finite-state accepters.

Every string in the language $\mathbf{L}_p$ has the property that each appearance of a left parenthesis is matched by a subsequent appearence of a right parenthesis. Although a counting accepter is able to test the simple matching structure of the parenthesis language, the recognition of some context-free languages requires the matching of several types of symbols and is beyond the capabilities of the counting accepters. An example is the double parenthesis language $\mathbf{L}_{dp}$. In $\mathbf{L}_{dp}$, each left parenthesis must be matched by a right parenthesis of the corresponding type. An accepter for $\mathbf{L}_{dp}$ must check not only that $\ell(\varphi) \geq r(\varphi)$ independently for the two types of parentheses, but must also keep a record showing the order in which unmatched left parentheses were scanned. We have seen that a pushdown accepter is able to maintain the necessary record, but no counting accepter is able to encode enough information into its count to recognize $\mathbf{L}_{dp}$.

**Theorem 8.7:** Counting accepters are intermediate in power between finite-state accepters and pushdown accepters. In particular, there is a counting accepter that recognizes the parenthesis language $\mathbf{L}_p$, but no counting accepter that recognizes the double parenthesis language $\mathbf{L}_{dp}$.

***Proof:*** We have constructed a counting accepter for $\mathbf{L}_p$ and a pushdown accepter for $\mathbf{L}_{dp}$. We must show that no counting accepter recognizes $\mathbf{L}_{dp}$.

Suppose that $\mathbf{M}$ is an $n$-state counting accepter such that $\mathbf{L}(\mathbf{M}) = \mathbf{L}_{dp}$. Without loss of generality, we may assume that $\mathbf{M}$ is proper. (The reader may verify that the construction of Section 8.2.1 is applicable to the class of counting accepters; no part of the construction involves the addition of stack symbols.) For each string $\omega \in \{(, [\}$, let $\hat{\omega}$ denote the string formed by reversing $\omega$ and substituting ) for ( and ] for [. Each such string $\omega\hat{\omega}$ is a symmetric string in $\mathbf{L}_{dp}$ formed through the use of the rules

1. ( ) and [ ] are in $\mathbf{L}_{dp}$.
2. If $\alpha$ is in $\mathbf{L}_{dp}$, then so are $(\alpha)$ and $[\alpha]$.

For each integer $r \geq 1$, let $\mathbf{L}_r$ be the language

$$\mathbf{L}_r = \{\omega\hat{\omega} \mid \omega \in \{(, [\} \text{ and } |\omega| = r\}$$

Each string $\omega\hat{\omega}$ in $\mathbf{L}_r$ must be accepted by at least one move sequence of $\mathbf{M}$, say

$$(q, \lambda, 0) \Longrightarrow (q_c, \omega, k_c) \Longrightarrow (q', \omega\hat{\omega}, 0) \qquad q \in \mathbf{I},\ q' \in \mathbf{F}$$

where $(q_c, \omega, k_c)$ is the configuration of $\mathbf{M}$ immediately after it scans the last symbol in $\omega$. Let us denote by $k(\omega)$ the smallest value of $k_c$ over all accepting move sequences of $\mathbf{M}$ for $\omega\hat{\omega}$.

We first show that there is a string $\omega \in \{(, [\}^r$ for which $k(\omega) \geq 2^r/n$. Suppose that $\omega_1\hat{\omega}_1$ and $\omega_2\hat{\omega}_2$ are distinct strings in $\mathbf{L}_r$. Then $\mathbf{M}$ has move sequences

$$\begin{aligned} &(q_1, \lambda, 0) \Longrightarrow (q_{c1}, \omega_1, k_{c1}) \Longrightarrow (q_1', \omega_1\hat{\omega}_1, 0) \\ &(q_2, \lambda, 0) \Longrightarrow (q_{c2}, \omega_2, k_{c2}) \Longrightarrow (q_2', \omega_2\hat{\omega}_2, 0) \end{aligned} \qquad \begin{cases} q_1, q_2 \in \mathbf{I} \\ q_1', q_2' \in \mathbf{F} \end{cases}$$

by which it accepts the strings. We cannot have $q_{c1}$ and $k_{c1}$ the same as $q_{c2}$ and $k_{c2}$, for then the strings $\omega_1\hat{\omega}_2$ and $\omega_2\hat{\omega}_1$ would also be accepted by **M**, and these are not well-formed parenthesis strings. Thus each string in $\{(, [\}^r$ must lead to a distinct combination of $q_c$ and $k_c$. Since there are $2^r$ distinct elements in $\{(, [\}^r$, there must exist at least one element $\omega$ with $n \cdot k(\omega) \geq 2^r$.

We now show that if **M** is a loop-free accepter, $k(\omega) < nr$. (The generalization of the argument for the case that **M** is not loop free is developed in the Problems.)

Let $\omega$ be as above, and consider **M**'s acceptance of $\omega\hat{\omega}$. Since $|\omega| = r$, $r$ scan moves are made during the scanning of $\omega$ by **M**. Consider now the number of write moves made during the scanning of $\omega$. Since **M** is proper, no write move may be immediately followed by a read move. Since **M** has $n$ states, no more than $n - 1$ consecutive write moves can be made if **M** is loopfree. Thus no more than $(n - 1)r$ moves can be made during the scanning of $\omega$ by a loop-free accepter, and $k(\omega) < nr$.

Since the choice of $r$ is arbitrary, the relation

$$\frac{2^r}{n} \leq k(\omega) < nr$$

must hold for all $r \geq 1$. However, for large enough $r$, $2^r/n > nr$, and thus **M** cannot be a counting accepter for $\mathbf{L}_{dp}$.

## 8.8 Ambiguity

In Chapter 3 we defined as ambiguous a grammar that provides more than one leftmost derivation of some terminal string. We found in Chapter 5 that every finite-state language has an unambiguous grammar in which leftmost derivations may be placed in one-to-one correspondence with the accepting state sequences of a deterministic finite-state accepter. For context-free languages, however, matters are not so simple. In fact, it is known that there are context-free languages which can be generated only by ambiguous context-free grammars. Such a language is said to be an *ambiguous language*.

It is natural to ask in what way the unambiguous context-free languages are related to the deterministic languages. Must an unambiguous language be deterministic? Must a deterministic language be unambiguous?

The answer to the first question is no, as shown by the following example. We know that the language

$$\mathbf{L}_{nd} = \{a^k b^k \mid k \geq 1\} \cup \{a^k b^{2k} \mid k \geq 1\}$$

is nondeterministic. However, the following grammar provides a unique derivation for each string in $\mathbf{L}_{nd}$:

$$\mathbf{G}_{nd}\colon\quad \Sigma \longrightarrow A \qquad \Sigma \longrightarrow B$$
$$A \longrightarrow aAb \qquad B \longrightarrow aBbb$$
$$A \longrightarrow ab \qquad B \longrightarrow abb$$

Thus there exist nondeterministic languages that are unambiguous.

The answer to the second question is yes, although a demonstration of the fact is a bit complicated. In Corollary 8.3, we noted the one-to-one correspondence between traverses in a nondeterministic pushdown accepter and leftmost derivations in the corresponding context-free grammar. We cannot immediately conclude that deterministic languages are unambiguous, because the accepting move sequences of deterministic accepters are not necessarily traverses. To prove that the deterministic languages are indeed unambiguous, we show that any deterministic accepter can be provided with stack-emptying instructions permitting it to accept each string by a unique traverse.

Let **M** be a deterministic pushdown accepter. Based on the results of Section 8.6.2, it is no restriction to assume that **M** is in complementable form, and that each final state of **M** labels only scan instructions. For each string $\omega \in \mathbf{L}(\mathbf{M})$, there is a unique accepting move sequence for **M** that terminates on the label of a scan instruction. Before constructing a grammar for **L**(**M**) using Table 8.3, we first convert **M** to a machine **M**′ that accepts the strings of **L**(**M**) with an empty stack. This is easily done by adding instructions to **M** as shown in Figure 8.32. Whenever **M** has an instruction whose successor state is a final state, we add a duplicate instruction in which the successor state is $q_A$, the single final state of **M**′. In state $q_A$, **M**′ empties its stack.

Although the new accepter is not deterministic, its accepting move

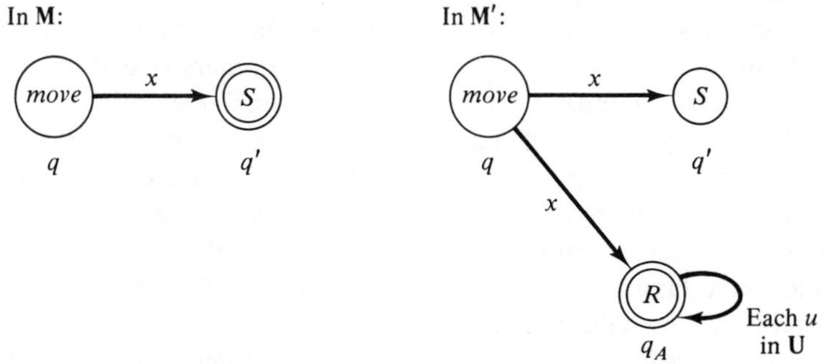


**Figure 8.32.** Modifying a DPDA to empty its stack.

sequence for any input string is still unique. A string $\omega$ that leads **M** to a final state $q'$ will lead **M**$'$ either to state $q'$ or to state $q_A$:

$$(q_I, \lambda, \lambda) \Longrightarrow (q, \varphi, \sigma) \begin{cases} \nearrow (q', \omega, \sigma) \xrightarrow{s} \ldots \\ \searrow (q_A, \omega, \sigma') \Longrightarrow (q_A, \omega, \lambda) \end{cases}$$

Acceptance of $\omega$ is only possible in the latter case, since in the former case the machine is in a nonfinal state and a scan move necessarily follows.

Now let **G**$'$ be the context-free grammar constructed from **M**$'$ according to Table 8.3. If **G**$'$ were ambiguous, there would be at least two distinct leftmost derivations of some terminal string $\omega$. But this would imply, by the correspondence given in Table 8.4, that **M**$'$ accepts $\omega$ by two or more distinct move sequences. From this contradiction we conclude the following:

**Theorem 8.8:** The class of deterministic context-free languages is a proper subclass of the unambiguous context-free languages.

In Chapter 9, we shall encounter languages for which no unambiguous grammar exists. Thus the class of unambiguous languages is a proper subclass of the context-free languages.

## Notes and References

The concept of a pushdown automaton was presented formally by Oettinger [1961] and Schutzenberger [1963], although the notion of a "pushdown" storage mechanism had been used for some years previously. The equivalence of PDA recognizable languages and context-free languages was demonstrated independently by Chomsky [1962] and Evey [1963].

The closure properties of context-free languages have been studied extensively. The closure of these languages under the set operations of union, concatenation, set closure, and reversal are established through straightforward constructions involving context-free grammars (see Problem 3.11). Their lack of closure under set intersection and complementation was demonstrated by Scheinberg [1960]. Bar-Hillel, Perles, and Shamir [1961] showed that context-free languages are closed under intersection with a regular set, and Ginsburg and Rose [1963] showed that they are closed under transduction and inverse transduction by generalized sequential machines. The closure of context-free languages under quotient with a regular set (Problem 8.15) was established by Ginsburg and Spanier [1963], and their closure under substitution (Problem 8.16) was shown by Bar-Hillel, Perles, and Shamir [1961].

Deterministic pushdown accepters have been studied by Fischer [1963], Schutzenberger [1963], Haines [1965], and Ginsburg and Greibach [1966]. The fact that each DPDA is equivalent to some complete DPDA was established by Schutzenberger [1963], and its consequence (that deterministic languages are closed under complementation) appears in Haines [1965] and in Ginsburg and Greibach [1966]. Many of the other closure properties of Theorem 8.6 appear in the latter work.

Ambiguity of context-free grammars has been studied by Cantor [1962], Floyd [1962], and Chomsky and Schutzenberger [1963]. The fact that each deterministic language is unambiguous is from Schutzenberger [1963], and the existence of inherently ambiguous context-free languages was noted by Parikh [1966].

## Problems

8.1. Construct pushdown accepters for the following languages:
   a. $\mathbf{L}_1 = \{0^n c 0^m \mid n, m > 0, n > m\}$.
   b. $\mathbf{L}_2 = \{0^n c 0^m \mid n > 0, m = 3n\}$.
   c. $\mathbf{L}_3 = \mathbf{L}_1 \cup \mathbf{L}_2$.
   d. $\mathbf{L}_4 = \mathbf{L}_1 \cdot \mathbf{L}_2$.

8.2. Construct a pushdown accepter for the language

$$\mathbf{L} = \{\omega \mid \omega \in \{0, 1\}^*, N_0(\omega) = N_1(\omega)\}$$

where $N_0(\omega)$ denotes the number of occurrences of symbol 0 in $\omega$, and similarly for $N_1(\omega)$.

8.3. Construct a pushdown accepter for the set of well-formed arithmetic expressions over the alphabet $\mathbf{T} = \{(, ), +, -, \times, \div, a, b\}$. Variable names are elements of $\{a, b\}^*$ and may be of any length greater than 0.

8.4. Construct a proper pushdown accepter equivalent to the accepter $\mathbf{M}$ (initial state 1, final states $\{1, 5\}$) with the following program:

1] **scan** $(a, 2), (b, 3)$
2] **write** $(x, 4), (x, 5), (y, 6)$
3] **scan** $(a, 3), (b, 4)$
4] **read** $(x, 7)$
5] **scan** $(a, 2), (b, 8)$
6] **read** $(x, 5)$
7] **write** $(x, 5)$
8] **read** $(x, 1)$

8.5. Let **M** be the PDA with initial states {1, 2}, final states {4, 8}, and the following program:

1] **scan** ($a$, 3), ($b$, 6)

2] **write** ($x$, 4), ($y$, 7)

3] **write** ($y$, 4)

4] **read** ($y$, 5)

5] **write** ($x$, 3)

6] **scan** ($b$, 2)

7] **scan** ($a$, 8), ($b$, 2)

8] **read** ($y$, 8)

Construct a proper, loop-free PDA equivalent to **M**.

**8.6.** Complete the *only if* portion of the proof of Proposition 8.1.

**8.7.** Suppose that we define a *generalized* PDA as a pushdown automaton in which states are allowed to label any number of the instruction types {scan, read, write}. Show that such generalized machines are no more powerful as language recognizers than PDA's as defined in Definition 8.1. (*Hint:* Describe how a generalized PDA can be converted into an equivalent PDA by splitting states, such that each new state labels at most one type of instruction.)

8.8. Let **G** be the context-free grammar with the following productions:

$$\Sigma \longrightarrow aYZ$$

$$X \longrightarrow abc$$

$$Y \longrightarrow aXb$$

$$Z \longrightarrow XY$$

$$Z \longrightarrow c$$

a. Construct a PDA **M** such that **L(M)** = **L(G)**.
b. Construct a leftmost derivation of the string $\omega = aaabcbc$, and show the sequence of configurations attained by **M** during the acceptance of $\omega$.

8.9. Let **G** be the grammar with the following productions:

$$\Sigma \longrightarrow aAA$$

$$A \longrightarrow bB$$

$$A \longrightarrow aB$$

$$A \longrightarrow a$$

$$B \longrightarrow aAA$$

Describe informally **L(G)**. Construct a pushdown accepter **M** such that **L(M)** = **L(G)**.

8.10. Complete the proof of Theorem 8.1. (That is, provide the argument for proposition 2 of the proof.)

8.11. Let **M** be the following PDA:

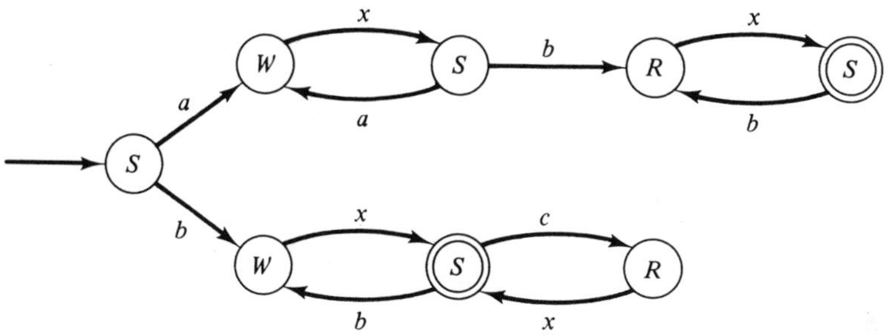


Using the construction of Section 8.3, construct a context-free grammar **G** such that **L(G)** = **L(M)**. Describe informally **L(G)**. Can you find a simpler grammar for the language?

8.12. Let **M** be the pushdown accepter (initial state 1, final state 5) with the following program:

1] **write** $(t, 1), (t, 2)$

2] **scan** $(a, 3), (a, 4)$

3] **read** $(t, 2)$

4] **write** $(u, 5)$

5] **scan** $(a, 4), (b, 6)$

6] **read** $(u, 5)$

Construct a context-free grammar **G** such that **L(G)** = **L(M)**.

***8.13.** In Section 8.4, we developed a procedure for the construction of a context-free grammar for the language recognized by an arbitrary proper PDA **M**. The construction is based on move sequences that connect any initial state to a specified state, and is analogous to the use of begin sets for the construction of a left-linear grammar from a finite-state machine.

Describe a procedure for constructing a context-free grammar for the language recognized by **M** based on move sequences that connect a specified state to some *final* state (analogous to the use of end sets in Chapter 5 for the construction of a right-linear grammar from a finite-state machine). In particular,

a. Describe the modifications to Proposition 8.7 necessary for the new procedure.

b. Verify that the traverse sets of interest are those ending in the set

$$\mathbf{E} = \mathbf{F} \cup \left\{ q \,\middle|\, \begin{array}{l} q]\ \textbf{read}\ (u, q') \text{ is an instruction in } \mathbf{M} \\ \text{for some } q' \in \mathbf{Q} \text{ and some } u \in \mathbf{U} \end{array} \right\}$$

c. Present a table of rules for the new construction analogous to Table 8.3.

d. Use the rules to construct from the PDA $\mathbf{M}_{dp}$ a context-free grammar for the double parenthesis language. (See Figure 8.17.) Can the grammar be simplified? How does it compare with the grammar constructed in Example 8.4?

**8.14.** Provide the missing arguments to complete the proof of Theorem 8.4. That is, show that the context-free languages are closed under the operations union, reversal, and set closure.

**8.15.** Let $\mathbf{L}_1$ and $\mathbf{L}_2$ be arbitrary languages. We define $\mathbf{L}_1/\mathbf{L}_2$, the *quotient of* $\mathbf{L}_1$ *with respect to* $\mathbf{L}_2$, to be the set

$$\mathbf{L}_1/\mathbf{L}_2 = \{\omega \mid \text{for some } \gamma \in \mathbf{L}_2, \omega\gamma \in \mathbf{L}_1\}$$

Show that the context-free languages are closed under quotient with a regular set; that is, show that if $\mathbf{L}_1$ is context free and $\mathbf{L}_2$ is regular, $\mathbf{L}_1/\mathbf{L}_2$ is context free.

**8.16.** Let $\mathbf{T}$ and $\mathbf{R}$ be finite alphabets. A *substitution* $f: \mathbf{T} \longrightarrow \mathbf{R}^*$ is a mapping of $\mathbf{T}$ onto subsets of $\mathbf{R}$ (that is, $f$ associates a language over $\mathbf{R}$ with each symbol of $\mathbf{T}$). We extend $f$ to strings in $\mathbf{T}^*$ as follows:

1. $f(\lambda) = \lambda$.
2. $f(x\omega) = f(x) \cdot f(\omega), \quad x \in \mathbf{T}, \quad \omega \in \mathbf{T}^*$.

Finally, we extend $f$ to each language $\mathbf{L} \subset \mathbf{T}^*$ by defining $f(\mathbf{L})$ to be

$$f(\mathbf{L}) = \bigcup_{\omega \in \mathbf{L}} f(\omega)$$

Show that the context-free languages are closed under substitution; that is, show that if $\mathbf{L} \subset \mathbf{T}^*$ is context free and $f(x) \subset \mathbf{R}^*$ is context free for each $x \in \mathbf{T}$, then $f(\mathbf{L})$ is a context-free language.

8.17. Show that the language

$$\mathbf{L}_{mi} = \{\omega\omega^R \mid \omega \in \{0, 1\}^*\}$$

is not deterministic. (*Hint:* Consider how a DPDA for the language must act on an input string of the form $\omega\omega^R$ when $\omega$ is itself of the form $\varphi\varphi^R$. In particular, what can be said about the configuration of the DPDA after scanning $\omega$?)

8.18. Consider the matching language with center marker

$$\mathbf{L}_{mc} = \{\omega c \omega^R \mid \omega \in \{0, 1\}^*\}$$

a. Draw the state diagram of a DPDA for $\mathbf{L}_{mc}$.
b. If the DPDA is not already in complementable form, convert it to complementable form.
c. Use the methods of Section 8.6.2 to construct a DPDA for the complement of $\mathbf{L}_{mc}$ with respect to the alphabet $\{0, 1, c\}$.

**8.19.** Prove that any DPDA can be modified to obtain an equivalent DPDA that is proper and loop free. Use this fact to prove Proposition 8.8.

**8.20.** Show that the deterministic context-free languages are closed under quotient with a regular set. (See Problem 8-15).

**8.21.** Show that the deterministic context-free languages are *not* closed under substitution. (See Problem 8-16.)

**8.22.** Suppose that $\mathbf{M}$ is a PDA with $n$ states, $m$ input tape symbols, and $k$ stack symbols. Let $\mathbf{G}$ be the grammar for $\mathbf{L}(\mathbf{M})$ constructed according to the rules of Table 8.3. In terms of $n$, $m$, and $k$, place a reasonable bound on the maximum number of productions in $\mathbf{G}$. Can your bound be improved if it is known that $\mathbf{M}$ is proper? If it is known that $\mathbf{M}$ is deterministic?

8.23. Construct a counting accepter for the language

$$\mathbf{L} = \{\alpha c \beta \mid \alpha, \beta \in \{0, 1\}^*, \alpha \neq \beta^R\}$$

(*Hint:* Construct a nondeterministic automaton.)

8.24. Prove that there exists no loop-free counting accepter for the language

$$\mathbf{L} = \{\alpha c \alpha^R \mid \alpha \in \{0, 1\}^*\}$$

(*Hint:* Use the validity, rather than the proof, of Theorem 8.7.)

***8.25.** Complete the proof of Theorem 8.7 by extending the arguments given to the case that $\mathbf{M}$ is not loop free. [*Hint:* Show that any counting accepter is equivalent to a counting accepter in which no read move immediately follows a write move, and no write move immediately follows a read move. Assume that $\mathbf{M}$ is such an accepter. Show that in scanning any string $\omega \in \{(, [\}^r$, $\mathbf{M}$ executes at least one loop of write instructions for each $rn$ symbols written in its stack. Conclude that if $k(\omega) \geq rn^3$, at least $n$ length $i$ loops of write instructions are executed during the scanning of $\omega$, $1 \leq i \leq n$. Similarly, show that if $k(\omega) \geq rn^3$, at least $n$ length $j$ loops of *read* instructions are executed during the subsequent scanning of the string $\hat{\omega}$, $1 \leq j \leq n$. Show that this implies $k(\omega) < rn^3$, and hence that $\mathbf{M}$ cannot be an accepter for $\mathbf{L}_{dp}$.]

**8.26.** Suppose that we permit a pushdown automaton to possess a special "empty stack state," which is entered via a $\lambda$-transition whenever the automaton attempts to read an empty stack. This special state may be a read, write, or scan state.

a. Show that permitting such states in pushdown automata does not increase their language-recognizing capabilities.

b. Show that permitting such states in counting automata *does* increase their language-recognizing capabilities, by describing a language that is not recognizable by any counting automaton but *is* recognizable by some such automaton containing an empty stack state. (*Hint:* Consider the language **L** of Problem 8-2.)

**8.27.** A "two-stack" PDA is a pushdown automaton with a pair of pushdown stacks. The instructions of the automaton are **scan**, **write** 1 (a write instruction for stack 1), **write** 2, **read** 1 (a read instruction for stack 1), and **read** 2.

a. Show that two-stack PDA's are more powerful than pushdown automata with a single stack. (*Hint:* Use the fact that the double matching language is not context free.)

b. Two-stack counting accepters are defined in a manner analogous to that for two-stack PDA's. Show that two-stack counting accepters are more powerful than counting accepters with a single stack. (*Hint:* See part a.)

*c. Show that the two-stack counting accepters are less powerful than two stack PDA's. (*Hint:* Modify the proof of Theorem 8.7 to show that the context-free language $\mathbf{L}_{dp}$ cannot be recognized by a two-stack counting accepter.)

# 9

# *Context-Free Languages*

The context-free model for language was the result of efforts by linguists to understand and characterize the structure of natural-language sentences. Although the model has profoundly influenced linguistic research, it has proved far more valuable as a model for programming languages than as a model for natural languages.

In processing a source language program, a compiler for a programming language acts in two roles: (1) to determine whether a program is syntactically correct, a compiler attempts to construct a derivation (structural description) of the program according to a formal grammar; in this role the compiler acts as an accepter. (2) To produce the object program, the compiler generates machine instructions from the structural description of a source program; in this role it acts as a transducer. Thus the choice of a method for forming structural descriptions of source programs—for performing *syntax analysis*—is a central problem in the design of compilers. Characterizing the valid sentences of a language as the set of strings generated by some context-free grammar has been an essential step in applying many practical methods of syntax analysis. The formal basis for several of these methods is studied in Chapter 10. In the present chapter, we develop a number of important results concerning context-free grammars and the languages that they define.

We begin with several transformations on context-free grammars that do not alter the language generated. These transformations permit removing inessential elements from grammars and converting grammars into canonical forms well suited to syntax analysis. We also prove some basic theorems about the structure of context-free languages. These theorems may be used to distinguish context-free from finite-state languages, and to show that certain languages are not context free.

The following are some definitions that are used frequently in this and the following chapter.

**Definition 9.1:** Let **G** be a context-free grammar. A production $A \longrightarrow \alpha$ in the grammar is called an *A rule* of **G**. The nonterminal letter $A$ is the *left part* of the rule; the string $\alpha$ is the *right part*. In a production of the form $A \longrightarrow x\beta$, the letter $x$ (which may be terminal or nonterminal) is called the *handle* of the production. A production of the form $A \longrightarrow B$, where $A$ and $B$ are nonterminals, is said to be a *nongenerative* production of **G**.

If **G** permits a derivation

$$A \overset{*}{\Longrightarrow} A\psi$$

then the nonterminal letter $A$ is *left recursive* in **G**; if **G** permits a derivation

$$A \overset{*}{\Longrightarrow} \varphi A$$

then $A$ is *right recursive* in **G**. If **G** permits a derivation

$$A \overset{*}{\Longrightarrow} A$$

of one or more steps, then $A$ is a *cyclic nonterminal* of **G**.

## 9.1 Transformation of Grammars

Thus far we have considered two grammars to be equivalent if they generate the same language. However, in studying the transformation of grammars into new forms, one is often interested in preserving the *structure* of the generated language as represented by the derivation trees for its sentences. For this reason, it is not always appropriate to regard two grammars as equivalent simply because they generate the same language. It may happen, for example, that one grammar for a language permits several derivations of some sentences, whereas another grammar for the same language permits only one derivation of each sentence in the language. In syntax analysis, the two grammars cannot be considered equivalent: one is ambiguous, the other is not. To study grammar transformations suitable for syntax analysis, we need a notion of equivalence that implies a correspondence between derivations in equivalent grammars.

### 9.1.1 Equivalence of Grammars

Example 9.1 shows that two grammars may generate the same language, yet provide quite different structural characterizations of sentences in the language.

**Example 9.1:** Consider the following grammars $\mathbf{G}_1$ and $\mathbf{G}_2$:

$$\mathbf{G}_1:\ \Sigma \longrightarrow S \qquad \mathbf{G}_2:\ \Sigma \longrightarrow S$$
$$S \longrightarrow S01 \qquad S \longrightarrow S0S$$
$$S \longrightarrow 1 \qquad S \longrightarrow 1$$

Both grammars generate the language $\mathbf{L} = \mathbf{1(01)^*}$. However, $\mathbf{G}_2$ is ambiguous, whereas $\mathbf{G}_1$ is not. We do not wish to consider $\mathbf{G}_1$ and $\mathbf{G}_2$ to be structurally equivalent, because $\mathbf{G}_2$ associates many distinct derivation trees with sentences of $\mathbf{L}$, whereas $\mathbf{G}_1$ provides a unique derivation tree for each sentence.

An equivalence definition suitable for grammar transformations should equate two grammars $\mathbf{G}_1$ and $\mathbf{G}_2$ only if the same sentences are ambiguous in each grammar. This can be met by requiring that the leftmost derivations of $\mathbf{G}_1$ and $\mathbf{G}_2$ be in one-to-one correspondence for each sentence generated. Yet this criterion may be too strict, for one form of structural ambiguity is trivial and easily removed.

**Example 9.2:**

$$\mathbf{G}_1:\ \Sigma \longrightarrow S \qquad \mathbf{G}_2:\ \Sigma \longrightarrow S$$
$$S \longrightarrow S01 \qquad S \longrightarrow S$$
$$S \longrightarrow 1 \qquad S \longrightarrow S01$$
$$S \longrightarrow 1$$

Grammar $\mathbf{G}_2$ has all the productions of $\mathbf{G}_1$ plus the rule $S \longrightarrow S$. Since this rule may be applied an arbitrary number of times to any sentential form containing $S$, any string generated by $\mathbf{G}_2$ has an infinity of distinct derivations. In contrast, $\mathbf{G}_1$ generates each string by a unique derivation. Although $\mathbf{G}_2$ is "very" ambiguous, the only difference between the structural descriptions of any sentence according to the two grammars is the number of repetitions of certain sentential forms in each derivation.

Derivations containing repetitions of a sentential form arise only from grammars having cyclic nonterminal letters. Since cyclic nonterminals are nonproductive, we would like to remove them; our criterion for equivalence must allow for removal of the associated ambiguity. Accordingly, we regard leftmost derivations containing no repeated sentential forms as providing the "correct" structural descriptions of sentences generated by a grammar.

> **Definition 9.2:** A leftmost derivation permitted by a context-free grammar is *minimal* if no sentential form is repeated in the derivation.

> **Definition 9.3:** Two context-free grammars $\mathbf{G}_1$ and $\mathbf{G}_2$ are *weakly equivalent* if $\mathbf{L}(\mathbf{G}_1) = \mathbf{L}(\mathbf{G}_2)$. They are *strongly equivalent* if they are weakly equivalent and, for each terminal string $\omega$, the minimal leftmost derivations of $\omega$ permitted by $\mathbf{G}_1$ can be placed in one-to-one correspondence with those permitted by $\mathbf{G}_2$.

The reader should convince himself that both weak and strong equivalence are truly equivalence relations on the class of all context-free grammars.

In grammars containing no cyclic nonterminals, every leftmost derivation is minimal; strong equivalence depends only on the existence of a one-to-one correspondence between leftmost derivations. The following examples illustrate strong equivalence:

**Example 9.3:** It is easily verified that both of the grammars

$$\begin{array}{llll} \mathbf{G}_1: & \Sigma \longrightarrow A & \mathbf{G}_2: & \Sigma \longrightarrow B \\ & A \longrightarrow 1B & & B \longrightarrow A1 \\ & A \longrightarrow 1 & & B \longrightarrow 1 \\ & B \longrightarrow 0A & & A \longrightarrow B0 \end{array}$$

can be derived from the same finite-state accepter, and that $\mathbf{L}(\mathbf{G}_1) = \mathbf{L}(\mathbf{G}_2) = \mathbf{1(01)^*}$. Since a state sequence in the accepter corresponds uniquely to a derivation in each grammar, the derivations in $\mathbf{G}_1$ and $\mathbf{G}_2$ are in one-to-one correspondence, and the grammars are strongly equivalent.

**Example 9.4:** Consider the grammars

$$\begin{array}{llllll} \mathbf{G}_1: & \Sigma \longrightarrow A & \mathbf{G}_2: & \Sigma \longrightarrow A & \mathbf{G}_3: & \Sigma \longrightarrow \mathrm{A} \\ & A \longrightarrow a & & A \longrightarrow a & & A \longrightarrow a \\ & A \longrightarrow aB & & A \longrightarrow abcA & & A \longrightarrow aB \\ & B \longrightarrow bC & & & & B \longrightarrow bC \\ & C \longrightarrow cA & & & & C \longrightarrow cA \\ & & & & & A \longrightarrow abcA \end{array}$$

Grammar $\mathbf{G}_2$ is obtained by replacing the rules of $\mathbf{G}_1$ used in the derivation

$$A \Longrightarrow aB \Longrightarrow abC \Longrightarrow abcA$$

with the single rule

$$A \longrightarrow abcA$$

Clearly, $\mathbf{L(G_1)} = \mathbf{L(G_2)}$. A unique derivation of a terminal string $\omega$ according to $\mathbf{G}_1$ can be constructed from a derivation of $\omega$ according to $\mathbf{G}_2$ by replacing each application of $A \longrightarrow abcA$ with applications of the rules

$$A \longrightarrow ab \qquad B \longrightarrow bC \qquad C \longrightarrow cA$$

Thus $\mathbf{G}_1$ and $\mathbf{G}_2$ are strongly equivalent. The productions of grammar $\mathbf{G}_3$ are the union of the productions in $\mathbf{G}_1$ and $\mathbf{G}_2$. Although $\mathbf{L(G_3)} = \mathbf{L(G_1)}$, $\mathbf{G}_3$ cannot be strongly equivalent to either $\mathbf{G}_1$ or $\mathbf{G}_2$, because $\mathbf{G}_3$ is ambiguous and free of cyclic nonterminals, whereas $\mathbf{G}_1$ and $\mathbf{G}_2$ are unambiguous.

In the next sections, we consider five elementary transformations of context-free grammars:

1. Substitution.
2. Expansion.
3. Removal of useless productions.
4. Removal of nongenerative productions.
5. Removal of left recursive nonterminal letters.

For each transformation, we describe the conditions under which a transformed grammar is equivalent to the original. The first four transformations are discussed presently; the last is discussed (when needed) in connection with standard-form grammars in Section 9.2.2.

### 9.1.2 Substitution and Expansion

A grammar is transformed by *substitution* when, for some nonterminal symbol $B$, the right parts of its $B$ rules are substituted for instances of $B$ in the right part of some other production in the grammar. For example, suppose that a context-free grammar $\mathbf{G}$ has the production

$$A \longrightarrow \varphi B \psi \qquad \begin{cases} B \in \mathbf{N}, \\ \varphi, \psi \in (\mathbf{N} \cup \mathbf{T})^* \end{cases}$$

and the $B$ rules

$$B \longrightarrow \beta_1, \ldots, B \longrightarrow \beta_n$$

The transformation of **G** by substitution for $B$ in the production $A \longrightarrow \varphi B \psi$ is the grammar **G**$'$ obtained according to the following rules:

*Rule 1:* The production $A \longrightarrow \varphi B \psi$ is not in **G**$'$.

*Rule 2:* All other productions of **G** are in **G**$'$.

*Rule 3:* Each production

$$A \longrightarrow \varphi \beta_i \psi, \qquad i = 1, 2, \ldots, n$$

is in **G**$'$.

**Example 9.5:** Consider the grammars

$$\begin{array}{llllll} \mathbf{G}_1: & \Sigma \longrightarrow S & \mathbf{G}_2: & \Sigma \longrightarrow S & & S \longrightarrow ST \\ & S \longrightarrow TT & & T \longrightarrow S & & S \longrightarrow aSbT \\ & T \longrightarrow S & & T \longrightarrow aSb & & S \longrightarrow cT \\ & T \longrightarrow aSb & & T \longrightarrow c & & \\ & T \longrightarrow c & & & & \end{array}$$

Grammar $\mathbf{G}_2$ is the result of substituting for the left instance of $T$ in the production $S \longrightarrow TT$ of $\mathbf{G}_1$. The production $S \longrightarrow TT$ is omitted in $\mathbf{G}_2$, but the $T$ rules of $\mathbf{G}_1$ are retained. Grammar $\mathbf{G}_2$ is strongly equivalent to $\mathbf{G}_1$. The reader may verify, for example, that the string *accbcc* has two leftmost derivations in each grammar.

If a production introduced by substitution is a duplicate of a production in the original grammar, the transformed grammar need not be strongly equivalent to the original. For instance, if a grammar **G** has productions

$$A \longrightarrow \varphi B \psi \qquad B \longrightarrow \beta \qquad A \longrightarrow \varphi \beta \psi$$

and we substitute for $B$ in the first $A$ rule, we obtain the productions

$$A \longrightarrow \varphi \beta \psi \qquad B \longrightarrow \beta$$

in the transformed grammar **G**$'$. Whereas **G** permits two derivations of the sentential form $\varphi \beta \psi$ from $A$

$$A \Longrightarrow \varphi B \psi \Longrightarrow \varphi \beta \psi$$
$$A \Longrightarrow \varphi \beta \psi$$

the second of these is the only such derivation permitted by **G**$'$.

**Example 9.6:** Let $\mathbf{G}_1$ and $\mathbf{G}_2$ be the grammars

$$\begin{array}{llll} \mathbf{G}_1: & \Sigma \longrightarrow S & \mathbf{G}_2: & \Sigma \longrightarrow S \\ & S \longrightarrow T & & S \longrightarrow a \\ & S \longrightarrow a & & T \longrightarrow a \\ & T \longrightarrow a & & \end{array}$$

Grammar $\mathbf{G}_2$ is the result of substituting for $T$ in the production $S \longrightarrow T$ of $\mathbf{G}_1$. The new production $S \longrightarrow a$ is already present in $\mathbf{G}_1$. Obviously, $\mathbf{G}_1$ permits two derivations of the string $a$, but only one derivation is permitted by $\mathbf{G}_2$.

**Proposition 9.1 (Substitution):** Let $\mathbf{G}$ be a context-free grammar, and let $\mathbf{G}'$ be formed from $\mathbf{G}$ by substituting for some nonterminal letter $B$ in a production $A \longrightarrow \varphi B \psi$ of $\mathbf{G}$. If no production of $\mathbf{G}'$ introduced through rule 3 of substitution has already been introduced through rule 2, then $\mathbf{G}$ and $\mathbf{G}'$ are strongly equivalent.

***Proof:*** To establish the strong equivalence of $\mathbf{G}$ and $\mathbf{G}'$, we must exhibit, for each terminal string $\omega$, a one-to-one correspondence between the minimal leftmost derivations of $\omega$ permitted by $\mathbf{G}$ and those permitted by $\mathbf{G}'$.

Let $\omega$ be some string in $\mathbf{L(G)}$, and consider a derivation of $\omega$ permitted by $\mathbf{G}$. If the derivation contains no application of the production $A \longrightarrow \varphi B \psi$, the derivation is permitted by $\mathbf{G}'$. If, on the other hand, the derivation contains an application of $A \longrightarrow \varphi B \psi$, then it contains a *last* application of $A \longrightarrow \varphi B \psi$, followed eventually by an application of some $B$ rule of $\mathbf{G}$:

$$\Sigma \Longrightarrow \ldots \Longrightarrow \eta A \xi \Longrightarrow \eta \varphi B \psi \xi \Longrightarrow \ldots$$
$$\Longrightarrow \sigma B \tau \Longrightarrow \sigma \beta \tau \Longrightarrow \ldots \Longrightarrow \omega$$

In the corresponding derivation of $\omega$ according to $\mathbf{G}'$, the step

$$\eta A \xi \Longrightarrow \eta \varphi B \psi \xi$$

is replaced with

$$\eta A \xi \Longrightarrow \eta \varphi \beta \psi \xi$$

and the step

$$\sigma B \tau \Longrightarrow \sigma \beta \tau$$

is omitted. If there are other applications of $A \longrightarrow \varphi B \psi$ in the original derivation, this argument must be iterated. The new derivation is minimal because no applications of nongenerative rules have been introduced; it is leftmost because no change has been made in the order of the derivation steps retained.

We can reverse the procedure above to obtain a unique minimal derivation according to $\mathbf{G}$ from any such derivation according to $\mathbf{G}'$. The details are left to the reader.

The converse of substitution is *expansion*. Suppose that we replace a production of the form

$$A \longrightarrow \varphi \psi, \qquad \varphi, \psi \in (\mathbf{N} \cup \mathbf{T})^* - \boldsymbol{\lambda}$$

in a context-free grammar with either

$$A \longrightarrow X\psi \qquad X \longrightarrow \varphi$$

or

$$A \longrightarrow \varphi X \qquad X \longrightarrow \psi$$

where $X$ is a new nonterminal symbol. In such a case, we have *expanded* the rule $A \longrightarrow \varphi\psi$. If a grammar $\mathbf{G}'$ is obtained from $\mathbf{G}$ by expansion of a rule $A \longrightarrow \varphi\psi$, then $\mathbf{G}$ may be obtained from $\mathbf{G}'$ by substituting for $X$ in the rule $A \longrightarrow X\psi$ or $A \longrightarrow \varphi X$. Hence, Proposition 9.1 and the symmetry of strong equivalence show that $\mathbf{G}$ and $\mathbf{G}'$ are strongly equivalent.

> **Proposition 9.2 (Expansion):** If the grammar $\mathbf{G}'$ is formed from the context-free grammar $\mathbf{G}$ by expanding some rule of $\mathbf{G}$, then $\mathbf{G}$ and $\mathbf{G}'$ are strongly equivalent.

### 9.1.3 Useless Productions and the Emptiness Test

A grammar may contain productions and nonterminals that are useless in that they cannot occur in the derivation of any terminal string.

> **Definition 9.4:** Let $\mathbf{G} = (\mathbf{N}, \mathbf{T}, \mathbf{P}, \Sigma)$ be any context-free grammar. A production $A \longrightarrow \alpha$ of $\mathbf{G}$ is *useful* if $\mathbf{G}$ permits a derivation
>
> $$\Sigma \stackrel{*}{\Longrightarrow} \varphi A \psi \Longrightarrow \varphi\alpha\psi \stackrel{*}{\Longrightarrow} \omega, \qquad \omega \in \mathbf{T}^*$$
>
> Otherwise $A \longrightarrow \alpha$ is *useless.*
>
> A nonterminal of $\mathbf{G}$ is *useful* if it is the left part of a useful production; otherwise, it is a *useless* nonterminal.

The useful productions of a context-free grammar $\mathbf{G}$ may be identified by applying two marking procedures. The **T**-*marking procedure*, performed first, marks each rule of $\mathbf{G}$ with the symbol $\mathbf{T}$ just if there is a derivation of a terminal string using the marked rule in the first step. The set of **T**-marked productions is denoted $\mathbf{P_T}$. In terms of $\mathbf{P_T}$, the set $\mathbf{N_T}$ of *terminal-connected* nonterminals is

$$\mathbf{N_T} = \{A \in \mathbf{N} \cup \{\Sigma\} \mid \text{there is a rule } A \longrightarrow \alpha \text{ in } \mathbf{P_T}\}$$

Obviously, each useful production of $\mathbf{G}$ must be in $\mathbf{P_T}$, and each useful nonterminal symbol must be terminal connected. However, the fact that a production is in $\mathbf{P_T}$ or a symbol is in $\mathbf{N_T}$ is not in itself sufficient to ensure that the production or symbol is useful; a nonterminal $A$ in $\mathbf{N_T}$ or a production $A \longrightarrow \alpha$ in $\mathbf{P_T}$ is not useful unless a sentential form containing the symbol $A$ can be derived from $\Sigma$. To determine whether such a form can be derived, we perform a second marking procedure.

The $\Sigma$-*marking procedure* marks each rule $A \longrightarrow \alpha$ in $\mathbf{P_T}$ with the symbol $\Sigma$ just if **G** permits a derivation

$$\Sigma \stackrel{*}{\Longrightarrow} \varphi A \psi$$

using only rules in $\mathbf{P_T}$. In such a case, **G** must permit a derivation

$$\Sigma \stackrel{*}{\Longrightarrow} \varphi A \psi \Rightarrow \varphi \alpha \psi \stackrel{*}{\Longrightarrow} \omega, \qquad \omega \in \mathbf{T}^*$$

since each nonterminal in $\varphi$ or $\psi$ is **T** connected. If we denote by $\mathbf{P}_\Sigma$ the set of $\Sigma$-marked productions, then $\mathbf{P}_\Sigma$ contains the useful productions of the grammar.

The **T**-marking and $\Sigma$-marking procedures are carried out as follows:

**T**-*marking procedure:* Let **G** be a context-free grammar with productions **P**. Construct a sequence $\mathbf{P}_0, \mathbf{P}_1, \ldots$ of subsets of **P** and a sequence $\mathbf{N}_0, \mathbf{N}_1, \ldots$ of subsets of **N** according to the following algorithm:

1. Let $\mathbf{P}_0$ and $\mathbf{N}_0$ be empty. Let $i = 0$.
2. Let $\mathbf{P}_{i+1} = \{A \longrightarrow \alpha \text{ in } \mathbf{P} \mid \alpha \text{ is in } (\mathbf{N}_i \cup \mathbf{T})^*\}$.
3. Let $\mathbf{N}_{i+1} = \{A \in \mathbf{N} \mid \mathbf{P}_{i+1} \text{ contains a rule } A \longrightarrow \alpha\}$.
4. If $\mathbf{P}_{i+1} \neq \mathbf{P}_i$, let $i = i + 1$, and go to step 2.
5. Let $\mathbf{P_T} = \mathbf{P}_{i+1}$ and $\mathbf{N_T} = \mathbf{N}_{i+1}$.

Each set $\mathbf{P}_i$ contains the nonterminals of **G** from which a terminal string is derivable within $i$ steps. Since $\mathbf{P}_i \subseteq \mathbf{P}_{i+1} \subseteq \mathbf{P}$ for each $i$, the procedure will terminate after a number of steps no greater than the number of rules in **G**.

$\Sigma$-*marking procedure:* Let **G** be a context-free grammar, and let $\mathbf{P_T}$ be the set of **T**-marked productions. Construct a sequence $\mathbf{Q}_1, \mathbf{Q}_2, \ldots$ of subsets of $\mathbf{P_T}$ according to the following algorithm:

1. Let $\mathbf{Q}_1 = \{\Sigma \longrightarrow \alpha \text{ in } \mathbf{P_T}\}$. Let $i = 1$.
2. Let $\mathbf{Q}_{i+1} = \mathbf{Q}_i \cup \{A \longrightarrow \alpha \text{ in } \mathbf{P_T} \mid \mathbf{Q}_i \text{ contains a rule } B \longrightarrow \varphi A \psi\}$.
3. If $\mathbf{Q}_{i+1} \neq \mathbf{Q}_i$, let $i = i + 1$, and go to step 2.
4. Let $\mathbf{P}_\Sigma = \mathbf{Q}_{i+1}$.

Each set $\mathbf{Q}_i$ contains a production $A \longrightarrow \alpha$ if and only if **G** permits a derivation $\Sigma \stackrel{*}{\Longrightarrow} \varphi A \psi \Longrightarrow \varphi \alpha \psi$ in no more than $i$ steps, using only productions in $\mathbf{P_T}$. Since $\mathbf{Q}_i \subseteq \mathbf{Q}_{i+1} \subseteq \mathbf{P_T}$, this procedure stops after a number of steps no greater than the number of productions in $\mathbf{P_T}$.

We have noted that a production is useful just if it is in $\mathbf{P}_\Sigma$ after the markings have been completed. Since the **T**-marking and $\Sigma$-marking procedures always terminate after a finite number of steps, we have the following:

> **Proposition 9.3:** Let **G** be a context-free grammar with productions **P**. For each production in **P**, it is possible to decide whether the production is or is not useful in **G**.

**Example 9.7:**

| | Rules | | Marking | |
|---|---|---|---|---|
| G: | $\Sigma \longrightarrow S$ | (1) | **T** | $\Sigma$ |
| | $S \longrightarrow AB$ | (2) | | |
| | $S \longrightarrow aS$ | (3) | **T** | $\Sigma$ |
| | $S \longrightarrow a$ | (4) | **T** | $\Sigma$ |
| | $B \longrightarrow Sb$ | (5) | **T** | |
| | $C \longrightarrow aC$ | (6) | | |

Applying the **T**-marking procedure to **G** marks the productions in the order 4, 1, 3, 5, and the **T**-connected nonterminals are thus

$$\mathbf{N_T} = \{\Sigma, S, B\}$$

The $\Sigma$-marking procedure marks rule 1, and then rules 3 and 4. Thus the useful rules of **G** are

$$\mathbf{P}_\Sigma = \{\Sigma \longrightarrow S, S \longrightarrow aS, S \longrightarrow a\}$$

Rule 5 is an example of a useless rule whose left part is **T** connected. Although $B$ is derivable from $\Sigma$ via $\Sigma \Longrightarrow S \Longrightarrow AB$, rule 5 is useless, because $A$ is not **T** connected; hence no terminal string derives from $AB$.

The **T**-marking procedure gives us a way of testing whether $\mathbf{L}(\mathbf{G}, A)$ is empty for any $A$ in $\mathbf{N} \cup \{\Sigma\}$. Indeed, $\mathbf{L}(\mathbf{G}, A)$ is nonempty if and only if $A$ is in $\mathbf{N_T}$. Thus we have the following important result:

**Theorem 9.1 (Emptiness Test):** For any context-free grammar **G**, one can decide whether $\mathbf{L}(\mathbf{G}, A) = \varnothing$ for any nonterminal symbol $A$ in **G**. In particular, one can decide whether the grammar generates any strings at all [that is, whether $\mathbf{L}(\mathbf{G}) = \mathbf{L}(\mathbf{G}, \Sigma) = \varnothing$].

It is trivially true that deleting useless productions from a grammar yields a new grammar strongly equivalent to the original.

**Proposition 9.4 (Removal of Useless Productions):** If the grammar **G′** is obtained from a context-free grammar **G** by removing useless productions, then **G** and **G′** are strongly equivalent.

### 9.1.4 Replacement of Nongenerative Productions

Removing nongenerative productions from a context-free grammar also eliminates cyclic nonterminals and is an important step in converting the grammar into canonical form. The procedure used is similar to that used in removing $\lambda$-transitions from a finite-state accepter. The following grammar will be used to illustrate the principle.

Let **G** be the grammar with productions

$$\Sigma \longrightarrow A \qquad A \longrightarrow B \qquad A \longrightarrow aB$$
$$\Sigma \longrightarrow B \qquad A \longrightarrow C \qquad A \longrightarrow b$$
$$B \longrightarrow C$$
$$C \longrightarrow B \qquad C \longrightarrow Aa$$

and consider the sequences of consecutive nongenerative derivation steps permitted by **G**. These sequences may be represented by a finite-state accepter **M(G)** having a state for each nonterminal that appears in a nongenerative production of **G**, as in Figure 9.1. Each of the $\lambda$-transitions of the machine corresponds to one nongenerative production of **G**, and the initial states and

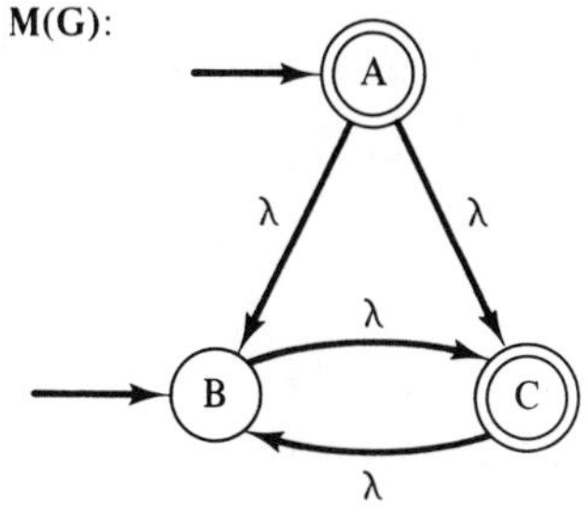


**Figure 9.1** Finite-state accepter representing the nongenerative productions of a grammar.

final states correspond to nonterminals on which a series of nongenerative steps can begin and end, respectively. For example, **M(G)** has a path from initial state A to final state C via the sequence of states

$$\mathrm{A} \longrightarrow \mathrm{B} \longrightarrow \mathrm{C} \longrightarrow \mathrm{B} \longrightarrow \mathrm{C}$$

This indicates that a sequence of steps

$$\varphi A \psi \Longrightarrow \varphi B \psi \Longrightarrow \varphi C \psi \Longrightarrow \varphi B \psi \Longrightarrow \varphi C \psi$$

can occur in a derivation permitted in **G**, such that the sequence is preceded and followed by generative steps. This is indeed the case in the derivation

$$\Sigma \Longrightarrow A \Longrightarrow B \Longrightarrow C \Longrightarrow B \Longrightarrow C \Longrightarrow Aa \Longrightarrow ba$$

of the terminal string *ba*.

In general, if $\mathbf{G} = (\mathbf{N}, \mathbf{T}, \mathbf{P}, \Sigma)$ is a context-free grammar with nongenerative rules, the associated finite-state accepter is $\mathbf{M(G)} = (\mathbf{Q}, \varnothing, \mathbf{P}', \mathbf{I}, \mathbf{F})$, where

$$\mathbf{Q} = \{\mathrm{A} \mid A \longrightarrow B \text{ or } B \longrightarrow A \text{ is a rule of } \mathbf{G}, \text{ for some } A, B \in \mathbf{N}\}$$

$$\mathbf{P}' = \{\mathrm{A} \xrightarrow{\lambda} \mathrm{B} \mid A \longrightarrow B \text{ is a rule of } \mathbf{G}\}$$

$$\mathbf{I} = \left\{ \mathrm{A} \in \mathbf{Q} \;\middle|\; \begin{array}{l} \Sigma \longrightarrow A \text{ is a rule of } \mathbf{G}, \text{ or} \\ B \longrightarrow \varphi A \psi \text{ is a rule of } \mathbf{G} \\ \text{with } \varphi\psi \neq \lambda \end{array} \right\}$$

$$\mathbf{F} = \{\mathrm{A} \in \mathbf{Q} \mid A \longrightarrow \beta \text{ is a rule of } \mathbf{G} \text{ with } \beta \notin \mathbf{N}\}$$

Note that the sets **I** and **F** include all nonterminal letters on which sequences of nongenerative derivation steps, *including the empty sequence*, can begin and end, respectively.

A grammar equivalent to **G**, but with no nongenerative productions, can be obtained by rewriting each generative production as several productions that incorporate the effect of the nongenerative derivation steps permitted by **G**. The new grammar $\mathbf{G}' = (\mathbf{T}, \mathbf{N}', \mathbf{P}'', \Sigma)$ includes a new nonterminal letter for each sequence of nongenerative steps that can occur as part of some minimal derivation in **G**. Each of these sequences corresponds to a loopfree path in **M(G)** from some initial state **X** to some final state **Y**:

$$\mathbf{N}' = \mathbf{N} \cup \{[X_1 X_2 \ldots X_n] \mid X_1 = \mathrm{X} \in \mathbf{I},\ X_n = \mathrm{Y} \in \mathbf{F},\ X_i \neq X_j$$
$$\text{for } i \neq j, \text{ and } X_1 \xrightarrow{\lambda} X_2 \xrightarrow{\lambda} \ldots \xrightarrow{\lambda} X_n \text{ in } \mathbf{M(G)}\}$$

The rules of the new grammar are designed so that whenever the sequence of derivation steps

$$A \Longrightarrow \varphi X \psi \Longrightarrow \ldots \Longrightarrow \varphi Y \psi \Longrightarrow \varphi \beta \psi$$

is permitted in a minimal derivation of **G**, the sequence

$$A \Longrightarrow \varphi[X \ldots Y]\psi \Longrightarrow \varphi\beta\psi$$

is permitted by **G**′. The productions of **G**′ are given by the following rules of construction:

*Rule 1:* If a production of **G** contains no symbol corresponding to a state in **Q**, that production is a production of **G**′.

*Rule 2:* If **G** contains a generative production

$$A \longrightarrow \alpha_0 B_1 \alpha_1 \ldots B_k \alpha_k, \qquad k \geq 1$$

in which $\{B_i \mid 1 \leq i \leq k\}$ are the symbols in the right-hand part of the production corresponding to members of **Q**, then **G**′ contains each production

$$U \longrightarrow \alpha_0 V_1 \alpha_1 \ldots V_k \alpha_k$$

such that

$$\mathbf{U} \in \begin{cases} \{A\} \text{ if A is not a final state of } \mathbf{M(G)} \\ \{[X \ldots Y] \mid Y = A\} \text{ if A is a final state of } \mathbf{M(G)} \end{cases}$$

$$\mathbf{V}_i \in \begin{cases} \{B_i\} \text{ if } \mathrm{B}_i \text{ is not an initial state of } \mathbf{M(G)} \\ \{[X \ldots Y] \mid X = B_i\} \text{ if } \mathrm{B}_i \text{ is an initial state of } \mathbf{M(G)} \end{cases}$$

**Example 9.8:** Consider the grammar **G** giving rise to the machine **M(G)** of Figure 9.1. Referring to the figure, we see that the new nonterminals required are

$$\{[AA], [AC], [BC], [ABC]\}$$

Following the rules of construction, we find that no rules of **G** are retained in the new grammar, because each rule has an appearance of some nonterminal corresponding to a state in **Q**. The productions of **G**′ resulting from rule 2 are as follows:

$$\begin{array}{rlrl}
\Sigma & \longrightarrow [AA] & [AA] & \longrightarrow b \\
\Sigma & \longrightarrow [AC] & [AA] & \longrightarrow a[BC] \\
\Sigma & \longrightarrow [BC] & [AC] & \longrightarrow [AA]a \\
\Sigma & \longrightarrow [ABC] & [ABC] & \longrightarrow [AA]a \\
[AC] & \longrightarrow [AC]a & [BC] & \longrightarrow [AA]a \\
[AC] & \longrightarrow [ABC]a & [BC] & \longrightarrow [AC]a \\
[ABC] & \longrightarrow [AC]a & [BC] & \longrightarrow [ABC]a \\
[ABC] & \longrightarrow [ABC]a & &
\end{array}$$

Given any minimal derivation permitted by **G**, we may construct a corresponding derivation according to **G**′ by replacing each sequence (including the empty sequence) of nongenerative steps with a single step identifying the replaced sequence. For example, **G** permits the derivation

$$\Sigma \Longrightarrow \underbrace{B \Longrightarrow C}_{[BC]} \Longrightarrow \underbrace{Aa \Longrightarrow Ba \Longrightarrow Ca}_{[ABC]} \Longrightarrow \underbrace{Aaa}_{[AA]} \Longrightarrow baa$$

containing three sequences of nongenerative steps (the last empty) seperated in each case by a generative step. The corresponding derivation according to **G**′ is

$$\Sigma \Longrightarrow [BC] \Longrightarrow [ABC]a \Longrightarrow [AA]aa \Longrightarrow baa$$

The correspondence of derivations illustrated by Example 9.8 applies to grammars **G** and **G**′ whenever **G**′ is obtained from **G** according to the rules given above. The demonstration of this fact is left to the reader.

**Proposition 9.5:** From any context-free grammar **G**, one can construct a strongly equivalent grammar **G**′ containing no nongenerative productions.

### 9.1.5 Well-Formed Grammars

Our ability to remove useless and nongenerative productions from context-free grammars motivates the following definition:

**Definition 9.5:** A context-free grammar $\mathbf{G} = (\mathbf{N}, \mathbf{T}, \mathbf{P}, \Sigma)$ is *well formed* if each production has one of the forms

$$\begin{array}{l} \Sigma \longrightarrow \lambda \\ \Sigma \longrightarrow B \\ A \longrightarrow \alpha \end{array} \quad \begin{cases} A, B \in \mathbf{N} \\ \alpha \in (\mathbf{N} \cup \mathbf{T})^* - \mathbf{N} \end{cases}$$

and each production is useful.

In a well-formed grammar, $\Sigma$ rules other than $\Sigma \longrightarrow \lambda$ are required to have the simple form $\Sigma \longrightarrow B$, and no nongenerative or useless productions are permitted. The absence of nongenerative productions ensures that each leftmost derivation permitted by such a grammar is minimal.

Now suppose that $\mathbf{G}$ is an arbitrary context-free grammar. By Proposition 9.2, we may expand all $\Sigma$ rules into the form $\Sigma \longrightarrow B$ and obtain a grammar strongly equivalent to the original. By Proposition 9.5 we can transform this grammar into a grammar without nongenerative rules, strongly equivalent to the original. By Proposition 9.4, the useless rules may be omitted, yielding a grammar strongly equivalent to the original. Therefore, we have the following:

**Theorem 9.2:** From any context-free grammar $\mathbf{G}$, one can construct a well-formed grammar strongly equivalent to $\mathbf{G}$.

In a well-formed grammar, each production other than the $\Sigma$ rules has the form

$$A \longrightarrow \alpha, \qquad \text{where } |\alpha| > 1 \quad \text{or} \quad \alpha \in \mathbf{T}^* - \boldsymbol{\lambda}$$

Thus each step in a derivation, other than the first, either increases the length of the sentential form or generates at least one letter of the terminal string. It follows that a derivation of a terminal string of length $n$ requires at most $2n$ steps, consisting of an initial step, at most $n - 1$ steps that generate $n$ instances of nonterminals, and at most $n$ steps that replace nonterminals with terminal symbols.

## 9.2 Canonical Forms of Grammars

By placing conditions on the form of productions permitted, we may define restricted forms of context-free grammars. If a strongly equivalent grammar in such a form can be obtained from an arbitrary context-free grammar, the restricted form is a *canonical form* for context-free grammars.

Canonical forms for context-free grammars are useful for two reasons: (1) it is often easier to establish some property for canonical-form grammars than for context-free grammars in general, and (2) representing context-free languages by canonical-form grammars may make it easier to devise methods of syntax analysis for the languages.

The well-formed grammars constitute a canonical form for context-free grammars that simplifies study by removing from consideration useless and nongenerative productions. Two other canonical forms for the grammars have been of widely recognized importance: (1) the *normal-form* grammar, which is particularly useful for theoretical work because the productions are restricted to a few very simple forms, and (2) the *standard-form* grammar, which is a useful form for syntax analysis because left recursion is not permitted. The reader should note that the Backus–Naur form (BNF), frequently used to represent the syntax of programming languages, is not a canonical form for context-free grammars; it is simply an alternative notation for the productions of an unrestricted context-free grammar.

### 9.2.1 Normal-Form Grammars

**Definition 9.6:** A context-free grammar $\mathbf{G} = (\mathbf{N}, \mathbf{T}, \mathbf{P}, \Sigma)$ is in *normal form* if each production has one of the following forms:

$$\begin{array}{lll} \Sigma \longrightarrow \lambda & A \longrightarrow BC & \left\{\begin{array}{l} A, B, C \in \mathbf{N} \\ a \in \mathbf{T} \end{array}\right. \\ \Sigma \longrightarrow A & A \longrightarrow a & \end{array}$$

This canonical form is also called *Chomsky normal form.*

Since it contains no nongenerative productions, a normal-form grammar is well formed if it contains no useless productions.

The principle for transforming a context-free grammar **G** into a strongly equivalent normal-form grammar **G′** is illustrated by Figure 9.2. In light of

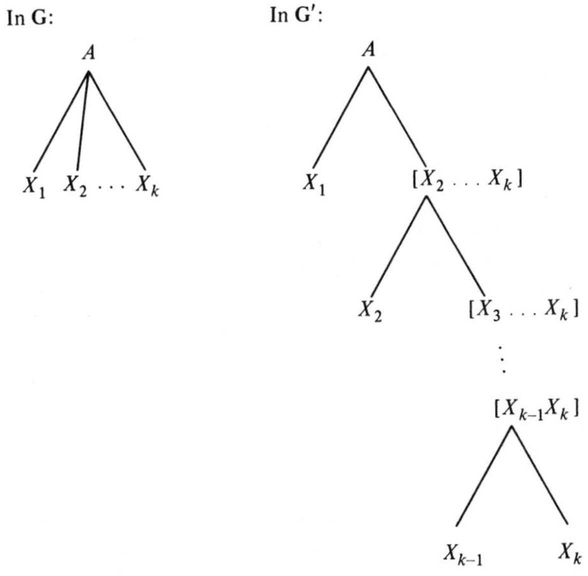


**Figure 9.2** Conversion to normal form.

Theorem 9.2, it is no restriction to assume that **G** is well formed. Thus each production of **G** has one of the following forms:

$$\begin{array}{lll} \Sigma \longrightarrow \lambda & A \longrightarrow \alpha & \begin{cases} A \in \mathbf{N} \\ \alpha \in (\mathbf{N} \cup \mathbf{T})^*, |\alpha| \geq 2 \\ a \in \mathbf{T} \end{cases} \\ \Sigma \longrightarrow A & A \longrightarrow a & \end{array}$$

Applying Proposition 9.2 to **G**, we may construct a grammar **G**′ by expanding each rule $A \longrightarrow \alpha$, with $|\alpha| > 2$, into a set of rules whose right parts each contain two symbols. For each rule

$$A \longrightarrow X_1X_2 \dots X_k, \qquad k > 2, X_i \in \mathbf{N} \cup \mathbf{T}$$

in **G**, we introduce $k - 2$ new nonterminals

$$[X_2 \dots X_k], [X_3 \dots X_k], \dots, [X_{k-1}X_k]$$

and replace $A \longrightarrow X_1X_2 \dots X_k$ with the set of productions

$$\begin{aligned} A &\longrightarrow X_1[X_2 \dots X_k] \\ [X_2 \dots X_k] &\longrightarrow X_2[X_3 \dots X_k] \\ &\vdots \\ [X_{k-1}X_k] &\longrightarrow X_{k-1}X_k \end{aligned}$$

Applying the production $A \longrightarrow X_1X_2 \dots X_k$ in **G** corresponds to applying these new productions in sequence, as shown in Figure 9.2. Each rule of **G**′ is now in one of the following forms:

$$\begin{array}{lll} \Sigma \longrightarrow \lambda & & \\ \Sigma \longrightarrow A & A \longrightarrow bC & \begin{cases} A, B, C \in \mathbf{N} \\ a, b, c \in \mathbf{T} \end{cases} \\ A \longrightarrow BC & A \longrightarrow Bc & \\ A \longrightarrow a & A \longrightarrow bc & \end{array}$$

The production types in the left column are in normal form, but those in the right column are not. The latter productions are put into normal form by introducing a nonterminal $[x]$ for each terminal letter $x$ in the grammar, and replacing each occurrence of $x$ in any production by $[x]$. The rule $[x] \longrightarrow x$ is then added to **G**′. For example, a production of the form $A \longrightarrow bC$ becomes the production $A \longrightarrow [b]C$, with the rule $[b] \longrightarrow b$ added to the grammar. By Proposition 9.3, the alterations we have described produce a new grammar strongly equivalent to the original. Thus we have the following:

> **Theorem 9.3 (Normal-Form Theorem):** From any context-free grammar, one can construct a strongly equivalent grammar in normal form.

**Example 9.9:** Consider the well-formed grammar

$$\mathbf{G}: \quad \Sigma \longrightarrow \lambda \qquad B \longrightarrow bCb$$
$$\Sigma \longrightarrow A \qquad A \longrightarrow a$$
$$A \longrightarrow ABBA \qquad C \longrightarrow c$$

Applying the procedure illustrated by Figure 9.2, we obtain the grammar

$$\mathbf{G}': \quad \Sigma \longrightarrow \lambda \qquad B \longrightarrow b[Cb]$$
$$\Sigma \longrightarrow A \qquad [Cb] \longrightarrow Cb$$
$$A \longrightarrow A[BBA] \qquad A \longrightarrow a$$
$$[BBA] \longrightarrow B[BA] \qquad C \longrightarrow c$$
$$[BA] \longrightarrow BA$$

Each production of $\mathbf{G}'$ is in normal form except for the rules $[Cb] \longrightarrow Cb$ and $B \longrightarrow b[Cb]$. Replacing these rules with the rules

$$[Cb] \longrightarrow C[b] \qquad B \longrightarrow [b][Cb]$$
$$[b] \longrightarrow b$$

yields a normal-form grammar strongly equivalent to $\mathbf{G}$.

### 9.2.2 Standard-Form Grammars

Context-free grammars in standard form have terminal letters as the handles of all rules. Because they are not left recursive, they play an important role in syntax analysis.

**Definition 9.7:** A context-free grammar $\mathbf{G} = (\mathbf{N}, \mathbf{T}, \mathbf{P}, \Sigma)$ is in *standard form* if each production has one of the forms

$$\begin{matrix} \Sigma \longrightarrow \lambda \\ \Sigma \longrightarrow A \\ A \longrightarrow a\beta \end{matrix} \qquad \begin{cases} A \in \mathbf{N} \\ a \in \mathbf{T} \\ \beta \in (\mathbf{N} \cup \mathbf{T})^* \end{cases}$$

This canonical form is also called *Greibach normal form.*

Since it cannot have rules of the form $A \longrightarrow B$, a standard-form grammar is well formed if it has no useless productions.

In a standard-form grammar, each step after the first in a leftmost derivation has the form

$$\varphi A \psi \Longrightarrow \varphi a \beta \psi$$

and generates at least one terminal letter. Therefore, the derivation of a terminal string of $n$ letters requires at most $n + 1$ steps. Left recursion is impossible in a standard-form grammar because no derivation of the form $A \stackrel{*}{\Longrightarrow} A\psi$ is permitted by the grammar.

Suppose that we wish to construct a standard-form grammar equivalent to some arbitrary context-free grammar **G**. Without loss of generality, we may assume that **G** is well formed. Each production of **G** will have one of the forms

$$\begin{array}{ll} \Sigma \longrightarrow \lambda & A \longrightarrow a\alpha \\ \Sigma \longrightarrow A & A \longrightarrow B\beta \end{array} \qquad \begin{cases} A, B \in \mathbf{N} \\ a \in \mathbf{T} \\ \alpha, \beta \in (\mathbf{N} \cup \mathbf{T})^*, \beta \neq \lambda \end{cases}$$

Each of these production types is in standard form except the type $A \longrightarrow B\beta$. Hence our task is to replace productions having nonterminal handles with productions in standard form.

Let $A$ be some nonterminal letter in **G**, and consider a leftmost derivation from $A$ in which each step applies a production having a nonterminal letter $X_i$ as its handle:

(1)
$$\begin{aligned} A &\Longrightarrow X_1\beta_1 \Longrightarrow X_2\beta_2\beta_1 \Longrightarrow \ldots \\ &\Longrightarrow X_k\beta_k \ldots \beta_2\beta_1 \Longrightarrow \ldots \end{aligned}$$

This derivation must be finite in length unless some nonterminal letter repeats in the sequence

$$A, X_1, X_2, \ldots, X_k, \ldots$$

Now if $X_i = X_j = X$ for some $i < j$, the derivation

$$X \stackrel{*}{\Longrightarrow} X\beta_j \ldots \beta_{i+1}$$

is permitted and $X$ is a left recursive nonterminal in **G**. On the other hand, if **G** has no left recursive nonterminals, each derivation of form (1) will produce a sentential form beginning with a terminal letter in a finite number of steps, and a finite number of substitutions will convert the rules of **G** into standard form.

**Example 9.10:** We shall transform the grammar $\mathbf{G}_1$ into standard form:

$$\begin{array}{lllll} \mathbf{G}_1\colon & \Sigma \longrightarrow A & A \longrightarrow Ba & B \longrightarrow Cb & C \longrightarrow cC \\ & & A \longrightarrow Ca & B \longrightarrow CAb & C \longrightarrow c \end{array}$$

This grammar has no left recursive nonterminals ($C$ is right recursive). Using Proposition 9.1, we may transform $\mathbf{G}_1$ by substituting for the handles of $A$ rules:

$$A \longrightarrow Ba \quad \text{becomes} \quad \begin{cases} A \longrightarrow Cba \\ A \longrightarrow CAba \end{cases}$$

$$A \longrightarrow Ca \quad \text{becomes} \quad \begin{cases} A \longrightarrow cCa \\ A \longrightarrow ca \end{cases}$$

The result is the grammar $\mathbf{G}_2$:

$$\mathbf{G}_2\colon\ \Sigma \longrightarrow A \qquad \begin{array}{ll} A \longrightarrow cCa & B \longrightarrow Cb \\ A \longrightarrow ca & B \longrightarrow CAb \\ A \longrightarrow Cba & C \longrightarrow cC \\ A \longrightarrow CAba & C \longrightarrow c \end{array}$$

The $B$ rules are now useless and may be deleted. Two of the new $A$ rules are not in standard form, but a second substitution completes the conversion. The result is $\mathbf{G}_3$:

$$\mathbf{G}_3\colon\ \Sigma \longrightarrow A \qquad \begin{array}{ll} A \longrightarrow cCa & A \longrightarrow cCAba \\ A \longrightarrow ca & A \longrightarrow cAba \\ A \longrightarrow cCba & C \longrightarrow cC \\ A \longrightarrow cba & C \longrightarrow c \end{array}$$

The construction of $\mathbf{G}_3$ from $\mathbf{G}_1$ satisfies the condition of Proposition 9.1: no transformed production duplicates any production already in the grammar. Hence $\mathbf{G}_3$ is strongly equivalent to $\mathbf{G}_1$.

Figure 9.3 shows in the form of a tree the substitutions involved in the construction of $\mathbf{G}_3$. The paths in the tree represent leftmost

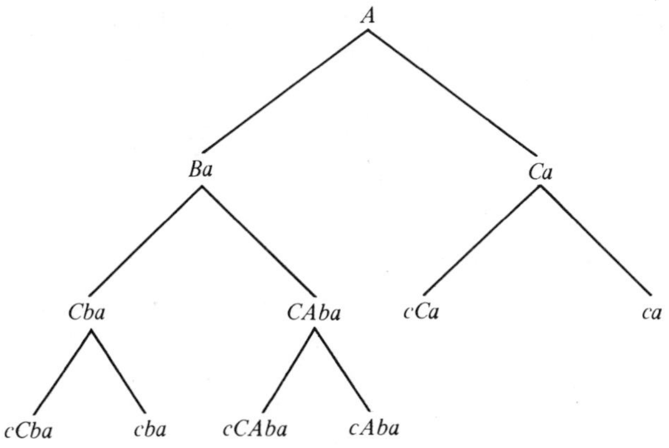


**Figure 9.3** Conversion of productions to standard form by substitution.

derivations from $A$ in $\mathbf{G}_1$ containing at least one application of a production with a nonterminal handle, and terminating with an application of one standard-form production. The replacement of $A$ rules with standard-form productions is equivalent to including in the new grammar $A$ rules whose right parts are the sentential forms labeling the leaves of the tree.

If the grammar to be converted into standard form has left recursive nonterminals, the procedure used in Example 9.10 never terminates. In Example 9.11, we illustrate the principle used in eliminating left recursive nonterminals from a grammar.

**Example 9.11:** Consider the grammar

$$\mathbf{G}_1\colon\ \Sigma \longrightarrow A \qquad A \longrightarrow AbA \qquad A \longrightarrow a$$

which has the left recursive production $A \longrightarrow AbA$. For simplicity, let $\mathbf{A}$ denote the set $\mathbf{L}(\mathbf{G}_1, A)$. According to the grammar, $\mathbf{A}$ must satisfy the equation

$$\mathbf{A} = \mathbf{A}(\mathbf{bA}) \cup \mathbf{a}$$

Arden's rule (Theorem 5.4) may be applied to obtain an alternative expression for $\mathbf{A}$:

$$\begin{aligned} \mathbf{A} &= \mathbf{a}(\mathbf{bA})^* \\ &= \mathbf{a} \cup \mathbf{abA}(\mathbf{bA})^* \end{aligned}$$

From this expression, it is easy to find standard-form productions that generate the strings in $\mathbf{A}$. The set $\mathbf{Z} = \mathbf{bA}(\mathbf{bA})^*$ is generated by the productions

$$Z \longrightarrow bAZ \qquad Z \longrightarrow bA$$

where $Z$ is a new nonterminal letter. Because the closure is realized through right recursion instead of left recursion, $Z$ does not appear as a handle in these rules; in fact, they are in standard form. The set

$$\mathbf{A} = \mathbf{a} \cup \mathbf{aZ}$$

is generated by the $A$ rules

$$A \longrightarrow aZ \qquad A \longrightarrow a$$

Thus the grammar

$$\begin{aligned} \mathbf{G}_2\colon\ \Sigma \longrightarrow A \qquad & A \longrightarrow aZ \qquad Z \longrightarrow bAZ \\ & A \longrightarrow a \qquad Z \longrightarrow bA \end{aligned}$$

describes the same language as $\mathbf{G}_1$. Moreover, each derivation in $\mathbf{G}_1$ using left recursion on $A$

$$\left.\begin{aligned} &\Sigma \Longrightarrow A \Longrightarrow AbA \Longrightarrow abA \Longrightarrow abAbA \Longrightarrow \cdots \\ &\Longrightarrow (ab)^k A \Longrightarrow (ab)^k a \end{aligned}\right\} k \geq 1$$

corresponds uniquely to the derivation

$$\left.\begin{aligned} &\Sigma \Longrightarrow A \Longrightarrow aZ \Longrightarrow abAZ \Longrightarrow \cdots \\ &\Longrightarrow a(ba)^{k-1}Z \Longrightarrow a(ba)^k \end{aligned}\right\} k \geq 1$$

using right recursion on $Z$ in $\mathbf{G}_2$. (This relation is illustrated by Figure 9.4.) Hence grammars $\mathbf{G}_1$ and $\mathbf{G}_2$ are strongly equivalent.

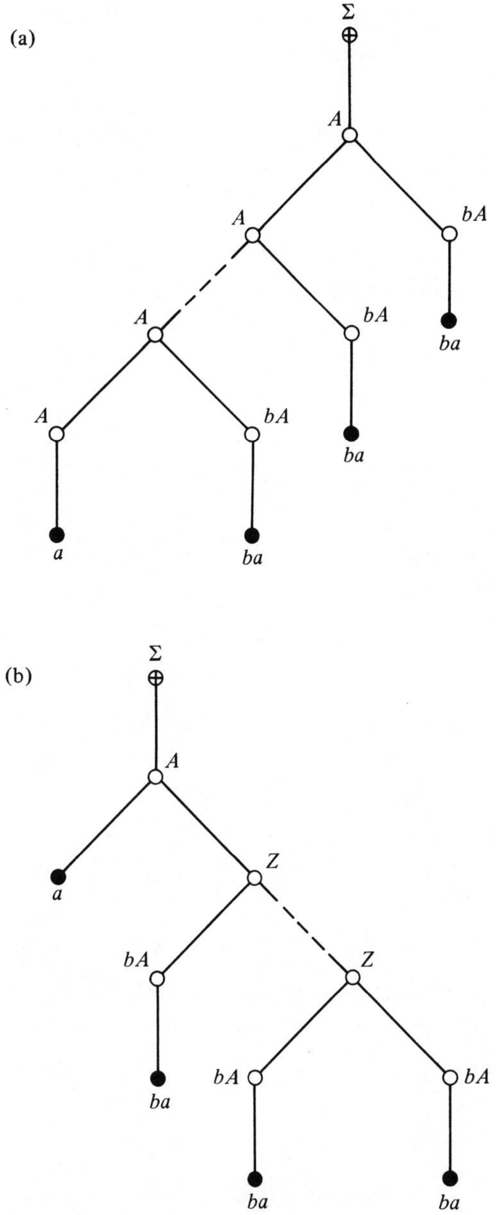


**Figure 9.4** Replacement of a left recursive rule.

To remove left recursion in some nonterminal $X$ from an arbitrary grammar, it may be necessary to handle many left recursive $X$ rules. This requires a simple generalization of the transformation just illustrated by Example 9.10.

**Propositon 9.6:** Let **G** be a context-free grammar, and suppose that the $X$ rules of **G** are

$$X \longrightarrow \alpha_1, \ldots, X \longrightarrow \alpha_n$$
$$X \longrightarrow X\beta_1, \ldots, X \longrightarrow X\beta_m$$

where the second group of rules includes each $X$ rule having $X$ as its handle. Let **G**′ be the grammar obtained by replacing the $X$ rules of **G** with the rules

$$X \longrightarrow \alpha_1, \ldots, X \longrightarrow \alpha_n$$
$$X \longrightarrow \alpha_1 Z, \ldots, X \longrightarrow \alpha_n Z$$
$$Z \longrightarrow \beta_1, \ldots, Z \longrightarrow \beta_m$$
$$Z \longrightarrow \beta_1 Z, \ldots, Z \longrightarrow \beta_m Z$$

where $Z$ is a new nonterminal letter. Then **G** and **G**′ are strongly equivalent.

***Proof:*** The set of strings denoted by $X$ in **G** is

$$\mathbf{X} = (\boldsymbol{\alpha}_1 \cup \ldots \cup \boldsymbol{\alpha}_n) \cup \mathbf{X}(\boldsymbol{\beta}_1 \cup \ldots \cup \boldsymbol{\beta}_m)$$

where $\boldsymbol{\alpha}_i$ and $\boldsymbol{\beta}_j$ denote the sets of strings derivable from the sentential forms $\alpha_i$ and $\beta_j$. Applying Arden's rule, we find

$$\mathbf{X} = (\boldsymbol{\alpha}_1 \cup \ldots \cup \boldsymbol{\alpha}_n)(\boldsymbol{\beta}_1 \cup \ldots \cup \boldsymbol{\beta}_m)^*$$

The set of strings denoted by **X** in **G**′ is

$$\mathbf{X} = (\boldsymbol{\alpha}_1 \cup \ldots \cup \boldsymbol{\alpha}_n) \cup (\boldsymbol{\alpha}_1 \cup \ldots \cup \boldsymbol{\alpha}_n)\mathbf{Z}$$

where

$$\mathbf{Z} = (\boldsymbol{\beta}_1 \cup \ldots \cup \boldsymbol{\beta}_m) \cup (\boldsymbol{\beta}_1 \cup \ldots \cup \boldsymbol{\beta}_m)\mathbf{Z}$$

Solving the second of these equations for **Z** using Arden's rule, and substituting the result in the first equation, yields

$$\begin{aligned}\mathbf{X} &= (\boldsymbol{\alpha}_1 \cup \ldots \cup \boldsymbol{\alpha}_n) \cup (\boldsymbol{\alpha}_1 \cup \ldots \cup \boldsymbol{\alpha}_n)(\boldsymbol{\beta}_1 \cup \ldots \cup \boldsymbol{\beta}_m)^* \\ &\quad (\boldsymbol{\beta}_1 \cup \ldots \cup \boldsymbol{\beta}_m) \\ &= (\boldsymbol{\alpha}_1 \cup \ldots \cup \boldsymbol{\alpha}_n)(\boldsymbol{\beta}_1 \cup \ldots \cup \boldsymbol{\beta}_m)^*\end{aligned}$$

Thus **X** denotes the same strings in both grammars and, since only the **X** rules of **G** have been changed, $\mathbf{L}(\mathbf{G}') = \mathbf{L}(\mathbf{G})$.

In addition, **G** and **G**′ are strongly equivalent because derivations of the form

$$X \Longrightarrow X\beta_{j_1} \Longrightarrow \ldots \Longrightarrow X\beta_{j_k} \ldots \beta_{j_1} \Longrightarrow \alpha_i\beta_{j_k} \ldots \beta_{j_1}$$

in **G** are in one-to-one correspondence with derivations of the form

$$X \Longrightarrow \alpha_i Z \Longrightarrow \alpha_i \beta_{j_k} Z \Longrightarrow \ldots \Longrightarrow \alpha_i \beta_{j_k} \ldots \beta_{j_1}$$

in **G**′.

Proposition 9.6 forms the basis of a procedure for converting any well-formed context-free grammar into an equivalent standard-form grammar. The description of the procedure is simplified by introducing the notion of subgrammars:

**Definition 9.8:** Let **G** be a context-free grammar, and let **M** be a subset of the nonterminal letters of **G**. The *subgrammar* **G(M)** has the set of productions

$$\{A \longrightarrow \alpha \mid A \in \mathbf{M} \text{ and } A \longrightarrow \alpha \text{ is a rule of } \mathbf{G}\}$$

Thus **G(M)** contains each rule of **G** whose left part is in **M**.

Suppose that **G** is any well-formed grammar. Let **M** be a set of nonterminals such that no element of **M** is left recursive in the subgrammar **G(M)**. Clearly, **M** cannot contain a nonterminal $A$ if there is a rule $A \longrightarrow A\alpha$ in **G**. Nevertheless, **M** may contain nonterminal letters that are left recursive in **G**.

**Example 9.12:** Let **G** be the grammar

$$\mathbf{G}\colon\ \Sigma \longrightarrow A \qquad A \longrightarrow Ba \qquad B \longrightarrow Ab$$
$$A \longrightarrow a$$

Both $A$ and $B$ are left recursive in **G**. However, $A$ is not left recursive in the subgrammar

$$\mathbf{G}(\{A\}) = \{A \longrightarrow Ba,\ A \longrightarrow a\}$$

and $B$ is not left recursive in the subgrammar

$$\mathbf{G}(\{B\}) = \{B \longrightarrow Ab\}$$

Now let **G** be a well-formed grammar containing left recursive nonterminals; we wish to put **G** into standard form. Let **G(M)** be a subgrammar of **G** in which no nonterminal letter is left recursive, and let $X$ be some nonterminal that is left recursive in **G**. Our procedure will transform **G** into an equivalent grammar **G**′ such that $\mathbf{G}'(\mathbf{M} \cup \{X\})$ has no left recursive nonterminals. By repeating this procedure for each left recursive nonterminal in **G**, we remove all left recursion from the grammar. Substitution may then be used to rewrite productions that are not in standard form.

There are two steps to the procedure for removing left recursion in $X$: in the first step, we use substitution to transform the $X$ rules of **G** so their handles are not members of **M**; in the second step, we use Proposition 9.6 to replace any left recursive $X$ rules.

*Step 1:* Consider any $X$ rule of **G** with its handle in **M**:

$$X \longrightarrow Y\beta, \qquad Y \in \mathbf{M}$$

Let the $Y$ rules of **G** be

$$Y \longrightarrow \alpha_1, \ldots, Y \longrightarrow \alpha_k$$

Using substitution, we replace the rule $X \longrightarrow Y\beta$ with the new rules

$$X \longrightarrow \alpha_1\beta, \ldots, X \longrightarrow \alpha_k\beta$$

and repeat the procedure until **G** has no $X$ rules with handles in **M**.

For each substitution made in the course of step 1, Proposition 9.1 ensures that the transformed grammar generates the same language as the original grammar. Since only $X$ rules are added to **G**, step 1 cannot introduce left recursion into the subgrammar **G**(**M**).

*Step 2:* Upon completion of step 1, the $X$ rules of **G** are

$X \longrightarrow \alpha_1, \ldots, X \longrightarrow \alpha_n$ (rules in which $X$ is not left recursive)

$X \longrightarrow X\beta_1, \ldots, X \longrightarrow X\beta_m$ (rules in which $X$ is left recursive)

in which no handle is a member of **M**. We replace these $X$ rules with the rules

$$X \longrightarrow \alpha_1, \ldots, X \longrightarrow \alpha_n$$
$$X \longrightarrow \alpha_1 Z, \ldots, X \longrightarrow \alpha_n Z$$
$$Z \longrightarrow \beta_1, \ldots, Z \longrightarrow \beta_m$$
$$Z \longrightarrow \beta_1 Z, \ldots, Z \longrightarrow \beta_m Z$$

where $Z$ is a new nonterminal letter.

Proposition 9.6 ensures that the replacement of step 2 does not change the language generated by **G**. Only $X$ rules and $Z$ rules are added, so all nonterminals in **M** remain non-left-recursive. Since $X$ and $Z$ do not appear as handles in any of the new rules, neither $X$ nor $Z$ is left recursive, thus $\mathbf{G}(\mathbf{M} \cup \{X\})$ contains no left recursive nonterminals.

When all left recursion has been removed from **G** through repeated application of steps 1 and 2, the nonterminal letters of the grammar will be $\mathbf{N} \cup \mathbf{R}$, where $\mathbf{R} = \{Z_1, \ldots, Z_p\}$ contains the nonterminal letters introduced through step 2 of the procedure. The grammar may still have rules with nonterminal letters as handles. Since no left recursion is present, these rules may be replaced with standard-form rules by finitely many substitutions. Some of the $Z$ rules introduced through step 2 may be nongenerative, because some of the strings $\beta_1, \ldots, \beta_m$ may consist of a single terminal letter. However, substituting for their handles will yield generative rules, because no element of **R** can be the handle of any $Z$ rule, and only $Z$ rules can be nongenerative.

We have shown how to convert any well-formed context-free grammar into standard form. In addition, Propositions 9.1 and 9.6 guarantee that the standard-form grammar is strongly equivalent to the given grammar unless, in substituting for a handle, we introduce a duplicate rule to the grammar. (In the latter case, we can avoid the duplication through the use of additional nonterminal symbols; the details are left to the Problems.) Thus we have the following:

**Theorem 9.4 (Standard Form Theorem):** If **G** is a context-free grammar, one can construct a grammar **G**′ in standard form such that **G** and **G**′ are strongly equivalent.

**Example 9.13:** We shall illustrate conversion into standard form using the grammar $\mathbf{G}_1$:

$$\mathbf{G}_1\colon\ \Sigma \longrightarrow A \qquad A \longrightarrow AaB \qquad B \longrightarrow BaC \qquad C \longrightarrow c$$
$$A \longrightarrow B \qquad B \longrightarrow C$$

Nonterminal letters $A$ and $B$ are left recursive in $\mathbf{G}_1$, but $C$ is not. Thus **M** initially contains the symbol $C$. We shall first remove the left recursion in $B$.

After substituting for the nonterminal handle of $B \longrightarrow C$, the grammar has the $B$ rules

$$B \longrightarrow BaC$$
$$B \longrightarrow c$$

After step 2 of the conversion procedure, the $B$ rules become

$$B \longrightarrow c$$
$$B \longrightarrow cZ$$
$$Z \longrightarrow aC$$
$$Z \longrightarrow aCZ$$

where $Z$ is a new nonterminal. The new grammar is still left recursive in $A$, but now **M** contains both $B$ and $C$. After substituting for $B$ in the rule $A \longrightarrow B$, the $A$ rules of the grammar are

$$A \longrightarrow AaB$$
$$A \longrightarrow c$$
$$A \longrightarrow cZ$$

After applying step 2, the first of these rules is replaced with the rules

$$A \longrightarrow cZ'$$

$$A \longrightarrow cZZ'$$
$$Z' \longrightarrow aB$$
$$Z' \longrightarrow aBZ'$$

where $Z'$ is a new nonterminal. The complete grammar, now in standard form, is $\mathbf{G}_2$:

$$\begin{array}{llll} \mathbf{G}_2: & \Sigma \longrightarrow A & A \longrightarrow cZZ' & B \longrightarrow cZ \\ & A \longrightarrow c & Z' \longrightarrow aB & Z \longrightarrow aC \\ & A \longrightarrow cZ & Z' \longrightarrow aBZ' & Z \longrightarrow aCZ \\ & A \longrightarrow cZ' & B \longrightarrow c & C \longrightarrow c \end{array}$$

## 9.3 Structure of Context-Free Languages

Context-free languages often contain collections of sentences in which phrases are nested in matched pairs. To illustrate, consider the production

$$A \longrightarrow \varphi A \psi$$

where $\varphi$ and $\psi$ are nonempty strings of terminal and nonterminal letters. This production permits the form of derivation shown in Figure 9.5; thus each of the sentential forms

$$\varphi^k A \psi^k, \qquad k \geq 0$$

is derivable from $A$. This property, the *self-embedding property*, is crucial: it distinguishes context-free languages from finite-state languages, and it provides a criterion by which we can show that certain languages are not context free. Three important theorems give formal expression to these facts.

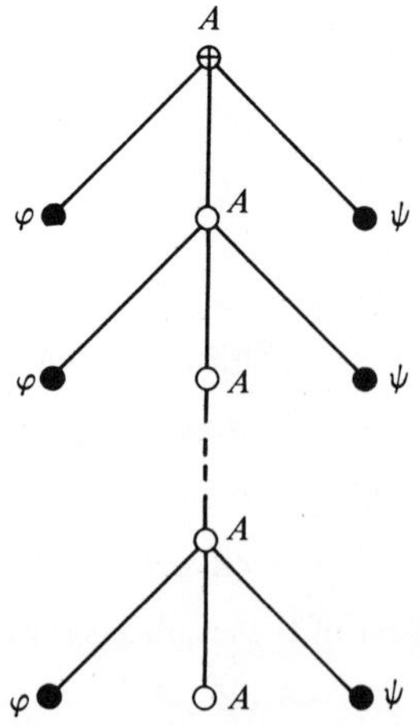


**Figure 9.5** Self-embedding derivation tree.

The *structure theorem* specifies the circumstances under which a context-free grammar generates an infinity of sentences. A corollary to the structure theorem, often called the *pumping lemma*, specifies conditions under which an infinite number of strings of a context-free language contain matched pairs of phrases. The *self-embedding theorem* specifies when the language generated by a context-free grammar is not a regular set.

### 9.3.1 Structure Theorem and the Pumping Lemma

**Theorem 9.5 (Structure Theorem):** Let $\mathbf{G} = (\mathbf{N}, \mathbf{T}, \mathbf{P}, \Sigma)$ be a well-formed context-free grammar. For any $A$ in $\mathbf{N} \cup \{\Sigma\}$, $\mathbf{L}(\mathbf{G}, A)$ is infinite if and only if $\mathbf{G}$ permits the following derivations for some nonterminal $B$:

1. $A \overset{*}{\Longrightarrow} \alpha B \beta,\ \alpha, \beta \in \mathbf{T}^*$.
2. $B \overset{*}{\Longrightarrow} \varphi B \psi,\ \varphi\psi \in \mathbf{T}^* - \boldsymbol{\lambda}$.
3. $B \overset{*}{\Longrightarrow} \sigma, \quad \sigma \in \mathbf{T}^* - \boldsymbol{\lambda}$.

(Note that $\sigma$ and at least one of $\varphi$, $\psi$ are nonempty.)

***Proof*** **(If):** Suppose that derivations 1, 2, and 3 are permitted. Then for each $k \geq 0$, the derivation

$$A \overset{*}{\Longrightarrow} \alpha B \beta \overset{*}{\Longrightarrow} \alpha\varphi B \psi\beta \overset{*}{\Longrightarrow} \alpha\varphi^k B \psi^k \beta \overset{*}{\Longrightarrow} \alpha\varphi^k \sigma \psi^k \beta$$

is permitted. Since $\varphi\psi$ is nonempty, each of these derivations gives rise to a distinct string in $\mathbf{L}(\mathbf{G}, A)$, and the language is therefore infinite.

(*Only If*): Let $n$ be the number of nonterminals of $\mathbf{G}$, and let $m$ be the length of the longest right part of any production in $\mathbf{G}$. Suppose that $\mathbf{L}(\mathbf{G}, A)$ is infinite. We claim that for a sufficiently long string $\omega$ in $\mathbf{L}(\mathbf{G}, A)$, there exists a path from the root node to some terminal node in the derivation tree for $A \overset{*}{\Longrightarrow} \omega$ on which some nonterminal $B$ is repeated (see Figure 9.6). To see this, consider the collection of nodes that can be reached from the root node of the tree by a path of length $k$ (or less). Since each right part of a production in $\mathbf{G}$ contains no more than $m$ symbols, this collection contains no more than $m^k$ nodes. Now suppose that no path in the tree contains the repetition of a nonterminal. Then each terminal symbol must be at a distance no greater than $n + 1$ from the root node (since $\mathbf{G}$ contains only $n$ nonterminals). But for any string $\omega \in \mathbf{L}(\mathbf{G}, A)$, the number of leaf nodes in the tree for $A \overset{*}{\Longrightarrow} \omega$ is equal to the length of $\omega$. Since $\mathbf{L}(\mathbf{G}, A)$ is infinite, we can choose $\omega$ such that $|\omega| > m^{n+1}$, and the tree for $A \overset{*}{\Longrightarrow} \omega$ will contain some path with repetitions of a nonterminal symbol.

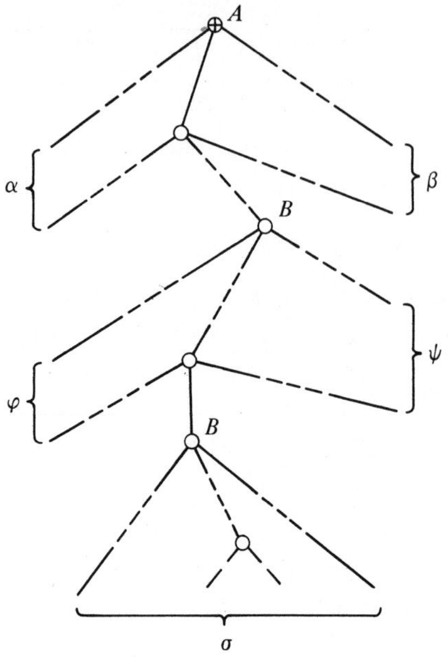


**Figure 9.6** Path with repeated nonterminal.

We have shown that, if $|\omega| > m^{n+1}$, the derivation tree for $A \overset{*}{\Longrightarrow} \omega$ has the form shown in Figure 9.6 for some nonterminal letter $B$; thus **G** permits derivations 1 to 3. The string $\sigma$ cannot be empty, because $B \overset{*}{\Longrightarrow} \lambda$ is not permitted in a context-free grammar. Also, since **G** is well formed, it cannot have $B \overset{*}{\Longrightarrow} B$, and therefore $\varphi\psi$ must be nonempty.

Theorem 9.5 provides a means for deciding whether a context-free grammar generates an infinite language.

**Theorem 9.6:** For any context-free grammar **G**, one can decide whether **L(G)** is finite or infinite.

***Proof:*** The existence of derivations of the form $B \overset{*}{\Longrightarrow} \sigma$ can be determined by the **T**-marking procedure described earlier, and the existence of derivations of the forms $\Sigma \overset{*}{\Longrightarrow} \alpha B \beta$ and $B \overset{*}{\Longrightarrow} \varphi B \psi$ can be determined by the $\Sigma$-marking procedure (with $B$ in place of $\Sigma$ in the case of the latter derivation).

The reasoning used in the second half of the proof of Theorem 9.5 can be extended to give a useful and important quantitative characterization of context-free languages. This result is called the "pumping lemma" because it asserts that, if one can find a certain string $\alpha\varphi\sigma\psi\beta$ in the language, one will find also the string $\alpha\varphi^k\sigma\psi^k\beta$ in the language for all $k \geq 0$. In other words, one can "pump" the $\varphi$–$\psi$ pairs in the string to generate arbitrarily many other strings of the language.

**Theorem 9.7 (Pumping Lemma):** If **L** is a context-free language, there exists a positive integer $p$ with the following properties: whenever $\omega$ is in **L** and $|\omega| > p$, there exist strings $\alpha$, $\varphi$, $\sigma$, $\psi$, and $\beta$, with $\varphi\psi$ and $\sigma$ nonempty and $|\varphi\sigma\psi| \leq p$, such that $\omega = \alpha\varphi\sigma\psi\beta$ and $\alpha\varphi^k\sigma\psi^k\beta$ is in **L** for all $k \geq 0$.

***Proof:*** Let **G** be a well-formed grammar that generates **L**. Suppose that **G** has $n$ nonterminals, and $m$ is the length of the longest right part of any rule. Take $p = m^{n+1}$. The proof of Theorem 9.5 shows that, if $\omega \in \mathbf{L}$ and $|\omega| > p$, then any derivation $\Sigma \stackrel{*}{\Longrightarrow} \omega$ has a tree of the form shown in Figure 9.6. Some path in this tree from $\Sigma$ to a leaf node must have at least $n + 1$ nodes labeled with nonterminals. Consider the longest such path. Tracing this path from the leaf node, one must encounter two instances of some nonterminal $B$ within $n + 1$ moves. Also, the instance of $B$ further from the leaf is at most the $(n + 1)$th node along *any* upward path from a leaf of the tree, because we are exploring the longest path containing multiple occurrences of a nonterminal. Thus the derivation $B \stackrel{*}{\Longrightarrow} \varphi\sigma\psi$ satisfies $|\varphi\sigma\psi| \leq p = m^{n+1}$. Since $\Sigma \stackrel{*}{\Longrightarrow} \alpha B\beta$, $B \stackrel{*}{\Longrightarrow} \varphi B\psi$ and $B \stackrel{*}{\Longrightarrow} \sigma$ must be permitted by **G**, and **L(G)** contains the strings $\alpha\varphi^k\sigma\psi^k\beta$ for all $k \geq 0$.

Theorem 9.7 can be used to show that certain languages are not context free.

**Example 9.14:** The language $\mathbf{L} = \{1^p | p \text{ is a prime}\}$ is not context free. To show this, we assume that **L** is context free and apply the pumping lemma. Since there are infinitely many distinct prime numbers, there is a prime number $p$ sufficiently large that

$$\alpha\varphi^k\sigma\psi^k\beta \in \mathbf{L}, \qquad \text{all } k \geq 0$$

where

$$\alpha\varphi\sigma\psi\beta = 1^p, \qquad \varphi\psi \neq \lambda, \sigma \neq \lambda$$

That is, there exist integers $a$, $b$, $c$, $d$, $e$ such that

$$1^a(1^b)^k1^c(1^d)^k1^e \in \mathbf{L}, \qquad \text{all } k \geq 0$$

where $b + d > 0$, $c > 0$, and $a + b + c + d + e = p$. Therefore,

$$(a + c + e) + (b + d)k$$

is prime for all $k \geq 0$; and if we let $x = a + c + e$ and $y = b + d$, we conclude that $x + ky$ is prime for all $k \geq 0$. Taking $k = x + y + 1$, we have

$$\begin{aligned} x + ky &= x + (x + y + 1)y \\ &= x + xy + y^2 + y \\ &= x(y + 1) + y(y + 1) \\ &= (x + y)(y + 1) \end{aligned}$$

which clearly is not prime, since both $x$ and $y$ are greater than 0 and primes cannot be factored. This contradiction shows that **L** is not context free.

**Example 9.15:** The double-matching language

$$\mathbf{L}_{dm} = \{a^n b^n c^n \mid n \geq 1\}$$

is not context free. To show this, we assume that $\mathbf{L}_{dm}$ is context free and obtain a contradiction. According to the pumping lemma, $\mathbf{L}_{dm}$ contains a string

$$\omega = \alpha\varphi\sigma\psi\beta, \qquad \varphi\psi \neq \lambda, \sigma \neq \lambda$$

such that

$$\omega_k = \alpha\varphi^k\sigma\psi^k\beta \in \mathbf{L}_{dm}, \qquad \text{all } k \geq 0$$

Each string $\omega_k$, being a member of $\mathbf{L}_{dm}$, consists of three subregions, the $a$ region, the $b$ region, and the $c$ region. The $\varphi$ portion of $\omega$ must lie entirely within one of the regions (that is, $\varphi \in \mathbf{a}^*$, $\varphi \in \mathbf{b}^*$, or $\varphi \in \mathbf{c}^*$), since otherwise $\omega_k$ would not consist of $a$'s followed by $b$'s followed by $c$'s for $k > 0$, and similarly for the $\psi$ portion.

Since at least one of $\varphi$ and $\psi$ is nonempty, the number of occurrences of at least one of the symbols $a, b, c$ in $\omega_k$ must be an increasing function of $k$. Since each $\omega_k$ is in $\mathbf{L}_{dm}$, it must therefore be the case that the number of occurrences of *each* of the three symbols in $\omega_k$ is an increasing function of $k$. But this cannot be the case unless either $\varphi$ or $\psi$ overlaps two regions of $\omega$, which we have shown is not possible. Thus $\mathbf{L}_{dm}$ is not context free.

Although $\mathbf{L}_{dm}$ is not context free, we know that $\mathbf{L}_{dm}$ is context sensitive by virtue of a grammar for the language given in Chapter 3. Therefore,

**Theorem 9.8:** The class of context-free languages is properly contained in the class of context-sensitive languages. In particular, $\mathbf{L}_{dm} = \{a^n b^n c^n \mid n \geq 1\}$ is context sensitive but not context free.

The pumping lemma is a powerful result (additional applications of the theorem are explored in the Problems), but it cannot always be used to show that a given language is not context free. For example, we have used the pumping lemma to show that one form of phrase structure is not representable in context-free grammar: structure requiring that two or more distinct phrases occur in equal numbers but in separate regions of a sentence (as typified by $\mathbf{L}_{dm}$ and illustrated by Figure 9.7). Another form of phrase structure

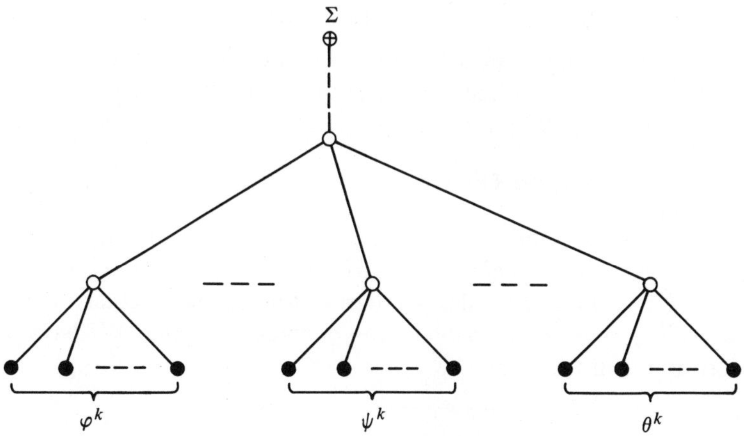


**Figure 9.7** Double-matching of phrases.

that cannot be represented in context-free grammar is that in which two or more pairs of phrase types [say ($\varphi$, $\psi$) and ($\eta$, $\xi$)] are neither separated nor nested in sentences of the language, but are required to match independently. This type of structure is illustrated by Figure 9.8, and typified by the *overlapped matching* language

$$\mathbf{L}_{om} = \{a^n b^m a^n b^m \mid m, n \geq 1\}$$

The reader may verify, however, that the pumping lemma does not provide an easy proof of the fact that $\mathbf{L}_{om}$ is not context free. A more powerful result, known as *Ogden's lemma*, can be used to establish this fact; details are left to the Problems.

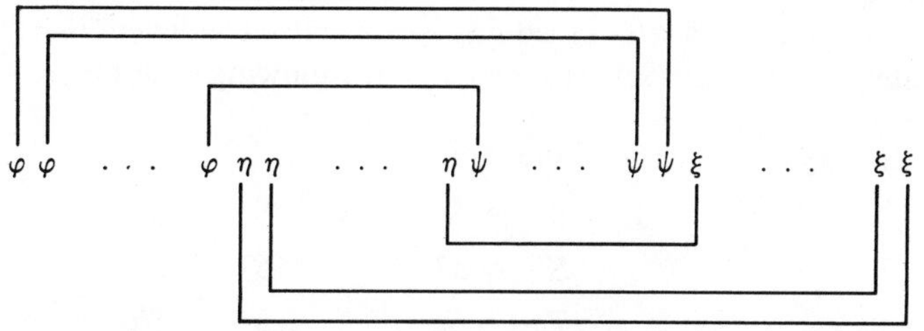


**Figure 9.8** Overlapped matches.

The closure properties of context-free languages established in Chapter 8, together with our knowledge of languages that are known to be non-context free, can be used to show that certain additional languages are non-context free. For example, the language $\{a^n b^n a^n \mid n \geq 1\}$ can be transformed into $\mathbf{L}_{dm}$ by a generalized sequential transducer, and is therefore not context free. Similarly, the language

$$\{\omega\omega \mid \omega \in (\mathbf{a} \cup \mathbf{b})^*\}$$

containing each string formed by concatenating two copies of some string in $(\mathbf{a} \cup \mathbf{b})^*$ is not context free: its intersection with the regular set $\mathbf{a}^*\mathbf{b}^*\mathbf{a}^*\mathbf{b}^*$ is the language $\{a^n b^m a^n b^m \mid m, n \geq 1\}$, which is not a context-free language.

### 9.3.2 Self-Embedding Theorem

A context-free grammar, although neither right nor left linear, may nonetheless generate a regular language. The self-embedding property of context-free grammars provides a criterion for testing whether or not the language represented by a context-free grammar is regular. We have noted that derivations of the form

$$A \Longrightarrow \varphi A \psi \Longrightarrow \ldots \Longrightarrow \varphi^k A \psi^k$$

are characteristic of context-free languages. If neither $\varphi$ nor $\psi$ is empty, such derivations are not possible in a left- or right-linear grammar. In a right-linear grammar, for example, only the rightmost symbol of a sentential form can be a nonterminal letter, and $\psi$ must be empty.

**Definition 9.9:** A context-free grammar $\mathbf{G}$ is *self-embedding* if, for some useful nonterminal letter $A$, there is a derivation

$$A \Longrightarrow \varphi A \psi$$

in $\mathbf{G}$, where both $\varphi$ and $\psi$ are nonempty terminal strings. In this case, $A$ is called an *embedding nonterminal* of $\mathbf{G}$.

If the grammar $\mathbf{G}$ is well formed, this definition can be weakened to allow nonterminal letters in the strings $\varphi$ and $\psi$, since each nonterminal in $\mathbf{G}$ must be $\mathbf{T}$ connected.

That a grammar is self-embedding is not in itself sufficient to ensure that it generates a nonregular set, as shown by the following example.

**Example 9.16:** The grammars

$$\begin{array}{llll} \mathbf{G}_1: & \Sigma \longrightarrow S & \mathbf{G}_2: & \Sigma \longrightarrow S \\ & S \longrightarrow aT & & S \longrightarrow aS \\ & T \longrightarrow Sa & & S \longrightarrow Sb \\ & S \longrightarrow aa & & S \longrightarrow ab \end{array}$$

are both embedding, as shown by the derivations

$$\mathbf{G}_1: \quad \Sigma \Longrightarrow S \Longrightarrow aT \Longrightarrow aSa$$
$$\mathbf{G}_2: \quad \Sigma \Longrightarrow S \Longrightarrow aS \Longrightarrow aSb$$

Yet the language

$$\mathbf{L}(\mathbf{G}_1) = \{a^k a^k \mid k \geq 1\} = \mathbf{aa(aa)^*}$$

is regular, as is the language

$$\mathbf{L}(\mathbf{G}_2) = \mathbf{a^*abb^*}$$

Since a self-embedding grammar does not necessarily generate a nonregular set, we can only hope to show that the absence of embedding ensures that the grammar generates a regular set. This is our immediate goal. Our approach is to provide a procedure for constructing an equivalent right-linear grammar $\mathbf{G}'$ from an arbitrary nonembedding context-free grammar $\mathbf{G}$. Since $\mathbf{G}$ may have both left and right recursive nonterminals, whereas the nonterminals of $\mathbf{G}'$ can only be right recursive, it is convenient to convert $\mathbf{G}$ to a standard-form grammar free from left recursion. We are obliged to show, however, that the conversion does not introduce embedding nonterminals.

**Proposition 9.7:** If $\mathbf{G}$ is a nonembedding context-free grammar, there is a nonembedding standard-form grammar strongly equivalent to $\mathbf{G}$.

***Proof:*** The reader may verify that the conversion of an arbitrary context-free grammar into a well-formed grammar does not introduce new embedding nonterminals. Hence we suppose that $\mathbf{G}$ is well formed. A standard-form grammar strongly equivalent to $\mathbf{G}$ is obtained by applying successive transformations of two types:

1. Substitution of right parts of rules for the handles of other rules.
2. Replacement of left recursive productions.

We must show that neither of these transformations can introduce embedding nonterminals. The demonstration for the replacement of left recursive productions is given here; the treatment of substitution is straightforward and is left to the reader.

The replacement of left recursive $X$ rules in $\mathbf{G}$ is accomplished by substituting rules of the forms

$$X \longrightarrow \alpha \qquad Z \longrightarrow \beta Z$$
$$X \longrightarrow \alpha Z \qquad Z \longrightarrow \beta$$

for rules of the forms

$$X \longrightarrow \alpha \qquad X \longrightarrow X\beta$$

where $Z$ is a new nonterminal letter. We must show that neither $X$ nor $Z$ is self-embedding in the resulting grammar $\mathbf{G}'$.

First we show that no derivation of the form

$$\beta \overset{*}{\Longrightarrow} \eta X \xi$$

is permitted by $\mathbf{G}$ or $\mathbf{G}'$. If a derivation $\beta \overset{*}{\Longrightarrow} \eta X \xi$ were permitted by $\mathbf{G}$, then the derivation

$$X \Longrightarrow X\beta \overset{*}{\Longrightarrow} X\eta X\xi \Longrightarrow X\eta X\beta\xi$$

would also be permitted, contradicting the premise that $X$ is nonembedding in $\mathbf{G}$. Now suppose that a derivation $\beta \overset{*}{\Longrightarrow} \eta X \xi$ is permitted by $\mathbf{G}'$. Since $\beta$ does not contain $Z$, the use of some $X$ rule in the derivation must precede the use of any $Z$ rule; thus $\mathbf{G}'$ must permit a derivation

$$\beta \overset{*}{\Longrightarrow} \eta' X \xi'$$

in which no $Z$ rule is used. But then this derivation is also permitted by $\mathbf{G}$, again contradicting the premise that $X$ is nonembedding in $\mathbf{G}$. An analogous argument can be used to show that no derivation of the form

$$\alpha \overset{*}{\Longrightarrow} \eta X \xi, \qquad \eta \neq \lambda$$

is permitted by either $\mathbf{G}$ or $\mathbf{G}'$.

Now, if $Z$ is an embedding nonterminal in $\mathbf{G}'$, then $\mathbf{G}'$ must permit a derivation

$$Z \overset{*}{\Longrightarrow} \varphi Z \psi$$

The embedded occurrence of $Z$ cannot be generated without the use of a rule $X \longrightarrow \alpha Z$; thus the above derivation must include the subderivation $\beta \overset{*}{\Longrightarrow} \eta X \xi$, which we have shown is not possible. We conclude that $Z$ is nonembedding in $\mathbf{G}'$.

Suppose that $X$ is embedding in $\mathbf{G}'$. Then one of the derivations

1. $X \Longrightarrow \alpha \overset{*}{\Longrightarrow} \varphi X \psi$
2. $X \Longrightarrow \alpha Z \overset{*}{\Longrightarrow} \varphi X \psi Z$
3. $X \Longrightarrow \alpha Z \overset{*}{\Longrightarrow} \alpha \varphi X \psi$

must be permitted by $\mathbf{G}'$. The third derivation implies $Z \overset{*}{\Longrightarrow} \varphi X \psi$ is permitted by $\mathbf{G}'$, but this necessarily includes the subderivation $\beta \overset{*}{\Longrightarrow} \eta X \xi$, which is impossible. Similarly, the first two derivations each include $\alpha \overset{*}{\Longrightarrow} \varphi X \xi$ with $\varphi \neq \lambda$, which is also impossible. Hence $X$ cannot be embedding in $\mathbf{G}'$.

In a standard-form grammar, each step in a leftmost derivation has the form

$$\varphi A \psi \Longrightarrow \varphi a \beta \psi$$

where $\varphi$ is a string of terminal letters and $A \longrightarrow a\beta$ is a production of the grammar. Since $\beta$, unless it is empty, always contains the leftmost nonterminal letter of the new sentential form, each step rewrites the first nonterminal introduced by the preceding step. If the grammar is nonembedding, we can show that only a finite number of distinct strings $\beta\psi$ may appear in a sentential form $\varphi a \beta \psi$. On the basis of this observation, we can construct a strongly equivalent right-linear grammar, and conclude that the language is regular.

**Proposition 9.8:** If a context-free grammar **G** is nonembedding and in standard form, one can construct a strongly equivalent right-linear grammar **G**′.

***Proof:*** Suppose that $A \longrightarrow a\beta$ is a production of **G** in which terminal letters appear in $\beta$. We may replace each appearance of a terminal letter $x$ in $\beta$ with the new nonterminal $[x]$, and add the rule $[x] \longrightarrow x$ to **G**. The resulting grammar is strongly equivalent to the given grammar, and is embedding if and only if the given grammar is. Thus there is no loss of generality in assuming that **G** has rules of the form

$$\left.\begin{aligned} \Sigma &\longrightarrow A \\ A &\longrightarrow a\beta \end{aligned}\right\} \qquad A \in \mathbf{N},\ a \in \mathbf{T},\ \beta \in \mathbf{N}^*$$

Let $n$ be the number of nonterminal symbols in **G**, and let $m$ be the length of the longest string of nonterminals in the right part of any production ($m$ is the maximum of $|\beta|$ over all rules $A \longrightarrow a\beta$ of **G**). Now consider any leftmost derivation in **G**

$$\begin{aligned} \Sigma &\Longrightarrow a_1 A_1 \psi_1 \\ &\Longrightarrow a_1 a_2 A_2 \psi_2 \\ &\quad\vdots \\ &\Longrightarrow a_1 a_2 \ldots a_r A_r \psi_r \end{aligned}$$

where the production applied in the $i$th step is

$$A_{i-1} \longrightarrow a_i\theta_i, \qquad A_0 = \Sigma,\ \theta_i \in \mathbf{N}^*,\ |\theta_i| \leq m,\ 1 \leq i \leq r$$

Note that some of the $\theta_i$ may be empty. We have

(1) $$\begin{aligned} |A_r\psi_r| &= 1 + (|\theta_1| - 1) + (|\theta_2| - 1) \\ &\quad + \cdots + (|\theta_r| - 1) \leq 1 + r(m-1) \end{aligned}$$

because each application of a production can replace a nonterminal letter with at most $m$ nonterminals. We claim that if **G** is nonembedding, $|A_r\psi_r| \leq mn$. Suppose otherwise; that is, suppose that $|A_r\psi_r| > mn$. From (1) we see that $r > n$, and at least $n$ steps in the derivation $\Sigma \stackrel{*}{\Longrightarrow} a_1 \ldots a_r A_r \psi_r$ must have $|\theta_i| > 1$. Since **G** has only $n$ nonterminals, at least two of these steps must replace the same nonterminal. Suppose that $A_i = A_j$ for $i < j$, where $|\theta_{i+1}| > 1$. Then the derivation $\Sigma \stackrel{*}{\Longrightarrow} a_1 \ldots a_r A_r \psi_r$ includes the steps

$$A_i \Longrightarrow a_{i+1}A_{i+1}\varphi_{i+1} \stackrel{*}{\Longrightarrow} a_{i+1} \ldots a_j A_j \varphi_j$$

where $A_{i+1}\varphi_{i+1} = \theta_{i+1}$. This shows that the nonterminal $A_i = A_j$ must be embedding in **G**, contradicting our premise.

We have shown that in every leftmost derivation

$$\Sigma \stackrel{*}{\Longrightarrow} \alpha A \psi, \qquad \alpha \in \mathbf{T}^*$$

permitted by a nonembedding grammar **G**, $|A\psi| \leq mn$. We define a new grammar **G**′ with nonterminals $[A\psi]$, and rules chosen so that $\Sigma \stackrel{*}{\Longrightarrow} \alpha[A\psi]$ if and only if **G** has $\Sigma \stackrel{*}{\Longrightarrow} \alpha A\psi$. The nonterminals of **G**′ are

$$\mathbf{N}' = \{[A\psi] \mid \Sigma \stackrel{*}{\Longrightarrow} \alpha A\psi \text{ in } \mathbf{G}, \text{ where } \alpha \in \mathbf{T}^*, A \in \mathbf{N}, \psi \in \mathbf{N}^*\}$$

The productions of **G**′ are

1. If **G** has $\Sigma \longrightarrow A$, **G**′ has $\Sigma \longrightarrow [A]$.
2. If **G** has $A \longrightarrow a$, **G**′ has $[A\psi] \longrightarrow a[\psi]$ for each $[A\psi]$ in **N**′.
3. If **G** has $A \longrightarrow a\beta$, **G**′ has $[A\psi] \longrightarrow a[\beta\psi]$ for each $[A\psi]$ in **N**′.

This construction is designed so that derivations of the form

$$\Sigma \Longrightarrow a_1A_1\psi_1 \Longrightarrow a_1a_2A_2\psi_2 \Longrightarrow \ldots \Longrightarrow a_1a_2 \ldots a_rA_r\psi_r$$

permitted by **G** are in one-to-one correspondence with derivations of the form

$$\Sigma \Longrightarrow a_1[A_1\psi_1] \Longrightarrow a_1a_2[A_2\psi_2] \Longrightarrow \ldots \Longrightarrow a_1a_2 \ldots a_r[A_r\psi_r]$$

permitted by **G**′. Thus **G**′ is equivalent to **G**; and since **G**′ is a right-linear grammar, **L(G)** = **L(G′)** is a regular set.

By Proposition 9.8, every nonembedding grammar generates a regular set, and a language having at least one nonembedding grammar is regular. Conversely, every regular set has a (nonembedding) right-linear grammar. We therefore have the following important result:

**Theorem 9.9 (Self-embedding Theorem):** A context-free language is nonregular if and only if every grammar generating the language is self-embedding.

## Notes and References

Early work on context-free grammars and languages appears in Chomsky [1956], Chomsky [1959], and Bar-Hillel, Perles, and Shamir [1961]. The latter work contains many of the results of this chapter, including Theorem 9.1 (emptiness test), Theorem 9.5 (structure theorem), and Theorem 9.7 (pumping lemma). Theorem 9.9 (self-embedding theorem) is from Chomsky [1959].

The normal-form grammars of Section 9.2.1 were proposed by Chomsky [1959], and the standard-form grammars of Section 9.2.2 were described by Greibach [1965]. A simple proof of Theorem 9.4 (standard-form theorem) appears in Rosenkrantz [1967].

Most of the results of this chapter, as well as many results concerning context-free languages that do not appear in this text, are discussed in Ginsburg [1966]; this work treats in detail the theory of context-free languages.

## Problems

9.1. Let **G** be the context-free grammar with productions

$$\begin{array}{ll} \Sigma \longrightarrow A & B \longrightarrow ByE \\ A \longrightarrow xBA & B \longrightarrow Cx \\ A \longrightarrow yB & B \longrightarrow CE \\ A \longrightarrow B & C \longrightarrow Dy \\ A \longrightarrow Ey & D \longrightarrow xCx \\ B \longrightarrow E & E \longrightarrow x \end{array}$$

Identify and remove the useless productions of **G** to obtain a strongly equivalent grammar in which all productions are useful.

**9.2.** Let **G** be a context-free grammar. Suppose that we apply the Σ-marking and **T**-marking procedures to **G** in an order reversed from that described in Section 9.1; that is, we first eliminate the productions that are not Σ connected, and then eliminate those containing nonterminals that are not **T** connected. Give an example of a grammar from which this method does not eliminate all useless productions.

9.3. Let **G** be the grammar of Problem 9.1. Construct from **G** a strongly equivalent grammar containing no nongenerative productions.

**9.4.** Let **G** be a context-free grammar, and suppose that all the productions of **G** are useful. Let **G**′ be the strongly equivalent grammar without nongenerative productions constructed from **G** according to the procedure outlined in Section 9.1.4. Show that all the productions of **G**′ must be useful.

**9.5.** Prove Proposition 9.5.

***9.6.** Let **G** be a context-free grammar with $n$ productions, and let **G**′ be an equivalent grammar without nongenerative productions constructed from **G** according to the procedure outlined in Section 9.1.4. In terms of $n$, place a reasonable bound on the maximum number of productions in grammar **G**′. (*Hint:* **G** contains no more than $n - 1$ useful nonterminals. How many may **G**′ contain?)

9.7. Let **G** be the grammar with productions

$$\begin{array}{lll} \Sigma \longrightarrow 0A & B \longrightarrow A & F \longrightarrow AF \\ \Sigma \longrightarrow 1B & B \longrightarrow C & F \longrightarrow 0D \\ A \longrightarrow C & B \longrightarrow 0 & D \longrightarrow 1D \\ A \longrightarrow D0 & C \longrightarrow EB & D \longrightarrow F \\ A \longrightarrow E0F & E \longrightarrow 1 & \end{array}$$

Construct from **G** a strongly equivalent, well-formed grammar.

**9.8.** Let **G** be an arbitrary context-free grammar. Describe an effective procedure for deciding, for any pair of sentential forms $\alpha$, $\beta$, whether or not **G** permits a derivation of $\beta$ starting from $\alpha$. Conclude that, if **G** has terminal symbols **T**, it is always possible to decide whether a given word $\omega \in \mathbf{T}^*$ is generated by **G**.

9.9. Construct a normal-form grammar strongly equivalent to the grammar **G** of Problem 9.1.

9.10. Construct a normal-form grammar strongly equivalent to the grammar **G** of Problem 9.7.

**9.11.** Suppose that **G** is a normal-form grammar and that $\omega$ is a length $n$ string in **L(G)**. How many steps may there be in a derivation of $\omega$ according to **G**?

9.12. Let **G** be the grammar with productions

$$\begin{array}{l} \Sigma \longrightarrow 0 \\ \Sigma \longrightarrow A1 \\ A \longrightarrow A1 \\ A \longrightarrow xAcAx \\ A \longrightarrow 0 \end{array}$$

Construct from **G** a strongly equivalent grammar in standard form.

9.13. Let **G** be the grammar with productions

$$\begin{array}{ll} \Sigma \longrightarrow A & C \longrightarrow AB \\ A \longrightarrow BC & C \longrightarrow 0 \\ B \longrightarrow CA & C \longrightarrow 1 \\ B \longrightarrow C & \end{array}$$

Construct from **G** a strongly equivalent grammar in standard form.

**9.14.** In constructing a strongly equivalent standard-form grammar from a well-formed context-free grammar as outlined in Section 9.2.2, why is step 1 essential to the procedure?

***9.15.** If we follow the procedure outlined in Section 9.2.2, we can construct from any context-free grammar **G** an equivalent standard-form grammar **G**′. Moreover, if no rule introduced through substitution during the procedure is already a rule in **G**, the grammar **G**′ is strongly equivalent to **G**. Prove that Theorem 9.4 is valid even if some substitution made during the procedure introduces a duplicate production. In particular, describe how additional productions involving new nonterminal symbols may be used in the event of such duplication to ensure strong equivalence of **G** and **G**′. (*Hint:* Any duplicate production introduced during the procedure must result from the substitution of a production $Y \longrightarrow \alpha$ into a production of the form $X \longrightarrow Y\beta$, where $\beta$ is a nonempty string. If the resultant production $X \longrightarrow \alpha\beta$ is already in the grammar, we may preserve strong equivalence by adding the productions

$$X \longrightarrow W\beta$$
$$W \longrightarrow \alpha$$

where $W$ is a new nonterminal. Show that while this procedure introduces new nonterminals to the grammar, only finitely many such nonterminals are introduced in constructing **G**′.)

9.16. Show that every context-free language can be generated by a context-free grammar in which each production is of one of the forms

$$\Sigma \longrightarrow \lambda \qquad \Sigma \longrightarrow A \qquad A \longrightarrow xB \qquad A \longrightarrow xBC \qquad \begin{cases} A, B, C \in \mathbf{N} \\ x \in \mathbf{T} \end{cases}$$

9.17. Show that every context-free language can be generated by a context-free grammar in which each production is of one of the forms

$$\Sigma \longrightarrow \lambda \qquad \Sigma \longrightarrow A \qquad A \longrightarrow \gamma x \qquad \begin{cases} A \in \mathbf{N} \\ x \in \mathbf{T} \\ \gamma \in \mathbf{N}^* \end{cases}$$

*9.18. Prove or disprove that every context-free language can be generated by a context-free grammar in which each production is of one of the forms

$$\Sigma \longrightarrow \lambda \qquad \Sigma \longrightarrow A \qquad A \longrightarrow \varphi B \gamma \qquad \begin{cases} A, B \in \mathbf{N} \\ \varphi, \gamma \in \mathbf{T}^* \end{cases}$$

**9.19.** Let **G** be a grammar containing productions of the form $\Sigma \longrightarrow A$ or $A \longrightarrow \gamma$, where $A$ is a nonterminal and $\gamma$ is a (possibly) empty string of terminals and nonterminals. Describe how to construct from **G** a context-free grammar **G**′ such that **L(G)** = **L(G′)**. Is it possible, in general, to construct a context-free grammar strongly equivalent to **G**?

9.20. Using the pumping lemma, prove that the language

$$\mathbf{L} = \{a^{n^2} \mid n > 0\}$$

is not context free.

9.21. Using the pumping lemma, prove that the language

$$\mathbf{L} = \{a^n c\omega \mid \omega \in \{0, 1\}^* \text{ is the binary representation of } n > 0\}$$

is not context free.

9.22. Which of the following languages are context free? Justify your answers.

a. $\mathbf{L}_1 = \{\alpha x \beta \mid \alpha = \beta,\ \alpha \in \{0, 1\}^*,\ \beta \in \{0, 1\}^*\}$.
b. $\mathbf{L}_2 = \{\alpha x \beta \mid \alpha \neq \beta,\ \alpha \in \{0, 1\}^*,\ \beta \in \{0, 1\}^*\}$.
c. $\mathbf{L}_3 = \{1^n \mid n \text{ not prime}\}$.
*d. $\mathbf{L}_4 = \{a^n x a^m \mid m = [\log_2 n],\ n > 0\}$.
(For any real number $r$, $[r]$ denotes the largest integer less than or equal to $r$.)

***9.23.** Prove that each context-free language over a unary alphabet is regular. (*Hint:* If the language is finite, it is regular. If it is infinite, each string of sufficient length can be used to "pump" an ultimately periodic set. Consider the possible periods of such sets.)

9.24. Prove that the language

$$\mathbf{L} = \{a^n b^n c^m \mid n \geq 0,\ m > n\}$$

is not context free. Note that the pumping lemma does not provide an easy proof of this result, but that closure properties do.

**9.25.** The following result is due to W. Ogden [1968]:
*Theorem* (Ogden's lemma): Let **G** be any context-free grammar. Then there exists a constant $k \geq 1$ such that if $\omega \in \mathbf{L(G)}$ with $|\omega| \geq k$, and if the symbols appearing at any $k$ or more distinct positions of $\omega$ are designated as "distinguished," then $\omega$ can be written as $\alpha\varphi\sigma\psi\beta$ such that

1. $\sigma$ contains at least one distinguished symbol.
2. Either $\alpha$ and $\varphi$ both contain distinguished symbols, or $\psi$ and $\beta$ both contain distinguished symbols.
3. The string $\varphi\sigma\psi$ contains at most $k$ distinguished symbols.

4. For some nonterminal symbol $A$, **G** permits the derivation

$$\Sigma \Longrightarrow \alpha A \beta \Longrightarrow \alpha\varphi A \psi \beta \stackrel{*}{\Longrightarrow} \alpha\varphi^i A \psi^i \beta \Longrightarrow \alpha\varphi^i \sigma \psi^i \beta$$

for each $i \geq 0$.

a. Show that the pumping lemma is a corollary to Ogden's lemma. Describe how the proof of the pumping lemma must be changed to provide a proof of Ogden's lemma.

b. Use Ogden's lemma to show that the language

$$\mathbf{L}_{om} = \{a^n b^m a^n b^m \mid n, m \geq 0\}$$

is not context free.

Ogden's lemma is a useful result for proving the existence of inherently ambiguous context-free languages (that is, languages which are generated by no unambiguous context-free grammar). The reader is referred to Aho and Ullman [1972] for details.

9.26. Which of the following grammars are self-embedding? For each grammar that is not self-embedding, find a regular grammar generating the same language.

| a. | b. | c. |
|---|---|---|
| $\Sigma \longrightarrow A$ | $\Sigma \longrightarrow A$ | $\Sigma \longrightarrow A$ |
| $A \longrightarrow 0BC1$ | $A \longrightarrow BC$ | $A \longrightarrow 1BC0$ |
| $A \longrightarrow 1$ | $B \longrightarrow A0$ | $B \longrightarrow C0$ |
| $C \longrightarrow 0BA$ | $C \longrightarrow 1A$ | $C \longrightarrow 0CD1$ |
| $B \longrightarrow AC$ | $A \longrightarrow 0$ | $D \longrightarrow 0D0$ |
| $B \longrightarrow 01$ | | $D \longrightarrow 0E$ |
| | | $E \longrightarrow 1CD$ |
| | | $C \longrightarrow 00$ |

**9.27.** Complete the proof of Proposition 9.7 by showing the following:

a. If **G** is a nonembedding context-free grammar and **G**′ is the well-formed grammar constructed from **G** as described in Section 9.1, **G**′ is nonembedding.

b. If **G** is a well-formed context-free grammar, no substitution performed in step 1 of the procedure for constructing a standard-form grammar from **G** (Section 9.2.2) can introduce embedding nonterminals.

# 10

# *Syntax Analysis*

The essence of syntax analysis, or *parsing*, is constructing a derivation of a sentence according to the rules of a specified grammar. A *syntax analyzer*, or *parser*, is a device or procedure for performing syntax analysis. We have seen how to construct a pushdown accepter that is a syntax analyzer for any given context-free grammar, the sentential forms of a derivation being determined by the successive configurations of an accepting move sequence. However, the direct simulation of a nondeterministic accepter by a computer program, although possible, is usually an inefficient method of syntax analysis. For example, certain grammatical constructions will lead a pushdown analyzer to waste effort exploring paths that cannot be part of a successful parse of a sentence. In practice, it is desirable to transform a given grammar into an equivalent form better suited to efficient syntax analysis, or to use an analysis procedure that recognizes unproductive paths and avoids them.

There are two basic approaches to building the structural description of a sentence $\omega$ according to a context-free grammar. *Top-down analysis* employs a series of *expansion* steps, each of which replaces a nonterminal of a current sentential form with the right part of a production; the analysis starts from $\Sigma$ and works toward the goal $\omega$. *Bottom-up analysis* employs a series of *reduction* steps, each of which replaces a substring of a current sentential form with the left part of a production having that substring as its right part; this type of analysis starts from $\omega$ and works toward the goal $\Sigma$. We introduce each approach by considering *parallel-form* algorithms that explore all possible sequences of derivation steps simultaneously. We then show how to construct *sequential* algorithms for the analyses that explore possible derivations one at a time until a successful derivation has been found or all possibilities have been exhausted. The sequential algorithms employ a technique called *backtracking*: each point at which a choice among alternatives has been made is flagged so that remaining alternatives can be explored later if the choices do not lead to a successful derivation.

*Deterministic analyzers* are sequential parsing algorithms in which backtracking is never used. We study two important methods of deterministic syntax analysis, *precedence analysis* and *left-to-right analysis*, and establish the classes of grammars to which they may be applied.

## 10.1 Top-Down Analysis

Parallel syntax analysis is conveniently discussed in terms of a chart containing lists of sentential forms. For top-down analysis, illustrated in Figure 10.1, column 0 contains only the starting sentential form $\Sigma$. Sentential form $\beta$ is placed in column $i$ of the chart whenever there is a sentential form $\alpha$ in column $i - 1$ such that $\beta$ is derived from $\alpha$ by applying one production of the grammar. Thus column $i$ will contain the sentential forms derivable from $\Sigma$ in exactly $i$ steps.

*Top-down analysis:* Given a context-free grammar **G**, and a string $\omega \in \mathbf{T}^*$, construct a chart with columns numbered $0, 1, \ldots, i, \ldots$, according to the following rules:

1. Enter $\Sigma$ in column 0. Let $i = 1$.
2. Place the sentential form $\varphi\alpha\psi$ in column $i$ whenever $\varphi A \psi$ appears in column $i - 1$ and $A \longrightarrow \alpha$ is a production of **G**.
3. If the goal $\omega$ does not appear in column $i$, let $i = i + 1$ and repeat step 2.
4. If $\omega$ appears in column $i$, then any sequence of sentential forms in columns $0, \ldots, i$ through which the goal is reached constitutes an $i$-step derivation of $\omega$.

As stated above, the top-down procedure will enter in column $i$ of the chart every sentential form generable by **G** in $i$ steps. Since the number of derivable forms usually proliferates rapidly as the lengths of derivations increase, this procedure is impractical unless some means can be found to limit the number of sentential forms generated. For this purpose three conditions may be imposed on a sentential form $\varphi\alpha\psi$ entered in the chart by step 2 of the procedure:

1. In the sentential form $\varphi\alpha\psi$, the string $\varphi$ must consist of terminal letters only.

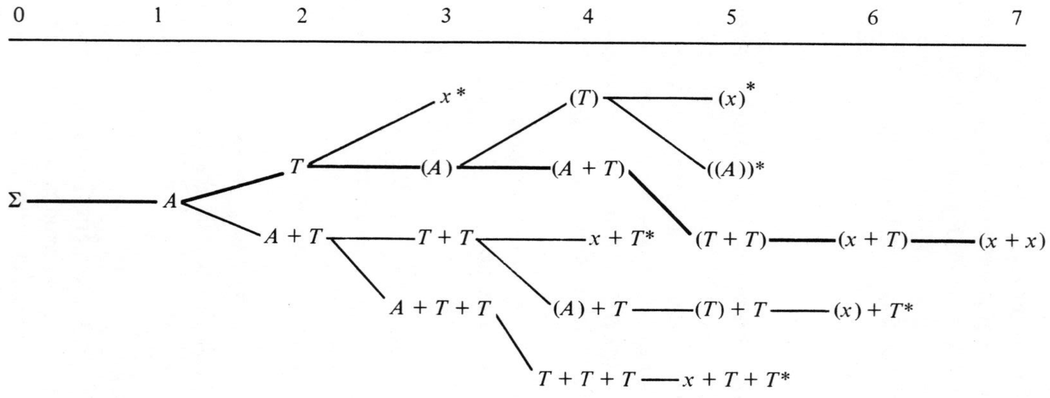


G: $\Sigma \to A$ $\quad A \to T$ $\quad T \to x$

$\quad A \to A + T$ $\quad T \to (A)$

**Figure 10.1** Top-down syntax analysis.

2. In the sentential form $\varphi\alpha\psi$, the string $\varphi$ must match a prefix of the sentence $\omega$.
3. The sentential form $\varphi\alpha\psi$ must not be longer than the sentence $\omega$.

Condition 1 limits sentential forms in column $i$ of the chart to those having $i$-step leftmost derivations in **G**. Unless the grammar is ambiguous, this condition ensures that each sentential form in column $i$ has a unique $i$-step derivation consisting of one entry from each column to its left in the chart. Condition 2 is stronger, removing from further consideration certain sentential forms from which the goal $\omega$ obviously cannot be reached. Condition 3 rules out sentential forms longer than the sentence $\omega$, since these cannot appear in any derivation of $\omega$.

A top-down analysis of the sentence $(x + x)$ is shown in Figure 10.1 for the grammar

$$\mathbf{G}:\quad \Sigma \longrightarrow A \qquad T \longrightarrow x$$
$$A \longrightarrow T \qquad T \longrightarrow (A)$$
$$A \longrightarrow A + T$$

which is a portion of the grammar for arithmetic expressions discussed in Chapter 3. The conditions above have been used to limit the proliferation of intermediate sentential forms in the figure. The points at which these conditions have been enforced are indicated by the starred sentential forms. The sequences of sentential forms that are leftmost derivations according to **G** are indicated in the chart, the darkened path being the leftmost derivation of $(x + x)$.

The top-down procedure enters in column $k$ of the chart each sentential form that has a $k$-step, leftmost derivation from $\Sigma$. Thus the analysis of each string $\omega$ in **L(G)** will terminate in a finite number of steps. Now suppose that a cyclic derivation is possible in **G**:

$$\Sigma \stackrel{*}{\Longrightarrow} \varphi A\psi \stackrel{*}{\Longrightarrow} \varphi A\psi$$

Should the top-down analyzer be presented with a sentence not in **L(G)** it may loop, since the cyclic derivation will cause a sentential form $\varphi A\psi$ to appear repeatedly in the chart, and none of conditions 1 to 3 can prevent this. Moreover, if a left recursive production

$$A \longrightarrow A\psi$$

is employed in the analysis of a sentence, the sequence of sentential forms containing the phrases

$$A,\ A\psi,\ A\psi\psi,\ \ldots,\ A\psi^k,\ \ldots$$

will be entered in successive columns of the chart, even though none may correspond to the phrase structure of the sentence. The sequence terminates only when the sentential forms become longer than the sentence, violating condition 3. (This problem does not arise with a right recursive production

$$A \longrightarrow \varphi A$$

when condition 2 is honored, because each instance of the phrase $\varphi$ must be expanded into a terminal string that matches the sentence before the right recursive production can be applied again.) Fortunately, the difficulties caused by cyclic nonterminals and left recursion in a grammar can be eliminated through transformation of the grammar by the methods developed in Chapter 9.

The syntactic analysis of a sentence is a fundamentally nondeterministic computation: at each derivation step, several productions of a grammar may be used to continue a particular leftmost or rightmost derivation. The parallel-form analyzer just described enumerates all possible derivations concurrently; a sequential procedure for top-down analysis pursues each alternative until it is either successful in reaching its goal or is found to fail. During forward operation, the analyzer marks where alternative choices of the next derivation step existed so that it can start at these points in subsequent forward operation. Should a path fail to reach the goal, the analyzer *backtracks* to take up the most recently discovered alternative not already followed; the analyzer rejects the given sentence only after all alternatives have been followed without success. An analyzer operating in this way is called a *backtracking* syntax analyzer.

Backtracking syntax analyzers are nearly always preferred to parallel analyzers for two reasons: (1) most contemporary computers are not organized to carry out highly parallel algorithms efficiently, and (2) the sentences analyzed (computer programs, for example) are typically long strings of symbols, and it is not usually practical to make an entire sentence directly assessible to the analyzer at once. A method of processing a sentence sequentially from left to right, forming as much as possible of its structural description after each new letter is examined, is thus very attractive.

Left-to-right processing of a sentence by top-down analysis requires that the leftmost nonterminal letter in a sentential form be the first nonterminal expanded by the analyzer. We shall consider the design of a top-down backtracking analyzer that honors conditions 1 and 2 and searches for leftmost derivations of an input sentence. We shall not require the analyzer to test condition 3, however, because it is often not practical for a left-to-right analyzer to know the length of the sentence being parsed.

Let **G** be a context-free grammar in which the productions are numbered 1, 2, . . . , $r$. Figure 10.2 defines a backtracking analyzer for sentences in **L(G)**. As successive sentential forms are generated, they are appended to a list that is very similar to the storage tape of a pushdown automaton. An entry is appended to the list by an operation called **push**; the most recent entry in the list is obtained by an operation called **pop**. Because items are added or removed from only one end of the list, this programming storage

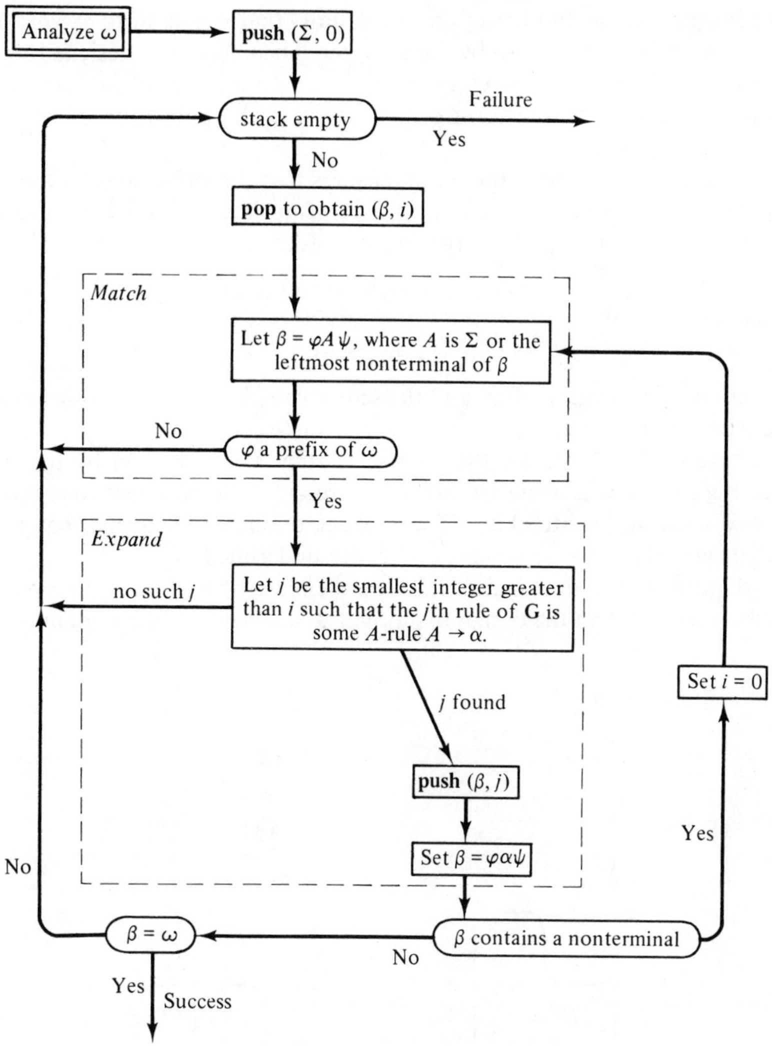


**Figure 10.2** Backtracking top-down parser.

structure is known as a *stack*; the last item appended is the *top* entry of the stack.

In Figure 10.2, each stack entry is a pair

$$(\varphi A\psi, i) \qquad \text{where} \begin{cases} 0 \leq i \leq r \\ A \in \mathbf{N} \cup \{\Sigma\} \\ \varphi \in \mathbf{T}^* \\ \psi \in (\mathbf{N} \cup \mathbf{T})^* \end{cases}$$

The integer $i$ is the number of the $A$ rule in **G** that was used to expand $\varphi A \psi$ in the most recent trial step by the analyzer. The analyzer is designed so that occurrence of the pair $(\varphi A \psi, i)$ in the stack means that all uninvestigated paths from the sentential form $\varphi A \psi$ continue with application of an $A$ rule numbered $j, j > i$.

The *match* routine in the parser ensures that the string $\varphi$ of each sentential form entered in the stack is a prefix of $\omega$. If the algorithm terminates successfully, and the stack entries in their order of generation are

$$(\Sigma, i_0), (\omega_1, i_1), \ldots, (\omega_k, i_k)$$

where $\omega_k = \omega$, then

$$\Sigma \Longrightarrow \omega_1 \Longrightarrow \omega_2 \Longrightarrow \ldots \Longrightarrow \omega_k$$

is a leftmost derivation of $\omega$, and the sequence $i_0, i_1, \ldots, i_{k-1}$ designates the sequence of rules used.

Figure 10.3 illustrates the analysis of the string $(x + x)$ by the backtracking analyzer. Downward arrows represent forward operation; upward arrows indicate backtracking. The prefixes of sentential forms that match initial symbols of the sentence $(x + x)$ are underlined.

Figure 10.2 is intended to illustrate the ideas of backtracking top-down analysis, rather than the design of a practical analyzer. If one were interested

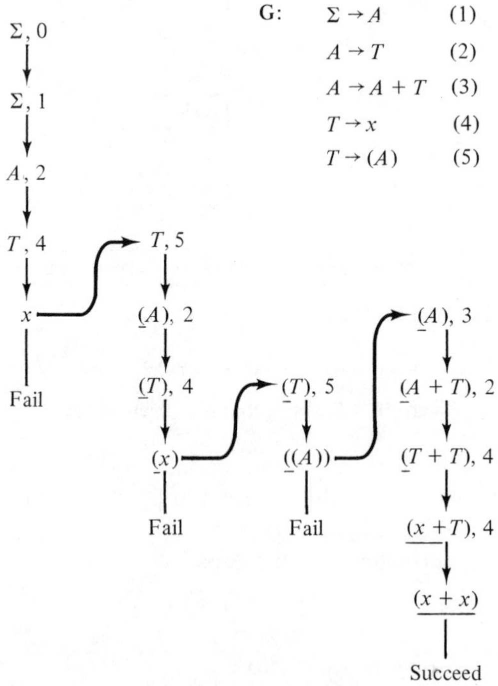


**Figure 10.3** Top-down analysis.

in implementing such an analyzer, many improvements to its design could be suggested. For example, rather than comparing the entire string $\varphi$ against $\omega$ in each match step, the parser need only match the portion of $\varphi$ introduced during the last expansion step, since the rest has been matched in previous match steps. This can be done by adding a component to each stack element that acts as an input pointer, indicating where in $\omega$ the matching of new symbols should begin. We leave the details to the reader.

If the parser for a grammar **G** terminates in its analysis of some input string $\omega$, the input will have been classified as in **L(G)** or not. However, if **G** contains left recursive nonterminals, the analysis of a string may never terminate, since no limit on the length of sentential forms has been implemented. Even if such a limit were implemented, the analysis might still fail for strings generated by grammars containing cyclic nonterminals. This problem may be overcome by converting a given grammar into a grammar in standard form (Chapter 9). A nonlooping backtracking analyzer can therefore be designed from any context-free grammar. However, the efficiency of such an analyzer is highly dependent on the given grammar, and in particular on the order in which the productions of the grammar are numbered.

## 10.2 Bottom-Up Analysis

In parallel bottom-up analysis, the sentence to be analyzed is entered in column 0 of a chart. A sentential form $\alpha$ is placed in column $i$ of the chart just if there is a sentential form $\beta$ in column $i - 1$ such that $\beta$ is derived from $\alpha$ through one application of a production of the grammar. Thus column $i$ of the chart will contain the sentential forms from which $\omega$ may be derived by exactly $i$ steps.

*Bottom-up analysis:* Given a context-free grammar **G**, and a string $\omega \in \mathbf{T}^*$, construct a chart with columns numbered $0, 1, \ldots, i, \ldots$, according to the following rules:

1. Enter $\omega$ in column 0. Let $i = 1$.
2. Place the sentential form $\varphi A \psi$ in column $i$ whenever $\varphi\alpha\psi$ appears in column $i - 1$ and $A \longrightarrow \alpha$ is a production of **G**.
3. If the goal $\Sigma$ does not appear in column $i$, let $i = i + 1$ and repeat step 2.
4. If $\Sigma$ appears in column $i$, then any sequence of sentential forms in columns $i, i - 1, \ldots, 0$ through which the goal is reached constitutes an $i$-step derivation of $\omega$.

Figure 10.4 shows the bottom-up analysis of the sentence $(x + x)$ according to the same grammar given earlier. All possible sentential forms from which $(x + x)$ may be derived appear in the chart. Because sentential forms

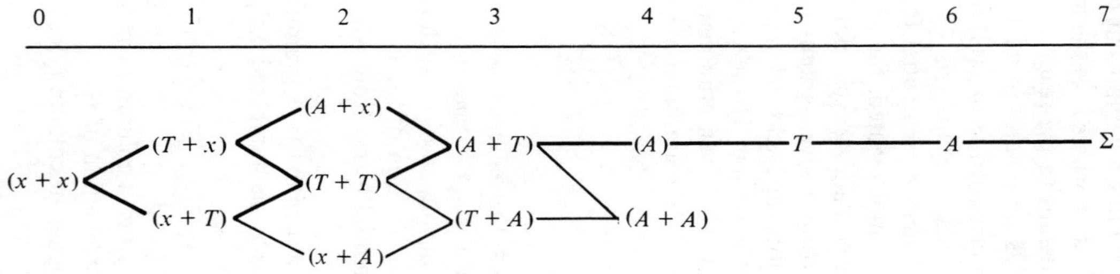


G: $\Sigma \to A \quad A \to T \quad T \to x$

$A \to A + T \quad T \to (A)$

**Figure 10.4** Bottom-up syntax analysis.

cannot grow in length as one proceeds to higher-numbered columns, the proliferation of intermediate sentential forms is far less than for top-down analysis. Constraint 3, used to limit the length of sentential forms generated in top-down analysis, is automatically satisfied in bottom-up analysis.

As in top-down analysis, it is useful to constrain the bottom-up procedure so that a unique derivation is found for each unambiguous sentence generated by the grammar:

In a sentential form $\varphi A \psi$ placed in the chart during step 2 of the bottom-up analysis, the string $\psi$ must comprise only terminal symbols.

We shall show this constaint ensures that the analyzer constructs just the rightmost derivations of the sentence $\omega$. For this purpose it is convenient to define the *handle* of a sentential form derivable in a context-free grammar:

**Definition 10.1:** Let **G** be a context-free grammar, and let $\omega = \varphi\alpha\psi$ be a sentential form. If $A \longrightarrow \alpha$ is a production of **G** and if $\psi \in \mathbf{T}^*$, then $\alpha$ is a *potential handle* of $\omega$. If, moreover, there is derivation of $\omega$ in **G** of the form

$$\Sigma \overset{*}{\Longrightarrow} \varphi A \psi \Longrightarrow \varphi\alpha\psi$$

then $\alpha$ is a *handle* of $\omega$.

The handle of a sentential form should not be confused with the handle of a production defined in Chapter 9.

Figure 10.5 illustrates the definition of a handle of a sentential form $\omega$ in terms of a derivation tree for $\omega$. The handle, being the right part of the last rule used in the derivation, must be a string of symbols that labels the leaves of a *simple subtree* (a subtree of depth 1). If the derivation is rightmost, the derivation tree can have no simple subtree with its leaves to the left of those of the handle, for such a subtree must correspond to a production $B \longrightarrow \beta$ used earlier in the derivation, and we would have

$$\Sigma \overset{*}{\Longrightarrow} \varphi_1 B \psi_1 \Longrightarrow \varphi_1 \beta \psi_1 \overset{*}{\Longrightarrow} \varphi_2 \beta \varphi_3 A \psi_2 \Longrightarrow \varphi_2 \beta \varphi_3 \alpha \psi_2,$$
$$\text{with } \varphi_2 \beta \varphi_3 = \varphi,\ \psi_2 = \psi$$

which is not a rightmost derivation. Thus, in the derivation tree corresponding to a rightmost derivation, the handle labels the lower leftmost simple subtree.

**Proposition 10.1:** Let **G** be a context-free grammar, and let

$$\omega_0 = \Sigma$$

$$\omega_i = \varphi_i \alpha_i \psi_i, \qquad i = 1, \ldots, k-1$$

$$\omega_k = \omega$$

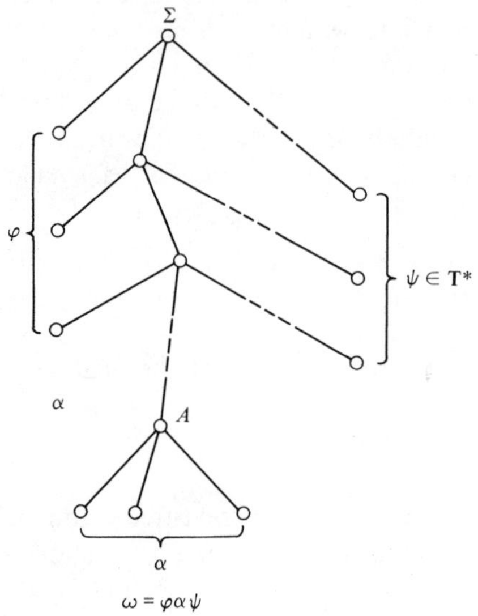


**Figure 10.5** Handle of a sentential form.

be a sequence of sentential forms such that

$$\omega_{i-1} = \varphi_i A_i \psi_i, \qquad i = 1, \ldots, k$$

where $A_i \longrightarrow \alpha_i$ is a production of **G** for each $i$. Then

$$\Sigma \Longrightarrow \omega_1 \Longrightarrow \omega_2 \Longrightarrow \ldots \Longrightarrow \omega_k$$

is a rightmost derivation of $\omega$ if and only if each $\alpha_i$ is a potential handle of $\omega_i$.

***Proof:*** If $A_i$ were not the rightmost nonterminal letter of some sentential form $\omega_{i-1} = \varphi_i A_i \psi_i$, then $\psi_i$ would have to contain a nonterminal letter, and $\alpha_i$ could not be a potential handle of $\omega_i = \varphi_i \alpha_i \psi_i$. Conversely, if $\alpha_i$ were not a potential handle of $\omega_i = \varphi_i \alpha_i \psi_i$, then $\psi_i$ would have to contain a nonterminal, and $A_i$ could not be the rightmost nonterminal in $\omega_{i-1} = \varphi_i A_i \psi_i$.

As does the top-down analyzer, the bottom-up analyzer requires the grammar to be free of cyclic nonterminals if its operation is to terminate for every sentence. The possibility of looping because of noncyclic left (or right) recursion does not arise in bottom-up analysis because successive sentential forms cannot increase in length.

To design a backtracking bottom-up analyzer, we assume as before that the sentence $\omega$ is being processed from left to right. At each point in its operation, we want the analyzer to build as much of the structural description of

$\omega$ as possible before examining further letters of the input string. Thus the analyzer will assemble the derivation tree by starting from its lower left-hand corner and working toward the goal $\Sigma$, gradually encompassing more terminal letters to the right. Each move of the analyzer will be a shift move or reduce move. A *shift move* advances the input pointer one letter to the right in the input string. A *reduce move* replaces the string immediately to the left of the input pointer with the left part of some rule having that string as its right part.

The construction of a derivation tree by bottom-up analysis is illustrated by the sequence of partial trees shown in Figure 10.6 for the sentence $(x + x)$. In each part of the figure, the symbols constituting the sentential form are written in a line, with the hypothesized handle underscored. At each stage, the partial derivation assigns structure to certain phrases within the sentence. The form of the remainder of the derivation tree is as yet unknown to the analyzer. In the example, each sentential form generated has a unique potential handle except the form

$$(A + T)$$

for which there are two potential handles:

$$T \quad \text{and} \quad A + T$$

A backtracking analyzer must choose which handle to replace; the first leads to failure, the second to success. This choice of which potential handle to use in generating the next sentential form is the basic choice among alternatives that must be made by such an analyzer.

Figure 10.7 specifies a backtracking bottom-up analyzer. [In the figure, *head*($\psi$) is the initial letter of the string $\psi$ and *tail*($\psi$) is the string formed from $\psi$ by deleting the initial letter.] As before, we assume that the productions of a context-free grammar **G** have been numbered $1, 2, \ldots, r$. The sentential form currently under consideration is represented by a triple $(\varphi, i, \psi)$ in which

$\varphi$ is the portion of the form so far analyzed, $\varphi \in (\mathbf{N} \cup \mathbf{T})^*$

$i$ is the number of the rule in **G** most recently used in a reduction from this form, $1 \leq i \leq r$

$\psi$ is the portion of the form not yet analyzed, $\psi \in \mathbf{T}^*$

At a given point in the analysis, the stack contains entries

$$(\varphi_1, i_1, \psi_1)(\varphi_2, i_2, \psi_2) \ldots (\varphi_k, i_k, \psi_k)$$

signifying that

$$\varphi_1\psi_1 \Longrightarrow \varphi_2\psi_2 \Longrightarrow \ldots \Longrightarrow \varphi_k\psi_k$$

is a rightmost derivation. The procedure terminates when the current sentential form has been reduced to $(\Sigma, \text{-}, \lambda)$.

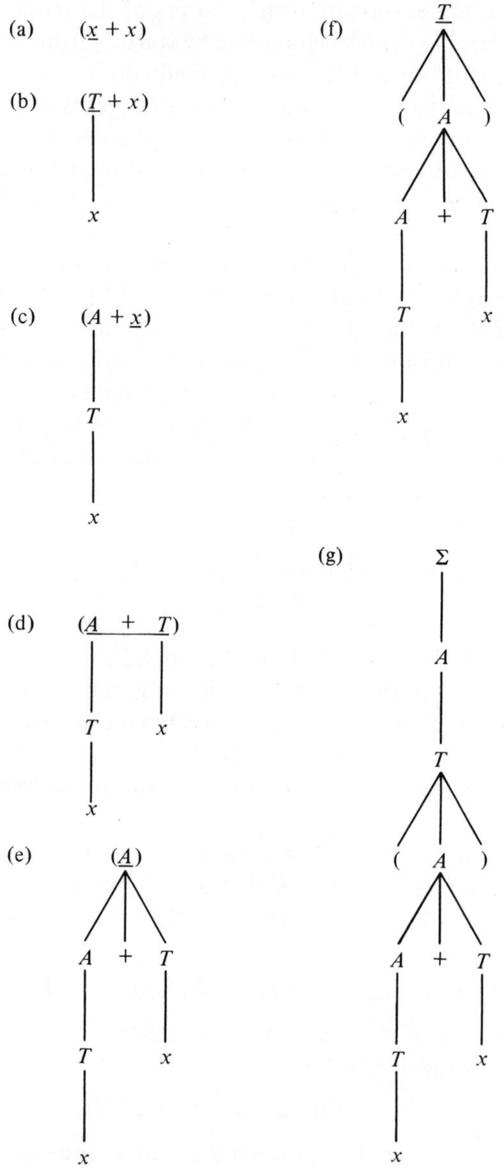


**Figure 10.6** Forming a rightmost derivation by bottom-up analysis.

Consider a typical move of the parser. Its object is to find the potential handle for $(\varphi, i, \psi)$ and replace it with the left part of a rule having that string as its right part. In other words, if $\varphi = \beta\alpha$ and the $k$th rule of **G** is $A \longrightarrow \alpha$, the analyzer reduces $(\varphi, i, \psi)$ to $(\beta A, k, \psi)$, and saves $(\varphi, k, \psi)$ on the

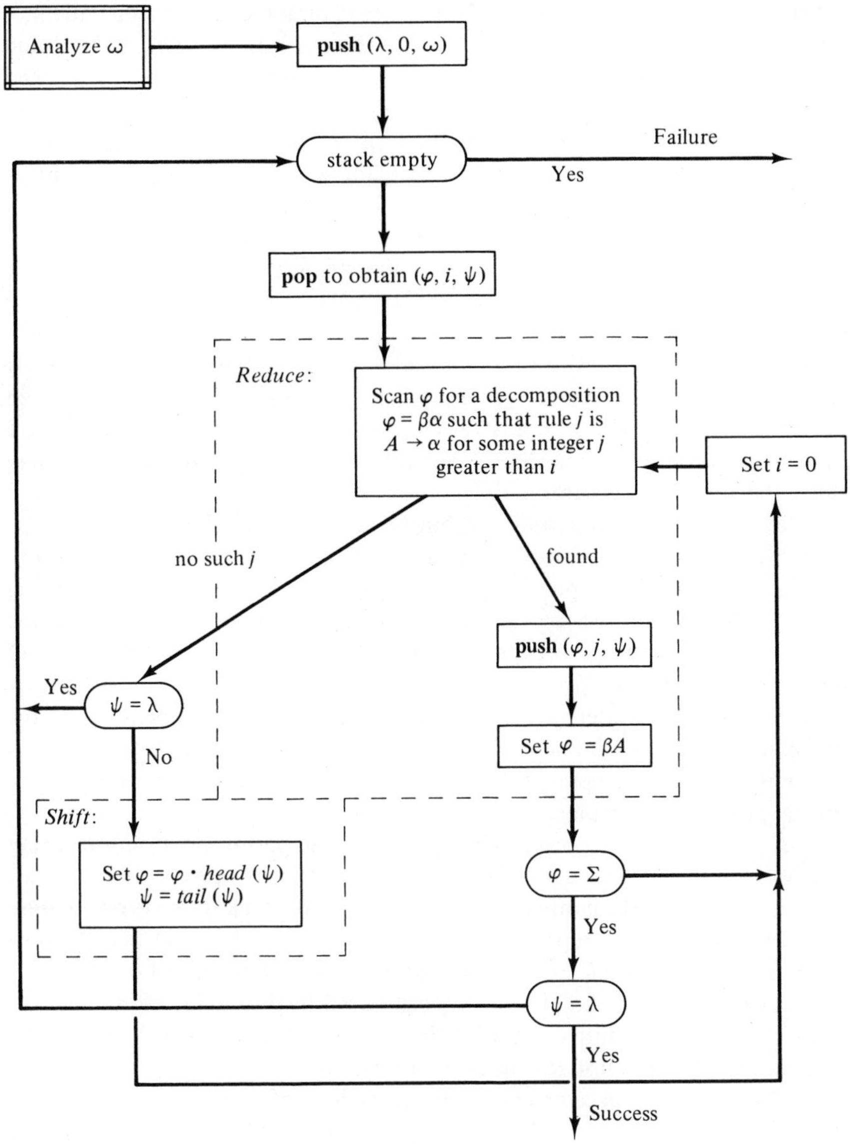


**Figure 10.7** Backtracking bottom-up syntax analyzer.

stack in case the potential handle $\alpha$ is not the actual handle. This reduction signifies that the step

$$\beta A \psi \Longrightarrow \beta\alpha\psi$$

is valid when rule $k$ is applied in a rightmost derivation. If the analyzer cannot find a suffix of $\varphi$ that is the right part of some rule, it must advance the input pointer [by replacing $\varphi$ with $\varphi \cdot head(\psi)$ and $\psi$ with $tail(\psi)$] and repeat the process; this is a shift move. If the end of the input is reached without a valid reduction, the stack is popped and the most recent reduction attempt replaced with another. The analysis reaches a successful termination only if the entire input has been processed and $\varphi = \Sigma$. On successful termination, the rule numbers in the stored stack elements give the order of application of the rules in a rightmost derivation of the input.

Figure 10.8 shows the analysis of the string $(x + x)$ according to the arithmetic subexpression grammar. In this analysis there is little backtracking because the rules of the grammar have unique right parts, only one of which is a suffix of another. Indeed, if most rules of a grammar are distinguishable by their right parts, there are generally few opportunities for backtracking in a bottom-up analysis. For this reason, bottom-up procedures often prove faster than top-down procedures, even though the top-down procedures may have the simpler structure.

Both the top-down and bottom-up analyses can be carried out by suitably designed pushdown accepters. In Chapter 8 we saw how to construct a pushdown accepter to perform top-down syntax analysis according to an arbitrary context-free grammar **G**. Given a sentence $\omega$ in **L(G)**, the pushdown accepter will recognize $\omega$ by progressing through a sequence of configurations $(\varphi_i, q_R, \beta_i^R A_i)$ corresponding to the sentential forms $\omega_i = \varphi_i A_i \beta_i$ of a leftmost derivation of $\omega$. The nondeterministic operation of the pushdown accepter eliminates the need for backtracking, and for this reason it is not necessary to represent the integer $i$ in Figure 10.2 in the configuration of the pushdown accepter.

A pushdown accepter may also be arranged to perform bottom-up syntax analysis of a sentence $\omega$ according to an arbitrary context-free grammar. Figure 10.9 shows the configuration of the pushdown accepter corresponding to the state of analysis represented by the pair $(\varphi, \psi)$. The string $\psi$ is the portion of the input sentence $\omega$ that has not yet been scanned, and $\varphi$ is the contents of the stack. As before, the integer $i$ used in the backtracking analysis of Figure 10.7 is omitted because the pushdown analyzer will pursue all alternatives through nondeterministic operation.

The pushdown accepter performs operations of two kinds:

1. *Shifting:* the current pair $(\varphi, s\psi)$ is replaced with $(\varphi s, \psi)$.

Shifting consists of reading the next symbol $s$ from the input tape and appending it to the string $\varphi$ held by the storage tape.

2. *Reducing:* The current pair $(\varphi, \psi)$ is replaced with $(\beta A, \psi)$, where **G** has the production $A \longrightarrow \alpha$, and $\varphi = \beta\alpha$.

To perform the reducing operation, the pushdown accepter compares the symbols of $\varphi$ (read in reverse order from the storage tape) with the symbols

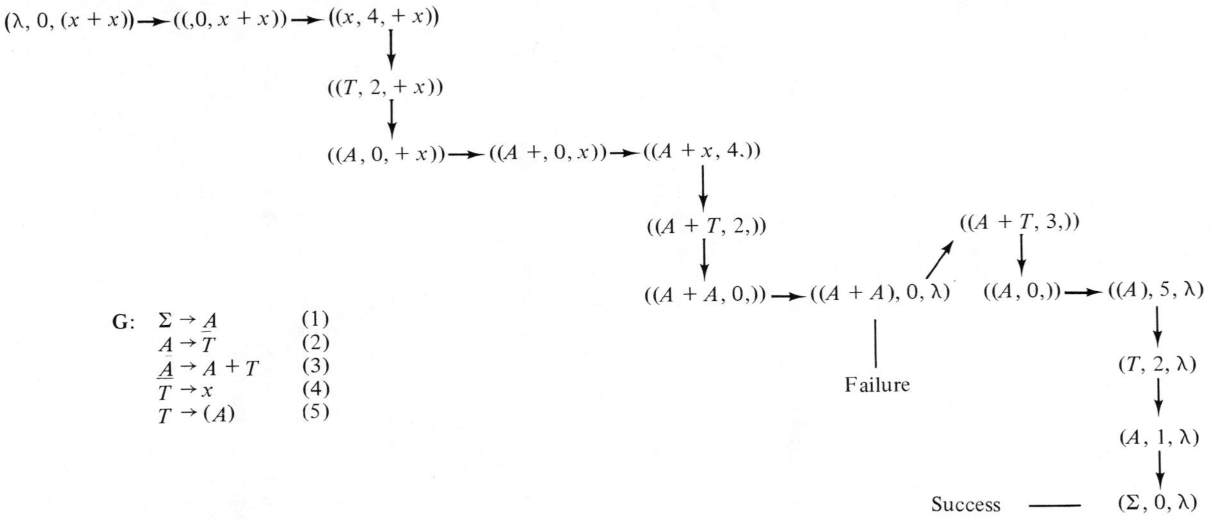


G:

| | | |
|---|---|---|
| | $\Sigma \rightarrow \underline{A}$ | (1) |
| | $\underline{A} \rightarrow T$ | (2) |
| | $\underline{A} \rightarrow A + T$ | (3) |
| | $T \rightarrow x$ | (4) |
| | $T \rightarrow (A)$ | (5) |

**Figure 10.8** Bottom-up analysis.

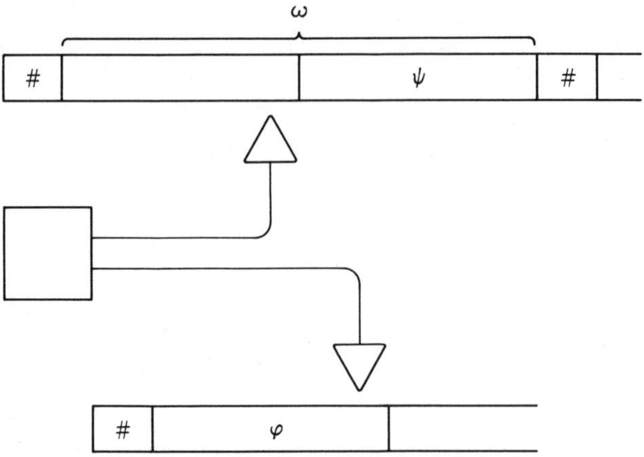


**Figure 10.9** Configuration of a pushdown accepter for performing bottom-up analysis.

of $\alpha$, the right part of the production. If a match is found, the nonterminal letter $A$ is written in the stack in place of $\alpha$. Through nondeterministic operation, this matching operation is carried out "concurrently" for all productions of **G**.

Acceptance of a sentence $\omega$ occurs if the accepter can reach, by some sequence of shifting and reducing operations, a configuration corresponding to the pair $(\Sigma, \lambda)$ when started in the configuration corresponding to the pair $(\lambda, \omega)$. For an accepted sentence, the sequence of configurations defines a rightmost derivation of $\omega$ according to **G**.

In a bottom-up analysis, if it is possible to determine without forward analysis the handle of each sentential form generated by a grammar, then backtracking will never be necessary, and the corresponding pushdown accepter may be designed to operate deterministically. Since practical grammars can often be transformed to permit deterministic analysis, deterministic bottom-up procedures have assumed great importance in the study of syntax analysis. Although many such procedures have been described, most of these procedures are, to a greater or lesser extent, refinements of two basic methods of analysis: *precedence analysis* and *LR*($k$) *analysis*. These methods are studied in the remainder of this chapter.

## 10.3 Precedence Analysis

Deterministic methods of bottom-up syntax analysis have long been known for two important classes of context-free grammars. In later sections of this chapter, we study the analysis for the *LR*($k$) *grammars* in which the handle of a sentential form may be determined by a left-to-right scan that examines no more than $k$ symbols to the right of the handle; presently, we study the analysis of *precedence grammars*, for which relations can be constructed on the symbols of a grammar so the handle of a sentential form may be identified immediately. We begin our study of precedence relations by considering their use in the evaluation of arithmetic expressions.

### 10.3.1 Arithmetic Expressions

Consider a class of arithmetic expressions represented as sentences

$$n_1 d_1 n_2 d_2 \ldots n_k d_k n_{k+1}$$

in which $n_1, \ldots, n_{k+1}$ are numerals, and $d_1, \ldots, d_k$ are delimiters in the set $\{+, -, \times, /, \uparrow\}$ that serve as infix arithmetic operators. A simple procedure for evaluating these expressions is based on associating a precedence level with each arithmetic operator:

| Precedence | | Operator |
|---|---|---|
| Lowest | $+$ | Addition |
| | $-$ | Subtraction |
| Intermediate | $\times$ | Multiplication |
| | $/$ | Division |
| Highest | $\uparrow$ | Exponentiation |

We write $d_1 \lessdot d_2$ to indicate that delimiter $d_2$ has higher precedence than delimiter $d_1$; we write $d_1 \doteq d_2$ if $d_1$ and $d_2$ have the same precedence; and we write $d_1 \mathrel{\dot{\geq}} d_2$ if the precedence of $d_1$ is at least equal to that of $d_2$. Note that these relations $\lessdot$ and $\mathrel{\dot{\geq}}$ are not converses, for $d_1 \mathrel{\dot{\geq}} d_2$ does not necessarily imply $d_2 \lessdot d_1$. Since it is convenient that even the first and last operator in an expression have a precedence defined with respect to their left and right context, we use a delimiter # to mark each end of an expression

$$\omega = \# n_1 d_1 \ldots n_k d_k n_{k+1} \#$$

and associate with # a precedence lower than that of any arithmetic operator:

$$\# \lessdot d \qquad d \mathrel{\dot{\geq}} \#, \qquad d \in \{\uparrow, \times, /, +, -\}$$

We summarize these precedence relations in the form of a *precedence matrix* **P**:

$\mathbf{P}(d_1, d_2)$:

| $d_1$ \ $d_2$ | $\uparrow$ | $\times$ | $/$ | $+$ | $-$ | $\#$ |
|---|---|---|---|---|---|---|
| $\uparrow$ | $\mathrel{\dot{\geq}}$ | $\mathrel{\dot{\geq}}$ | $\mathrel{\dot{\geq}}$ | $\mathrel{\dot{\geq}}$ | $\mathrel{\dot{\geq}}$ | $\mathrel{\dot{\geq}}$ |
| $\times$ | $\lessdot$ | $\mathrel{\dot{\geq}}$ | $\mathrel{\dot{\geq}}$ | $\mathrel{\dot{\geq}}$ | $\mathrel{\dot{\geq}}$ | $\mathrel{\dot{\geq}}$ |
| $/$ | $\lessdot$ | $\mathrel{\dot{\geq}}$ | $\mathrel{\dot{\geq}}$ | $\mathrel{\dot{\geq}}$ | $\mathrel{\dot{\geq}}$ | $\mathrel{\dot{\geq}}$ |
| $+$ | $\lessdot$ | $\lessdot$ | $\lessdot$ | $\mathrel{\dot{\geq}}$ | $\mathrel{\dot{\geq}}$ | $\mathrel{\dot{\geq}}$ |
| $-$ | $\lessdot$ | $\lessdot$ | $\lessdot$ | $\mathrel{\dot{\geq}}$ | $\mathrel{\dot{\geq}}$ | $\mathrel{\dot{\geq}}$ |
| $\#$ | $\lessdot$ | $\lessdot$ | $\lessdot$ | $\lessdot$ | $\lessdot$ | $\doteq$ |

The matrix specifies that the end marker # satisfies the relation $\# \doteq \#$. This provides a convenient means of testing if the evaluation of an expression has been completed.

When a numeral appears between operators of different precedence, the numeral is an operand of the operator having higher precedence. Thus the expression

$$2 + 3 \times 5$$

is evaluated as

$$2 + (3 \times 5)$$

and not

$$(2 + 3) \times 5$$

When adjacent operators have equal precedence, as in the case of + and − or / and ×, the precedence matrix associates a numeral with the operator to its left. Thus the expression

$$4 - 3 + 1$$

has the customary interpretation

$$(4 - 3) + 1$$

rather than

$$4 - (3 + 1)$$

A combination of operator and operands in an expression may be evaluated to yield a simpler expression. This is done according to the usual evaluation rule:

*Step 1:* Scan the arithmetic expression from left to right for the first delimiter $d_i$ such that $d_{i-1} \lessdot d_i \gtrdot d_{i+1}$. Then $n_i d_i n_{i+1}$ is the *prime subexpression* of the given arithmetic expression.

The reduced expression to be considered next is obtained thus:

*Step 2:* Replace the prime subexpression $n_i d_i n_{i+1}$ by the numeral that is the result of applying operator $d_i$ to operands $n_i$ and $n_{i+1}$.

The complete evaluation of an arithmetic expression is done by repeating steps 1 and 2 until an expression $\# n \#$ is obtained. The numeral $n$ is the value of the given expression.

**Example 10.1:** In the expression

$$\# 3 \times 5 - 2 \uparrow 3 / 4 \times 3 + 1 \#$$

adjacent operators are related as follows:

$$\# \lessdot \times \gtrdot - \lessdot \uparrow \gtrdot / \gtrdot \times \gtrdot + \gtrdot \#$$

By locating the leftmost occurrence of $\gtrdot$, the prime subexpression is found to be $3 \times 5$; its evaluation reduces the expression to

$$\# \; 15 - 2 \uparrow 3 \, / \, 4 \times 3 + 1 \; \#$$

The complete evaluation is shown below with the prime subexpression underscored in each line.

| Expression | Operator Precedence |
|---|---|
| $\# \; \underline{3 \times 5} - 2 \uparrow 3 / 4 \times 3 + 1 \; \#$ | $\# \lessdot \times \gtrdot - \lessdot \uparrow \gtrdot / \gtrdot \times \gtrdot + \gtrdot \#$ |
| $\# \; 15 - \underline{2 \uparrow 3} / 4 \times 3 + 1 \; \#$ | $\# \lessdot - \lessdot \uparrow \gtrdot / \gtrdot \times \gtrdot + \gtrdot \#$ |
| $\# \; 15 - \underline{8 / 4} \times 3 + 1 \; \#$ | $\# \lessdot - \lessdot / \gtrdot \times \gtrdot + \gtrdot \#$ |
| $\# \; 15 - \underline{2 \times 3} + 1 \; \#$ | $\# \lessdot - \lessdot \times \gtrdot + \gtrdot \#$ |
| $\# \; \underline{15 - 6} + 1 \; \#$ | $\# \lessdot - \gtrdot + \gtrdot \#$ |
| $\# \; \underline{9 + 1} \; \#$ | $\# \lessdot + \gtrdot \#$ |
| $\# \; 10 \; \#$ | $\# \doteq \#$ |

The evaluation of arithmetic expressions containing parentheses, such as

$$2 \times (1 + 1) \uparrow (4 - 2)$$

requires a different use of operator precedence. All operators appearing within a pair of matched parentheses must be performed before the parentheses may be deleted without changing the meaning of the expression. This can be done by making the parentheses appear to the evaluation procedure as end markers of the subexpression that they enclose:

$$( \lessdot d \gtrdot ), \quad \text{each operator } d$$
$$( \doteq )$$

We must also force the evaluator to replace a parenthesized subexpression with its numeric value before attempting to use it as an operand. For this purpose we give the parentheses high precedence relative to operators that are adjacent and outside:

$$) \gtrdot d \lessdot (, \qquad \text{each operator } d$$
$$( \lessdot ($$
$$) \gtrdot )$$

The complete precedence matrix is displayed in Figure 10.10.

In the case of expressions containing parentheses, the prime subexpression will have one of two forms calling for different treatment by the evaluator.

*Step 1:* Scan the delimiters of the expression to find the leftmost delimiter $d_j$ such that $d_j \gtrdot d_{j+1}$.

| | ( | ↑ | / | × | + | − | ) | # |
|---|---|---|---|---|---|---|---|---|
| ) | | $\gtrdot$ | $\gtrdot$ | $\gtrdot$ | $\gtrdot$ | $\gtrdot$ | $\gtrdot$ | $\gtrdot$ |
| ↑ | $\lessdot$ | $\gtrdot$ | $\gtrdot$ | $\gtrdot$ | $\gtrdot$ | $\gtrdot$ | $\gtrdot$ | $\gtrdot$ |
| / | $\lessdot$ | $\lessdot$ | $\gtrdot$ | $\gtrdot$ | $\gtrdot$ | $\gtrdot$ | $\gtrdot$ | $\gtrdot$ |
| × | $\lessdot$ | $\lessdot$ | $\gtrdot$ | $\gtrdot$ | $\gtrdot$ | $\gtrdot$ | $\gtrdot$ | $\gtrdot$ |
| + | $\lessdot$ | $\lessdot$ | $\lessdot$ | $\lessdot$ | $\gtrdot$ | $\gtrdot$ | $\gtrdot$ | $\gtrdot$ |
| − | $\lessdot$ | $\lessdot$ | $\lessdot$ | $\lessdot$ | $\gtrdot$ | $\gtrdot$ | $\gtrdot$ | $\gtrdot$ |
| ( | $\lessdot$ | $\lessdot$ | $\lessdot$ | $\lessdot$ | $\lessdot$ | $\lessdot$ | $\doteq$ | |
| # | $\lessdot$ | $\lessdot$ | $\lessdot$ | $\lessdot$ | $\lessdot$ | $\lessdot$ | | $\doteq$ |

**Figure 10.10** Precedence matrix for arithmetic expressions with parentheses.

*Step 2:* Scan left from $d_j$ to locate the rightmost delimiter $d_i$ such that $d_{i-1} \lessdot d_i$. (It will usually be true that $i = j$.) Let $\alpha = d_i \ldots d_j$.

*Step 3a:* If $\alpha$ is a single operator symbol, the prime subexpression is $n \, \alpha \, n'$, where $n$ and $n'$ are the numerals to the left and right of $\alpha$ in the given expression. Replace the prime subexpression with the numeral that is its value.

*Step 3b:* If $\alpha = (\ )$, the prime subexpression is $(n)$. Replace it with the numeral $n$.

If the reduced expression is $\# \, n \, \#$, then the numeral $n$ is its value. Otherwise, steps 1, 2, and 3 are repeated until such an expression is obtained.

**Example 10.2:** The evaluation of a parenthesized expression using the precedence matrix in Figure 10.10 is shown below. Again the prime subexpression is underscored in each line.

| Expression | Precedence |
|---|---|
| $\# \, 2 \times (\underline{1+1}) \uparrow (4-2) \, \#$ | $\# \lessdot \times \lessdot ( \underline{\lessdot + \gtrdot} ) \gtrdot \uparrow \lessdot ( \lessdot - \gtrdot ) \gtrdot \#$ |
| $\# \, 2 \times \underline{(2)} \uparrow (4-2) \, \#$ | $\# \lessdot \times \underline{\lessdot ( \doteq ) \gtrdot} \uparrow \lessdot ( \lessdot - \gtrdot ) \gtrdot \#$ |
| $\# \, 2 \times 2 \uparrow (\underline{4-2}) \, \#$ | $\# \lessdot \times \lessdot \uparrow \lessdot ( \underline{\lessdot - \gtrdot} ) \gtrdot \#$ |
| $\# \, 2 \times 2 \uparrow \underline{(2)} \, \#$ | $\# \lessdot \times \lessdot \uparrow \underline{\lessdot ( \doteq ) \gtrdot} \#$ |
| $\# \, 2 \times \underline{2 \uparrow 2} \, \#$ | $\# \lessdot \times \underline{\lessdot \uparrow \gtrdot} \#$ |
| $\# \, \underline{2 \times 4} \, \#$ | $\# \underline{\lessdot \times \gtrdot} \#$ |
| $\# \, 8 \, \#$ | $\# \doteq \#$ |

Figure 10.11 presents an *expression evaluator* in the form of a flow chart. First, end markers are added to the given expression $\omega$, and the right end marker is made the initial contents of a delimiter stack $\sigma$. A separate stack $\tau$

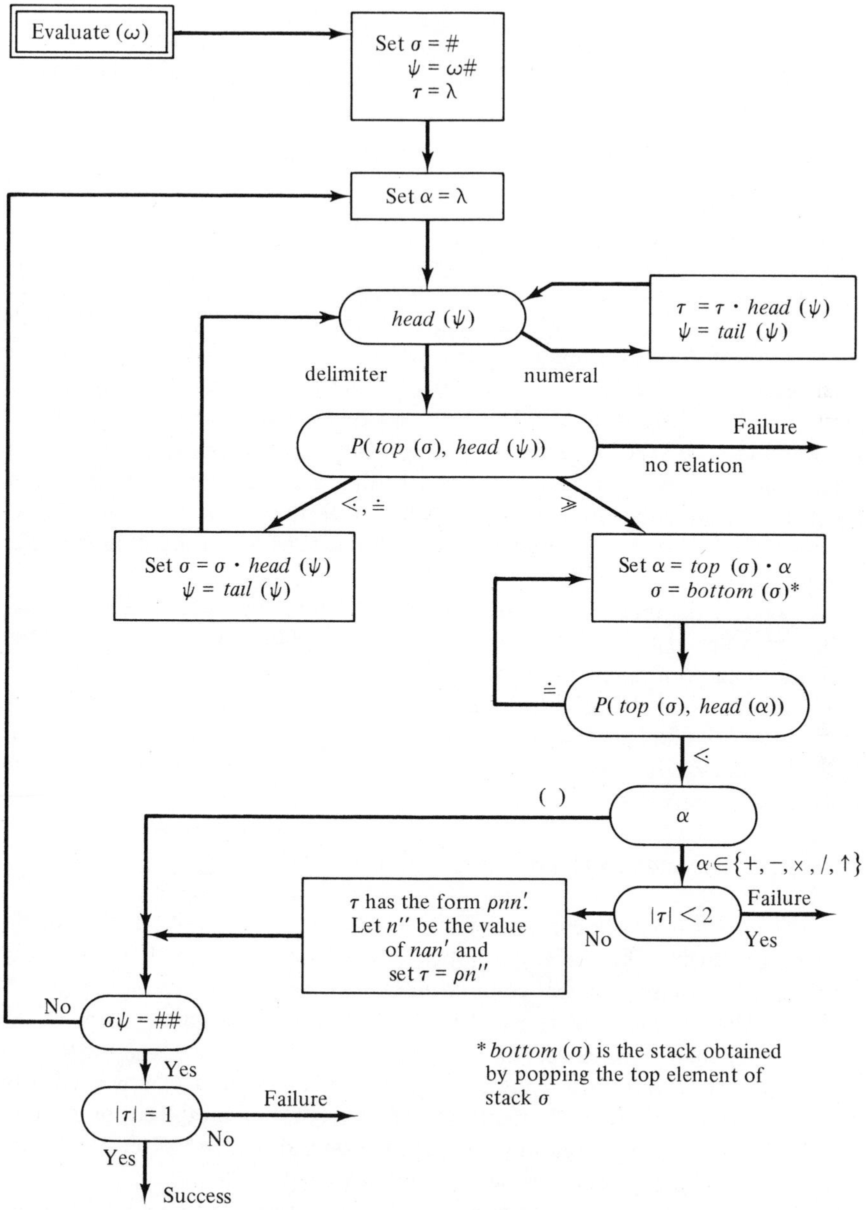


* *bottom* (σ) is the stack obtained by popping the top element of stack σ

**Figure 10.11** Precedence evaluator for arithmetic expressions.

is initially empty, but later stores numeric values of subexpressions until they are required as operands. The delimiters are moved from the string $\psi$ into the stack until the next delimiter $head(\psi)$ and the top delimiter of the stack $top(\sigma)$ satisfy

$$top(\sigma) \gtrdot head(\psi)$$

(During this process, numerals encountered in $\psi$ are pushed into $\tau$.) Then delimiters are popped from the stack into a string variable $\alpha$ until

$$top(\sigma) \lessdot head(\alpha)$$

At this point, we have satisfied the relations

$$top(\sigma) \lessdot head(\alpha), \qquad top(\alpha) \gtrdot head(\psi)$$

Thus $\alpha$ contains the delimiters of the prime subexpression, and must be either a single operator or a pair of parentheses if the given expression is well formed.

Once the above relations are satisfied, the prime subexpression is replaced. If $\alpha$ is an operator, the prime subexpression is $n\,\alpha\,n'$, where $n$ and $n'$ are the top two numerals in $\tau$. These two numerals are removed from $\tau$ and replaced by the value of the subexpression. The delimiters of the prime subexpression are then discarded by resetting $\alpha$ to the empty string. If $\alpha$ is ( ), the prime subexpression is $(n)$, where $n$ is the top numeral in $\tau$. This numeral is left in $\tau$, and the parentheses are discarded by resetting $\alpha$ to the empty string.

The algorithm succeeds when the expression has been reduced to $\#\ n\ \#$, that is, when $\sigma\psi = \#\#$. The value of the original expression is then the single numeral $n$ remaining in the list $\tau$.

Note that if the original expression is not well formed (if, for example, the expression has too few or too many numerals, or a pair of adjacent delimiters are not related by $\lessdot$, $\doteq$, or $\gtrdot$) the evaluator will fail to obtain a value for the expression.

### 10.3.2 Precedence Grammars

The concept of precedence just illustrated for the evaluation of arithmetic expressions has been developed into an important method of syntax analysis for a large class of context-free languages. For this purpose, precedence relations are used to identify the handle of a sentential form in the same way that precedence was used to identify the prime subexpression of an arithmetic expression being evaluated. The application of precedence to parsing, however, requires precedence relations defined on the entire vocabulary $\mathbf{V} = \mathbf{N} \cup \mathbf{T}$ of a grammar, rather than on a special set of terminal symbols, such as the operator symbols of expressions.

In this section, we show how precedence analysis can be applied to the parsing of an important subclass of the deterministic languages. In the following section, we develop a generalized method of precedence analysis that encompasses *all* deterministic context-free languages.

For the present development, we assume that the productions of a grammar **G** under consideration are numbered 1, 2, . . . , $r$. Recall that any rightmost derivation permitted by **G** is of the form

$$\Sigma \overset{*}{\Longrightarrow} \varphi A \psi \Longrightarrow \varphi \alpha \psi$$

in which $\psi$ is a string of terminals and $\alpha$ is a handle of $\varphi\alpha\psi$. We say for convenience that $\varphi\alpha\psi$ is a *right sentential form* of **G** and that it *reduces to* $\varphi A \psi$ *by rule* $p$ of **G** if rule $p$ is $A \longrightarrow \alpha$. Suppose that

$$\omega_n \Longrightarrow \omega_{n-1} \Longrightarrow \ldots \Longrightarrow \omega_1, \qquad \omega_n = \Sigma, \qquad \omega_1 = \omega$$

is a rightmost derivation of $\omega$. The corresponding bottom-up *parse* of $\omega$ is the sequence of production numbers

$$p_1, \ldots, p_{n-1}$$

such that each $\omega_i$ reduces to $\omega_{i+1}$ by application of rule $p_i$.

Parsing by precedence analysis is performed according to the following outline: three precedence relations $\lessdot$, $\doteq$, and $\gtrdot$ are defined on the vocabulary of the grammar $\mathbf{V} = \mathbf{N} \cup \mathbf{T}$ so that at most one of the three relations holds for each pair of symbols in $\mathbf{V} \times \mathbf{V}$, and exactly one of the relations holds for each pair of symbols that can appear adjacent in some sentential form of the grammar. Given such relations, the handle of a right sentential form is located as follows:

1. Scan the sentential form from left to right until $\gtrdot$ holds between adjacent symbols.
2. From this point, scan to the left until $\lessdot$ holds between adjacent symbols.
3. The string of symbols $\alpha$ between the points where $\lessdot$ and $\gtrdot$ hold is the handle of the sentential form.

Let the sentential form be

$$\underbrace{X_1 \ldots X_k}_{\varphi} \;\; \underbrace{Y_1 \ldots Y_m}_{\alpha} \;\; \underbrace{a_1 \ldots a_n}_{\psi}$$

where $\alpha$ is the handle and $\psi \in \mathbf{T}^*$. If the procedure given above locates the handle of $\varphi\alpha\psi$, then adjacent pairs of symbols in the sentential form must be related thus:

$$X_k \lessdot Y_1 \doteq \ldots \doteq Y_m \gtrdot a_1$$

Since $(Y_m, a_1)$ is the first pair satisfying $\gtrdot$ in the left-to-right scan, $\gtrdot$ must not hold for any pair of symbols within the string $\varphi\alpha$. Similarly, $(X_k, Y_1)$ is the first pair satisfying $\lessdot$ found in scanning to the left; hence $\lessdot$ must not hold for any pair occurring within the handle $\alpha$.

To justify the precedence analysis procedure, we must show how to construct the relations $\lessdot$, $\doteq$, and $\gtrdot$, and we must prove that the steps specified uniquely determine the production to be used in reducing any right sentential form.

The precedence relations are derived by analyzing the grammar to find symbol pairs that may appear together in sentential forms of the grammar. If the two symbols occur adjacent in the right part of some production, they are related by $\doteq$; if they can straddle the right boundary of the handle of a sentential form, they are related by $\gtrdot$; if they can straddle the left boundary of a handle, they are related by $\lessdot$. If these three relations are disjoint, the grammar is called a *precedence* grammar.

**Definition 10.2:** Let $\mathbf{G}$ be a context-free grammar, let $\mathbf{V} = \mathbf{N} \cup \mathbf{T}$ be the vocabulary of $\mathbf{G}$, and let $\lessdot$, $\doteq$, and $\gtrdot$ be the *precedence relations* for $\mathbf{G}$ defined as follows:

1. $Y_1 \doteq \ldots \doteq Y_m$ if $\mathbf{G}$ has a rule $A \longrightarrow Y_1 \ldots Y_m$.
2. $X \lessdot Y$ whenever $\Sigma \overset{*}{\Longrightarrow} \varphi' X A \psi$ and $A \longrightarrow Y\beta$ is a rule of $\mathbf{G}$.
3. $Y \gtrdot a$, $a \in \mathbf{T}$, whenever $\Sigma \overset{*}{\Longrightarrow} \varphi A a \psi'$ and $A \longrightarrow \beta Y$ is a rule of $\mathbf{G}$.

If at most one of the relations $\lessdot$, $\doteq$, and $\gtrdot$ holds for each pair in $\mathbf{V} \times \mathbf{V}$, then $\mathbf{G}$ is a *precedence grammar.*

It is not difficult to transform a normal-form context-free grammar into a precedence grammar (see the Problems). Since every context-free grammar can be put in normal form (Theorem 9.3), it follows that a precedence grammar can be constructed for any context-free language. However, the existence of a precedence grammar for a language does not guarantee that a deterministic precedence analyzer for the language can be found. The problem is that a precedence grammar may have distinct rules $A \longrightarrow \alpha$ and $B \longrightarrow \alpha$ with identical right parts. Even though the precedence relations may locate $\alpha$ as the handle of a sentential form, there is no way of knowing which of the two rules is to be used in the reduction. This problem is eliminated if we insist that no two productions have identical right parts.

**Definition 10.3:** A context-free grammar $\mathbf{G}$ is *invertible* if, whenever $A \longrightarrow \alpha$ and $B \longrightarrow \beta$ are productions of $\mathbf{G}$, $\alpha = \beta$ implies $A = B$. A language generated by an invertible precedence grammar is called a *simple precedence language*.

We can describe a deterministic parsing procedure for simple precedence languages. For this purpose it is convenient to bound each sentential form by end markers so that the procedure will work even if the handle occurs at the extreme left or right of the sentential form. Given a grammar **G**, an *end marked grammar* **G**$'$ is formed by adding the production

$$\Sigma' \longrightarrow \# \, \Sigma \, \#$$

to the rules of **G**, and making $\Sigma'$ the sentence symbol of **G**$'$. (The end marker $\#$ is a new terminal symbol, and $\Sigma$ is a nonterminal symbol in **G**$'$.) Clearly, $\omega$ is a right sentential form of **G** if and only if $\# \, \omega \, \#$ is a right sentential form of **G**$'$. The *precedence matrix* of a precedence grammar **G** consists of the three precedence relations $\lessdot$, $\doteq$, and $\gtrdot$ defined by the corresponding end-marked grammar **G**$'$. Thus the end marker $\#$ satisfies

$$\# \doteq \Sigma \doteq \#$$

and

$$\# \lessdot X \qquad \text{if } \Sigma \overset{*}{\Longrightarrow} X\psi \text{ in } \mathbf{G}$$

$$X \gtrdot \# \qquad \text{if } \Sigma \overset{*}{\Longrightarrow} \varphi X \text{ in } \mathbf{G}$$

Neither $X \lessdot \#$ nor $\# \gtrdot X$ holds for any $X$ in $\mathbf{N} \cup \mathbf{T}$.

**Example 10.3:** Consider the following grammar for arithmetic expressions, in which each appearance of the terminal letter $x$ denotes an arbitrary numeral.

$$\begin{array}{llll} \mathbf{G}: & \Sigma \longrightarrow A & A \longrightarrow A + T & F \longrightarrow (\, A \,) \\ & & A \longrightarrow T & F \longrightarrow x \\ & & T \longrightarrow T \times F & \\ & & T \longrightarrow F & \end{array}$$

As it stands, **G** is not a precedence grammar because the precedence relations obtained from **G** contain conflicts:

1. The rule $F \longrightarrow (\, A \,)$ implies that $( \doteq A$, but the derivation $\Sigma \overset{*}{\Longrightarrow} (\, A \,) \Longrightarrow (\, A + T \,)$ implies $( \lessdot A$.
2. The rule $A \longrightarrow A + T$ implies that $+ \doteq T$, but the derivation $\Sigma \overset{*}{\Longrightarrow} A + T \Longrightarrow A + T \times F$ implies $+ \lessdot T$.

These conflicts may be removed by introducing extra nonterminal letters, as in the following grammar **G**$'$:

$$\begin{array}{lllll} \mathbf{G}': & \Sigma \longrightarrow B & B \longrightarrow A & T \longrightarrow P & F \longrightarrow (\, B \,) \\ & & A \longrightarrow A + T & P \longrightarrow P \times F & F \longrightarrow x \\ & & A \longrightarrow T & P \longrightarrow F & \end{array}$$

To construct the precedence matrix for **G**$'$, it is convenient to define certain sets of symbols for each symbol $X$ in $\mathbf{N}' \cup \{\Sigma\}$.

**ℓ**($X$): symbols that may appear immediately left of a phrase denoted by $X$.

**i**($X$): symbols that may be initial symbols of a phrase denoted by $X$.

**f**($X$): symbols that may be final symbols of a phrase denoted by $X$.

**r**($X$): symbols that may appear immediately right of a phrase denoted by $X$.

For **G**′, these sets are shown in Figure 10.12a. Note that if $X \longrightarrow Y\beta$ is a rule of **G**′, then $\boldsymbol{\ell}(X) \subseteq \boldsymbol{\ell}(Y)$ and $\mathbf{i}(X) \supseteq \mathbf{i}(Y)$. Similarly, if $X \longrightarrow \beta Y$ is a rule, then $\mathbf{f}(X) \supseteq \mathbf{f}(Y)$ and $\mathbf{r}(X) \subseteq \mathbf{r}(Y)$. In terms of these sets, the relations $\lessdot$ and $\gtrdot$ are defined by

$$X \lessdot Y \quad \text{if } X \in \boldsymbol{\ell}(Z) \text{ and } Y \in \mathbf{i}(Z) \text{ for some } Z \in \mathbf{N}' \cup \{\Sigma\}$$

$$X \gtrdot Y \quad \text{if } X \in \mathbf{f}(Z) \text{ and } Y \in \mathbf{r}(Z) \text{ for some } Z \in \mathbf{N}' \cup \{\Sigma\}$$

The precedence matrix for **G**′ is given in Figure 10.12b.

| | **ℓ** | **i** | **f** | **r** |
|---|---|---|---|---|
| Σ | # | *BATPF*(*x* | *BATPF*)*x* | # |
| *B* | #( | *ATPF*(*x* | *ATPF*)*x* | )# |
| *A* | #( | *ATPF*(*x* | *TPF*)*x* | +)# |
| *T* | #(+ | *PF*(*x* | *PF*)*x* | +)# |
| *P* | #(+ | *PF*(*x* | *F*)*x* | ×+)# |
| *F* | #(+× | (*x* | )*x* | ×+)# |

(a)

| | *B* | *A* | *T* | *P* | *F* | ( | *x* | × | + | ) | # |
|---|---|---|---|---|---|---|---|---|---|---|---|
| *B* | | | | | | | | | | $\doteq$ | $\gtrdot$ |
| *A* | | | | | | | | | $\doteq$ | $\gtrdot$ | $\gtrdot$ |
| *T* | | | | | | | | | $\gtrdot$ | $\gtrdot$ | $\gtrdot$ |
| *P* | | | | | | | | $\doteq$ | $\gtrdot$ | $\gtrdot$ | $\gtrdot$ |
| *F* | | | | | | | | $\gtrdot$ | $\gtrdot$ | $\gtrdot$ | $\gtrdot$ |
| ) | | | | | | | | $\gtrdot$ | $\gtrdot$ | $\gtrdot$ | $\gtrdot$ |
| *x* | | | | | | | | $\gtrdot$ | $\gtrdot$ | $\gtrdot$ | $\gtrdot$ |
| × | | | | | $\doteq$ | $\lessdot$ | $\lessdot$ | | | | |
| + | | | $\doteq$ | $\lessdot$ | $\lessdot$ | $\lessdot$ | $\lessdot$ | | | | |
| ( | $\doteq$ | $\lessdot$ | $\lessdot$ | $\lessdot$ | $\lessdot$ | $\lessdot$ | $\lessdot$ | | | | |
| # | $\lessdot$ | $\lessdot$ | $\lessdot$ | $\lessdot$ | $\lessdot$ | $\lessdot$ | $\lessdot$ | | | | |

(b)

**Figure 10.12** Construction of the precedence matrix for the arithmetic expression grammar.

A complete algorithm for parsing sentences of a simple precedence language is given in Figure 10.13. The variable $\psi$ holds the portion of the end-marked sentence $\# \omega \#$ that has not yet been scanned. Letters from $\psi$ are pushed into a stack $\sigma$ until a position within $\# \omega \#$ is reached at which $\gtrdot$ is satisfied; then symbols are popped from the stack to form the handle $\alpha$ until a position is reached at which $\lessdot$ holds. Since **G** is invertible, $\alpha$ uniquely determines the rule $A \longrightarrow \alpha$ to be used in reducing the form $\sigma\alpha\psi$ to $\sigma A \psi$. The nonterminal $A$ is pushed into the stack, and scanning to the right is continued. Note that $top(\sigma) \gtrdot A$ cannot hold, because the right boundary of the handle in the right sentential form $\sigma A \psi$ must be to the right of $A$.

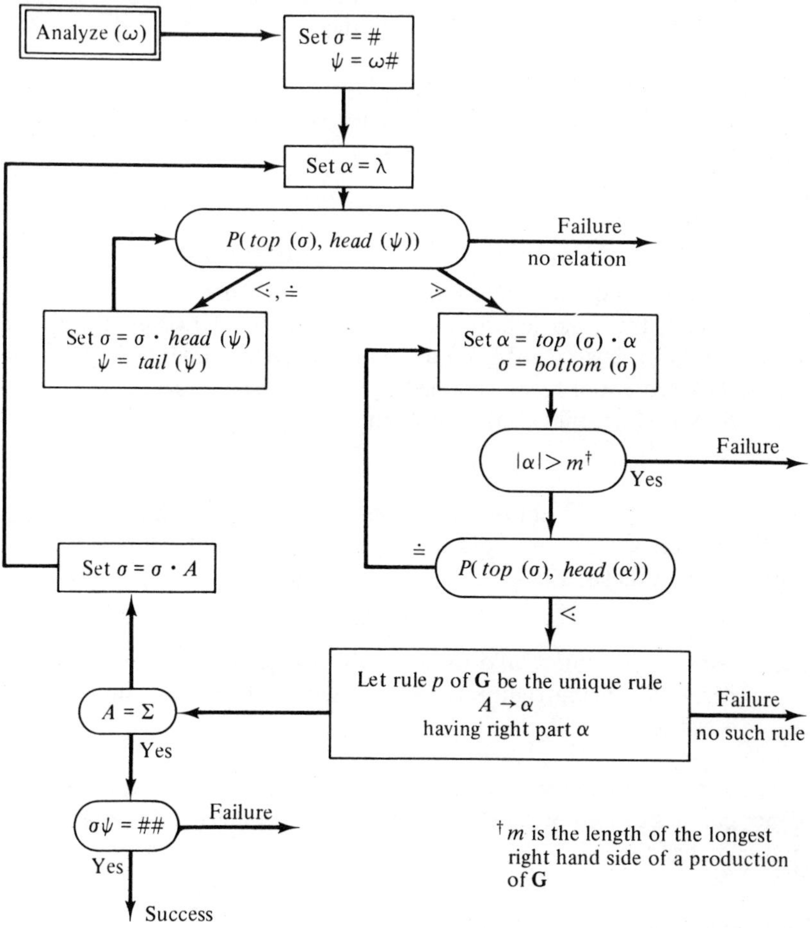


**Figure 10.13** Precedence analyzer.

**Example 10.3 (continued):** Figure 10.14 shows how the precedence analysis algorithm parses the sentence $x \times (x \times x + x)$ using the precedence matrix for $\mathbf{G}'$.

The following theorem verifies that the precedence analysis algorithm locates the handle of any right sentential form.

**Theorem 10.1:** Let $\mathbf{G} = (\mathbf{N}, \mathbf{T}, \mathbf{P}, \Sigma)$ be a precedence grammar, and let $\lessdot, \doteq$, and $\gtrdot$ denote the precedence relations on $(\mathbf{V} \cup \#) \times (\mathbf{V} \cup \#)$ defined by the associated end-marked grammar $\mathbf{G}'$. If

$$\Sigma' \Longrightarrow \# \Sigma \# \overset{*}{\Longrightarrow} \varphi A \psi \Longrightarrow \varphi \alpha \psi$$

is a rightmost derivation in $\mathbf{G}'$ in which $\varphi = X_1 \ldots X_k$, $\psi = a_1 \ldots a_n$, and the handle is $\alpha = Y_1 \ldots Y_m$, then

1. $X_k \lessdot Y_1 \doteq \ldots \doteq Y_m \gtrdot a_1$.
2. $X_i \lessdot X_{i+1}$ or $X_i \doteq X_{i+1}$ for each pair of adjacent symbols within $\varphi$.

***Proof:*** Let

$$\Sigma' \Longrightarrow \# \Sigma \# \overset{*}{\Longrightarrow} \varphi A \psi \Longrightarrow \varphi \alpha \psi$$

be a rightmost derivation in $\mathbf{G}'$. Condition 1 of the theorem follows directly from the definition of the precedence relations. To show that condition 2 is satisfied, we use an inductive argument. Suppose that each sentential form obtained by an $(r - 1)$-step rightmost derivation in $\mathbf{G}$ satisfies condition 2, and let

$$\Sigma \overset{*}{\Longrightarrow} \varphi \alpha \psi \Longrightarrow \varphi' \beta \psi'$$

be an $r$-step rightmost derivation, where $\alpha$ and $\beta$ are handles. The relation $\gtrdot$ does not hold for any pair of adjacent symbols within $\varphi$ by hypothesis. Let $\varphi = X_1 \ldots X_k$ and $\alpha = Y_1 \ldots Y_m$. Since

$$X_k \lessdot Y_1 \doteq \ldots \doteq Y_m$$

relation $\gtrdot$ cannot hold for any pair of adjacent symbols in $\varphi\alpha$. The derivation being rightmost, $\varphi'$ is a prefix of $\varphi\alpha$ and condition 2 is satisfied.

Certain grammars would be precedence grammars were it not for a precedence conflict caused by a left or right recursive nonterminal. Suppose that a grammar has the rule

$$B \longrightarrow XA$$

and permits a derivation

$$A \overset{*}{\Longrightarrow} A\alpha$$

(a) Analyzer Configurations

| Stack $\sigma$ | Handle $\alpha$ | Input $\psi$ | Production |
|---:|---:|---|---|
| $\#$ | $\lessdot x \gtrdot$ | $\times\ (x \times x + x)\#$ | $F \to x$ |
| $\#$ | $\lessdot F \gtrdot$ | $\times\ (x \times x + x)\#$ | $P \to F$ |
| $\# P \times ($ | $\lessdot x \gtrdot$ | $\times\ x + x)\#$ | $F \to x$ |
| $\# P \times ($ | $\lessdot F \gtrdot$ | $\times\ x + x)\#$ | $P \to F$ |
| $\# P \times (P \times$ | $\lessdot x \gtrdot$ | $+ x)\#$ | $F \to x$ |
| $\# P \times ($ | $\lessdot P \times F \gtrdot$ | $+ x)\#$ | $P \to P \times F$ |
| $\# P \times ($ | $\lessdot P \gtrdot$ | $+ x)\#$ | $T \to P$ |
| $\# P \times ($ | $\lessdot T \gtrdot$ | $+ x)\#$ | $A \to T$ |
| $\# P \times (A +$ | $\lessdot x \gtrdot$ | $)\#$ | $F \to x$ |
| $\# P \times (A +$ | $\lessdot F \gtrdot$ | $)\#$ | $P \to F$ |
| $\# P \times (A +$ | $\lessdot P \gtrdot$ | $)\#$ | $T \to P$ |
| $\# P \times ($ | $\lessdot A + T \gtrdot$ | $)\#$ | $A \to A + T$ |
| $\# P \times ($ | $\lessdot A \gtrdot$ | $)\#$ | $B \to A$ |
| $\# P \times$ | $\lessdot (B) \gtrdot$ | $\#$ | $F \to (B)$ |
| $\#$ | $\lessdot P \times F \gtrdot$ | $\#$ | $T \to P \times F$ |
| $\#$ | $\lessdot T \gtrdot$ | $\#$ | $A \to T$ |
| $\#$ | $\lessdot A \gtrdot$ | $\#$ | $B \to A$ |
| $\#$ | $\lessdot B \gtrdot$ | $\#$ | $\Sigma \to B$ |

(b) Derivation Tree

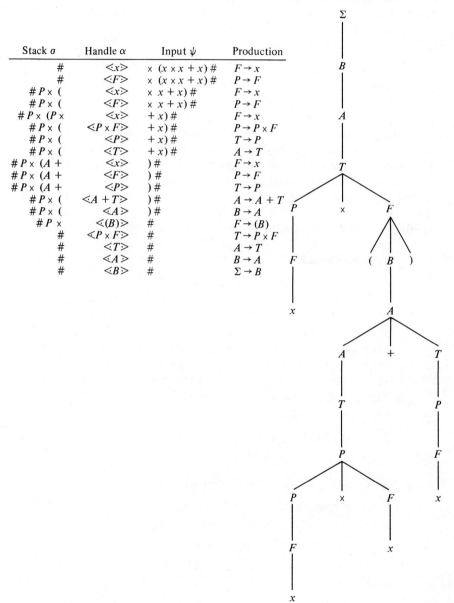

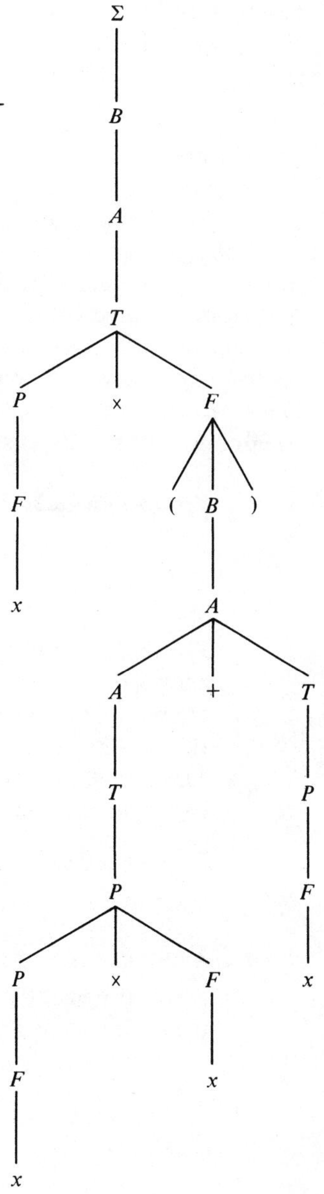


**Figure 10.14** Precedence analysis of the sentence $x \times (x \times x + x)$.

Since the definition of the precedence relations require that $X \doteq A$ and $X \lessdot A$, the grammar is not a precedence grammar. This precedence conflict may be removed by introducing a new nonterminal $A'$, and replacing the rule $B \longrightarrow XA$ with

$$B \longrightarrow XA' \quad \text{and} \quad A' \longrightarrow A$$

We then have $X \doteq A'$ and $X \lessdot A$, and there is no conflict. Thus precedence conflicts arising from recursive nonterminals may be removed by introducing nongenerative productions, as was done in Example 10.3 to obtain the precedence grammar $\mathbf{G}'$.

The class of simple precedence languages is included in the class of deterministic languages, as may be seen by noting that a DPDA can be designed to perform the precedence analysis algorithm of Figure 10.13. (The technique is similar to that discussed at the end of Section 10.2, but the finite-state control must contain the precedence matrix as well as the rules of the grammar.) However, the invertible precedence grammars fail to generate *all* deterministic language, as shown next:

**Proposition 10.2:** The language

$$\mathbf{L} = \{a\, 0^n 1^n \mid n \geq 1\} \cup \{b\, 0^n\, 1^{2n} \mid n \geq 1\}$$

is deterministic, but is not a simple precedence language.

***Proof:*** The reader may verify that **L** is deterministic by constructing a DPDA that recognizes **L**. Now suppose that **G** is a simple precedence grammar that generates **L**. Since **L** is the union of the infinite sets $\mathbf{L}_a = \{a\, 0^n\, 1^n \mid n \geq 1\}$ and $\mathbf{L}_b = \{b\, 0^n\, 1^{2n} \mid n \geq 1\}$, the argument of Theorem 9.5 may be applied to derivations in each set. Thus **G** must have nonterminals $X$ and $Y$ such that

$$\Sigma \overset{*}{\Longrightarrow} \eta_1 X \xi_1 \overset{*}{\Longrightarrow} \eta_1 \varphi_1^k X \psi_1^k \xi_1 \overset{*}{\Longrightarrow} \eta_1 \varphi_1^k \sigma_1 \psi_1^k \xi_1, \qquad \eta_1 \varphi_1^k \sigma_1 \psi_1^k \xi_1 \in \mathbf{L}_a$$

and

$$\Sigma \overset{*}{\Longrightarrow} \eta_2 Y \xi_2 \overset{*}{\Longrightarrow} \eta_2 \varphi_2^k Y \psi_2^k \xi_2 \overset{*}{\Longrightarrow} \eta_2 \varphi_2^k \sigma_2 \psi_2^k \xi_2, \qquad \eta_2 \varphi_2^k \sigma_2 \psi_2^k \xi_2 \in \mathbf{L}_b$$

Since strings of 0's and strings of 1's are matched with each other in the sentences of $\mathbf{L}_a$ and $\mathbf{L}_b$, we must have

$$\varphi_1, \varphi_2 \in \mathbf{0}^* - \boldsymbol{\lambda}$$
$$\psi_1, \psi_2 \in \mathbf{1}^* - \boldsymbol{\lambda}$$
$$\sigma_1, \sigma_2 \in \mathbf{0}^*\mathbf{1}^*$$

Also, $X$ and $Y$ must be distinct, for otherwise **G** would generate strings not in **L**. Furthermore, since

$$X \overset{*}{\Longrightarrow} 0^i X 1^j, \qquad i \geq 1, j \geq 1$$

we must have $0 \lessdot 0$ and $1 \gtrdot 1$. We shall now show that any string derived from $X$ or $Y$ can have only one nonterminal letter:

Suppose otherwise; that is, **G** permits

$$X \overset{*}{\Longrightarrow} \alpha A \beta B \gamma \overset{*}{\Longrightarrow} 0^m 1^n, \qquad A, B \in \mathbf{N}$$

where $\beta$ contains no nonterminal letters, $\beta \in \mathbf{0^*1^*}$. There are three cases to be considered:

1. $\beta = \lambda$. Let the final letter of some phrase denoted by $A$ be $c$ (either $c = 0$ or $c = 1$), and let the initial letter of some phrase denoted by $B$ be $d$. By definition of $\lessdot$ and $\gtrdot$, we must have both $c \lessdot d$ and $c \gtrdot d$, a conflict.
2. $\beta \in \mathbf{00^*1^*}$. Then the final letter of each phrase denoted by $A$ must be 0, and we have $0 \gtrdot 0$, which is a conflict since we have already established $0 \lessdot 0$.
3. $\beta \in \mathbf{0^*1^*1}$. Then the initial letter of each phrase denoted by $B$ must be 1, and we have $1 \lessdot 1$, again a conflict since we have established $1 \gtrdot 1$.

Consider now the derivations

$$X \overset{*}{\Longrightarrow} \alpha \qquad Y \overset{*}{\Longrightarrow} \beta, \qquad \alpha, \beta \in \mathbf{0^*1^*}$$

and suppose that the sets of nonterminals occurring in the two derivations are disjoint. Since $0 \lessdot 0$ and $1 \gtrdot 1$, no rule of **G** may have adjacent 0's or adjacent 1's in its right part, and the last pair of rules used in the derivations must be one of the following:

| In $X \overset{*}{\Longrightarrow} \alpha$ | | In $Y \overset{*}{\Longrightarrow} \beta$ |
|---|---|---|
| $U \longrightarrow 0$ | $0 \gtrdot 1$ | $V \longrightarrow 0$ |
| $U \longrightarrow 1$ | $0 \lessdot 1$ | $V \longrightarrow 1$ |
| $U \longrightarrow 01$ | $0 \doteq 1$ | $V \longrightarrow 01$ |

The presence of one of these rules in **G** implies the precedence relation for (0, 1) shown on the same line. Thus only rules on the same line may appear in **G**, but the rules on the same line have identical right parts. This is not possible, because **G** is invertible and we have assumed $U \neq V$.

Finally, suppose that some nonterminal appears in both derivations. Let $Z$ be the first nonterminal appearing in $X \overset{*}{\Longrightarrow} \alpha$ that also appears in $Y \overset{*}{\Longrightarrow} \beta$, and consider the rules that generate $Z$:

| In $X \overset{*}{\Longrightarrow} \alpha$ | In $Y \overset{*}{\Longrightarrow} \beta$ |
|---|---|
| $U \longrightarrow \omega Z \varphi$ | $V \longrightarrow \psi Z \delta$ |

Neither $\omega$ nor $\psi$ can end in 1, for then $Z$ could generate only 1's and $1 \lessdot 1$ would have to hold. Similarly, neither $\varphi$ nor $\delta$ can begin with 0. Since no string derived from $X$ or $Y$ can have more than one nonterminal, the only possibilities left are

| In $X \overset{*}{\Longrightarrow} \alpha$ | | In $Y \overset{*}{\Longrightarrow} \beta$ |
|---|---|---|
| $U \longrightarrow Z$ | $0 \lessdot Z \gtrdot 1$ | $V \longrightarrow Z$ |
| $U \longrightarrow 0Z1$ | $0 \doteq Z \doteq 1$ | $V \longrightarrow 0Z1$ |
| $U \longrightarrow 0Z$ | $0 \doteq Z \gtrdot 1$ | $V \longrightarrow 0Z$ |
| $U \longrightarrow Z1$ | $0 \lessdot Z \doteq 1$ | $V \longrightarrow Z1$ |

which imply the indicated precedence. Only rules on the same line may appear in **G**, but such rules have identical right parts. Since **G** is invertible, we must have $U = V$, contradicting that $Z$ is the first nonterminal appearing in $X \overset{*}{\Longrightarrow} \alpha$ that also appears in $Y \overset{*}{\Longrightarrow} \beta$.

## 10.4 Generalized Precedence Grammars

The precedence analyzer of Section 10.3 identifies the handle of a sentential form in two steps: first, it shifts the symbols of the sentential form onto its stack until the relation $\gtrdot$ is encountered; then it scans down the stack until the relation $\lessdot$ is encountered. The string thus identified on top of the stack is the right part of a production. Because the grammar is required to be invertible, a unique left part can be substituted during the subsequent reduction step. This method can be generalized (sufficiently to include all the deterministic languages) by relaxing the requirement of invertibility, without giving up the ability to identify the unique production for reducing the top stack symbols.

The *generalized precedence analyzer* also operates in two steps: it shifts symbols from a sentential form onto the stack until the relation $\gtrdot$ is encountered, then scans the stack until a string matching some production's right part is found. If that right part is unique in the grammar, it can be immediately replaced by the left part of the production. Otherwise, the parser looks one symbol farther into the stack, determining the unique reduction from this single symbol of *left context*. If a grammar allows such a parser, it is called a *generalized precedence grammar*. Note that in addition to relaxing the requirement of invertibility, this parsing procedure also relaxes the precedence requirements: the relations $\lessdot$ and $\doteq$ need not be disjoint, since they are not used to determine the left end of a handle. For this reason, we merge these relations into a single relation $\lessdot\!\!\!\!\!\leq$, and require only that $\lessdot\!\!\!\!\!\leq$ be disjoint from $\gtrdot$.

Suppose that $\varphi X\alpha\psi$ is a right sentential form of a grammar and that both $A \longrightarrow \alpha$ and $B \longrightarrow \alpha$ are rules of the grammar. A parser, having encountered $\alpha$ on top of the stack, must be able to decide from the next stack symbol $X$ which of these rules should be used in the reduction step. To formalize this decision, we define the set $\ell(N)$, which contains all possible symbols that can appear immediately to the left of the nonterminal $N$ in a right sentential form:

$$\ell(N) = \{X \in \mathbf{V} \cup \{\#\} \mid \varphi XN\psi \text{ is a right sentential form of } \mathbf{G}\}$$

If $\ell(A)$ is disjoint from $\ell(B)$, and if $X$ is in $\ell(A)$, then $\varphi XB\psi$ cannot be a right sentential form, and the parser may correctly use $A \longrightarrow \alpha$ for the reduction of $\varphi X\alpha\psi$.

In a generalized precedence grammar, we require that $\ell(A)$ and $\ell(B)$ be disjoint for nonterminals $A$ and $B$ whenever $A$ and $B$ have rules with identical right parts. However, this condition alone does not guarantee the most general deterministic parser, for if the grammar has rules of the form $A \longrightarrow \theta$ and $B \longrightarrow \theta'\theta$, the stack scanning step may stop after recognizing $\theta$ on top of the stack even though $B \longrightarrow \theta'\theta$ provides the proper reduction. We can eliminate this problem by requiring $X \notin \ell(A)$ whenever the grammar has rules

$$A \longrightarrow \theta \quad \text{and} \quad B \longrightarrow \alpha X\theta$$

If $X$ is not in $\ell(A)$, the rule $A \longrightarrow \theta$ cannot be used to reduce a sentential form if $X$ appears immediately left of a potential handle $\theta$. Thus $\theta$ found atop the stack is the handle of a sentential form just if the next stack symbol is in $\ell(A)$; if the next stack symbol is not in $\ell(A)$, the parser must scan farther into the stack to find the handle.

These ideas are summarized in Definition 10.4. We show shortly that they are sufficient to guarantee that every deterministic language has a generalized precedence analyzer.

**Definition 10.4:** Let $\mathbf{G} = (\mathbf{N}, \mathbf{T}, \mathbf{P}, \Sigma)$ be a context-free grammar, and let $\mathbf{V} = \mathbf{N} \cup \mathbf{T}$. Define precedence relations $\lessdot$ on $\mathbf{V} \times \mathbf{V}$ and $\gtrdot$ on $\mathbf{V} \times \mathbf{T}$ by

1. $Y_1 \lessdot \ldots \lessdot Y_m$ if $\mathbf{G}$ has a rule $A \longrightarrow Y_1 \ldots Y_m$.
2. $X \lessdot Y$ if $\mathbf{G}$ has a rightmost derivation $\Sigma \overset{*}{\Longrightarrow} \varphi XA\psi$ and a rule $A \longrightarrow Y\beta$.
3. $X \gtrdot a$ if $\mathbf{G}$ has a rightmost derivation $\Sigma \overset{*}{\Longrightarrow} \varphi Aa\psi$ and a rule $A \longrightarrow \beta X$.

Then $\mathbf{G}$ is a *generalized precedence grammar* if

1. Relations $\lessdot$ and $\gtrdot$ are disjoint.
2. $\ell(A) \cap \ell(B) = \varnothing$ whenever $A \longrightarrow \alpha$ and $B \longrightarrow \alpha$ are distinct rules of $\mathbf{G}$.

3. $X \notin \ell(B)$ whenever $A \longrightarrow \alpha XY\beta$ and $B \longrightarrow Y\beta$ are both rules of **G**.

The description of a parsing algorithm for generalized precedence analysis is simplified by defining a *reduction function* $f$ for the grammar **G**. Let **G**′ be the end-marked version of **G**, and consider any right sentential form of **G**′

$$X_1 \ldots X_k \underbrace{Y_1 \ldots Y_m}_{\alpha} a_1 \ldots a_n$$

in which $Y_m \gtrdot a_1$. The arguments of the reduction function are a string $\alpha = Y_1 \ldots Y_m$, conjectured to be the handle of the sentential form, and the symbol $X_k$ immediately left of $\alpha$. The value $f(X_k, \alpha)$ is 0 if $\alpha$ is not the handle, or $p$ if $\alpha$ is the handle, where $p$ is the rule of **G** to be used in reducing the sentential form. Thus the reduction function for **G** is a mapping

$$f\colon\ (\mathbf{V} \cup \{\#\}) \times \mathbf{V}^* \longrightarrow \{0, 1, \ldots, r\}$$

where the rules of **G** are numbered $1, \ldots, r$. It is defined by

$$f(X, Y_1 \ldots Y_m) = \begin{cases} p & \text{if rule } p \text{ of } \mathbf{G} \text{ is } A \longrightarrow Y_1 \ldots Y_m \text{ and } X \in \ell(A) \\ 0 & \text{otherwise} \end{cases}$$

It should be clear from the conditions of Definition 10.4 that this definition assigns a unique value to each pair of arguments for which $f$ is defined. Since the reduction function is only defined for strings $Y_1 \ldots Y_m$ that are not longer than the longest right part of any rule in **G**, the domain of $f$ is a finite set.

Figure 10.15 is a flow chart for generalized precedence analysis. The right end of the handle is located by shifting input symbols onto the stack until $\gtrdot$ holds between the top stack symbol and the next input symbol. The parser then scans the stack until the string $\alpha$ and the left context symbol $X$ satisfy $f(X, \alpha) = p > 0$. Production $p$ is used to reduce the sentential form, and shifting of input symbols is resumed. If the reduction function is undefined at any point in the analysis, no reduction of the current sentential form is possible, and the analysis has failed.

**Example 10.4:** In Figure 10.16, the precedence matrix and reduction function for the arithmetic expression grammar are shown. Every rule of this grammar is invertible. The right part of $A \longrightarrow T$ is a suffix of the right part of $A \longrightarrow A + T$, but $+$ is not in $\ell(A)$ in accordance with condition 3 of Definition 10.4; similarly, the right part of $T \longrightarrow F$ is a suffix of the right part of $T \longrightarrow T \times F$, but $\times$ is not in $\ell(T)$. Therefore, this grammar is a generalized precedence grammar.

**Example 10.5:** The grammar in Figure 10.17a generates the language $\mathbf{L(G)} = \{a0^n1^n \mid n \geq 1\} \cup \{b0^n1^{2n} \mid n \geq 1\}$, which, as we have seen, is not a simple precedence language. Nevertheless, **G** is a generalized

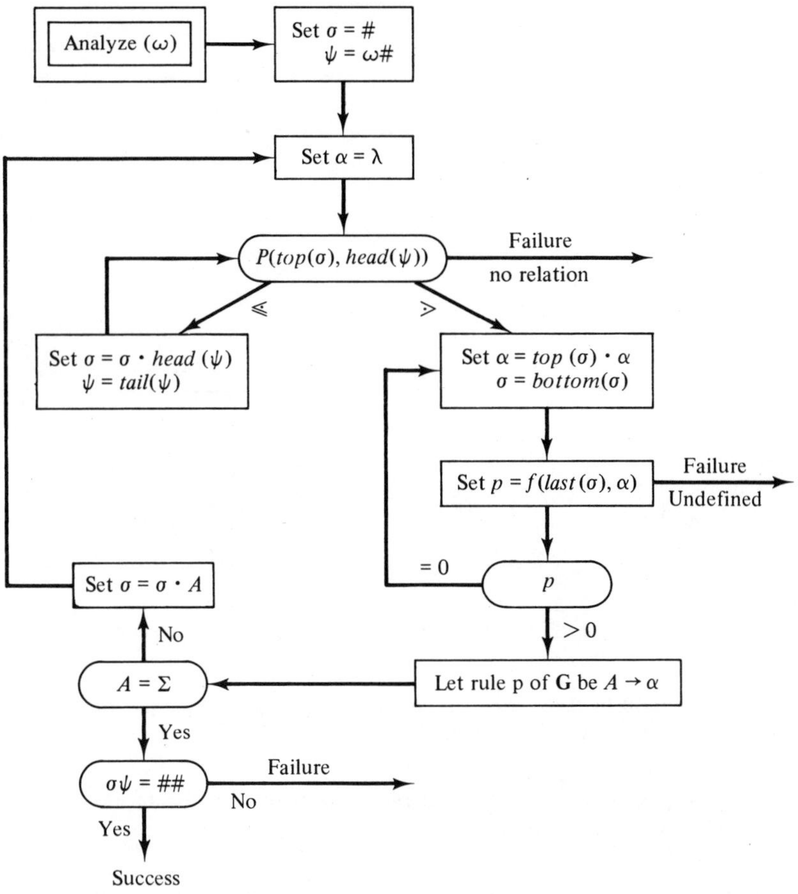


**Figure 10.15** Generalized precedence analyzer.

precedence grammar: the grammar has rules $C \longrightarrow 0$ and $D \longrightarrow 0$, but $\ell(C) = \{C, a\}$ and $\ell(D) = \{D, b\}$, so $\ell(C) \cap \ell(D) = \varnothing$. Thus condition 2 of Definition 10.4 is satisfied. The right part of the rule $E \longrightarrow 1$ is a suffix of the right parts of four rules in **G**, but the following listing shows that each pair of rules satisfies condition 3 of the definition:

| Rules | | Requirement |
|---|---|---|
| $A \longrightarrow CA1$ | $E \longrightarrow 1$ | $A \notin \ell(E) = \{B, D\}$ |
| $A \longrightarrow C1$ | $E \longrightarrow 1$ | $C \notin \ell(E)$ |
| $A \longrightarrow DBE1$ | $E \longrightarrow 1$ | $E \notin \ell(E)$ |
| $A \longrightarrow DE1$ | $E \longrightarrow 1$ | $E \notin \ell(E)$ |

(a) grammar

| | | |
|---|---|---|
| **G**: | $\Sigma \longrightarrow A$ | (1) |
| | $A \longrightarrow T$ | (2) |
| | $A \longrightarrow A + T$ | (3) |
| | $T \longrightarrow F$ | (4) |
| | $T \longrightarrow T \times F$ | (5) |
| | $F \longrightarrow (A)$ | (6) |
| | $F \longrightarrow x$ | (7) |

(c) reduction function

| $X$ | $\alpha$ | $f(X, \alpha)$ |
|---|---|---|
| # | $A$ | 1 |
| #,( | $T$ | 2 |
| #,( | $A + T$ | 3 |
| #,(,+ | $F$ | 4 |
| #,(,+ | $T \times F$ | 5 |
| #,(,+,× | $(A)$ | 6 |
| #,(,+,× | $x$ | 7 |

(b) precedence matrix

| | $A$ | $T$ | $F$ | ( | $x$ | × | + | ) | # |
|---|---|---|---|---|---|---|---|---|---|
| $A$ | | | | | | | $\underline{\lessdot}$ | $\underline{\lessdot}$ | $\gtrdot$ |
| $T$ | | | | | | $\underline{\lessdot}$ | $\gtrdot$ | $\gtrdot$ | $\gtrdot$ |
| $F$ | | | | | | $\gtrdot$ | $\gtrdot$ | $\gtrdot$ | $\gtrdot$ |
| ) | | | | | | $\gtrdot$ | $\gtrdot$ | $\gtrdot$ | $\gtrdot$ |
| $x$ | | | | | | $\gtrdot$ | $\gtrdot$ | $\gtrdot$ | $\gtrdot$ |
| × | | | $\underline{\lessdot}$ | $\underline{\lessdot}$ | $\underline{\lessdot}$ | | | | |
| + | | $\underline{\lessdot}$ | $\underline{\lessdot}$ | $\underline{\lessdot}$ | $\underline{\lessdot}$ | | | | |
| ( | $\underline{\lessdot}$ | $\underline{\lessdot}$ | $\underline{\lessdot}$ | $\underline{\lessdot}$ | $\underline{\lessdot}$ | | | | |
| # | $\underline{\lessdot}$ | $\underline{\lessdot}$ | $\underline{\lessdot}$ | $\underline{\lessdot}$ | $\underline{\lessdot}$ | | | | |

**Figure 10.16** Precedence matrix and reduction function for the arithmetic expression grammar.

The precedence matrix and reduction function for **G** are shown in Figures 10.17b and c.

The importance of generalized precedence grammars lies in their ability to generate all deterministic languages.

**Theorem 10.2:** A context-free language is deterministic if and only if it is generated by a generalized precedence grammar.

***Proof*** (*If*)**:** As in the case of invertible precedence grammars, a DPDA can be constructed from any generalized precedence grammar. (Note that the reduction function defined above has a finite domain and can thus be represented in the finite-state control unit of the DPDA.) The details of the construction are left to the reader.
(*Only If*): Let **M** be a DPDA, and assume that **M** is proper and loop free. We shall show that the context-free grammar **G** constructed from **M** using the rules of Table 8.3 is a generalized precedence grammar. Let $\underline{\lessdot}$ and $\gtrdot$ be the precedence relations for **G** according

(a) grammar

| | | |
|---|---|---|
| **G**: | $\Sigma \longrightarrow aA$ | (1) |
| | $A \longrightarrow CA1$ | (2) |
| | $A \longrightarrow C1$ | (3) |
| | $C \longrightarrow 0$ | (4) |
| | $\Sigma \longrightarrow bB$ | (5) |
| | $B \longrightarrow DBE1$ | (6) |
| | $B \longrightarrow DE1$ | (7) |
| | $D \longrightarrow 0$ | (8) |
| | $E \longrightarrow 1$ | (9) |

(b) precedence matrix

| | $A$ | $B$ | $C$ | $D$ | $E$ | $a$ | $b$ | 0 | 1 | # |
|---|---|---|---|---|---|---|---|---|---|---|
| $A$ | | | | | | | | | $\lessdot$ | $\gtrdot$ |
| $B$ | | | | | $\lessdot$ | | | | $\lessdot$ | $\gtrdot$ |
| $C$ | $\lessdot$ | | $\lessdot$ | | | | | $\lessdot$ | $\lessdot$ | |
| $D$ | | $\lessdot$ | | $\lessdot$ | $\lessdot$ | | | $\lessdot$ | $\lessdot$ | |
| $E$ | | | | | | | | | $\lessdot$ | |
| $a$ | $\lessdot$ | | $\lessdot$ | | | | | $\lessdot$ | | |
| $b$ | | $\lessdot$ | | $\lessdot$ | | | | $\lessdot$ | | |
| 0 | | | | | | | | $\gtrdot$ | $\gtrdot$ | |
| 1 | | | | | | | | | $\gtrdot$ | $\gtrdot$ |
| # | | | | | | $\lessdot$ | $\lessdot$ | | | |

(c) reduction function

| $X$ | $\alpha$ | $f(X, \alpha)$ |
|---|---|---|
| # | $aA$ | 1 |
| $C,a$ | $CA1$ | 2 |
| $C,a$ | $C1$ | 3 |
| $C,a$ | 0 | 4 |
| # | $bB$ | 5 |
| $b,D$ | $DBE1$ | 6 |
| $b,D$ | $DE1$ | 7 |
| $b,D$ | 0 | 8 |
| $B,D$ | 1 | 9 |

**Figure 10.17** Precedence matrix and reduction function for parsing strings of the language $\{a0^n1^n \mid n \geq 1\} \cup \{b0^n1^{2n} \mid n \geq 1\}$.

to Definition 10.4; three facts must be established:

1. Relations $\lessdot$ and $\gtrdot$ are disjoint.
2. $\ell(A) \cap \ell(B) = \varnothing$ whenever $A \longrightarrow \alpha$ and $B \longrightarrow \alpha$ are rules of **G**.
3. $X \notin \ell(B)$ whenever $A \longrightarrow \alpha XY\beta$ and $B \longrightarrow Y\beta$ are rules of **G**.

For convenience, the four correspondences between traverse patterns in **M** and types of productions in **G** are shown again in Figure 10.18. Here we use the simplified notation $q \longrightarrow q'$ for a traverse of **M** from state $q$ to state $q'$ and use the letters $S$, $R$, and $W$ to indicate scan, read, and write moves, respectively.

The following preliminary fact is used at several points in the proof: if $N(q_1, q_1')N(q_2, q_2')$ occurs in a right sentential form of **G**, then **M** has the behavior

$$q_1 \longrightarrow q_1' \; W \ldots W q_2 \longrightarrow q_2'$$

| | traverse of **M** | production in **G** |
|---|---|---|
| (1) | $qSq'$ | $N(q, q') \longrightarrow a$ |
| (2) | $q \longrightarrow q''Sq'$ | $N(q, q') \longrightarrow N(q, q'')a$ |
| (3) | $q \longrightarrow q''Wp \longrightarrow p'Rq'$ | $N(q, q') \longrightarrow N(q, q'')N(pp')$ |
| (4) | $qWp \longrightarrow p'\,Rq'$ | $N(q, q') \longrightarrow N(p, p')$ |

**Figure 10.18** Relation of traverses of a DPDA to productions of a grammar.

In particular, $q_1'$ is a state from which **M** makes only write moves prior to entering state $q_2$. To see this, consider the production that introduces $N(q_1, q_1')$ in the rightmost derivation

$$\Sigma \overset{*}{\Longrightarrow} \varphi N(q_1, q_1')N(q_2, q_2')\psi$$

Of the four possibilities indicated by Figure 10.18, (1) cannot apply, and (2) would introduce a terminal letter to the right of $N(q_1, q_1')$. The form (4) is not possible because the reduced sentential form must contain at least one nonterminal to the right of $N(q_1, q_1')$ from which $N(q_2, q_2')$ derives, and this cannot occur in a rightmost derivation. Thus the production that introduces $N(q_1, q_1')$ must be of the form

$$N(q_1, q_1'') \longrightarrow N(q_1, q_1')N(q_3, q_3')$$

and the derivation has the form

$$\Sigma \overset{*}{\Longrightarrow} \varphi N(q_1, q_1'')\psi' \Rightarrow \varphi N(q_1, q_1')N(q_3, q_3')\psi' \overset{*}{\Longrightarrow} \varphi N(q_1, q_1')N(q_2, q_2')\psi$$

It must be the case, then, that $q_1'$ is a write state of **M**. After arriving at state $q_1'$, the DPDA, being proper, can make no read move until some terminal letter is scanned. Since no terminals occur between $N(q_1, q_1')$ and $N(q_2, q_2')$, **M** executes only write moves until state $q_2$ is entered.

We are now ready to establish the three facts stated earlier:

1. Suppose that $N(q_1, q_1') \gtrdot a$ holds in **G** for some nonterminal $N(q_1, q_1')$. Then **G** permits a derivation

$$\Sigma \overset{*}{\Longrightarrow} \varphi A a \psi \Longrightarrow \varphi \beta N(q_1, q_1') a \psi$$

where $A \longrightarrow \beta N(q_1, q_1')$ is a rule of **G**. According to Figure 10.18, this rule must have the form

$$N(q_2, q_2') \longrightarrow N(q_2, q_2'')N(q_1, q_1')$$

corresponding to the traverse

$$q_2 \longrightarrow q_2''\, W\, q_1 \longrightarrow q_1'\, R\, q_2'$$

or the form

$$N(q_2, q_2') \longrightarrow N(q_1, q_1')$$

corresponding to the traverse

$$q_2 \; W \; q_1 \longrightarrow q_1' \; R \; q_2'$$

In either case, $q_1'$ is a read state of **M**.

Now suppose that $N(q_1, q_1') \lessdot a$ also holds. Then **G** must permit a derivation

$$\Sigma \overset{*}{\Longrightarrow} \varphi N(q_1, q_1')A\psi \Longrightarrow \varphi N(q_1, q_1')a\beta\psi$$

where $A \longrightarrow a\beta$ is a rule of **G**, implying that $q_1'$ is a write state and contradicting the fact that $q_1'$ must be a read state of **M**. Thus the relations $\lessdot$ and $\gtrdot$ must be disjoint.

2. Suppose that **G** has productions

$$N(q_1, q_1') \longrightarrow \alpha \qquad N(q_2, q_2') \longrightarrow \alpha, \qquad N(q_1, q_1') \neq N(q_2, q_2')$$

and suppose further that $N(q, q') \in \ell(N(q_1, q_1')) \cap \ell(N(q_2, q_2'))$. It follows that **G** permits rightmost derivations

$$\Sigma \overset{*}{\Longrightarrow} \varphi_1 N(q, q')N(q_1, q_1')\psi_1$$

and

$$\Sigma \overset{*}{\Longrightarrow} \varphi_2 N(q, q')N(q_2, q_2')\psi_2$$

and by our earlier argument, **M** has the behavior

$$q \longrightarrow q' \; W \ldots W \; q_1$$

and

$$q \longrightarrow q' \; W \ldots W \; q_2$$

Since **M** is deterministic, either $q_1 = q_2$, or $q_2$ occurs in the sequence $q' \; W \ldots W q_1$, or $q_1$ occurs in the sequence $q' \; W \ldots W q_2$. In either of the last two cases, at least one of the states $q_1, q_2$ is a write state of **M**.

First suppose that $q_1 \neq q_2$. According to Figure 10.18, there are four possibilities for the right part $\alpha$ of the productions:

1. If $\alpha = a$ for some terminal letter $a$, $q_1$ and $q_2$ are both scan states of **M**, contradicting that at least one of the two states must be a write state.
2. If $\alpha = N(q_3, q_3')a$, we have $q_3 = q_1$ and $q_3 = q_2$, contradicting that $q_1 \neq q_2$.
3. If $\alpha = N(q_3, q_3')N(p, p')$, we again have $q_3 = q_1$ and $q_3 = q_2$, a contradiction.
4. If $\alpha = N(p, p')$, **M** has the behavior

$$q' \; W \ldots W \; q_1 \; W \; p \longrightarrow p' \; R$$

and also

$$q'\ W \ldots W\ q_2\ Wp \longrightarrow p'\ R$$

We know that either $q_2$ occurs in the sequence $q'\ W \ldots W q_1$ or $q_1$ occurs in $q'\ W \ldots W q_2$. Suppose, for example, that the former is the case. Then we have

$$q'\ W \ldots W\ q_2\ Wp\ W \ldots W\ q_1\ Wp$$

and since $p$ occurs twice in the sequence, **M** has a loop of write states contrary to the assumption that **M** is loop free.

Now suppose that $q_1 = q_2$. Because **M** is deterministic, it follows from Figure 10.18 that $q_1' = q_2'$ regardless of which of the four possibilities we choose for $\alpha$. But then we have $N(q_1, q_1') = N(q_2, q_2')$, contradicting our original assumption that $N(q_1, q_1') \neq N(q_2, q_2')$.

3. Suppose that **G** has two productions

$$A \longrightarrow \alpha XY\beta \qquad B \longrightarrow Y\beta$$

where the combination $XB$ occurs in some right sentential form. From Figure 10.18 there are two possibilities:

1. $N(q_1, q_1') \longrightarrow N(q_1, q_1'')a$ and $N(q_2, q_2') \longrightarrow a$, where $XB = N(q_1, q_1'')N(q_2, q_2')$ and $Y = a$.

Since $XB$ occurs in some right sentential form, $q_1''$ must be a write state of **M**. But the first production implies that $q_1''$ is a scan state, a contradiction.

2. $N(q_1, q_1') \longrightarrow N(q_1, q_1'')N(p, p')$ and $N(q_2, q_2') \longrightarrow N(p, p')$, where $XB = N(q_1, q_1'')N(q_2, q_2')$ and $Y = N(p, p')$.

Again $q_1''$ must be a write state of **M**. From Figure 10.18, **M** has the traverse patterns

$$q_1 \longrightarrow q_1''\ Wp \longrightarrow p'\ R\ q_1'$$

and

$$q_2\ Wp \longrightarrow p'\ \mathrm{R}\ q_2'$$

If $N(q_1, q_1'')N(q_2, q_2')$ occurs in a right sentential form, we must have

$$q_1''\ W \ldots W\ q_2$$

and consequently **M** has the behavior

$$q_1 \longrightarrow q_1''\ Wp\ W \ldots W\ q_2\ Wp$$

Thus **M** has a loop, contrary to assumption.

## 10.5 Generalized Left-to-Right Analysis

In precedence analysis, a parser looks at one symbol to the left and one symbol to the right of a string conjectured to be the handle of a right sentential form. An important generalization of this idea lets the parser use the entire left context and $k$ symbols of right context to decide whether a string is the handle of a right sentential form. This generalization is natural, because a left-to-right analyzer, when considering whether $\alpha$ is the handle, will have already examined all symbols left of $\alpha$ in the sentential form In examining $k$ symbols to the right of a potential handle, a left-to-right parser is "looking ahead" of the site of which a reduction will be made. Therefore, the method studied in this section is called *left-to-right analysis with k-symbol look-ahead*, or simply *LR*($k$) *analysis*.

Looking ahead $k$ symbols may exhaust the remaining terminal letters of a right sentential form. So that it will not be necessary to treat this situation as a special case, it is convenient to use sentential forms having $k$ end markers appended on the right. An end-marked sentential form $\omega\#^k$ has a rightmost derivation from $\Sigma\ \#^k$ by the same sequence of rules as in the rightmost derivation of $\omega$ from $\Sigma$.

**Definition 10.5:** Let $\mathbf{G} = (\mathbf{N}, \mathbf{T}, \mathbf{P}, \Sigma)$ be a well-formed context-free grammar with productions numbered $1, 2, \ldots, r$. Let the relation

$$g \subseteq \mathbf{V}^* \times (\mathbf{T} \cup \#)^k \times \{1, \ldots, r\}, \qquad \mathbf{V} = \mathbf{N} \cup \mathbf{T}$$

be defined as follows: if

$$\Sigma\ \#^k \overset{*}{\Longrightarrow} \varphi' A\theta\psi \Longrightarrow \varphi'\alpha\theta\psi, \qquad |\theta| = k$$

is any rightmost derivation in $\mathbf{G}$, where $A \longrightarrow \alpha$ is rule $p$ of $\mathbf{G}$, then

$$(\varphi, \theta, p) \in g, \qquad \text{where } \varphi = \varphi'\alpha$$

Grammar $\mathbf{G}$ is said to be *left-to-right analyzable with lookhead k*, or simply *LR*($k$), if the relation $g$ satisfies two conditions:

1. If $(\varphi, \theta, p_1)$ and $(\varphi, \theta, p_2)$ are both in $g$, then $p_1 = p_2$.
2. If $(\varphi, \theta, p) \in g$, then there is no $(\varphi', \theta', p') \in g$ such that $\varphi\theta$ is a proper prefix of $\varphi'\theta'$.

If $\mathbf{G}$ is *LR*($k$), the relation $g$ defines a function

$$f\colon\ \mathbf{V}^* \times (\mathbf{T} \cup \#)^k \longrightarrow \{0, \ldots, r\}$$

where

$$f(\varphi, \theta) = \begin{cases} p & \text{if } (\varphi, \theta, p) \in g \text{ for some } p \in \{1, \ldots, r\} \\ 0 & \text{otherwise} \end{cases}$$

This function is the *reduction function* of the *LR*($k$) grammar.

Figure 10.19 shows how the reduction function is used in a parsing procedure for an $LR(k)$ grammar. The parser performs actions of two kinds: shifting and reducing. Before each action, the right sentential form being analyzed is $\varphi\theta\psi$, where $\theta$ is the $k$-symbol lookahead string. Initially, $\varphi$ is the empty string and $\theta\psi$ is the entire input string $\omega$ with $k$ end markers appended. Whether shifting or reducing is performed is determined by the reduction function:

1. *Shift:* If $f(\varphi, \theta) = 0$, the lookahead string is advanced one symbol to the right within the sentential form. One letter from the left end of $\psi$ is appended to $\theta$, and the leftmost letter of $\theta$ is appended to $\varphi$.
2. *Reduce:* If $f(\varphi, \theta) = p > 0$, then rule $p$ of **G** is used to obtain the new sentential form $\varphi' A\theta\psi$, where rule $p$ is $A \longrightarrow \alpha$ and $\varphi = \varphi'\alpha$.

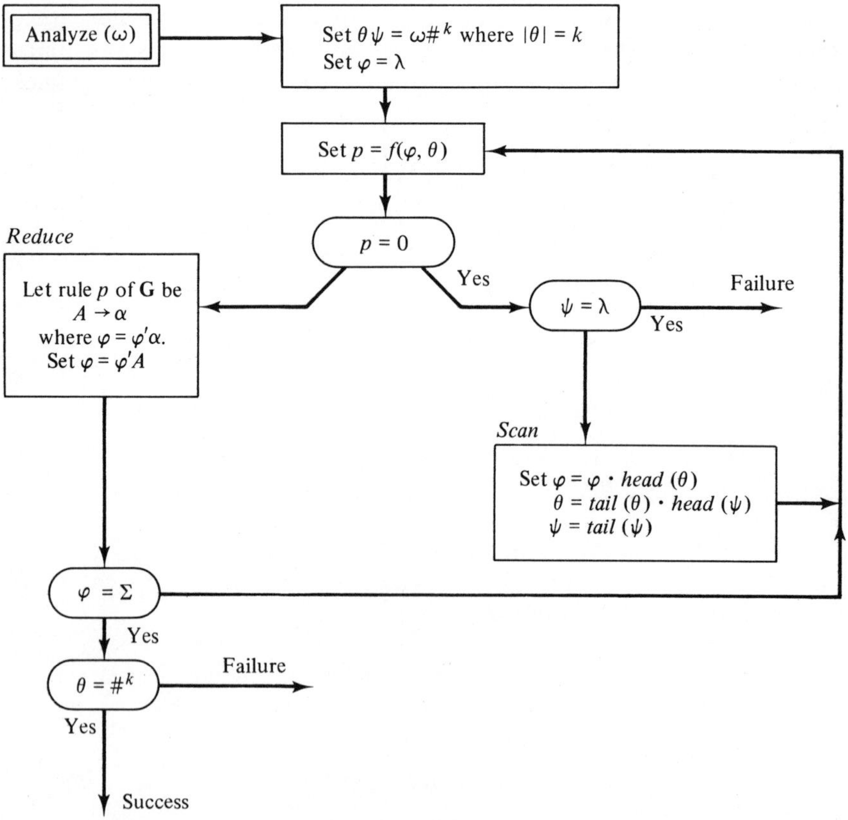


**Figure 10.19** Parsing procedure for $LR(k)$ grammars.

The procedure terminates when reduction is performed using some $\Sigma$-rule of **G** and $\theta = \#^k$, indicating that all letters of $\omega$ have been scanned. The numbers of the rules used in reduction steps form a parse of $\omega$.

From the parsing procedure it may be seen that the two conditions in the definition of *LR*($k$) grammars are both essential to correct operation of the parser. If condition 1 were not met, there would be right sentential forms for which the reduction function could not designate a unique rule. If condition 2 were not met, there would be sentential forms within which the parser would find potential handles at two distinct positions. Since it scans from left to right, the parser would always choose the handle farther to the left, and would fail for sentential forms in which the handle farther to the right is the correct choice.

The reduction function of an *LR*($k$) grammar has an infinite domain, so it appears that the evaluation of $f(\varphi, \theta)$ in the parsing procedure would be beyond the capability of a finite-state device. However, the grammar **G** has finitely many productions; hence, for each different lookahead string, the set $\mathbf{V}^*$ is partitioned into finitely many equivalence classes in correspondence with the productions that must be used to reduce the sentential forms. In the following development we obtain two key results about *LR*($k$) analysis. First we show that a finite-state machine may be designed that analyzes a right sentential form $\varphi\theta\psi$ and determines $p = f(\varphi, \theta)$. Then we show how this finite-state machine may be used to construct a deterministic pushdown accepter that carries out the parsing procedure given by Figure 10.19. These results show that the class of *LR*($k$) languages is the same as the class of deterministic languages and the class of generalized precedence languages.

For this development, we associate a *characteristic string* with each rightmost derivation in a grammar. Let **G** be a well-formed context-free grammar with productions numbered $1, 2, \ldots, r$, and suppose that we wish to construct an *LR*($k$) parser for some specified $k \geq 0$. Let

$$\Sigma \#^k \overset{*}{\Longrightarrow} \varphi' A \theta\psi \Longrightarrow \varphi' \alpha\theta\psi, \qquad \theta\psi \in \mathbf{T}^* \#^k, \qquad |\theta| = k$$

be any rightmost derivation permitted by **G**, where the last rule used, $A \longrightarrow \alpha$, is rule $p$ of **G**. The *k-characteristic string* for this derivation is

$$\varphi\theta\Delta_p$$

where $\varphi = \varphi'\alpha$ and $\Delta_p$ is a special symbol associated with rule $p$ of **G**.

Suppose that $\mathbf{L}_c$ is the set of all $k$-characteristic strings for **G**. From the construction of the relation $g$ in Definition 10.5, we see that

$$(\varphi, \theta, p) \text{ in } g \qquad \text{if and only if } \varphi\theta\Delta_p \in \mathbf{L}_c$$

From this property it is easy to show that the two conditions in the following proposition hold just if the relation $g$ for the grammar satisfies the conditions of Definition 10.5.

**Proposition 10.3:** Let **G** be a well-formed context-free grammar, and let $\mathbf{L}_c$ be the set of $k$-characteristic strings for all rightmost derivations permitted by **G**. Then **G** is an $LR(k)$ grammar if and only if $\mathbf{L}_c$ satisfies the following conditions:

1. If $\omega\Delta_p \in \mathbf{L}_c$ and $\omega\Delta_q \in \mathbf{L}_c$, then $p = q$.
2. If $\omega_1\Delta_{p_1} \in \mathbf{L}_c$ and $\omega_2\Delta_{p_2} \in \mathbf{L}_c$, then $\omega_1$ is not a proper prefix of $\omega_2$.

If we can determine that $\omega\Delta_p$ is a $k$-characteristic string of a right sentential form $\omega\psi$, then we know that rule $p$ of the grammar may be used to reduce the form

$$\varphi\alpha\theta\psi$$

to the form

$$\varphi A\theta\psi$$

where $\omega = \varphi\alpha\theta$, $|\theta| = k$, and rule $p$ is $A \longrightarrow \alpha$. Moreover, if there is only one $k$-characteristic string for each right sentential form, then the characteristic strings of the grammar determine a unique parse of any sentence.

The set $\mathbf{L}_c$ of $k$-characteristic strings of a context-free grammar is a regular set. We shall establish this fact by showing how to construct a finite-state accepter for $\mathbf{L}_c$, and shall then show how this accepter may be used to derive a deterministic parser for **L(G)** if **G** is an $LR(k)$ grammar. We begin our study with $LR(0)$ grammars, and then generalize to $LR(k)$ grammars for arbitrary $k$.

Let **G** be a well-formed context-free grammar, and consider any rightmost derivation permitted by **G**

$$\Sigma \stackrel{*}{\Longrightarrow} \varphi A_n \psi \Longrightarrow \varphi\alpha\psi$$

Figure 10.20 illustrates the form of the corresponding derivation tree. Let $\Sigma$ and the nonterminal letters $A_1, \ldots, A_n$ label the nodes on the path from the root node $\Sigma$ to the node $A_n$ associated with the final step of the derivation. From the figure we see that a rightmost derivation of $\varphi\alpha\psi$ has the following form:

(1)
$$\begin{aligned}
\Sigma &\Longrightarrow \alpha_1 A_1 \beta_1 \stackrel{*}{\Longrightarrow} \alpha_1 A_1 \beta_1' \\
&\Longrightarrow \alpha_1\alpha_2 A_2 \beta_2 \beta_1' \stackrel{*}{\Longrightarrow} \alpha_1\alpha_2 A_2 \beta_2' \beta_1' \\
&\qquad \vdots \qquad\qquad\qquad \vdots \\
&\Longrightarrow \alpha_1 \ldots \alpha_n A_n \beta_n \ldots \beta_1' \stackrel{*}{\Longrightarrow} \alpha_1 \ldots \alpha_n A_n \beta_n' \ldots \beta_1' \\
&\Longrightarrow \underbrace{\alpha_1 \ldots \alpha_n}_{\varphi} \alpha \underbrace{\beta_n' \ldots \beta_1'}_{\psi}
\end{aligned}$$

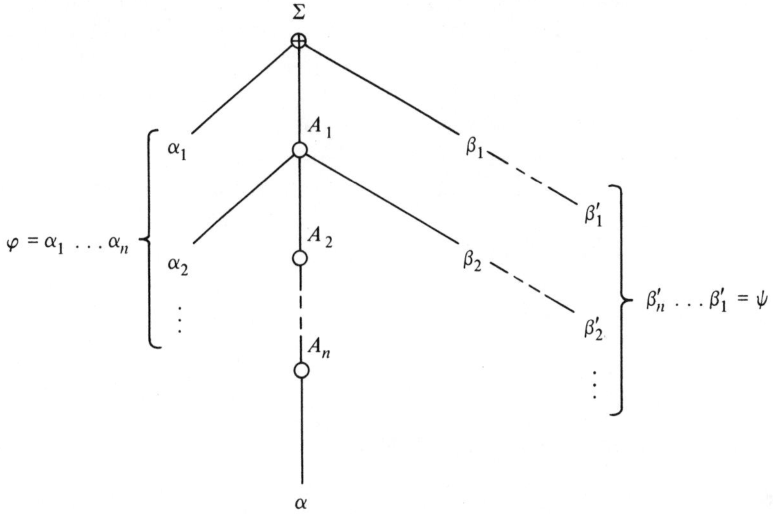


**Figure 10.20** Form of derivation tree for $\Sigma \overset{*}{\Longrightarrow} \varphi\alpha\psi$.

The productions used in this derivation include

$$\Sigma \longrightarrow \alpha_1 A_1 \beta_1 \tag{2}$$
$$A_{i-1} \longrightarrow \alpha_i A_i \beta_i, \qquad i = 2, \ldots, n$$
$$A_n \longrightarrow \alpha$$

and other productions by which each terminal string $\beta_i'$ is derived from $\beta_i$.

Let **M** be the finite-state accepter derived from **G** by the construction given in Table 10.1. The input alphabet of **M** includes the symbols that may

**Table 10.1** Construction of an accepter for the characteristic strings of a grammar

*Given:* a well-formed context-free grammar $\mathbf{G} = (\mathbf{N}, \mathbf{T}, \mathbf{P}, \Sigma)$
*To construct:* a finite-state accepter $\mathbf{M} = (\mathbf{Q}, \mathbf{V}, \mathbf{P}', \{q_\Sigma\}, \{q_F\})$ such that $\mathbf{L}(\mathbf{M})$ is the set of 0-characteristic strings for **G**
*Let:* $\mathbf{Q} = \{q_A | A \in \mathbf{N}\} \cup \{q_\Sigma\} \cup \{q_p | p = 1, \ldots, r\} \cup \{q_F\}$
$\mathbf{V} = \mathbf{N} \cup \mathbf{T} \cup \{\Delta_p | p \text{ is a rule of } \mathbf{G}\}$

| If rule $p$ of **G** has the form | then **M** has |
|---|---|
| $A \longrightarrow \alpha$, $\alpha \in \mathbf{V}^* - \lambda$ | $q_A \overset{\alpha}{\longrightarrow} q_p \overset{\Delta_p}{\longrightarrow} q_F$ |
| $A \longrightarrow \alpha B \beta$, $\alpha, \beta \in \mathbf{V}^*$, $B \in \mathbf{N}$ | $q_A \overset{\alpha}{\longrightarrow} q_B$ |

appear in sentential forms of **G**, plus the symbol $\Delta_p$ for each rule $p$ of **G**. Machine **M** has a single initial state $q_\Sigma$, a state $q_A$ for each nonterminal $A$ of **G**, a state $q_p$ for each rule $p$ of **G**, and a single accepting state $q_F$. For convenience, we have permitted transitions of **M** to be labeled with strings of more than one symbol. (This implies the existence of unnamed intermediate states of **M**.) Also, the construction may require use of $\lambda$-transitions, as will be seen in the examples. We claim that **M** accepts the 0-characteristic strings of **G**, and only these strings.

Corresponding to the productions (2) in **G**, **M** has the transitions

(3)
$$q_\Sigma \xrightarrow{\alpha_1} q_{A_1}$$
$$q_{A_{i-1}} \xrightarrow{\alpha_i} q_{A_i}, \qquad i = 2, \ldots, n$$
$$q_{A_n} \xrightarrow{\alpha} q_p \xrightarrow{\Delta_p} q_F$$

Thus **M** accepts the characteristic string $\varphi\alpha\Delta_p$ by the move sequence

(4)
$$q_\Sigma \xrightarrow{\alpha_1} q_{A_1} \xrightarrow{\alpha_2} q_{A_2} \xrightarrow{\alpha_3} \cdots$$
$$\xrightarrow{\alpha_n} q_{A_n} \xrightarrow{\alpha} q_p \xrightarrow{\Delta_p} q_F$$

Conversely, any string in **L(M)** corresponds to some path in **M** from $q_\Sigma$ to $q_F$, and the associated move sequence has the form (4). Hence **M** must have transitions as in (3), and **G** must have corresponding rules as in (2). Since **G** is well formed, **G** permits a derivation of some terminal string $\beta_i'$ from each string $\beta_i$. Therefore, **G** has a rightmost derivation of the form (1) in which the last step uses rule $p$ of **G**; thus each string in **L(M)** is the characteristic string of some rightmost derivation permitted by **G**.

By converting **M** into a deterministic accepter using the methods developed in Chapter 5, we obtain a machine $\mathbf{M}_c$ called the *0-characteristic finite-state accepter* (0-CFSA) for the grammar **G**.

**Example 10.6:** Consider the following grammar for the simple matching language $\{a^k b^k \mid k > 0\}$:

$$\mathbf{G}: \quad \Sigma \longrightarrow A \qquad (1)$$
$$A \longrightarrow aAb \qquad (2)$$
$$A \longrightarrow ab \qquad (3)$$

A finite-state accepter **M** for the 0-characteristic strings of **G** is shown in Figure 10.21a. Converting **M** into a deterministic accepter yields $\mathbf{M}_c$, the 0-CFSA for **G**, shown in Figure 10.21b. The trap state of $\mathbf{M}_c$ and its associated transitions have been omitted for simplicity.

Note that a characteristic accepter will have a single accepting state, because the reachable set for any characteristic string is $\{q_F\}$. If an accepter **M** is

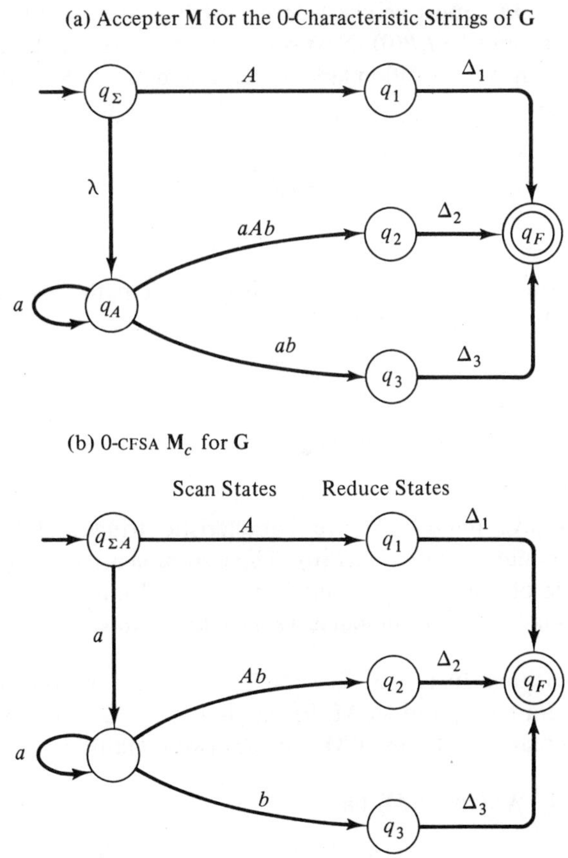


**Figure 10.21** Construction of the characteristic accepter of an *LR*(0) grammar.

constructed according to Table 10.1 from a well-formed grammar, there will be a path in **M** from each named state $q_A$ or $q_p$ to $q_F$, because the grammar, being well formed, has at least one $A$ rule for each nonterminal symbol $A$. It follows that there is a path from each state of the characteristic accepter (other than its trap state) to the accepting state.

Now suppose that there are two Δ-transitions leaving some state $q$ of a characteristic accepter $\mathbf{M}_c$. Then for some string $\varphi$, $\mathbf{M}_c$ has

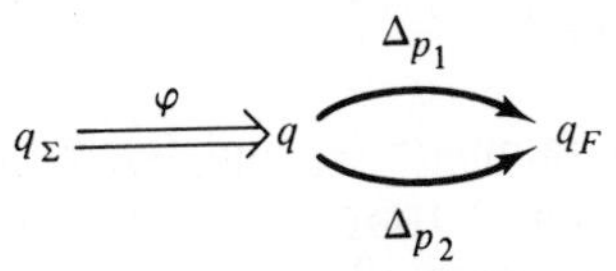

Both $\varphi\Delta_{p_1}$ and $\varphi\Delta_{p_2}$ must be characteristic strings and, by Proposition 10.3, the grammar cannot be $LR(0)$. Next suppose that there is a $\Delta$-transition leaving state $q$ and also a transition labeled $X$ for some $X \in \mathbf{N} \cup \mathbf{T}$:

$$q_\Sigma \overset{\varphi}{\Longrightarrow} q \overset{\Delta_{p_1}}{\underset{X}{\diagup\diagdown}} \begin{matrix} q_F \\ q'' \end{matrix}$$

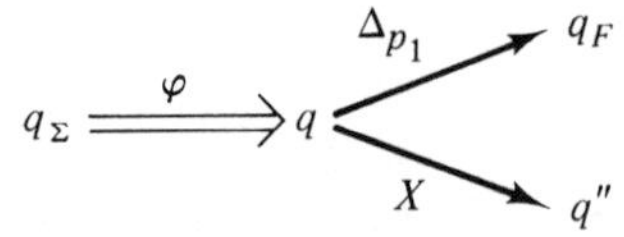

By construction, every transition in $\mathbf{M}_c$ is on some path to $q_F$. Thus there is a string $\beta$ and a state $q'$ such that

$$q_\Sigma \overset{\varphi}{\Longrightarrow} q \overset{\Delta_{p_1}}{\underset{X}{\diagup\diagdown}} \begin{matrix} q_F \\ q'' \overset{\beta}{\Longrightarrow} q' \overset{\Delta_{p_2}}{\Longrightarrow} q_F \end{matrix}$$

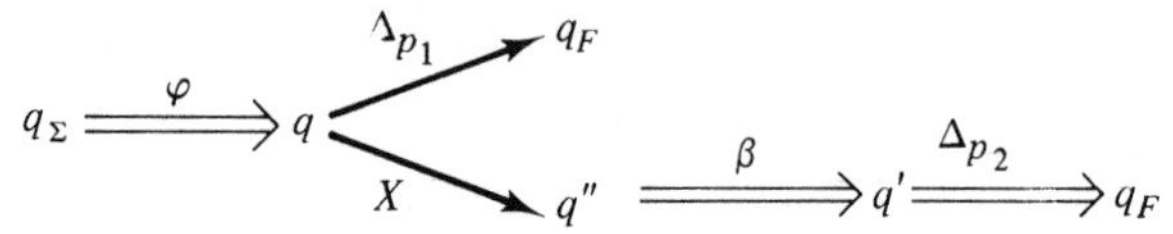

But then both $\varphi\Delta_{p_1}$ and $\varphi X \beta\Delta_{p_2}$ are characteristic strings and, by Proposition 10.3, the grammar cannot be $LR(0)$. These arguments may be reversed to show that one of the two situations just described must occur in $\mathbf{M}_c$ if the grammar is not $LR(0)$. In summary, we have the following:

**Proposition 10.4:** Let $\mathbf{G} = (\mathbf{N}, \mathbf{T}, \mathbf{P}, \Sigma)$ be a well-formed context-free grammar, and let $\mathbf{M}_c$ be the 0-CFSA for $\mathbf{G}$. Then $\mathbf{G}$ is an $LR(0)$ grammar if and only if $\mathbf{M}_c$ satisfies two conditions:

1. Whenever $\mathbf{M}_c$ has

$$q \overset{X}{\longrightarrow} q', \qquad X \in \mathbf{N} \cup \mathbf{T}$$

no $\Delta$-transition leaves state $q$.
2. Whenever $\mathbf{M}_c$ has

$$q \overset{\Delta_p}{\longrightarrow} q_F$$

this is the only transition leaving state $q$.

Thus, if $\mathbf{G}$ is an $LR(0)$ grammar, the states of the characteristic accepter, other than the trap state and the accepting state, fall into two disjoint groups.

1. *Shift states:* states with no $\Delta$-transitions leaving them.
2. *Reduce states:* states with one $\Delta$-transition to $q_F$, and no other transitions leaving them.

**Example 10.7:** Grammars $\mathbf{G}_1$ and $\mathbf{G}_2$ both generate the language $\{a^{2k+1}b \mid k \geq 0\}$; the corresponding 0-CFSA's are shown in Figure 10.22. From Proposition 10.4, $\mathbf{G}_1$ is an $LR(0)$ grammar, but $\mathbf{G}_2$ is

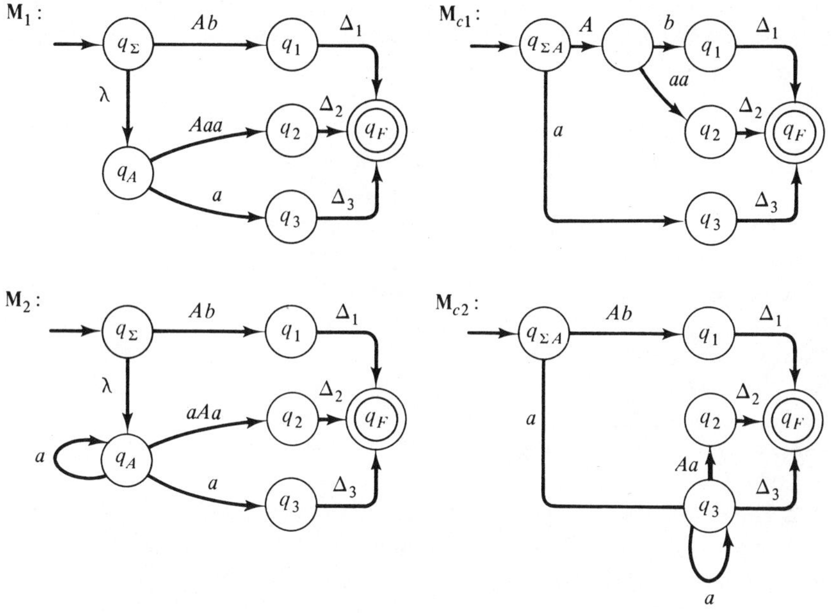


**Figure 10.22** Two characteristic accepters for an $LR(0)$ language.

not. This example illustrates the point that an $LR(k)$ language may be generated by a grammar that is not $LR(k)$.

$$\begin{array}{llll} \mathbf{G}_1: & \Sigma \longrightarrow Ab & (1) \qquad \mathbf{G}_2: & \Sigma \longrightarrow Ab \quad (1) \\ & A \longrightarrow Aaa & (2) & A \longrightarrow aAa \quad (2) \\ & A \longrightarrow a & (3) & A \longrightarrow a \quad (3) \end{array}$$

If **G** is an $LR(0)$ grammar, its characteristic accepter $\mathbf{M}_c$ may be used to design a deterministic parser for **G**. Given a sentence $\omega$, the parser will construct a sequence of sentential forms $\omega_1, \omega_2, \ldots, \omega_n$ such that $\omega_1 = \omega$, $\omega_n = \Sigma$, and the sequence is a rightmost derivation of $\omega$. The construction of $\omega_k$ from $\omega_{k-1}$ is done as follows:

1. Initialize $\mathbf{M}_c$ and apply symbols of $\omega_{k-1}$ until $\mathbf{M}_c$ enters a reduce state $q$.
2. Since **G** is $LR(0)$, the only transition leaving state $q$ is labeled $\Delta_p$, where rule $p$ of **G** is $A \longrightarrow \alpha$. At this point, $\omega_{k-1}$ has the form $\varphi\alpha\psi$, where $\psi$ is the suffix of $\omega_k$ that has not been presented to $\mathbf{M}_c$.
3. The new sentential form is $\omega_k = \varphi A \psi$.

These steps are repeated until the sentence is reduced to $\Sigma$. The sequence of rules used is a parse of $\omega$.

If this procedure fails because a symbol presented to $\mathbf{M}_c$ does not label a transition from its current state, then the string $\omega$ cannot be a sentence of **L(G)**. This is also the case if the symbols of $\omega_{k-1}$ are exhausted before $\mathbf{M}_c$ enters a reduce state.

The parsing procedure may be improved by permitting the characteristic accepter to begin its analysis of a new sentential form $\omega_k = \varphi A \psi$ at the first symbol in which it differs from $\omega_{k-1} = \varphi \alpha \psi$, that is, the nonterminal letter $A$. To do this, the parser must be able to return $\mathbf{M}_c$ to the state in which the first symbol of $\alpha$ was presented; for this purpose we use a stack into which state names for scan states of $\mathbf{M}_c$ are written as the symbols of a sentential form are read. When $\mathbf{M}_c$ enters a reduce state calling for reduction of $\varphi \alpha \psi$ using a rule $A \longrightarrow \alpha$, the top $|\alpha| - 1$ state names in the stack are removed, and the next entry remaining in the stack names the scan state from which operation of $\mathbf{M}_c$ should be resumed upon presentation of symbols of $\psi$. This process can be carried out by a deterministic pushdown accepter, whose construction we now describe.

The construction rules for a deterministic parser $\mathbf{M}_p$ are given in Table 10.2, where **G** is an $LR(0)$ grammar and $\mathbf{M}_c$ is its characteristic accepter. The parser has states corresponding to the shift and reduce states of $\mathbf{M}_c$, and auxiliary states as required to implement the parsing procedure. The stack alphabet contains a distinct symbol $u_i$ for each shift state $q_i$ of $\mathbf{M}_c$. These symbols are the state names used to direct resumption of shifting after a reduction is performed.

The construction of Table 10.2 uses three elementary routines. The **shift** $t$ routine begins at a scan state $q_i$, pushes the state name $u_i$ into the stack, and performs a shift move leading to state $q'$ if the letter $t$ is read from the input tape. Routine **top** $u_i$ tests the state name at the top of the stack and enters state $q_i'$ if the state name is $u_i$. The **pop** $n$ routine reads and discards $n$ state names from the stack.

If $\mathbf{M}_p$ is in a scan state $q_i$, it writes the associated state name $u_i$ into the stack, and reads a letter from the input tape. When $\mathbf{M}_p$ enters a reduce state $q_p$, a reduction is performed according to rule $p$ of the grammar, say $A \longrightarrow \alpha$. The effect of replacing $\alpha$ by $A$ in the current sentential form is achieved by reading and discarding the last $|\alpha| - 1$ state names written into the stack. The symbol then at the top of the stack is the name of the state $q_i$ at which $\mathbf{M}_p$ scanned the first symbol of $\alpha$; $\mathbf{M}_p$ makes a transition to the state $q_i'$ corresponding to the transition $\mathbf{M}_c$ would make if it were presented in state $q_i$ with the nonterminal symbol $A$. The relationship of the behavior of $\mathbf{M}_p$ to the behavior of $\mathbf{M}_c$ is illustrated by Figure 10.23. When $\mathbf{M}_p$ enters state $q_i'$, the top symbol in the stack is still $u_i$; thus scanning is, in effect, resumed in state $q_i$ with the presentation of $A$. Note that scanning of a nonterminal letter $A$ by $\mathbf{M}_c$ is replaced by a series of moves of $\mathbf{M}_p$ (including perhaps many reduction steps) that processes a phrase of type $A$ scanned from the input tape.

**Table 10.2** Construction of a DPDA for an $LR(0)$ grammar.

Given: The 0-CFSA $\mathbf{M}_c$ for an $LR(0)$ Grammar $\mathbf{G}$.

To Construct: A DPDA $\mathbf{M}_p$ such that $\mathbf{L}(\mathbf{M}_p) = \mathbf{L}(\mathbf{G})$.

$\mathbf{G} = (\mathbf{N}, \mathbf{T}, \mathbf{P}, \Sigma)$ $\quad \mathbf{M}_c = (\mathbf{Q}_c, \mathbf{N} \cup \mathbf{T}, \mathbf{P}_c, q_I, q_F)$ $\quad \mathbf{M}_p = (\mathbf{Q}_p, \mathbf{T}, \mathbf{P}_p, q'_I, q'_F)$

| If $\mathbf{M}_c$ has | then $\mathbf{M}_p$ has |
|---|---|
| 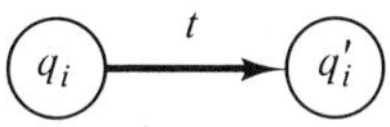<br>$q_i$ a scan state, $t \in \mathbf{T}$ | 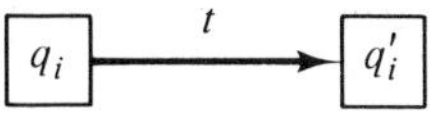 |
| 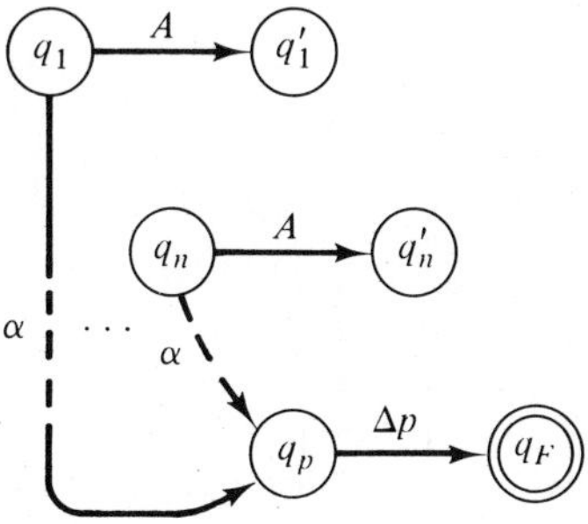<br>Rule $p$ of $\mathbf{G}$ is $A \to \alpha$ | 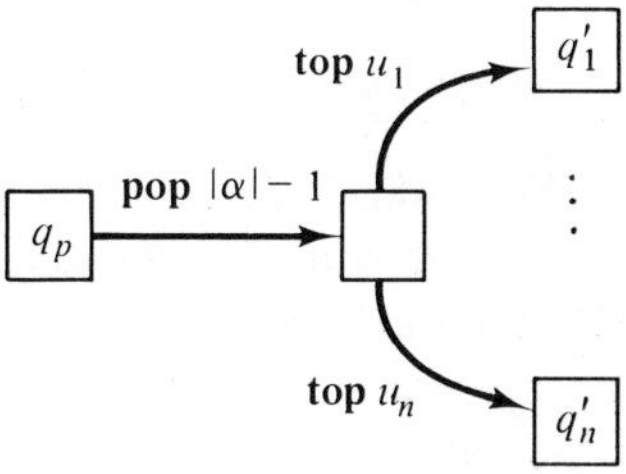 |
| 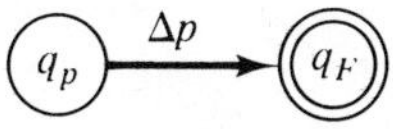<br>Rule $p$ of $G$ is $\Sigma \to \alpha$ | 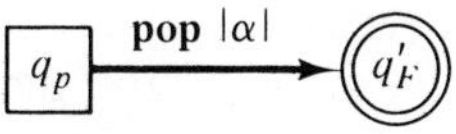 |

| | Notation | DPDA Routine |
|---|---|---|
| **shift** | 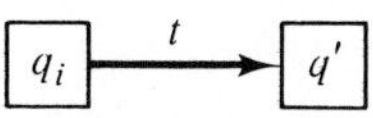 | 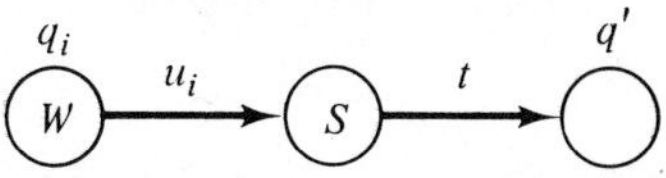 |
| **top** |  | 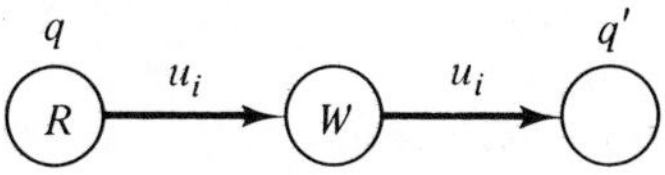 |
| **pop** | 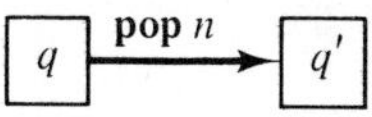 | 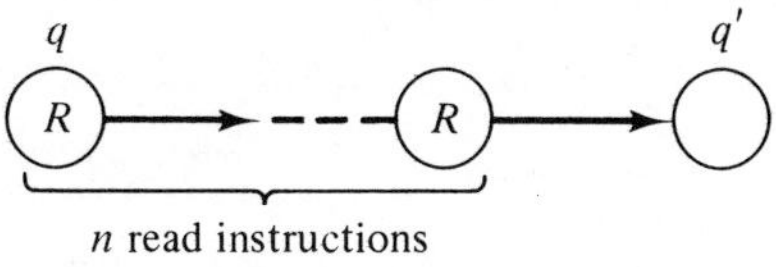 |

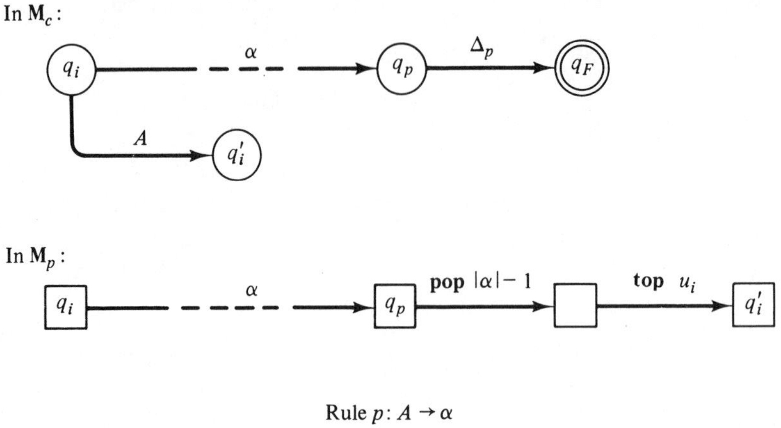


**Figure 10.23** Behavior of $\mathbf{M}_c$ and $\mathbf{M}_p$ for reduction by rule $p$.

Figure 10.24 shows the construction of a deterministic pushdown accepter from the characteristic accepter of Example 10.6. The figure also shows the sequence of configurations by which the string $a^2b^2$ is accepted.

Let us summarize the development to this point. With each context-free grammar we can associate the set of characteristic strings of its rightmost derivations. Since this set is regular, we can construct a finite-state accepter, the characteristic accepter, that accepts precisely these strings. The grammar is $LR(0)$ if and only if the states of the characteristic accepter can be partitioned into shift states and reduce states. If so, we can construct a deterministic pushdown accepter for the $LR(0)$ grammar by a straightforward transformation of the characteristic accepter.

To generalize these steps to $LR(k)$ parsing, we investigate the construction of a finite-state accepter for the $k$-characteristic strings of a well-formed grammar. Consider a rightmost derivation

$$\Sigma \,\#^k \stackrel{*}{\Longrightarrow} \varphi A_n \theta \psi \Longrightarrow \varphi \alpha \theta \psi$$

where $A_n \longrightarrow \alpha$ is rule $p$ of $\mathbf{G}$, and $\theta$ is the length $k$ lookahead string. Figure 10.25 shows the form of the corresponding derivation tree when the lookahead strings $\theta_1, \ldots, \theta_n$ associated with nonterminals $\Sigma, A_1, \ldots, A_n$ are made explicit. Thus the rightmost derivation has the form

$$\begin{aligned}
(1) \quad \Sigma\theta_0 &\Longrightarrow \alpha_1 A_1 \beta_1 \theta_0 \stackrel{*}{\Longrightarrow} \alpha_1 A_1 \theta_1 \beta_1' \\
&\Longrightarrow \alpha_1 \alpha_2 A_2 \beta_2 \theta_1 \beta_1' \stackrel{*}{\Longrightarrow} \alpha_1 \alpha_2 A_2 \theta_2 \beta_2' \beta_1' \\
&\Longrightarrow \alpha_1 \ldots \alpha_n A_n \beta_n \theta_{n-1} \beta_{n-1}' \ldots \beta_1' \stackrel{*}{\Longrightarrow} \alpha_1 \ldots \alpha_n A_n \theta_n \beta_n' \ldots \beta_1' \\
&\Longrightarrow \underbrace{\alpha_1 \ldots \alpha_n}_{\varphi} \underbrace{\alpha \theta_n \beta_n \ldots \beta_1}_{\psi}
\end{aligned}$$

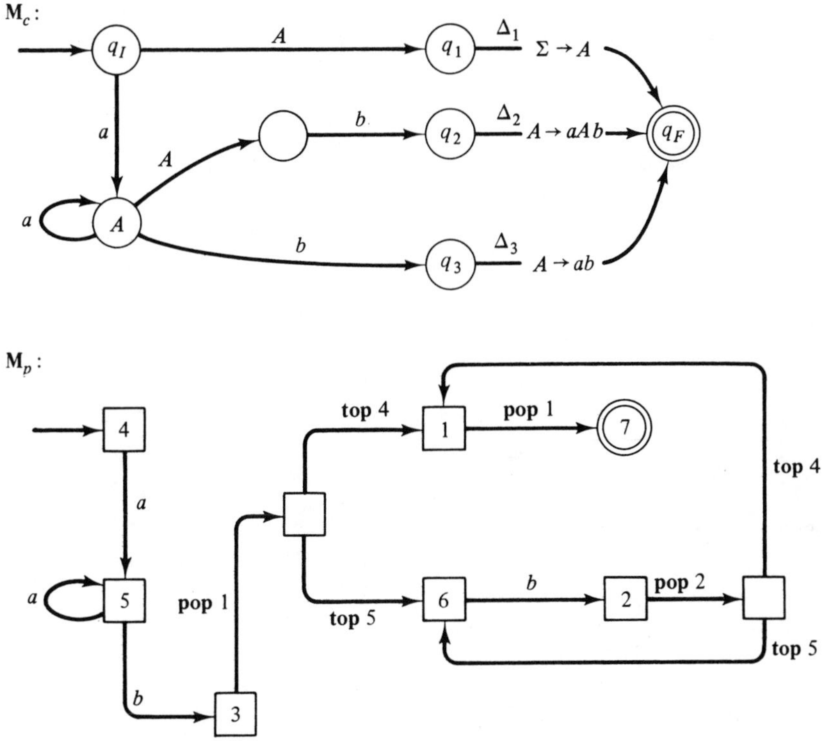


$(4, \lambda, \lambda) \longrightarrow (5, a, 4) \longrightarrow (5, aa, 45)$

$(3, aab, 455) \longrightarrow (6, aab, 45)$

$(2, aabb, 456) \longrightarrow (1, aabb, 4) \longrightarrow (7, aabb, \lambda)$

**Figure 10.24** A DPDA for an $LR(0)$ grammar.

The lookahead strings satisfy

$$\theta_0 = \#^k$$
$$|\theta_i| = k, \qquad i = 0, \ldots, n$$

and each string $\theta_i \beta_i'$ is a string of terminal letters derived from the string $\beta_i \theta_{i-1}$.

The $k$-characteristic string of this derivation is

$$\varphi\alpha\theta_n\Delta_p = \alpha_1 \ldots \alpha_n\alpha\theta_n\Delta_p$$

To obtain an accepter **M** for the $k$-characteristic strings of **G**, it is no longer sufficient to associate states with the nonterminal letters of **G**. Instead we associate a state $[A\theta]$ with each string $A\theta$ (where $A$ is a nonterminal and $\theta$

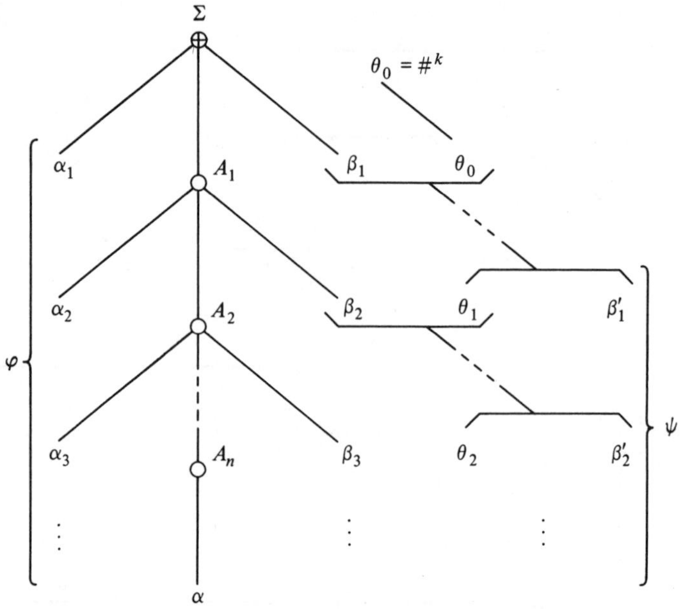


**Figure 10.25** Derivation tree for $\Sigma\#^k \overset{*}{\Longrightarrow} \varphi\alpha\theta\psi$.

is a $k$-symbol lookahead string), such that $A\theta$ occurs in some end-marked right sentential form of **G**. In correspondence with derivation (1), **M** will accept the characteristic string $\alpha_1 \ldots \alpha_n\alpha\theta_n A_p$ by the move sequence

$$\Sigma\,\theta_0 \xrightarrow{\alpha_1} [A_1\theta_1] \xrightarrow{\alpha_2} [A_2\theta_2] \xrightarrow{\alpha_3} \ldots$$
$$\xrightarrow{\alpha_n} [A_n\theta_n] \xrightarrow{\alpha\theta_n} q_p \xrightarrow{\Delta_p} q_F$$

The construction of **M** from **G** is specified in Table 10.3, and the proof that **M** accepts precisely the $k$-characteristic strings of **G** parallels the argument given earlier in connection with 0-characteristic strings. The *k-characteristic finite-state accepter* ($k$-CFSA) for **G** is obtained by converting **M** into a deterministic accepter.

**Example 10.8:** Consider the grammar

$$\mathbf{G}:\quad \Sigma \longrightarrow A \quad (1) \qquad \Sigma \longrightarrow B \quad (4)$$
$$A \longrightarrow aA \quad (2) \qquad B \longrightarrow aBb \quad (5)$$
$$A \longrightarrow a \quad (3) \qquad B \longrightarrow ab \quad (6)$$

This grammar is clearly not $LR(0)$ since it is necessary to see whether the last $a$ of a sentence is followed by $\#$ or $b$ to determine whether

**Table 10.3** Construction of an accepter for the $k$-characteristic strings of a grammar

*Given:* a well-formed context-free grammar $\mathbf{G} = (\mathbf{N}, \mathbf{T}, \mathbf{P}, \Sigma)$
*To construct:* a finite-state accepter $\mathbf{M} = (\mathbf{Q}, \mathbf{V}, \mathbf{P}', \{q_\Sigma\}, \{q_F\})$ such that $\mathbf{L}(\mathbf{M})$ is the set of $k$-characteristic strings of $\mathbf{G}$
*Let:* $\mathbf{Q_N} = \{[A\theta] \mid A \in \mathbf{N} \cup \{\Sigma\}, \theta \in \mathbf{T}^*\#^*, |\theta| = k\}$
$\mathbf{Q} = \mathbf{Q_N} \cup \{q_p \mid p = 1, \ldots, r\} \cup \{q_F\}$
$\mathbf{V} = \mathbf{N} \cup \mathbf{T} \cup \{\Delta_p \mid p \text{ is a rule of } \mathbf{G}\}$

| If rule $p$ of $\mathbf{G}$ has the form | then $\mathbf{M}$ has |
|---|---|
| $A \longrightarrow \alpha$<br>$\alpha \in \mathbf{V}^* - \lambda$ | $[A\theta] \xrightarrow{\alpha\theta} q_p \xrightarrow{\Delta_p} q_F$,<br>each $[A\theta]$ in $\mathbf{Q_N}$ |
| $A \longrightarrow \alpha B \beta$<br>$\alpha, \beta \in \mathbf{V}^*$<br>$B \in \mathbf{N}$ | $[A\theta] \xrightarrow{\alpha} [B\theta']$<br>each $[A\theta] \in \mathbf{Q_N}$ and<br>each $[B\theta'] \in \mathbf{Q_N}$ such that<br>$\beta\theta \stackrel{*}{\Longrightarrow} \theta'\gamma$ in $\mathbf{G}$<br>for some $\gamma \in \mathbf{T}^*\#^*$ |

reduction via rules 1 to 3 or via rules 4 to 6 is required. In Figure 10.26, $\mathbf{M}$ is a nondeterministic accepter for the 1-characteristic strings of $\mathbf{G}$, and $\mathbf{M}_c$ is the 1-CFSA.

The discussion leading to Proposition 10.4 applies without modification to the $k$-characteristic accepter $\mathbf{M}_c$ of a grammar $\mathbf{G}$: the states of $\mathbf{M}_c$ other than $q_F$ and the trap state form disjoint sets of shift states and reduce states just if $\mathbf{G}$ is $LR(k)$. Thus we can always decide whether an arbitrary context-free grammar is $LR(k)$ for a specified value of $k$.

**Theorem 10.3:** Given any context-free grammar $\mathbf{G}$, one can determine, for any $k \geq 0$, whether $\mathbf{G}$ is an $LR(k)$ grammar.

This result does not assert solvability of a slightly more general problem: given the context-free grammar $\mathbf{G}$, can one decide whether there is some $k \geq 0$ for which $\mathbf{G}$ is $LR(k)$? Using Theorem 10.3, the best one can do is to test whether $\mathbf{G}$ is $LR(k)$ for successive values $k = 0, 1, \ldots$. If $\mathbf{G}$ is an $LR(k)$ grammar, the sequence of tests will eventually yield a positive result. If it happens that $\mathbf{G}$ is not $LR(k)$, this procedure will never end, and we will never know how far testing should be continued. The fact is, this is an unsolvable decision problem; in Chapter 12 we develop the tools needed to establish this fact.

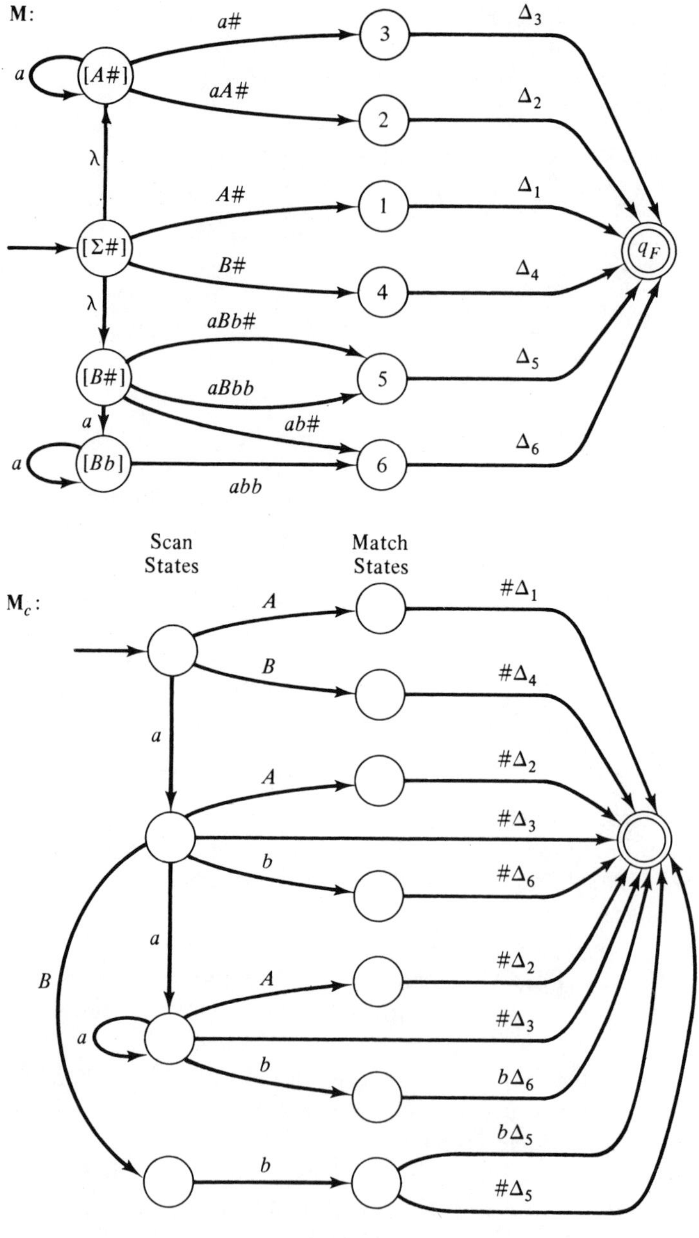


**Figure 10.26** Construction of the 1-CFSA of an $LR(1)$ grammar.

The $k$-characteristic accepter for an $LR(k)$ grammar is the basis for the deterministic parsing device **M** shown in Figure 10.27. This device is a deterministic pushdown accepter equipped with a special head that senses the string of $k$ terminal letters immediately right of the scan head on the input tape. In the configuration shown, the device is ready to perform the reduction

$$\varphi\alpha\theta\psi \quad \text{reduces to} \quad \varphi A\theta\psi \quad \text{by some rule} \quad A \longrightarrow \alpha$$

To specify the operation of **M**, we make a slight modification of the characteristic accepter $\mathbf{M}_c$. The modified accepter $\mathbf{M}'_c$ is obtained from $\mathbf{M}_c$ in two steps:

1. Whenever $\mathbf{M}_c$ has

$$q \overset{\theta}{\Longrightarrow} q_p$$

where $q_p$ is a reduce state, add the transition

$$q \overset{\theta\Delta_p}{\longrightarrow} q_F$$

State $q$ is then a *match state* of $\mathbf{M}'_c$.

2. Delete all reduce states of $\mathbf{M}_c$ and their associated transitions.

In the modified accepter, each transition into the final state $q_F$ is labeled by $\theta\Delta_p$, where $|\theta| = k$. It should be clear that $\mathbf{M}_c$ and $\mathbf{M}'_c$ accept the same set of strings.

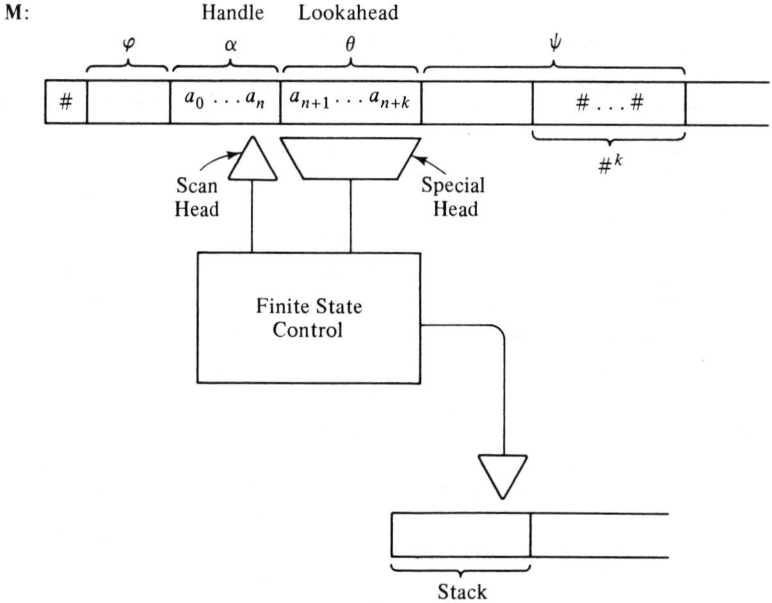


**Figure 10.27** $LR(k)$ parsing device.

Operation of **M** is identical to that of the deterministic parser for an $LR(0)$ grammar except for matching the lookahead string. If $\mathbf{M}'_c$ is in a scan state, **M** writes the current state name into the stack and advances the two input tape heads one square. The next state of $\mathbf{M}_c$ is determined by the letter now seen by the scan head. Whenever $\mathbf{M}'_c$ enters a match state $q$, **M** tests whether $\mathbf{M}'_c$ has a transition of the form

$$q \xrightarrow{\theta\Delta_p} q_F$$

such that $\theta$ matches the lookahead string sensed by the special head. If there is no match, **M** continues as if $q$ were a scan state. If there is a match, it must be unique if the grammar is $LR(k)$, and the rule $A \longrightarrow \alpha$ to be used in reducing $\varphi\alpha\theta\psi$ is rule $p$ of **G**. The top $|\alpha| - 1$ stack symbols are then discarded by **M**, and the next stack symbol is the name of the state of $\mathbf{M}'_c$ at whose $A$-successor scanning is resumed. The parsing is complete when reduction by a rule $\Sigma \longrightarrow \alpha$ occurs, and deleting $|\alpha|$ state names leaves the stack empty.

**Example 10.9:** Figure 10.28 shows the construction of the 0-CFSA for a simple arithmetic expression grammar

$$\mathbf{G}\!: \quad \Sigma \longrightarrow A \quad (1) \qquad A \longrightarrow T \quad (2) \qquad T \longrightarrow (A) \quad (4)$$
$$A \longrightarrow A + T \quad (3) \qquad T \longrightarrow x \quad (5)$$

This characteristic accepter violates the $LR(0)$ conditions because there is a $+$ transition leaving state 1 and also a $\Delta$-transition; an $LR(0)$ parser would not know whether to scan or reduce upon entering this state. This difficulty is resolved if the parser can look ahead one symbol. The sentential form $A$ is the only string that puts $\mathbf{M}_c$ in state 1, and examination of the grammar shows that $\#$, ), and $+$ are the only letters that can appear immediately right of $A$ in an end-marked right sentential form. If the parser arrives at state 1 and the next input symbol is $\#$, the current sentential form can only be $A\#$, and rule 1 must be used to reduce. Similarly, if the next symbol is ), rule 4 must be used. If the next symbol is $+$, the sentential form cannot be $A\#$ or $A$) and scanning must be continued. The need for this test by the parser may be specified in the CFSA by replacing the $\Delta_1$-transition with transitions labeled $\#\Delta_1$ and $)\Delta_4$.

We conclude this study of $LR(k)$ grammars by showing that the languages they define are exactly the deterministic languages, and that $LR(1)$ grammars are equal in language-defining ability to the whole class of $LR(k)$ grammars.

**Theorem 10.4:** (1) Every deterministic context-free language is generated by some $LR(1)$ grammar. (2) Every $LR(k)$ language is deterministic.

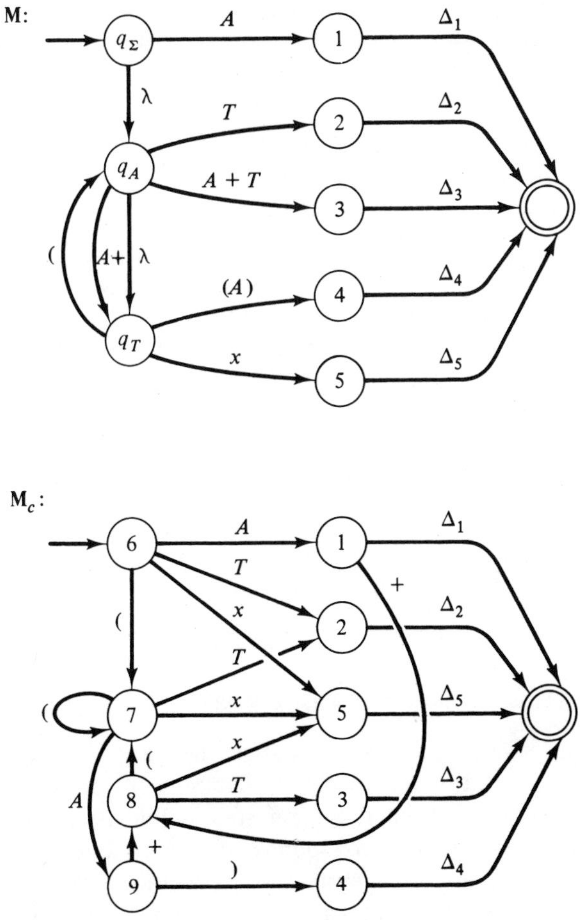


**Figure 10.28** Characteristic accepter for an arithmetic expression grammar.

***Proof:*** Statement 1 follows from Theorem 10.2: each deterministic language is generated by some generalized precedence grammar, and any generalized precedence grammar is an $LR(1)$ grammar. For statement 2, we outline the construction of a deterministic pushdown accepter $\mathbf{M}'$ that simulates the $LR(k)$ parsing machine of Figure 10.27. Since the number of distinct strings of $k$ terminal letters and end markers is finite, the DPDA can maintain a record of the $k$ look-ahead symbols in its control unit. As shown in Figure 10.29, we may imagine the control unit of $\mathbf{M}'$ as containing a $k$-position shift register. The machine begins operation by marking the bottom of its stack and making $k$ scan moves to fill its shift register with the

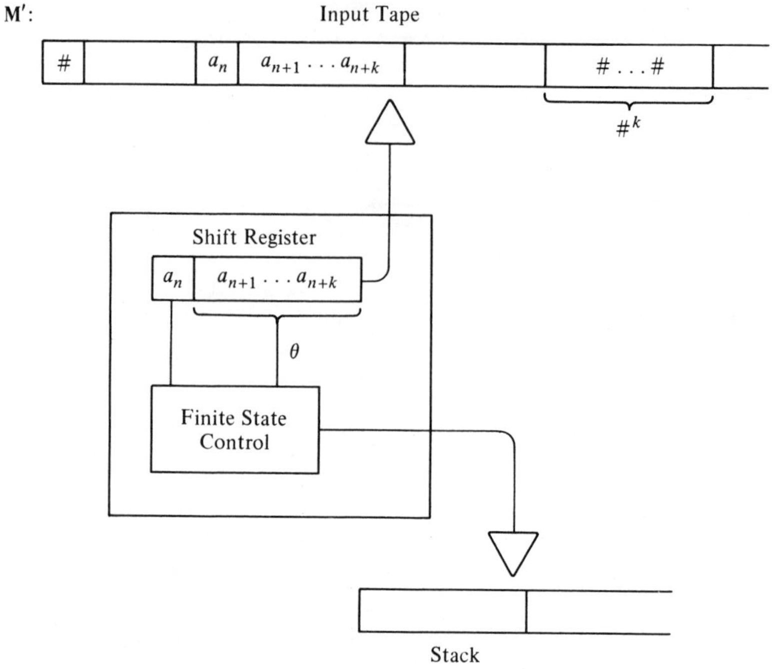


**Figure 10.29** Converting the $LR(k)$ parser into a DPDA.

initial lookahead string. Thereafter, the state of the control unit is sufficient information to detect matching of the lookahead string and determine which reduction step should be performed. If the configuration of **M′** corresponds to a shift state of **M′** the DPDA writes the name of its current state on the stack tape, executes a scan move, shifts the lookahead string one position left, and enters a new state in accordance with the letter moved out of the shift register. If the configuration of **M′** corresponds to a match state of **M**, the contents of the shift register determine whether a match exists and, if so, which rule $A \longrightarrow \alpha$ applies to the reduction of the current sentential form. The DPDA pops $|\alpha| - 1$ state names from the stack and enters a new state according to the state name now at the top of the stack. When reduction by a rule $\Sigma \longrightarrow \alpha$ takes place, the DPDA pops $|\alpha|$ items from the stack. If this action just empties the stack (as indicated by the bottom stack marker), the string of scanned letters has been parsed, and **M′** enters a final state.

Although every $LR(k)$ language is generated by some $LR(1)$ grammar, we cannot hope to find an $LR(0)$ grammar for an arbitrary deterministic language. Consider any deterministic language **L** having the *prefix property*: there are nonempty strings $\omega$ and $\varphi$ such that both $\omega$ and $\omega\varphi$ are sentences of **L**. Assume that there is an $LR(0)$ grammar for **L**, and let $\mathbf{M}'$ be the deterministic pushdown accepter for **L** constructed from the characteristic accepter for the $LR(0)$ grammars. If $\mathbf{M}'$ is presented with the sentence $\omega\varphi$, it will scan the symbols of $\omega$ and, since $\omega \in \mathbf{L}$, will halt without testing whether $\omega$ is followed by # or more terminal symbols. Therefore, **M** cannot accept the string $\omega\varphi$. The language of Example 10.8 illustrates this point.

## Notes and References

Working compilers existed for Fortran (Backus *et al* [1957] and Algol 60 (Naur *et al* [1963]) prior to the first theoretical work on syntax analysis. These early successes stimulated the research on parsing techniques.

Top-down, or *recursive descent*, parsers were motivated by the recursive structure of BNF productions. Irons' [1961] syntax-directed compiler for Algol 60 demonstrated the method and showed that a compiler could be written in its own language. Schorre [1964] and Reynolds [1965] carried the techniques further, and Kuno and Oettinger [1962] applied them in natural language analysis. Earley [1968] showed that these methods could be used to build parsers capable of analyzing an $n$-symbol input in time proportional to $n^2$ for an unambiguous grammar, or $n^3$ for an ambiguous grammar. Lewis and Stearns [1968] introduced the class of $LL(k)$ *grammars*, whose $k$-symbol lookahead parsers model the full class of deterministic top-down analyzers. These analyzers are "incomplete", however, for there are deterministic languages which are not $LL(k)$ for any $k$.

The principal attraction of top-down parsers is their simplicity; the quest for faster parsing methods, even at the expense of more complex parsers, led to the study of bottom-up techniques. Using analogies with arithmetic expression evaluation, Floyd [1963] devised the deterministic "operator precedence" method; he quickly improved the method by allowing for a bounded left and right context of the potential handle [1964]. Knuth [1965] generalized further, introducing $LR(k)$ analysis which encompasses all the deterministic languages. A few years later, DeRemer [1969, 1971] and Korenjak [1969] showed how to build efficient $LR(k)$ parsers. (Our treatment of the topic is based on DeRemer's.)

Wirth and Weber [1966] generalized Floyd's precedence grammars, obtaining the simple precedence grammars. Fischer [1969] showed that every context-free language is generated by some precedence grammar (but not necessarily by an invertible grammar). Aho, Denning, and Ullman [1972] described mixed strategy precedence parsing, which combined ideas from simple precedence grammars and bounded left context; the result extended precedence analysis to the full class of deterministic languages. They also showed how to express a bottom-up parser in the "shift-reduce" formalism.

Many good surveys of parsing techniques have been published. Cheatham and Sattley [1964] studied early top-down methods, and Floyd [1963, 1964] surveyed early bottom-up methods. Griffiths and Petrick [1965] compared the two approaches. Even today, Feldman and Gries [1968] is one of the most comprehensive overviews available. The tutorial by Aho and Johnson [1974] is one of the most intuitive presentations of $LR(k)$ parsing.

There are also many good texts in the field. Aho and Ullman [1972, 1973] is unequaled for coverage of the theory, and the collection of papers edited by Bauer and Eickel [1976] presents a good picture for the mid 1970's. Cheatham [1967], Gries [1971], McKeeman et al [1970], and, to a lesser extent, Lewis et al [1976], aim toward practical implementations of compilers.

## Problems

10.1. Let **G** be the context-free grammar with productions

$$\Sigma \longrightarrow X$$
$$\Sigma \longrightarrow Y$$
$$X \longrightarrow Y$$
$$X \longrightarrow X0Y$$
$$Y \longrightarrow c$$
$$Y \longrightarrow 1Y1$$
$$Y \longrightarrow 1X1$$

a. Illustrate a parallel top-down syntax analysis of the string $\omega = 1c01c0c11$. How many such analyses are there?
b. Illustrate a parallel bottom-up analysis of $\omega$.

10.2. Let **G** be the grammar of Problem 10.1 with productions numbered as ordered in that problem.
a. Illustrate a backtracking top-down analysis of the string $\omega = 1c01c0c11$.
b. Illustrate a backtracking bottom-up analysis of $\omega$.

**10.3.** Let **G** be the grammar of Problems 10.1 and 10.2, and suppose that we perform a top-down analysis of a string $\alpha$ in **L(G)** as described in Section 10.1. As a function of the length of $\alpha$, how many sentential forms may appear in any column of the analysis if we impose the three conditions indicated in that section to limit the proliferation of sentential forms? How many may appear if we do not impose the conditions?

Now suppose that we perform an analysis of a string $\alpha$ generated by some arbitrary context-free grammar with $k$ productions. How many sentential forms may appear in a column of a top-down analysis of $\alpha$ if we impose the three conditions? If we do not impose the conditions? How many sentential forms may appear in any column of a bottom-up analysis of $\alpha$?

10.4. Illustrate the evaluation of the arithmetic expression

$$\# \; 3 + 5 \uparrow 6 \uparrow 2 \times 3 - 4 \,/\, 5 + 3 \; \#$$

using the operator precedence matrix of Section 10.3.1. Repeat for the expression

$$\# \; 3 + (3 \,/\, 4 - (5 \uparrow 6) + 1 \uparrow 7) + (1 - 3) \; \#$$

What happens if we try to evaluate the expression

$$\# \; (4 \,/\, 5 - 1) \,/\, (3 + 4 \times (3 - 1)) \uparrow 3) \uparrow 2 \; \#$$

10.5. Let **G** be the grammar of Problem 10.1. If **G** is a precedence grammar, exhibit the precedence matrix for **G**. Otherwise, exhibit a precedence conflict in the grammar.

10.6. Three grammars each generate the same language:

| $\mathbf{G}_1$: | $\mathbf{G}_2$: | $\mathbf{G}_3$: |
|---|---|---|
| $\Sigma \longrightarrow A$ | $\Sigma \longrightarrow A$ | $\Sigma \longrightarrow A$ |
| $A \longrightarrow BC$ | $A \longrightarrow BX$ | $A \longrightarrow BX$ |
| $B \longrightarrow 0B1$ | $B \longrightarrow 0B1$ | $B \longrightarrow 0BX$ |
| $B \longrightarrow c$ | $B \longrightarrow c$ | $B \longrightarrow c$ |
| $C \longrightarrow 1C$ | $X \longrightarrow C$ | $X \longrightarrow C$ |
| $C \longrightarrow 1$ | $C \longrightarrow C1$ | $C \longrightarrow 1C$ |
| | $C \longrightarrow 1$ | $C \longrightarrow 1$ |

Informally, describe the language generated by the grammars. Which of the grammars are precedence grammars? For each such grammar, exhibit the precedence matrix, and show how the precedence analyzer of Figure 10.13 parses the sentence $00c1111$.

**10.7.** Prove that any context-free grammar can be converted into a precedence grammar. (*Hint:* Assume that the grammar is in normal form; see Theorem 9.3.)

*10.8. Prove that the language

$$\mathbf{L} = \{0^i 1^j 0^k \mid i = j \text{ or } j = k\}$$

is not a simple precedence language.

10.9. Let **G** be the grammar with productions:

$$\Sigma \longrightarrow A$$
$$\Sigma \longrightarrow B$$
$$A \longrightarrow B$$
$$A \longrightarrow AcB$$
$$B \longrightarrow 0$$
$$B \longrightarrow aBa$$

$$B \longrightarrow aAI$$

$$I \longrightarrow a$$

Show that **G** is a generalized precedence grammar by displaying its precedence matrix. Is **L(G)** a simple precedence language?

10.10. Construct a generalized precedence grammar for the language

$$\mathbf{L} = \{\omega \mid \omega \in \{0, 1\}^*, N_0(\omega) = N_1(\omega)\}$$

where $N_0(\omega)$ is the number of occurences of 0 in $\omega$, and similarly for $N_1(\omega)$.

**10.11.** Prove that if **G** is any generalized precedence grammar, a deterministic pushdown accepter can be constructed for **L(G)**. (This is the "if" portion of Theorem 10.2.)

10.12. Construct an $LR(0)$ grammar for the language $\mathbf{L} = \{c0^n1^n \mid n \geq 1\} \cup \{0^n1^{2n} \mid n \geq 1\}$. Prove that the grammar is $LR(0)$ by constructing the 0-CFSA for the grammar, and showing that the states are partitioned into shift and reduce states as required by Proposition 10.4.

10.13. Construct an $LR(1)$ grammar for the language $\mathbf{L} = \{a^nb^m \mid n \geq m \geq 0\}$, and prove that it is $LR(1)$ by constructing the 1-CFSA for the grammar.

10.14. Which of the grammars $\mathbf{G}_1$, $\mathbf{G}_2$, $\mathbf{G}_3$ of Problem 10.6 are $LR(0)$? Which are $LR(1)$?

**10.15.** Show that if **L** is an $LR(k)$ language over an alphabet **T**, and $x$ is some terminal symbol not in **T**, then $\mathbf{L} \cdot \mathbf{x}$ is an $LR(0)$ language.

10.16. Show that these grammars are not $LR(k)$ for any $k$:

| | |
|---|---|
| $\mathbf{G}_1$: $\Sigma \longrightarrow A$ | $\mathbf{G}_2$: $\Sigma \longrightarrow A$ |
| $A \longrightarrow 0A1$ | $A \longrightarrow 0A1$ |
| $A \longrightarrow A1$ | $A \longrightarrow 01$ |
| $A \longrightarrow 1$ | $A \longrightarrow Cc$ |
| | $C \longrightarrow 0CD$ |
| | $C \longrightarrow 0D$ |
| | $D \longrightarrow 1E$ |
| | $E \longrightarrow 1E$ |
| | $E \longrightarrow 1$ |

(*Hint:* Show strings in which no bounded lookahead can distinguish the handle.)

# 11

# *Turing Machines*

In 1936, Allan M. Turing published the first study of an abstract machine model for computation. He desired to devise a mathematically precise notion for the informal concept of "algorithm," or "step-by-step procedure". His success is confirmed by the continuing acceptance of his startling thesis that *every algorithmic problem solution may be represented by the program of instructions for some Turing machine*. The remainder of this book studies this seemingly presumptuous claim.

The theory of algorithms arising from the work of Turing and many others has a unique consequence: *there are well-formulated problems for which no algorithmic solution can exist*! This concept is studied in Chapter 12, where its application to problems in the theory of formal languages is emphasized. The equivalence of Turing machines to mathematical systems for dealing with computations on integers is studied in Chapter 13, and to systems for manipulating strings of symbols in Chapter 14. The equivalence of these seemingly different systems for studying computation is strong evidence in support of Turing's thesis.

## 11.1 Definitions

The fundamental feature of a Turing machine is its ability to store and retrieve unlimited amounts of information. Many varieties of such automata have been devised; one simple form is a tape automaton (Figure 11.1) that is

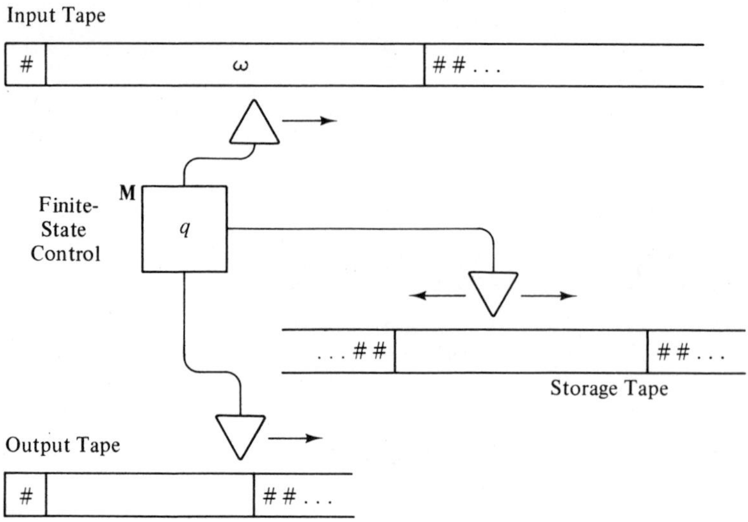


**Figure 11.1** Unrestricted tape automaton.

allowed to read and write symbols on a storage tape with no restriction other than that the head may move only one square at a time. As we shall see, no generality is lost by omitting the input and output tapes, or by assuming that the storage tape extends indefinitely only to the right. Accordingly, we use the one-tape automaton shown in Figure 11.2 as our basic form of Turing machine.

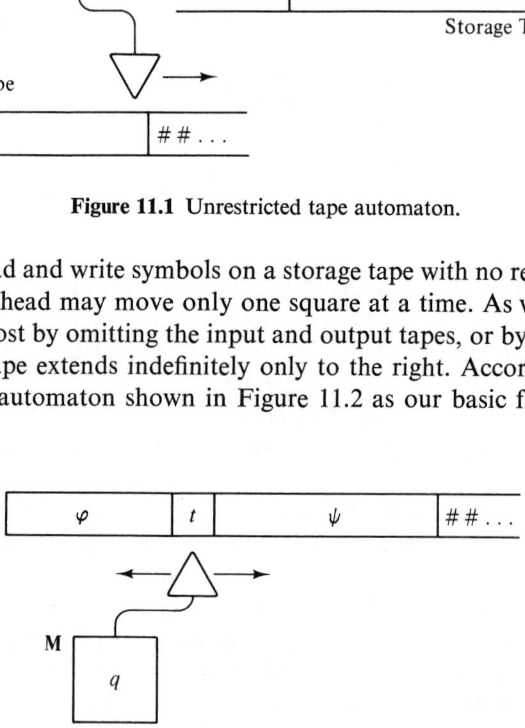


**Figure 11.2** Turing machine in configuration $(\varphi, q, t, \psi)$.

**Definition 11.1:** A *Turing machine* (TM) is a four-tuple

$$\mathbf{M} = (\mathbf{Q}, \mathbf{T}, \mathbf{P}, q_I)$$

in which **Q** is a finite set of control states including an initial state $q_I$, **T** is an alphabet of tape symbols, and **P** is a finite program of instructions. Each instruction of **P** has one of two forms,

$$\begin{array}{ll} q]\ \textbf{right}\ (t/t', q') & \\ q]\ \textbf{left}\ (t/t', q') & \end{array} \quad \text{where} \begin{cases} t, t' \in \mathbf{T} \cup \{\#\} \\ q, q' \in \mathbf{Q} \end{cases}$$

and each state labels instructions of one form only. (The symbol # is the special *blank symbol* used by **M**.)

A *configuration*, or *instantaneous description*, of **M** is a four-tuple

$$(\varphi, q, t, \psi), \qquad \varphi\psi \in (\mathbf{T} \cup \{\#\})^*, t \in \mathbf{T} \cup \{\#\}, q \in \mathbf{Q}$$

in which the rightmost symbol of $\psi$ is not #. The string of symbols $\varphi t \psi$ is called the *tape* of the configuration. If $\varphi = \lambda$ and $q = q_I$, the configuration is an *initial configuration* of **M**.

Figure 11.2 shows a Turing machine in configuration $(\varphi, q, t, \psi)$. The control is in state $q$, and the tape head is positioned at a square containing the symbol $t$. The portion of the tape to the left of this square contains the string $\varphi$, and the portion to the right of this square contains the string $\psi$. The remainder of the tape is blank. (That is, each square outside the region containing $\varphi t \psi$ is inscribed with #.) In any reachable configuration $(\varphi, q, t, \psi)$, the string $\varphi t \psi$ is the string of symbols on the tape from the leftmost square through the rightmost nonblank square or the square under the head, whichever is farther to the right.

**Definition 11.2:** The right and left *moves* of a Turing machine from a given configuration are shown in Figure 11.3. (There are four cases, depending on the position of the head relative to the rightmost nonblank symbol.) If a machine has no moves from a given configuration, the configuration is *dead*.

We say that

$$(\lambda, q_I, t, \psi) \Longrightarrow (\varphi', q', t', \psi')$$

is a *computation* of **M**, if **M** has a sequence of moves leading from the initial configuration $(\lambda, q_I, t, \psi)$ to the configuration $(\varphi', q', t', \psi')$. In such a case, we refer to the latter configuration as the *final configuration* of the computation, and call the computation *halted* if the final configuration is dead.

A Turing machine is *deterministic* if at most one move is possible from each configuration; this can be determined from the TM's instruction set. For most purposes, it is sufficient to consider only deterministic Turing machines; unless otherwise stated, the machines we study are assumed deterministic. (In fact, we shall show that no power is gained from nondeterministic operation.)

A deterministic Turing machine defines a function from initial tapes into final tapes, as shown in Figure 11.4.

1. Right move $q]$ **right** $(\#/t', q')$ into blank tape:

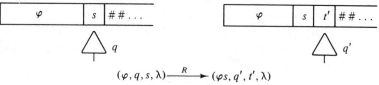

$$(\varphi, q, s, \lambda) \xrightarrow{R} (\varphi s, q', t', \lambda)$$

2. Right move $q]$ **right** $(t/t', q')$ into nonblank tape:

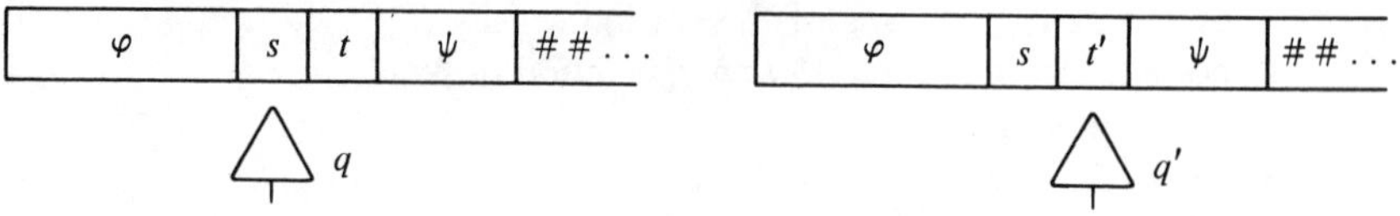


$$(\varphi, q, s, t\psi) \xrightarrow{R} (\varphi s, q', t', \psi)$$

3. Left move $q]$ **left** $(t/t', q')$ from blank tape:

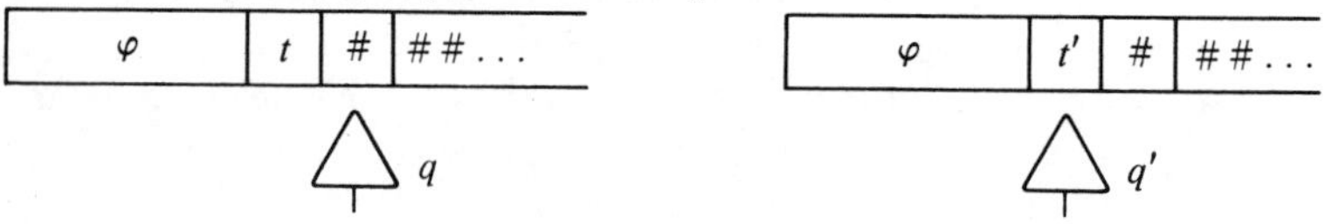


$$(\varphi t, q, \#, \lambda) \xrightarrow{L} (\varphi, q', t', \lambda)$$

4. Left move $q]$ **left** $(t/t', q')$ from nonblank tape:

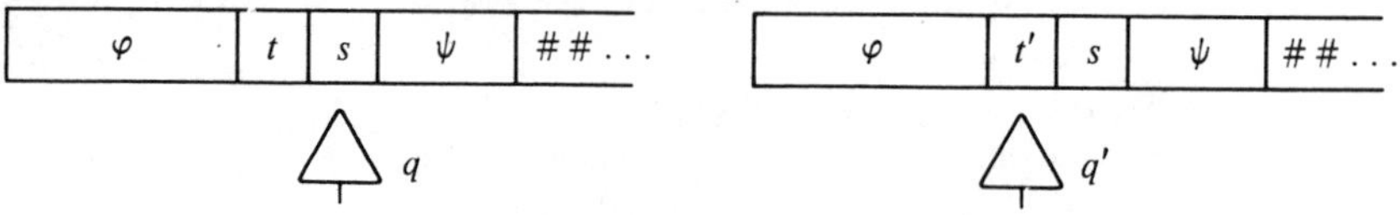


$$(\varphi t, q, s, \psi) \xrightarrow{L} (\varphi, q', t', s\psi)$$

**Figure 11.3** Moves of a Turing machine.

**Definition 11.3:** For a deterministic Turing machine **M**, define the function $f_{\mathbf{M}}: (\mathbf{T} \cup \{\#\})^* \longrightarrow (\mathbf{T} \cup \{\#\})^*$ by

$$f_{\mathbf{M}}(\omega) = \begin{cases} \omega' & \text{if } (\lambda, q_I, t, \psi) \Longrightarrow (\varphi', q', t', \psi') \text{ is a halted computation of } \mathbf{M}\text{, where } \omega = t\psi \text{ is the } \textit{initial tape} \text{ of } \mathbf{M}\text{, and } \omega' = \varphi' t' \psi' \text{ is the } \textit{final tape} \\ \text{undefined} & \text{otherwise} \end{cases}$$

Then $f_{\mathbf{M}}$ is the *function defined by* **M**. If a function $f$ is $f_{\mathbf{M}}$ for some Turing machine **M**, then $f$ is a *Turing-definable* function.

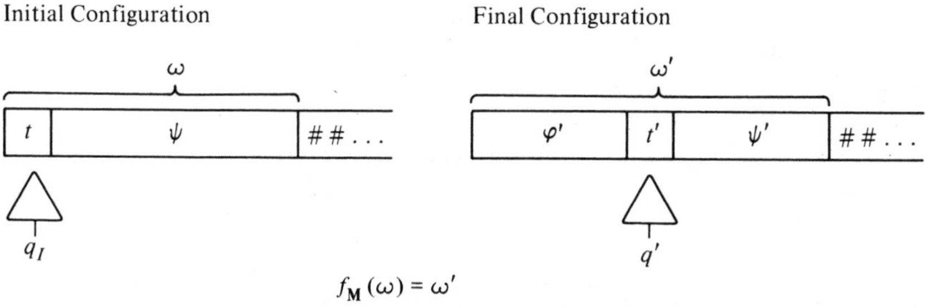


**Figure 11.4** Function defined by a Turing machine.

The function defined by a Turing machine is generally partial, since the machine may fail to halt for some initial tapes. It is not always possible to convert a Turing machine into one that always halts without modifying the machine's function.

We are often interested in using Turing machines already designed as components in more complex machines. To facilitate their use as component machines, we adopt the output convention shown in Figure 11.5: a Turing

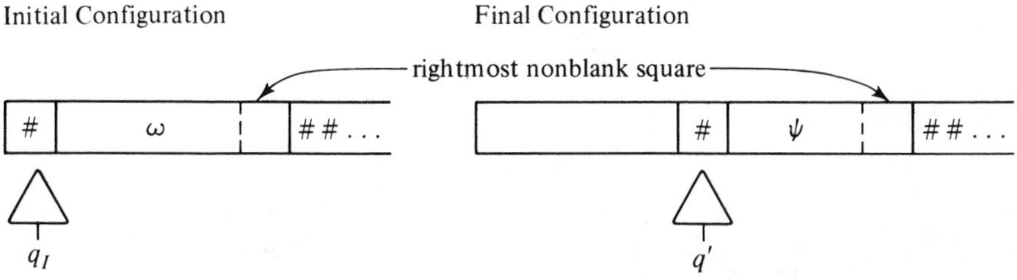


**Figure 11.5** Definition of Turing-realizable function.

machine will stop on a square containing #, with the output string immediately to the right of the square. In addition, the machine will never have moved left of the sharp on which its computation began. With these conventions, Turing machines may be combined in such a way that the output of one becomes the input of another: at the conclusion of the first computation, the combined machine is "restarted," using the former output as its new input. Functions that can be computed in this way are called *Turing realizable*.

**Definition 11.4:** A function $f$: $\mathbf{V}^* \longrightarrow \mathbf{V}^*$ is *Turing realizable* if there exists a Turing machine **M** such that **M** has a halted computation

$$(\lambda, q_I, \#, \omega) \Longrightarrow (\varphi, q, \#, \psi)$$

if and only if $f(\omega) = \psi$, and **M** fails to halt for an input tape $\#\omega$ if and only if $f(\omega)$ is undefined.

Turing realizability is a satisfactory basic notion of Turing machine capability, because any Turing-definable function is also Turing realizable (see the Problems). The converse does not hold, however, because the empty string cannot be in either the domain or range of a Turing-definable function. (Note that in Definition 11.3, each of $\omega$ and $\omega'$ contain at least one, possibly blank, symbol.)

Since the class of functions $f$: $\mathbf{V}^* \longrightarrow \mathbf{V}^*$ is uncountable, and the class of Turing machines, just as other classes of automata, *is* countable, not every such function is Turing realizable. Examples of functions realizable by no Turing machine will be studied in Chapter 12.

Following are examples of Turing machines. For each machine, we give a state diagram or program of instructions, and illustrate the initial and final configurations. We recommend that the reader be not content merely to inspect the figures. To enhance his understanding of the machines, the reader should trace the sequence of configurations with pencil and paper for several interesting cases.

Our first example is a Turing machine that constructs a copy of a given input string.

**Example 11.1:** We shall design a TM that realizes the function

$$f\colon \mathbf{A}^* \longrightarrow \mathbf{A}^* \# \mathbf{A}^*$$

where $\mathbf{A} = \{0, 1\}$ and

$$f(\omega) = \omega\#\omega,\ \omega \in \mathbf{A}^*$$

Figure 11.6a illustrates the desired behavior in terms of initial and final configurations. The copier machine cannot store the string $\omega$ in its control unit, for we could always choose an $\omega$ that would exhaust the finite storage capacity of the control. Therefore, our machine must duplicate $\omega$ by making many trips up and down the tape. The simplest machine is one that copies one symbol at a time, and such a TM is specified by the state diagram of Figure 11.6b (and the program of Figure 11.6c). In the program, instructions of the form

$$q]\ \textbf{left}\ (t/t, q') \quad \text{or} \quad q]\ \textbf{right}\ (t/t, q')$$

which do not change the printed symbol are abbreviated to

$$q]\ \textbf{left}\ (t, q') \quad \text{or} \quad q]\ \textbf{right}\ (t, q')$$

Otherwise, the state diagram and program follow our usual conventions for tape automata.

The machine marks the square being copied by printing $x$ in place of 0 or $y$ in place of 1. It moves right until it has passed one blank square, and prints the symbol (0 or 1) in the next blank square found. The machine then moves left to the square containing $x$ or $y$

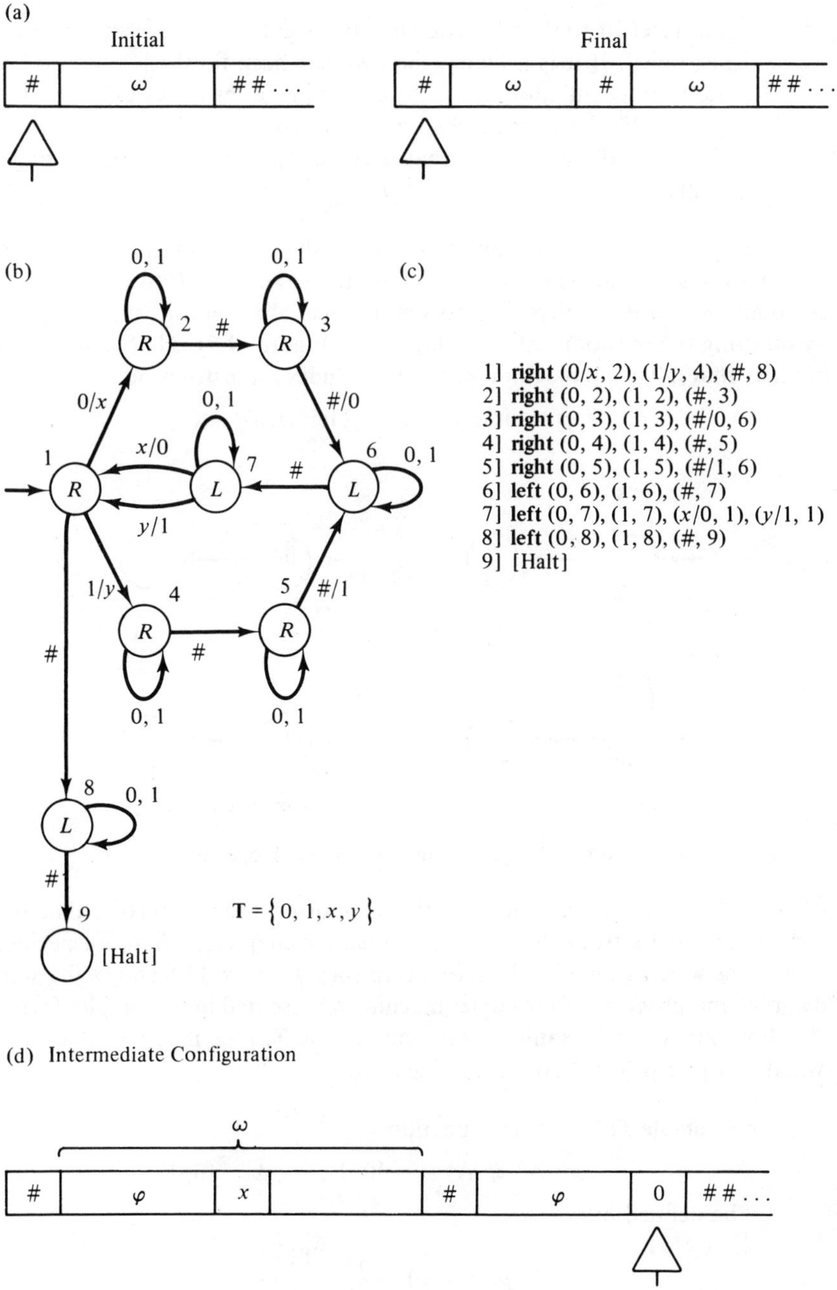


**Figure 11.6** Copier Turing machine.

and resets it to 0 or 1. A single move right finds the next symbol to be copied. If it is a blank, the task has been finished. Figure 11.6d shows the configuration of the copier just after it has printed a 0 in state 3; the letter $x$ marks the square from which the 0 was read. Note that this machine behaves correctly even if the given string is empty.

Turing machines often employ *searching*: the operation of moving left or right until a specified symbol is located on the tape. In fact, this operation is so common that it is convenient to simplify its description in state diagrams by omitting the self-loops at each state (as in Figure 11.7). That is, it shall be implicit that a Turing machine program includes an instruction

$$q] \textbf{ right } (t, q) \quad \text{or} \quad q] \textbf{ left } (t, q)$$

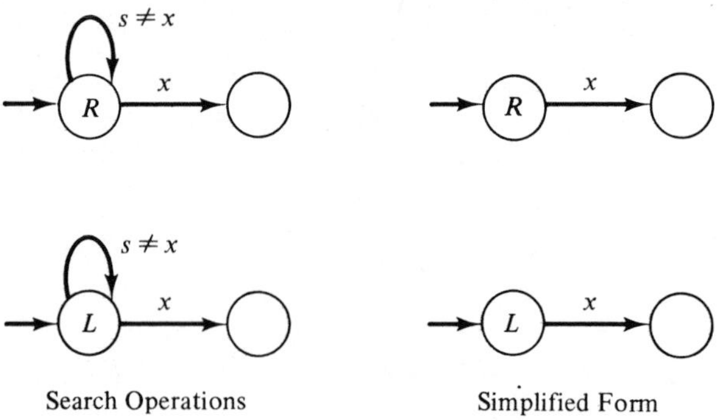


**Figure 11.7** Simplified notation for search operations.

whenever no move is specified for the symbol $t$ in state $q$. (Note that this convention differs from that adopted in earlier chapters, where unspecified transitions were assumed to lead to a trap state.) Figure 11.8 shows the state diagram and program of the copier machine represented in the simpler form.

For our second example, we construct a Turing machine that tests whether a pair of input strings are identical.

**Example 11.2:** Let the function

$$p: \mathbf{A}^* \# \mathbf{A}^* \longrightarrow \{0, 1\}, \qquad \mathbf{A} = \{0, 1\}$$

be defined by

$$p(\omega \# \varphi) = \begin{cases} 1 & \text{if } \omega = \varphi \\ 0 & \text{otherwise} \end{cases}$$

The equality tester TM in Figure 11.9 realizes the function $p$ by matching successive letters of $\omega$ and $\varphi$, and overwriting them with

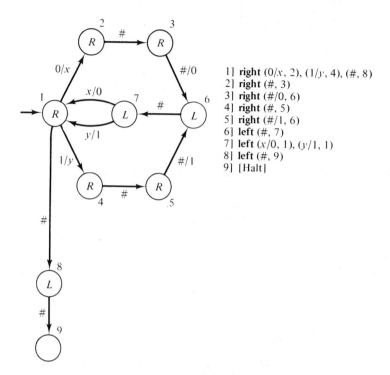

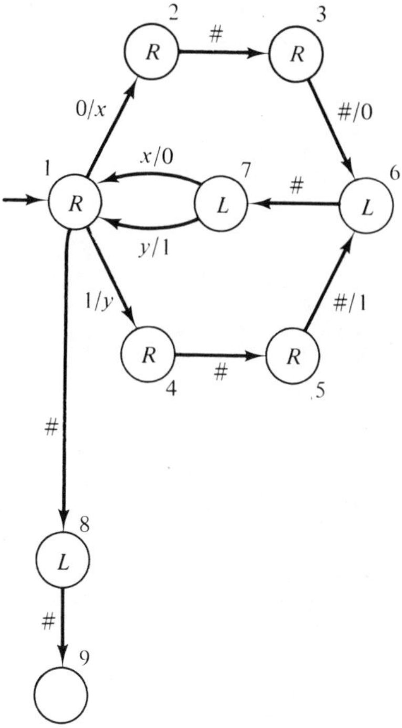


1] **right** (0/$x$, 2), (1/$y$, 4), (#, 8)
2] **right** (#, 3)
3] **right** (#/0, 6)
4] **right** (#, 5)
5] **right** (#/1, 6)
6] **left** (#, 7)
7] **left** ($x$/0, 1), ($y$/1, 1)
8] **left** (#, 9)
9] [Halt]

**Figure 11.8** Simplified form of copier machine.

$a$'s to record the progress of the computation. If the strings are identical, the TM writes a 1 two squares to the right of the second string; otherwise, it writes a 0. In either case, the final tape-head position is just left of the output symbol.

## 11.2 Simulation of Other Automata

The Turing machines are only one of many classes of abstract computing machines. However, it has been found that for each proposed class of automata a Turing machine can be devised that will carry out the computations of any member of the class. Although it is possible that some formulation of abstract machines may prove more powerful than the Turing machines, no one has yet found such a class. Indeed, the possibility that such a class exists must be considered quite remote.

To show that a class of automata $\mathfrak{M}$ is as powerful as a class of automata $\mathfrak{M}'$, it suffices to show how, given an arbitrary machine in $\mathfrak{M}'$, we can construct a machine in $\mathfrak{M}$ that performs the same computations. This method of

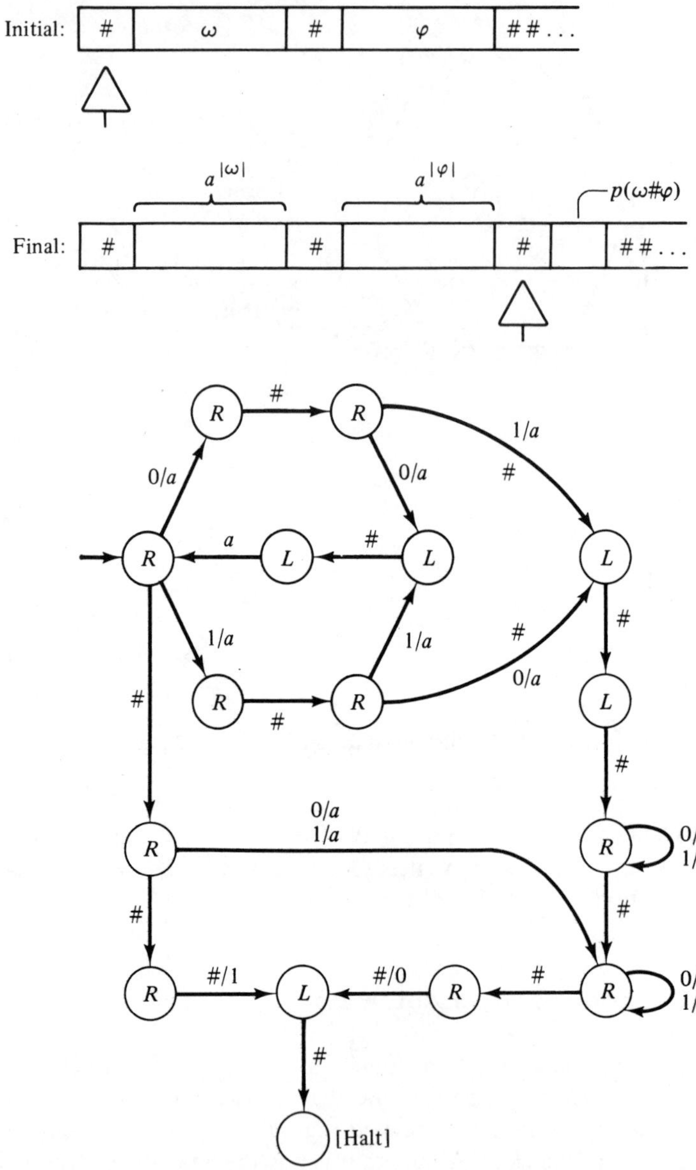


**Figure 11.9** Equality-tester Turing machine.

simulating a machine in one class by a machine in another is sometimes called *emulation*.

Another method of showing $\mathfrak{M}$ to be as powerful as $\mathfrak{M}'$ is to design a *single* machine in $\mathfrak{M}$ that can carry out the computations of *any* machine in

$\mathfrak{M}'$. Such a simulator is presented with a description of the machine to be simulated and a description of its initial configuration; it then generates descriptions of successive configurations of the simulated machine, halting just if that machine halts. This method of simulation is sometimes called *interpretation*.

In the following paragraphs, we exhibit Turing machines that emulate automata of apparently greater computational power. In Section 11.6, we exhibit a Turing machine that is capable of interpreting any other Turing machine and thus, indirectly, of simulating any other known automaton. This simulation has advanced the thesis that Turing machines are universal in the computing ability; indeed, the existence of a "universal simulator" is the foundation of the theory of computability.

### 11.2.1 Turing Transducers

A *Turing transducer* is a Turing machine equipped with an input and an output tape, in addition to its storage tape (Figure 11.1). The program of a Turing transducer may contain, in addition to the instructions by which it manipulates its storage tape, instructions of the forms

$$q]\ \textbf{scan}\ (s, q') \qquad q]\ \textbf{print}\ (r, q')$$

where $s$ and $r$ are letters in an input alphabet $\mathbf{S}$ and an output alphabet $\mathbf{R}$, respectively, that do not contain the blank symbol $\#$. Scan and print instructions are defined for Turing transducers as they were for the generalized sequential machines of Chapter 7; each transducer state is allowed to label no more than one type of instruction. Such a transducer $\mathbf{M}$ defines a function $f_{\mathbf{M}}: \mathbf{S}^* \longrightarrow \mathbf{R}^*$, where $f_{\mathbf{M}}(\omega) = \psi$ just if $\mathbf{M}$ halts with $\psi$ on its output tape when started with $\omega$ on its input tape.

It is easy to construct a Turing transducer $\mathbf{M}'$ that emulates an arbitrary Turing machine $\mathbf{M}$. Machine $\mathbf{M}'$ first copies its input string from its input tape onto its storage tape; it then obeys the program of $\mathbf{M}$ until it reaches a storage-tape configuration for which $\mathbf{M}$ would halt; when and if such a configuration is reached, $\mathbf{M}'$ copies the output string from its storage tape onto its output tape. If $\mathbf{T}$ is the tape alphabet of $\mathbf{M}$, the alphabet $\mathbf{T} \cup \{\Delta, \#\}$ is used on all three tapes of $\mathbf{M}'$, where $\#$ is the blank symbol of $\mathbf{M}'$ and is initially written in all squares of each tape. The symbol $\Delta$ is used to represent the blank symbol of $\mathbf{M}$, and the instructions of $\mathbf{M}$ are modified in $\mathbf{M}'$ so that $\mathbf{M}'$ writes $\Delta$ whenever $\mathbf{M}$ would write $\#$. This substitution makes it possible for $\mathbf{M}'$ to identify the end of its storage tape string when copying it onto its output tape.

It follows from this emulation that Turing transducers are at least as powerful as Turing machines: each function realizable by a Turing machine is also definable by some Turing transducer. To show that Turing transducers are no more powerful than Turing machines, a more elaborate construction is required.

Let **M** be any Turing transducer. We can represent configurations of **M** on the tape of a Turing machine **M′** by the correspondence illustrated in Figure 11.10. The three regions of the Turing machine tape hold representations of the three tapes of the transducer—input tape, storage tape, and output tape, in that order—each region separated from the next by the special symbol □. As in the emulation described above, the symbol Δ is used for the blank symbol of **M** so it may be distinguished from the blank symbol # of **M′**. Since **M′** must move its head over all three regions of its tape, whereas

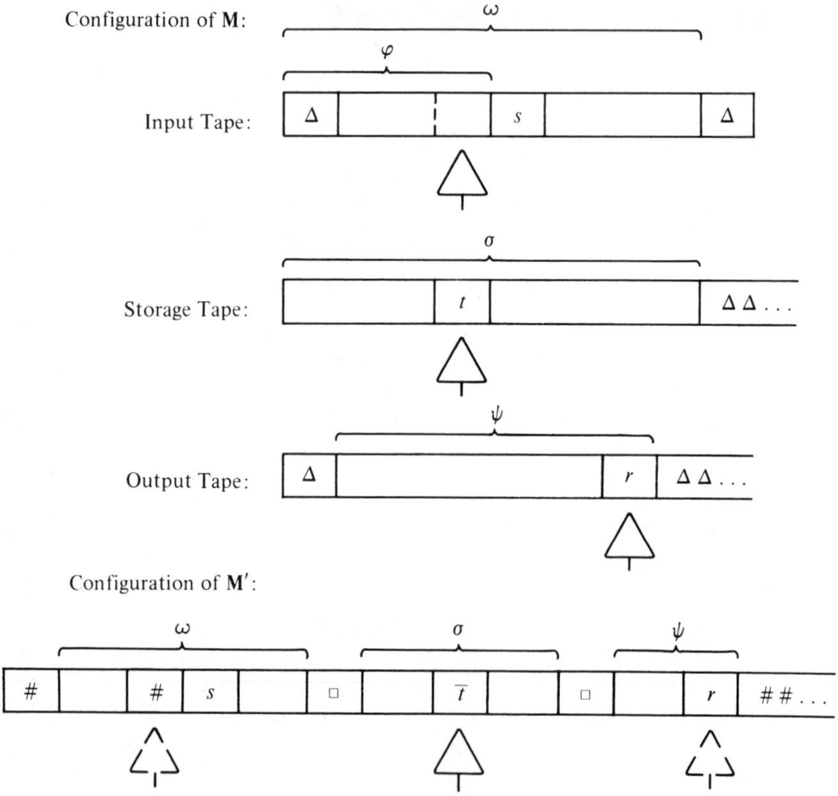


**Figure 11.10** Representation of transducer configuration on the tape of a TM.

**M** has a separate head for each tape, some scheme must be adopted by which the positions of the three heads of **M** are identified for later reference in configurations of **M′**. A convenient scheme is the following:

1. *Input tape:* each input symbol is replaced by # when it is scanned.

2. *Output tape:* the first # in the output tape region is the square for printing the next output symbol.

3. *Storage tape:* two sets of storage-tape symbols **T** and $\bar{\mathbf{T}}$ are used, a symbol from $\bar{\mathbf{T}}$ indicating that the storage-tape head of **M** is positioned at that square.

According to this scheme, the tape alphabet of **M′** is

$$\mathbf{T}' = \mathbf{S} \cup \mathbf{R} \cup \mathbf{T} \cup \bar{\mathbf{T}} \cup \{\Delta, \bar{\Delta}, \square\}$$

where

$$\bar{\mathbf{T}} = \{\bar{t} \mid t \in \mathbf{T}\}$$

The state set of **M′** includes an initial state $q_0$ and a state corresponding to each state of **M**. For each of the latter states, the Turing machine has instructions that make changes in its configuration corresponding to the moves of **M**. These instructions are specified in Figure 11.11, where $q$ denotes both an arbitrary state of **M** and the corresponding state of **M′**, and **X** is the set of states that label left or right instructions in **M**. Observe that the instructions of **M′** are designed so that the symbol under the storage-tape head of **M** is represented by an element of $\mathbf{T} \cup \{\Delta\}$ if **M** is about to perform a left or right instruction, and is an element of $\bar{\mathbf{T}} \cup \{\bar{\Delta}\}$ if **M** is about to perform a scan or print. This convention results in a simpler program for **M′**.

What happens when the storage-tape region of **M′** must be enlarged? Our strategy here is simply to move each symbol of the output-tape region one position to the right to make room for a new storage-tape square in which Δ is written. This routine is shown in Figure 11.11e, and is entered whenever **M′** encounters the symbol □ in simulating a right move of **M**. The instructions required in **M** to set up the three-region storage-tape format are given in Figure 11.11f.

It may seem that our Turing machine must do a lot of work just to simulate one right move of **M** that writes on a blank square. This is true, but in designing Turing machines one is always concerned only with the *possibility* of doing some task and not with the efficiency with which the task is performed. Thus, we shall always prefer the most convincing design.

In formulating these rules of construction, we have shown that Turing transducers are no more powerful than Turing machines. The simpler, single-tape model may be used with no loss of generality.

### 11.2.2 Variations on Storage Tapes

The catalog of abstract automata includes a variety of schemes for providing unbounded storage capacity; yet no automaton has proved more powerful than the single-tape Turing machine of Figure 11.2. A simple variation on the Turing machine uses a storage tape extending indefinitely

(a) If state $q$ labels the instruction $q$] **scan** $(s, q')$, $\mathbf{M}'$ has:

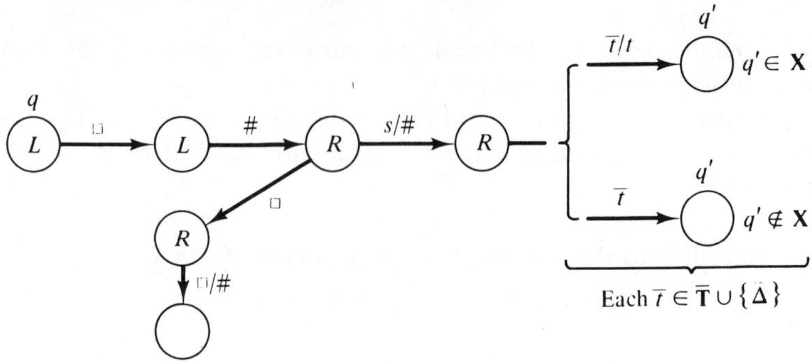


(b) If state $q$ labels the instruction $q$] **print** $(r, q')$, $\mathbf{M}'$ has:

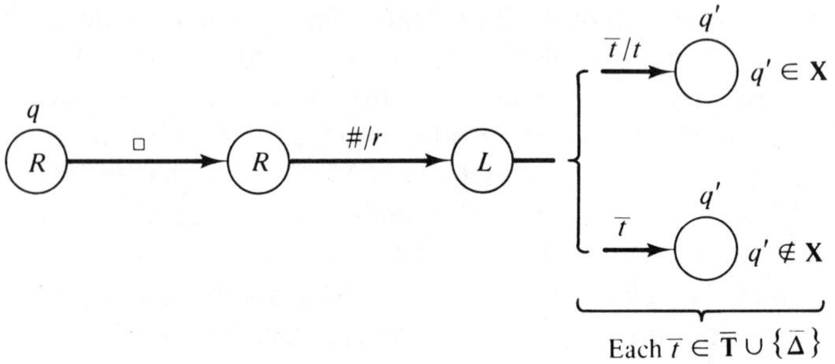


(c) If state $q$ labels the instruction $q$] **left** $(t/t', q')$, $\mathbf{M}'$ has:

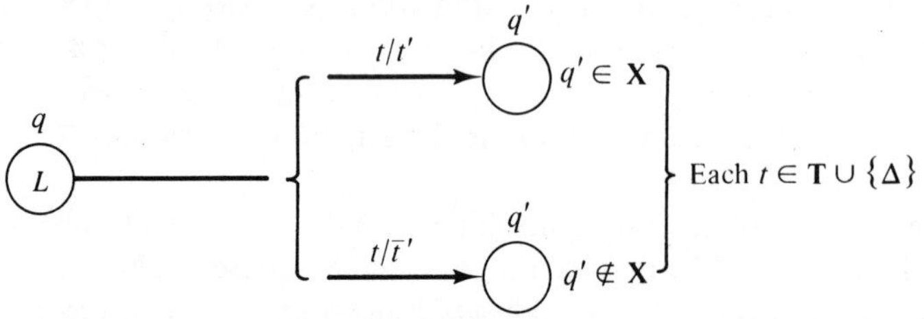


(d) If state $q$ labels the instruction $q$] **right** $(t/t', q')$, $\mathbf{M}'$ has:

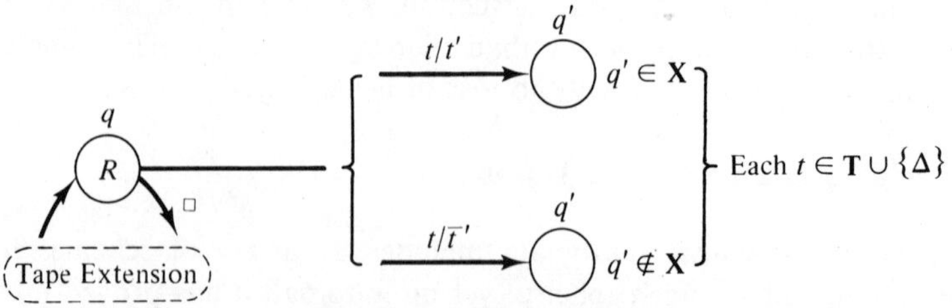


**Figure 11.11** Simulation of a Turing transducer by a Turing machine.

(e) For each state $q$ that labels right instructions, $\mathbf{M}'$ has:

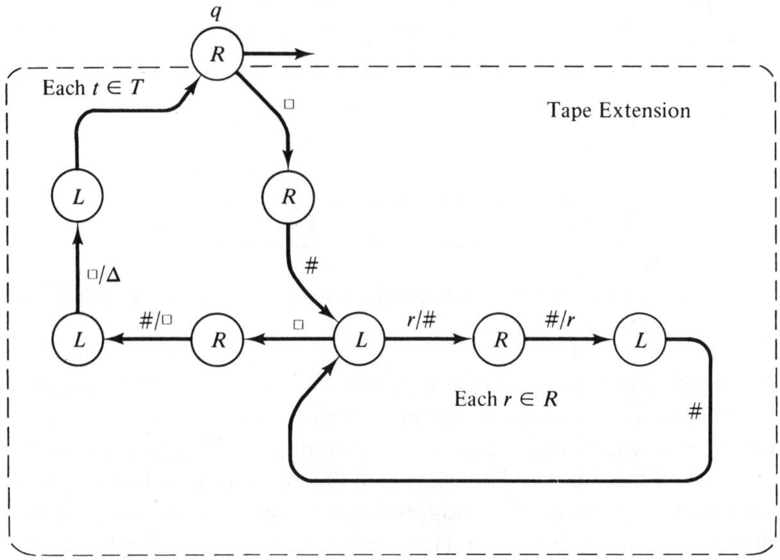


(f) To initialize tape regions, $\mathbf{M}'$ has:

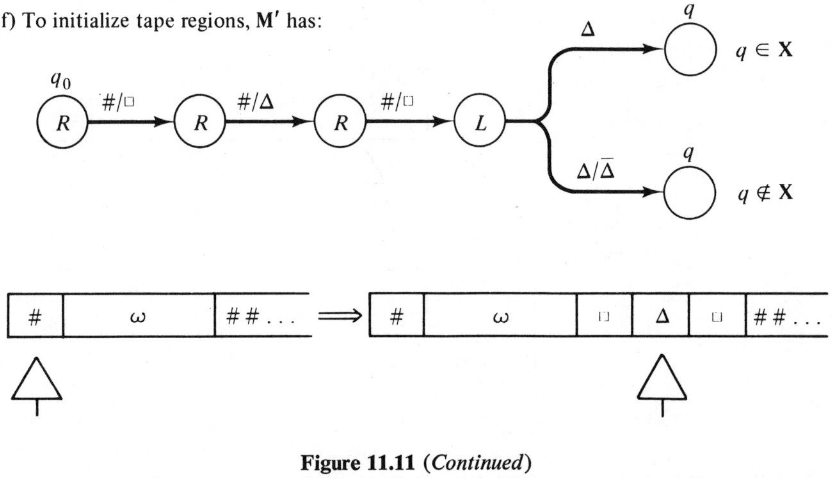


**Figure 11.11** (*Continued*)

both left and right. Figure 11.12 shows how the squares of the doubly-infinite tape may be placed in one-to-one correspondence with those of a singly infinite tape. After fixing an arbitrary point on the doubly infinite tape as the "center," we assign successive even numbers to squares on the right and odd numbers to squares on the left. This correspondence may be used to devise a

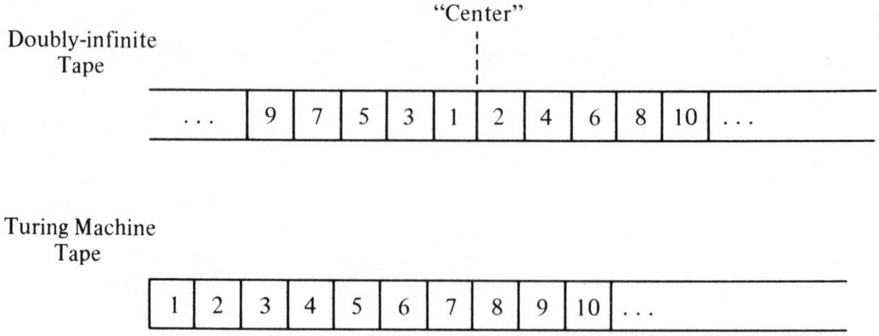


**Figure 11.12** Mapping a doubly infinite tape onto a Turing machine tape.

Turing machine program for emulating a machine with a doubly infinite tape: we make two copies of the machine's control, one in use when the simulated machine is operating in the even-numbered region of its tape, the other when the simulated machine is in the odd-numbered region. So that the simulator stays on even- or odd-numbered squares, each left (or right) move in the original machine is replaced with a pair of left (or right) moves in the simulator. Left and right moves are interchanged in the copy of the control used for odd-numbered squares, and each copy is modified to switch to the other whenever the simulator reaches the left end of its tape.

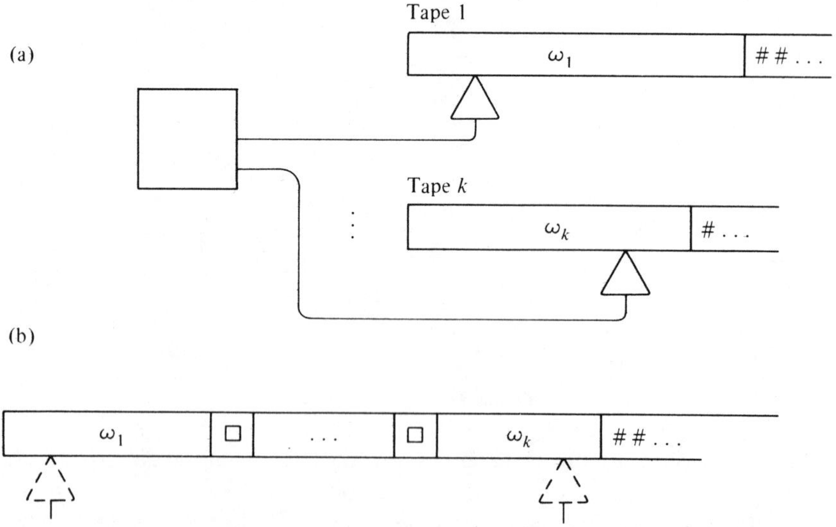


**Figure 11.13** Turing machine representation for configurations of a multitape automaton.

Another variation on the Turing machine is a machine with several storage tapes, each with its own read–write head. Figure 11.13a shows a multitape machine. Figure 11.13b shows how the $k$ tapes of the machine may be represented on the single tape of a Turing machine. The scheme used earlier to simulate a Turing transducer may be adopted here to simulate configuration changes of the multitape machine.

Other storage-tape variations, such as multitrack tapes or tapes with many heads, may also be simulated straightforwardly by the Turing machines defined in this chapter. Several such variations are explored in the Problems.

### 11.2.3 Nondeterministic Turing Machines

A nondeterministic Turing machine (NDTM) may generate many distinct computations that terminate in dead configurations. For these machines, we must regard the output string defined by the final configuration of each halted computation as a legitimate output string of the machine; thus an NDTM realizes a relation, not a function, between input and output strings. Example 11.3 shows that the set of output strings for some input strings may be infinite.

**Example 11.3:** The machine shown in Figure 11.14 is a slightly modified version of the copier TM constructed earlier. Note that it is nondeterministic because two successor states exist if # is read on a right move from the initial state. After copying its input string, this machine may either halt or proceed to make a copy of the copy just completed. Thus, for any input string $\omega$, this machine has an infinity of output strings

$$\omega\#\omega, \omega\#\omega\#\omega, \omega\#\omega\#\omega\#\omega, \ldots$$

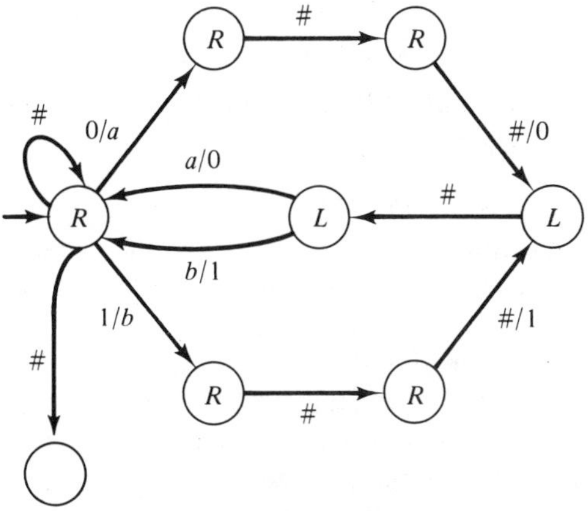


**Figure 11.14** Nondeterministic Turing machine.

and realizes the relation $g$, where

$$(\omega, \omega(\#\omega)^k) \in g, \qquad \text{each } \omega \in \{0, 1\}^*, \text{ each } k \geq 1$$

How can we compare the computational power of deterministic and nondeterministic Turing machines, when one of these forms produces a single output for a given input while the other may produce an infinity of outputs? Two approaches are possible. Given an NDTM $\mathbf{M}$, we can carry out all its computations for a given input "simultaneously," by representing on the tape of a Turing machine, in the $k$th phase of its operation, the set of all configurations of $\mathbf{M}$ reachable from its initial configuration in exactly $k$ moves. Alternatively, we can simulate one computation by $\mathbf{M}$ to completion, making a copy of its configuration at each point where more than one choice of next move is possible. If and when a dead configuration is reached, the output string is recorded, and simulation of some other computation of $\mathbf{M}$ is begun.

The second, or backtracking, approach has a serious flaw: if our simulator attempts a computation of $\mathbf{M}$ that never reaches a dead configuration, it will never simulate any remaining computations, even though these might produce output strings in finitely many steps! To avoid the difficulties caused by nonhalting computations, we use the first approach.

A nondeterministic machine $\mathbf{M}$ realizes a relation

$$g_{\mathbf{M}} = \left\{ (\omega, \psi) \;\middle|\; \begin{array}{l} \omega \in (\mathbf{T} \cup \mathbf{\Delta})^*, \\ (\lambda, q_I, \Delta, \omega) \Longrightarrow (\varphi, q, \Delta, \psi) \\ \text{is a halted computation of } \mathbf{M} \end{array} \right\}$$

where $\Delta$ is the blank symbol of $\mathbf{M}$. We wish to describe a Turing machine $\mathbf{M}'$ which, given a list of configurations that $\mathbf{M}$ may reach in $k$ moves, constructs a list of the configurations $\mathbf{M}$ may reach in $k + 1$ moves. Let

$$\mathbf{C}_k = \{\alpha_1, \ldots, \alpha_m\}$$

be the set of configurations of $\mathbf{M}$ reachable from an initial configuration $\alpha_0$ in exactly $k$ moves, where

$$\alpha_i = (\varphi_i, q_i, t_i, \psi_i)$$

The set of configurations $\mathbf{C}_k$ may be represented on the tape of a Turing machine as in Figure 11.15a. The special symbol □ separates configurations on the tape.

It is convenient for $\mathbf{M}'$ to construct the description of $\mathbf{C}_{k+1}$ on blank tape to the right of $\mathbf{C}_k$, as shown in Figure 11.15b, where the symbol ⬡ indicates the end of the tape description of $\mathbf{C}_k$. For each configuration $\alpha_i$ in $\mathbf{C}_k$, $\mathbf{M}'$ computes the successor configuration for each possible move of $\mathbf{M}$ and appends it to the new list. When $\mathbf{M}$ has finished processing all elements of $\mathbf{C}_k$, it begins processing the new list in the same manner.

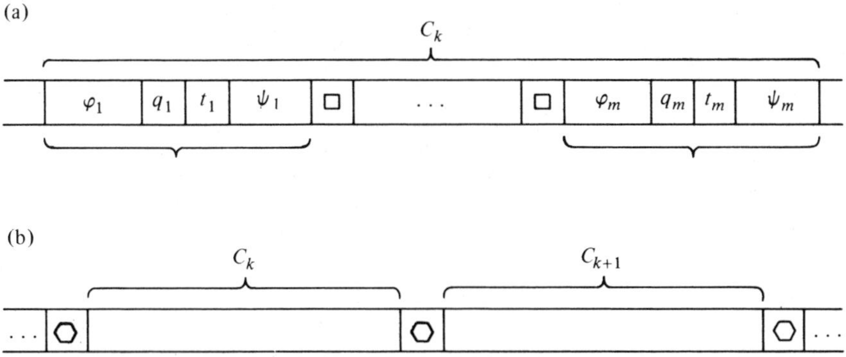


**Figure 11.15** Representation of NDTM configurations on a TM tape.

This describes how a Turing machine **M**′ can generate descriptions of all configurations reachable by **M** in finitely many steps. How can **M**′ display the output strings of **M**? Since these may be infinite in number, there is no way to list them all in finitely many steps; thus we must be satisfied with a method of enumerating all possible outputs. An output string of **M** is defined by each dead configuration it can reach, and each such configuration will eventually appear on the tape of **M**′. Consider constructing from **M**′ a Turing machine **M**″ whose input strings are of the form

$$\omega\#1^n, \qquad \omega \in (\mathbf{T} \cup \mathbf{\Delta})^*,\ n \geq 0$$

and whose output is the tape of the $n$th dead configuration written on the tape of **M**′. In this way **M**″ associates an output string of **M** with each whole number $n$, and each output string of **M** will be produced by **M**″ for some choice of $n$. We say that the Turing machine **M**″ *enumerates* the output strings of **M** for any input string $\omega$.

> **Proposition 11.1:** Let **M** be any NDTM. One can construct a TM **M**″ such that, for each input string $\omega \in (\mathbf{T} \cup \mathbf{\Delta})^*$, **M**″ enumerates the output strings of **M**.

In Section 11.7 we shall return to Turing machine enumerations of sets.

## 11.3 Turing Accepters

A Turing machine can be regarded as *accepting* a string just if it performs a halted computation when given the string as input. The set of strings accepted by a Turing machine is therefore the domain of the machine's input–output function.

**Definition 11.5:** A language **L** is *Turing recognizable* if it is the domain of a Turing-realizable function.

Note that by this definition every Turing machine is an accepter for some language.

**Example 11.4:** Figure 11.16 shows a TM that recognizes the double-matching language $\mathbf{L}_{dm} = \{a^k b^k c^k \mid k \geq 1\}$. The machine operates by crossing off one letter from each section of the input string until all letters are crossed off or a disagreement in number is discovered.

Note that the definition of Turing-realizable language is no more general if "function" is changed to "relation" in Definition 11.5. Given any NDTM **M**, it is easy to construct a Turing machine **M**′ such that **M**′ accepts a string $\omega$ just if **M** may perform some halted computation when presented $\omega$ as its input string. To see this, let **M**′ be the deterministic machine that simulates **M** by the construction given in the preceding section. If we alter **M**′ to halt as soon as it finds a dead configuration of **M**, then the language recognized by **M**′ is precisely the domain of the relation realized by **M**.

**Theorem 11.1:** The domain of the relation realized by any NDTM is a Turing-recognizable language.

Since a pushdown automaton is a restricted form of NDTM, it is easy to simulate a given pushdown accepter with a Turing machine. Thus the class of languages defined by Turing accepters includes the context-free languages. Since we know that the language $\mathbf{L}_{dm}$ is not context free, Example 11.4 shows this inclusion to be proper.

**Theorem 11.2:** The class of Turing-recognizable languages properly includes the class of context-free languages.

We shall see that Turing machines form the most powerful class of language recognizers known, and there is no reason to suppose that more powerful accepters exist. There is, however, a class of accepters called *linear-bounded accepters* intermediate in power between pushdown accepters and Turing accepters. A linear-bounded accepter is a Turing transducer restricted to using a length of storage tape that is some fixed multiple of the length of its input string. (The adjective "linear" is used in describing the machine because the amount of storage permitted is related linearly to the length of an input string.) It is known that a language is context sensitive just if it is recognized by some nondeterministic linear-bounded accepter, but it is not known whether each such language can be recognized by some deterministic

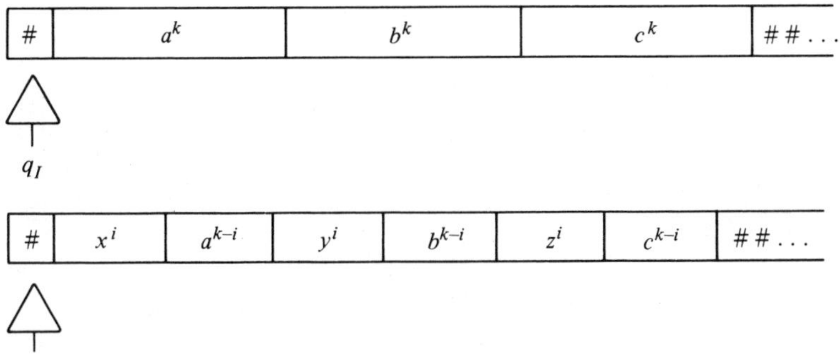


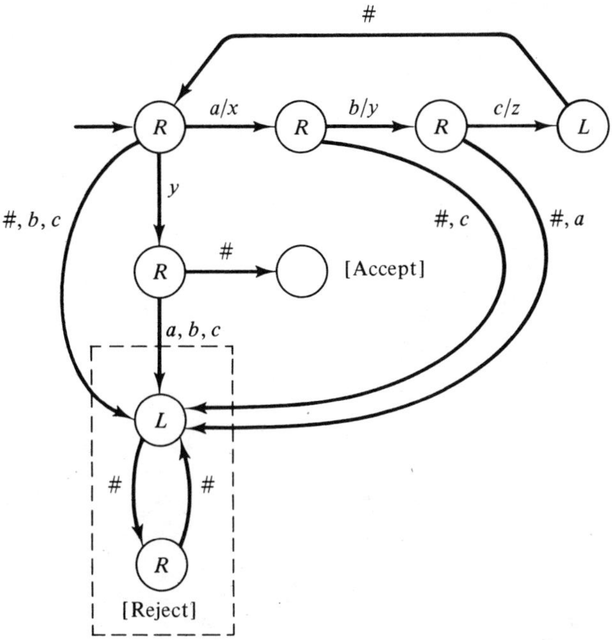


**Figure 11.16** Turing accepter for $\mathbf{L}_{dm}$.

linear-bounded accepter. Indeed, many of the questions we have answered for other classes of automata have remained unanswered for linear-bounded automata. Since the theory of context-sensitive languages has had little impact on programming languages, linear-bounded automata are not studied in this book.

## 11.4 Computable Functions and Predicates

We now study Turing machines as evaluators of functions on the natural numbers {0, 1, 2, . . .}. Our immediate objective is to indicate the enormous variety of functions that can be computed, by showing how Turing machines that define simple number-theoretic functions and predicates may be combined to yield machines that define more complex functions. (Our approach is similar to that used in computer programming, where simple routines are combined to construct routines of greater complexity.) This study further supports the thesis that Turing computability is a general formalization of the concepts of "algorithm" and "effective procedure."

Since our goal is an understanding of the computational power of Turing machines, economy of time and space is immaterial; we are free to represent numbers in the way that affords the simplest exposition. We shall use *unary notation*, in which an integer $x$ is represented by $1^x$, a string of 1's having length $x$. An $m$-tuple of integers,

$$\mathbf{x} = (x_1, \ldots, x_m)$$

is represented by the unary codes for $x_1, \ldots, x_m$ separated by sharps:

$$1^{x_1} \# 1^{x_2} \# \ldots \# 1^{x_m}$$

For example,

$$1 \# \# 1 1 1 \# 1 1$$

represents the four-tuple

$$(1, 0, 3, 2)$$

### 11.4.1 Functions on Natural Numbers

A number-theoretic function is *computable* if there is a Turing machine that can evaluate the function when the argument and result are expressed in the unary notation just described. The following definition is illustrated by Figure 11.17.

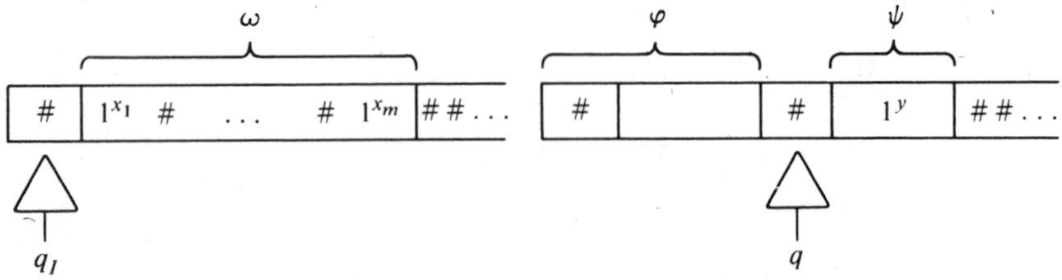


$$(\lambda, q_I, \#, \omega) \Rightarrow (\varphi, q, \#, \psi)$$

**Figure 11.17** Evaluation of a Turing-computable function.

**Definition 11.6:** Let $\mathbf{N} = \{0, 1, 2, \ldots\}$ denote the natural numbers. A function

$$f\colon \mathbf{N}^m \longrightarrow \mathbf{N}$$

is *Turing computable* if there exists a TM that realizes the function $g\colon \{\#, 1\}^* \longrightarrow \mathbf{1}^*$, where

$$g(1^{x_1} \# \ldots \# 1^{x_m}) = \begin{cases} 1^y & \text{if } f(x_1, \ldots, x_m) = y \\ \text{undefined} & \text{if } f(x_1, \ldots, x_m) \text{ is undefined} \end{cases}$$

A Turing machine that computes $f$ will perform the computation

$$(\lambda, q_I, \#, 1^{x_1} \# \ldots \# 1^{x_m}) \Longrightarrow (\varphi, q, \#, 1^y)$$

whenever $y = f(x_1, \ldots, x_m)$, and will fail to halt if $f(x_1, \ldots, x_m)$ is undefined. Such a machine will also perform the computation

$$(\xi, q_I, \#, 1^{x_1} \# \ldots \# 1^{x_m}) \Longrightarrow (\xi\varphi, q, \#, 1^y)$$

for any string of symbols $\xi$, since an attempt to perform a left move from the initial head position would cause the machine to halt erroneously if $\xi$ were the empty string. It is quite convenient that the machine leaves undisturbed the portion of the tape to the left of the initial head position, since this allows us to easily combine Turing machines to implement complex functions.

**Example 11.5:** Ordinary integer addition is computable. Figure 11.18 shows the state diagram of a Turing machine **add** that computes

$$f(x, y) = x + y$$

for nonnegative integers $x$ and $y$. The machine operates by changing the # separating $x$ and $y$ to a 1, and then deleting the final 1.

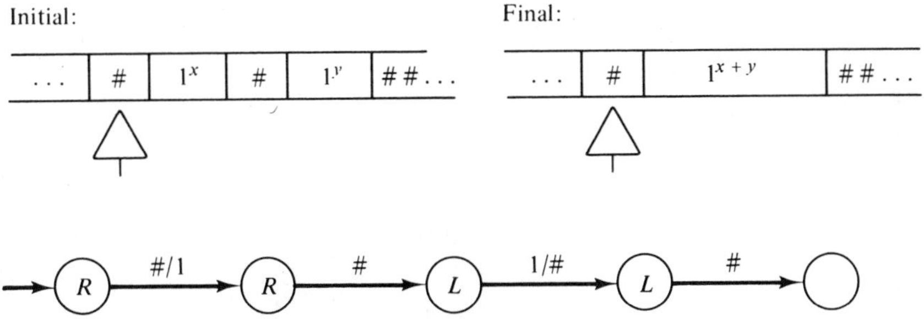


**Figure 11.18 add** Turing machine.

The **add** machine of Figure 11.18 has certain important properties. In particular,

1. The head starts and finishes at the same square, which is blank.

2. The arguments, written in unary notation to the right of the initial head position, are followed by completely blank tape.

3. The computed result, written in unary notation to the right of the final head position, is followed by completely blank tape.

4. The machine never attempts to move left of its initial head position.

Each machine we construct for computing functions and predicates will have these characteristics.

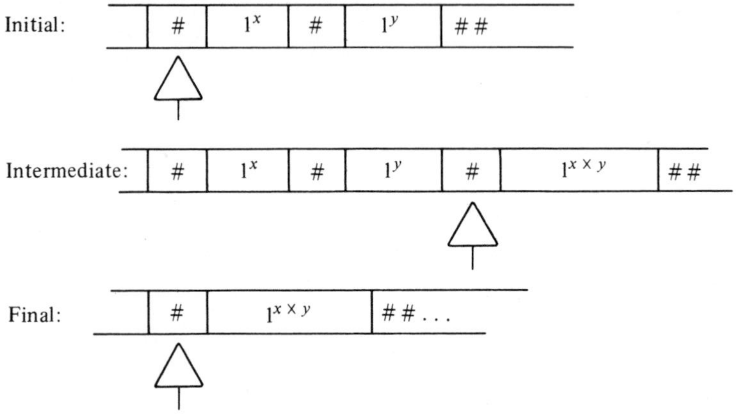


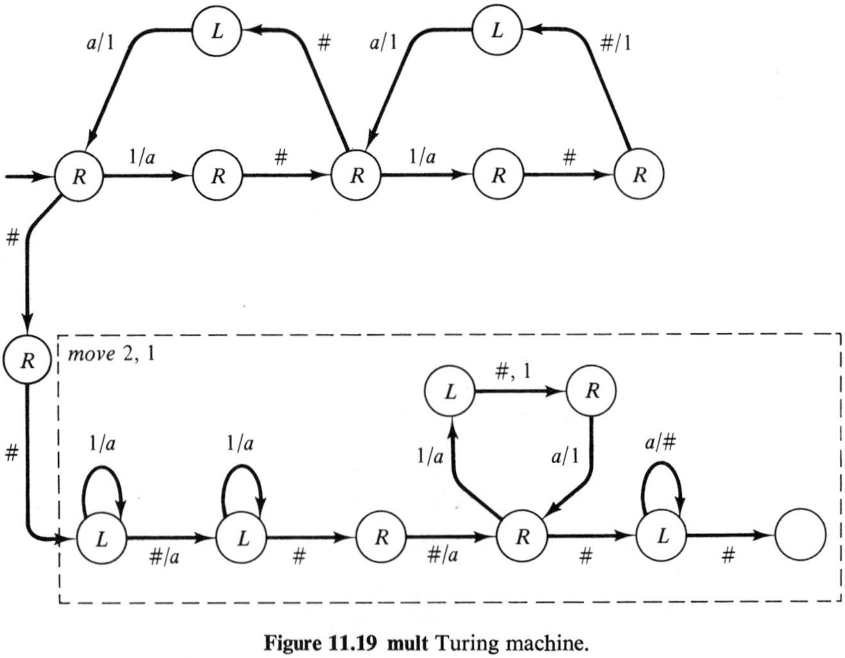


**Figure 11.19 mult** Turing machine.

**Example 11.6:** The machine **mult** in Figure 11.19 computes

$$f(x, y) = x \times y$$

It consists of two parts. The first part performs the multiplication by copying the $y$ block to the right $x$ times. When this is done, the tape contains $1^x \# 1^y \# 1^{x \times y}$. The second part of the machine (enclosed in the dashed box) erases the $x$ and $y$ blocks and copies the result $x \times y$ into the proper position just right of the initial head position.

**Example 11.7:** The second part of the **mult** machine is an instance of the class of Turing machines designated **move** $m, n$, where $m$ and $n$ are whole numbers. As shown in Figure 11.20, the machine **move** $m, n$ erases $m$ numbers to the left of the initial head position, then moves $n$ numbers leftward to close up the gap. The tape to the right of the $n$ numbers is assumed to be initially blank, and is also blank after the copying has been completed.

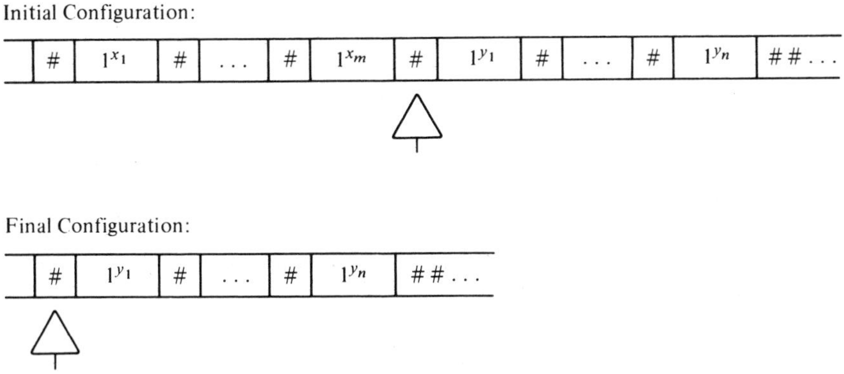


**Figure 11.20** Operation of the **move** $m, n$ machine.

**Example 11.8:** Because there are no negative natural numbers, subtraction of the natural numbers is not the ordinary subtraction of integers. Let

$$f(x, y) = \begin{cases} x - y & \text{if } x \geq y \\ 0 & \text{otherwise} \end{cases}$$

This function is known variously as *positive difference*, *proper subtraction*, or *monus* (as distinct from "minus"), and is usually written

$$f(x, y) = x \dot{-} y$$

with a dot over the minus sign. The machine **monus** of Figure 11.21 computes this function.

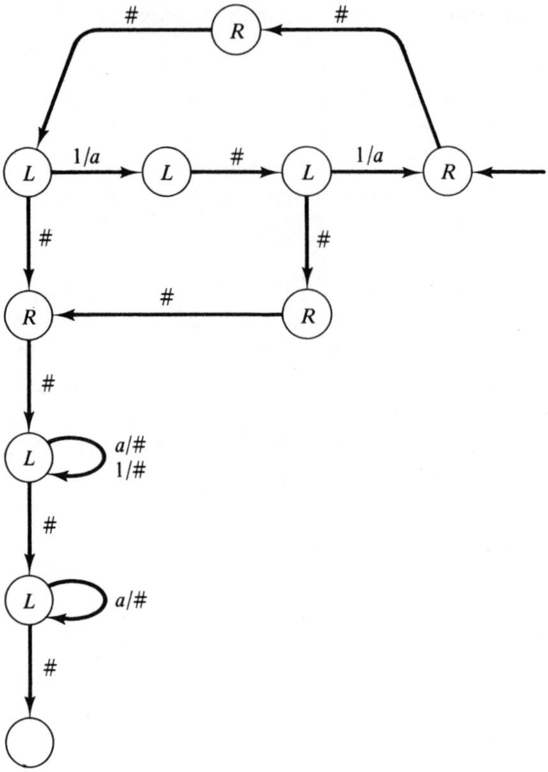


**Figure 11.21** **monus** machine.

### 11.4.2 Predicates on Natural Numbers

We next consider several simple number-theoretic predicates that can be evaluated by Turing machines.

**Definition 11.7:** A predicate $p\colon \mathbf{N}^m \longrightarrow \{true, false\}$ is *Turing decidable* if the function $f = \mathbf{N}^m \longrightarrow \{0, 1\}$ is Turing computable, where

$$f(\mathbf{x}) = \begin{cases} 0 & \text{if } p(\mathbf{x}) = \mathit{false} \\ 1 & \text{if } p(\mathbf{x}) = \mathit{true} \end{cases}$$

A set $\mathbf{M} \subseteq \mathbf{N}$ is *Turing decidable* if the predicate

$$x \in \mathbf{M}$$

is Turing decidable.

**Example 11.9:** The machine **greater** in Figure 11.22 decides the predicate

$$p(x, y) = true \qquad \text{if and only if } x > y$$

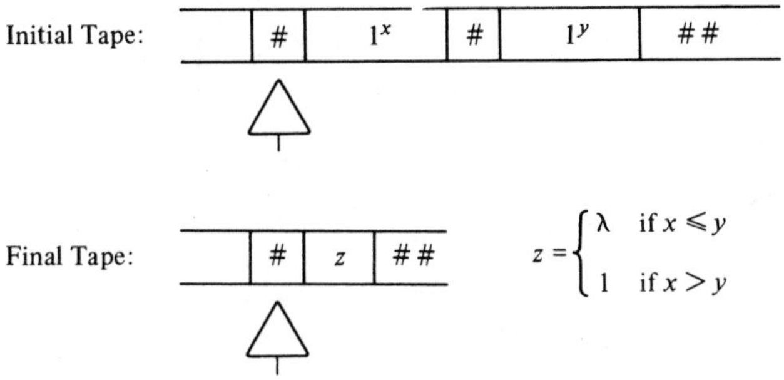


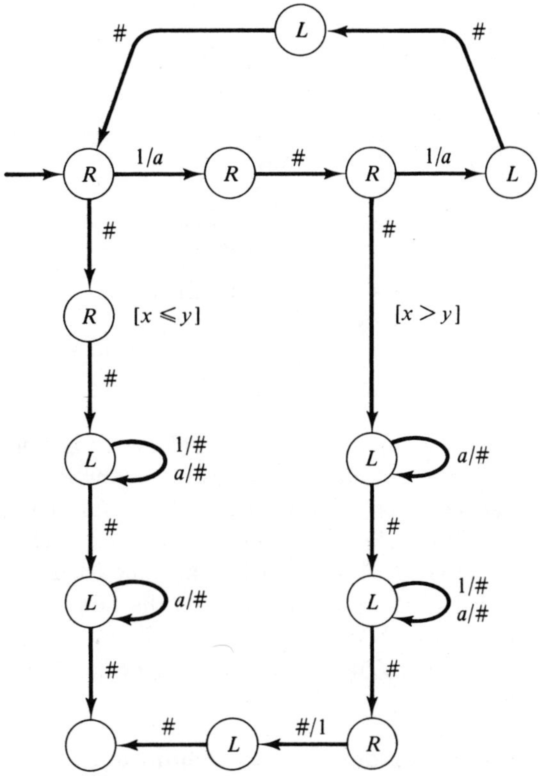


**Figure 11.22** **greater** machine.

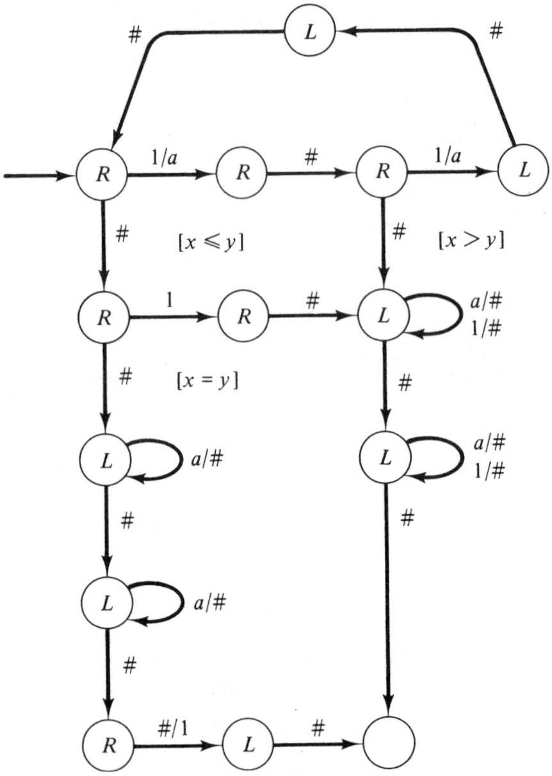


**Figure 11.23 equal** machine.

The machine **equal** in Figure 11.23 decides

$$p(x, y) = true \qquad \text{if and only if } x = y$$

For building compound Turing machines, it is convenient to use component machines that decide predicates by halting in one of two final states, $q_t$ if the predicate is *true*, $q_f$ if it is *false*, after returning the head to its initial position with blank tape to the right. Figure 11.24a shows the construction of such a machine **M**′ from a Turing machine **M** that decides predicate $p$. (It is assumed that **M** starts and halts on the same square of its tape.) The reverse construction of **M** from **M**′ is illustrated in Figure 11.24b, showing that the two forms of Turing machines for deciding predicates are computationally equivalent.

### 11.4.3 Combinations of Turing Machines

Our next example shows how complex functions are shown computable by combining simple Turing machines. Consider computing the greatest common divisor (gcd) of two natural numbers $x$ and $y$. The value of gcd $(x, y)$

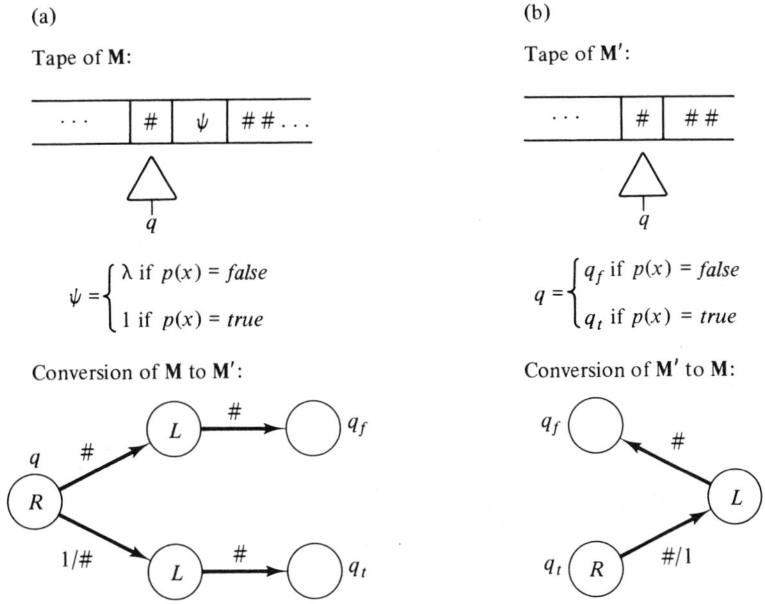


**Figure 11.24** Equivalent forms of TM for deciding predicate $p$.

is the largest natural number $z$ that divides evenly into both $x$ and $y$. For example,

$$\gcd(12, 4) = 4 \qquad \gcd(12, 10) = 2$$
$$\gcd(12, 5) = 1 \qquad \gcd(12, 12) = 12$$

We are not concerned with the value of gcd $(x, y)$ when either $x = 0$ or $y = 0$. The well-known *Euclidean algorithm* for evaluating gcd is given as a flow chart in Figure 11.25, and is based on the following facts:

1. If $x > y$, then gcd $(x, y) =$ gcd $(x - y, y)$.
2. If $x = y$, then gcd $(x, y) = x$.
3. If $x < y$, then gcd $(x, y) =$ gcd $(x, y - x)$.

To prove (1), suppose that $d =$ gcd $(x, y)$. Then we can express $x$ and $y$ in the forms

$$x = d \times x'$$
$$y = d \times y'$$

If $x > y$, then $x - y = d \times (x' - y')$; thus $d$ divides both $x - y$ and $y$. The truth of (2) is obvious. The truth of (3) follows from the fact that gcd $(x, y) =$ gcd $(y, x)$. To compute gcd $(x, y)$, we apply (1) and (3) repeatedly to reduce the problem, until the condition of (2) holds.

The Euclidean algorithm may also be expressed as a computational *procedure* using notation similar to the programming language Algol:

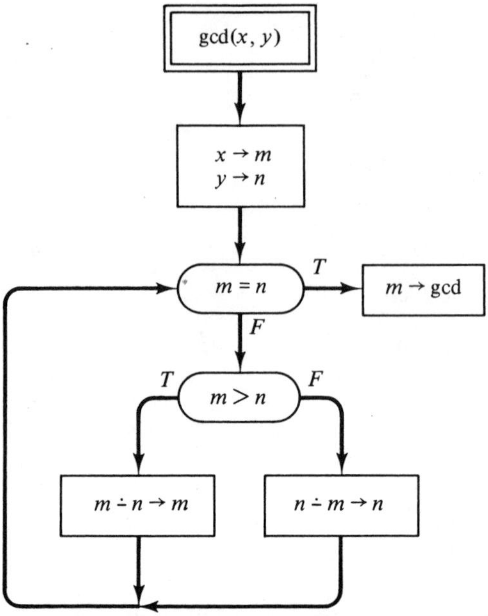


**Figure 11.25** Euclidean algorithm.

**procedure** gcd $(x, y)$
**begin**
  $m := x; n := y;$
  **while** $m \neq n$ **do** {**if** $m > n$ **then** $m := m - n$ **else** $n := n - m$};
  gcd $= m;$
**end**

The *body* of a procedure is a sequence of *statements* enclosed by the symbols **begin** and **end**. The statements will have the following forms:

1. *Assignment:* a statement of the form $a := b$ associates the value of the expression $b$ with the variable $a$.
2. *Iteration:* a statement **while** $P$ **do** $\{S_1 ; \ldots ; S_k\}$ causes the predicate $P$ to be evaluated and the statements $S_1, \ldots, S_k$ to be performed if the result is *true*. This action is repeated until evaluation of $P$ yields *false*.
3. *Conditional:* a statement **if** $P$ **then** $S_1$ **else** $S_2$ causes the predicate $P$ to be evaluated. If the result is *true*, $S_1$ is performed; if *false*, $S_2$ is performed.

In the remainder of this book, it will be convenient to demonstrate Turing computability by giving procedures of the form just described. For this approach to be valid, we must show how such procedures may be implemented in the form of Turing machine programs. This is done by adjoining suitable primitive Turing machines and arranging for control to transfer from one machine to another according to the requirements of the procedure being implemented. In addition to the Turing machines already presented for evaluating simple functions and predicates, we need elementary machines that perform certain clerical operations. These are described next, and their action is illustrated in Figure 11.26:

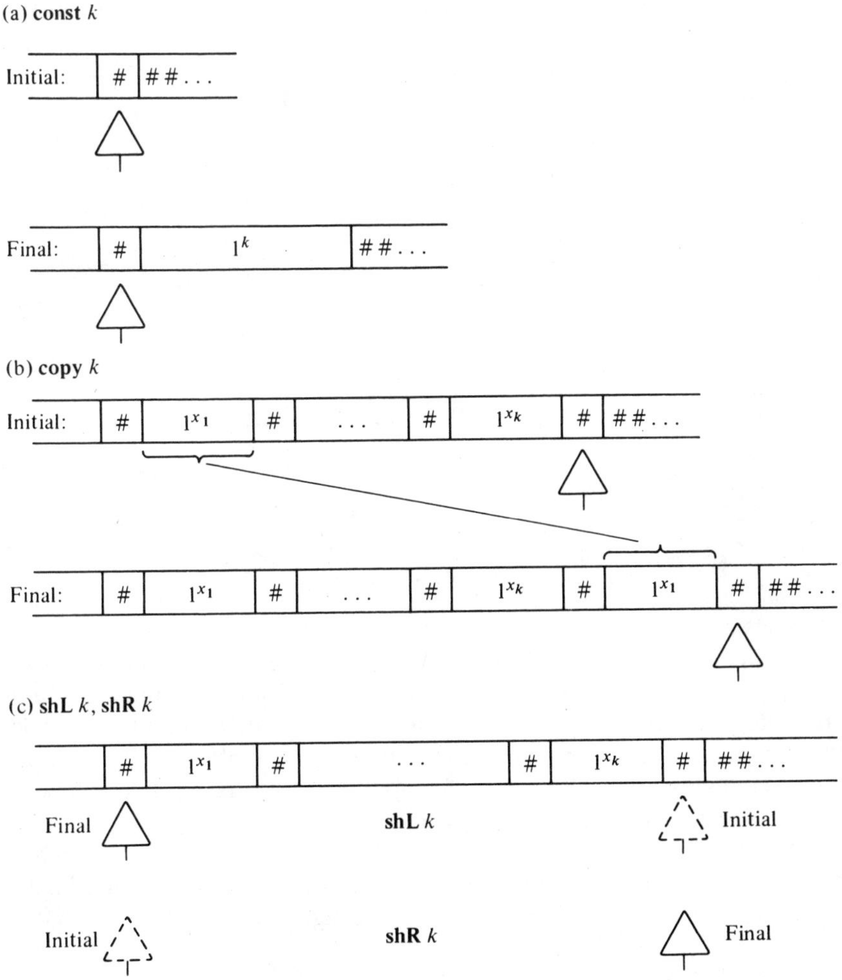


**Figure 11.26** Elementary TM's for clerical operations.

**const** $k$: print the string $1^k$ to the right of the initial head position, and return the head to its initial position.

**copy** $k$: locate the $k$th block of 1's counting left from the initial head position, and copy this block into blank tape to the right of the initial head position. The head is positioned at the first sharp to the right of the new copy.

**shL** $k$: shift the head left past $k$ blocks of 1's.

**shR** $k$: shift the head right past $k$ blocks of 1's.

Figure 11.27 shows, in terms of elementary Turing machine programs, a composite Turing machine that implements the Euclidean algorithm. The state diagram of the composite machine is formed from those of elementary

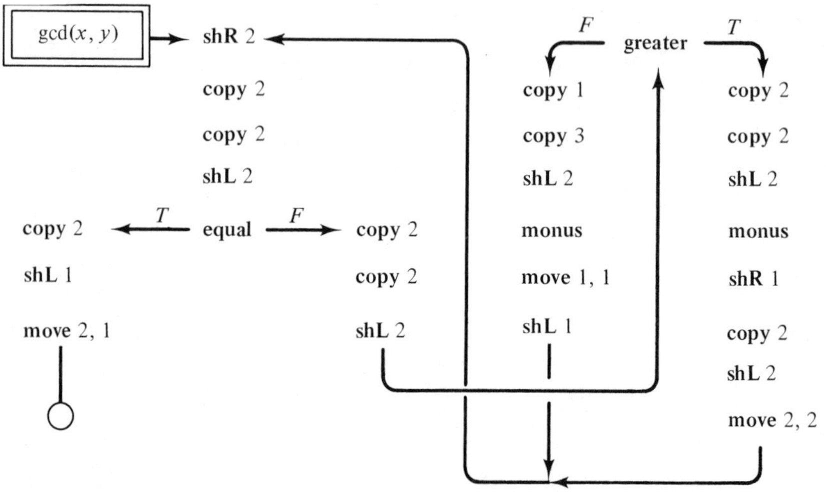


**Figure 11.27** **gcd** machine constructed from elementary TM's.

machines by merging each final state of an elementary machine with the initial state of the appropriate successor machine. The **copy** and **shift** machines are used to set up operands for the applications of primitive functions and predicates, and the move machines delete unneeded blocks of 1's, while maintaining the condition that the tape is completely blank to the right of the block holding the most recently computed result. The **equal** and **greater** machines were discussed in Example 11.9.

Figure 11.28 gives a flow chart that describes a partial function and a corresponding Turing machine **sqrt** synthesized from elementary machines. Expressed as a computational procedure, the algorithm is

**procedure** sqrt ($x$)
**begin**
  $k := 1; y := k \times k;$
  **while** $x \neq y$ **do** $\{k := k + 1; y := k \times k\};$
  sqrt $:= y$
**end**

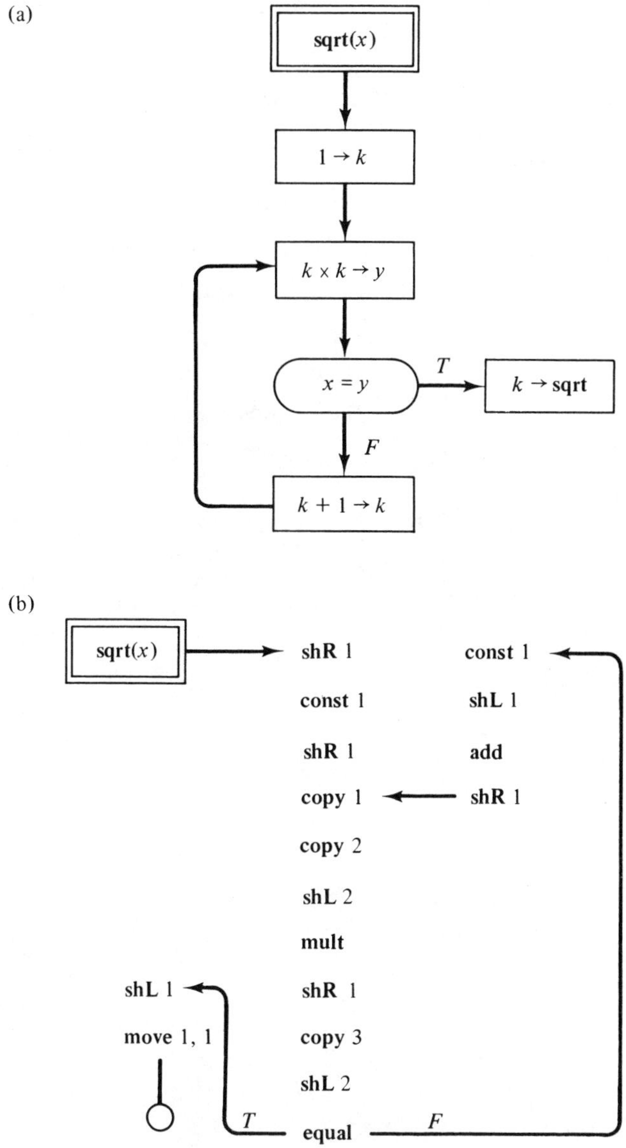


**Figure 11.28** **sqrt** machine constructed from elementary TM's.

The machine **sqrt** finds the square root of $x$ if $x$ is a perfect square; otherwise, the predicate $x \neq y$ will always be satisfied and the machine will fail to halt. Note that by Definition 11.5 the set

$$\{1^k \mid k \text{ is a perfect square}\}$$

is a Turing-recognizable language.

### 11.4.4 Interrelation of Functions and Predicates

With each function

$$f: \mathbf{N}^m \longrightarrow \mathbf{N}$$

we may associate a predicate

$$p: \mathbf{N}^m \times \mathbf{N} \longrightarrow \{true, false\}$$

defined by

$$p(x, y) = \begin{cases} true & \text{if } y = f(\mathbf{x}) \\ false & \text{otherwise} \end{cases}$$

The domain of $p$ is $\mathbf{N}^m \times \mathbf{N}$ if $f$ is total, or $\mathbf{D}_f \times \mathbf{N}$ if $f$ is a partial function with domain $\mathbf{D}_f$.

If $f$ is a total function, then $f$ is Turing computable if and only if $p$ is Turing decidable, as demonstrated by these procedures:

```
procedure p(x, y)
begin
  w := f(x);
  if w = y then p := true else p := false;
end
```

```
procedure f(x)
begin
  y := 0;
  while p(x, y) = false do {y := y + 1};
  f := y
end
```

## 11.5 Algorithms and Effective Computability

### 11.5.1 Turing's Thesis and Church's Thesis

Our study of Turing machines has shown them to be very powerful computing devices; many simple functions may be evaluated by Turing machines, and the programs of Turing machines may be combined to build machines that realize successively more complex functions. In addition, we know that Turing machines can simulate all other known abstract machines.

The broad capabilities of the Turing machine suggest that it might represent an inherent limit on computational ability. Indeed, the brilliance of Turing's work is that he conceived his abstract machine model with exactly this concept in mind.† Turing proposed that *any computation one might naturally regard as possible to carry out can be performed by some Turing machine having a suitable set of instructions.* This proposal, that Turing machines are a formal counterpart to the informal notion of algorithms, has become known as *Turing's thesis.*

How is it possible to validate Turing's thesis? The fundamental difficulty lies in the informal concept of algorithm: there is no way of describing formally a property of the class of all algorithms unless one has a precise formal notion of what an algorithm is. But then, this is exactly what Turing's abstract machines are claimed to be! Since it is an assertion about informal algorithms, Turing's thesis must remain formally unproved. Nevertheless, it is generally accepted as an empirical truth.

Accepting the impossibility of a formal proof, we may argue informally in favor of Turing's claim. An algorithm is commonly said to be a "step-by-step procedure for solving a problem." Let us try to be more explicit. In describing an algorithm, we imply the existence of some *computing agent* capable of carrying out successive steps of the algorithm. Furthermore, we regard an algorithm as incomplete unless each step to be taken by the computing agent is clear and unambiguous. Let us call the portion of an algorithm used by the agent to determine the next step of its action an *instruction.* The agent must know what action to take for each possible instruction and how the execution of instructions should be sequenced.

"Solving a problem" normally means that the computing agent, presented with a statement of the problem, obeys the instructions of the algorithm and eventually produces an answer. We call the problem description an *input* to the algorithm and the answer an *output.*

We wish our informal notion of algorithm to be such that we can readily imagine its execution by a human or mechanical agent. Therefore, we insist that the objects the computing agent must examine in any step be elements from finite sets. But we also wish to represent problem statements and answers that require the agent to distinguish among arbitrarily many possibilities; even so elementary an operation as adding 1 to an integer requires our agent to distinguish among the infinity of integers. This requirement is met by constructing inputs, outputs, and intermediate values from discrete symbols chosen from finite sets. The instructions of the algorithm must also be constructed from finite sets of symbols; moreover, an algorithm may only have

†Remember that Turing did this work ten years before the idea of a practical stored program computer was realized. Subsequently, Turing contributed to the development of practical digital computers.

finitely many instructions if one expects to prepare a list of instructions for the computing agent!

This analysis of the nature of informal algorithms is nicely summed up by the following quotation from Rogers†:

> Consider a box *B* inside of which we have a man *L* with a desk, pencils, and paper. On one side *B* has two slots, marked *input* and *output*. If we write a number on paper and pass it through the input slot, *L* takes it and begins performing certain computations. If and when he finishes, he writes down a number obtained from the computation and passes it back to us through the output slot. Assume further that *L* has with him explicit deterministic instructions of finite length as to how the computation is to be done. We refer to these instructions as *P*. Finally, assume that the supply of paper is inexhaustible, and that *B* can be enlarged in size so that an arbitrarily large amount of paper work can be stored in it in the course of any single computation. (Indeed, this elasticity might be needed just to store the input number, if that number were sufficiently large.) I think we had better assume, too, that *L* himself is inexhaustible, since we do not care how long it takes for an output to appear, provided that it does eventually appear after a finite amount of computation.

From this picture of a computing agent working with finite alphabets of symbols, finite sets of instructions, and unbounded memory for notes to himself, many formal models have been invented for the activity of the computing agent. In each scheme there is a specified representation for the instructions of the algorithm and precise rules of interpretation for each possible instruction.

Turing's abstract machine model is the result of one line of reasoning. The control unit and the rules for obeying the instructions of its program are a precise model of the computing agent, while the storage tape provides unbounded memory and also holds the problem statement and answer encoded as arbitrarily long strings of symbols.

Two other models are also studied in this book: the recursive partial functions introduced by Church and Kleene as a formalization of "algorithmically computable function" are studied in Chapter 13; the symbol-manipulation systems devised by Post are treated in Chapter 14. Each of these formal schemes defines a class of functions that can be described by a finite set of "instructions" given to the "computing agent" of the scheme. It happens that all three formal systems define precisely the same class of functions! This result is a powerful argument for accepting Turing's thesis, since

†Rogers [1959].

all three systems are in complete agreement as to what functions are computable. These functions are generally known as the *recursive partial functions*, or, for convenience, the *recursive functions*.

Alonzo Church was quick to recognize that all formalizations of algorithms were destined to yield the same class of computable functions, and he asserted that the notion of recursive functions is a satisfactory formalization of "effectively computable functions". This assertion is now known as *Church's thesis*.

The equivalence of the models of Turing, Church–Kleene, and Post is proved in Chapters 13 and 14. Although Church's and Turing's theses are unprovable, the equivalence of the various models has the status of a formal result: the models dealt with are precise mathematical objects.

### 11.5.2 Recursive Invariance

Church's thesis is sometimes called a *principle of recursive invariance*, since the main results of the theory of algorithms are invariant over all approaches to the formalization of algorithms: all approaches identify the same class of functions as being effectively calculable.

A second notion of invariance arises in connection with the representation of problem statements and answers for a particular formal model. We have already mentioned that the formal models must use finitely many distinct symbols to represent inputs and outputs. Turing reasoned that there would be no loss of generality if the symbols are arranged in a linear sequence, as on the tape of a Turing machine. Of course, there are many ways of encoding a problem statement as a string of symbols. Is it possible that our formalization of algorithm will demonstrate the existence of an algorithm for one choice of representation, but no algorithm for some other choice? Recursive invariance asserts that the choice of representation makes no difference: *the existence of a formal algorithm for a problem is invariant with respect to the encoding of statements and answers as finite strings of symbols.*

In asserting this second principle of recursive invariance, we must place an important restriction on the nature of encoding: the process of encoding the problem statement and the process of decoding the answer must be algorithmic in the informal sense. If we did not insist that these processes be algorithmic, we could envision an encoding scheme in which each problem statement contains an encoding of its answer! We would be left with a rather uninteresting theory of effective computability.

As in the case of Church's thesis, this second principle of recursive invariance cannot be proved; it is accepted on the basis of the overwhelming evidence in its favor. Part of this evidence is the fact that encoded problem statements can be transformed in very complex ways without affecting the existence of formal algorithms for the problems.

Suppose that we are interested in whether an informal algorithm exists for some problem. Let **S** be a set of informally expressed problem statements, and let **R** be the set of possible answers. We wish to know whether or not the function $A: \mathbf{S} \longrightarrow \mathbf{R}$ that correctly associates answers with problem statements is algorithmic. Let **T** be some finite alphabet, and let $g_1$ and $g_2$ be encodings of the elements of **S** into strings in $\mathbf{T}^*$:

$$g_1: \mathbf{S} \longrightarrow \mathbf{T}^* \qquad g_2: \mathbf{S} \longrightarrow \mathbf{T}^*$$

Similarly, let $h_1$ and $h_2$ be decodings of strings in $\mathbf{T}^*$ into answers in **R**:

$$h_1: \mathbf{T}^* \longrightarrow \mathbf{R} \qquad h_2: \mathbf{T}^* \longrightarrow \mathbf{R}$$

Figure 11.29 shows the relationship among these mappings. If $g_1$ and $h_1$ are chosen as the encoding and decoding rules, then, using Turing's thesis, $A$ is an algorithmic function if and only if there exists a Turing-realizable function $f_1$ such that $A = h_1 \circ f_1 \circ g_1$

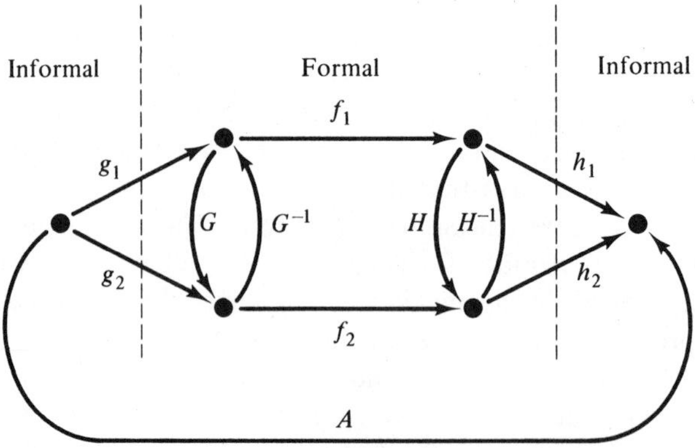


**Figure 11.29** Recursive invariance for two schemes of encoding and decoding problem statements and answers.

Likewise, using $g_2$ and $h_2$ as the encoding and decoding rules, $A$ is algorithmic just if there exists a Turing-realizable function $f_2$ such that

$$A = h_2 \circ f_2 \circ g_2$$

Now suppose that we can devise Turing machines that translate between the two encoding schemes; that is, suppose that there is a one-to-one function $G$, where $G$ and $G^{-1}$ are both Turing realizable, such that

$$g_2 = G \circ g_1 \qquad g_1 = G^{-1} \circ g_2$$

Also, suppose that $H$ and $H^{-1}$ are Turing-realizable functions such that

$$h_2 = h_1 \circ H^{-1} \qquad h_1 = h_2 \circ H$$

Since $f_1 = H^{-1} \circ f_2 \circ G$ and $f_2 = H \circ f_1 \circ G^{-1}$, we conclude that $f_1$ is Turing realizable if and only if $f_2$ is Turing realizable.

Thus we see that any realizable and reversible transformation of encoded problem statements can have no effect on the existence of formal algorithms for the problems.

### 11.5.3 Effective Computability

In describing an informal algorithm for a problem, one often asserts (as we have throughout this book) that he has given an *effective procedure* for solving the problem, and therefore an answer to any problem statement is *effectively computable*. In saying this, one is claiming the existence of a formal algorithm corresponding to the informal algorithm he has described. Since constructing the formal counterpart to the informal algorithm is usually accompanied by loss of conciseness and clarity, this is generally left undone; one merely relies on Church's thesis and is prepared to back up his claim with further details if challenged. It is much the same as in mathematical proofs, where one may omit steps if he is confident that the reader will be able to fill in the formal details of the argument.

### 11.5.4 Arithmetization

Much work on the formalization of algorithms has been based on the assumption that the algorithmic solutions of problems may be expressed as computable number-theoretic functions. (In particular, the theory of recursive functions introduced by Church and Kleene is concerned exclusively with number-theoretic functions.) This assumption is justified because there are conversion rules for reversibly mapping symbol strings into integers.

Given any set $\mathbf{X}$ of strings, an effective procedure for mapping $\mathbf{X}$ onto the integers is called a *Gödel numbering* of $\mathbf{X}$, in honor of the logician Kurt Gödel. The mapping we use here to associate unique integers with arbitrary symbol strings is somewhat simpler than that used by Gödel.

Suppose that $\mathbf{X} \subseteq \mathbf{V}^*$ for some alphabet $\mathbf{V}$ containing $p$ distinct symbols. We associate with each symbol $a$ in $\mathbf{V}$ a unique integer $h(a)$ in $\mathbf{J}_p = \{1, 2, \ldots, p\}$, so that $h: \mathbf{V} \longrightarrow \mathbf{J}_p$ is one to one. Then $G_p(\omega)$, the Gödel number of the string $\omega \in \mathbf{V}^*$, is defined by

$$G_p(\lambda) = 0$$

$$G_p(\varphi a) = h(a) + p \times G_p(\varphi)$$

The function $G_p: \mathbf{V}^* \longrightarrow \mathbf{N}$ is a one-to-one correspondence between members of $\mathbf{V}^*$ and $\mathbf{N}$. Below we give procedures for coding strings into Gödel numbers and decoding Gödel numbers into strings:

```
procedure G_p(ω)                 procedure G_p^{-1}(n)
begin                            begin
  n := 0                           ω := λ
  while ω ≠ λ do                   while n ≠ 0 do
    begin                            begin
    x := head(ω)                     q := rem(n − 1, p) + 1
    ω := tail(ω)                     n := quo(n − 1, p)
    n := h(x) + p × n                ω := h^{-1}(q)·ω
    end                              end
  G_p := n                         G_p^{-1} := ω
end                              end
```

In the procedure $G_p^{-1}$, the abbreviations quo $(x, y)$ and rem $(x, y)$ denote the quotient and remainder that result from dividing $x$ by $y$. Both procedures, $G_p$ and $G_p^{-1}$, can be performed by suitably programmed Turing machines using unary notation for the Gödel numbers. Using these machines, we show how Turing computability is related to Turing realizability.

> **Proposition 11.2:** Let $G\colon \mathbf{V}^* \longrightarrow \mathbf{N}$ be a Gödel numbering of the strings in $\mathbf{V}^*$. Let $f\colon \mathbf{V}^* \longrightarrow \mathbf{V}^*$ be some function, not necessarily total, and let $g\colon \mathbf{N} \longrightarrow \mathbf{N}$ be the corresponding function on Gödel numbers; that is $g = G \circ f \circ G^{-1}$. Then $g$ is Turing computable if and only if $f$ is Turing realizable.

The proof, which involves constructing composite Turing machines that perform the computations illustrated in Figure 11.30, is left to the reader.

In Chapter 13, we show how all actions of a Turing machine may be translated into simple arithmetic operations on Gödel numbers of its configurations. In this way, all aspects of the behavior of a symbol-manipulating device can be reduced to questions about numerical computations. The translation of a symbolic model of computation into the language of arithmetic is called *arithmetization* of the symbolic model.

## 11.6 A Universal Turing Machine

One of Turing's most remarkable findings was that a single fixed machine could be designed to carry out the computations of any Turing machine. Such a machine, which is called a *universal Turing machine*, is presented with descriptions of the machine to be simulated and its initial configuration; it then generates descriptions of successive configurations of the machine, using each description to determine the next move the machine would make. These descriptions must be expressed within the fixed tape alphabet of the universal machine, regardless of the number of distinct symbols and states of the simu-

(a) Computability of $g$ implies realizability of $f$:

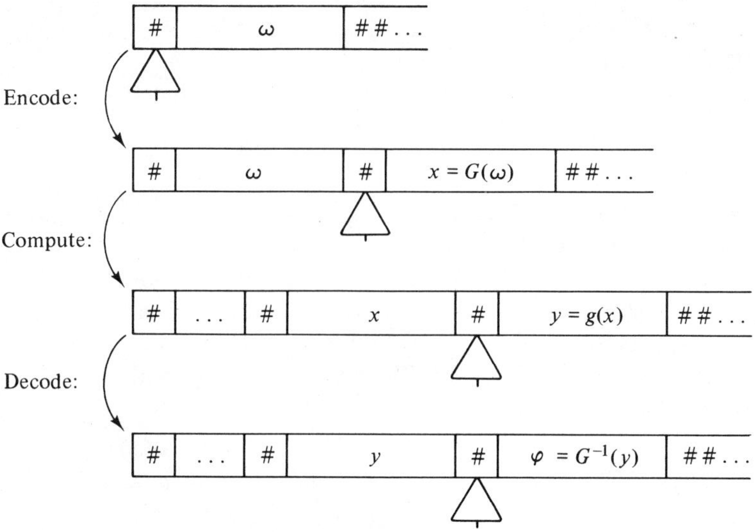


(b) Realizability of $f$ implies computability of $g$:

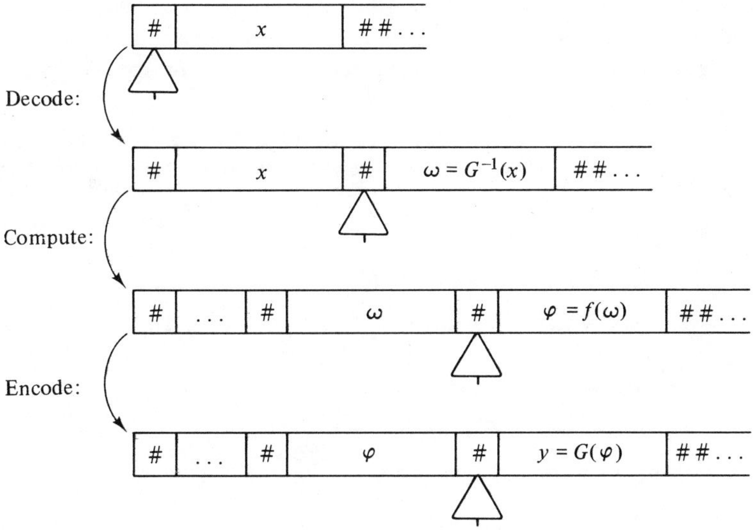


**Figure 11.30** Relationship of Turing realizability and computability.

lated machine; that is, the universal machine must deal with encoded descriptions of machines and configurations.

Let **M** be an arbitrary Turing machine, and let $D(\mathbf{M})$ denote an encoded description of **M**. Suppose that **M** realizes the function

$$f_{\mathbf{M}}: \mathbf{T}^* \longrightarrow \mathbf{T}^*$$

for some alphabet **T**, and let $\alpha_0 = (\lambda, q_I, \#, \omega)$ be an initial configuration of **M** for some $\omega \in \mathbf{T}^*$. Let $T_m(\omega)$ denote an encoding of $\omega$, and let $C_{m,n}(\alpha)$ denote an encoding of any configuration $\alpha$ of **M**. [The subscripts $m$ and $n$ refer to the lengths of the codes for symbols and states of **M**, respectively, as a reminder that the encoding of $\omega$ and $\alpha$ must be consistent with that of symbols and states in $D(\mathbf{M})$.] We shall construct a Turing machine **U** which realizes a function $f_{\mathbf{U}}$ such that

$$f_{\mathbf{U}}(D(\mathbf{M}) \# T_m(\omega)) = \begin{cases} C_{m,n}(\alpha) & \text{if } \mathbf{M} \text{ has a halted} \\ & \text{computation } \alpha_0 \Longrightarrow \alpha \\ \text{undefined} & \text{otherwise} \end{cases}$$

As illustrated by Figure 11.31, **U** first constructs the encoding $C_{m,n}(\alpha_0)$ from $T_m(\omega)$, and then repeatedly transforms each encoded configuration $C_{m,n}(\alpha_i)$ into its successor encoded configuration $C_{m,n}(\alpha_{i+1})$. The universal machine uses the fixed tape alphabet

$$\mathbf{A} = \{0, 1, a, b, P, I, X, Q, S, M, B, E, H\}$$

where symbols 0 and 1 are used in encoding the states and symbols of **M**, symbols $a$ and $b$ are substituted for 0 and 1 as a convenient means of indexing through a code being copied or compared, and the remaining symbols serve as field separaters and as markers of particular fields on the tape. The descrip-

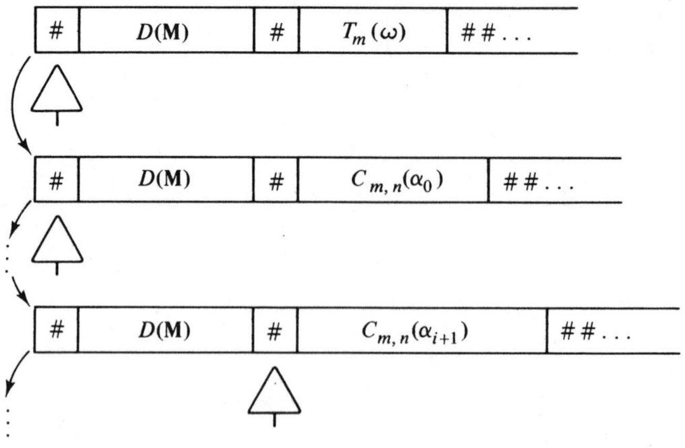


**Figure 11.31** Operation of a universal Turing machine.

tion of the Turing machine being simulated has the form

$$D(\mathbf{M}) = PI\sigma_1 I\sigma_2 \ldots I\sigma_p$$

where each string $\sigma_i$ is the encoding of one instruction of **M**, each $I$ marks the beginning of an instruction code, and $P$ marks the beginning of the program of instructions. The representation of an instruction

$$q] \textbf{ right } (t/r, q') \quad \text{or} \quad q] \textbf{ left } (t/r, q')$$

must include codes for $q$, $t$, $q'$, $r$, and the direction of move. It is convenient to use binary notation: assuming that **M** has no more than $2^n$ states and no more than $2^m$ symbols, we encode each instruction as a string $\sigma_i$ in the set

$$\underset{q}{\{0, 1\}^n} X \underset{t}{\{0, 1\}^m} X \underset{q'}{\{0, 1\}^n} X \underset{r}{\{0, 1\}^m} X \underset{\text{move}}{\{0, 1\}}$$

where symbol $X$ serves to separate the components of the instruction code. We use the "move" component of the instruction code to indicate the direction of move associated with state $q'$, rather than with state $q$. This is done because **U** must know, at each step in its simulation of **M**, the symbol scanned by **M** at its new head position before it can determine which instruction is applicable to a configuration. Thus it is convenient to have an instruction code identify the move of the successor state, rather than the current state.

In our encoding of an arbitrary Turing machine **M**, the code $0^n$ is reserved for the initial state of **M**, and the code $0^m$ is assigned to the blank symbol of **M** (so the code for the blank symbol of **M** is distinct from the blank symbol of **U**). We use the symbol 0 to indicate a right move in an instruction code, and 1 to indicate a left move.

> **Example 11.10:** Figure 11.32 shows a Turing machine **M** which, when started on a blank tape, generates the sequence of strings $\lambda$, 1, 11, 111, . . . , $1^k$, . . . . The description of **M** according to the conventions just discussed is also shown. Note that every instruction in the program of **M** must be included in $D(\mathbf{M})$, not just the instructions corresponding to the explicit transitions of our simplified state diagrams.

The encoding of a configuration of **M** must identify the current state of **M**, must represent the tape of **M**, and must locate the position of **M**'s tape head. Our encoded form for a tape of **M** is a *pseudotape* of the form

$$T_m(\omega) = BX\tau_1 X\tau_2 \ldots X\tau_k E$$

where the strings

$$\tau_i \in \{0, 1\}^m$$

(a)

**M**:

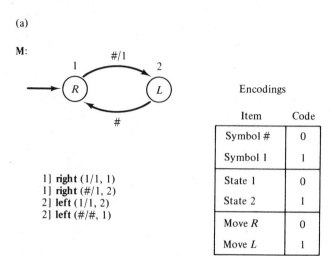

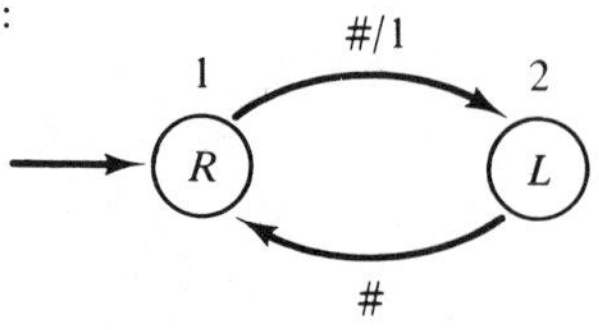


1] **right** (1/1, 1)
1] **right** (#/1, 2)
2] **left** (1/1, 2)
2] **left** (#/#, 1)

Encodings

| Item | Code |
|---|---|
| Symbol # | 0 |
| Symbol 1 | 1 |
| State 1 | 0 |
| State 2 | 1 |
| Move *R* | 0 |
| Move *L* | 1 |

(b) Encoding $D(\mathbf{M})$:

$$P\ \ I\,0\,X\,1\,X\,0\,X\,1\,X\,0\ \ I\,0\,X\,0\,X\,1\,X\,1\,X\,1\ \ I\,1\,X\,1\,X\,1\,X\,1\,X\,1\ \ I\,1\,X\,0\,X\,0\,X\,0\,X\,0$$

**Figure 11.32** Encoding the instructions of a Turing machine.

are the codes for successive symbols on the tape of **M**, and the symbols $B$ and $E$ mark the beginning and end of the pseudotape. A configuration

$$\alpha = (\varphi, q, t, \psi)$$

is represented by a string

$$C_{m,n}(\alpha) \in \underbrace{Q\{0,1\}^n}_{q}\underbrace{S\{0,1\}^m}_{t}\underbrace{M\{0,1\}}_{\text{move}}\overbrace{B\,\underbrace{X\tau_1 \ldots}_{\varphi} \underbrace{H\tau_i}_{t} \underbrace{\ldots X\tau_k}_{\psi} E}^{\text{pseudotape}}$$

consisting of a pseudotape prefixed by markers and codes for the current state, symbol, and direction of move. We represent the head position in $\alpha$ by replacing the appropriate delimiter $X$ by a marker $H$ in the pseudotape. The direction of move is 0 if $q$ is a right-moving state of **M**, and 1 if $q$ is a left-moving state.

The state diagram of the universal Turing machine is shown in Figure 11.33. The program of **U** consists of routines that perform the various steps required to simulate execution of one instruction of **M**. Each cycle through the routines transforms $C_{m,n}(\alpha_i)$ on the tape of **U** into $C_{m,n}(\alpha_{i+1})$; that is,

$$D(\mathbf{M}) \# C_{m,n}(\alpha_i) \Longrightarrow D(\mathbf{M}) \# C_{m,n}(\alpha_{i+1})$$

The following is a brief description of the function of each routine:

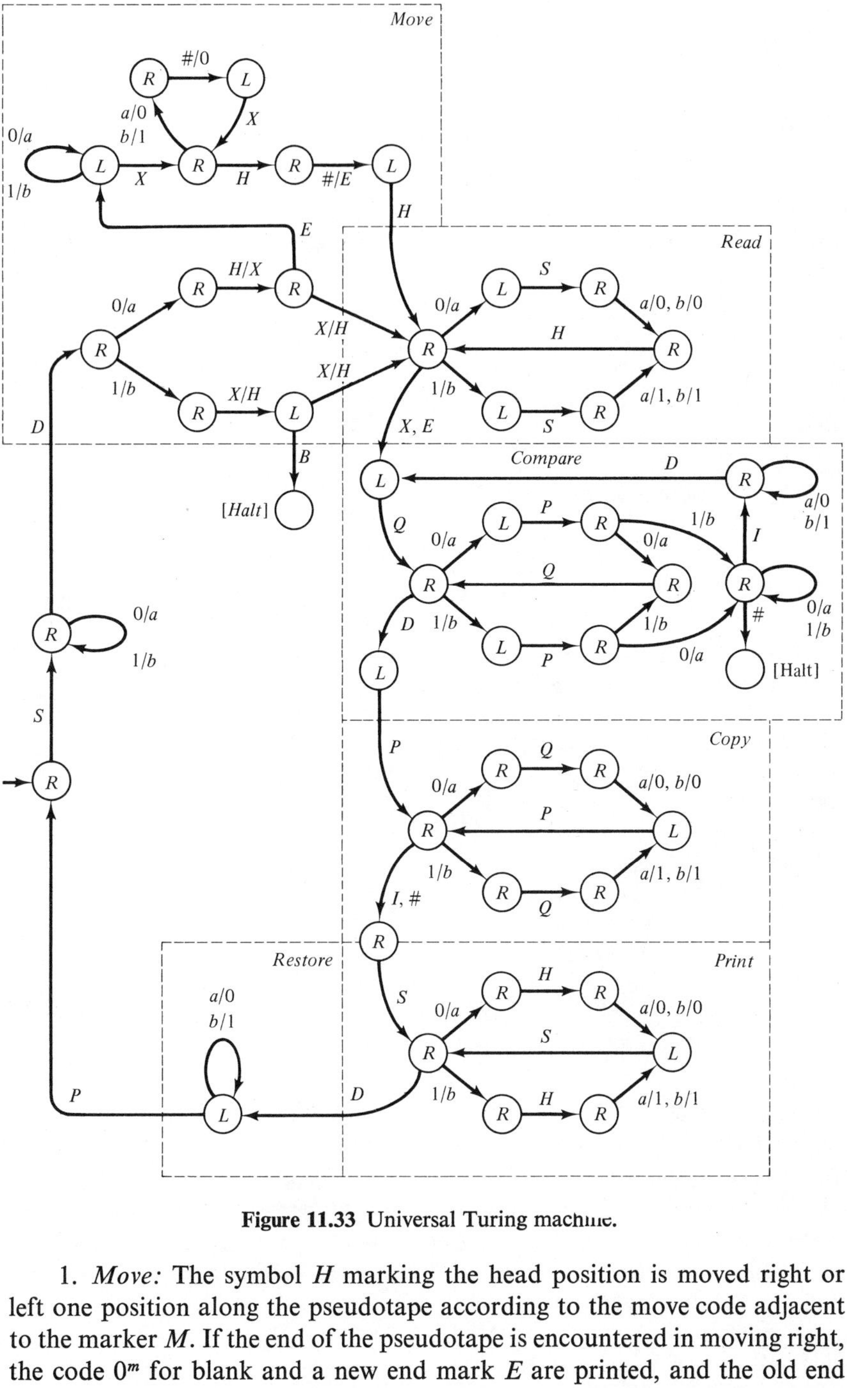


**Figure 11.33** Universal Turing machine.

1. *Move:* The symbol $H$ marking the head position is moved right or left one position along the pseudotape according to the move code adjacent to the marker $M$. If the end of the pseudotape is encountered in moving right, the code $0^m$ for blank and a new end mark $E$ are printed, and the old end

mark is changed to $X$. Note that **U** determines the number of zeros in the code for blank by measuring the length of the final symbol code on the pseudotape. In this way, the program of **U** is independent of $m$.

2. *Read:* The new symbol scanned by **M** is printed over the current symbol. In copying the symbol, its code on the pseudotape is converted from 0, 1 code into $a$, $b$ code. It will be translated back by the print routine.

3. *Compare:* The instruction applicable to configuration $\alpha_i$ is found by comparing the codes for the current state and symbol with the first $m + n$ bits of each instruction. The progress of the search through $D(\mathbf{M})$ is recorded by translating from 0, 1 code into $a$, $b$ code. If no match is found, $\alpha_i$ is a dead configuration of **M** and exit is made to the *halt* routine.

4. *Copy:* The new state–symbol pair and direction of move code (for the new state) are copied from $D(\mathbf{M})$ into the spaces marked by $Q$, $S$, and $M$.

5. *Print:* The new symbol is printed in 0, 1 code in the position of the pseudotape marked by $H$.

6. *Restore:* **U** returns to the initial square of its tape, translating $D(\mathbf{M})$ back into 0, 1 code on the way.

In Figure 11.33, we have not shown the instructions of **U** for constructing $C(\alpha_0)$ from $T_m(\omega)$. Also, when **U** discovers there is no applicable instruction in the description of **M**, it must return the head of **M** to the proper square of the pseudotape in order to halt with the correct final configuration of **M**. The instructions to do this have not been shown.

**Theorem 11.3:** One can construct a universal Turing machine **U** that realizes a function

$$f_{\mathbf{U}}: \mathbf{A}^* \longrightarrow \mathbf{A}^*$$

such that for any Turing machine **M** with tape alphabet **T** and any string $\omega \in \mathbf{T}^*$, we have

$$f_{\mathbf{U}}(D(\mathbf{M}) \# T(\omega)) = \begin{cases} C(\alpha) & \text{if } \mathbf{M} \text{ has a halted computation } \alpha_0 \Longrightarrow \alpha \\ \text{undefined} & \text{otherwise} \end{cases}$$

where $\alpha_0 = (\lambda, q_I, \#, \omega)$, and $D(\mathbf{M})$, $T(\omega)$, and $C(\alpha)$ are specific encodings of **M**, $\omega$, and $\alpha$ in the finite alphabet **A**.

The existence of the universal Turing machine shows that there is a certain minimal level of computational ability that is sufficient for any algorithmic computation. In other words, there is a single set of instructions for a computing agent that allows the agent to carry out any algorithmetic procedure when presented with appropriate input (a problem statement and encoded instructions). Our universal Turing machine is a formal example of such a computing agent, although we have used a large alphabet and state set to make its operation clear. Minsky [1967] has shown how the essential requirements for all effective computation are met by very simple formal systems, including a Turing machine with four symbols and seven states.

## 11.7 Effective Enumerability

### 11.7.1 Enumeration of Sets

Let **X** be any set. Is it possible to devise an algorithm that generates the elements of **X**? We shall find that this question plays a central role in characterizing the limitations of Turing machines.

Informally, "generating the elements of **X**" means listing the elements of **X**, and just those elements, is some definite order:

$$x_0, x_1, x_2, \ldots, x_k, \ldots$$

It does not matter if some elements are repeated in this list, but it does matter that each element is $x_k$ for some choice of $k$. Since such a listing is nothing more than a mapping of the natural numbers **N** onto **X**, generating the elements of **X** is equivalent to providing an algorithm which, given any $k$ in **N**, will produce the $k$th member in some complete listing of **X**. Such an algorithm is said to *enumerate* the set **X**, and **X** is called an *effectively enumerable set* if such an algorithm exists. For a precise definition of enumerable sets, we use Turing computability in place of the informal notion of algorithm.

> **Definition 11.8:** A subset **K** of the natural numbers $\mathbf{N} = \{0, 1, 2, \ldots\}$ is *Turing enumerable* if either (1) $\mathbf{K} = \varnothing$, or (2) there exists a Turing computable function $f$: $\mathbf{N} \longrightarrow \mathbf{K}$ that maps **N** onto **K**. In the latter case, we say that $f$ is an *enumeration* of **K**.

Using the notion of a Gödel numbering, we can extend Definition 11.8 to an arbitrary set $\mathbf{X} \subseteq \mathbf{V}^*$, where **V** is any alphabet: set **X** is *Turing enumerable* if the set $\{G(\omega) \mid \omega \in \mathbf{X}\}$ is Turing enumerable, where $G$ is a Gödel numbering of $\mathbf{V}^*$.

Note the difference between a countable set and an enumerable set of natural numbers: both sets are defined in terms of a function $f$ that maps **N** onto the set, but enumerability requires that $f$ be computable. Thus the class of countable sets includes the class of enumerable sets, but we shall find that many countable sets are not enumerable. In particular, every subset of a countable set is countable, but an enumerable set may contain nonenumerable subsets.

Theorem 11.4 is a fundamental result about enumerable sets.

> **Theorem 11.4:** A set $\mathbf{X} \subseteq \mathbf{N}$ is Turing enumerable if and only if **X** is the domain of a Turing computable function.

***Proof (Only If):*** Suppose that **X** is enumerated by the Turing-computable function $g$. Consider the following procedure:

> **procedure** $p(n)$
> **begin**
> $i := 0$
> $m := g(i)$
> **while** $m \neq n$ **do** $\{i := i + 1;\ m := g(i)\}$
> $p := 1$
> **end**

Evidently, $p$ is a Turing-computable function having **X** as its domain.

*If:* If **X** is the empty set, **X** is enumerable by definition. Suppose that **X** is not empty. Let $f$ be a Turing-computable function with domain **X** and let **M** be a Turing machine that computes $f$. We describe the operation of a Turing machine **M**′ that enumerates **X** by simulating the behavior of **M** for every natural number. Since **M** will fail to halt for any number not in **X**, all these simulations must be carried out concurrently. This is done by having **M**′ keep a list of configurations of **M**: at the $k$th stage of simulation, **M**′ adds to its list the initial configuration of **M** for input $k$; it then simulates one move of **M** for each configuration on its list. Presented an integer $n$, **M**′ performs this behavior for $k = 0, 1, 2, \ldots$ until $n$ dead configurations on **M** have been found (that is, until $n$ simulated computations have halted). It then produces as output the input associated with the last computation to halt.

The scheme just described fails if **X** is finite, for **M**′ will fail to halt for values of $n$ greater than the cardinality of **X**. But if **X** is finite it is regular, and thus trivially enumerable by some Turing machine.

In Definition 11.7, we defined a Turing-decidable set **M** to be one for which the predicate $n \in \mathbf{M}$ is decidable, that is, for which an effective procedure exists that determines whether $n$ is in **M** for any natural number $n$. Such sets are of interest in later chapters. Also of interest are sets that are *semidecidable* in that $n \in \mathbf{M}$ is computable whenever $n$ *is* in **M**, but not when $n$ is *not* in **M**.

**Definition 11.9:** A predicate $p\colon \mathbf{N}^m \longrightarrow \{true, false\}$ is *Turing semidecidable* if there is a Turing-computable function $f\colon \mathbf{N}^m \longrightarrow \{1\}$ such that

$$f(\mathbf{x}) = \begin{cases} 1 & \text{if } p(\mathbf{x}) = true \\ \text{undefined} & \text{otherwise} \end{cases}$$

A set $\mathbf{M} \subseteq \mathbf{N}$ is *Turing semidecidable* if $x \in \mathbf{M}$ is a Turing-semidecidable predicate.

Theorem 11.5 follows directly from the proof of Theorem 11.4.

**Theorem 11.5:** A set $\mathbf{X} \subseteq \mathbf{N}$ is Turing semidecidable if and only if it is Turing enumerable.

Clearly, any decidable set is also semidecidable; thus the decidable sets are contained in the class of enumerable sets. In Chapter 13, we shall see that this containment is proper.

Using Theorem 11.5, we can show that the ability to enumerate the strings of a language is the same as the ability to recognize the language.

**Theorem 11.6:** A set is Turing recognizable if and only if it is Turing enumerable.

**Proof**: Let $\mathbf{V}$ be a finite alphabet, and let $\mathbf{X}$ be any subset of $\mathbf{V}^*$. Let $G$ be a Gödel numbering of $\mathbf{V}^*$, and let $\mathbf{M} = \{G(\omega) \mid \omega \in \mathbf{X}\}$. The procedures rec and sdec show that $\mathbf{X}$ is Turing recognizable if and only if $\mathbf{M}$ is Turing semidecidable.

```
procedure rec (ω)                  procedure sdec (n)
begin                              begin
  n := G(ω)                          ω := G⁻¹(n)
  while not p(n) do { }              m := f(ω)
end                                end
```

The left procedure recognizes $\mathbf{X}$ if $p$ is a semidecidable predicate such that $\mathbf{M} = \{n \mid p(n) = true\}$. The procedure on the right is a semidecision procedure for $\mathbf{M}$ if $f$ is a Turing-realizable function with domain $\mathbf{X}$. The theorem then follows from Theorem 11.5.

### 11.7.2 Enumeration of Turing Machines

An important tool for arguments developed in the next two chapters is an enumeration of the set of all Turing machines. Let us consider how such an enumeration may be constructed. For our universal Turing machine, we devised a scheme for encoding an arbitrary Turing machine as a string in the finite alphabet $\mathbf{A}$. With each string $\omega$ in $\mathbf{A}^*$ we may associate a Gödel number $z = G_r(\omega)$, where $\mathbf{A}$ has $r$ letters and $G_r\colon \mathbf{A}^* \longrightarrow \mathbf{N}$ is the one-to-one function defined in Section 11.5. We noted that both $G_r$ and $G_r^{-1}$ may be implemented by Turing machine programs.

We can construct a Turing machine **test** $(z)$ which, given any natural number $z$ written in unary notation on its tape, transforms $z$ into the string

$\omega = G_r^{-1}(z)$. The machine then checks whether $\omega$ is a valid encoding of a Turing machine description. To do this, it checks that $\omega$ has the form

$$\omega = PI\sigma_1 I\sigma_2 \ldots I\sigma_k$$

where

$$\sigma_i \in \{0, 1\}^n X\{0, 1\}^m X\{0, 1\}^n X\{0, 1\}^m X\{0, 1\}, \qquad 1 \leq i \leq k$$

Also, since we are only considering deterministic Turing machines, **test** must check that the first $m + n$ binary digits of each instruction are unique to that instruction. As the reader may verify, these checks are readily performed by a Turing machine. Thus the set

$$\mathbf{Z} = \{z \in \mathbf{N} \mid G_r^{-1}(z) \text{ is a valid TM description}\}$$

is a Turing-decidable set. Moreover, we can construct a Turing machine that enumerates the set $\{\omega \in \mathbf{A}^* \mid G_r(\omega) \in \mathbf{Z}\}$ of valid Turing machine descriptions by implementing the following procedure:

**procedure** mach $(z)$
**begin**
  $m := 0$; $n := 0$
  **while** $n < z$ **do**
    **begin**
    $\omega := G_r^{-1}(m)$
    **if** test $(m)$ **then** $\{n := n + 1\}$
    $m := m + 1$
    **end**
  mach $:= \omega$
**end**

Interestingly, the Gödel number of this Turing machine is somewhere among the members of **Z**.

Since we can enumerate the set of all Turing machines descriptions, we can build a Turing machine that computes a function $W: \mathbf{N} \times \mathbf{N} \to \mathbf{N}$ according to the following procedure:

**procedure** $W(z, x)$
**begin**
  $\omega :=$ mach $(z)$
  $m := d(\omega)$
  $\varphi := E_m(x)$
  $\psi := f_{\mathrm{U}}(\omega \# \varphi)$
  $W := F_m(\psi)$
**end**

This procedure first obtains the description $\omega$ of the $z$th Turing machine in our enumeration. The function $d$ obtains from $\omega$ the number of digits $m$ used to encode symbols in the description of $\mathbf{M}_z$. The function $E_m$ produces a pseudotape $\varphi$ containing the encoded string $1^x$. The function $f_U$ is that computed by our universal Turing machine, which produces $\psi$, an encoding of the final configuration of $\mathbf{M}_z$, if $\mathbf{M}_z$ halts for input $1^x$. Finally, the function $F_m$ produces the integer represented on the pseudotape of $\psi$. The reader should be convinced by now that each of these functions and their compositions may be implemented by Turing machines.

Through the procedure outlined above, we have shown there is a Turing machine that computes

$$y = W(z, x)$$

if and only if

$$y = f_z(x)$$

where $f_z$ is the function computed by the $z$th machine $\mathbf{M}_z$ in an enumeration of Turing machines.

> **Theorem 11.7:** There exists a Turing computable function
>
> $$W: \mathbf{N} \times \mathbf{N} \longrightarrow \mathbf{N}$$
>
> such that for all $z, x, y$
>
> $$W(z, x) = y$$
>
> if and only if machine $\mathbf{M}_z$ in an enumeration of Turing machines computes
>
> $$f_z(x) = y$$

## Notes and References

The concept of the Turing machine, and the notion of computation by such a machine, is due to A. M. Turing [1936]. Since the publication of that work, Turing machines have been studied extensively. Many studies (Shannon [1956], Wang [1957], Minsky [1961], Fischer [1965], and others) have dealt with the simulation of Turing machines by seemingly less powerful automata, or the simulation by Turing machines of seemingly more powerful automata. Minsky [1967], Arbib [1969], and Hopcroft and Ullman [1969] contain discussions of several of these simulations.

The concept of effective computability is fundamental to the branch of mathematics known as recursive function theory. This theory is studied in Chapter 13; detailed treatments can be found in Davis [1958] and Rogers [1967]. Kleene [1952] and Davis [1958] contain discussions of Church's thesis. A precise formulation of recursive invariance and a discussion of the arithmetization of computable functions can be found in Rogers [1967]. The existence of a universal Turing machine was established by Turing [1936], and these machines were studied by Shannon [1956], who demonstrated the existence of a two-state universal machine and a two-symbol universal machine, and by Minsky [1967]. The concepts of recursive enumerability and the enumerability of the Turing machines are from Turing [1936].

## Problems

11.1. Construct a Turing machine which, started on blank tape, generates successive natural numbers in unary notation, that is, generates the tape

| | | | | | | | | | | | | | | | |
|---|---|---|---|---|---|---|---|---|---|---|---|---|---|---|---|
| # | 1 | # | 1 | 1 | # | 1 | 1 | 1 | # | 1 | 1 | 1 | 1 | # | ... |

11.2. Construct a Turing machine that realizes the function $f\colon \{0, 1\}^* \longrightarrow \{0, 1\}^*$ defined by

$$f(\omega) = \omega\omega^R$$

11.3. Construct a Turing machine that realizes the function $f\colon \{0, 1\}^* \longrightarrow \{0, 1\}$ defined by

$$f(\omega) = \begin{cases} 1 & \text{if } \omega \text{ is a mirror-image string, that is, if } \omega = \omega^R \\ 0 & \text{otherwise} \end{cases}$$

**11.4.** Show that every Turing-definable function is Turing realizable.

11.5. Consider a Turing machine variation in which we permit, for any $n \geq 1$, $n$ heads on the Turing machine tape. The machine will have separate right and left moves for each head. Show how such a *multi-head* machine can be simulated by a Turing machine as defined in Section 11.1.

11.6. Consider a Turing machine variation in which we permit, for any $n \geq 1$, $n$ distinct *tracks* on the Turing machine tape. The tape head of the machine may read and write symbols on any track of the tape, and the moves of the machine are of the form **left** $i$ and **right** $i$, $1 \leq i \leq n$, where $i$ indicates the track of the tape on which the move is performed. Show how such a *multitrack* machine can be simulated by a Turing machine as defined in Section 11.1.

11.7. Show how a Turing machine, as defined in Section 11.1, can simulate a variation in which the Turing machine tape is replaced by a semi-infinite plane, as follows:

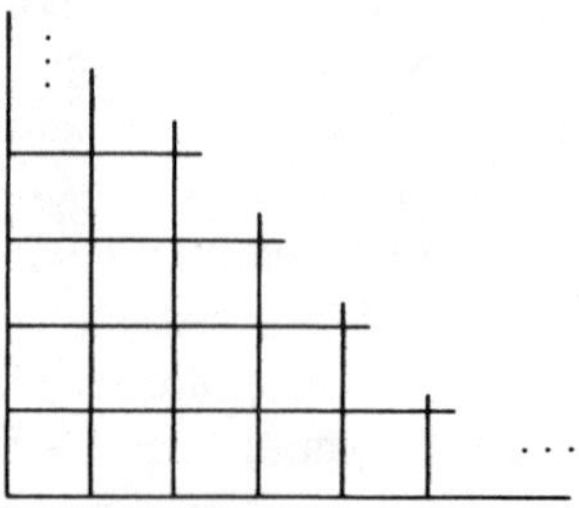

In addition to left and right moves, the variation will have *up* and *down* moves, permitting its head to move vertically in the plane as well as horizontally.

11.8. Construct a Turing accepter for the overlapping matching language

$$\mathbf{L}_{om} = \{a^n b^m a^n b^m \mid n, m \geq 1\}$$

11.9. Construct a Turing accepter for the language

$$\mathbf{L} = \{a^k b^n c^m \mid k, n, m \geq 0, k = n \text{ or } k = m \text{ or } n = m\}$$

11.10. Show that the language

$$\mathbf{L} = \{1^{n_1} \$ 1^{n_2} \$ \ldots \$ 1^{n_k} \$\$ 1^i \$ 1^{n_i} \mid n_1, \ldots, n_k > 0, \quad k > 0, 1 \leq i \leq k\}$$

is Turing recognizable. (*Hint:* Use the Turing machine variation of Problem 11.5.)

***11.11.** In Problem 8.27, we defined two-stack PDA's and demonstrated that such accepters are more powerful than PDA's with a single stack. Show that any language recognizable by a Turing machine can be recognized by a two-stack PDA. [*Hint:* A two-stack PDA can represent a Turing machine configuration $(\varphi, q, s, \psi)$ by storing $\varphi^R$ in one stack, $\psi$ in the other, and "remembering" $q$ and $s$ in finite-state control. Describe how a two-stack PDA that represents configurations in this manner can simulate a left or a right move of a Turing machine.]

11.12. Construct a Turing machine that computes the function $f\colon \mathbf{N} \longrightarrow \mathbf{N}$ defined by

$$f(n) = [\log_2 n]$$

where, for any real number $x$, $[x]$ denotes the greatest whole number less than or equal to $x$.

11.13. Construct a Turing machine that computes the function $f\colon \mathbf{N} \longrightarrow \mathbf{N}$ defined by

$$f(n) = 2^n$$

11.14. Construct a Turing machine that decides the predicate $p\colon \mathbf{N} \longrightarrow \{true, false\}$ defined by

$$p(n) = \begin{cases} true & \text{if } n \text{ is prime} \\ false & \text{otherwise} \end{cases}$$

11.15. Let $p\colon \mathbf{N} \times \mathbf{N} \longrightarrow \{true, false\}$ be the predicate defined by

$$p(m, n) = \begin{cases} true & \text{if } m \text{ is the } n\text{th perfect square} \\ false & \text{otherwise} \end{cases}$$

Show that $p$ is Turing decidable.

11.16. If $n$ and $n + 2$ are natural numbers such that each is prime, we refer to the numbers as *twin primes*. It has been conjectured that for any $m \geq 0$, there exists $n \geq m$ such that $n$ and $n + 2$ are twin primes. Show that, whether or not the conjecture is true, the predicate $p: \mathbf{N} \longrightarrow \{true, false\}$ defined by

$$p(k) = \begin{cases} true & \text{if there exists } n \geq k \text{ such that } n \text{ and} \\ & n + 2 \text{ are twin primes} \\ false & \text{otherwise} \end{cases}$$

is Turing decidable. (*Hint:* To show that a predicate is Turing decidable, we need only show that *some* Turing machine decides the predicate; we need not specify which one.)

***11.17.** Show that there exists a universal Turing machine that utilizes a single nonblank tape symbol. (*Hint:* Let 0 and 1 represent the machine's blank and nonblank tape symbols, respectively. Encode the symbols of the universal machine **U** of Section 11.6 as binary strings of some fixed length $k$. Each move of **U** is simulated by $k$ moves of the new universal machine.)

11.18. Show that the following sets are Turing enumerable:

a. $\{n \mid n \text{ is a perfect square}\}$.

b. $\{n \mid n, n + 2 \text{ are twin primes}\}$ (see Problem 11.16).

c. $\{n \mid \text{a string of at least } n \text{ consecutive 1's appears in the decimal expansion of } \pi\}$.

**11.19.** Let **A** be a recursively enumerable set such that $\mathbf{A}^c$ is also recursively enumerable. Show that **A** is Turing decidable.

**11.20.** Let **A** be an infinite recursively enumerable set. Show that **A** is the range of a one-to-one Turing computable function. (Thus there exists some Turing machine that can enumerate **A** without repeating elements.)

# 12

# *Unsolvable Problems*

A most significent event in the study of fundamental mathematics was Turing's discovery, published in 1936, that there are well-defined problems that cannot be solved by any effective procedure. Basing his conclusion on a study of the machines now associated with his name, Turing showed that, if one accepts the thesis that any algorithmic procedure can be represented as a set of instructions for some Turing machine, one must admit the existence of problems without algorithmic solutions. This result marked the beginning of the formal study of algorithms and computation.

Initially, Turing's work met with skepticism as well as praise. Logicians had searched for a "universal" algorithm which, presented with the axioms and rules of inference of a logic system, could determine whether a given proposition is a theorem. Reluctant to end their long quest, many felt that Turing's formulation was incomplete, and that more general systems must exist for representing algorithmic procedures. Indeed, many other mathematical systems, including the logic systems of Church and Post and the recursive functions of Kleene, were proposed as entirely different systems in which procedures could be expressed. That all these systems were shown equivalent to Turing's formulation provides overwhelming empirical evidence in support of his thesis, and strengthens the significence of his work.

In this chapter, we study the basis for Turing's conclusions and explore the consequences of his results, particularly as they relate to the study of formal grammars and the languages that they define. In the remaining chapters, we show how the study of other mathematical systems yields parallel results.

## 12.1 Computable and Noncomputable Functions

As defined in Chapter 11, a function $f: \mathbf{N}^r \longrightarrow \mathbf{N}$ is *computable* if there is a Turing machine which, started in the initial configuration $(\lambda, q_I, \#, 1^{x_1} \# 1^{x_2} \# \ldots \# 1^{x_r})$, halts in the final configuration $(\omega, q, \#, 1^y)$ whenever $y = f(x_1, x_2, \ldots, x_r)$, and fails to halt when $f(x_1, x_2, \ldots, x_r)$ is undefined. If no such Turing machine exists, we say that $f$ is *noncomputable*. Similarly, we say that the predicate $p: \mathbf{N}^r \longrightarrow \{true, false\}$ is *decidable* if the function $f: \mathbf{N}^r \longrightarrow \{0, 1\}$ defined as

$$f(x_1, x_2, \ldots, x_r) = \begin{cases} 0 & \text{if } p(x_1, x_2, \ldots, x_r) \text{ is } \textit{false} \\ 1 & \text{if } p(x_1, x_2, \ldots, x_r) \text{ is } \textit{true} \end{cases}$$

is computable; otherwise, $p$ is *undecidable*.

When we say that a problem is *unsolvable*, we mean, by Turing's thesis, that its solution cannot be defined in terms of a computable function or a decidable predicate. For instance, we shall see that the problem of determining whether $\mathbf{L}_1 \cap \mathbf{L}_2$ is empty for arbitrary context-free languages $\mathbf{L}_1$ and $\mathbf{L}_2$ is an unsolvable problem: no Turing machine exists which, presented with descriptions of the languages, decides whether they have strings in common.

It is important to note that when we speak of a problem's being unsolvable we mean that no Turing machine can solve the problem in *every* case. There may, however, exist Turing machines that solve the problem in *some* cases. (The problem we have just considered, for example, is solvable in many cases, such as when one or both of $\mathbf{L}_1$ and $\mathbf{L}_2$ are regular or when $\mathbf{L}_1$ and $\mathbf{L}_2$ are over disjoint alphabets.) In fact, the unsolvability of a problem need not be a practical restriction at all, since we may be able to solve the problem in all cases of practical interest. However, knowing that a problem is unsolvable does assure us that no general solution can be found, and explains why solutions to particular cases are often hard to find. Later in this chapter, we show that the question, *Is a given a context-free grammar*, $\mathbf{G}$, *ambiguous*? is undecidable; when we bemoan the difficulty of deciding whether a given grammar is ambiguous, we can at least be sure that we have not overlooked some effective decision procedure.

## 12.2 Halting Problem

It is easy to establish the existence of functions that cannot be computed by any Turing machine. In Chapter 11, we showed that the set of all Turing machines is countable, since the machines can be enumerated and placed in one-to-one correspondence with the integers. On the other hand, we know that the set of all functions $f: \mathbf{N} \longrightarrow \mathbf{N}$ has the same cardinality as the power set of the integers, and is uncountable. Thus the Turing machines can compute only a subset of the number-theoretic functions.

This argument is rather unsatisfying, however, since it establishes the existence of noncomputable functions without providing an example of such a function. After all, might it not be the case that such functions are so bizarre as to be of little use in the theory of practical computation? Turing showed that this is *not* the case; he exhibited well-defined and meaningful problems beyond the capabilities of the Turing machines. Accepting his thesis, we must deny the existence of algorithms for solving these problems.

Certainly the best known of all unsolvable problems is the *halting problem* for Turing machines: *Given a Turing machine* **M** *and an initial tape T, does* **M** *halt when started on tape T*? To show that this problem is unsolvable, we show that no Turing machine computes the function

$$h(\mathbf{M}, T) = \begin{cases} 1 & \text{if Turing machine } \mathbf{M} \text{ halts for initial tape } T \\ 0 & \text{otherwise} \end{cases}$$

Our approach is rather informal, since our primary objective is an understanding of Turing's original methods. The reader who so desires should have little difficulty in formalizing our arguments.

Suppose that the halting problem is solvable; that is, some Turing machine **H** computes the function $h$ defined above. Since a given machine may have an arbitrary number of states and tape symbols, whereas **H** has a fixed alphabet and fixed number of states, **H** must deal with *descriptions* of machines and tapes expressed within its alphabet. We have seen how such descriptions may be constructed in connection with the design of a universal Turing machine in Chapter 11: machines were described by concatenating strings of symbols representing individual instructions (using binary codes for the states and symbols of the encoded machines), while tapes were represented by the sequence of binary codes for the symbols of the tape, each code separated from the next by some fixed delimiting letter. Of course other descriptions of machines and tapes are possible (using Gödel numberings or or other methods), but by Turing's thesis the encoding used by **H** must be effective; otherwise, we would have no way of verifying that **H** really does compute $h$.

Let $\mathfrak{M}$ and $\mathfrak{T}$ be the sets of machine and tape descriptions, respectively, in the encoding scheme used by **H**. Suppose that we denote by $D(\mathbf{M})$ the description of machine **M** in $\mathfrak{M}$, and by $\hat{D}(T)$ the description of tape $T$ in $\mathfrak{T}$. Then **H** must behave as illustrated in Figure 12.1: starting in the configuration of part a, **H** halts in the configuration of part b or c, according as **M** does or does not halt for tape $T$. (The behavior of **H** when presented with invalid machine or tape descriptions is immaterial.)

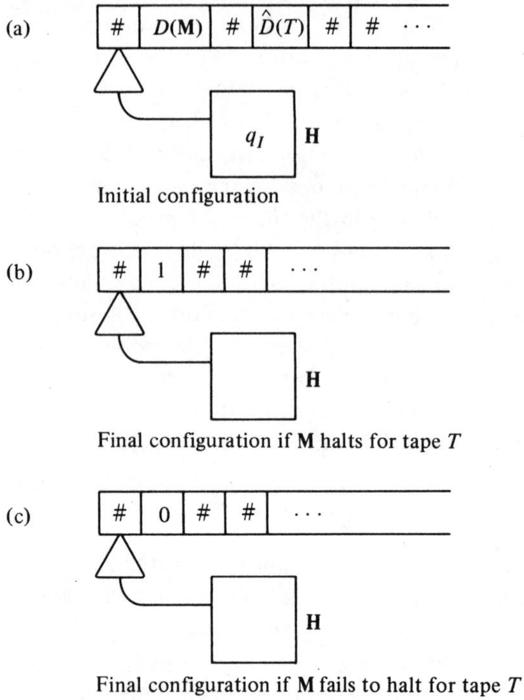


**Figure 12.1** Turing machine for the halting problem.

If **H** behaves correctly for all pairs of input descriptions $(D(\mathbf{M}), \hat{D}(T))$, then in particular it behaves correctly for those pairs in which $T$ is $D(\mathbf{M})$, that is, for pairs that represent a Turing machine started on a description of itself. For such a tape, $\hat{D}(T) = \hat{D}(D(\mathbf{M}))$; since the translation of $D(\mathbf{M})$ into $\hat{D}(D(\mathbf{M}))$ is Turing computable, the tape contains *redundant* information: the second component of the tape can be effectively obtained from the first. By restricting attention to machines whose initial tapes are their own descriptions, we can construct a machine **H**′ which, when presented $D(\mathbf{M})$, constructs $\hat{D}(D(\mathbf{M}))$ and then computes $h(\mathbf{M}, D(\mathbf{M}))$. Then **H**′ computes

$$h'(\mathbf{M}) = \begin{cases} 1 & \text{if } \mathbf{M} \text{ halts when started on a description of itself} \\ 0 & \text{otherwise} \end{cases}$$

The behavior of **H**′ is suggested in Figure 12.2. After constructing $\hat{D}(D(\mathbf{M}))$ on its tape, **H**′ returns the head to the initial square and passes control to machine **H**. Given that **H** solves the halting problem, **H**′ solves the *self-computability problem: Given an arbitrary Turing machine* **M**, *does* **M** *halt when started on a tape containing its own description*? Suppose that we now construct a machine **H**″ that differs from **H**′ only in that it enters a loop

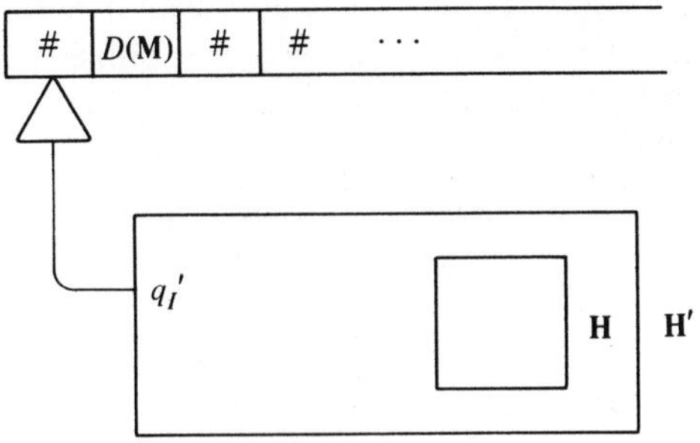


Initial configuration of **H**′

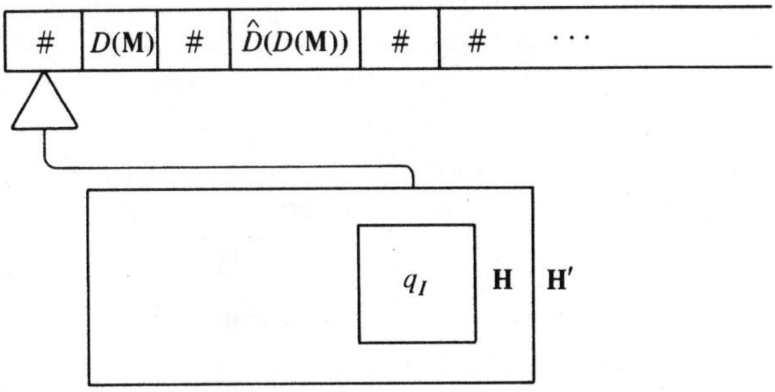


Configuration of **H**′ when control is passed to **H**

**Figure 12.2** Turing machine for the self-computability problem.

whenever **H**′ would have halted with output 1. What happens if we start **H**″ on a description of itself? If we suppose that **H**″ halts for *D*(**H**″), then **H**′ must halt with 0 for *D*(**H**″); but this implies **H**″ does *not* halt for *D*(**H**″). On the other hand, if we suppose that **H**″ does not halt for *D*(**H**″), then **H**′ halts with 1 for *D*(**H**″); but this implies that **H**″ *does* halt for *D*(**H**″). Thus we see that **H**″ *halts for D*(**H**″) *just if* **H**″ *does not halt for D*(**H**″)! This absurdity follows from our assumption that **H** solves the halting problem; thus,

> **Theorem 12.1:** The halting problem for Turing machines is unsolvable.

The reader may object to our calling this result a theorem, since its validity depends on the validity of Turing's thesis. Indeed, we have only shown that no *Turing machine* solves the halting problem for Turing machines. But although Turing's thesis can never be proved, it is universally accepted; results such as this have the stature of theorems, and we shall refer to them as such without qualification.

## 12.3 Busy-Beaver Function

Let us denote by $\mathcal{B}$ the class of Turing machines with binary tape alphabet $\{0, 1\}$. If we start any machine **M** in $\mathcal{B}$ on an empty tape, then **M**, being deterministic, either fails to halt for the tape or it halts with some unique final tape. In the latter case, only a finite number of nonblank symbols can appear on the tape, since **M** can have visited only a finite portion of the tape during its computation. The exact number of symbols on the final tape is related to the "complexity" of the machine, and is bounded by a value that depends on the number of states in its control.

For each $n \geq 0$, let $\mathcal{B}_n$ be the class of $n$-state Turing machines in $\mathcal{B}$, and let $b(n)$ be the maximum number of nonblank symbols on the final tape of any member of $\mathcal{B}_n$ that halts when started on blank tape. The function $b$: $\mathbf{N} \longrightarrow \mathbf{N}$ is called the *busy-beaver function* since, for a given argument $n$, it indicates how many symbols an $n$-state machine can possibly print, that is, how "busy" it can be, before halting for blank tape. It is easy to verify that the busy-beaver function satisfies the property

$$b(n_1) \geq b(n_2) \qquad \text{just if } n_1 \geq n_2 \geq 0$$

That is, the busy-beaver function is monotonic increasing.

In fact, the busy-beaver function is a very rapidly increasing function. Some of the known values are as follows

| Argument $n$ | $b(n)$ |
|---|---|
| 0 | 0 |
| 1 | 0 |
| 3 | $\geq 5$ |
| 5 | $\geq 17$ |
| 7 | $\geq 20{,}000$ |
| 8 | $\geq 10^{40}$ |

When $n$ equals 7, the function experiences a sharp jump, because 7 states are sufficient to perform exponentiation. With more than 7 states, Turing machines can compute functions of such complexity that the value of $b$ virtually defies description! Intuitively, $b$ is not computable because its value for a given $n$ is related to the maximum complexity possible in an $n$-state machine, and no single Turing machine (with a fixed number of states) can have built into it the combined complexity of all Turing machines.

**Theorem 12.2:** The busy-beaver function $b$: $\mathbf{N} \longrightarrow \mathbf{N}$ is noncomputable.

***Proof:*** Suppose that $b$ is computable by some Turing machine $\mathbf{M}_b$ with $m$ states. For simplicity, we shall assume that $\mathbf{M}_b$ computes $b$ in unary notation; that is, presented with a tape containing $n$ 1's, $\mathbf{M}_b$ halts with a final tape containing $b(n)$ 1's. We shall show how $\mathbf{M}_b$ can be combined with familiar Turing machines to demonstrate a logical absurdity.

For any $k \geq 1$, we can construct a $(2k + 3)$-state Turing machine that prints $k$ 1's on an initially blank tape, returns the head to its initial position, and halts. The form of the machine is shown in Figure 12.3a, and it halts for blank tape with the final tape shown

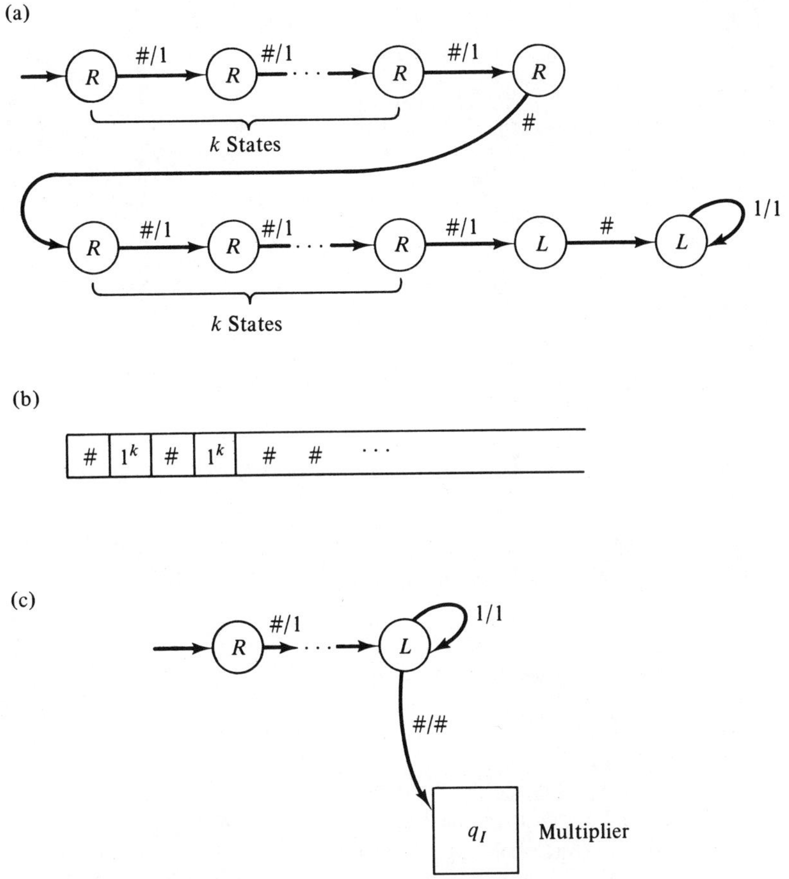


**Figure 12.3** Construction for Theorem 12.2.

in part b. If this machine is combined as in part c of the figure with the multiplier machine of Example 11.6, we obtain a $(2k + 19)$-state machine, which, started on blank tape, halts with $k^2$ 1's on its tape. What happens if we combine this final machine with the machine $\mathbf{M}_b$ as shown in Figure 12.4? The resultant machine has $2k + 19 + m$ states and halts with $b(k^2)$ 1's when started on blank tape. Thus $b(k^2)$ is a lower bound on $b(2k + 19 + m)$:

$$b(2k + 19 + m) \geq b(k^2)$$

But since $b$ is monotonic increasing, this implies that

$$2k + 19 + m \geq k^2$$

which, by construction, must be true for each value of $k$. From this absurdity, we conclude that $\mathbf{M}_b$ cannot exist and that $b$ is noncomputable.

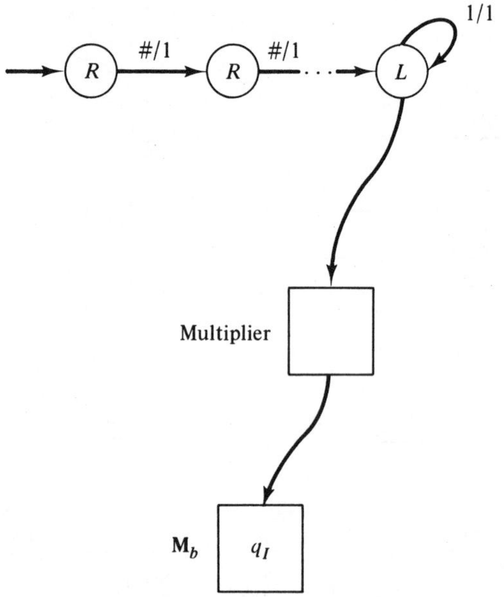


**Figure 12.4** Machine that computes $b(k^2)$ for blank tape.

## 12.4 Reducibility

An important concept in the theory of computation is that of problem *reducibility*. We say that problem $P$ is *reducible* to problem $P'$ if a solution to $P'$ implies a solution to $P$. In practice, we often demonstrate reducibility by constructions involving Turing machines: to show that $P$ is reducible to $P'$, we show how to construct a Turing machine that solves $P$ from one that solves $P'$. If it happens that $P$ is unsolvable, this construction establishes the unsolvability of $P'$; thus reducibility is an important proof technique in the theory of computation.

In the preceding sections, we gave separate proofs of the unsolvability of the halting problem and the noncomputability of the busy-beaver function. To illustrate problem reducibility, we shall show that either problem is reducible to the other.

First, suppose that we were able to construct a Turing machine **H** that solves the halting problem. Using **H** as a component, we could construct a machine $\mathbf{M}_b$ that computes the busy-beaver function as follows.

Given an initial tape containing some integer $n \geq 1$, $\mathbf{M}_b$ constructs on its tape the descriptions of all $n$-state Turing machines with alphabet $\{0, 1\}$. (Since there are only a finite number of such machines, this task is eventually completed.) Using the machine **H**, each description is tested in turn to determine whether the machine described halts for blank tape. If so, the description is retained; otherwise, it is discarded. After all descriptions have been tested, the machines whose descriptions remain are simulated for blank tape, and a record is kept of each final tape. When the simulations are completed, the final tapes are compared to determine which tape has the greatest number of nonblank symbols. This number is recorded, all other records are erased, and the machine halts with $b(n)$ on its tape.

Reducing the halting problem to the busy-beaver function is less straightforward. The difficulty is that we cannot determine whether a given machine will halt for blank tape merely by observing the number of symbols it writes during its computation, even if we know the value of $b$ for the machine's number of states. A machine may fail to halt, for example, without ever writing a symbol at all. Or a machine may write a great number of symbols during its computation, but erase them before halting. To deal with these problems, we must modify the Turing machines we consider so that the number of symbols ultimately printed is proportional to the number of moves made during a computation. In this way, we can place a limit on the number of symbols a machine can write if it is to halt for blank tape, and be assured that the machine will exceed this limit if it fails to halt.

Let **M** be an arbitrary Turing machine. We can construct from **M** a machine $\mathbf{M}' \in \mathcal{B}$ that simulates **M**, but writes the symbol 1 in a special *move count* region of its tape each time it completes a move of the original machine. (Of course, this region may have to be moved from time to time, but we have seen how this can be done in Chapter 11.) If **M** has $n$ states, machine $\mathbf{M}'$ can be designed with $kn$ states for some constant $k$ independent of $n$; its description is readily constructed from a description of **M**.

Now suppose that we were able to construct a Turing machine $\mathbf{M}_b$ that computes the busy-beaver function. Using this machine as a component, we could construct a machine $\mathbf{H}_b$ that operates as follows: given the description of an $n$-state Turing machine $\mathbf{M}$, $\mathbf{H}_b$ constructs the description of the machine $\mathbf{M}'$ described above. Using $\mathbf{M}_b$, $\mathbf{H}_b$ computes $b(kn)$ and then simulates $\mathbf{M}'$ on blank tape until $\mathbf{M}'$ halts or prints more than $b(kn)$ 1's in the move count region of its tape. In the latter case, $\mathbf{M}'$ (and hence $\mathbf{M}$) cannot halt for blank tape, since $\mathbf{M}'$ never erases the symbols in its move count region. If we design $\mathbf{H}_b$ to halt in each case, as illustrated in Figure 12.5, $\mathbf{H}_b$ solves the *blank tape halting problem* for Turing machines: *given a Turing machine* $\mathbf{M}$, *does* $\mathbf{M}$ *halt when started on blank tape*?

We have thus shown that the blank tape halting problem is reducible to the busy-beaver function. To reach our original goal, we must show that the general halting problem can be reduced to that for blank tape.

Suppose that we have a Turing machine $\mathbf{H}_b$ that solves the blank tape halting problem. Let $\mathbf{M}$ be an arbitrary Turing machine and $T$ an arbitrary tape, and consider the construction of a Turing machine $\mathbf{M}'$, which, started on blank tape, writes the symbols of $T$ onto its tape and then simulates $\mathbf{M}$. Obviously, $\mathbf{M}'$ halts for blank tape just if $\mathbf{M}$ halts for tape $T$, and a description of $\mathbf{M}'$ is readily constructed from a description of $\mathbf{M}$ and a description

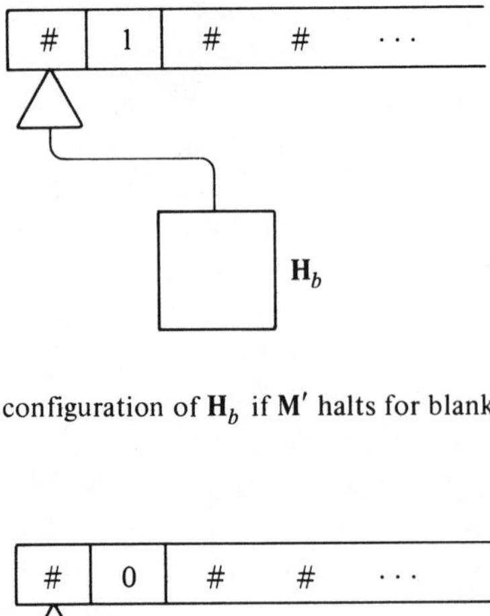


Final configuration of $\mathbf{H}_b$ if $\mathbf{M}'$ halts for blank tape.

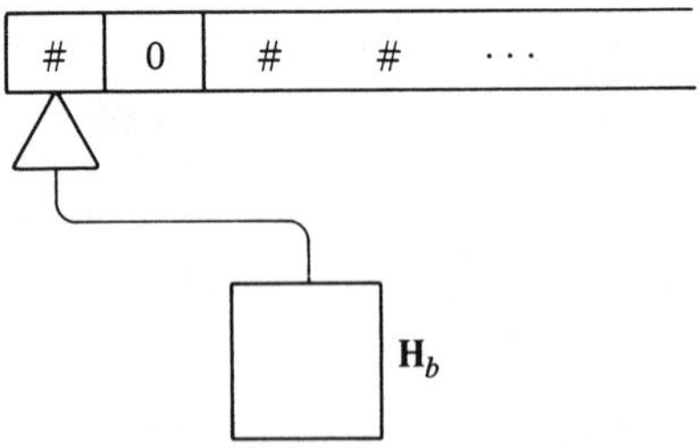


Final configuration of $\mathbf{H}_b$ if $\mathbf{M}'$ prints more than $b(kn)$ "move count" symbols.

**Figure 12.5** Final configurations of $\mathbf{H}_b$.

of $T$. Thus we may construct a Turing machine **H** that solves the halting problem as follows: given a description of **M** and $T$, **H** constructs a description of the corresponding machine **M**′, erases the rest of its tape, and passes control to machine $\mathbf{H}_b$. If $\mathbf{H}_b$ has output conventions as in Figure 12.5, **H** halts with 1 or 0 according as **M** does or does not halt for tape $T$.

Using reducibility arguments similar to those above, many other interesting problems can be shown unsolvable.

**Example 12.1:** The *number of moves* function $m$: $\mathbf{N} \longrightarrow \mathbf{N}$ is defined, for each $n \geq 0$, to be the greatest number of moves that can be executed by an $n$-state Turing machine that eventually halts when started on blank tape. Since at least one move is required to print a symbol on a tape, we have

$$m(n) \geq b(n), \qquad \text{all } n \in \mathbf{N}$$

where $b$ is the busy-beaver function. If $m$ were computable, the blank tape halting problem would be also. To determine if a given machine halts for blank tape, we could simulate the machine on blank tape and keep a count of the number of moves it makes; if the machine has $n$ states, it would have to halt within $m(n)$ moves or not halt at all.

**Example 12.2:** It is undecidable whether a given state in a Turing machine is ever entered. It is easy to construct, from an arbitrary Turing machine **M**, a Turing machine **M**′ that simulates **M** but halts in a unique state $q_h$ just if **M** halts at all. If we could decide whether a Turing machine enters a particular state, we could decide whether an arbitrary Turing machine halts for a given tape.

Using similar arguments, we can show that it is undecidable whether a Turing machine ever executes a given instruction or ever prints a given tape symbol.

**Example 12.3:** The *configuration problem* for Turing machines is the problem of deciding, for a given Turing machine **M**, whether **M** has a sequence of moves

$$\alpha \Longrightarrow \beta$$

where $\alpha$ and $\beta$ are arbitrary configurations of **M**. A solution to the configuration problem would be an effective prcedure for evaluating the predicate

$$p(\mathbf{M}, \alpha, \beta) \begin{cases} \mathit{true} & \text{if } \mathbf{M} \text{ has a move sequence } \alpha \Longrightarrow \beta \\ \mathit{false} & \text{otherwise} \end{cases}$$

We shall show that if the configuration problem were solvable, the halting problem for Turing machines would also be solvable.

Suppose that we modify the universal Turing machine of Chapter 11 to obtain a machine **U**′, which, started on a description of a machine **M** and a tape $T$, simulates **M** for $T$, and, if the simulation ever terminates, erases its tape and halts in some specific final state $q$. (To enable **U**′ to erase its tape at the end of a simulation, we design **U**′ so that it marks the end of the nonblank region of its tape with a special end-mark symbol \$. This symbol is moved to the right as needed to make space available during a computation. At the conclusion of a simulation, **U**′ moves its head right until it scans \$, and then moves it left to the initial square, erasing any symbols encountered along the way.) By construction, **U**′ performs the computation

$$(\lambda, q_I, \#, D(\mathbf{M})\#\hat{D}(T)) \Longrightarrow (\lambda, q, \#, \lambda)$$

just if **M** halts for $T$. If a solution to the configuration problem existed, we could solve the halting problem for arbitrary **M** and $T$ by evaluating the predicate

$$p(\mathbf{U}', (\lambda, q_I, \#, D(\mathbf{M})\#\hat{D}(T)), (\lambda, q, \#, \lambda))$$

Since we know that the halting problem is unsolvable, we conclude that the configuration problem is unsolvable.

In each of these examples, we reduced the halting problem for Turing machines to a given problem and thereby established the unsolvability of the problem. The reader may verify that the converse reducibilities also hold: in each case the given problem is reducible to the halting problem. These problems are equivalent in the sense that a solution to any one of them implies a solution to each of the others. Do there exist unsolvable problems that are not equivalent to the halting problem for Turing machines? To answer such a question, one might postulate an "oracle" for the halting problem and then characterize the class of problems that could be solved if Turing machines were allowed to consult this oracle. It turns out that there are problems that cannot be solved even with this oracle; in fact, there is an infinite hierarchy of equivalence classes of unsolvable problems, corresponding to oracles postulated to resolve undecidable questions at lower levels. This hierarchy is used to define a concept of *degrees of unsolvability*, the halting problem being of first degree. All the unsolvable problems studied in this book exhibit the same degree of unsolvability as the halting problem; for a discussion of problems exhibiting greater degrees of unsolvability, the reader is referred to Rogers [1967].

## 12.5 Word Problem and Correspondence Problem

In this section, we study two well-known unsolvable problems: the word problem for formal grammars, and the correspondence problem of Emil Post. These problems provide our first examples of unsolvable problems expressed within the framework of mathematical systems other than the Turing machines; however, the proofs of their unsolvability follow readily from Turing's results.

### 12.5.1 Word Problem

The *word problem* for formal grammars is the problem of deciding, for an arbitrary grammar **G** and arbitrary strings $\omega$ and $\varphi$, whether $\varphi$ can be derived from $\omega$, that is, whether

$$\omega \stackrel{*}{\Longrightarrow} \varphi$$

is permitted by **G**.

Suppose that a derivation of a string $\varphi$ from a string $\omega$ is permitted by a grammar **G**. Since the derivation consists of a finite number of steps and **G** has a finite number of productions, we can certainly design a procedure for constructing such a derivation if one exists. However, such a procedure is not a decision procedure for the word problem unless it provides a means of deciding, after some finite number of steps, when *no* such derivation exists. This difficulty is the same as that encountered in designing an algorithm for the Turing machine halting problem. Using the universal Turing machine, we can design an effective procedure for determining the move sequence by which an arbitrary Turing machine halts, if indeed it does halt; yet we cannot design a procedure that solves the halting problem for Turing machines, because there is no general procedure for determining that a given machine will fail to halt.

We shall prove that the word problem is unsolvable by constructing a type 0 grammar with derivation steps in one-to-one correspondence with the moves of an arbitrary Turing machine. In this way, we show that the type 0 grammars have sufficient power to describe Turing machine computations, and are thus subject to the same limitations as the Turing machines. This technique, reducing problems in one formal system to those in another, is used extensively in the theory of computability.

**Theorem 12.3:** The word problem for type 0 grammars is unsolvable.

***Proof:*** Let $\mathbf{M} = (\mathbf{Q}, \mathbf{S}, \mathbf{P}, q_I)$ be an arbitrary Turing machine. We shall construct from **M** an instance of the word problem that is *true* just if **M** halts for blank tape.

Without loss of generality we may assume that **M** has a unique state $q_H$ that is entered just if **M** halts (as in Example 12.2). If, for convenience, we represent a configuration $(\varphi, q, s, \psi)$ of **M** by the string of symbols

$$\$ \, \varphi q s \psi \, \$$$

(where \$ is a special end-mark symbol), then **M** enters a configuration of the form $\$ \, \varphi q_H s \psi \, \$$ for blank tape if and only if **M** halts for blank tape. Let **G** be a type 0 grammar with the following productions:

| | | |
|---|---|---|
| $qts \longrightarrow tpr$ | all $t \in \mathbf{S} \cup \{\#\}$ | if **M** has $q]$ **right** $(s/r, p)$ |
| $sq \longrightarrow pr$ | | if **M** has $q]$ **left** $(s/r, p)$ |
| $qt\$ \longrightarrow qt\#\$$ | all $t \in \mathbf{S} \cup \{\#\}$, $q \in \mathbf{Q}$ | (to lengthen configuration rightward) |
| $q_H t \longrightarrow q_H$ | all $t \in \mathbf{S} \cup \{\#\}$ | (to erase configuration rightward) |
| $tq_H \longrightarrow q_H$ | all $t \in \mathbf{S} \cup \{\#\}$ | (to erase configuration leftward) |

Of course, the first two types of productions are not, strictly speaking, valid in a formal grammar. However, we have seen in Chapter 3 how such productions can be replaced with sets of valid productions, containing new nonterminals, that accomplish the desired interchange of symbols; thus we permit their inclusion in **G**.

The machine **M** begins in the initial configuration $\$ \, q_I \# \, \$$, and each move by **M** modifies the configuration according to a single rule in **G**. A right move of **M**

$$(\varphi, q, t, s\psi) \Longrightarrow (\varphi t, p, r, \psi)$$

corresponds to the derivation step

$$\$\varphi qts\psi \, \$ \Longrightarrow \$ \, \varphi tpr\psi\$$$

in **G**; a left move of **M**

$$(\varphi s, q, t, \psi) \Longrightarrow (\varphi, p, r, t\psi)$$

corresponds to the derivation step

$$\$ \, \varphi sqt\psi \, \$ \Longrightarrow \$ \, \varphi prt\psi \, \$$$

in **G**. The rules $qt\,\$ \longrightarrow qt\#\,\$$ permit the addition of blank symbols to a configuration, corresponding to a right move by **M** into the unused region of its tape. The rules $q_H t \longrightarrow q_H$ and $tq_H \longrightarrow q_H$ permit the derivation of the string $\$ \, q_H \, \$$ from that representing the configuration of **M** after entering state $q_H$.

Now **M** halts for blank tape just if there are strings $\varphi, \psi \in \mathbf{S}^*$ such that **M** has the move sequence

$$(\lambda, q_I, \#, \lambda) \Longrightarrow (\varphi, q_H, s, \psi)$$

for some $s \in \mathbf{S}$. But this is the case just if the derivation

$$\$q_I\#\$ \overset{*}{\Longrightarrow} \$\varphi q_H s\psi\$ \overset{*}{\Longrightarrow} \$q_H\$$$

is permitted by **G**. Thus a procedure for solving the word problem could be used to decide whether an arbitrary Turing machine halts for blank tape. Since the blank tape halting problem is unsolvable, the word problem is unsolvable.

No theorem analogous to Theorem 12.3 can be established for grammars of types 1, 2, or 3; the erasing productions of grammar **G** are essential to the proof of the theorem. In fact, it is straightforward to design a procedure for solving the word problem for formal grammars containing no length-decreasing productions. The procedure enumerates derivations until one is found to satisfy the word problem, or until only strings longer than the target string $\psi$ can be generated (see Problem 12.8).

### 12.5.2 Correspondence Problem

A powerful result in the theory of computability is the unsolvability of Post's correspondence problem. Although it has had many important applications, our interest in the problem stems primarily from its utility in establishing unsolvability results for context-free languages and grammars.

**Definition 12.1:** A *correspondence pair* is a pair $\mathbf{C} = (\mathbf{A}, \mathbf{B})$ in which **A** and **B** are ordered, finite sets of strings on an alphabet **V**, each set having $n \geq 1$ elements:

$$\mathbf{A} = (\alpha_1, \alpha_2, \ldots, \alpha_n)$$
$$\mathbf{B} = (\beta_1, \beta_2, \ldots, \beta_n)$$

We say that the finite sequence of integers

$$i_1, i_2, \ldots, i_m, \qquad 1 \leq i_j \leq n,\ 1 \leq j \leq m$$

is a *solution* for the correspondence pair **C** if and only if the strings

$$\varphi = \alpha_{i_1}\alpha_{i_2}\ldots\alpha_{i_m}$$

and

$$\psi = \beta_{i_1}\beta_{i_2}\ldots\beta_{i_m}$$

are identical. The *correspondence problem* is that of deciding, for any given correspondence pair **C**, whether **C** has a solution.

Figure 12.6 provides an intuitive interpretation of the correspondence problem. Presented with an integer $i$, transducers $\mathbf{M_A}$ and $\mathbf{M_B}$ produce strings $\alpha_i$ and $\beta_i$ from sets **A** and **B**, respectively. The correspondence problem is to decide whether there is an input sequence of integers that causes $\mathbf{M_A}$ and $\mathbf{M_B}$ to produce the same output sequence. (A given integer may appear more than once in such an input sequence.) It is important to note that the responses of $\mathbf{M_A}$ and $\mathbf{M_B}$ to an integer need not be of the same length; thus $\varphi$ and $\psi$ may be identical without having $\alpha_i$ identical to $\beta_i$ for each $i$.

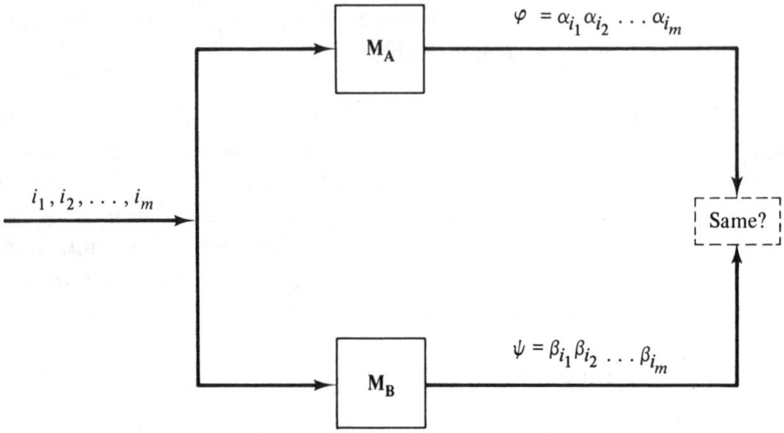


**Figure 12.6** Interpretation of Post's correspondence problem.

**Example 12.4:** Let $\mathbf{C} = (\mathbf{A}, \mathbf{B})$ be the correspondence pair in which

$$\mathbf{A} = (ba, ab, bb, aabb)$$
$$\mathbf{B} = (a, abbb, aa, bbb)$$

Although each element of **A** is different from the corresponding element of **B**, the pair **C** does have a solution. In particular, if the elements of the sets are concatenated in the order 2, 3, 4, 1, both sets yield the string *abbbaabbba.* Note that if a sequence of integers **I** is a solution to a correspondence pair, then so is $\mathbf{I}^n$ for each $n \geq 1$. Thus **C** also has solutions

2, 3, 4, 1, 2, 3, 4, 1

2, 3, 4, 1, 2, 3, 4, 1, 2, 3, 4, 1

and so on.

**Example 12.5:** Consider the correspondence pair $\mathbf{C} = (\mathbf{A}, \mathbf{B})$, where

$$\mathbf{A} = (0011, 010, 0110, 011)$$
$$\mathbf{B} = (1110, 10, 01, 110)$$

Any solution for **C** must begin with integer 3; otherwise, the string formed from the elements of **A** would begin with 0, while that formed from the elements of **B** would begin with 1. But if we start a solution with 3, the length of the string formed from **A** is longer than that formed from **B**, and it must remain longer since no element of **B** is longer than the corresponding element of **A**. Thus **C** can have no solution.

To show that the correspondence problem is unsolvable, we use a technique analogous to that used for the word problem: we devise a method of representing the behavior of any Turing machine in the format of a correspondence pair. In particular, we show how to construct, from an arbitrary Turing machine **M**, a pair **C** = (**A**, **B**) that has a solution just if **M** halts for blank tape. If the correspondence problem were solvable, we could decide whether any such pair has a solution and thus solve the blank tape halting problem for Turing machines.

Suppose that **C** = (**A**, **B**) is a correspondence pair, where

$$\mathbf{A} = \alpha_1, \ldots, \alpha_n$$

and

$$\mathbf{B} = \beta_1, \ldots, \beta_n$$

It is convenient to think of the pairs $(\alpha_i, \beta_i)$, $1 \leq i \leq n$, as being written on dominoes of $n$ types:

$$\begin{pmatrix}\alpha_1\\ \beta_1\end{pmatrix}, \ldots, \begin{pmatrix}\alpha_n\\ \beta_n\end{pmatrix}$$

The set of domino types is said to have a *solution* if there is a finite sequence of dominoes, each being of one of the $n$ types, such that the upper and lower rows of the dominoes spell out the same word. Since each correspondence pair corresponds to a finite set of dominoes, and vice versa, the problem of deciding whether a given finite set of dominoes has a solution is an alternative formulation of the correspondence problem. For notational convenience, we shall use this alternative formulation in the arguments that follow.

Let **M** = (**Q**, **S**, **P**, $q_I$) be an arbitrary Turing machine. We shall represent configurations of **M** as we did in proving the unsolvability of the word problem (Theorem 12.3), and shall assume as we did there that **M** has a unique state $q_H$ that is entered just if **M** halts. Consider the "grammar" **G(M)** with the infinite set of rules

| | | |
|---|---|---|
| $\$\,\omega q t s \varphi\,\$ \longrightarrow \$\,\omega t p r \varphi\,\$$ | all $t \in \mathbf{S} \cup \{\#\}$ | if **M** has $q]$ **right** $(s/r, p)$ |
| $\$\,\omega s q \varphi\,\$ \longrightarrow \$\,\omega p r \varphi\,\$$ | | if **M** has $q]$ **left** $(s/r, p)$ |
| $\$\,\omega q t\,\$ \longrightarrow \$\,\omega q t \#\,\$$ | all $t \in \mathbf{S} \cup \{\#\}$, $q \in \mathbf{Q}$ | |
| $\$\,\omega q_H t \varphi\,\$ \longrightarrow \$\,\omega q_H \varphi\,\$$ | all $t \in \mathbf{S} \cup \{\#\}$ | |
| $\$\,\omega t q_H\,\$ \longrightarrow \$\,\omega q_H\,\$$ | all $t \in \mathbf{S} \cup \{\#\}$ | |

for all $\omega, \varphi \in \mathbf{S}^*$. The reader may verify that **G(M)** permits the derivation of $\$\, q_H\, \$$ from $\$\, q_I\#\, \$$ just if **M** halts for blank tape.

Now let $\mathfrak{D}$(**M**) be the infinite set of dominoes

$$\mathfrak{D}(\mathbf{M}) = \left\{\begin{pmatrix} \$ \\ \$\, q_I\# \end{pmatrix}, \begin{pmatrix} q_H\, \$ \\ \$ \end{pmatrix}\right\} \cup \left\{\begin{pmatrix} \gamma\$ \\ \$\gamma' \end{pmatrix} \middle| \$\gamma\$ \longrightarrow \$\gamma'\$ \text{ is a rule of } \mathbf{G(M)}\right\}$$

and suppose that $\mathfrak{D}$(**M**) has a solution

$$\begin{pmatrix} \$ \\ \$\, q_I\, \# \end{pmatrix}\begin{pmatrix} \gamma_1\, \$ \\ \$\, \gamma_1' \end{pmatrix}\begin{pmatrix} \gamma_2\, \$ \\ \$\, \gamma_2' \end{pmatrix} \cdots \begin{pmatrix} \gamma_n\, \$ \\ \$\, \gamma_n' \end{pmatrix}\begin{pmatrix} q_H\, \$ \\ \$ \end{pmatrix}$$

of $n + 2$ dominoes, for some $n \geq 0$. [Note that any such solution *must* begin and end with

$$\begin{pmatrix} \$ \\ \$\, q_I\# \end{pmatrix} \quad \text{and} \quad \begin{pmatrix} q_H\, \$ \\ \$ \end{pmatrix}$$

respectively; otherwise, the end symbols \$ in the upper and lower rows cannot match.] The substrings enclosed between successive pairs of \$'s must satisfy

$$\begin{aligned} \gamma_1 &= q_I\# & \$\gamma_1\,\$ &\longrightarrow \$\gamma_1'\,\$ \\ \gamma_1' &= \gamma_2 & \$\gamma_2\,\$ &\longrightarrow \$\gamma_2'\,\$ \\ &\ \ \vdots \\ \gamma_{n-1}' &= \gamma_n & \$\gamma_n\,\$ &\longrightarrow \$\gamma_n'\,\$ \\ \gamma_n' &= q_H \end{aligned}$$

Thus the sequence $\gamma_1, \gamma_2, \ldots, \gamma_n$ in the upper (and lower) row is in one-to-one correspondence with the steps in a derivation of $\$\, q_H\, \$$ from $\$\, q_I\#\, \$$, and $\mathfrak{D}$(**M**) has a solution just if **M** halts for blank tape.

We cannot yet conclude that the blank tape halting problem for Turing machines is reducible to the corrrespondence problem, because $\mathfrak{D}$(**M**), being infinite, does not correspond to a valid correspondence pair. However, we shall show how to construct from $\mathfrak{D}$(**M**) a finite set of dominoes $\mathfrak{D}_f$(**M**) that has a solution if and only if $\mathfrak{D}$(**M**) has a solution.

Let $\triangle$ and $\square$ be special symbols not in $\mathbf{S} \cup \mathbf{Q} \cup \{\$\}$. For each configuration $\$\, \omega q s \varphi\, \$$ of **M**, we modify strings $\omega$ and $\varphi$ so that $\triangle$ follows each symbol in $\omega$, and $\square$ precedes each symbol in $\varphi$. If $\omega$ and $\varphi$ are the strings

$$t_1 t_2 \ldots t_n \quad \text{and} \quad u_1 u_2 \ldots u_m$$

respectively, then the modified strings are

$$t_1 \triangle t_2 \triangle \ldots t_n \triangle \quad \text{and} \quad \square u_1 \square u_2 \ldots \square u_n$$

and the configuration $\$\,\omega q s \varphi\,\$$ becomes

$$\$\, t_1\triangle t_2\triangle \ldots t_n\triangle q\square s\square u_1\square u_2 \ldots \square u_m\, \$$$

Note that in this modified configuration, every second symbol between the end marks is $\triangle$ until a state symbol $q$ is encountered, and $\square$ thereafter.

Now $\mathfrak{D}(\mathbf{M})$ is infinite because, for each state $q$ and each tape symbol $s$, $\mathfrak{D}(\mathbf{M})$ contains a domino for each pair of strings $\omega, \varphi \in \mathbf{S}^*$. If we provide $\mathfrak{D}_f(\mathbf{M})$ with dominoes that have particular subsolutions in one-to-one correspondence with individual dominoes of $\mathfrak{D}(\mathbf{M})$, then the solutions of $\mathfrak{D}(\mathbf{M})$ will be in one-to-one correspondence with those of $\mathfrak{D}_f(\mathbf{M})$. With $\omega$ and $\varphi$ as above, the subsolutions corresponding to individual dominoes of $\mathfrak{D}(\mathbf{M})$ are shown in Table 12.1; based on these subsolutions, the dominoes of $\mathfrak{D}_f(\mathbf{M})$ are given in Table 12.2. (The last three domino types in the table are required for the case in which either or both of $\omega$ and $\varphi$ are empty.)

Clearly, $\mathfrak{D}_f(\mathbf{M})$ is finite. Also, from the correspondence exhibited by Table 12.1, $\mathfrak{D}(\mathbf{M})$ has a solution only if $\mathfrak{D}_f(\mathbf{M})$ has a solution. Conversely, any solution of $\mathfrak{D}_f(\mathbf{M})$ must contain, between each pair of \$'s, a domino containing a state symbol in accord with Table 12.1; thus if $\mathfrak{D}_f(\mathbf{M})$ has a solution, so must $\mathfrak{D}(\mathbf{M})$.

We have shown how to construct, corresponding to an arbitrary Turing machine **M**, a finite set of dominoes that has a solution just if **M** halts for blank tape. Since an algorithm for the correspondence problem would enable us to decide whether such a set of dominoes has a solution, we have the following:

**Theorem 12.4:** The correspondence problem is unsolvable.

There are several solvable problems similar in statement to the correspondence problem, and the reader should be careful to distinguish them.

**Table 12.1** Correspondence of $\mathfrak{D}$ and $\mathfrak{D}_f$

| Domino in $\mathfrak{D}$ | Corresponding Subsolution in $\mathfrak{D}_f$ |
|---|---|
| $\binom{\omega q t s \varphi\,\$}{\$\,\omega t p r \varphi}$ | $\binom{t_1\triangle}{\$\,t_1}\binom{t_2\triangle}{\triangle t_2}\cdots\binom{t_n\triangle}{\triangle t_n}\binom{q\square t\square s\square}{\triangle t\triangle p\square r}\binom{u_1\square}{\square u_1}\cdots\binom{u_m\square}{\square u_m}$ |
| $\binom{\omega s q \varphi\,\$}{\$\,\omega p r \varphi}$ | $\binom{t_1\triangle}{\$\,t_1}\binom{t_2\triangle}{\triangle t_2}\cdots\binom{t_n\triangle}{\triangle t_n}\binom{s\triangle q\square}{\triangle p\square r}\binom{u_1\square}{\square u_1}\cdots\binom{u_m\,\$}{\square u_m}$ |
| $\binom{\omega q t\,\$}{\$\,\omega q t\,\#}$ | $\binom{t_1\triangle}{\$\,t_1}\binom{t_2\triangle}{\triangle t_2}\cdots\binom{t_n\triangle}{\triangle t_n}\binom{q\square t\square\$}{\triangle q\square t\square\#}$ |
| $\binom{\omega q_H s \varphi\,\$}{\$\,\omega q_H \varphi}$ | $\binom{t_1\triangle}{\$\,t_1}\binom{t_2\triangle}{\triangle t_2}\cdots\binom{t_n\triangle}{\triangle t_n}\binom{q_H\square s\square}{\triangle q_H}\binom{u_1\square}{\square u_1}\cdots\binom{u_m\square}{\square u_m}$ |
| $\binom{\omega s q_H\,\$}{\$\,\omega q_H}$ | $\binom{t_1\triangle}{\$\,t_1}\binom{t_2\triangle}{\triangle t_2}\cdots\binom{t_n\triangle}{\triangle t_n}\binom{s\triangle q_H\,\$}{\triangle q_H}$ |

**Table 12.2** Domino types in $\mathfrak{D}_f$

| Basic Domino Types | Reason |
|---|---|
| $\begin{pmatrix} \$ \\ \$q_I\square\# \end{pmatrix}$, $\begin{pmatrix} q_H\$ \\ \$ \end{pmatrix}$ | Initial and final dominoes |
| $\begin{pmatrix} t\triangle \\ \triangle t \end{pmatrix}$, all $t \in \mathbf{S}$ | To construct $\omega$ region of modified configurations |
| $\begin{pmatrix} u\square \\ \square u \end{pmatrix}$, all $u \in \mathbf{S}$ | To construct $\varphi$ region of modified configurations |
| $\begin{pmatrix} q\square t\square s\square \\ \triangle t\triangle p\square r \end{pmatrix}$ | Local configuration change due to instruction of $\mathbf{M}$ $q]$ **right** $(s/r, p)$ |
| $\begin{pmatrix} s\triangle q\square \\ \triangle p\square r \end{pmatrix}$ | Local configuration change due to instruction of $\mathbf{M}$ $q]$ **left** $(s/r, p)$ |
| $\begin{pmatrix} q\square t\,\$ \\ \triangle q\square t\square\# \end{pmatrix}$, all $t \in \mathbf{S}$, $q \in \mathbf{Q}$ | To lengthen configuration rightward |
| $\begin{pmatrix} q_H\square s\square \\ \triangle q_H \end{pmatrix}$, all $s \in \mathbf{S}$ | To erase symbols rightward |
| $\begin{pmatrix} s\triangle q_H\$ \\ \triangle q_H \end{pmatrix}$, all $s \in \mathbf{S}$ | To erase symbols leftward |

Additional Domino Types

| If in $\mathfrak{D}_f$ | Add to $\mathfrak{D}_f$ | |
|---|---|---|
| $\begin{pmatrix} \alpha \\ \triangle\beta \end{pmatrix}$ | $\begin{pmatrix} \alpha \\ \$\beta \end{pmatrix}$ | Add end marks if $\omega$ or $\varphi$ is empty |
| $\begin{pmatrix} \alpha\square \\ \beta \end{pmatrix}$ | $\begin{pmatrix} \alpha\$ \\ \beta \end{pmatrix}$ | |
| $\begin{pmatrix} \alpha\square \\ \triangle\beta \end{pmatrix}$ | $\begin{pmatrix} \alpha\$ \\ \$\beta \end{pmatrix}$ | |

Two are of particular note. Let

$$\mathbf{A} = \{\alpha_1, \alpha_2, \ldots, \alpha_n\}$$

and

$$\mathbf{B} = \{\beta_1, \beta_2, \ldots, \beta_n\}$$

be sets of strings on some alphabet $\mathbf{V}$. The question, *do there exist sequences of integers* $i_1, i_2, \ldots, i_k$ *and* $j_1, j_2, \ldots, j_l$ *such that* $\alpha_{i_1}\alpha_{i_2}\ldots\alpha_{i_k} = \beta_{j_1}\beta_{j_2}\ldots\beta_{j_l}$?, can always be answered, since it is tantamount to asking whether the regular set $\mathbf{A}^* \cap \mathbf{B}^*$ is empty. Similarly, suppose that $\mathbf{A}$ is the set of strings

$$\mathbf{A} = \{\alpha_1, \alpha_2, \ldots, \alpha_n\}$$

The problem of deciding whether there exist distinct sequences of integers $i_1, i_2, \ldots, i_k$ and $j_1, j_2, \ldots, j_l$ such that $\alpha_{i_1}\alpha_{i_2}\ldots\alpha_{i_k} = \alpha_{j_1}\alpha_{j_2}\ldots\alpha_{j_l}$ is solvable, since it too reduces to questions about regular languages; details are left to the Problems.

## 12.6 Unsolvable Problems for Context-Free Languages

Many interesting problems that can be posed about context-free languages are unsolvable, and can be shown so by arguments involving Post's correspondence problem. In most cases, the proofs of these results depend on the construction of grammars or languages that have a given property just if an arbitrary correspondence pair has a solution. Using Theorem 12.4, we can then conclude that the problem of deciding whether a grammar or language has the particular property is unsolvable.

Let $\mathbf{C} = (\mathbf{A}, \mathbf{B})$ be an arbitrary correspondence pair on some alphabet $\mathbf{V}$:

$$\mathbf{A} = \{\alpha_1, \ldots, \alpha_n\}, \qquad \alpha_i \in \mathbf{V}^*, 1 \leq i \leq n$$

$$\mathbf{B} = \{\beta_1, \ldots, \beta_n\}, \qquad \beta_i \in \mathbf{V}^*, 1 \leq i \leq n$$

and let $\mathbf{G_A}$ and $\mathbf{G_B}$ be the grammars

$$
\begin{array}{llll}
\mathbf{G_A}: & \Sigma \longrightarrow A & \mathbf{G_B}: & \Sigma \longrightarrow B \\
& A \longrightarrow (1)A\alpha_1 & & B \longrightarrow (1)B\beta_1 \\
& \quad\vdots & & \quad\vdots \\
& A \longrightarrow (n)A\alpha_n & & B \longrightarrow (n)B\beta_n \\
& A \longrightarrow (1)\$\alpha_1 & & B \longrightarrow (1)\$\beta_1 \\
& \quad\vdots & & \quad\vdots \\
& A \longrightarrow (n)\$\alpha_n & & B \longrightarrow (n)\$\beta_n
\end{array}
$$

Each string generated by $\mathbf{G_A}$ or $\mathbf{G_B}$ has the form

$$(i_m) \ldots (i_2)(i_1)\$\varphi_{i_1}\varphi_{i_2} \ldots \varphi_{i_m}$$

where $\varphi_i$ is $\alpha_i$ or $\beta_i$, according as the string is generated by $\mathbf{G_A}$ or $\mathbf{G_B}$. Such a string consists of a sequence of elements from $\mathbf{A}$ or $\mathbf{B}$, preceded by the reversed sequence of corresponding subscripts. The symbol \$ is a special symbol not in $\mathbf{V}$, and is used to separate subscripts from elements. The reader may verify that a string

$$(i_m) \ldots (i_2)(i_1)\$\varphi_{i_1}\varphi_{i_2} \ldots \varphi_{i_m}$$

is generated by both $\mathbf{G_A}$ and $\mathbf{G_B}$ just if $i_1, i_2, \ldots, i_m$ is a solution for the correspondence pair $\mathbf{C}$. This fact is the basis of a number of important unsolvability results.

**Theorem 12.5:** The problem of deciding, for arbitrary context-free languages $\mathbf{L}$ and $\mathbf{L}'$, whether $\mathbf{L} \cap \mathbf{L}'$ is empty (or infinite) is unsolvable.

***Proof:*** Let $\mathbf{L} = \mathbf{L}(\mathbf{G_A})$ and $\mathbf{L}' = \mathbf{L}(\mathbf{G_B})$. The language $\mathbf{L} \cap \mathbf{L}'$ is empty just if $\mathbf{C}$ has no solution; thus a procedure for deciding whether $\mathbf{L} \cap \mathbf{L}' = \varnothing$ would solve the correspondence problem. Similarly, since $\mathbf{I}^n$ is a solution for the correspondence pair $\mathbf{C}$ whenever $\mathbf{I}$ is a solution for $\mathbf{C}$, $\mathbf{L} \cap \mathbf{L}'$ contains an infinity of elements just if $\mathbf{C}$ does have a solution. Thus a procedure for deciding whether $\mathbf{L} \cap \mathbf{L}'$ is infinite would also solve the correspondence problem.

The fact that $\mathbf{G_A}$ and $\mathbf{G_B}$ generate deterministic languages allows us to establish similar unsolvability results for the complements of context-free languages:

**Theorem 12.6:** The problem of deciding, for an arbitrary context-free language $\mathbf{L}$, whether $\mathbf{L}^c$ is empty (or infinite) is unsolvable.

***Proof:*** Since $\mathbf{L}(\mathbf{G_A})$ and $\mathbf{L}(\mathbf{G_B})$ are deterministic, their complements are context free. So is the union of their complements. If we take $\mathbf{L} = (\mathbf{L}(\mathbf{G_A}))^c \cup (\mathbf{L}(\mathbf{G_B}))^c$, then $\mathbf{L}^c = \mathbf{L}(\mathbf{G_A}) \cap \mathbf{L}(\mathbf{G_B})$, and the required results follow from those of Theorem 12.5.

In Chapter 9, we hinted at the difficulty of deciding whether a given context-free language is regular. We are now in a position to show that the problem is unsolvable.

**Theorem 12.7:** There is no effective procedure for deciding whether a given context-free language is regular.

***Proof:*** Let $\mathbf{L} = (\mathbf{L}(\mathbf{G_A}))^c \cup (\mathbf{L}(\mathbf{G_B}))^c$, as in the proof of Theorem 12.6. The problem of deciding whether $\mathbf{L}$ is regular is that of deciding whether $\mathbf{L}(\mathbf{G_A}) \cap \mathbf{L}(\mathbf{G_B})$ is regular, since the complement of any regular set is regular.

Now $\mathbf{L}(\mathbf{G_A}) \cap \mathbf{L}(\mathbf{G_B})$ is regular if the correspondence pair $\mathbf{C}$ has no solution, since in that case the set is the empty set $\varnothing$. If $\mathbf{C}$ has a solution, then $\mathbf{L}(\mathbf{G_A}) \cap \mathbf{L}(\mathbf{G_B})$ contains some string

$$\eta\$\gamma$$

and must in fact contain the string

$$\eta^k\$\gamma^k$$

for each $k > 0$, since any solution for $\mathbf{C}$ can be repeated arbitrarily many times to yield additional solutions for $\mathbf{C}$. But if $\mathbf{L}(\mathbf{G_A}) \cap \mathbf{L}(\mathbf{G_B})$ is regular, the set must then contain strings of the form

$$\eta^i\$\gamma^j$$

with $i \neq j$, which is impossible since $\eta^i$ cannot in that case be the sequence of subscripts corresponding to $\gamma^j$. Thus $\mathbf{L}(\mathbf{G_A}) \cap \mathbf{L}(\mathbf{G_B})$ is regular if and only if it is empty, which by Theorem 12.5 cannot be decided.

The next result follows from the preceding theorem and the intricate result of Stearns [1967] that regularity is decidable for deterministic context-free languages.

**Theorem 12.8:** There is no effective procedure for determining whether a given context-free language is deterministic.

***Proof:*** Suppose that such a procedure exists. Given an arbitrary context-free language **L**, we could apply the procedure to determine whether **L** is deterministic. If so, we could apply Stearns's procedure to determine whether **L** is regular; otherwise, we could conclude that **L** is nonregular, since every regular set is a deterministic language. If such a procedure exists, we could decide whether an arbitrary context-free language is regular, contradicting Theorem 12.7.

We now show that the problem of deciding whether a given context-free grammar is ambiguous is an unsolvable problem. Note that this result is *not* an immediate consequence of the preceding result, since deterministic languages may be generated by ambiguous grammars.

**Theorem 12.9:** There is no effective procedure for deciding, given any context-free grammar **G**, whether **G** is ambiguous.

***Proof:*** Let **G** be the grammar formed by combining the productions of grammars $\mathbf{G_A}$ and $\mathbf{G_B}$. Since $\mathbf{G_A}$ and $\mathbf{G_B}$ are unambiguous and have no nonterminals in common, the grammar **G** is ambiguous just if $\mathbf{G_A}$ and $\mathbf{G_B}$ generate some common element; that is, just if $\mathbf{L}(\mathbf{G_A}) \cap \mathbf{L}(\mathbf{G_B}) \neq \varnothing$. Since there is no procedure for deciding whether the intersection of arbitrary context-free languages is empty, there can be no procedure for deciding whether a given context-free grammar is ambiguous.

In light of Theorem 12.9, it is not surprising that the problem of deciding whether a given context-free grammar generates an inherently ambiguous language is unsolvable. We leave the proof of this result to the reader (see Problem 12.16).

Our final result asserts the impossibility of designing an effective procedure to determine when two context-free grammars generate the same language.

**Theorem 12.10:** The problem of deciding whether **L(G)** = **L(G′)** for arbitrary context-free grammars **G** and **G′** is unsolvable.

***Proof:*** Let **L** be an arbitrary context-free language, and let **T** be the alphabet of **L**. Let **G** be a context-free grammar generating **L**, and let **G′** be a context-free grammar generating **T***. (Since **T*** is regular, it is an easy matter to construct such a grammar **G′**.) Then **G** and **G′** generate the same language just if $\mathbf{L}^c$ is empty; any procedure for deciding whether arbitrary context-free grammars generate the same language would enable us to determine whether the complement of an arbitrary context-free language is empty, contradicting Theorem 12.6.

## Notes and References

The unsolvability of the halting problem for Turing machines was established by Turing [1936]; the noncomputability of the busy beaver function was shown by Rado [1962]. The correspondence problem was shown unsolvable by Post [1946]. (An alternative proof appears in Floyd [1964].) The unsolvability of the word problem for formal grammars follows from the equivalence, established by Chomsky [1959], of the type 0 languages and the Turing recognizable languages.

Many of the results in Section 12.6 concerning unsolvable problems for context-free languages are from Bar-Hillel, Perles, and Shamir [1961]. Additional results (for example, that of Problem 12.15) appear in Ginsburg and Rose [1963]. The undecidability of ambiguity of a context-free grammar was established independently by Cantor [1962], Floyd [1962], and Chomsky and Schutzenberger [1963]; the undecidability of inherent ambiguity (Problem 12.16) is from Ginsburg and Ullian [1966]. Unsolvability results for deterministic languages appear in Ginsburg and Greibach [1966].

For a discussion of problems exhibiting greater degrees of unsolvability than the halting problem, as well as rigorous treatment of the notion of reducibility, the reader is referred to Rogers [1967].

## Problems

12.1. The enumerability of the Turing machines provides a very simple proof of the unsolvability of the halting problem. For each $i$, let $\mathbf{M}_i$ be the $i$th machine in an enumeration of the Turing machines, and let $f_i$ be the function computed by $\mathbf{M}_i$. Show how to construct, given a Turing machine **H** that solves the halting problem, a machine **M** that computes a function $f$ differing from that computed by any Turing machine in the enumeration. Since **M** must itself be in the enumeration, this contradicts the existence of **H**. [*Hint:* Construct **M** so that, for each $i \geq 0$, $f(i)$ differs from $f_i(i)$.]

***12.2.** Let **E** be some enumeration of the Turing machines, and, for each $i \geq 0$, let $\mathbf{M}_i$ be the $i$th machine in **E**. Show that the function $s: \mathbf{N} \longrightarrow \mathbf{N}$ defined by

$$s(i) = \begin{cases} n & \text{if } \mathbf{M}_i \text{ halts for blank tape and } n \text{ is the rightmost tape square reached by } \mathbf{M}_i \text{ during its computation} \\ 0 & \text{otherwise} \end{cases}$$

is noncomputable. Show that the predicate $p$: $\mathbf{N} \times \mathbf{N} \longrightarrow \{true, false\}$ defined by

$$p(i, j) = \begin{cases} true & \text{if } \mathbf{M}_i \text{ halts for blank tape without ever reaching the } j\text{th tape square} \\ false & \text{otherwise} \end{cases}$$

*is* decidable.

12.3. Show that the problems of Examples 12.1 to 12.3 are each reducible to the halting problem.

**12.4.** a. Show that there is no algorithm for deciding, given an arbitrary Turing machine **M**, whether the function computed by **M** is total (that is, whether **M** halts for every tape).

b. Show that there is no algorithm for deciding, given an arbitrary Turing machine **M**, whether the function computed by **M** is everywhere undefined (that is, whether **M** fails to halt for every tape).

**12.5.** For a given Turing machine **M**, let $\mathfrak{T}(\mathbf{M})$ denote the set of tapes for which **M** halts. Show that it is undecidable whether $\mathfrak{T}(\mathbf{M})$ is finite. Show that it *is* decidable whether $\mathfrak{T}(\mathbf{M})$ is a *nonempty* finite set.

**12.6.** Show that there is no procedure for deciding, for an arbitrary Turing machine **M** and an arbitrary tape $T$, whether or not **M** halts with final tape $T$ for some initial tape. (Thus there is no method of deciding, for arbitrary $n \in \mathbf{N}$, whether $n$ is in the range of a given computable function.)

**12.7.** Let $\mathbf{M} = (\mathbf{Q}, \mathbf{S}, \mathbf{P}, q_I)$ be an arbitrary Turing machine, and let $\mathfrak{C}(\mathbf{M}) = \mathbf{S}^* \times \mathbf{Q} \times \mathbf{S} \times \mathbf{S}^*$ be the set of configurations of **M**. We can construct a one-to-one function $g$: $\mathfrak{C}(\mathbf{M}) \longrightarrow \mathbf{N}$ that maps configurations of **M** into the natural numbers, and use this mapping to define a (partial) number-theoretic function $f$:

$$f(i) = \begin{cases} n & \text{if } \mathbf{M}\text{, started in } g^{-1}(i)\text{, halts in } g^{-1}(n) \\ \text{undefined} & \text{otherwise} \end{cases}$$

a. Show that there is no algorithm for deciding, for arbitrary **M** and arbitrary $\alpha \in \mathfrak{C}(\mathbf{M})$, whether or not $f(g(\alpha))$ is defined.

b. Show that it *is* possible to decide, for arbitrary **M**, whether or not $f$ is *everywhere* undefined. (Compare this result with that of Problem 12.4b.)

**12.8.** Show that the word problem is solvable for type 1 grammars. (*Hint:* Note that, for a type 1 grammar, no terminal string derives from a sentential form longer than the string.)

12.9. Let $\mathbf{C} = (\mathbf{A}, \mathbf{B})$ be a correspondence pair with lists

$$\mathbf{A} = (ab,\ aba,\ bba,\ b)$$
$$\mathbf{B} = (aba,\ bab,\ abb,\ ba)$$

Exhibit a solution for **C** or prove that **C** has no solution.

***12.10.** The *modified Post's correspondence problem* is the problem of deciding, for an arbitrary correspondence pair $\mathbf{C} = (\mathbf{A}, \mathbf{B})$ in which

$$\mathbf{A} = (\alpha_1, \alpha_2, \ldots, \alpha_n)$$
$$\mathbf{B} = (\beta_1, \beta_2, \ldots, \beta_n)$$

whether there exists a sequence of integers $i_1, i_2, \ldots, i_k$ such that

$$\alpha_1 \alpha_{i_1} \alpha_{i_2} \ldots \alpha_{i_k} = \beta_1 \beta_{i_1} \beta_{i_2} \ldots \beta_{i_k}$$

(The difference between the correspondence problem and the modified correspondence problem is that a solution for a correspondence pair in the modified problem is required to start with the first element of each list.) Show that the modified problem reduces to the correspondence problem.

**12.11.** Let $\mathbf{A} = (\alpha_1, \alpha_2, \ldots, \alpha_n)$ be an ordered set of strings over some alphabet **V**. Show that it is decidable whether there exist distinct sequences of integers $i_1, i_2, \ldots, i_k$ and $j_1, j_2, \ldots, j_l$ such that $\alpha_{i_1}\alpha_{i_2} \ldots \alpha_{i_k} = \alpha_{j_1}\alpha_{j_2} \ldots \alpha_{j_l}$. This shows that, given a finite set of "code words," it is decidable whether each string formed by concatenating code words is uniquely decipherable.

**12.12.** Show that it is undecidable whether the complement of a context-free language is a context-free language.

**12.12.** Show that it is undecidable for arbitrary context-free languages $\mathbf{L}_1$ and $\mathbf{L}_2$ whether $\mathbf{L}_1 \subseteq \mathbf{L}_2$. Is the question decidable if $\mathbf{L}_1$ is regular? if $\mathbf{L}_2$ is regular? if both $\mathbf{L}_1$ and $\mathbf{L}_2$ are deterministic languages?

**12.14.** Show that it is undecidable whether the union of two deterministic context-free languages is a deterministic language.

***12.15.** Show that it is unsolvable, for arbitrary context-free languages $\mathbf{L}_1$ and $\mathbf{L}_2$, whether $\mathbf{M}(\mathbf{L}_1) = \mathbf{L}_2$ for some GST **M**.

***12.16.** Show that it is undecidable whether an arbitrary context-free grammar generates an inherently ambiguous language. [*Hint*: Use the facts, which we have not demonstrated in this book, that the language

$$\mathbf{L} = \{a^n b^n c^m d^m \mid n, m \geq 1\} \cup \{a^n b^m c^m d^n \mid n, m \geq 1\}$$

is inherently ambiguous, and that the class of unambiguous languages is closed under inverse transduction by deterministic GST's. Let $\mathbf{G_A}$ and $\mathbf{G_B}$ be the grammars of Section 12.6, let $\mathbf{L_{AB}}$ be the language

$$\mathbf{L_{AB}} = \mathbf{L(G_A)} \cdot ¢ \cdot \mathbf{L(G_B)}$$

where ¢ is a new symbol not used in $\mathbf{G_A}$ or $\mathbf{G_B}$, and let $\mathbf{L'_{AB}}$ be the language

$$\mathbf{L'_{AB}} = \{\omega ¢ \omega^R \mid \omega \in \mathbf{V}^*\{(1), (2), \ldots, (n)\}^*\}$$

Show that $\mathbf{L_{AB}} \cup \mathbf{L'_{AB}}$ is inherently ambiguous just if $\mathbf{L_{AB}} \cap \mathbf{L'_{AB}}$ is not empty.]

**12.17.** a. Show that the set of tapes for which an arbitrary Turing machine halts is enumerable.

b. Show that the set of tapes for which an arbitrary Turing machine does not halt is not enumerable.

# 13

# *Recursive Functions*

The recursive functions (introduced by Kleene in 1936) are a class of number theoretic functions that can be evaluated algorithmically. Like Turing, Kleene set out to formalize the intuitive notion of "effective procedure" applied to numeric quantities. When eventually it was discovered that Kleene's functions and Turing's machines were equivalent formulations—that is, that an algorithm can be realized by a Turing machine if and only if it can be expressed as a recursive function—Turing's thesis acquired considerable stature and credibility.

We have already seen several instances in which *recursion* plays a central role: proof by induction (Chapter 2), the construction of trees and derivations according to formal grammars (Chapter 3), the definition of regular expressions (Chapter 5). Most readers are probably familiar with function definitions that involve recursion. For example, for each $n \geq 0$, let $A_n$ denote the amount of money in a bank account after $n$ years, when the initial principal is $p$ and the yearly interest rate is $r$. Then

(1) $$A_0 = p$$

(2) $$A_{n+1} = A_n + rA_n$$

Equation 1 is the *basis* of the recursive definition of $A_n$, and equation 2 shows how to construct $A_{n+1}$ from $A_n$ and $r$. It is easily verified that the formula

(3) $$A_n = (1 + r)^n p$$

is equivalent to equations 1 and 2.

In the above example, it is clear that the algebraic solution 3 is equivalent to the recursive definition 1 and 2. However, recursive definitions are often easier to use or to understand than equivalent algebraic equations. As an example, consider the *Fibonacci number sequence*, a portion of which is

$$1, 1, 2, 3, 5, 8, 13, 21, 34, 55, 89, \ldots$$

The first two terms in the sequence are both 1, and the $n$th term in the sequence ($n \geq 3$) is obtained by adding the preceding two terms. Let $F(n)$ denote the $n$th term in the sequence. A recursive definition of $F$ is

$$\begin{aligned} F(0) &= 1 \\ F(1) &= 1 \\ F(n+2) &= F(n+1) + F(n) \end{aligned} \tag{4}$$

While it is known that

$$F(n) = \frac{1}{\sqrt{5}}\left(\frac{1+\sqrt{5}}{2}\right)^{n+1} - \frac{1}{\sqrt{5}}\left(\frac{1-\sqrt{5}}{2}\right)^{n+1}$$

it is not at all obvious how one obtains the algebraic formula 5 from the recursive definition 4. Certainly the recursive definition provides a clearer understanding of the nature of the sequence.

To further demonstrate the power of recursive definitions, we consider an example of a number sequence which is generated by a simple procedure but for which there is no known algebraic expression for the $n$th term. Let $k \geq 1$ be given, and consider the procedure

1. If $k = 1$, stop.
2. If $k$ is even, set $k = k/2$ and go to step 1.
3. If $k$ is odd, set $k = 3k + 1$ and go to step 1.

The following are some examples of the sequences of values generated by this procedure, in terms of the starting value of $k$:

| *k* | *sequence* |
|---|---|
| 1 | 1 |
| 2 | 2, 1 |
| 3 | 3, 10, 5, 16, 8, 4, 2, 1 |
| 4 | 4, 2, 1 |
| 5 | 5, 16, 8, 4, 2, 1 |
| 6 | 6, 3, 10, 5, 16, 8, 4, 2, 1 |
| 7 | 7, 22, 11, 34, 17, 52, 26, 13, 40, 20, 10, 5, 16, 8, 4, 2, 1 |

For each $k, n \geq 1$, let $f(k, n)$ denote the $n$th term in the sequence beginning with $k$ (we take $f(k, n) = 0$ if the sequence has fewer than $n$ terms). There is no known algebraic expression for $f(k, n)$. Yet there is a simple recursive definition of $f$, as follows:

$$f(k, 1) = k$$

$$f(1, n) = \begin{cases} 1 & \text{if } n = 1 \\ 0 & \text{if } n > 1 \end{cases}$$

$$f(k, n + 1) = \begin{cases} f(k/2, n) & \text{if } k \text{ is even} \\ f(3k + 1, n) & \text{if } k \text{ is odd} \end{cases}$$

Note that this definition allows us to compute a given element of a number sequence without requiring us to generate the sequence itself.

In each example above, the three basic elements of a recursive function definition are evident:

1. A *basis* (equivalently, "axioms" or "boundary conditions") which states that certain numbers are, by definition, values of the function for given arguments.
2. A *recursive construction rule* while tells how to determine other values of the function from the known values.
3. An understanding (or statement) that the function takes on only those values that result from finitely many applications of the recursive construction rule to the basis function values.

As will be made clearer below, a recursive definition is so formulated that it specifies an effective procedure for evaluating a function whenever the function is defined. Recursive definitions can also be used to define sets, whenever the elements of the set can be effectively enumerated. In such a case, the basis specifies that certain elements are by definition members of the set, and the recursive construction rule tells how to identify additional members by performing specified operations on the known members. Our understanding is that the set contains just those elements that can be obtained by applying the construction rule to the known members.

The recursive functions are a class of functions on the natural numbers, each of which has a recursive definition and each of which is computable by an effective procedure. The class itself has a recursive definition. We begin by defining certain functions, known as *base functions*, which we agree are members of the class and which are (obviously) computable by an effective procedure. We then define three construction rules—composition, primitive recursion, and minimalization—which define new functions in terms of those already defined. The functions so defined are called the *general recursive functions*.

We begin our studies by considering the class of functions generated from the base functions by using only the first two construction rules—

composition and recursion. This class is known as the *primitive recursive functions.*

## 13.1 Primitive Recursive Functions

We are interested in functions mapping $n$-tuples of natural numbers into natural numbers; that is, functions of the form

$$f: \mathbf{N}^n \longrightarrow \mathbf{N}, \quad n \geq 1$$

For convenience, we let

$$\mathbf{x} = (x_1, \ldots, x_n)$$

denote an element of $\mathbf{N}^n$, so that we can write $f(\mathbf{x})$ instead of $f(x_1, \ldots, x_n)$. The primitive recursive functions are a class of functions of the form $f: \mathbf{N}^n \longrightarrow \mathbf{N}$, comprising a set of *base functions* together with all other functions that can be constructed from base functions by finitely many applications of composition and recursion rules. The following base functions are primitive recursive by definition:

1. The *zero function*: $Z(x) = 0$ for all $x$ in $\mathbf{N}$. Informally, we write 0 instead of $Z(x)$.
2. The *successor function*: $S(x) = x + 1$ for all $x$ in $\mathbf{N}$. Informally, we write $x + 1$ or $x'$ instead of $S(x)$.
3. The *projection functions*: $I_k(\mathbf{x}) = x_k$, where $x = (x_1, \ldots, x_n)$ and $1 \leq k \leq n$. Informally, we write $x_k$ instead of $I_k(\mathbf{x})$. If $n = 1$, we write $I(x) = x$ and refer to $I$ as the *identify function.*

The set of base functions is countably infinite, and each is a total function.

The rules for composition and (primitive) recursion are:

1. *Composition:* Suppose the functions $g_1, \ldots, g_m$, $h$ are primitive recursive, where the domain of each $g_i$ is $\mathbf{N}^n$, and the domain of $h$ is $\mathbf{N}^m$. Then

$$f(\mathbf{x}) = h(g_1(\mathbf{x}), \ldots, g_m(\mathbf{x})) \qquad \mathbf{x} = (x_1, \ldots, x_n)$$

is primitive recursive. Since $g_1, \ldots, g_m$, $h$ are all total functions, $f$ is a total function with domain $\mathbf{N}^n$.

2. *Recursion:* Suppose $g$ and $h$ are primitive recursive functions, where the domain of $g$ is $\mathbf{N}^n$ and the domain of $h$ is $\mathbf{N}^{n+2}$. Then the pair of equations

(1) $$f(\mathbf{x}, 0) = g(\mathbf{x})$$

(2) $$f(\mathbf{x}, y + 1) = h(\mathbf{x}, y, f(\mathbf{x}, y))$$

defines a primitive recursive function with domain $\mathbf{N}^{n+1}$. Equation 1 is the *boundary condition* of the definition, and equation 2 is the *recursion equation.* Given that $g$ and $h$ are total, $f$ must also be total: note that $f(\mathbf{x}, 0) = g(\mathbf{x})$ is defined, and once $f(\mathbf{x}, y)$ has been found the value of $f(\mathbf{x}, y + 1)$ is obtained by evaluating the total function $h$. In the case $n = 0$, equations 1 and 2 assume the form

(1) $$f(0) = k, \quad \text{some fixed integer } k \geq 0$$

(2) $$f(y + 1) = h(y, f(y))$$

Since the notations $y'$ and $y + 1$ are alternatives for the successor of $y$, we often use $f(x, y')$ in place of $f(x, y + 1)$ in equation 2 of the recursion rules.

**Definition 13.1:** The class $\mathfrak{C}$ of primitive recursive functions is the smallest class of functions on the natural numbers such that:

1. Each base function is in $\mathfrak{C}$.
2. $\mathfrak{C}$ is closed under composition and recursion.

This definition provides a basis for proving that a particular function $f$ is primitive recursive: we construct a sequence of functions $f_1, \ldots, f_n$ such that $f_n = f$ and each $f_i$ is either a base function or is obtained from some subset of the functions $f_1, \ldots, f_{i-1}$ through composition or recursion. In such a case, it is easy to prove that $f$ is computable (in the informal sense), starting from the assumption that the base functions are effectively computable. One supposes by induction that algorithms for evaluating $f_1, \ldots, f_{i-1}$ have been constructed; then, according to the rules for composition and recursion, one may construct an algorithm for evaluating $f_i$ using the algorithm for $f_1, \ldots, f_{i-1}$ as subroutines. A similar argument can be used to demonstrate that the primitive recursive functions are total. However, we shall show later that primitive recursiveness is a sufficient but not a necessary condition for totality: there exist total functions that are not primitive recursive.

The following are examples of primitive recursive functions. To simplify the presentation, we use informal notation for the zero, successor, and projection functions.

**Example 13.1:** The *constant function* $C_k$ defined by

$$C_k(x) = k, \qquad \text{all } x \in \mathbf{N}$$

is primitive recursive for any $k \in \mathbf{N}$, being obtained through $k$ applications of the successor function to the zero function via composition. Formally,

$$C_k(x) = S^k(Z(x))$$

where $S^k$ denotes the $k$-fold composition of $S$ with itself.†

†For a function $f$, $f^0(x) = x$ and $f^k(x) = f(f^{k-1}(x))$, $k \geq 1$.

**Example 13.2:** Ordinary addition of integers, add $(x, y) = x + y$, is primitive recursive. An informal definition is

$$\text{add}\ (x, 0) = x$$
$$\text{add}\ (x, y + 1) = \text{add}\ (x, y) + 1$$

A formal definition is

$$\text{add}\ (x, 0) = I(x)$$
$$\text{add}\ (x, y + 1) = h(x, y, \text{add}\ (x, y))$$
$$h(x, y, z) = S(I_3(x, y, z))$$

**Example 13.3:** Ordinary multiplication of integers, mul $(x, y) = xy$, is primitive recursive. An informal definition is

$$\text{mul}\ (x, 0) = 0$$
$$\text{mul}\ (x, y + 1) = \text{mul}\ (x, y) + x$$

A formal definition is

$$\text{mul}\ (x, 0) = Z(x)$$
$$\text{mul}\ (x, y + 1) = g(x, y, \text{mul}\ (x, y))$$
$$g(x, y, z) = \text{add}\ (I_1(x, y, z), I_3(x, y, z))$$

These examples demonstrate the convenience of informal definitions for primitive recursive functions, and we shall use such definitions frequently in this chapter.

The evaluation of a primitive recursive function can be displayed conveniently as an *evaluation tree*. Suppose $\mathbf{a} = (a_1, \ldots, a_n)$ is an argument to a function $f$, where $f$ is defined by the composition

$$f(\mathbf{x}) = h(g_1(\mathbf{x}), \ldots, g_m(\mathbf{x}))$$

The subtree of Figure 13.1a illustrates the evaluation of $f(\mathbf{a})$. We evaluate each of $g_1(\mathbf{a}), \ldots, g_m(\mathbf{a})$, and substitute the results $\Delta_1, \ldots \Delta_m$ as arguments to $h$, whose evaluation yields the value $f(\mathbf{a})$. Now, suppose $f(\mathbf{a}, b)$ is to be evaluated, where $f$ is defined by recursion

$$f(\mathbf{x}, 0) = g(\mathbf{x})$$
$$f(\mathbf{x}, y + 1) = h(\mathbf{x}, y, f(\mathbf{x}, y))$$

If $b = 0$, we know immediately that $f(\mathbf{a}, b) = g(\mathbf{a})$. Otherwise, the evalution of $f(\mathbf{a}, b)$ is defined by the subtree of Figure 13.1b. We evaluate $f(\mathbf{a}, b - 1)$ and the result $\Delta$ is made the third argument to $h$, whose subsequent evaluation yields $f(\mathbf{a}, b)$. Figure 13.2 shows an evaluation of add (2, 3) and Figure 13.3 shows an evaluation of mul (2, 3).

(a) Composition

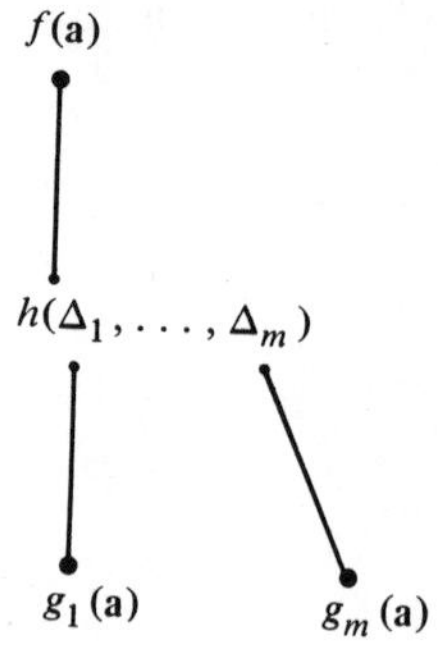


(b) Recursion

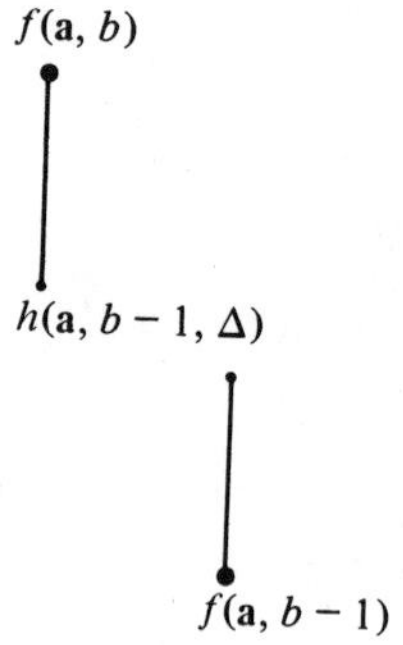


**Figure 13.1** Evaluation subtrees for primitive recursive functions.

We conclude this section with further examples of primitive recursive functions.

**Example 13.4:** The *factorial function* $\text{fac}(x) = x!$ is primitive recursive:

$$\text{fac}(0) = 1$$

$$\text{fac}(x + 1) = \text{mul}(x + 1, \text{fac}(x))$$

Thus fac is primitive recursive because mul is primitive recursive.

**Example 13.5:** The *predecessor function* prd is defined by

$$\text{prd}(x) = \begin{cases} x - 1 & \text{if } x < 0 \\ 0 & \text{if } x = 0 \end{cases}$$

This function is expressible directly by recursion:

$$\text{prd}(0) = 0$$

$$\text{prd}(x + 1) = x$$

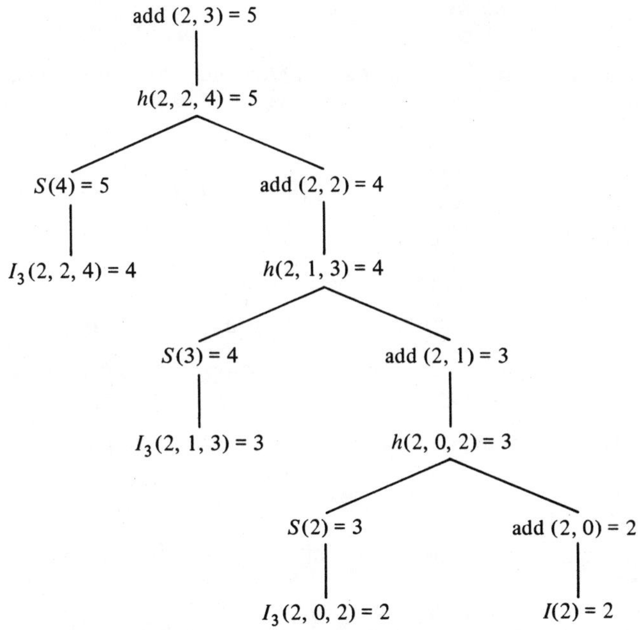


**Figure 13.2** Evaluation tree for add (2, 3).

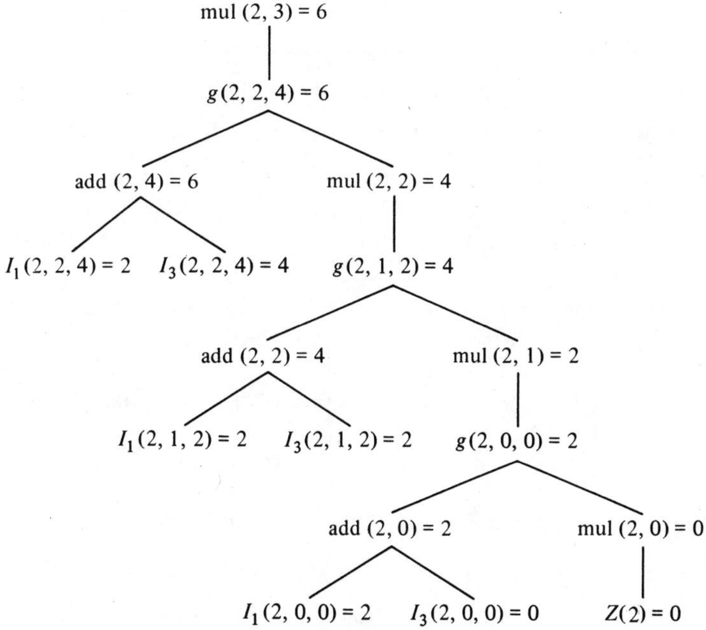


**Figure 13.3** Evaluation tree for mul (2, 3).

**Example 13.6:** The *proper subtraction operation*, or monus, is defined by

$$\text{mon}(x, y) = \begin{cases} x - y & \text{if } x > y \\ 0 & \text{if } x \leq y \end{cases}$$

Using recursion,

$$\text{mon}(x, 0) = x$$
$$\text{mon}(x, y + 1) = \text{prd}(\text{mon}(x, y))$$

To understand this last expression, suppose $x > y$ so that $x - y > 0$. Then

$$\begin{aligned} \text{mon}(x, y + 1) &= x - (y + 1) = (x - y) - 1 = \text{prd}(x - y) \\ &= \text{prd}(\text{mon}(x, y)) \end{aligned}$$

**Example 13.7:** Each of the following functions is primitive recursive:

$$\text{exp}(x, y) = x^y$$
$$\text{abs}(x, y) = |x - y|$$
$$\text{zer}(x) = \begin{cases} 1 & \text{if } x = 0 \\ 0 & \text{if } x > 0 \end{cases} \qquad \text{[zero test]}$$
$$\text{min}(x, y) = \text{smaller of } x \text{ and } y$$
$$\text{max}(x, y) = \text{larger of } x \text{ and } y$$
$$\text{rem}(x, y) = \text{remainder after dividing } x \text{ by } y$$
$$\text{quo}(x, y) = \text{quotient after dividing } x \text{ by } y$$
$$\text{equ}(x, y) = \begin{cases} 1 & \text{if } x = y \\ 0 & \text{otherwise} \end{cases} \qquad \text{[equality test]}$$

The demonstration that each of these functions is primitive recursive is left to the reader. (See Problem 13.2).

**Example 13.8:** The number of divisors of $x$ other than 1 and $x$ is

$$\text{div}(x) = \sum_{y=2}^{x-1} \text{zer}(\text{rem}(x, y))$$

which is primitive recursive because it can be defined as

$$\text{div}(x) = f(x, 2, x - 2)$$
$$f(u, v, w + 1) = f(u, v + 1, w) + \text{zer}(\text{rem}(u, v))$$
$$f(u, v, 0) = 0$$

Now, $x$ is a prime number if and only if div $(x) = 0$. Thus the *prime test* function

$$\text{prm}(x) = \begin{cases} 1 & \text{if } x \text{ is prime} \\ 0 & \text{otherwise} \end{cases}$$

is primitive recursive because

$$\text{prm}(x) = \text{zer}(\text{div}(x))$$

**Example 13.9:** A rational number is one expressible as some fraction $x/y$, where $y \neq 0$; we can represent such a rational by the pair $(x, y)$. All of the common arithmetic operations on the rational numbers are primitive recursive. For example, the product of the rationals $(a, b)$ and $(c, d)$ is the pair $(ac, bd)$. This is represented by the function mulr defined by

$$\text{mulr}((a, b), (c, d)) = (\text{mul}(a, c), \text{mul}(b, d))$$

Similarly, the sum of the rationals $(a, b)$ and $(c, d)$ is the pair $(ad + bc, bd)$. This is represented by the function sumr defined by

$$\text{sumr}((a, b), (c, d)) = (\text{add}(\text{mul}(a, d), \text{mul}(b, c)), \text{mul}(b, d))$$

These examples show the primitive recursive functions to be a rather rich class of functions. This class contains all of the common arithmetic operations on integers and rational numbers, and most functions of practical interest are known to be primitive recursive. In fact, it is so difficult to find *total* functions which are not primitive recursive that it was once thought that all total functions are primitive recursive. This is not the case, as we shall see in the following section.

## 13.2 Incompleteness of the Primitive Recursive Functions

In this section we demonstrate the existence of total functions which are not primitive recursive.† We present two arguments: a *nonconstructive* argument that demonstrates the existence of such a function without exhibiting one; and a *constructive* argument that proves that a specific, well-defined function is total but not primitive recursive. The latter argument is considerably more involved than the former.

The nonconstructive argument proceeds as follows: first, we show that there is an effective enumeration of the primitive recursive functions; then we apply a diagonalization argument to this enumeration to construct a total function that is not in the enumeration.

†This is sometimes referred to as the *incompleteness property* of the primitive recursive functions.

The definition of primitive recursive functions implies that each such function may be described by a finite system of equations. By adopting suitable encoding for variable and function symbols, for numerals, for subscripts and punctuation marks, we can express any system of equations as a single string over a finite alphabet. Once an encoding scheme has been agreed upon, it makes sense to talk about the $z$th primitive recursive function: we systematically generate all strings of lengths 1, 2, 3, . . . over the encoding alphabet, testing each in turn to determine whether it is the string representing some primitive recursive equation system; we denote by $f_z$ the function defined by the $z$th such string.

For our present purpose, it is sufficient to consider functions of one variable; we may index these so that $f_z$ as the $z$th single-variable primitive recursive function. Consider now the function $g$ defined by

$$g(z) = f_z(z) + 1, \qquad z \in \mathbf{N}$$

Certainly, $g$ is total since $f_z$ denotes some function for every $z$ and each such function is total. But $g$ cannot be in the enumeration, otherwise we would have

$$g = f_y$$

for some $y$, and hence would have

$$f_y(y) = g(y) = f_y(y) + 1$$

which is a contradiction. Thus $g$ is not primitive recursive. The reader should note the similarity between this argument and that given in Chapter 2 to establish the uncountability of the real numbers.

The diagonalization argument just given is straightforward but nonconstructive: it establishes the existence of a total function that is not primitive recursive, but gives no hint as the nature of such a function. The following argument is constructive: we give a specific system of equations and show that it defines a total function; we then show that this function "grows too fast" to be primitive recursive.

Consider the function $H$ defined by the system

(1) $$H(n', x') = H(n, H(n', x))$$

(2) $$H(n', 0) = H(n, 1)$$

(3) $$H(0, x) = x + 1$$

This system assigns values consistent with

(4) $$H(1, x) = x + 2$$

(5) $$H(2, x) = 2x + 3$$

(6) $$H(3, x) = 2^{x+3} - 3$$

(7) $$H(4, x) = 2^{2^{\cdot^{\cdot^{\cdot^{2^{16}}}}}} - 3$$

where the "height" of the exponential expression in equation 7 is $x + 1$. As suggested by equations 4—7, the first argument of $H$ regulates the rate of growth of the function: the larger this argument, the faster the function grows with $x$. The validity of equations 4—7 can be established by induction on $n$ and $x$, the basis being $H(0, x) = x + 1$ (equation 3). For example, consider equation 6 for $n = 3$. Assuming the equations hold for $n < 3$, for $x = 0$ we have

$$\begin{aligned} H(3, 0) &= H(2, 1) && \text{[equation 2]} \\ &= 2 \cdot 1 + 3 && \text{[equation 5]} \\ &= 5 \\ &= 2^{0+3} - 3 \end{aligned}$$

Now, suppose equation 6 holds for $x - 1$. Then it also holds for $x$, as follows,

$$\begin{aligned} H(3, x) &= H(2, H(3, x - 1)) && \text{[equation 1]} \\ &= 2 \cdot H(3, x - 1) + 3 && \text{[equation 5]} \\ &= 2(2^{x-1+3} - 3) + 3 && \text{[induction]} \\ &= 2^{x+3} - 6 + 3 \\ &= 2^{x+3} - 3 \end{aligned}$$

The other equations can be proved similarly.

Evidently, $H(n, x)$ grows very rapidly with $x$ for all but the smallest values of $n$. This results from $H$ being equivalent to a composition of functions. Let $f_0, f_1, \ldots, f_n, \ldots$ be a sequence of functions such that $H(n, x) = f_n(x)$ for all $n$ and $x$, and suppose $f_{n+1}(x + 1)$ is the $(x + 1)$-fold composition of $f_n$ on some argument $a$:

(8) $$f_{n+1}(x + 1) = f_n^{x+1}(a)$$

Since $f^{x+1}(a) = f(f^x(a))$, equation 8 can be rewritten

(9) $$f_{n+1}(x + 1) = f_n(f_n^x(a)) = f_n(f_{n+1}(x))$$

Substituting $H(n', x')$ for $f_{n+1}(x + 1)$ in equation 9, we see that equation 9 is equivalent to equation 1. The function $H$ is called *Ackermann's function.*

The proof that $H$ is total is a straightforward induction on $n$ and $x$, similar to that used to prove equation 6. For $n = 0$, equation 3 shows that $H(n, x) = x + 1$ is defined for all $x$. Given that $H(n, x)$ is defined for all $x$, we show that $H(n', x)$ is defined for all $x$ by induction on $x$: the basis of the induction is equation 2, and the induction step follows from equation 1. We leave the details to the reader.

The fact that $H$ is not primitive recursive follows from the following result.

**Proposition 13.1:** For every primitive recursive function $f$, there exists an integer $q$ such that, for all $\mathbf{x}$,

$$f(\mathbf{x}) < H(q, \langle \mathbf{x} \rangle)$$

where $\mathbf{x} = (x_1, \ldots, x_n)$ and

$$\langle \mathbf{x} \rangle = \sum_{i=1}^{n} x_i$$

***Proof:*** We make use of certain properties of the function $H$, stated by the following relations 10–15. After each equation we indicate the induction step required in its proof.

(10) $$H(n, x) \geq x + 1 \quad \text{all } n, x$$

Suppose $H(n, x) \geq x + 1$ for all $x$, and $H(n', x) \geq x + 1$ for all $x \leq a$. Then $H(n', a') = H(n, H(n', a)) \geq H(n', a) + 1 \geq a + 2 = a' + 1$.

(11) $$H(n, x') > H(n, x) \quad \text{all } n, x$$

Suppose $H(n, x') > H(n, x)$, all $x$, whenever $n \leq k$. Then $H(k', x') = H(k, H(k', x)) \geq H(k', x) + 1 > H(k', x)$, where equation 10 is used for the first inequality.

(12) $$H(n', x) \geq H(n, x') \quad \text{all } n, x$$

Suppose $H(n', x - 1) \geq H(n, x)$, for all $x \leq a$. Then $H(n', a) = H(n, H(n', a - 1)) \geq H(n, H(n, a)) \geq H(n, a')$, where the second inequality follows from applying equation 10 to $H(n, a)$.

(13) $$H(n', x) > H(n, x) \quad \text{all } n, x$$

By equations 11 and 12, $H(n', x) \geq H(n, x') > H(n, x)$.

(14) $H(n_1, x) + H(n_2, x) < H(q, x), \quad q = \max(n_1, n_2) + 4$, all $x$

This inequality is proved as follows:

$$\begin{aligned} H(n_1, x) + H(n_2, x) &\leq 2H(q - 4, x) && \text{[equation 13]} \\ &< 2H(q - 4, x) + 3 \\ &< H(2, \mathrm{H}(q - 4, x)) && \text{[equation 5]} \\ &< H(q - 2, \mathrm{H}(q - 1, x)) && \text{[equations 11, 13]} \\ &< H(q - 1, x + 1) && \text{[equation 1]} \\ &< H(q, x) && \text{[equation 12]} \end{aligned}$$

Finally, for all $\mathbf{x}$

(15) $$f(\mathbf{x}) < H(q, \langle \mathbf{x} \rangle) \Rightarrow (f(\mathbf{x}) + \langle \mathbf{x} \rangle) < H(q + 4, \langle \mathbf{x} \rangle)$$

This follows from equations 3 and 14:

$$f(\mathbf{x}) < H(q, \langle \mathbf{x} \rangle) \Rightarrow f(\mathbf{x}) + \langle \mathbf{x} \rangle < H(q, \langle \mathbf{x} \rangle) + \langle \mathbf{x} \rangle + 1$$
$$< H(q, \langle \mathbf{x} \rangle) + H(0, \langle \mathbf{x} \rangle) \quad \text{[equation 3]}$$
$$< H(q + 4, \langle \mathbf{x} \rangle) \quad \text{[equation 14]}$$

We turn now to the proof of the proposition. From Definition 13.1, a function $f$ is primitive recursive only if it can be derived from base functions by $k$ applications of the composition and/or recursion rules, for some $k \geq 0$. Suppose it has been proved that Proposition 13.1 holds for all primitive recursive functions derived from base functions by fewer than $k_0$ applications of composition and recursion, and suppose $f$ is derived by $k_0$ such applications. Then either

(16) $$f(\mathbf{x}) = h(g_1(\mathbf{x}), \ldots, g_m(\mathbf{x}))$$

or

(17) $$f(\mathbf{x}, 0) = g(\mathbf{x})$$
$$f(\mathbf{x}, y') = h(\mathbf{x}, y, f(\mathbf{x}, y))$$

In the case of (16), there exist by induction integers $p, r_1, \ldots, r_m$ such that, for all $\mathbf{x}$,

(18) $$g_i(\mathbf{x}) < H(r_i, \langle \mathbf{x} \rangle) \quad 1 \leq i \leq m$$

(19) $$h(\mathbf{x}) < H(p, \langle \mathbf{x} \rangle)$$

We must show that there exists an integer $q$ such that, for all $\mathbf{x}$,

(20) $$h(g_1(\mathbf{x}), \ldots, g_m(\mathbf{x})) < H(q, \langle \mathbf{x} \rangle)$$

This follows from the properties of $H$:

$$h(g_1(\mathbf{x}), \ldots, g_m(\mathbf{x})) < H(p, \sum_{i=1}^{m} g_i(\mathbf{x})) \quad \text{[equation 19]}$$
$$< H(p, \sum_{i=1}^{m} H(r_i, \langle \mathbf{x} \rangle)) \quad \text{[equations 11, 18]}$$
$$< H(p, H(r, \langle \mathbf{x} \rangle))$$
$$r = \max(r_1, \ldots, r_m) + 4(m - 1) \quad \text{[equation 14]}$$
$$< H(t, H(t + 1, \langle \mathbf{x} \rangle))$$
$$t = \max(p, r) \quad \text{[equations 11, 13]}$$
$$< H(t + 1, \langle \mathbf{x} \rangle + 1) \quad \text{[equation 1]}$$
$$< H(t + 2, \langle \mathbf{x} \rangle) \quad \text{[equation 12]}$$

Letting $q = t + 2$, we have equation 20. In the case of 17, there exist by induction integers $p$ and $r$ such that for all $\mathbf{x}, y, z$

(21) $$g(\mathbf{x}) < H(p, \langle \mathbf{x} \rangle)$$

(22) $$h(\mathbf{x}, y, z) < H(r, \langle \mathbf{x} \rangle + y + z)$$

and we must show that there exists $q$ such that for all $\mathbf{x}, y$

(23) $$f(\mathbf{x}, y) < H(q, \langle \mathbf{x} \rangle + y)$$

We prove a slightly stronger result:

(24) $$(f(\mathbf{x}, y) + \langle \mathbf{x} \rangle + y) < H(q, \langle \mathbf{x} \rangle + y) \quad \text{all } \mathbf{x}, y$$

Let $q = \max(p, r) + 5$, so that $q - 1 \geq r + 4$ and $q > p + 4$; the proof of 24 proceeds by induction on $y$. For $y = 0$:

$$\begin{aligned} f(\mathbf{x}, 0) + \langle \mathbf{x} \rangle &= g(\mathbf{x}) + \langle \mathbf{x} \rangle \\ &< H(p, \langle \mathbf{x} \rangle) + \langle \mathbf{x} \rangle && \text{[equation 21]} \\ &< H(p + 4, \langle \mathbf{x} \rangle) && \text{[equation 15]} \\ &< H(q, \langle \mathbf{x} \rangle) \end{aligned}$$

For some $y > 0$, assume $(f(\mathbf{x}, y) + \langle \mathbf{x} \rangle + y) < H(q, \langle \mathbf{x} \rangle + y)$. Then

$$\begin{aligned} f(x, y') + \langle \mathbf{x} \rangle + y + 1 &= h(\mathbf{x}, y, f(\mathbf{x}, y)) + \langle \mathbf{x} \rangle + y + 1 \\ &\leq H(r, \langle \mathbf{x} \rangle + y + f(\mathbf{x}, y)) \\ &\quad + \langle \mathbf{x} \rangle + y && \text{[equation 22]} \\ &\leq H(r, \langle \mathbf{x} \rangle + y + f(\mathbf{x}, y)) \\ &\quad + \langle \mathbf{x} \rangle + y + f(\mathbf{x}, y) \\ &< H(r + 4, \langle \mathbf{x} \rangle + y + f(\mathbf{x}, y)) \\ &&& \text{[equation 15]} \\ &< H(r + 4, H(q, \langle \mathbf{x} \rangle + y)) \\ &&& \text{[induction]} \\ &< H(q - 1, H(q, \langle \mathbf{x} \rangle + y)) \\ &< H(q, \langle \mathbf{x} \rangle + y') && \text{[equation 1]} \end{aligned}$$

This completes the proof of Proposition 13.1.

The fact that $H$ is not primitive recursive follows readily from the preceding result.

**Proposition 13.2:** The function $H$ is not primitive recursive.

***Proof:*** Suppose $H$ is primitive recursive. Then the function $f(x) = H(x, x)$ is also primitive recursive. But by Proposition 13.1, there exists $q$ such that $f(x) < H(q, x)$ for all $x$; when $x = q$, a contradiction results.

## 13.3 Mu-Recursive Functions

The class of recursive functions can be greatly enlarged by introducing the *$\mu$-operator*, or *minimalization operator*, as the basis of a third rule for constructing recursive functions.

*Minimalization*: Let $g: \mathbf{N}^{n+1} \longrightarrow \mathbf{N}$ be a total function, not necessarily primitive recursive. Define the function $f: \mathbf{N}^n \longrightarrow \mathbf{N}$ so that

$$f(\mathbf{x}) = \mu y[g(\mathbf{x}, y) = 0]$$

is the least integer $y \geq 0$ for which $g(\mathbf{x}, y) = 0$. Then $f$ is obtained from $g$ by *minimalization*.

The function $f$ can be evaluated, for a given argument $\mathbf{a}$, by evaluating $g(\mathbf{a}, y)$ for $y = 0, 1, 2, \ldots$; that is, by computing sequentially the values

$$g(\mathbf{a}, 0), g(\mathbf{a}, 1), g(\mathbf{a}, 2) \ldots$$

If $y_0$ is the first value of $y$ for which $g(\mathbf{a}, y) = 0$, we assign $f(\mathbf{a}) = y_0$. Since for some choices of $\mathbf{a}$ there may be *no* value of $y$ such that $g(\mathbf{a}, y) = 0$, it is possible that the sequence of subcomputations may be carried on indefinitely without producing a value of $f(\mathbf{a})$; thus $f$ need not be a total function. Note that if $g$ is computable, the evaluation of $f$ terminates just if $f$ is defined at the argument given.

**Definition 13.2:** The class $\mathfrak{T}$ of *$\mu$-recursive functions* is the smallest class of number theoretic functions with the following membership:

1. Every primitive recursive function is in $\mathfrak{T}$.
2. If $g$ is a total function in $\mathfrak{T}$, then the function

$$f(\mathbf{x}) = \mu y[g(\mathbf{x}, y) = 0]$$

obtained by minimalization from $g$ is in $\mathfrak{T}$.

Note that Definition 13.2 does *not* imply that the recursive functions are closed under minimalization, since $\mathfrak{T}$ may contain nontotal functions and part 2 of the definition requires that $g$ be total.

We give three examples involving the use of the $\mu$-operator. The first example demonstrates the method of evaluation, the second shows how a function may be defined by minimalization on a predicate, and the third shows that a $\mu$-recursive function need not be primitive recursive.

**Example 13.10:** The function max $(x, y)$ is primitive recursive since

$$\max(x, y) = y + (x \dot{-} y)$$

It can also be expressed using the $\mu$-operator:

$$\max(x, y) = \mu z[(x \dot{-} z) + (y \dot{-} z) = 0]$$

The function $g(x, y, z) = (x \dot{-} z) + (y \dot{-} z)$ is zero only if $z =$

max $(x, y)$. To evaluate max $(x, y)$ we evaluate $g(x, y, z)$ for $z = 0, 1, 2, \ldots$ until we obtain the value 0. For example, the evaluation of max (2, 4) requires the evaluations

$$g(2, 4, 0) = 6$$
$$g(2, 4, 1) = 4$$
$$g(2, 4, 2) = 2$$
$$g(2, 4, 3) = 1$$
$$g(2, 4, 4) = 0$$

The argument $z = 4$ is the least $z$ such that $g(2, 4, z) = 0$; thus, max $(2, 4) = 4$.

**Example 13.11:** A logical predicate can be used to define a function using the $\mu$-operator. Let $p$ be a predicate such that

$$p'(\mathbf{x}, y) = \begin{cases} 1 & \text{if } p(\mathbf{x}, y) \text{ is } \textit{true} \\ 0 & \text{if } p(\mathbf{x}, y) \text{ is } \textit{false} \end{cases}$$

is a total $\mu$-recursive function. Then the function $f$ defined by

$$f(\mathbf{x}) = \text{least } y \text{ such that } p(\mathbf{x}, y) \text{ is } \textit{true}$$

is $\mu$-recursive since $f$ can be defined

$$f(\mathbf{x}) = \mu y[g(\mathbf{x}, y) = 0]$$

where $g$ is the function

$$g(\mathbf{x}, y) = \text{abs}\,(p'(\mathbf{x}, y), 1)$$

In such a case, we usually write

$$f(\mathbf{x}) = \mu y[p(\mathbf{x}, y)]$$

For example, suppose $p$ is the predicate

$$p(x, y) = \begin{cases} \textit{true} & \text{if } y \text{ is a prime number greater than } x \\ \textit{false} & \text{otherwise} \end{cases}$$

Then the function

$$f(x) = \mu y[p(x, y)]$$

is the function which, for argument $x$, returns the least prime number greater than $x$.

**Example 13.12:** The previous two examples defined total $\mu$-recursive functions. The function

$$f(x) = \mu y[\text{rem}\,(x, 2) + y = 0]$$

is a simple example of a partial function, being

$$f(x) = \begin{cases} 0 & \text{if } x \text{ is even} \\ \text{undefined} & \text{if } x \text{ is odd} \end{cases}$$

Since $f$ is partial, $f$ is not primitive recursive.

Later in this chapter, we show that recursive functions are Turing computable. However, for this to be the case, we must insist that the $\mu$-operator be applied only to total functions. To see this, let $h(z)$ denote the result of applying to blank tape the $z$th Turing machine in some enumeration of Turing machines:

$$h(z) = \begin{cases} \omega & \text{if } \mathbf{M}_z \text{ halts with tape } \omega \text{ when started on blank tape} \\ \text{undefined} & \text{otherwise} \end{cases}$$

Define a function $g$ so that $g(z, y) = 0$ if $y = 1$ or if both $y = 0$ and $h(z)$ is defined; $g(z, y)$ is undefined otherwise. Clearly, $g$ is computable: $g(z, 0)$ is computed by simulating $\mathbf{M}_z$ on blank tape, and $g(z, y)$ is trivially computable for all $y \neq 0$. Now define a function $f$ as follows:

$$f(z) = \mu y[g(z, y) = 0]$$

The function $f$ is total: $f(z) = 0$ if $g(z, 0) = 0$ (that is, if $\mathbf{M}_z$ halts on blank tape), otherwise $f(z) = 1$. But $f$ cannot be computable, for we could then use $f$ to solve the blank tape halting problem, which we know is unsolvable. Thus, applying the $\mu$-operator to nontotal functions may yield noncomputable functions.

## 13.4 Multiple-Recursive Functions

According to our earlier remarks, a function is recursive just if it is the last in a sequence of functions, each of which is a base function or is obtained from its predecessors in the sequence by the rules of composition, recursion, or minimalization. In our examples, we have displayed such functions as systems of equations. We consider now an approach in which we specify directly the structure of an equation system that defines a recursive function. One aspect of this approach is that a function may be defined in terms of itself, something not permitted in our earlier formulation.

As a generalization of our notion of recursion, we shall permit recursion simultaneously on more than one variable in a function definition. If a function has recursion defined on $k$ of its variables, we say that $f$ is *k-fold recursive*, or simply *multiple recursive*. As we shall see, multiple recursion allows us to define partial recursive functions without the use of the $\mu$-operator.

An example should clarify the nature of the new formulation. Consider the system of equations

(1) $$f(x', y', z) = z + f(x, y, z)$$

(2) $$f(x', 0, z) = 0$$

(3) $$f(0, y', z) = 1$$

(4) $$f(0, 0, z) = 2$$

Equation 1 is called the *principal equation* for $f$, and equations 2–4 are called the *boundary equations* for $f$. This function is defined using 2-fold recursion on the variables $x$ and $y$. The boundary equations account for the three possible ways in which a boundary condition—either or both of $x$ and $y$ become zero—can occur during an evaluation. (In general, a $k$-fold recursive definition requires as many as $2^k - 1$ boundary equations.) The reader may verify that

$$f(x, y, z) = z \min(x, y) + \begin{cases} 1 & \text{if } y > x \\ 0 & \text{if } y < x \\ 2 & \text{if } y = x \end{cases}$$

The equation systems which define multiple-recursive functions have the following constituents:

variable symbols $x_1, x_2, \ldots$

vectors of variable symbols $\mathbf{x}_1, \mathbf{x}_2, \ldots$

function symbols $f_1, f_2, \ldots$

base function applications $Z(x)$, $S(x)$, $I_k(\mathbf{x})$

An *equation* is an expression of the form

$$f(\mathbf{w}) = h(g_1(\mathbf{x}), \ldots, g_m(\mathbf{x}))$$

where $f, h, g_1, \ldots, g_m$ are function symbols and $\mathbf{x}$ is a vector consisting of those variable symbols $x_i$ for which $w_i \neq 0$ (that is, $\mathbf{x} = (x_{i_1}, \ldots, x_{i_r})$ where $w_{i_1}, \ldots, w_{i_r}$ are the nonzero elements of $\mathbf{w}$). Such an equation is called a *declaration* of the function $f$. An *equation system* **E** is a finite set of equations; the function declared in the first equation of **E** is the function *defined by* **E**. An equation system is *closed* if each function symbol in the right part of an equation is declared in the system or is a base function symbol.

A closed equation system is analogous to a closed collections of subroutines in a programming language, the collection being closed under the operation of subroutine call. In subsequent discussions, we assume that all equation systems are closed.

Let $\mathbf{a} = (a_1, \ldots, a_n)$ be an $n$-tuple of natural numbers, let **E** be an equation system defining a $k$-fold recursive function $f$, $k \geq 0$, and suppose $f(\mathbf{a})$ is to be evaluated. An equation $f(\mathbf{w}) = h(g_1(\mathbf{x}), \ldots, g_m(\mathbf{x}))$ *applies to* $f(\mathbf{a})$ whenever

$$\begin{aligned} w_i = x_i' &\Rightarrow a_i > 0 \\ w_i = x_i &\Rightarrow a_i \geq 0 \qquad 1 \leq i \leq n \\ w_i = 0 &\Rightarrow a_i = 0 \end{aligned}$$

In equations 1–4, for example, the applicable equation to each of the following cases is

| $f(\mathbf{a})$ | equation |
|---|---|
| $f(0, 4, 2)$ | 3 |
| $f(0, 0, 3)$ | 4 |
| $f(4, 1, 2)$ | 1 |
| $f(3, 0, 1)$ | 2 |
| $f(3, 0, 0)$ | 2 |

A function $f\colon \mathbf{N}^n \to \mathbf{N}$ is *properly defined* in a system if, for each $\mathbf{a} \in \mathbf{N}^n$, exactly one equation applies to $f(\mathbf{a})$. If $\mathbf{E}$ is an equation system defining a $k$-fold recursive function, then function $f$ is properly defined in $\mathbf{E}$ only if $\mathbf{E}$ contains a principal equation for $f$ and at most $2^k - 1$ boundary equations for $f$. We say that $\mathbf{E}$ is *proper* if all functions declared in $\mathbf{E}$ are properly defined; hereafter, we assume that all equation systems are proper.

The evaluation of a function $f$ in an equation can be illustrated by evaluation trees as discussed earlier. Suppose we have determined that

$$f(\mathbf{w}) = h(g_1(\mathbf{x}), \ldots, g_m(\mathbf{x}))$$

is applicable to $f(\mathbf{a})$. Let $w_{i_1}, \ldots, w_{i_r}$ be the nonzero elements of $\mathbf{w}$. (Thus $\mathbf{x}$ is an $r$-tuple.) Define the $r$-tuple $\mathbf{b} = (b_1, \ldots, b_r)$ in which

$$b_j = \begin{cases} a_{i_j} & \text{if } w_{i_j} = x^{i}{}_{j} \\ a_{i_j} - 1 & \text{if } w_{i_j} = x'_{i_j} \end{cases} \quad 1 \le j \le r$$

We evaluate $g_1(\mathbf{b}), \ldots, g_m(\mathbf{b})$, constructing the $m$-tuple $\mathbf{c} = (c_1, \ldots, c_m)$ in which

$$c_i = g_i(\mathbf{b}) \quad 1 \le i \le m$$

We then evaluate $h(\mathbf{c})$ and assign

$$f(\mathbf{a}) = h(\mathbf{c})$$

Figure 13.4 illustrates this procedure as a step in the construction of an evaluation tree.

The system of equations 1–4 clearly defines a total function because, for each choice of numerical elements, the evaluation tree is finite. However, the system

$$f(x') = g(x)$$

$$f(0) = 0$$

$$g(x') = f(x)$$

$$g(0) = f(1)$$

defines the partial function

$$f(x) = \begin{cases} 0 & \text{if } x \text{ is even} \\ \text{undefined} & \text{if } x \text{ is odd} \end{cases}$$

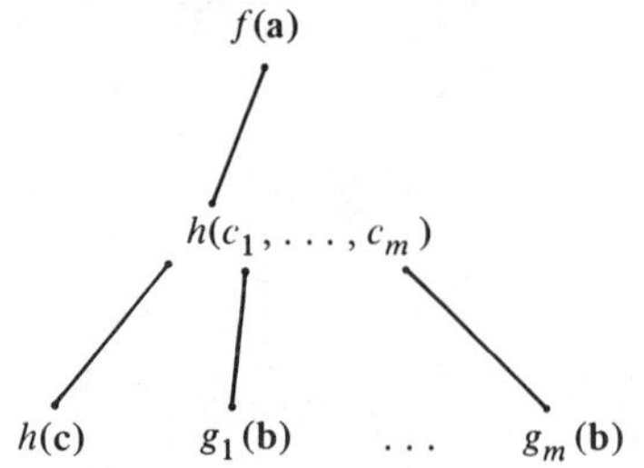


**Figure 13.4** Evaluation of a multiple recursive function.

When $x$ is odd, an evaluation tree for $f(x)$ will eventually contain $g(0)$; thereafter, the evaluation loops between $g(0)$ and $f(1)$, never terminating. Since these equation systems may define partial functions even under 1-fold recursion, 1-fold recursive functions are not necessarily primitive recursive. (The reason is that a 1-fold recursive function may be defined in terms of itself, which is not permitted by the rules of primitive recursion.)

**Definition 13.3:** The class of *multiple-recursive functions*, denoted $\mathfrak{T}_m$, is the smallest class of functions defined by proper, closed recursive equation systems.

As before, we make liberal use of informal notation in these equation systems with the understanding that we could, if so desired, construct a corresponding formal representation. For example, equations 1–4 could be expressed formally as

$$\begin{aligned} f(x', y', z) &= \text{add}\,(I_3(x, y, z), f(x, y, z)) \\ f(x', 0, z) &= Z(I_1(x, z)) \\ f(0, y', z) &= S(Z(I_1(y, z)) \\ f(0, 0, z) &= S(S(Z(z))) \\ \text{add}(x', y) &= S(\text{add}(x, y)) \\ \text{add}\,(0, y) &= I(I(y)) \end{aligned}$$

For larger equation systems, the formal notation can become extremely unwieldy!

We show now that the class of recursive functions is contained in the class of multiple-recursive functions. We state this as

**Proposition 13.3:** Let $\mathfrak{T}$ be the class of $\mu$-recursive functions (Definition 13.2), and let $\mathfrak{T}_m$ be the class of multiple-recursive functions (Definition 13.3). Then $\mathfrak{T} \subseteq \mathfrak{T}_m$.

***Proof:*** Clearly, the operations of composition and (1-fold) primitive recursion are directly expressible in the formalism of multiple-recursive equation systems. Thus, we need only show how to express an equation of the form

$$(6) \qquad f(\mathbf{x}) = \mu y[g(\mathbf{x}, y) = 0]$$

within the framework of multiple recursion. Let equation 6 be replaced by the equations

$$(7) \qquad \begin{aligned} f(\mathbf{x}) &= h(g(\mathbf{x}, 0), \mathbf{x}, 0) \\ h(0, \mathbf{x}, y) &= y \\ h(u', \mathbf{x}, y) &= h(g(\mathbf{x}, y'), \mathbf{x}, y') \end{aligned}$$

where $h$ is a new function symbol. Suppose $\mathbf{a}$ is given, $f(\mathbf{a})$ is to be evaluated, and $y_0$ is the smallest value of $y$ for which $g(\mathbf{a}, y) = 0$. We must show that $f(\mathbf{a}) = y_0$ is assigned by equation 7. The evaluation tree for $f(\mathbf{a})$ takes the form shown in Figure 13.5. As long as $g(\mathbf{a}, y) > 0$, the principal $h$ equation is applicable and the tree for $f(\mathbf{a})$ progresses one level deeper; the last argument $y$ of $h$ counts the depth of the tree. As soon as $g(\mathbf{a}, y) = 0$, the depth of the tree is $y_0$, the boundary condition $h$ equation becomes applicable, and the

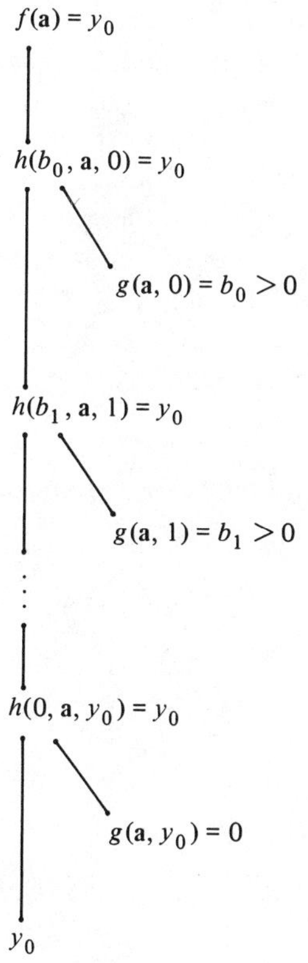


**Figure 13.5** Simulation of the $\mu$-operator.

value $y_0$ is assigned to $f(\mathbf{a})$. If there is no $y$ such that $g(\mathbf{a}, y) = 0$, the evaluation tree will not terminate and $f(\mathbf{a})$ is undefined as required by equation 6.

## 13.5 Evaluation of Recursive Functions by Turing Machines

Our objective in this section is to show that every multiple recursive function can be evaluated by some Turing machine.

> **Proposition 13.3:** Let $\mathfrak{F}_T$ be the class of Turing-computable functions, and $\mathfrak{F}_m$ the class of multiple-recursive functions. Then $\mathfrak{F}_m \subseteq \mathfrak{F}_T$.

Let **E** be an equation system defining a recursive function $f$. We must show that $f$ is computed by some Turing machine **M**. The technique we use in the construction of **M** is similar to that used in implementing recursive procedures in such programming languages as Algol. For each function declared in **E**, **M** will have a *procedure* (subroutine) which carries out an evaluation according to the function's definition in **E**. During an evaluation, a procedure in **M** may call other procedures, itself included; thus we require mechanisms for procedure call, procedure return, and argument passing. The Turing machine tape will be used to provide private storage for the instances of procedure calls (that is, for procedure *activations*).

Let **E** be the given equation system, and let the equations of **E** be numbered 1, 2, 3, . . . with equation 1 being the declaration of the function defined by **E**. Let $g$ be a $k$-fold recursive function, $k \geq 0$, declared in **E**. Without loss of generality, we suppose that the first $k$ variables of $g$ are the recursion variables, that is, that the left part of the principal $g$ equation is of the form

$$g(x'_1, \ldots, x'_k, x_{k+1}, \ldots, x_n)$$

The procedure for evaluating $g(\mathbf{a})$ for a given argument $\mathbf{a}$ consists of these steps:

*Step 1:* Construction of the vector $\mathbf{b}$ whose components are

$$(1) \qquad b_j = \begin{cases} a_j - 1 & \text{if } a_j > 0, \quad 1 \leq j \leq k \\ \text{omitted} & \text{if } a_j = 0, \quad 1 \leq j \leq k \\ a_j & \qquad\qquad\quad k < j \leq n \end{cases}$$

*Step 2:* Determination of the $g$ equation

$$g(\mathbf{w}) = h(g_1(\mathbf{x}), \ldots, g_n(\mathbf{x}))$$

applicable to $\mathbf{a}$.

*Step 3:* The computation of $c_j = g_j(\mathbf{b})$, for $j = 1, \ldots, n$.

*Step 4:* The computation of $h(\mathbf{c})$, $\mathbf{c} = (c_1, \ldots, c_n)$, and the assignment of $h(\mathbf{c})$ to $g(\mathbf{a})$.

An integer $x \geq 0$ will be represented by the notation $01^{x+1}$, and the vector $\mathbf{x} = (x_1, \ldots, x_n)$ by the string

(2) $$01^{x_1+1}01^{x_2+1} \ldots 01^{x_n+1}$$

As we shall see, the machine **M** occasionally erases parts of a number's representation; it does this by overprinting the special symbol $\Delta$. All routines of **M** will ignore the symbol $\Delta$, which is thus an "invisible" symbol. A string over $\{0, 1, \Delta\}$ is a valid representation of **x** if, when invisible symbols are ignored, the resulting string is of the form 2. Figure 13.6 shows the notation used in diagrams of the machine's operation.

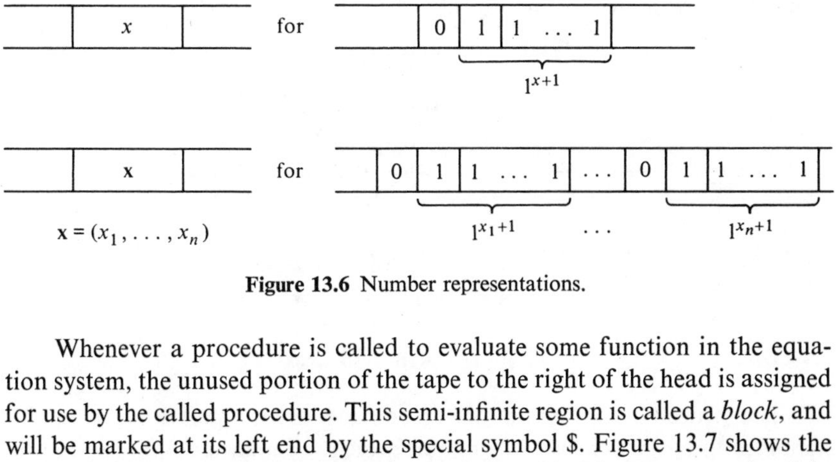


**Figure 13.6** Number representations.

Whenever a procedure is called to evaluate some function in the equation system, the unused portion of the tape to the right of the head is assigned for use by the called procedure. This semi-infinite region is called a *block*, and will be marked at its left end by the special symbol \$. Figure 13.7 shows the conventions for calling procedure $g$ to evaluate $g(\mathbf{a})$. The square to the right of \$ contains $q$, the name of the Turing machine state to which control will be returned when evaluation of $g(\mathbf{a})$ is complete. The operation

**setup** $(q, \mathbf{a})$

causes a block to be allocated for $g$ with return state $q$ and argument **a**. The operation

**goto** $q_g$

causes **M** to enter state $q_g$, the initial state of procedure $g$. When execution of $g$ is completed, a return routine is executed which erases the pair (\$, $q$) and leaves **M** in state $q$; the result $g(\mathbf{a})$ will then be to the right of the tape head.

(a) To initiate procedure activation: **setup**($q$, **a**); **goto** $q_g$.

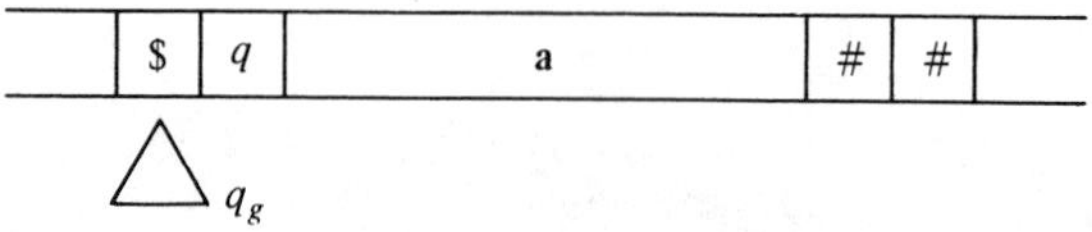


(b) To complete procedure activation: **return**.

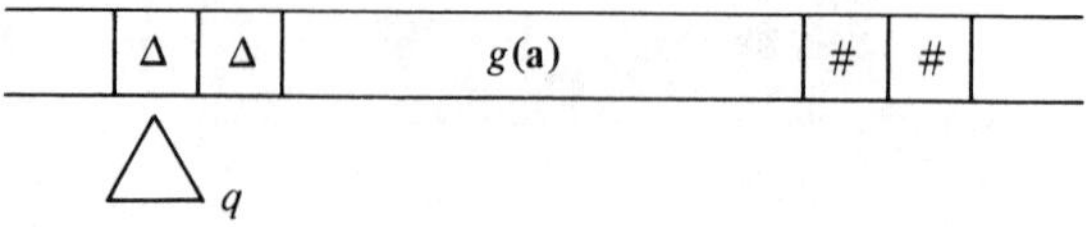


**Figure 13.7** Procedure activation.

The return routine is shown in Figure 13.8.† The initial and final configurations of **M** are shown in Figure 13.9.

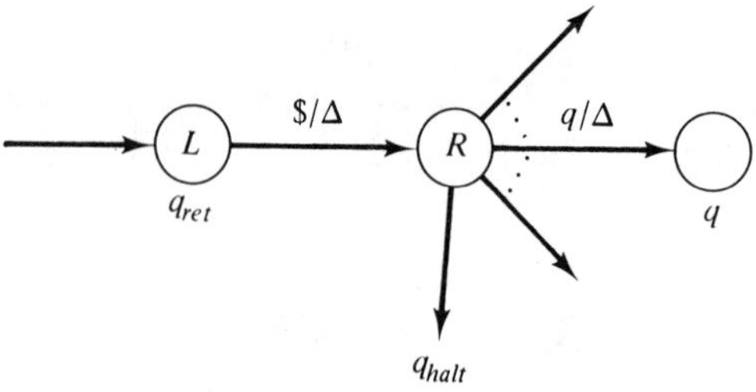


**Figure 13.8** Return routine.

The procedure for evaluating $g$ consists of two parts: the *preamble* examines the argument **a** to determine which $g$ equation applies to **a**, and transforms **a** into the vector **b** of equation 1; the *evaluator* evaluates $f$(**a**) according to the applicable equation of **E**.

The execution of the preamble is suggested by Figure 13.10, where we have used a binary decision tree consisting of decision routines **D**. The initial state of the procedure for $g$ is the initial state of the routine at the root of the tree. The routines at the $j$th level from the root, $1 \leq j \leq k$, test whether or not $a_j = 0$, and the path followed through the tree determines which $g$ equation is applicable to the given argument **a**. If the applicable $g$ equation is

†Recall that missing transitions in a Turing machine state diagram are assumed to be self-loops: the machine remains in a given state, moving in the direction indicated, until it detects a symbol labelling an exit transition.

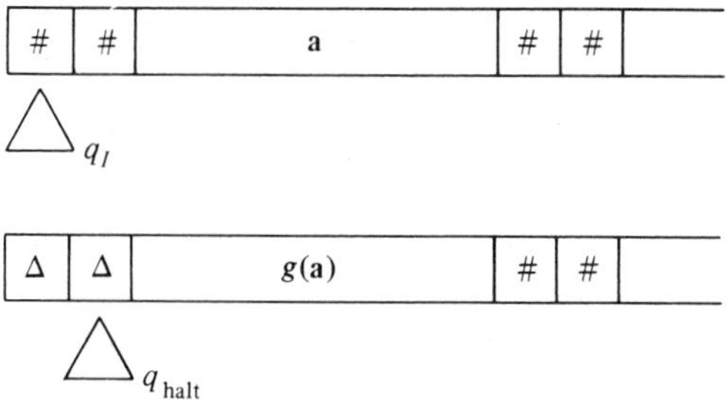


**Figure 13.9** Initial and final configurations of **M**.

equation $i$, the path terminates in state $p_i$, the initial state of the routine in the evaluator corresponding to the $i$th equation. During the testing of $a_1$, . . . , $a_k$, the routines perform the steps of transforming **a** into the vector **b**. If $a_j > 0$, the reduction of $a_j$ to $a_j - 1$ is effected by erasing the first 1 in the representation of $a_j$. If $a_j = 0$, the variable $x_j$ does not appear in the right side of the $i$th equation, and the entire representation 01 must be erased. The state diagram of a routine **D** is shown in Figure 13.10b, and the effect of performing the computation of **D** on $a_j$ is shown in Figure 13.10c.

The evaluator portion of procedure $g$ consists of a routine for each $g$ equation in **E**. Suppose the $i$th equation of **E** is

$$g(\mathbf{w}) = h(g_1(\mathbf{x}), \ldots, g_n(\mathbf{x}))$$

We associate with this equation the special states of the machine

$$p_i, q_{i,0}, q_{i,1}, \ldots, q_{i,n}, r_i$$

Figure 13.11 shows the appearances of these states in machine configurations arising in the evaluation of $f(\mathbf{a})$. The figure shows that these routines are required in the machine:

| Initial State | Description | Purpose |
|---|---|---|
| $p_i$ | **initialize**($*$, $r_i$)<br>**goto** $q_{i,0}$ | Mark by $*$ the end of vector **b**, enter state $q_{i,0}$. |
| $q_{i,j-1}$  $1 \leq j \leq n$ | **setup**($q_{i,j}$, **b**);<br>**goto** $q_{g_j}$ | Call procedure $g_j$ with argument **b**, compute $c_j = g_j(\mathbf{b})$. |
| $q_{i,n}$ | change $*$ to \$;<br>**goto** $q_h$ | Call procedure $h$ with argument **c**. |
| $r_i$ | copy result;<br>**goto** $q_{ret}$ | Move $h(\mathbf{c})$ into the proper position, enter initial state of return routine. |

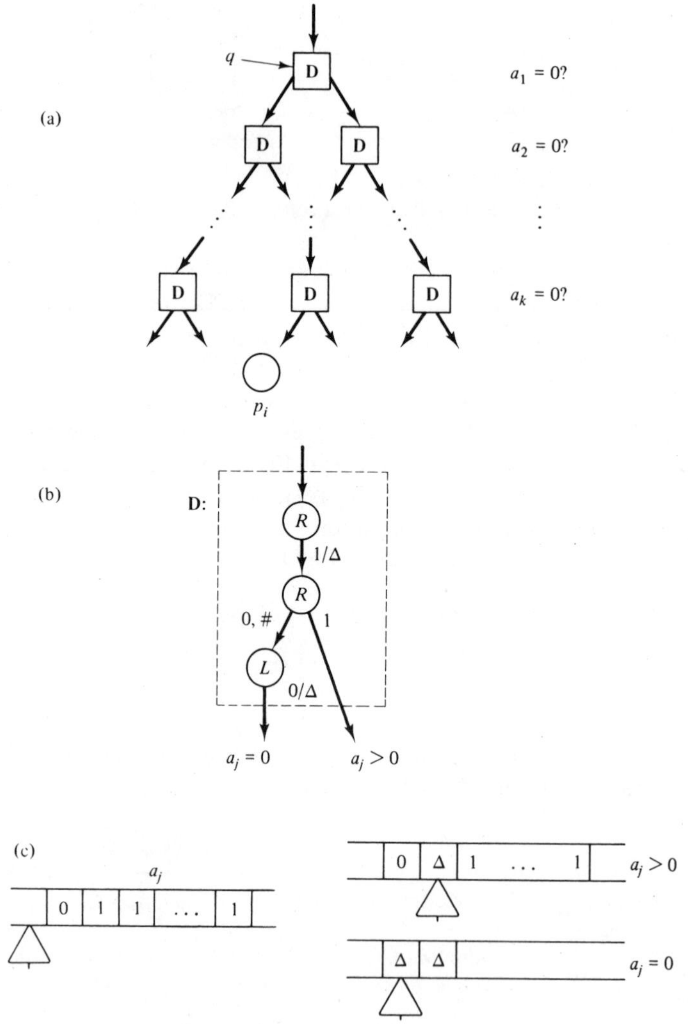


**Figure 13.10** Preamble portion of procedure *g*.

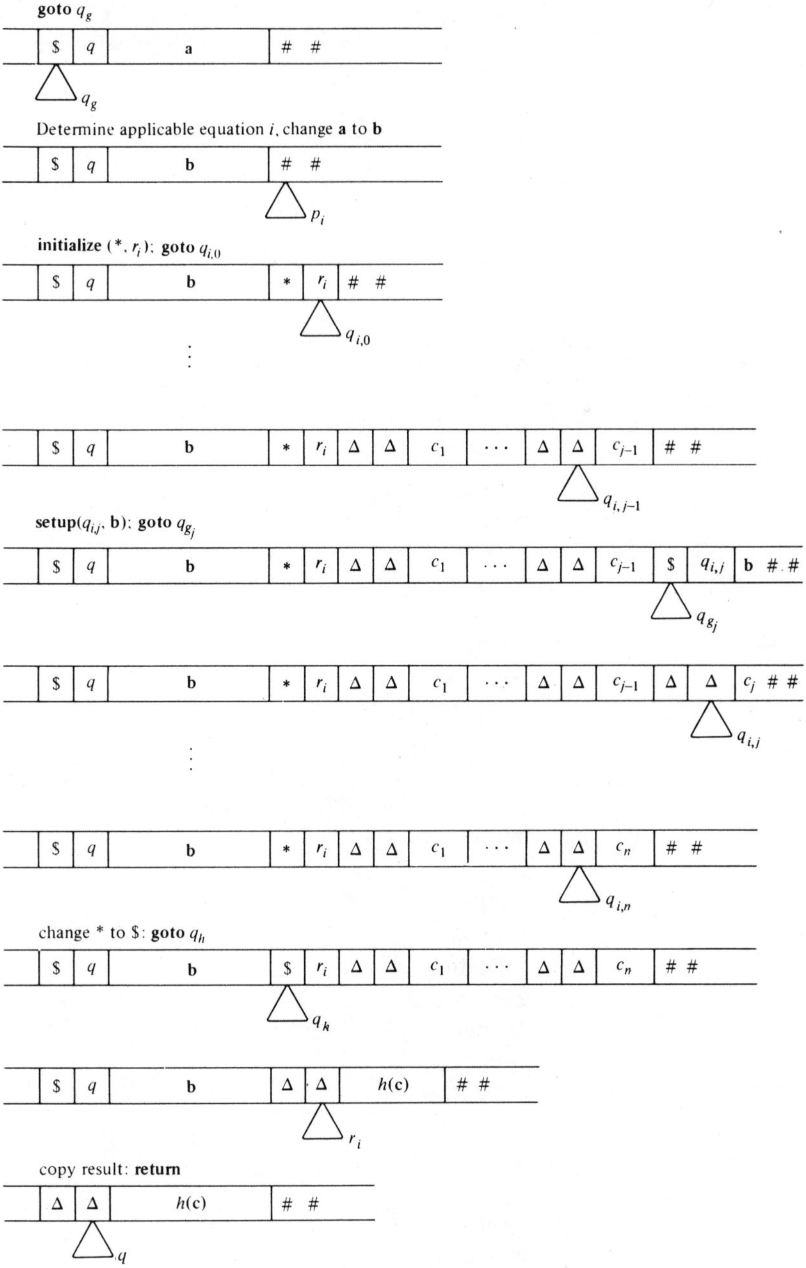


**Figure 13.11** Machine configurations.

The state diagrams for these routines are given in Figure 13.12. The construction of **M** is completed with the routines shown in Figure 13.13, which implement the base functions.

**Example 13.13:** Consider this equation system, which defines the function $f(x, y) = xy' = xy + x$:

(1) $f(x, y) = \text{add}(\text{mul}(x, y), I_1(x, y))$
(2) $\text{mul}(x', y) = \text{add}(\text{mul}(x, y), I_2(x, y))$
(3) $\text{mul}(0, y) = Z(I(y))$

For convenience, we treat add as a base function. The routines for evaluating $f$ are summarized as the sequence of statements below and the evaluation of $f(1, 2) = 3$ is shown in Figure 13.14.

$q_f$: **goto** $p_1$;
$p_1$: **initialize** $(*, r_1)$;
**goto** $q_{1,0}$
$q_{1,0}$: **setup** $(q_{1,1}, \mathbf{b})$;
**goto** $q_{\mathbf{mul}}$;
$q_{1,1}$: **setup** $(q_{1,2}, \mathbf{b})$;
**goto** $q_{I_1}$;
$q_{1,2}$: change $*$ to \$;
**goto** $q_{\mathbf{add}}$;
$r_1$: copy result;
**return;**
$q_{\mathbf{mul}}$: **if** $a_1 > 0$ **then** $\{a_1 := a_1 - 1$; **goto** $p_2\}$
**else** {erase $a_1$; **goto** $p_3$}
$p_2$: **initialize** $(*, r_2)$;
**goto** $q_{2,0}$;
$q_{2,0}$: **setup** $(q_{2,1}, \mathbf{b})$;
**goto** $q_{\mathbf{mul}}$;
$q_{2,1}$: **setup** $(q_{2,2}, \mathbf{b})$;
**goto** $q_{I_2}$;
$q_{2,2}$: change $*$ to \$;
**goto** $q_{\mathbf{add}}$;
$r_2$: copy result;
**return;**
$p_3$: **initialize** $(*, r_3)$;
**goto** $q_{3,0}$;
$q_{3,0}$: **setup** $(q_{3,1}, \mathbf{b})$;
**goto** $q_{I_1}$;
$q_{3,1}$: change $*$ to \$;
**goto** $q_Z$;
$r_3$: copy result;
**return**

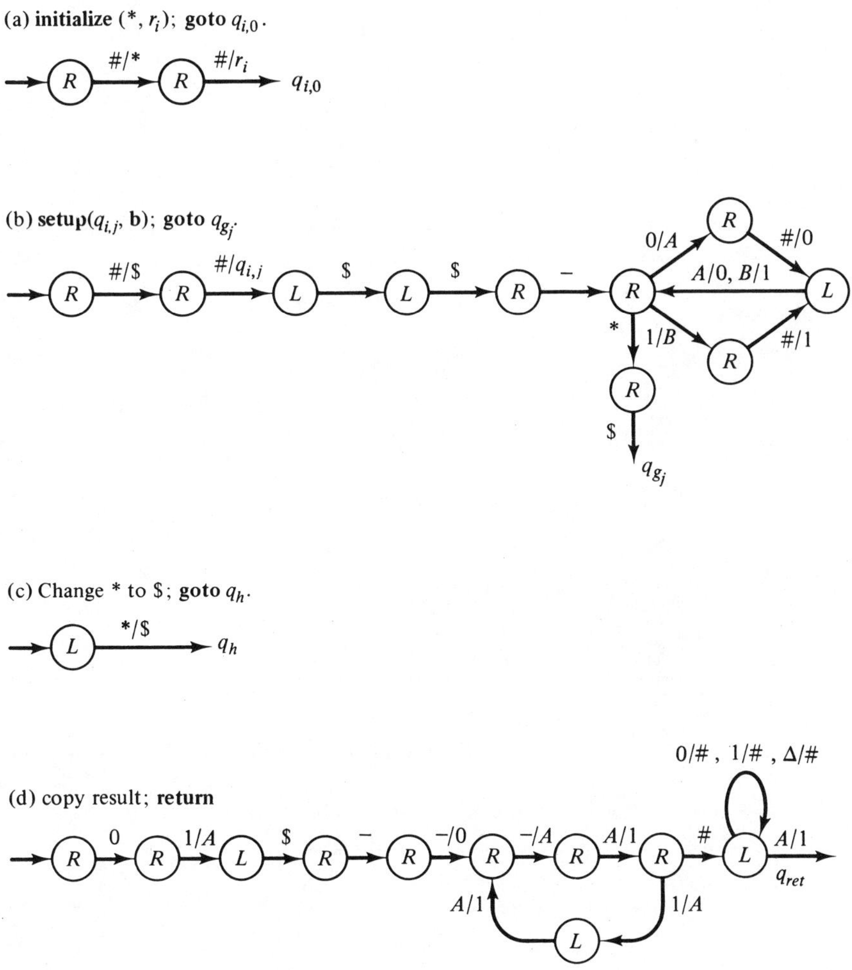


**Figure 13.12** State diagrams of evaluator routines.

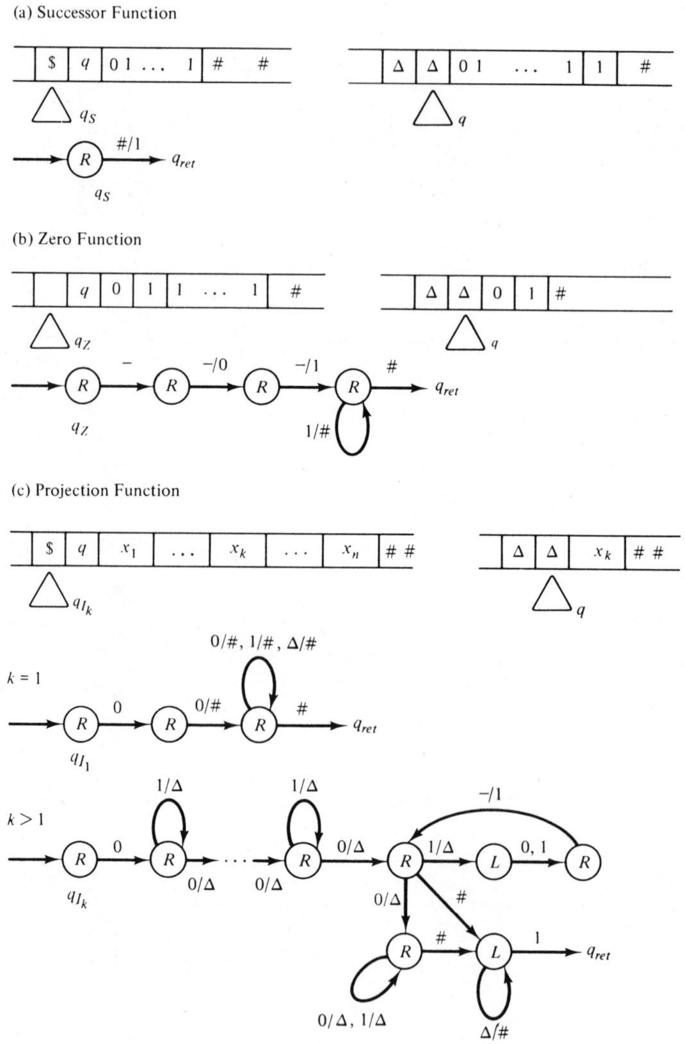


**Figure 13.13** Base functions.

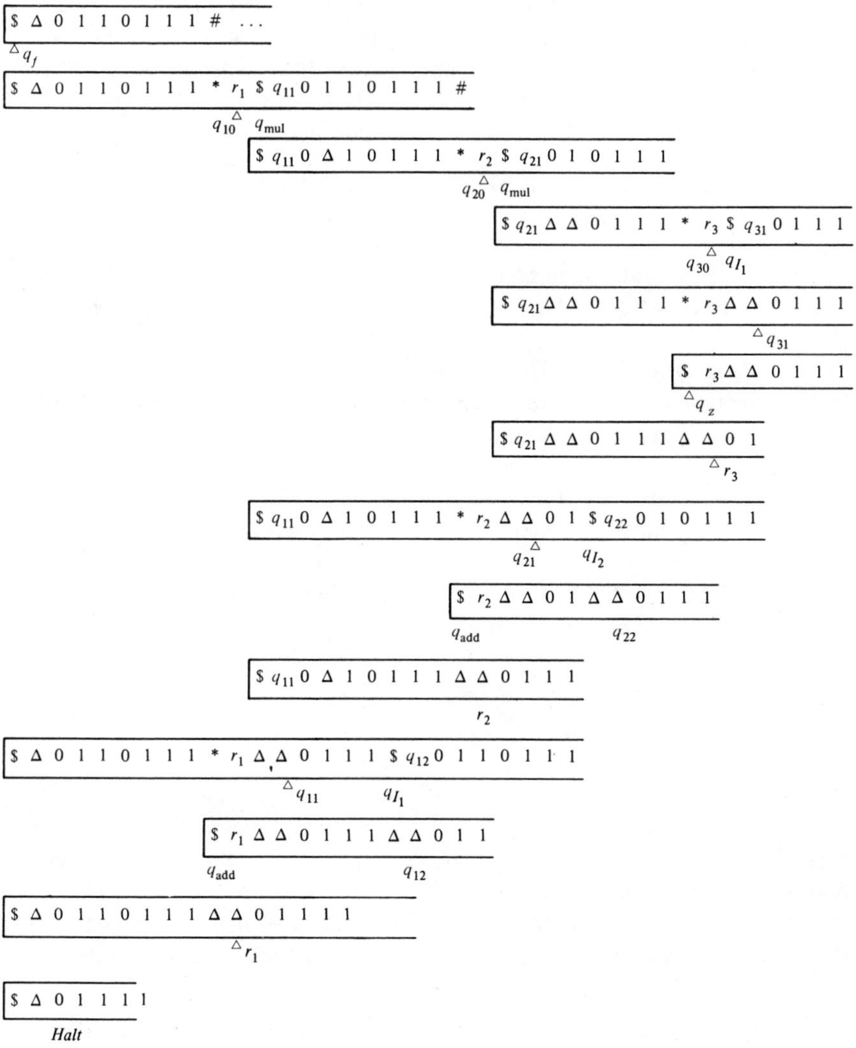

**Figure 13.14** Evaluation of a recursive function.

## 13.6 Simulation of Turing Machines by Recursive Functions

Suppose $\mathbf{M} = (\mathbf{Q}, \mathbf{S}, \mathbf{P}, q_I)$ is an $n$-state Turing machine. Without loss of generality, we may assume that $\mathbf{M}$ uses just the symbols $\{0, 1\}$, with 0 being the blank symbol of the machine, and that $\mathbf{M}$ has a special state which it enters just if it halts (see Problem 11.17 and Example 12.1). We have seen that $\mathbf{M}$ computes a function $f_{\mathbf{M}}\colon \mathbf{S}^* \longrightarrow \mathbf{S}^*$ defined by

$$(1) \qquad f_{\mathbf{M}}(\omega) = \begin{cases} \gamma & \text{if } \mathbf{M}\text{, started on tape } \omega\text{, halts with tape } \gamma \\ \text{undefined} & \text{if } \mathbf{M}\text{, started on tape } \omega\text{, fails to halt} \end{cases}$$

We shall show that there exists a recursive function whose definition is equivalent to equation 1. That is, we shall establish the following result:

> **Proposition 13.4:** The function defined by any Turing machine is recursive. If $\mathfrak{T}_T$ is the class of Turing computable functions and $\mathfrak{T}$ is the class of $\mu$-recursive functions, then $\mathfrak{T}_T \subseteq \mathfrak{T}$.

Since recursive functions map natural numbers into natural numbers, whereas Turing machines map tapes into tapes, we must represent Turing machine tapes by natural numbers that will be arguments to corresponding recursive functions. To construct a recursive function equivalent to $f_{\mathbf{M}}$, we require mappings $d$ and $e$ to complete this diagram:

$$\begin{array}{ccc} \mathbf{N} & \xrightarrow{\;f\;} & \mathbf{N} \\ {\scriptstyle e}\uparrow & & \downarrow{\scriptstyle d} \\ \{0, 1\}^* & \xrightarrow[f_{\mathbf{M}}]{} & \{0, 1\}^* \end{array}$$

In the diagram, $e$ is an encoding function mapping tapes into natural numbers, $f$ is a recursive function equivalent to $f_{\mathbf{M}}$, and $d$ is a decoding function mapping natural numbers into tapes.

The encoding and decoding functions can be specified independently of the Turing machine $\mathbf{M}$. If $s_0, s_1, \ldots, s_k, \ldots$ is the sequence of symbols on a tape of $\mathbf{M}$, then the integer

$$(2) \qquad x = \sum s_k 2^k$$

uniquely represents the tape. The encoding function $e\colon \{0, 1\}^* \longrightarrow \mathbf{N}$ maps binary strings into integers according to equation 2; expressed in the form of a recursive function it is

$$(3) \qquad \begin{aligned} e(s \cdot \omega) &= s + 2e(\omega) \\ e(\lambda) &= 0 \end{aligned}$$

where $\omega$ is a binary string and $s \in \{0, 1\}$.† The decoding function $d\colon \mathbf{N} \longrightarrow \{0, 1\}^*$ maps integers into binary strings with the least significent digits leftmost; the function $d$ can be expressed

$$d(x') = \text{rem}(x', 2) \cdot d\left(\left[\frac{x'}{2}\right]\right)$$

$$d(0) = \lambda$$

where the dot $(\cdot)$ is concatenation, and, for any real number $x$, $[x]$ is the least integer $\leq x$.

The recursive function equivalent to $f_{\mathbf{M}}$ will simulate $\mathbf{M}$'s moves on encodings of $\mathbf{M}$'s configurations. We encode a configuration $(\omega, q, t, \psi)$ of $\mathbf{M}$ by the triple $(x, y, z)$ of integers in which

$x = e(\omega t \psi)$ represents the Turing machine tape

$y \in \{0, 1, \ldots, n - 1\}$ represents $\mathbf{M}$'s state $q$

$z = |\omega|$ represents the position of $\mathbf{M}$'s tape head

In the constructions that follow, we assume that $\mathbf{M}$'s initial state is represented by the integer 0 and $\mathbf{M}$'s special halting state by the integer 1.

The construction of the recursive function $f$ is straightforward. We begin by defining three functions

$$\text{(4)} \qquad \text{direction}\,(y) = \begin{cases} 1 & \text{if } y \text{ is a right state of } \mathbf{M} \\ 0 & \text{if } y \text{ is a left state of } \mathbf{M} \end{cases}$$

$$\text{(5)} \qquad \text{symbol}\,(y, s) = r, \quad \text{if } \mathbf{M} \text{ prints } r \text{ when scanning symbol } s \text{ in state } y \text{ of } \mathbf{M}$$

$$\text{(6)} \qquad \text{state}\,(y, s) = x, \quad \text{if } \mathbf{M} \text{ enters state } x \text{ after scanning symbol } s \text{ in state } y$$

The functions are undefined whenever $y$ does not represent a state of $\mathbf{M}$ or $s$ is not one of the symbols $\{0, 1\}$. Since they are defined only for a finite number of initial arguments, the functions can be defined by a finite number of boundary equations; thus each is recursive.

Next, we define a function that extracts from an encoded configuration $(x, y, z)$ the tape symbol currently under scan by $\mathbf{M}$ (that is, the $z$th symbol in the binary expansion of $x$). The function

$$\text{(7)} \qquad \text{head}\,(x, y, z) = z\text{th symbol in } d(x)$$

†Of course, we wish to encode only the "used" portion of a Turing machine's tape, and thus we require some means of identifying this portion. The simplest approach is to equip the machine with a special end mark which is moved right each time the used region is enlarged.

is defined by

(8) $$\text{head}(x, y, z) = \left[\frac{x}{2^z}\right] \dot{-} 2\left[\frac{x}{2^{z+1}}\right]$$

To see this, note that if $d(x) = s_0 s_1 \ldots s_z s_{z+1} \ldots$ then

$$d\left(\left[\frac{x}{2^z}\right]\right) = s_z s_{z+1} s_{z+2} \ldots$$

and

$$d\left(2\left[\frac{x}{2^{z+1}}\right]\right) = 0 s_{z+1} s_{z+2} \ldots$$

Hence

$$d\left(\left[\frac{x}{2^z}\right] \dot{-} 2\left[\frac{x}{2^{z+1}}\right]\right) = s_z 00 \ldots$$

and

$$\left[\frac{x}{2^z}\right] \dot{-} 2\left[\frac{x}{2^{z+1}}\right] = s_z$$

as required. Since

$$\left[\frac{x}{y}\right] = \text{quo}(x, y)$$

is primitive recursive (Example 13.7), it follows that "head" is primitive recursive.

Now, suppose that $(x, y, z)$ is an encoded configuration of **M**. Using the direction function, the recursive *next head position* function is defined by

(9) $$\text{nexthead}(x, y, z) = z + \text{equ}(\text{direction}(y), 1) \dot{-} \text{equ}(\text{direction}(y), 0)$$

The next state is determined by the symbol under the head at its new position; the recursive *next state* function is defined by

(10) $$\text{nextstate}(x, y, z) = \text{state}(y, \text{head}(x, y, \text{nexthead}(x, y, z)))$$

Finally, the recursive *next tape* function is defined by

(11) $$\text{nexttape}(x, y, z) = 2^z\left(2\left[\frac{x}{2^{z+1}}\right] + \text{symbol}(y, \text{head}(x, y, \text{nexthead}(x, y, z)))\right) + x \dot{-} 2^z\left[\frac{x}{2^z}\right]$$

To prove 11, suppose $\text{head}(x, y, \text{nexthead}(x, y, z)) = s$ and $\text{symbol}(y, s) = r$. Then

$$\begin{aligned} 2^z\left(2\left[\frac{x}{2^{z+1}}\right] + r\right) &= 2^z(e(0 s_{z+1} s_{z+2} \ldots) + r) \\ &= 2^z(e(r s_{z+1} s_{z+2} \ldots)) \\ &= e(\underbrace{0 \ldots 0}_{z-1\ 0\text{'s}} r s_{z+1} s_{y+2} \ldots) \end{aligned}$$

and

$$\begin{aligned} x \dot{-} 2^z\left[\frac{x}{2^z}\right] &= e(s_0 \ldots s_{z-1} s_z s_{z+1} \ldots) \dot{-} e(\underbrace{0 \ldots 0}_{z-1\ 0\text{'s}} s_z s_{z+1} \ldots) \\ &= e(s_0 \ldots s_{z-1} 00 \ldots) \end{aligned}$$

Thus

$$\text{nexttape}\,(x, y, z) = e(s_0 \ldots s_{z-1} r s_{z+1} \ldots)$$

as required.

In terms of the functions 9–11, the *move function m* is given by

$$m(x, y, z) = (\text{nexttape}\,(x, y, z), \text{nextsymbol}\,(x, y, z), \text{nexthead}\,(x, y, z))$$

The value of $m(x, y, z)$ is the encoding of **M**'s configuration after one move from the configuration represented by $(x, y, z)$. The *configuration function c* is defined in terms of $m$ using recursion:

$$c(x, y, z, 0) = (x, y, z)$$

$$c(x, y, z, t') = m(c(x, y, z, t))$$

The value of $c(x, y, z, t)$ is the encoded configuration of **M** at time $t$, given that the encoded configuration of **M** at time 0 is $(x, y, z)$. Finally, the *halting time function h* is defined using the $\mu$-operator

$$h(x, y, z) = \mu t[I_2(c(x, y, z, t)) = 1]$$

The value of $h(x, y, z)$ is the time at which **M** halts, given that the encoded configuration of **M** at time 0 is $(x, y, z)$. (Recall that **M**'s halting state is represented by the integer 1.) Note that if **M** fails to halt when started in configuration $(x, y, z)$, $h$ will be undefined at $(x, y, z)$. Thus $h$ need not be total.

Since the functions 9–11 are recursive, the move, configuration, and halting time functions are recursive. In terms of these functions, the required recursive function $f$ is

$$f(x) = I_1(c(x, 0, 0, h(x, 0, 0)))$$

This completes the proof of Proposition 13.4.

## 13.7 The Equivalence Theorem

Propositions 13.3 and 13.4 establish the following equivalence result:

> **Theorem 13.1:** The $\mu$-recursive functions, the multiple-recursive functions, and the Turing-computable functions are equivalent classes of functions.

An important consequence of Theorem 13.1 is that every problem we have proved unsolvable in terms of Turing machines can be proved unsolvable in terms of recursive functions. (For this reason, unsolvable problems are often referred to as *recursively* unsolvable problems.) This theorem provides flexibility in establishing unsolvability results, since it allows us to establish results for Turing machines in terms of recursive functions and *vice versa.*

Consider, for example, the Turing machine halting problem. By Theorem 13.1, this problem is equivalent to that of deciding, for arbitrary $x$ and $z$, whether $f_z(x)$ is defined ($f_z$ being the $z$th recursive function in some enumeration of these functions). Since $f_z(x)$ is undefined just if its evaluation tree extends indefinitely, this problem is sometimes known as the *immortality problem* for recursive functions. Accepting Church's thesis, the immortality problem is solvable just if the function

$$g(x, z) = \begin{cases} 1 & \text{if } f_z(x) \text{ is defined} \\ 0 & \text{otherwise} \end{cases}$$

is recursive. To show that $g$ is not recursive, we assume that $g$ *is* recursive and define the recursive function $h$ by

$$h(z) = \begin{cases} 0 & \text{if } g(z, z) = 0 \\ 1 + f_z(z) & \text{if } g(z, z) = 1 \end{cases}$$

Since $h$ is recursive, $h = f_y$ for some $y$. Also, since $h$ is total, $g(z, y) = 1$ for all $z$ and, in particular, $g(y, y) = 1$. But then

$$f_y(y) = h(y) = 1 + f_y(y)$$

which is an absurdity; thus $g$ cannot be recursive. The reader should compare this argument with Turing's proof of the unsolvability of the halting problem, outlined in Section 12.1.

## 13.8 Recursive and Recursively Enumerable Sets

In Chapter 11, we mentioned two basic concepts of set theory—decidability of membership in a set and the effective enumerability of a set's elements. In Chapter 12, we saw that the first of these is subject to fundamental limitations: set membership is not always decidable, even if we restrict attention to countable sets. Shortly, we shall show that the second is subject to similar limitations. Before demonstrating this fact, it is instructive to reexamine the membership and enumeration problems in light of the theory of recursive functions.

Deciding membership in a set means deciding, by some effective procedure, whether a given object is or is not in the set. We have seen sets in which membership is not decidable: the set of Turing machines that halt for blank tape (or, equivalently, the set of recursive functions defined at the argument zero) is an example. A set in which membership is decidable is called a *recur-*

*sive set*, since, by Turing's thesis and Theorem 13.1, it is one for which the *characteristic function*

$$c(x) = \begin{cases} 1 & \text{if } x \text{ is in the set} \\ 0 & \text{if } x \text{ is not in the set} \end{cases}$$

is total and recursive.

Enumerating a set means listing its elements (repetition allowed) by some effective procedure. There are sets, including countable sets, which cannot be so enumerated. (The total recursive functions form such a set: if we assume that these functions can be enumerated, we can derive a contradiction by applying a diagonalization argument to construct a total recursive function not in the enumeration.) A set which can be effectively enumerated is called a *recursively enumerable set* (or an *r.e.* set) since, by Definition 11.8 and Theorem 13.1, it is either empty or the range of a total recursive function.

Note that if **A** is a set with a total recursive characteristic function $c_{\mathbf{A}}$, the algorithm for computing $c_{\mathbf{A}}$ is also the algorithm for deciding membership in **A**. If **A** is the range of a total recursive function $f$, the algorithm for computing $f$ provides an algorithm for enumerating **A**: we need only compute in order $f(0), f(1), f(2), \ldots$. The reader may verify that the recursive and r.e. sets defined in this way are the Turing-definable and Turing-enumerable sets, respectively, of Chapter 11.

**Example 13.14:** These sets are recursive:

1. The set of odd integers.
2. The sets **N** and $\varnothing$.
3. The set of prime numbers.
4. The set of Turing machine descriptions.
5. Each finite set.
6. Each set with finite complement.
7. Each regular set.
8. Each context free language.

Sets 5 and 6 are recursive because a list of the elements in the appropriate finite set can be used as the basis of an algorithm for deciding membership: an element is in 5 just if it is in the finite list, and is in 6 just if it is not in the list. Sets 7 and 8 are recursive because finite state accepters and pushdown accepters represent effective procedures for deciding set membership.

**Example 13.15:** Each context-sensitive grammar (and thus each context-free or regular grammar) generates a recursive set. Let **G** be such a grammar and let **M** be a Turing machine which, presented with some terminal string $\omega$, constructs sets $\mathbf{A}_0, \mathbf{A}_1, \ldots, \mathbf{A}_k, \ldots$ defined as follows:

$$\mathbf{A}_0 = \{\Sigma\}$$
$$\mathbf{A}_k = \{\beta \mid \mathbf{G} \text{ permits } \alpha \Longrightarrow \beta \text{ for some } \alpha \text{ in } \mathbf{A}_{k-1}, \; |\beta| \leq |\omega|, \text{ and } \beta \notin \mathbf{A}_{k-1}\}$$

Note that for each $i$, $\mathbf{A}_i$ is the set of strings no longer than $\omega$ which have $i$-step, but no $(i-1)$-step, derivations in **G**. Since **G** has no length decreasing productions, **M** must eventually construct either a set containing $\omega$ or a set that is empty. In the former case, **M** halts indicating $\omega \in \mathbf{L}(\mathbf{G})$; in the latter case, **M** halts indicating $\omega \notin \mathbf{L}(\mathbf{G})$.

**Example 13.16:** Each of the sets in Example 13.14 is recursively enumerable; we leave it to the reader to devise enumeration procedures.

The set of tapes for which a Turing machine halts need not be recursive, for otherwise the halting problem would be solvable. However, we shall see that this set is always recursively enumerable.

Although the set of all recursive function descriptions (corresponding to the set of all Turing machine descriptions) is recursive, the set of all total recursive function descriptions (corresponding to the descriptions of Turing machines that halt for every tape) is neither recursive nor recursively enumerable.

**Example 13.17:** The intersection and the union of recursive sets are recursive sets. If **A** and **B** are recursive sets with characteristic functions $c_{\mathbf{A}}$ and $c_{\mathbf{B}}$, then the characteristic function of $\mathbf{A} \cap \mathbf{B}$ is defined by

$$c_{\mathbf{A}\cap\mathbf{B}}(x) = c_{\mathbf{A}}(x)c_{\mathbf{B}}(x)$$

Similarly, the characteristic function of $\mathbf{A} \cup \mathbf{B}$ is defined by

$$c_{\mathbf{A}\cup\mathbf{B}}(x) = 1 \dot{-} (1 \dot{-} c_{\mathbf{A}}(x))(1 \dot{-} c_{\mathbf{B}}(x))$$

The union of r.e. sets is r.e. Suppose **A** and **B** are the ranges of total recursive functions $f$ and $g$, respectively. We may define a total recursive function $h$ by

$$h(x) = \begin{cases} f(x/2) & \text{if } x \text{ is even} \\ g((x-1)/2) & \text{if } x \text{ is odd} \end{cases}$$

Then $\mathbf{A} \cup \mathbf{B}$ is the range of $h$. We leave it to the reader to show that $\mathbf{A} \cap \mathbf{B}$ is also r.e.

We summarize in the following theorem important relations between recursiveness and recursive enumerability

**Theorem 13.2:** Let $\mathbf{A} \subseteq \mathbf{N}$ and $\mathbf{A}^c = \mathbf{N} - \mathbf{A}$. Then:

(1) **A** is recursive if and only if $\mathbf{A}^c$ is recursive.

(2) **A** is recursive only if **A** is r.e.

(3) **A** is recursive just if both **A** and $\mathbf{A}^c$ are r.e.

***Proof:***

(1) Suppose **A** is recursive with characteristic function $c_\mathbf{A}$. Then the characteristic function of $\mathbf{A}^c$ is defined by

$$c_{\mathbf{A}^c}(x) = 1 \dot{-} c_\mathbf{A}(x)$$

(2) If $\mathbf{A} = \varnothing$, then **A** is by definition r.e. If **A** is finite, then $\mathbf{A} = \{x_0, \ldots, x_n\}$ for some $n \geq 0$. The function

$$f(k) = \begin{cases} x_k & \text{if } k \leq n \\ x_n & \text{if } k > n \end{cases}$$

is a total recursive function with range **A**. If **A** is infinite, its characteristic function $c_\mathbf{A}$ may be used to enumerate **A**: we generate in order $c_\mathbf{A}(0)$, $c_\mathbf{A}(1)$, $c_\mathbf{A}(2), \ldots$ and add $i$ to the output list whenever $c_\mathbf{A}(i) = 1$. Since $c_\mathbf{A}$ is total, each element of **A** will eventually appear in the list; thus **A** is r.e.

(3) *Only if:* By 1 and 2, **A** recursive implies that **A** and $\mathbf{A}^c$ are r.e.

*If*: If either **A** or $\mathbf{A}^c$ is empty, then **A** is either **N** or $\varnothing$, and is therefore recursive. Suppose both **A** and $\mathbf{A}^c$ are nonempty, and let $f$ and $g$ be total recursive functions such that **A** is the range of $f$ and $\mathbf{A}^c$ is the range of $g$. Given any $x$, we determine whether or not $x$ is in **A** by generating the sequence of values

$$f(0), g(0), f(1), g(1), f(2), g(2), \ldots$$

If $x$ appears as a value of $f$ for some argument, then $x$ is in **A**. If $x$ appears as a value of $g$ for some argument, then $x$ is in $\mathbf{A}^c$. Since $\mathbf{A} \cup \mathbf{A}^c = \mathbf{N}$, $x$ must eventually appear as an argument of either $f$ or $g$; thus this decision procedure eventually terminates.

In Chapter 11, we showed that a set is Turing enumerable just if it is the domain of a Turing-computable function. This result is restated as

**Theorem 13.3:** A set **A** is recursively enumerable if and only if **A** is the domain of a Turing-computable function. Equivalently, **A** is recursively enumerable if and only if **A** is the domain of a (partial) recursive function.

The theorem follows immediately from Theorems 11.4 and 13.1.

**Example 13.18:** The set of tapes for which a Turing machine fails to halt need not be recursively enumerable, otherwise the set of tapes for which a Turing machine halts would necessarily be recursive (by Theorem 13.2 and Theorem 13.3). This would contradict the unsolvability of the Turing machine halting problem.

**Example 13.19:** Let **G** be an arbitrary type 0 grammar, and let **M** be a Turing machine which, presented with some terminal string $\omega$, performs this procedure:

1. Set $k = 1$ and set $\mathbf{A}_0 = \{\Sigma\}$.
2. Set $\mathbf{A}_k = \{\beta \mid \alpha \Longrightarrow \beta$ for some $\alpha$ in $\mathbf{A}_{k-1}\}$.
3. Determine whether $\omega$ is in the (finite) set $\mathbf{A}_k$: if so, go to step 4; otherwise, set $k = k + 1$ and go to step 2.
4. Halt.

Clearly, **M** halts on $\omega$ if and only if $\omega \in \mathbf{L}(\mathbf{G})$. By Theorem 13.2, **G** generates a recursively enumerable set.

We used a procedure similar to that of Example 13.19 to show that the context-sensitive grammars generate recursive sets (Example 13.15). We were able to demonstrate that the procedure for deciding membership in such sets always halts, because the noncontracting property of these grammars permits us to bound the length of derivations of a given string. The contracting property of type 0 grammars, on the other hand, means that a string generated by such a grammar might require an arbitrary number of steps for its derivation. We cannot, therefore, extend the procedure of Example 13.15 to type 0 grammars. Indeed, type 0 grammars need not generate recursive sets.

In Section 13.2, we used a diagonalization argument to establish the "incompleteness" of the primitive recursive functions. Very similar arguments can be used to establish the following important results:

**Theorem 13.4:** The class of total recursive functions cannot be effectively enumerated.

***Proof:*** Let **M** be any Turing machine that enumerates some set of total recursive functions

$$f_1, f_2, \ldots, f_z, \ldots$$

Define the function $g$ by

$$g(z) = 1 + f_z(z)$$

The function $g$ is recursive because, for each $z$, we may use **M**'s enumeration to determine $f_z$, compute $f_z(z)$, then add 1 to this result. Also, the function $g$ is total because each function $f_z$ is total. But the function $g$ is not in the enumeration produced by **M**, for if it were we would have $g = f_y$ for some $y$. By definition of $g$, we would then have

$$f_y(y) = g(y) = 1 + f_y(y)$$

which is a contradiction. Thus **M** cannot enumerate all total recursive functions.

**Example 13.20:** Let $\mathfrak{M}_t$ denote the class of Turing machines that halt for all tapes. Then $\mathfrak{M}_t$ is not a recursively enumerable set: by Theorem 13.1, the class of functions computed by such machines is the class of total recursive functions. Thus an effective procedure for enumerating $\mathfrak{M}_t$ would contradict Theorem 13.4.

**Theorem 13.5:** No recursively enumerable class of recursive sets contains every recursive set.

***Proof:*** Suppose **M** is a Turing machine that enumerates recursive sets

$$\mathbf{E}_1, \mathbf{E}_2, \ldots, \mathbf{E}_z, \ldots$$

with characteristic functions

$$c_{\mathbf{E}_1}, c_{\mathbf{E}_2}, \ldots, c_{\mathbf{E}_z}, \ldots$$

We construct a characteristic function $c_{\mathbf{E}}$ defined by

$$c_{\mathbf{E}}(x) = 1 \dot{-} c_{\mathbf{E}_x}(x)$$

Evidently, $c_{\mathbf{E}}$ is a total recursive function that defines the recursive set

$$\mathbf{E} = \{x \mid x \notin \mathbf{E}_x\}$$

But the set **E** cannot be in **M**'s enumeration: if it were, we would have $\mathbf{E} = \mathbf{E}_y$ for some $y$, and must then accept the contradiction that $y \in \mathbf{E}_y$ just if $y \notin \mathbf{E}_y$.

**Example 13.21:** We have seen that each context-sensitive grammar generates a recursive set. Since the class of context-sensitive grammars is recursively enumerable (why?), Theorem 13.5 implies that there are recursive sets that are not context sensitive languages.

Figure 13.15 shows the relations of the recursive and recursively enumerable sets to the hierarchy of abstract languages. The fact that the recursive sets properly contain the type 1 languages follows from Examples 13.15 and

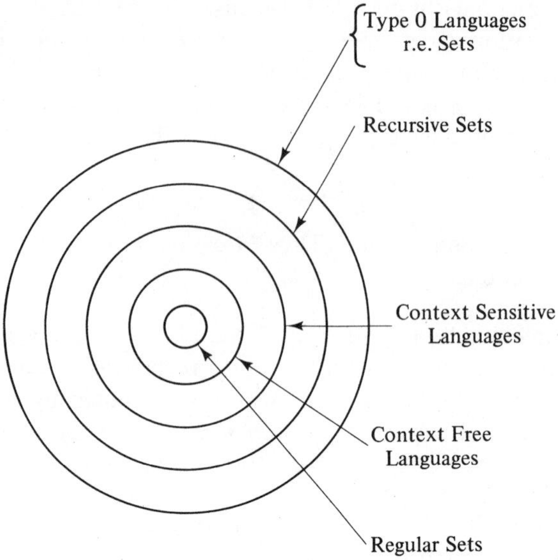


**Figure 13.15** Hierarchy of language types.

13.21. The equivalence of the r.e. sets and the type 0 languages follows from Theorem 13.3 and the simulation of Turing machines by type 0 grammars, outlined in Chapter 11.

## Notes and References

Although the term *primitive recursive function* was first used by Kleene in 1936, the class of functions described in Section 13.1 had been recognized decades earlier. (Indeed, the incompleteness of these functions had been established years before Kleene's work. The constructive proof of Section 13.2 is due to the mathematician Ackermann [1928], and the function $H$ has come to be known as *Ackermann's function.*)

The general classes of recursive functions described in Sections 13.3 and 13.4 were studied by Gödel [1931] and by Kleene [1936]; the characterizations used in this chapter are essentially those found in the latter work. The equivalence of the recursive functions and the Turing machines as models of effective computability follows from work of Kleene [1936] and Turing [1937].

A variety of other schemes for defining recursive functions have been studied. Hennie [1977] contains discussions of several such schemes.

The concepts presented in this chapter, including those in the last section of the chapter, are the starting point of a branch of mathematics known as *recursive function theory*. The reader who wishes to explore this theory in detail is referred to Davis [1958] or Rogers [1967].

## Problems

13.1. Show that the functions sign: $\mathbf{N} \longrightarrow \{0, 1\}$ and $\overline{\text{sign}}$: $\mathbf{N} \longrightarrow \{0, 1\}$ defined by

$$\text{sign}(x) = \begin{cases} 0 & \text{if } x = 0 \\ 1 & \text{if } x > 0 \end{cases}$$

and

$$\overline{\text{sign}}(x) = \begin{cases} 1 & \text{if } x = 0 \\ 0 & \text{if } x > 0 \end{cases}$$

are primitive recursive.

13.2. Show that each function of Example 13.7 is primitive recursive.

13.3. Show that the predicates ls: $\mathbf{N}^2 \longrightarrow \{0, 1\}$ and gr: $\mathbf{N}^2 \longrightarrow \{0, 1\}$ defined by

$$\text{ls}(x, y) = \begin{cases} 1 & \text{if } x < y \\ 0 & \text{if } x \geq y \end{cases}$$

$$\text{gr}(x, y) = \begin{cases} 1 & \text{if } x > y \\ 0 & \text{if } x \leq y \end{cases}$$

are primitive recursive.

13.4. Show that the monus operation is primitive recursive when extended to the rational numbers.
(Hint: Give an informal definition using any of the primitive recursive functions and predicates defined in the chapter or in Problems 13.1–13.3.)

13.5. Let $f$: $\mathbf{N} \longrightarrow \mathbf{N}$ be a total function such that $f(x) = 0$ for all but finitely many values of $x$. Show that $f$ is primitive recursive.
(Hint: Suppose that $f(x) = 0$ for all $x$ other than $x_1, \ldots, x_n$, and let $y_i$ denote the value of $x_i$ for each $i$, $1 \leq i \leq n$. Define the predicate ne: $\mathbf{N}^2 \longrightarrow \{0, 1\}$ by

$$\text{ne}(x, y) = \begin{cases} 1 & \text{if } x \neq y \\ 0 & \text{if } x = y \end{cases}$$

and show that "ne" is primitive recursive. Use this predicate and the predicate "equ" of Example 13.7 to define $f$.)

**13.6.** Suppose we add to the composition and recursion rules of Section 13.1 the *summation* rule
*Summation:* If $g$: $\mathbf{N}^n \longrightarrow \mathbf{N}$ is a primitive recursive function, then the function $f$: $\mathbf{N}^n \longrightarrow \mathbf{N}$ defined by

$$f(x_1, x_2, \ldots, x_n) = \sum_{i=0}^{x_1} g(i, x_2, \ldots, x_n)$$

is primitive recursive. [If $x_1 = 0$, we take $f(x_1, x_2, \ldots, x_n) = 0$.]

Show that the addition of this rule does not change the class of primitive recursive functions. Now, suppose we add the additional rule

*Product:* If $g: \mathbf{N}^n \longrightarrow \mathbf{N}$ is a primitive recursive function, then the function $f: \mathbf{N}^n \longrightarrow \mathbf{N}$ defined by

$$f(x_1, x_2, \ldots, x_n) = \prod_{i=0}^{x_1} g(i, x_2, \ldots, x_n)$$

is primitive recursive. [If $x_1 = 0$, we take $f(x_1, x_2, \ldots, x_n) = 1$.]

Again, show that the addition of this rule does not change the class of primitive recursive functions.

13.7. In Section 13.2, we used a diagonalization argument to demonstrate nonconstructively the existence of total, non-primitive recursive functions. As an alternate nonconstructive proof, show that there exists just a countable infinity of primitive recursive functions and conclude from this the existence of total non-primitive recursive functions.

13.8. Show that the function $f: \mathbf{N} \longrightarrow \mathbf{N}$ defined by

$$f(n) = \begin{cases} x & \text{if } x \text{ is a perfect square} \\ \text{undefined} & \text{otherwise} \end{cases}$$

is a $\mu$-recursive function.

13.9. Show that the predicate $p: \mathbf{N} \longrightarrow \{0, 1\}$ is $\mu$-recursive, where $p$ is

$$p(n) = \begin{cases} 1 & \text{if there exist integers } i, j, k > 0 \\ & \text{such that } i^n + j^n = k^n \\ \text{undefined} & \text{otherwise} \end{cases}$$

At this writing, it is unknown whether $p(n) = 1$ for any $n$ greater than 1. It is often far easier to construct a recursive definition of a function than it is to carry out the corresponding evaluation procedure!

***13.10.** Suppose we replace the minimalization rule of Section 13.3 with a rule of "bounded minimalization":

*Bounded Minimalization:* Let $g: \mathbf{N}^n \longrightarrow \mathbf{N}$ be a total function. Define the function $f: \mathbf{N}^n \longrightarrow \mathbf{N}$ so that

$$f(x, z) = \mu y[g(x, y) = 0]$$

is the least integer $y$, $z \geq y \geq 0$, for which $g(x, y) = 0$, or $z + 1$ if no such integer exists. Then $f$ is obtained from $g$ by *bounded minimalization.*

Let $\mathfrak{T}_b$ be the smallest class of number theoretic functions such that:

i) Every primitive recursive function is in $\mathfrak{T}_b$.

ii) $\mathfrak{T}_b$ is closed under bounded minimalization.

Show that $\mathcal{T}_b$ is precisely the class of primitive recursive functions. (Hint: For any primitive recursive function $h$: $\mathbf{N}^n \longrightarrow \mathbf{N}$ let the function $g$: $\mathbf{N}^n \longrightarrow \mathbf{N}$ be defined by

$$g(x, y) = \begin{cases} 1 & \text{if } h(x, i) \neq 0, \text{ all } i, 1 \leq i \leq y \\ 0 & \text{otherwise} \end{cases}$$

Show that $g$ is primitive recursive, and obtain the required result by applying the results of Problem 13.6.)

13.11. Let $f$: $\mathbf{N}^2 \longrightarrow \mathbf{N}$ be the function whose value for argument $(x, y)$ is the binomial coefficient $\binom{x+y}{x}$. Show that $f$ is a multiple recursive function.

13.12. a. Define the function of Problem 13.8 using a multiple recurisve equation system.
b. Define the predicate of Problem 13.9 using a multiple recursive equation system.

13.13. The function gcd: $\mathbf{N}^2 \longrightarrow \mathbf{N}$ is defined by

$$\text{gcd}\,(x, y) = \text{greatest common divisor of } x \text{ and } y$$

Construct a multiple recursive definition of gcd.

13.14. The function rem: $\mathbf{N}^2 \longrightarrow \mathbf{N}$ is defined by

$$\text{rem}\,(x, y) = \text{remainder after dividing } x \text{ by } y$$

Construct a multiple recursive definition of rem.

***13.15.** Show that each multiple recursive function is equivalent to a $\mu$-recursive function whose definition contains at most a single application of the $\mu$-operator.
(Hint: Use theorem 13.1 and consider the simulation of Turing machines described in Section 13.6.)

13.16. Consider the system of equations provided as an example in Section 13.4:

(1) $f(x', y', z) = z + f(x, y, z)$
(2) $f(x', 0, z) = 0$
(3) $f(0, y', z) = 1$
(4) $f(0, 0, z) = 2$

Present the routines for a Turing machine evaluation of $f$ (as in Example 13.13) and show, as a sequence of Turing machine configurations, the evaluation of $f(2, 2, 1)$.

***13.17.** Let **M** be any Turing machine with binary alphabet. Show that **M** can be simulated by a multiple recursive function defined by a system of no more than $cn$ equations, where $c$ is a constant and $n$ is the number of states in the machine. Show that the dependency on $n$ cannot be eliminated; that is, show that there is no constant $c$ which necessarily bounds the length of the equation system.

13.18. Which of the following sets are recursive? Recursively enumerable?

i) $\{n \in \mathbf{N} \mid n \text{ is a perfect square}\}$
ii) $\{n \in \mathbf{N} \mid n, n + 2 \text{ are each prime}\}$
iii) $\{n \in \mathbf{N} \mid$ the $n$th digit in the decimal expansion of $\pi = 3.141592 \ldots$ is zero$\}$
iv) $\{n \in \mathbf{N} \mid$ no zero appears after the $n$th digit in the decimal expansion of $\pi\}$

13.19. In each of the following sets, $f_n$ denotes the $n$th function in some enumeration of the Turing machines. Which of the sets are recursive? Which are recursively enumerable?

i) $\{n \in \mathbf{N} \mid f_n(n) \text{ is defined}\}$
ii) $\{n \in \mathbf{N} \mid f_n \text{ is a constant function}\}$
iii) $\{n \in \mathbf{N} \mid f_n \text{ is a monotonic increasing function}\}$
iv) $\{n \in \mathbf{N} \mid f_n \text{ has infinite domain}\}$
v) $\{n \in \mathbf{N} \mid f_n \text{ has finite domain}\}$
vi) $\{n \in \mathbf{N} \mid f_n \text{ has empty domain}\}$
vii) $\{n \in \mathbf{N} \mid f_n \text{ has nonempty domain}\}$
viii) $\{n \in \mathbf{N} \mid f_n \text{ has finite range}\}$

(Hint: Recall that every recursive function is computed by some Turing machine. In terms of corresponding Turing machines, what are the sets (i)–(viii)?)

**13.20.** Describe a set which is not recursively enumerable and whose complement is not recursively enumerable.

**13.21.** Show that the intersection of two recursively enumerable sets is a recursively enumerable set.

**13.22.** Let $\mathbf{X} \subseteq \mathbf{N}$ be a finite set, $\mathbf{Y} \subseteq \mathbf{N}$ a recursive set, and $\mathbf{Z} \subseteq \mathbf{N}$ a recursively enumerable set.

a) Let $f$ be a total recursive function, let $\mathbf{X}'$ be the set $\{n \mid n = f(m)$ for some $m \in \mathbf{X}\}$, and let $\mathbf{Y}'$ and $\mathbf{Z}'$ be defined analogously. Need $\mathbf{X}'$ be recursive? Need $\mathbf{Y}'$? Need $\mathbf{Z}'$? Need $\mathbf{X}'$ be recursively enumerable? Need $\mathbf{Y}'$? Need $\mathbf{Z}'$?

b) Suppose we let $f$ be an arbitrary (partial) recursive function. Need $\mathbf{X}'$ be recursive? Need $\mathbf{Y}'$? Need $\mathbf{Z}'$? Need $\mathbf{X}'$ be recursively enumerable? Need $\mathbf{Y}'$? Need $\mathbf{Z}'$?

**13.23.** Let $f, g$ be recursive functions such that, for all $x \in \mathbf{N}$, we have

$$f(x) \geq g(x)$$

Show that if $f$ is one-to-one and the range of $f$ is a recursive set, then the range of $g$ is a recursive set. Need the range of $g$ be a recursive set if $f$ is not one-to-one?

***13.24.** Prove that any infinite recursively enumerable set has an infinite recursive subset.

(Hint: Suppose **X** is such a set. Let $f$ be a recursive function such that **X** is the range of $f$, and define a function $g$ by

$$g(0) = f(0)$$

$$g(x') = f(\mu y[f(y) > g(x)])$$

Show that the range of $g$ is an infinite recursive subset of **X**.)

# 14

# *Post Systems*

In Chapters 11 and 12 we studied a theory of computability based on the notion of machines obeying instructions. In Chapter 13 we studied an equivalent theory based on the notion of functions being evaluated. In this chapter we study yet another theory of computability, based on the notion of symbol string manipulation.

The logician Emil Post studied the processes by which one makes logical deductions, and he developed a model for representing any formal system in which logical deductions are performed. Post reasoned that any such system must consist of a set of axioms and a finite set of rules of inference, the latter specifying the ways in which valid statements, or *theorems*, may be deduced from the axioms. Abstractly, the axioms are strings of symbols over some alphabet, and the rules of inference are means of specifying that certain strings are derivable from others. The strings that can be derived in a finite number of steps from the axioms are the theorems *provable* in the system, and the sequences of deduction steps constitute proofs of these theorems. It is important to note that the foregoing ideas depend in no way on the semantics of the axioms and theorems.

The model proposed by Post has come to be known as a *Post system*, and we shall see that it is equivalent to the Turing machine in its ability to model computation; this fact constitutes the last of three powerful arguments in support of Turing's thesis.

## 14.1 Definitions and Examples

A Post system is a finite set of rewriting rules for strings of symbols. These rules resemble the productions of formal grammars but contain, in addition to terminal and nonterminal symbols, *string variables* that stand for arbitrary strings of terminal letters that may appear in derivations permitted by the system.

**Definition 14.1:** A *Post system* is a quadruple

$$\mathbf{P} = (\mathbf{T}, \mathbf{U}, \mathbf{V}, \mathbf{R})$$

in which

**T** is a finite set of *terminal symbols*, $\mathbf{T} = \{a, b, c, \ldots\}$

**U** is a finite set of *auxiliary symbols*, $\mathbf{U} = \{A, B, C, \ldots\}$

**V** is a finite set of *string variables*, $\mathbf{V} = \{\alpha, \beta, \gamma, \ldots\}$

**R** is a finite set of *rewriting rules*, each of which is an ordered pair of strings in $(\mathbf{T} \cup \mathbf{U} \cup \mathbf{V})^*$. If $(\omega, \varphi)$ is a rule in **R** we write $\omega \longrightarrow \varphi$. Each rule is of the form

$$X_0\alpha_1X_1 \ldots \alpha_nX_n \longrightarrow Y_0\beta_1Y_1 \ldots \beta_mY_m$$

in which

$$X_i,\ Y_j \in (\mathbf{T} \cup \mathbf{U})^*, \quad 1 \le i \le n,\ 1 \le j \le m$$
$$\alpha_i,\ \beta_j \in \mathbf{V}, \quad 1 \le i \le n,\ 1 \le j \le m$$
$$\alpha_i \ne \alpha_j \quad \text{whenever } i \ne j$$

and for each $j$ there is an $i$ such that $\beta_j = \alpha_i$ (that is, each string variable appearing in the righthand side of the rule appears in the lefthand side of the rule).

Just as the rules of a formal grammar permit the derivation of terminal strings from a starting symbol, the rules of a Post system permit the deduction of theorems from a given set of axioms. Let **P** be as above, and suppose that $\sigma$ and $\sigma'$ are strings

$$\sigma = X_0\omega_1X_1\omega_2X_2 \ldots \omega_nX_n$$
$$\sigma' = Y_0\varphi_1Y_1\varphi_2Y_2 \ldots \varphi_mY_m$$

where each $X_i$ and $Y_j$ is in $(\mathbf{T} \cup \mathbf{U})^*$, and each $\omega_i$ and $\varphi_j$ is a terminal string. If

$$X_0\alpha_1X_1\alpha_2X_2 \ldots \alpha_nX_n \longrightarrow Y_0\beta_1Y_1\beta_2Y_2 \ldots \beta_mY_m$$

is a rule in **R** such that $\varphi_j = \omega_i$ whenever $\beta_j = \alpha_i$, we say that $\sigma'$ is *immediately deducible* from $\sigma$, and we write $\sigma \Longrightarrow \sigma'$. If $\sigma_1, \sigma_2, \ldots, \sigma_k$ are strings such that $\sigma_1 \Longrightarrow \sigma_2 \Longrightarrow \ldots \Longrightarrow \sigma_k$, we say that $\sigma_k$ is (*ultimately*) *deducible* from $\sigma_1$, and we write $\sigma_1 \overset{*}{\Longrightarrow} \sigma_k$. (In the latter case, the sequence of strings

$\sigma_1, \sigma_2, \ldots, \sigma_k$ constitutes a *proof* of $\sigma_k$ from $\sigma_1$.) If **A** is a finite set of strings in **T***, then **A** is a valid set of *axioms* for **P** and the set

$$T(\mathbf{P}, \mathbf{A}) = \{\varphi \in \mathbf{T}^* \mid \omega \stackrel{*}{\Longrightarrow} \varphi \text{ for some } \omega \text{ in } \mathbf{A}\}$$

is the set of *theorems provable from the axioms* **A**.

The reader should note an important difference between these concepts and those associated with derivations in a formal grammar. Whereas the rules of a formal grammar specify that certain *substrings* of a given string may be rewritten in certain ways during a derivation step, the rules of a Post system specify (by means of string variables) the form of the *entire* string at each step in the deduction of a theorem. Since each string variable denotes an arbitrary terminal string, each rule of a Post system stands for the infinite collection of grammatical rules that could be obtained by substituting terminal strings for the string variables.

**Example 14.1:** We shall construct a Post system which, starting from the axiom $1 + 1 = 11$, proves valid unary addition statements of the form $1^i + 1^j = 1^{i+j}$. For example, statements such as

$$1 + 11 = 111$$

$$11 + 111 = 11111$$

are valid, but the statement

$$1 + 11 = 11$$

is not. Let $\mathbf{P} = (\mathbf{T}, \mathbf{U}, \mathbf{V}, \mathbf{R})$ be the Post system with

$$\mathbf{T} = \{1, +, =\}, \quad \mathbf{U} = \varnothing, \quad \mathbf{V} = \{\alpha, \beta, \gamma\}$$

$$\mathbf{R}: \quad \alpha + \beta = \gamma \longrightarrow \alpha 1 + \beta = \gamma 1 \qquad (1)$$

$$\alpha + \beta = \gamma \longrightarrow \alpha + \beta 1 = \gamma 1 \qquad (2)$$

We prove the statement $11 + 111 = 11111$ as follows:

| | |
|---|---|
| $1 + 1 = 11$ | [axiom] |
| $11 + 1 = 111$ | [rule 1] |
| $11 + 11 = 1111$ | [rule 2] |
| $11 + 111 = 11111$ | [rule 2] |

It should be clear that

$$T(\mathbf{P}, \mathbf{A}) = \{1^i + 1^j = 1^k \mid i + j = k\}$$

where **A** is the axiom $1 + 1 = 11$.

**Example 14.2.** We shall construct a Post system which, starting from the axiom $1 \times 1 = 1$, proves valid unary multiplication statements of the form $1^i \times 1^j = 1^{ij}$. That is, we shall construct **P** so that

$$T(\mathbf{P}, \mathbf{A}) = \{1^i \times 1^j = 1^k \mid ij = k\}$$

where $\mathbf{A} = \{1 \times 1 = 1\}$. The Post system **P** has

$$\mathbf{T} = \{1, \times, =\}, \mathbf{U} = \varnothing, \mathbf{V} = \{\alpha, \beta, \gamma\}$$

and rewriting rules

$$\mathbf{R}: \quad \alpha \times \beta = \gamma \longrightarrow \alpha 1 \times \beta = \gamma\beta \qquad (1)$$

$$\alpha \times \beta = \gamma \longrightarrow \alpha \times \beta 1 = \gamma\alpha \qquad (2)$$

A proof of $11 \times 111 = 111111$ is:

$$1 \times 1 = 1 \qquad \text{[axiom]}$$

$$11 \times 1 = 11 \qquad \text{[rule 1]}$$

$$11 \times 11 = 1111 \qquad \text{[rule 2]}$$

$$11 \times 111 = 111111 \qquad \text{[rule 2]}$$

Evidently, **P** is the desired Post system.

The reader has no doubt concluded from these examples that Post systems are a generalization of formal grammars. Indeed, let $\mathbf{G} = (\mathbf{N}, \mathbf{T}, \mathbf{P}, \Sigma)$ be a formal grammar and let $\mathbf{P}'$ be the Post system with terminals $\mathbf{T} \cup \{\Sigma\}$, auxiliary symbols $\mathbf{U} = \varnothing$, string variables $\mathbf{V} = \{\omega, \varphi\}$, and rewriting rules containing $\omega\alpha\varphi \longrightarrow \omega\beta\varphi$ whenever $\alpha \longrightarrow \beta$ is a rule of **G**. The reader may verify that

$$T(\mathbf{P}', \{\Sigma\}) = \mathbf{L}(\mathbf{G})$$

Thus each formal grammar can be simulated by some Post system.

In constructing Post systems, it is often convenient to permit deductions from infinite axiom sets. Suppose **P** is a Post system with terminals **T** and $\mathbf{A} \subseteq \mathbf{T}^*$ is an infinite set of strings generated by some grammar **G**. By augmenting the rules of **P** with rules corresponding to those of **G**, as described above, we obtain a Post system $\mathbf{P}'$ such that

$$T(\mathbf{P}', \{\Sigma\}) = T(\mathbf{P}, \mathbf{A})$$

Hence we permit, when convenient, any formal language as the axiom set for a Post system.

**Example 14.3:** We shall construct a Post system that proves statements of the form $\eta = \xi$, in which $\eta$ is the unary representation of some natural number $n$ (that is, $\eta = 1^n$ for some $n \geq 1$), and $\xi$ is the binary representation of $n$ with the most significant digits to the left. Specifically, the system is to prove statements such as

$$1111 = 100$$

$$111111 = 110$$

$$111111111 = 1001$$

The axioms will be the set $\mathbf{A} = \mathbf{11}^*$. We shall represent, in the rewriting rules, a standard algorithm for converting a number to binary:

Successively divide the number by 2, and save the sequence of remainders. When the number is represented in unary, division by 2 consists of discarding every second 1; thus an appropriate Post system is

$$\mathbf{T} = \{1, 0, =\}, \mathbf{U} = \{A, B, C\}, \mathbf{V} = \{\alpha, \beta, \gamma, \delta\}$$

$$\mathbf{R}: \quad \alpha \longrightarrow \alpha AB\alpha C \tag{1}$$

$$\alpha A\gamma B11\delta C\beta \longrightarrow \alpha A\gamma 1B\delta C\beta \tag{2}$$

$$\alpha A\gamma BC\beta \longrightarrow \alpha AB\gamma C0\beta \tag{3}$$

$$\alpha A\gamma B1C\beta \longrightarrow \alpha AB\gamma C1\beta \tag{4}$$

$$\alpha ABC\beta \longrightarrow \alpha = \beta \tag{5}$$

Rule 1 starts with a given axiom $\alpha$ and sets up the string $\alpha AB\alpha C$ on which manipulations are subsequently performed. The $\alpha$ between auxiliary symbols $B$ and $C$ will be successively divided by 2, this being done by using $B$ to replace every second 1 (rule 2). If symbols $B$ and $C$ become adjacent after repeated applications of rule 2, the original string contained an even number of 1's; accordingly, rule 3 records the remainder 0 and moves the $B$ back to the start of the string between $A$ and $C$ for the next division by 2. Rule 4 handles the case in which the remainder of the division is 1, and rule 5 removes the auxiliary symbols after the conversion to binary is complete. A proof of the theorem $111111 = 110$ according to $\mathbf{P}$ is:

| | |
|---|---|
| $111111$ | [axiom] |
| $111111AB111111C$ | [rule 1] |
| $111111A1B1111C$ | [rule 2] |
| $111111A11B11C$ | [rule 2] |
| $111111A111BC$ | [rule 2] |
| $111111AB111C0$ | [rule 3] |
| $111111A1B1C0$ | [rule 2] |
| $111111AB1C10$ | [rule 4] |
| $111111ABC110$ | [rule 4] |
| $111111 = 110$ | [rule 5] |

The reader should prove a few theorems on his own to be sure he understands the operation of this Post system.

## 14.2 Equivalence of Post Systems and Turing Machines

In this section, we establish the equivalence of Post systems and Turing machines as abstract models of computation. Specifically, we show that the deductions of any Post system can be carried out by an appropriate Turing machine, and that the computations of any Turing machine can be represented as the deductions of some Post system.

We have seen that for each Post system **P** and axiom set **A**, there exists a Post system **P**′ such that

$$T(\mathbf{P}', \{\Sigma\}) = T(\mathbf{P}, \mathbf{A})$$

Thus, in constructing a Turing machine that simulates a given Post system, it is sufficient to consider Post systems whose deductions begin from the single axiom Σ. Consider, then, a nondeterministic TM with a two-track tape, initially containing the lone symbol Σ in the leftmost square of its upper track. The TM will execute a series of "cycles", each of which performs a single deduction according to a given Post system. At the start of the $k$th cycle, the upper track of the tape will contain a string $\sigma$ derivable from Σ in exactly $k$ steps, and the lower track will be blank; at the end of the cycle, the upper track will contain a string $\sigma'$ such that $\sigma \Longrightarrow \sigma'$, and the lower track will again be blank. During a cycle, the TM performs the following operations:

It scans the string in the upper track and halts in a *success* state if that string is a theorem (that is, a terminal string). Otherwise, it nondeterministically chooses some one of its rewriting rules, say $X_0\alpha_1X_1 \ldots \alpha_nX_n \longrightarrow Y_0\beta_1Y_1 \ldots \beta_mY_m$, and executes a routine that examines the string in the upper track to determine whether its form matches the left part of the chosen rewriting rule. If it does not find such a match, the TM erases its tape and halts in a state indicating *failure*. If it does find such a match, the upper track must contain a string of the form

$$X_0\gamma_1X_1 \ldots \gamma_nX_n$$

where $\gamma_1, \ldots, \gamma_n$ are terminal strings. In such a case, the TM performs, for $j = 1, 2, \ldots, m$, the following routine:

1. It writes $Y_{j-1}$ into the leftmost blank portion of the lower track.
2. It determines the $i$ for which $\alpha_i = \beta_j$ in the chosen rewriting rule.
3. It copies $\gamma_i$ from the upper track into the leftmost blank region of the lower track.

The TM then writes $Y_m$ onto the lower track, copies the contents of the lower track onto the upper track, erases the lower track, and begins the next cycle. Whenever $\sigma_1 \Longrightarrow \sigma_2 \ldots \Longrightarrow \sigma_n$ is a deduction according to the Post system, there will exist a sequence of TM configurations which construct the strings $\sigma_i$ on the upper track in successive cycles. If $\sigma_n$ is a terminal string (a theorem), this sequence of configurations will leave the TM halted in its *success* state.

This argument shows that any deduction expressible in a given Post system can be carried out by a Turing machine; thus the Turing machines are at least as powerful as Post systems. To prove the converse of this statement, we must show that any Turing machine computation can be expressed as a deduction in a corresponding Post system. To prove this fact, let $\mathbf{M} = (\mathbf{Q}, \mathbf{T}, \mathbf{P}, q_I)$ be an arbitrary TM. We construct a Post system with terminal symbols $\mathbf{T}$, auxiliary symbols $\mathbf{Q}$, string variables $\omega$ and $\varphi$, and rewriting rules as follows:

$$\omega q t \varphi \longrightarrow \omega t' q' \varphi \qquad \text{if } \mathbf{M} \text{ has } q] \ \textbf{right} \ (t/t', q')$$

$$\omega q \longrightarrow \omega t' q' \qquad \text{if } \mathbf{M} \text{ has } q] \ \textbf{right} \ (\#/t', q')$$

$$\omega t q \varphi \longrightarrow \omega q' t' \varphi \qquad \text{if } \mathbf{M} \text{ has } q] \ \textbf{left} \ (t/t', q')$$

The left parts of these rewriting rules correspond to configurations of the Turing machine:

$$\omega q t \varphi \text{ to } (\omega', q, s, t\varphi), \text{ where } \omega = \omega' s$$

$$\omega q \quad \text{to } (\omega', q, s, \lambda), \text{ where } \omega = \omega' s$$

$$\omega t q \varphi \text{ to } (\omega t, q, s, \varphi'), \text{ where } \varphi = s\varphi'$$

Now, if $\mathbf{M}$ is started on initial tape $t\alpha$ its initial configuration is $(\lambda, q_I, t, \alpha)$; accordingly, we take as an axiom the string $q_I t\alpha$. It is not difficult to see that successive deductions of this Post system from the axiom $q_I t\alpha$ are in one-to-one correspondence with successive TM configurations from $(\lambda, q_I, t, \alpha)$. Thus the computations of the TM are representable as deductions in the Post system, and we conclude that Post systems are as powerful a model of computation as Turing machines.

**Theorem 14.1:** Post systems and Turing machines are equivalent representations of effective computability. That is, the deductions of a given Post system can be represented as the computations of some Turing machine, and the computations of a given Turing machine can be represented as the deductions of some Post system.

Theorems 13.1 and 14.1 show that Turing machines, recursive functions, and Post systems are equivalent mathematical models. Consequently, any result established within the context of one of these models implies equivalent results expressible within the context of the others. The following examples illustrate this point. Of course, the results established in these examples could be demonstrated by means of appropriate Post system constructions, but Theorems 13.1 and 14.1 render such exercises unnecessary.

**Example 14.4:** Let $\mathbf{X} \subseteq \mathbf{N}$ be a recursive set. Then there exists a Post system $\mathbf{P}$ such that $\boldsymbol{T}(\mathbf{P}, \mathbf{N}) = \{0, 1\}$ and $n \overset{*}{\Longrightarrow} 1$ is a deduction in $\mathbf{P}$ just if $n \in \mathbf{X}$. Similarly, let $\mathbf{Y} \subseteq \mathbf{N}$ be a recursively enumerable set. Then there exists a Post system $\mathbf{P}'$ such that $\boldsymbol{T}(\mathbf{P}', \{n\}) = \{n\text{th element of } \mathbf{Y}\}$, each $n \in \mathbf{N}$.

**Example 14.5:** We have seen that there exists a universal Turing machine which, given the descriptions of an arbitrary Turing machine and an arbitrary initial tape, simulates that machine on that tape. Thus there exists a *universal Post system* which, given as axioms the descriptions of an arbitrary Post system and axiom set, permits the deductions of that system from that set of axioms.

Similarly, the equivalence of nondeterministic TM's to deterministic TM's assures us that every Post system—which in general is nondeterministic since it may contain several rewriting rules with identical left parts—has a deterministic equivalent in which each rewriting rule has a unique left part. (Such systems are called *monogenic* systems.)

**Example 14.6:** Each problem unsolvable for Turing machines has an unsolvable analog in terms of Post systems. For example, the analog of the halting problem for Turing machines is the *immortality problem* for Post systems: *Does a given Post system, starting from an arbitrary axiom, permit the deduction of some other theorem within a finite number of steps*? Similarly, the configuration problem for Turing machines becomes the problem of deciding, for a given Post system **P** and given terminal strings $\omega$ and $\varphi$, whether or not $\omega \stackrel{*}{\Longrightarrow} \varphi$ is permitted by **P**. The reader will notice that this is a generalization of the word problem for formal grammars, shown unsolvable in Chapter 12.

## 14.3 On the Power of Computing Machines

In the last four chapters we have studied three distinct mathematical systems, each proposed as an appropriate formalization of the imprecise notion of "algorithm". We have seen that these systems, outwardly so different from each other, are equivalent in their ability to express effective computation. This fact lends substantial credibility to the thesis that there is a fundamental limit on the power of computating machines, and that this limit is reached by the Turing machine. Turing's work is thus assured a place among the great works of modern mathematics.

### Notes and References

The Post system was introduced by Emil Post [1943], who showed that any such system could be transformed into one in a simple normal form (see Problem 14.6). The reader is referred to Minsky [1967] for a more detailed discussion of Post systems.

## Problems

14.1. Given the Post system and axiom set of Example 14.3, prove the theorem $1111111 = 111$.

14.2. Construct a Post system **P** which, starting from the axiom $1 \dot{-} 1 = \#\#$ proves unary monus; that is, construct a system such that

$$T(\mathbf{P}, \mathbf{A}) = \begin{cases} 1^i \dot{-} 1^j = \#1^{i-j}\#, \text{ if } i \geq j \\ \#\# \text{ otherwise} \end{cases}$$

where **A** is $\{1 \dot{-} 1 = \#\#\}$.

14.3. Construct a Post system which, starting from some finite set of axioms, proves unary exponentiation. If **A** is the set of axioms, we desire

$$T(\mathbf{P}, \mathbf{A}) = \{1^i \uparrow 1^j = 1^{i^j}\}$$

for the Post system **P**.

**14.4.** Prove that there is no effective procedure for deciding, given a Post system **P** and a set of axioms **A**, whether a given axiom is *redundant* (that is, whether it can be deduced according to **P** from the remaining axioms in **A**). Specifically, show that it is undecidable whether a given $\alpha \in \mathbf{A}$ is in $T(\mathbf{P}, \mathbf{A} - \{\alpha\})$.

**14.5.** Prove that there is no effective procedure for deducing, given an arbitrary Post system **P** and arbitrary axiom set **A**, the elements of **T(P, A)** in order of increasing length.

***14.6.** A Post system is said to be in *Post normal form* if each of its rewriting rules is of the form

$$X\alpha \longrightarrow \alpha Y$$

where $\alpha$ is a string variable and $X$, $Y$ are auxiliary variables. Prove that each Post system is equivalent to some system in Post normal form.

# Afterword

What should you have learned from your studies in this book?

We hope you have learned to appreciate the most significant aspects of theoretical computer science. We have emphasized the hierarchy among abstract machines and the corresponding languages. These models extend the notation and methods of set theory and mathematical logic to study the fundamental limits of the discrete systems arising in the practice of computers—algorithms, language analyzers and interpreters, and the software and hardware parts of computer systems.

The hierarchy of machines and languages forms a natural progression in the capabilities of machines. The finite-state machine represents computations with a fixed, prior bound on the information storage available to solve a problem. These machines can recognize only the regular sets, which are generated by right- (or left-) linear grammars whose productions correspond one-to-one with a machine's internal state transitions.

The pushdown machine represents computations with an unbounded stack as the store. These machines can recognize context-free languages, which are generated by grammars whose productions are in one-to-one correspondence with certain configuration sequences (traverses) of a machine. Pushdown machine theory has led to highly efficient compilers for programming languages. The concept of evaluating arithmetic expressions using a pushdown stack is rapidly becoming familiar to everyone because of pocket calculators that use this storage mechanism.

The Turing machine represents computations using an unbounded, random-access store. These machines can recognize language representable by a grammar. According to Turing's thesis, no further generalization is possible because every effective procedure can be programmed on a Turing machine (and thus on any computer having sufficient storage). This unprovable thesis is now accepted as empirical fact—because the universal machine can emulate any other machine, because no more general machine has been found (though many proposals have been studied), and because every other system of representing effective computation can be simulated using Turing machines. We devoted the final chapters of the book to the recursive functions and to Post's logical systems: each is a self-contained, formal theory of effective computation—a theory equivalent to Turing's.

Our progression through the hierarchy of machines and languages was formulated on well-defined problems beyond the capabilities of each class of machines. No finite-state machine can multiply arbitrarily large numbers; no pushdown machine can analyze programming languages containing overlapping, matched pairs of phrases; no Turing machine can determine whether an arbitrary program halts. That there are problems beyond the capabilities of these particular classes of machines is neither surprising nor perplexing. What is surprising is the thesis that we cannot expect ever to find a class of machines to perform computations that Turing machines cannot. Supporting this conclusion is an extensive formal theory, perhaps the most significant achievement of mathematics in the twentieth century.

Our treatment of automata theory, formal linguistics, and computability is eclectic. There is much advanced, specialized literature in these areas. The "Notes and References" at the end of each chapter can guide you to these materials and acquaint you with their history.

* * *

How will you use the knowledge of this book?

The concepts you have explored are applied throughout theoretical computer science; you will need these fundamentals to talk effectively with others working in advanced computer science and to read what they have written. Contemporary theoretical computer science is trying to understand the design and use of algorithms, programming languages, computer hardware, and software systems. The most active areas of research are:

program verification
formal semantics
analysis of algorithms
complexity theory

Do not let our relative silence about these subject mislead you: each has an extensive literature. Indeed, entire books have been written about each.

**Program verification** studies formal methods for demonstrating that programs meet their specifications. Such a demonstration consists of describing the intent of a program with a logical assertion about its input and output values—providing a *specification*—and proving that this assertion holds in every execution of the program. Floyd [1967] is often credited with early work on labelling program flow charts with assertions, but McCarthy [1963] discussed the demonstration of correctness some time earlier, and A. Perlis and S. Gorn studied some of the methods in 1959.

The main subjects of study are deductive logic systems for constructing proofs (Manna and Waldinger [1977]), the implementation of program verification systems based on such deductive theories (Luckham [1977]), proof rules or axiom schemes for particular features of programming languages (Hoare [1969]; London *et al.* [1978]), and properties of programming languages that make programs easier to verify (Pratt [1975]). An important focus of this research is on structuring programs in such a way that the proofs of parts can be completed independently of the proof that the combination of the parts into a whole is correct.

**Formal Semantics** studies the *meanings* of programs—the effects of executing programs expressed in a given programming language. Three styles of formal semantics for a programming language have been used: operational, denotational, and axiomatic. A system of *operational* semantics defines a program's meaning in terms of the computation carried out by an abstract interpreter (Wegner [1972]). A system of *denotational* semantics views the meaning of a program as a function composed from simpler functions which express the meanings of the program's parts (Scott and Strachey [1971]; Tennent [1976]; Stoy [1977]). A system of *axiomatic* semantics characterizes meanings of program statements in terms of assertions among values of program variables before and after each statement is executed (Hoare [1969]; Dijkstra [1976]).

The three styles of semantic definition are convenient for different purposes. An operational definition is easiest to relate to an implementation. A denotational definition is usually the most direct expression of the input/output properties of a program. An axiomatic definition gives the most constructive method of formulating proof rules for program verification. Besides these three themes, semantic theories based on abstract algebra have been used with abstract data types (Liskov and Zilles [1975]).

These studies have influenced the design of programming languages by showing which constructs have the simplest formal descriptions, give the easiest proof rules, or are the most amenable to separating program development into independent components. Examples of this influence include the languages Pascal (Wirth [1971]), Euclid (London *et al.* [1978]), CLU (Liskov *et al.* [1977]), Alphard (Wulf and Shaw [1977]), and Lucid (Ashcroft and Wadge [1977]).

**Analysis of Algorithms** seeks to characterize the amount of time and space a given program takes to solve a problem of given size. ("Size" is the number of symbols required to describe an instance of the problem to the algorithm.) It also seeks to characterize the best possible time for a class of problems and, possibly, to find an optimal algorithm. The theorems typically give lower or upper bounds on the running time of algorithms for classes of problems. For example, we know that the best possible time to sort $n$ items is proportional to $n \log n$ in the worst case; because the bast known algorithm does no worse than this, it is optimal. Weide [1977] has surveyed the kinds of results and methods used to prove them. Baase [1978] wrote an undergraduate text for a course in this subject, while Aho *et al.* [1974] wrote a graduate text. Knuth's volumes are encyclopedic [1968, 1969, 1972].

**Complexity theory**, in both its "abstract" and "concrete" forms, deals with the intrinsic time (and space) required to solve classes of problems. *Abstract complexity theory* is a branch of recursive function theory. If the running time of a program is a recursive function of the size of the input data set, there are solvable problems so incredibly complex that their algorithms, no matter how efficient, can always be made arbitrarily more efficient. Ackermann's function, as fast growing as it is, is far too simple to be streamlined in this way. Indeed, most of abstract complexity theory has been of little practical use—real programs do not approach a relevant degree of complexity.

**Concrete complexity theory** deals with classes of problems (usually combinatorial) that arise frequently in practice. A class of problems is considered *tractable* if the running time of an algorithm for that type of problem is never worse than a polynomial function of the size of the given instance of the problem. Thus an algorithm that takes at least $2^n$ steps to solve a problem of size $n$, is considered *intractable*. (Of course, an algorithm of running time $n^{10}$ is not really tractable either; but most problems which are tractable in the polynomial sense turn out to be no worse than $n^3$.) All algorithms whose running times are bounded by a polynomial in $n$ are members of the class designated "P".

There is another class of problems, designated "NP", for which *nondeterministic* algorithms can provide solutions in polynomial-bounded time. This class includes the NP-complete problems, which are mutually reducible in the sense that a fast deterministic algorithm for any one of them could be used to construct such an algorithm for any of the others. The NP-complete class includes such well known combinatorial problems as the traveling salesman problem, the knapsack packing problem, the job-shop scheduling problem, and the Boolean-function satisfiability problem. In 1978, it was an open question whether P = NP—that is, whether there is a fast deterministic algorithm for any NP-complete problem. That no one has ever found a fast algorithm for any NP-complete problem is accepted by many researchers as empirical evidence that no fast algorithm for any of these problems exists. For this reason, there has been much research into *approximation* (heuristic) *algorithms*—fast algorithms that solve the problem correctly in some, but not all, the cases.

Young and Machtey [1978] cover all of modern complexity theory at a graduate level. Baase [1978] covers some topics in concrete complexity theory at an undergraduate level, including examples of approximation algorithms. Borodin and Munro [1975] examine these topics specifically for algebraic and numerical problems. Savage [1976] complements these approaches with a theory based on the number of gates in the logic circuits which would implement the Boolean function representing an algorithm.

* * *

As you grow in knowledge and experience, we hope you will find that this book has increased your appreciation of the strong role played by theory in practical computation. You should also be prepared for further insights through the works of others, including the masters of computer science. We offer you our best wishes in your work with machines, languages, and computation.

# Bibliography

ACKERMANN, W. [1928] *Zum Hilbertschen Aufbau der reellen Zahlen. Mathematische Annalen*, **99**, 118–133.

AHO, A. V., P. J. DENNING, AND J. D. ULLMAN [1972] Weak and mixed strategy precedence parsing. *J. ACM.*, **19**:2, 225–243.

AHO, A. V., J. E. HOPCROFT, AND J. D. ULLMAN [1974] *Design and Analysis of Computer Algorithms*. Reading, Mass.: Addison-Wesley.

AHO, A. V., AND S. C. JOHNSON [1974] *LR* Parsing. *Computing Surveys*, **6**:2, 99–124.

AHO, A. V., AND J. D. ULLMAN [1972] *Theory of Parsing, Translation, and Compiling*, Vol. 1. Englewood Cliffs, N.J.: Prentice-Hall.

AHO, A. V., AND J. D. ULLMAN [1973] *Theory of Parsing, Translation, and Compiling*, Vol. 2. Englewood Cliffs, N.J.: Prentice-Hall.

ARBIB, M. A., (ed.) [1968] *The Algebraic Theory of Machines, Languages, and Semigroups*. New York: Academic Press.

ARBIB, M. A. [1969] *Theories of Abstract Automata*. Englewood Cliffs, N.J.: Prentice-Hall.

ASHCROFT, E. A., AND W. W. WADGE [1977] LUCID, a nonprocedural language with iteration. *Comm. ACM*, **20**:7, 519–526.

BAASE, S. [1978] *Computer Algorithms: Introduction to Design and Analysis*. Reading, Mass.: Addison-Wesley.

BACKUS, J. W., ET AL. [1957] The FORTRAN automatic coding system. *Proc. West. Joint Comp. Conf.*, **11**, 188–198.

BAR-HILLEL, Y. [1964] *Language and Information*. Reading, Mass.: Addison-Wesley.

BAR-HILLEL, Y., C. GAIFMAN, AND E. SHAMIR [1960] On categorical and phrase-structure grammars. *Bull. Res. Council Israel*, **9F**, 155–166.

BAR-HILLEL, Y., M. PERLES, AND E. SHAMIR [1961] On formal properties of simple phrase structure grammars. *Z. Phonetik. Sprach. Kommunikationsforsch.*, **14**, 143–172. (Also in Bar-Hillel [1964], chap. 9.)

BAUER, F. L. AND J. EIKEL (eds.) [1976] *Compiler Construction, An Advanced Course*. Berlin: Springer-Verlang.

BIRKHOFF, G., AND S. MACLANE [1967] *Algebra*. New York: Macmillan.

BORODIN, A. AND I. MUNRO [1975] *The Computational Complexity of Algebraic and Numeric Problems*. New York: Elsevier North-Holland.

BRAFFORT, P., AND D. HIRSCHBERG (eds.) [1963] *Computer Programming and Formal Systems*. Amsterdam: North-Holland.

BRZOZOWSKI, J. A. [1962] A survey of regular expressions and their applications. *IRE Trans. on Electronic Computers*, **11**:3, 324–335.

BRZOZOWSKI, J. A. [1962] Canonical regular expressions and minimal state graphs for definite events. *Proc. Symp. Math. Theory of Automata*, Brooklyn, N.Y., 529–561.

BRZOZOWSKI, J. A. [1964] Derivatives of regular expressions. *J. ACM*, **11**:4, 481–494.

BRZOZOWSKI, J. A. [1964] Regular expressions from linear sequential circuits. *IEEE Trans. Elec. Comp. EC-13*, 741–744.

CALDWELL, S. H. [1958] *Switching Circuits and Logical Design*. New York: Wiley.

CANTOR, D. C. [1962] On the ambiguity problem of Backus systems. *J. ACM*, **9**:4, 477–479.

CHEATHAM, T. E. [1967] *The Theory and Construction of Compilers* (2nd ed.) Wakefield, Mass.: Computer Associates.

CHEATHAM, T. E., AND K. SATTLEY [1964] Syntax directed compiling. *Proc. AFIPS Spring Joint Comp. Conf.*, **25**, Spartan, New York, 31–57.

CHOMSKY, N. [1956] Three models for the description of language. *IEEE Trans. on Information Theory*, **2**:3, 113–124.

CHOMSKY, N. [1959] On certain formal properties of grammars. *Inf. and Control*, **2**:2, 137–167.

CHOMSKY, N. [1959] A note on phrase structure grammars. *Inf. and Control*, **2**:4, 393–395.

CHOMSKY, N. [1962] Context-free grammars and pushdown storage. *Quart. Prog. Rept. No.* **65**, 187–194. MIT Res. Lab. Electronics, Cambridge, Mass.

CHOMSKY, N., AND G. A. MILLER [1958] Finite state languages. *Inf. and Control*, **1**:2, 91–112.

CHOMSKY, N. AND M. P. SCHUTZENBERGER [1963] The algebraic theory of context-free languages. In BRAFFORT AND HIRSCHBERG [1963], 118–161.

CHURCH, A. [1936] An unsolvable problem of elementary number theory. *Amer. J. Math.*, **58**, 345–363.

DAVIS, M. [1958] *Computability and Unsolvability*. New York: McGraw-Hill.

DAVIS, M. (ed.) [1965] *The Undecidable*. New York: Raven Press.

DEREMER, F. L. [1969] "Practical Translators for LR(k) Languages." Doctoral thesis, MIT, Cambridge, Mass.

DEREMER, F. L. [1971] Simple LR(k) grammars. *Comm. ACM*, **14**:7, 453–460.

DIJKSTRA, E. W. [1976] *A Discipline of Programming*. Englewood Cliffs, N.J.: Prentice-Hall.

EARLEY, J. [1968] "An Efficient Context-Free Parsing Algorithm." Doctoral Thesis, Carnegie-Mellon University, Pittsburgh.

EVEY, R. J. [1963] Theory and application of pushdown-store machines. *Proc. AFIPS Fall Joint Comp. Conf.*, **24**, Spartan, New York, 215–227.

FELDMAN, J. A., AND D. GRIES [1968] Translator writing systems. *Comm. ACM*, **11**:2, 77–113.

FISCHER, M. J. [1969] Some properties of precedence languages. *Proc. ACM Symp. Theory of Computing*, 181–190.

FISCHER, P. C. [1963] On computability of certain classes of restricted Turing machines. *Proc. 4th Ann. Symp. Switching Circuit Theory and Logic Des.*, Chicago, 23–32.

FISCHER, P. C. [1965] Multitape and infinite state automata—a survey. *Comm. ACM*, **8**:12, 799–805.

FLOYD, R. W. [1962] On ambiguity in phrase structure languages. *Comm. ACM*, **5**:10, 526–534.

FLOYD, R. W. [1963] Syntactic analysis and operator precedence. *J. ACM*, **10**:3, 316–333.

FLOYD, R. W. [1964] New proofs and old theorems in logic and formal linguistics. Wakefield, Mass.: Computer Associates, Inc.

FLOYD, R. W. [1964] Bounded context syntactic analysis. *Comm. ACM*, **7**:2, 62–67.

FLOYD, R. W. [1967] Assigning meanings to programs. *Proc. Symp. Appl. Math.*, **19**, 19–31. Amer. Math. Soc., Providence, R.I.

GINSBURG, S. [1966] *The Mathematical Theory of Context-Free Languages.* New York: McGraw-Hill.

GINSBURG, S., AND S. A. GREIBACH [1966] Deterministic context-free languages. *Inf. and Control*, **9**:6, 620–648.

GINSBURG, S., AND S. A. GREIBACH [1967] Abstract families of languages. *IEEE Conf. Record of 8th Ann. Symp. Switching and Automata Theory*, Austin, Texas.

GINSBURG, S., S. A. GREIBACH, AND M. A. HARRISON [1967] Stack automata and compiling. *J. ACM*, **14**:1, 172–201.

GINSBURG, S., AND G. F. ROSE [1963] Some recursively unsolvable problems in ALGOL-like languages. *J. ACM*, **10**:1, 29–47.

GINSBURG, S., AND G. F. ROSE [1963] Operations which preserve definability in languages. *J. ACM*, **10**:2, 175–195.

GINSBURG, S., AND G. F. ROSE [1966] Preservation of languages by transducers. *Inf. and Control*, **9**, 153–176.

GINSBURG, S., AND E. H. SPANIER [1963] Quotients of context-free languages. *J. ACM*, **10**:4, 487–492.

GINSBURG, S., AND J. S. ULLIAN [1966] Ambiguity in context-free languages. *J. ACM*, **13**:1, 62–89.

GINZBURG, A. [1968] *Algebraic Theory of Automata*. New York: Academic Press.

GÖDEL, K. [1931] Über formal unentscheidbare Sätze der Principia Mathematica und verwandter Systeme, I. *Monatschefte für Mathematik und Physik*, **38**, 173–198. (English translation in Davis [1965].)

GREIBACH, S. A. [1965] A new normal-form theorem for context-free phrase structure grammars. *J. ACM*, **12**:1, 42–52.

GREIBACH, S. A., AND J. E. HOPCROFT [1967] Independence of AFL operations. SDC Document TM 738/034/00.

GRIES, D. [1971] *Compiler Construction for Digital Computers.* New York: Wiley.

GRIFFITHS, T. V. AND S. R. PETRICK [1965] On the relative efficiencies of context-free grammar recognizers. *Comm. ACM*, **8**:5, 289–300.

HAINES, L. H. [1965] "Generation and Recognition of Formal Languages." Doctoral Thesis, MIT, Cambridge, Mass.

HALMOS, P. [1960] *Naive Set Theory*. New York: Van Nostrand Reinhold.

HARTMANIS, J., AND H. SHANK [1968] On the recognition of primes by automata. *J. ACM*, **15**, 382–389.

HARTMANIS, J., AND R. E. STEARNS [1966] *Algebraic Theory Sequential Machines*. Englewood Cliffs, N.J.: Prentice-Hall.

HENNIE, F. C. [1968] *Finite-State Models for Logical Machines*. New York: Wiley.

HENNIE, F. C. [1977] *Introduction to Computability*. Reading, Mass.: Addison-Wesley.

HERMES, H. [1965] *Enumerability-Decidability-Computability*. New York: Academic Press.

HOARE, C. A. R. [1969] An axiomatic basis for computer programming. *Comm. ACM*, **12**:10, 576–580.

HOPCROFT, J. E., AND J. D. ULLMAN [1969] *Formal Languages and Their Relation to Automata*. Reading, Mass: Addison-Wesley.

HUFFMAN, D. A. [1954] The synthesis of sequential switching circuits. *J. Franklin Institute*, **257**:3–4, 161–190, 275–303.

IBARRA, O. [1967] On the equivalence of finite-state sequential machine models. *IEEE Trans. Electronic Computers EC-16*, 88–90.

IRONS, E. T. [1961] A syntax directed compiler for ALGOL 60. *Comm. ACM*, **4**:1, 51–55.

JONES. N. [1973] *Computability Theory: An Introduction*. New York: Academic Press.

KAIN, R. Y. [1972] *Automata Theory: Machines and Languages*. New York: McGraw-Hill.

KLEENE, S. C. [1936] General recursive functions of natural numbers. *Mathematische Annalen*, **112**, 727–742.

KLEENE, S. C. [1936] $\lambda$-definability and recursiveness. *Duke Math. J.*, **2**, 340–353.

KLEENE, S. C. [1956] Representation of events in nerve nets and finite automata. In SHANNON AND MCCARTHY [1956], 3–42.

KNUTH, D. E. [1965] On the translation of languages from left to right. *Inf. and Control*, **8**:6, 607–639.

KNUTH, D. E. [1968] *The Art of Computer Programming*, Vol. 1. Reading, Mass.: Addison-Wesley.

KNUTH, D. E. [1969] *The Art Computer Programming*, Vol. 2. Reading, Mass.: Addison-Wesley.

KNUTH, D. E. [1972] *The Art of Computer Programming*, Vol. 3. Reading, Mass: Addison-Wesley.

KORENJAK, A. J. [1969] A practical method for contructing LR(k) processors. *Comm. ACM*, **12**:11, 613–623.

KUNO, S., AND A. G. OETTINGER [1962] Multiple-path syntactic analyzer. *Information Processing 62*, 306–311. North-Holland, Amsterdam.

KURMIT, A. A. [1974] *Information Lossless Automata of Finite Order*. New York: Wiley.

KURODA, S. Y. [1964] Classes of languages and linear-bounded automata. *Inf. and Control*, **7**:2, 207–223.

LANDWEBER, P. S. [1963] Three theorems on phrase structure grammars of type 1. *Inf. and Control*, **6**:2, 131–136.

LEWIS, P. M., D. J. ROSENKRANTZ, AND R. E. STEARNS [1976] *Compiler Design Theory*. Reading, Mass.: Addison-Wesley.

LEWIS, P. M. AND R. E. STEARNS [1968] Syntax directed transduction. *J. ACM*, **15**:3, 464–488.

LISKOV, B., A. SNYDER, R. ATKINSON, C. SHAFFERT [1977] Abstraction mechanisms in CLU. *Comm. ACM*, **20**:8, 564–576.

LISKOV, B., AND S. ZILLES [1975] Specification techniques for data abstractions. *IEEE Trans. on Software Eng. SE-1*, **1**, 7–19.

LONDON, R. L. ET AL. [1978] Proof rules for the programming language EUCLID. *Acta Informatica* (to appear).

LUCKHAM, D. C. [1977] Program verification and verification oriented programming. *Proc. IFIP Congress* 1977, 783–793. North-Holland, Amsterdam.

MANNA, Z., AND R. WALDINGER [1977] The logic of computer programming. *Tech. Rpt., Art. Int. Lab.*, Stanford University, Stanford, Calif.

MARGARIS, A. [1967] *First Order Mathematical Logic*. Lexington, Mass.: Blaisdell Publishing.

MCCARTHY, J. [1963] Towards a mathematical science of computation. *Proc. IFIP Congress 1962*, 21–28. North-Holland, Amsterdam.

MCCULLOCH, W. S., AND W. PITTS [1943] A logical calculus of the ideas immanent in nervous activity. *Bull. Math. Biophysics*, **5**, 115–133.

MCKEEMAN, W. M., J. J. HORNING, AND D. B. WORTMAN [1970] *A Compiler Generator*. Englewood Cliffs, N.J.: Prentice-Hall.

MCNAUGHTON, R., AND H. YAMADA [1960] Regular expressions and state graphs for automata. *IRE Trans. on Electronic Computers*, **9**:1, 39–47. Also in MOORE [1964], 157–174.

MEALY, G. H. [1955] A method for synthesising sequential circuits. *Bell System Tech. J.*, **34**, 1045–1079.

MENDELSON, E. [1964] *Introduction to Mathematical Logic*. New York: Van Nostrand Reinhold.

MEYER, A. R. AND M. J. FISCHER [1971] Economy of description by automata, grammars and formal systems. *IEEE Conf. Record 12th Ann. Symp. Switching and Automata Theory*, 188–191.

MINSKY, M. L. [1961] Recursive unsolvability of Post's problem of 'Tag' and other topics in the theory of Turing machines. *Annals of Math.*, **74**:3, 437–455.

MINSKY, M. L. [1967] *Computation: Finite and Infinite Machines*. Englewood Cliffs, N.J.: Prentice-Hall.

MINSKY, M., AND S. PAPERT [1966] Unrecognizable sets of numbers. *J. ACM*, **31**, 281–286.

MOORE, E. F., [1956] Gedanken experiments on sequential machines. In SHANNON AND MCCARTHY [1956], 129–153.

MOORE, E. F. (ed.) [1964] *Sequential Machines: Selected Papers*. Reading, Mass.: Addison-Wesley.

MYHILL, J. [1957] Finite automata and the representation of events. *Wright Air Development Command Tech. Rept.*, 57–624. Wright-Patterson Air Force Base, Ohio.

MYHILL, J. [1960] Linear bounded automata. *Wright Air Development Division Tech. Note*, 60–165. Wright-Patterson Air Force Base, Ohio.

NAUR, P. (ed.) [1963] Revised report on the algorithmic language ALGOL 60. *Comm. ACM*, **6**:1, 1–17.

NERODE, A. [1958] Linear automaton transformations. *Proc. Amer. Math. Soc.*, **9**, 541–544.

OETTINGER, A. [1961] Automatic syntactic analysis and the pushdown store. *Proc. Symp. Appl. Math.*, **12**, 104–129. Amer. Math. Soc., Providence, R.I.

OGDEN, W. [1968] A helpful result for proving inherent ambiguity. *Math. Systems Theory*, **2**:3, 191–194.

OTT, G. H., AND N. H. FEINSTEIN [1961] Design of sequential machines from their regular expressions. *J. ACM*, **8**, 585–600.

PARIKH, R. J. [1961] Language generating devices. *Quart. Prog. Rept.*, **60**, MIT Res. Lab. Electronics, 199–212.

PARIKH, R. J. [1966] On context-free languages. *J. ACM*, **13**:4, 570–581.

POST, E. L. [1936] Finite combinatory processes-formulation I. *J. Symb. Logic*, **1**, 103–105.

POST, E. L. [1943] Formal reductions of the general combinatorial decision problem. *Amer. J. Math.*, **65**, 197–215.

POST, E. L. [1946] A variant of a recursively unsolvable problem. *Bull. Amer. Math. Soc.*, **52**, 264–268.

PRATT, T. W. [1975] *Programming Languages: Design and Implementation.* Englewood Cliffs, N.J.: Prentice-Hall.

RABIN, M. O., AND D. SCOTT [1959] Finite automata and their decision problems. *IBM J. Res.*, **3**:2, 115–125. Also in MOORE [1964], 63–91.

RADO, T. [1962] On non-computable functions. *Bell System Tech. J.*, **41**, 877–884.

RANDELL, B., AND L. J. RUSSELL [1964] *ALGOL 60 Implementation.* New York: Academic Press.

REYNOLDS, J. C. [1965] An introduction to the COGENT programming system. *Proc. ACM National Conf.*, 422.

RITCHIE, R. W. [1963] Finite automata and the set of squares. *J. ACM*, **10**, 528–531.

ROGERS, H. [1959] The present theory of Turing machine computability. *J. SIAM*, **7**, 114–130.

ROGERS, H. [1967] *Theory of Recursive Functions and Effective Computability.* New York: McGraw-Hill.

ROSENKRANTZ. D. J. [1967] Matrix equations and normal forms for context-free grammars. *J. ACM.*, **14**:3, 501–507.

SAVAGE, J. E. [1976] *The Complexity of Computing.* New York: Wiley.

SCHEINBERG, S. [1960] Note on the Boolean properties of context-free languages. *Inf. and Control*, **3**:4, 372–375.

SCHORRE, D. V. [1964] META II, a syntax oriented compiler writing language. *Proc. ACM National Conf.*, **19**, D1.3-1-D1.3-11.

SCHUTZENBERGER, M. P. [1963] On context-free languages and pushdown automata. *Inf. and Control*, **6**:3, 246–264.

SCOTT, D. AND C. STRACHEY [1971] Toward a mathematical semantics of computer languages. *Proc. Symp. Computers and Automata*, Polytechnic Institute of Brooklyn, N.Y.

SHANNON, C. E. [1938] A symbolic analysis of relay and switching circuits. *Trans. Amer. Inst. Elec. Eng.*, **57**:1, 1–11.

SHANNON, C. E. [1956] A Universal Turing machine with two internal states. In SHANNON AND MCCARTHY [1956], 129–153.

SHANNON, C. E., AND J. MCCARTHY (eds.) [1956] *Automata Studies*. Princeton, N.J.: Princeton University Press.

SHAW, M. A. AND W. A. WULF [1977] Abstraction and verification in Alphard: defining and specifying iteration and generators. *Comm. ACM*, **20**:8, 553–564.

SHEPHERDSON, J. C. [1959] Reduction of two-way automata to one-way automata. *IBM J. Res.*, **3**, 198–200.

STEARNS, R. E. [1967] A regularity test for pushdown machines. *Inf. and Control*, **11**:3, 323–340.

STOLL, R. R. [1963] *Set Theory and Logic*. San Francisco: Freeman.

STOY, J. E. [1977] *Denotational Semantics*. Cambridge, Mass.: MIT Press.

TENNENT, R. D. [1976] The denotational semantics of programming languages. *Comm. ACM*, **19**:8, 437–453.

TURING, A. M. [1936] On computable numbers, with an application to the Entscheidungsproblem. *Proc. London Math. Soc.*, **2-42**, 230–265. (Correction, *ibid.*, **2-43**, 544–546.)

TURING, A. M. [1937] Computability and $\lambda$-definability. *J. Symb. Logic*, **2**, 153–163.

WANG, H. [1957] A variant to Turing's theory of computing machines. *J. ACM*, **4**:1, 63–92.

WEGNER, P. [1972] The Vienna definition language. *Computing Surveys*, **4**:1, 5–63.

WEIDE, B. [1977] A survey of analysis techniques for combinatorial algorithms. *Computing Surveys*, **9**:4, (to appear).

WIRTH, N. [1971] The programming language Pascal. *Acta Informatica*, **1**:1, 35–63.

WIRTH, N., AND H. WEBER [1966] EULER—a generalization of ALGOL and its formal definition, Parts 1 and 2. *Comm. ACM*, **9**:1–2, 13–23, 89–99.

YED, R. T. (ed.) [1977] *Current Trends in Programming Methodology*, Vol. 1. Englewood Cliffs, N.J.: Prentice-Hall.

YOUNG, P. AND M. MACHTEY [1978] *An Introduction to the General Theory of Algorithms*. New York: Elsevier North-Holland.

# Author Index

# Subject Index